THE CRAFT
OF PUBLIC
ADMINISTRATION

DUE

THE CRAFT
OF PUBLIC
ADMINISTRATION

160201

EIGHTH EDITION

George Berkley • *University of Massachusetts*

John Rouse • *Ball State University*

Boston   Burr Ridge, IL   Dubuque, IA   Madison, WI   New York   San Francisco   St. Louis
Bangkok   Bogotá   Caracas   Lisbon   London   Madrid
Mexico City   Milan   New Delhi   Seoul   Singapore   Sydney   Taipei   Toronto

McGraw-Hill Higher Education

A Division of The **McGraw-Hill** *Companies*

THE CRAFT OF PUBLIC ADMINISTRATION, EIGHTH EDITION

Copyright © 2000, 1997 by The McGraw-Hill Companies, Inc. All rights reserved. Printed in the United States of America. Except as permitted under the United States Copyright Act of 1976, no part of this publication may be reproduced or distributed in any form or by any means, or stored in a data base or retrieval system, without the prior written permission of the publisher.

This book is printed on acid-free paper.

1 2 3 4 5 6 7 8 9 0 DOC/DOC 0 9 8 7 6 5 4 3 2 1 0

ISBN 0–697–38590–6

Editorial director: *Jane E. Vaicunas*
Sponsoring editor: *Monica Eckman*
Developmental editor: *Hannah Glover*
Senior marketing manager: *Suzanne Daghlian*
Project manager: *Marilyn M. Sulzer*
Production supervisor: *Laura Fuller*
Supplement coordinator: *Sandra M. Schnee*
Compositor: *Shepherd, Inc.*
Typeface: *10/12 Palatino*
Printer: *R. R. Donnelley & Sons Company/Crawfordsville, IN*

Cover designer: *Trudi Gershenov*
Cover photo: © *Mel Curtis, Photonica*

Library of Congress Cataloging-in-Publication Data

Berkley, George E.
      The craft of public administration / George Berkley, John Rouse. — 8th ed.
          p.   cm.
      Includes bibliographical references and index.
      ISBN 0–697–38590–6
      1. Public administration.   I. Rouse, John Edward,   1942– .
      II.   Title.
      JF1351.B47   2000
      351—dc21   99–18621
                                                                                      CIP

www.mhhe.com

CONTENTS

PREFACE

FOUR PEDAGOGICAL SEGMENTS

The Craft of Public Administration is not just a textbook; it is a pedagogical gathering of pertinent yet limited literature, assembled to inform and interest college students in the dynamics of the public, or government, sector in the United States. The literature is limited because we choose not to write a book that is "everything one wants to know about public administration but is afraid to ask." Local, state, regional, and federal governments are too overwhelming and far-reaching to attempt a dictionary approach to the field. To comprehend projected federal government spending of more than $1.87 trillion in 2002 (state and local government spending not included), the literature of public administration is divided into four pedagogical segments:

- *federalism* (craft of public administration, relationships to economic development, political and bureaucratic culture, the structure of politics, partisan, policy, and systems politics, equality, efficiency, synergy, formal organization, human relations). Chapters 1 through 4 focus upon the structure of American politics, or issues of U.S. federalism. Chapter 1 concerns "The Administrative Craft"; Chapter 2 deals with "The Ecology of the Administrative Craft"; Chapter 3 investigates "The Anatomy of Public Organization"; Chapter 4 studies "The Physiology of Organization."
- *public personnel administration* (people, patronage, merit, equal opportunity, affirmative action, job classifications, labor relations, leadership, charisma, communication, technology). Chapters 5 through 8 address matters of public personnel administration. Chapter 5 explores "People and Personnel";

Chapter 6 reviews "Public Sector Labor-Management Relations"; Chapter 7 develops the role of "Leadership"; Chapter 8 relates the importance of "Communication" in government bureaucracies.

- *budgets* (taxing, appropriations, spending, productivity, efficiency, effectiveness, motivation, privatization of government functions, planning, program evaluation). Chapters 9 and 10 examine priorities of taxing, budgeting, spending, productivity, and program evaluation. Chapter 9 addresses "Taxing, Budgeting, and Spending" and points out how partisan, policy, and systems politics impact the likelihood of higher taxes but fewer government programs and services. Chapter 10 probes "The Productivity Challenge" and outlines the pressures for government employees to do more with less resources.

- *regulations* (administrative law, administrative controls, administrative law judges, ethics, discretion, rules, procedures, administrative responsibility, administrative state, clientele relations). Chapters 11 and 12 explain administrative law, clientele relations, and government regulations. Chapter 11 outlines issues of "Administrative Law and Control" and describes the impact of administrative growth on democratic ideals, outlines traditional and contemporary cornerstones of American administrative law, notes the expanding role of administrative law judges, and probes how much law and control is enough. Chapter 12 develops the impacts of "Government Regulations and Regulatory Behaviors" and illustrates how economic, social, and subsidiary regulations are affected by administrative rules and rule-making.

The narrative and case studies allow students to learn from analyzing the literature in conjunction with specific illustrations. Case studies force us to think about how the general (literature) affects the particular (case study) and how specific illustrations amend our perceptions of public administration literature. Examination of case study facts brings out the dynamic nature of the literature.

Public administration constitutes the "chemistry" of the United States. The two key principles that have come to embody the American ideal, equality and efficiency, are likewise the crucial determinants of how well the public, or government, sector functions in the United States. Democratic capitalism does not flourish if public infrastructures, such as schools, highways, institutions of public safety, and similar taxpayer funded government operations are devalued and rendered ineffective.

Public sector functions, programs, and activities represent the "bottom line" expectations that society guarantees citizens. The domestic and military spending priorities of the 1980s have forced public administration as a field to be more accountable, adjust to economic realities, and evolve in unforseen ways. The field is dynamic. The efficacy of *The Craft of Public Administration* depends upon people *effectively* relating to other people in the exchange of partisan, policy, and systems politics.

The attempts of the Clinton administration to reduce the number of government jobs is recognized. The actions and reactions of Democrat *Bill Clinton*, as president in charge of the federal bureaucracy, and Republican *Denny Hastert*, as speaker of the House of Representatives, bring to life the "chemistry" of equality and efficiency and of public and private relations in the United States. Professors Berkley and Rouse encourage feedback from professors and students on the effectiveness of *The Craft of Public Administration*. Your contributions will make future editions of this text reflect the dynamic "chemistry" of U.S. life as it is played out in everyday relations between the "equality" of government programs and services and the "efficiency" of private opportunities.

CONFLICTS OF VALUES

The dynamics of public administration cannot be removed from the increasing diversity—and disparity—of American life and its many value systems. The development, implementation, and evaluation of public administration programs and services reflect not only a diversity of values but conflicts in values. As we study federalism, personnel, budgeting, and regulations, we do so realizing conflicts in values—and economic disparity—dominate our thinking of how government should function.

What conflicts in values should we keep in mind as we engage the dynamics of public administration?

- *Individualism versus Collectivism.* Individualism is represented by private initiative, personal choice, self-sufficiency, pursuit of materialism, and the private-enterprise economic system. The responsibility of individuals to themselves contrasts with responsibility of the individual to society. Collectivism is represented by government, the nation, states, government bureaucracies, public goods, and the "common good." Public administration consists of public goods, which are widely distributed to citizens. Governments implement public programs for the many, not the few.

- *Materialism versus Spiritualism.* Materialism, as a doctrine, espouses that comfort, pleasure, and wealth are the only or highest goals or values. Achievement of the "good life" is what many believe the American dream is about. The good life perhaps includes a home, yard, automobile, appliances, and the necessities that go with climbing ladders of economic success. Materialism incorporates the consumer society of shop and buy. American elections are contested primarily on economic, or materialistic values, not spiritual values. Spiritualism finds its origins in religious or moral thoughts. Materialism remains dominant in United States society, but spiritual values are not dismissed. Material well-being permits governments to offer programs to citizens for private use. Despite materialistic demands, moral authorities, or traditionalists, struggle against modernization and its manifestations.

- *Modernization versus Traditionalism.* Modernism sympathizes with modern ideas. Modern thinkers conform to present-day practices, standards, and tastes. Modernization designates certain contemporary tendencies. Traditionalism honors stories, beliefs, customs, conventions, and proverbs observed by generations throughout the ages. Conflicts over the functions of governments confront modernization and traditionalism. Modernization may mean "progressive" change. Modernization implies opposition to traditional values. Modernization has lead to industrialization and secularization. Traditionalism may be best defined as the desire to maintain values, customs, mores, and living patterns that have been established over time. Computer technology, feminist workforce values, video games, and government administrative systems may also reflect modernization. If governments emphasize modernization, they may be in conflict with traditional groups in their society. Modern public administration reflects modernization, but values espoused by Max Weber and other theorists are traditional, classic, and timeless.

- *Centralization versus Decentralization.* There are approximately 80,000 units of public administration systems, or governments, in the United States. The most prevalent ones, of course, are the 50 American states. Counties, cities, townships, and special districts incorporate an administrative system that is fragmented and decentralized. The government in Washington may propose, but the people in the boonies dispose.

If authority is concentrated, advocates of centralization argue, more efficient decision-making and policy-implementation can be achieved. Decisions can be reached quickly. Policy can be implemented with fewer people at cross-purposes. Decentralization philosophy claims to be more democratic, and responsive, as it brings more people into decision-making and policy-implementing processes. The possibility of a decision-making error is minimized.

- *Moral Value versus Opposed Moral Value.* In a country as large as the United States there are a wide range of values. Individualism and collectivism; materialism and spiritualism; modernization and traditionalism; and the legitimacy of opposed moral values impact public administration programs and units.[1]

The many dimensions of American public administration occur within these frameworks of philosophical thought.

- In a society that emphasizes individual freedoms, how does the "body politic" organize collective priorities for public services made available to individuals?
- How do material values effect the development of public programs?
- If public administration programs result in modernistic values, what role does traditionalism play?

Centralization and decentralization values are realized daily as more than 80,000 units of government collaborate in the craft of American public administration. Partisan, policy, and system politics are distinctive in programs and services of the national government, states, counties, cities, townships, and other special districts. And one moral value opposed by another or other moral values?

- Should government/s be involved?
- What level of government should accomplish the tasks?
- How should the collective society pay for these programs and services?
- How strong is the private economy, which must be taxed to provide public programs and services?

[1]Daniel S. Papp, *Contemporary International Relations: Frameworks for Understanding,* 3d ed. (New York: Macmillan Publishing Co., 1991), 578–593.

- Consumerism is part of the materialistic culture. From the productivity of materialism comes taxation, or revenues for public programs and services. Should collective programs and services be implemented by private means or through government agencies?

The Craft of Public Administration, in its zillions of substantive and procedural facets, is manifest in such conflicts of values.

ACKNOWLEDGMENTS

As principal author of the eighth edition of *The Craft of Public Administration*, I wish to express my thanks and appreciation to:

- George Berkley, author of the first four editions of this textbook, for the opportunity to coauthor the fifth, sixth, seventh, and eighth editions;
- Monica Eckman, Hannah Glover, Anne Scroggin, and Marilyn Sulzer, McGraw-Hill Companies, for their encouragement and feedback on the development and evaluation of various stages of the writing and production;
- Ray Scheele, chairman and professor, Department of Political Science, Ball State University, for his leadership in promoting a working environment conducive to integrating the tasks of teaching and research;
- faculty colleagues in the Department of Political Science, Ball State University, for creating an atmosphere where consensus is valued and productivity is recognized;
- Mike Corbett, professor, Department of Political Science, Ball State University, for his assistance in my adjustment to out-of-date computer software;
- Stephanie Painter and Gretchen Buckles, administrative assistants to chairman Scheele, who facilitated in many ways with telephone calls, faxes, and photocopying;
- employees of the more than 80,000 units of government in the United States, whose craft constitutes the challenges of federalism, personnel, budgets, and government regulations;
- thousands of Ball State University graduate and undergraduate students, past and present, who continually force me to think and rethink the dynamics of the public sector in the United States;
- the generous taxpayers of the State of Indiana, my employer, for access to a professional career that bridges the worlds of partisan, policy, and systems politics with the rich and varied literature of public administration; and
- Barbara Maves, my wife, and for many years, executive director of a government-funded, not-for-profit east central Indiana health-care agency, which daily confronts the challenges of the craft of public administration.

These contributions in many ways enhanced my research and writing of this edition of *The Craft of Public Administration*.

John Rouse
00jerouse@bsuvc.bsu.edu

1

THE ADMINISTRATIVE CRAFT

The words *public administration* express a concept that at first glance may seem abstract and nondescript. However, a closer look at the phrase helps take away the ambiguity.

Public means the citizens of a given area—the people of a town, county, state, or country. If an issue is considered in the public domain, information and discussion about that issue are open to, or shared by, the people and can be known to all. The word *public* also refers to activities administered by the state in the name of the entire community.

Public administrators serve the people. Organized collectives of citizens constitute a variety of public communities in the United States. These publicly organized communities include national, state, and local governments. They include townships, state recreation areas, and public utilities. They include school, sanitary, and water districts. There are also public libraries, public parks, public defenders (police, fire, legal), public roadways, and public servants. In the event of war, citizens may be called upon to make the ultimate sacrifice to their national community—their lives. However, in peacetime, Americans are required only to pay taxes and obey the laws. When April 15th rolls around, citizens have a definitive economic opportunity to be patriotic by meeting their financial obligation to society. The one thing all public programs have in common is they are financed by taxpayers, most of whom want a voice in how those dollars are spent. The breakdown of government employees is 14.8 percent federal, 24.2 percent state, and 61.0 percent local. In 1996, there were 2,895,000 federal, 4,719,000 state, and 11,906,000 local government employees in the United States, or a total of 18,236,000 government employees.[1]

How big is government? Annual expenditures (1996) for all levels of government are approximately the following: federal, $1,600 billion; state; $850 billion; and local, $750 billion. In 1996, the nation's gross domestic product (GDP) was approximately $7,000 billion. Government spends about half what the nation "earns" each year. Is this amount excessive? A comparison of the percentage of GDP spent by the U.S. government with that of other countries indicates that the size of the U.S. government is, in proportion to its economy, smaller than that of nearly any other industrialized nation.[2]

The pressure from U.S. taxpayers is to reduce personnel and expenses for services. (There is correspondingly less demand to reduce services to citizens.) Since most services are delivered by local governments and their employees, the reduction of personnel and expenses must come at the local level of operations, less so at the state level, and much less so at the centers of federal government operations. So, as we study *public administration,* the abstract, nondescript, colorless images of public bureaucracies will fade away. They will be replaced by more concrete concerns about the development, evaluation, and implementation of how we spend our tax dollars. Such decisions are usually political decisions. A major function of politics is to allocate importance to numerous and often conflicting values in society. Public administration is the process of implementing those diverse values in our complex and ever-changing society and therefore plays a vital role in the daily lives of all citizens.

A NEW SPIRIT OF COMMUNITY

William Jefferson Clinton, taking the presidential oath of office for a second term on January 20, 1997, issued an urgent call to end political and racial disharmony in America and outlined a vision for a smaller, more compassionate government to provide "a new spirit of community."

Source: Ann Scales, "Clinton Speaks of his Dream," *Boston Globe*, 21 January 1997 , p. A1.

TABLE 1–1 Total Tax Receipts as Percent of Gross Domestic Product

Nation	Percent
Denmark	51.6
Sweden	51.0
Finland	47.3
Czech Republic	47.3
Belgium	46.6
Netherlands	45.9
Luxembourg	45.0
France	44.1
Poland	43.2
Austria	42.8
Greece	42.5
Italy	41.7
Norway	41.2
Hungary	41.0
Germany	39.3
Ireland	37.5
New Zealand	37.0
Canada	36.1
Spain	35.8
United Kingdom	34.1
Switzerland	33.9
Portugal	33.0
Iceland	30.9
Australia	29.9
Japan	27.8
United States	27.6
Turkey	22.2
Mexico	18.8

Source: OECD (1997, 46–47).

The Heart of the Matter

In a classic textbook, Herbert Simon, Donald Smithburg, and Victor Thompson define *administration* simply but graphically in this opening sentence: "When two men cooperate to roll a stone that neither could have moved alone, the rudiments of administration have appeared."[3] That illustrates much about what administration is and what it is not. The first and foremost ingredient of administration is *people*. A stone by itself on a hill is not involved in any form of administration. If that stone rolls down the hill by some act of nature, administration is not involved. People have to be present before administration can take place.

The second ingredient of administration is *action*. Two people looking at the stone are not, in that act alone, involved in administration. They must take some action regarding the stone before administration can enter the picture. There is no such thing as inactive administration (although many who have dealt with administrative agencies sometimes believe otherwise).

The third ingredient is *interaction*. If one person moves the stone, administration does not occur. At least two people must combine their efforts to move the stone for the activity to involve administration. The essence of administration is *people relating to people*.

People interacting with people to accomplish tasks—this is what administration is about, although not all activity involving human interaction can bear the label "administration." The line that separates administration from other types of human interaction often becomes blurred. For example, a biology class lecture is not, in itself, a form of administration. The students are there to obtain a product and the professor is there to dispense that product. Consequently, the students, as learners, are no more engaged in an administrative relationship with their teacher than department store customers are with a sales clerk.

If the professor and students undertake a joint project, however, such as investigating pollution levels in a nearby river and reporting the results to the state legislature, the relationship changes. Now they are *mutually* involved in an endeavor, and their joint activity is an essential part of all administration. This joint activity need not be voluntary. A young man may be drafted against his will into the army. He may be sent, even more unwillingly, to a foreign base. Yet, in performing whatever role he is assigned, he is participating in administration. Like it or not, he is involved with others in the common effort to maintain the nation's security.

To sum up, administration is a process involving human beings jointly engaged in working toward common goals. Administration thus covers many, if not most, of the more exciting activities that take place in human society.

FIRST ENCOUNTERS OF THE BUREAUCRATIC KIND

The ability to adapt to a bureaucratic system is necessary to be able to function in the American society. Most young people first experience bureaucracy as college freshmen. Their views regarding bureaucracy reveal the process of socialization that lead to the acceptance of or resistance to a system that can be inefficient or, at times, dysfunctional. Although the students experience frustration with the long lines and waiting as well as with the impersonality of the administrative staff, they develop coping mechanisms that enable them to accept the system and conform in the long run.

Source: Glen J. Godwin and William T. Markham, "First Encounters of the Bureaucratic Kind: Early Freshman Experiences with a Campus Bureaucracy," *Journal of Higher Education* 67, no. 6 (November–December, 1996):660–692.

ART, SCIENCE, OR CRAFT?

The title of this book clearly proposes that administration is a craft. Why this classification instead of another? Why should we not consider administration a science or an art?

Science is characterized by precision and predictability. A scientific rule is one that works all the time. Rules in science are so rigid and final that they are not called rules at all, but laws. Two parts of hydrogen combined with one part of oxygen will *always* give us water, steam, or ice, depending on the temperature. While it is true that some sciences, particularly the social sciences, do not achieve such a 100 percent predictability level, it is also true that any scientific theory must stand up to rigorous, repeated tests to be considered valid. Administration uses scientific data, laws, and theories. An obvious example is the use of mathematics and computers to keep a government agency's financial records. However, administration itself is not a science.

Although administrators use scientific laws, techniques, and data, they do so in ways that allow free rein to individual imagination and temperament. Usually a variety of successful solutions exist for dealing with a particular administrative problem, and a creative administrator may even devise a new solution on the spot. Administrative problems are rarely identical and it is impossible to derive scientific equations that work the same way every time for such problems.

Administration shares traits with the arts as well as the sciences. Administrators often work in highly imaginative ways, employing a mix of methods, including intuition. Like painters and composers, administrators often find their own moods and personalities reflected in their work. There is, however, a vital difference that keeps administration from being characterized as an art: Artists create works of aesthetics; administrators attempt to solve problems. The respective end products and the criteria for evaluating them differ as a result.

Public administration shares traits with both science and art, therefore categorizing the field as one or the other paints an incomplete picture. There is, however, a category more suitable than these—or at least more comfortable and workable. That category is *craft*.

Let us assume a city is divided, for trash collection, into two distinct and equal districts. One team of sanitation workers under an assistant sanitation commissioner is assigned to each section with the objective of keeping the streets clean. One of the assistant commissioners may choose to have his or her people work straight eight-hour shifts five days a week. The other may choose to bunch the efforts of his or her crew at key times in the week and work them for longer periods of time on fewer days. One may try to improve the conditions of work by conducting a promotional campaign designed to persuade the residents of his or her section to switch from garbage cans to plastic bags. The other may deem it more fruitful to ask the police to crack down on litter under the street litter law. One may offer his or her workers extra inducements if they do their jobs successfully, while the other may hold out to his or her crew the prospect of more time off for a job well done.

The way each team works may differ, depending on the personalities of the administrative leaders, the personalities of the workers, and a variety of other factors. In every case, however, an objective standard exists for comparing the relative efficiency of each: Which team produces cleaner streets? In the example, and in most administrative situations, an objective standard lurks somewhere. This standard, however objective, is often shadowy, elusive, and hard to apply. At the same time, there is never a precise formula that will invariably work best in all situations. Not only do situations vary, but ideas for handling them are almost as infinite as the human mind. The objective standard, lack of precise formula, changing situations, and problem solving are traits that best fall under the classification of craft. Another example will further support the contention that administration may be more easily categorized as a craft rather than as an art or science.

As the New Deal was reaching its height, Harry Hopkins and Harold Ickes emerged as Franklin Roosevelt's most valued and trusted aides. Each man was given a substantial chunk of the federal public works and relief programs to administer. As they acquired power, however, they became increasingly suspicious and jealous of each other. Word of their growing rivalry and animosity soon leaked out, causing their respective partisans or opponents in the government, in the press, and in the public to leap to their attack or defense. Washington was abuzz with rumors of the feud, and that so many people were choosing sides was producing disruption throughout the government. The situation placed Roosevelt in a quandary. If he fired or encouraged the resignation of either man, he would not only lose a tried-and-tested aide but would also alienate and antagonize the aide's admirers and supporters. On the other hand, if Roosevelt issued a statement denying the feud, he would only succeed in acknowledging and giving credence to the rumors. Here was an administrator with a problem.

OUR LOVE-HATE RELATIONSHIP WITH GOVERNMENT

"Broadly speaking, President Clinton's nemesis is the modern welfare state. By welfare state, I mean something beyond the usual narrow concept: *government as helper of the poor*. The modern welfare state differs radically from that. It touches all of us, providing us with benefits of various types and claiming a huge part of our incomes. It creates a vast web of dependency on government that is the ultimate source of huge budget deficits and, quite perversely, distrust of government.

. . . we have no public philosophy by which to judge government. By public philosophy, I mean widely shared beliefs about what government should—and should not—do. . . . In an arithmetic sense, the budget deficits result from our over-optimistic economic assumptions and a loose concept of government. . . . But in a larger sense, the deficits stem from an inadequate public philosophy. We lack the popular consensus that would enable the political process to cut some spending programs—because they're not deemed worthy of government support—and raise taxes to cover the rest. . . .

Sooner or later, we need to come to terms with the welfare state. We need more rigorous standards for judging whose welfare is being advanced and why. As it is now, the welfare state is too big and intertwined in our social fabric for conservatives to dismantle. But it is too expensive and unpopular for liberals to expand endlessly. The irony is that the welfare state arose in the 1930s as an antidote to the insecurities of free markets. More than 50 years later, it has itself become a wellspring of anxiety and contention."

Source: Robert J. Samuelson, "Clinton's Nemesis," *Newsweek*, 1 February 1993, 51; "Our Love-Hate Relationship with Government," *The Washington Post*, 27 January 1993, p. A19.

Roosevelt decided to solve his problem by embarking on one of his famous conservation tours and taking Hopkins and Ickes with him. For nine days and nights the trio wound their way by train and automobile through the American countryside, inspecting dam sites, forestry projects, and other New Deal undertakings. At every opportunity, Roosevelt lavished public praise on his two associates and played up their importance in his administration. Every night he sat down with them for a poker game. By the time the presidential party arrived back in Washington, the rumors of the feud were dissolving.

The steady stream of news and pictures of the men standing shoulder to shoulder had worked. And, in fact, the two men appeared to have ended the junket on much better terms. One administrator had solved a pressing problem. Roosevelt used a great deal of artistry and imagination in dealing with this situation. Yet he was not creating a work of art; he was resolving a difficult problem. He was not acting as a scientist because what he did would not lend itself to concrete formulation. His solution, although it might provide some ideas for other administrators in similar dilemmas, certainly does not provide an all-embracing equation.

Public administration, then, requires a mixture of artistic and scientific elements. It uses artistry but is not an art. It uses science but is not a science. It is more properly thought of as a craft, seeking to achieve goals and to meet standards, and in so doing, often demanding all the creativity, capability, and civility that its harried practitioners can muster. In the current administrative state, the challenges of the craft of public administration are more demanding than ever before.

WHATEVER HAPPENED TO POLITICS?

Garry Wills, writing in *The New York Times Magazine*, concludes that "for two generations, Government elites defined the great issues. Now, a tidal change in the culture is sweeping away traditional geopolitics."[4] According to Wills, Washington is not where it's at. The vast majority of government employees do work at the state and local jurisdictions. Less than one in five government employees works for the federal government.

Wills offers the following insights for why politics is no longer serious.

- There are no great debates on the issues.
- Both the President and Congress seem like sailors in a dead calm.
- The current prosperity cannot explain a falling off of political debate that precedes it.
- . . . conservatives have won the political war but lost the cultural war. Politics with no cultural impact is a feckless exercise.
- This Establishment (agenda-setting elite) was not liberal but centrist.
- Religion was a private matter except when seen as a prop for the Establishment.
- The family, like religion, was a civil institution making for stability.
- Television brought alternative life styles into every living room.
- Conservatives like to treat the 60s as the end of civilization as we knew it, but the right, too, had a role in bringing a "marginal" cultural activity—religion—into politics.
- The restriction of politics to "the system," which meant primarily the electoral system, can no longer be enforced.
- But women's status changed, more than ever in human history, over the last three decades.
- The fall of the Soviet Union shattered the cold-war consensus on foreign policy.
- Real change—sweeping, unprecedented change—has not been taking place because of the electoral system. The electoral system is, instead, a lagging and imperfect indicator of such changes.
- Republicans, not Democrats, are our new superdemocrats, the defenders of elections as the sole arbiters of political life.
- . . . the old Establishment favored its own kind, excluding Jews or blacks or Catholics or Asians.

- . . . conservatives, in order to wrest short-term gains against affirmative action, have become strict meritocrats.
- The brightest side of American history has been the slow but persistent spread of egalitarianism.
- The civil rights movement is our modern epic, the great social achievement of our time.
- Not reporting the advances of feminism now would be like not reporting the Civil War in the 1860s because ending slavery had its unpleasantness.
- . . . whites will be a minority by early in the next century.
- Women will keep changing the shape of family life.
- People who deplore "rights politics" ain't seen nothin' yet.
- What is America as a social entity going to make of itself?

PARTISAN POLITICS, POLICY POLITICS, AND SYSTEM POLITICS

American government employees exercise their skills, knowledge, and expertise within the framework of Wills' insights into a fast-paced and ever-changing U.S. society. Three of the dynamic forces at work in our organized society are partisan politics, policy politics, and system politics. Partisan politics is concerned with which political party wins office. Policy politics deals with deciding which policies to adopt. System politics examines how administrative systems (decision structures) are set up.[5]

Public administration emphasizes two of the three forms of politics: policy and system politics. However, it originates from partisan politics. Minimum wage increases and tax cuts originated as Democratic and Republican partisan issues, respectively. Although the minimum wage is a core Democratic Party issue, moderate Republicans accept some version of the minimum wage as a legitimate policy. Members of both parties argue over what particular minimum wage policy may best be implemented by the Department of Labor. Although tax cuts are a core Republican Party issue, Democrats accept the notion that certain groups—students, the elderly, the disadvantaged—may need some tax incentives. Members of both parties argue over what particular tax reduction may best be implemented by the Department of Treasury. Therefore, the minimum wage and tax cuts are partisan, policy, and system issues.

Meanwhile, Social Security is mainly a policy and system issue. Social Security is usually not hotly debated in an election campaign because most politicians from both political parties accept the necessity of Social Security. Social Security is not a partisan issue. But the policy and system issues that arise from Social Security cause heated debates. In 1998, however, President Clinton advocated the financial solvency of Social Security over any proposed GOP tax cut. Policy politics, which provides the means for carrying out the strategic use of resources to alleviate problems, is an integral part of public administration.

REPUBLICAN "CONTRACT WITH AMERICA"

The ten-point platform for House Republicans, unveiled by then House Minority Whip Newt Gingrich (R-GA), and aimed at reviving former president Ronald Reagan's political agenda:

- **Propose** constitutional amendment requiring balanced federal budgets. Expand presidential power to veto budgetary line items.
- **Rewrite** recent crime bill to create law enforcement block grants, delete most crime prevention programs and add provisions to streamline death row appeals.
- **Revise** welfare to impose work requirements and two year limit on benefits, deny payments to teenage mothers and prohibit benefit increases for additional children.
- **Grant** tax benefits for adoption and dependent care. Require parents who do not make child support payments to work for state.
- **Grant** families $500 tax credit per child and ease tax burden on married couples. Expand uses and tax benefits available for Individual Retirement Accounts.
- **Restrict** funding and participation in United Nations peacekeeping. Deploy antiballistic missile defense, including "Star Wars."
- **Ease** taxes on upper-income and working recipients of Social Security. Create tax incentives to purchase insurance for nursing home and other long-term care.
- **Cut** and index capital gains tax. Loosen federal regulations and ban unfunded federal mandates on state and local governments.
- **Require** loser in frivolous lawsuits to pay legal costs of winner. Revise laws on liability for defective products.
- **Propose** constitutional amendments to limit terms of senators to twelve years and representatives to either twelve or six years.

Source: *The Washington Post,* 30 September 1994, p. A10.

In a nutshell, the intertwining of partisan, policy, and system politics works like this: citizens elect political partisans to public office; partisans establish regulatory, distributive, redistributive, and constituent policies; administrative systems implement policies adopted by partisans. System politics is the core of public administration.

Who's in Charge of Central Park?

Partisan, policy, and system politics are not separate, exclusive applications of the craft in practice. Politics to many is the "touchy, feely stuff"—the intangible relations among cronies, the ever-changing ways of doing the public's business. Things political may not mirror system accountability because in a public system everyone is accountable and yet practically no one is.

Central Park in New York City is a public park. Located in the middle of Manhattan, the park runs from 59th Street to 110th Street, from 5th Avenue to 8th Avenue. In the midst of some of the most expensive private real estate in the world, the park somehow survives the marketplace values of New York City. Central Park affords the citizens of New York a wide variety of playgrounds, bicycle paths, wooded areas, jogging paths, swimming pools, picturesque lakes, and other natural scenery. The facilities of Central Park are offered to the public on a first come, first served basis.

Who's in charge of Central Park? Are the politicians in charge? Are the police in charge? Are the bureaucrats from the parks department in charge? These types of questions demonstrate the subtleties of how politics shapes life in the public sector. Similar analogies may be made to federal lands, state parks, and municipal buildings. So who is really responsible for the upkeep of the facilities of Central Park? In a general sense, the people of New York are responsible. In a more direct way, the New York parks department, the police, and the mayor are responsible because they are the custodians of this public interest.

Whereas the concept of political responsibility is often abstract, administrative aspects such as hierarchy, chain of command, unity of command, span of control, due process, regulations, rules, and even bureaucratic ineptness are more definitive and recognizable by citizens. Politics, in its varied definitions, may be vague to many citizens; on the other hand, citizens have concrete experiences with bureaucracies.

How is the study of public bureaucracy different from the study of elections, executives, legislatures, or the courts? The study of bureaucracy focuses upon obeying authority; the study of elections, executives, legislatures, or the courts relates to the institutionalizing of democratic values. The study of public administration tells us what actually happens to policies after enactment by legislatures and approval by executives.

Decisions by government officials, representing departments and agencies, reflect the policy and system politics that occur in public bureaucracies. Such decisions are monitored by political partisans within the framework of majority rule and minority rights.

LEGALISM

On a visit to the United States in 1830, France's Count Alexis de Tocqueville was startled by the prominence of lawyers and the predominance of legal processes. He noted with amazement how in the United States nearly every political issue of importance ends up in a courtroom. This tendency has not abated, but instead has accelerated in the century and a half since de Tocqueville's visit. This country harbors two-thirds of the world's lawyers, while its courts have extended their reach into nearly all areas of political life. Judges now decide not only major policy disputes but also minor details of

---

YEAR 2000 LEGAL PROBLEMS?

State governments face potential legal issues and the problem of retaining staff as they address the year 2000 transition. States worry that suits could be filed over missing benefit checks or traffic lights that do not work properly. Governments also have to be wary of the documents they circulate about the problem. Any memo that points out potential system failures can be used in court to show that a state did not fix the problem even though it knew of it. States IT managers should meet with legal advisors to determine how they themselves and their states could be sued.

Nevada is taking an unusual step and has passed a law that claims the year 2000 problem is comparable to an act of God, so the state cannot be sued for related problems. The state claims that taxes pay for the computer fix and would have to be increased to pay for a lawsuit. States have a hard time recruiting staff because private companies can pay more.

Source: Patrick Thibodeau, "Year 2000 Legal Issues, Staffing Are Top Worries of State CIOs," *Computerworld*, 31, no. 41 (13 October 1997): 29.

---

policy execution. The 1970s saw a federal judge in Boston determine how many basketballs a local high school may have and another federal judge in Alabama determined the right temperature for hot water in a state mental hospital. In no other land do the bench and bar figure so formidably in the workings of everyday life.

The consequences of this state of affairs for public managers are many and great. Public administration by its nature enjoys, or suffers (depending on one's point of view), a close relationship with the law. Laws set up public agencies, prescribe and proscribe agency activities, and supply agencies with resources. The relationship has become much closer. David Bazelon notes that "as the constitutional right to due process of law expands, more and more administrators will find themselves locked into an involuntary partnership with the courts."[6]

For most administrators that time has arrived, and the partnership is not only involuntary but unpleasant. Although at times they look to and depend on the courts to help them dispose of disruptive issues or to back them up on controversial matters, in most instances they view the court's role in their affairs from a quite different perspective. To the average administrator, the increasing legalization of the U.S. policy has meant harassment and hindrance in the fulfillment of administrative responsibilities.

Reductions in the size of the executive branch of the federal government have so far passed over the lawyers, whose numbers have increased. In 1993, the executive branch had 2,200,000 workers, 17,557 of them lawyers. The Internal Revenue Service, Department of Justice, and Securities and Exchange Commission employ the most lawyers, and all have increased legal staff.

ADVERSARIAL LEGALISM

Compared to other economically advanced democracies, the United States is uniquely prone to adversarial, legalistic modes of policy formulation and implementation, shaped by the prospect of judicial review. While adversarial legalism facilitates the expression of justice—claims and challenges to official dogma—its costs are often neglected or minimized.

A survey of existing research indicates the extent to which adversarial legalism causes (or threatens) enormous dispute-resolving costs and procedural delays, which in turn distort policy outcomes. Adversarial legalism, moreover, has increased in recent decades, as Americans have attempted to implement the ambitious, socially transformative policies of activist government through political structures, forms of legislation, and legal procedures that reflect deep suspicion of governmental authority.

Source: Robert A. Kagan, "Adversarial Legalism and American Government," *Journal of Policy Analysis & Management,* 10, no. 3 (summer 1991): 369–407.

However, further reductions will include more pink slips, which may start targeting attorneys.[7]

One need not roam too far or wide to find reasons for such sentiments. The hiring and firing of employees, the purchase of equipment, and the adoption or even adjustment of a simple operational guideline have produced costly and frustrating litigation. To activist administrators, the law and its practitioners often seem to exist merely to tie their hands. Aggravating the problem for many public administrators is that their craft is becoming increasingly result-oriented. This contrasts sharply with the legalistic approach, which stresses the correctness of procedure. To the legal mind, justice is not a product but a process.[8]

Public administrators rely on, and are vulnerable to, the law. Legalism in general, and laws in particular, tend to limit and influence the operation of a public institution much more than they do a private one. "This pervasive legal context is among the principal distinctions between public and private enterprise," note John M. Pfiffner and Robert Presthus. "In private management one is assured that he can do anything not specifically forbidden. In public administration, on the other hand, discretion is limited by a great number of laws, rules, and regulations."[9] To put it more succinctly, in private administration the law generally tells administrators only what they *cannot* do; in public administration, the law tells them what they *can* do.

The legal limitations placed on public agencies contribute to or create many of the other differences between them and private enterprise. As illustrated, government organizations must usually operate in a goldfish bowl, subject to scrutiny from politicians, the public, and the press. They must be ready to open

---

LAWSUIT.COM

The Internet is facilitating increasing numbers of lawsuits. In fact, with the 49 million American Internet users expected to double by the year 2000, according to Jupiter Communications, the number of litigations via the Internet is bound to multiply. Angry consumers who are frustrated with combatitive efforts against large, unresponsive enterprises are finding solace in the Internet's simplicity. These consumers are hooking up with other angry buyers who have also been unsuccessful in obtaining customer satisfaction and in turn with lawyers to force companies to listen to their gripes.

Many law firms are even programming their Web sites to accommodate key word searches for phrases such as personal injury and toxic chemical lawyer. While lawyer's Web sites must comply with legal services advertising rules, state bar associations treat the Internet comparably to billboard and television advertising and require only that the information be factually correct.

Source: Susan Adams and David Lipschultz, "Lawsuit.com," *Forbes*, 160, no. 12 (1 December 1997): 47–49.

---

their doors and their books to almost any outsider, even though the outsider's interest in the agency may be prompted by no more than idle curiosity.

The legal context within which the public sector functions also helps explain why its employees usually enjoy greater rights—and face greater obligations. Public agencies frequently possess less flexibility than private ones. The public organization must hold itself accountable. *Responsiveness* and *responsibility* are the hallmarks of public administration in a democratic society.[10]

THE CRAFT AND THE AMERICAN POLITICAL SYSTEM

The craft of public administration is influenced by factors other than partisan, policy, and system politics and legalism. Our republican form of government, federalism, separation of powers, and constitutionalism—all of which will be discussed on the following pages—help put the craft into a larger perspective. Much is said pejoratively about public bureaucrats and their perceived power to operate without constraints in the American political system. However, a public administrator receives his or her authority for administrative decision making from certain constitutional principles. What are these constitutional principles?

C. Herman Pritchett cites four constitutional principles, embodied in the document signed September 17, 1787, that influence the lives of Americans every day.[11]

First, the Constitution established a *republican* form of government. Many Americans hold on to their grade school conceptions of democracy in America, believing that we have a democratic form of government. We do have a democratic philosophy of government; however, the structure of our government is republican. What *is* a republican form of government? Simply stated, we send representatives—legislators and executives—to city hall, the general assembly, Congress, the governor's mansion, and the White House because it would be impractical for all citizens to vote and decide public policy on every issue. Although Article 4 of the Constitution guarantees "a republican form of government," the definition thereof was left open-ended for future generations of Americans. Democratic values characterize our system of periodic elections; however, once elected, politicians select administrative leaders, using values of bureaucracy—such as specialization, hierarchy, chain of command, authority, and so on—to get legislative mandates implemented by public and private organizations. Elected leaders, employing bureaucratic values, administer the collective will of a certain community of citizens, who may reside in a municipality, a state, or the nation.

Second, the Constitution created a *federal* system. The original U.S. government set up in 1776 was a confederation or a mere league of states in which each state retained its sovereign powers. Under the auspices of the 1787 Constitutional Convention in Philadelphia, the delegates formed a stronger central government that was to receive its authority from the people. Powers not transferred to the new national government were to be retained by the states. As the cornerstone of the U.S. governmental system, federalism encompassed a two-level structure of government that divided power between the central government and state governments, allocating independent authority to respective levels. The federal concept contributed to the eventual organization of Congress. The larger states, represented by Virginia, Massachusetts, and Pennsylvania, saw an advantage to the new political system. The smaller states, led by New Jersey, fearing the political reorganization, sought protection of their interests. By a narrow vote, the Convention agreed to equal state representation in the U.S. Senate with senators to be elected by the state legislatures. The House of Representatives would be elected directly by the people with its membership proportionate to the population of each state. The Seventeenth Amendment, ratified in 1913, transferred the franchise for electing U.S. senators to the people of the respective states.

The condition of U.S. federalism has been altered by political conflicts and economic crises. The Civil War ended the political aspirations of those who wanted a confederate political system, and the economic collapse of the 1930s brought down a dual form of federalism where states had been somewhat independent of the central government. Events culminating in the 1860s (Civil War) and 1930s (economic collapse) can be seen as signposts for a more centralized American political economy in the twenty-first century. The Civil War was a crisis in federalism, as its effects caused the influence of the states and political decentralization to decline. The Great Depression of the 1930s was also a crisis in federalism, as the effects of such an economic collapse resulted in the central government's intervention on behalf of the private economy. The Civil War and the economic depression had centralizing effects upon federalism. The federal government's influence expanded, as did the expertise, skills, and knowledge of public administrators. Contrary to what the name implies, the United States are far from united on matters of politics and economics. A lack of consensus among

Americans concerning political economy produces a corresponding lack of agreement on the development, implementation, and evaluation of public administration. Federalism, then, is the structure of politics in the United States.

Reelected in 1996, President Clinton continued the trend of passing some federal powers and programs over to the states, such as telecommunications. Legislation from 1996—decentralizing drinking water standards and the welfare system—showed that the relationship between the federal and state governments was being redefined. The next generation will face a renewed federal-state debate over such issues as the federal gasoline tax, the Superfund toxic waste cleanup program, federal highway funds, clean water standards, Medicare, and Medicaid. A new era of demographic federalism will emerge if the shift in federal-state relations observed during the 104th Congress continues. Demographic federalism makes the federal government accountable for the health and financial security of the elderly and disabled. The states will be responsible for human capital and programs for workers, families, and children. These changes will have a significant impact on decision-making concerning economic and social policies.[12/13]

Our political culture promotes diversity, not consensus. Many claim that the United States is in the midst of a "culture war" that deals with moral values and life-styles, but the primary attacks come from the political right and left while much of the public remains apathetic. This apathy stirs the activists to more stridency.[14]

The Constitution also advocates the *separation-of-powers* principle. Each branch of government is assigned a particular task: Congress makes the law, the executive branch administers the law, and the judicial system enforces and interprets the law. The separation-of-powers concept operates in tandem with the goal of limited government powers. Separation-of-powers doctrine restrains one branch from usurping the powers of the others; the limitation of government powers inhibits the national government from overpowering the rights of the states and restricts the intrusion of government into private lives. A system of checks and balances enables each branch to have some influence on the operation of the others. Congress regulates the kinds of cases to be heard by the Supreme Court and the Senate ratifies treaties and approves executive appointments. The president appoints federal judges and vetoes laws, but the Senate must approve of his judicial appointments. The courts pass judgment on the validity of executive acts and interpret congressional statutes. With these checks and balances in place, abuse of power is less likely.

Finally, basic to the concepts of republicanism, federalism, and separation-of-powers is the idea of *constitutionalism.* Constitutionalism includes such ideas as rule of law, representative institutions, and guaranteed individual liberty. Two important elements of American constitutionalism are majority rule and minority rights. What happens when people disagree? The answer customarily given is "majority rule." It is here, however, that we must exercise caution. If 51 percent of the people voted to put the other 49 percent into concentration camps, we would hardly call this an exercise in democracy. When we think of constitutional democracy in American political culture, therefore, we must think not only of majority rule, but also of minority rights. This tenuous balance between the wishes of the majority and the rights of the few enormously complicates democracy, especially for public sector managers who must carry out the majority's mandate while simultaneously safeguarding basic minority interests. Public administration in a democratic society is a delicate and difficult task, requiring its practitioners to possess generous amounts of tolerance and tact. Those lacking such capacities may well do better in other fields.

The majorities in the U.S. Senate after the 1992 and 1994 elections illustrate the roles of majority and minority. After the 1992 election, numerically the Democrats had the votes in Congress. Because of the rules, the majority can work its way more easily in the House of Representatives than in the Senate. In the Senate, regardless of which political party maintains a majority of U.S. senators, the leadership needs a sufficient number of senators to reach sixty to cut off debate. Until the magic number of sixty is reached, a minority of the minority can stall legislation. As the loyal opposition, the minority has responsibilities to offer amendments to the suggested programs of the majority.

As previously emphasized, public administration uses art and science, but is especially a craft. Considering public administration's grounding in constitutional principles incorporating majority rule and minority rights, the use of the term craft to refer to public administration is appropriate and realistic. With the limitations and diversity of constitutional guidelines, public administrators need to be "crafty."

In constitutional terms, then, public bureaucrats exercise power within the framework of a republican form of government, a federal system, the separation-of-powers principle, and constitutionalism. Federalism is the basis of the American constitutional system and American public administration. A constitution is federal when two levels of government rule the same land and people. Each level must have at least one area of action in which it is autonomous. There is some guarantee of each level's autonomy in its own sphere of influence. However, the character of federalism, or political power, has changed in the United States.

What is this change, and how has it affected public policy and administration? Americans commonly perceive that the federal government is powerful and that state and local jurisdictions have lesser influence and fewer responsibilities. The nation and states sometimes are seen as competitors, as they reflect diverse communities of citizens with a variety of economic, political, and cultural interests. As sovereign communities, states promote their own economic interests, seeking political advantage over each other; this sometimes results in a state public sector being able to offer a better quality of life to its citizens. For example, the "sunbelt" states, with lower wages and "right-to-work" laws, may try to lure "rustbelt" corporations to move south and west. All states seek foreign investments and, in this manner, they compete for such outside private investments as Japanese automobile companies. New investments boost the local economy, which provides more revenues for politicians to disperse as public services.

William S. Livingston illustrates three ways in which the changing pattern of modern federalism has affected political bureaucracy.[15] First, he describes a cooperative federalism where the *centralization of power* is not accompanied by the *centralization of governmental function*. The central government makes policy, then delegates the function of implementing this policy to other levels of government. Since the New Deal era, the decentralization of governmental function has followed the centralization of governmental authority and power. According to this perspective, state and national governments supplement each other and jointly perform a variety of functions. The federal food stamp program illustrates centralization of power with decentralization of administrative function.

Monies to finance the food stamp program are collected under the auspices of the federal purse and the sixteenth Amendment. Congress authorizes the Department of Agriculture to organize the food stamp program—to pen its varied regulations and to monitor its progress—but depends upon the county welfare offices in the fifty states for administration. So the national government, with its enlarged powers, supplements rather than supplants the performance of functions by the states and local jurisdictions.

After the 1998 elections, Republican state governors illustrated how the centralization of federal power is not accompanied by the centralization of government function. The 1998 elections gave powerful endorsements to GOP governors. Thirty-one Republican executives lead states that are home to approximately 70 percent of the U.S. population. Democrats control 17 state executive mansions including that of California, the nation's largest commonwealth. Former professional wrestler Jesse "The Body" Ventura scored a stunning third-party upset in Minnesota. The country's other independent governor is Maine's Augus King.

The Republican governors are increasingly known for their political moderation and administrative skills, knowledge, and expertise. This assembly of Republican state leaders includes Lincoln C. Almond (R.I.), George W. Bush (Tex.), Jeb Bush (Fla.), Paul Celluci (Mass.), John Engler (Mich.), Bill Owens (Co.), George E. Pataki (N.Y.), Tom Ridge (Pa.), John Rowland (Ct.), George H. Ryan (Ill.), Robert Taft (Ohio), Tommy G. Thompson (Wis.), and Christine Todd Whitman (N.J.). Asked to define his political philosophy, Thompson replied: "Activism—and common sense."

Republican governors differ on social issues that split the ranks of the GOP—including abortion rights. But no Republican governor offers legislation to abolish a woman's access to abortion. Despite cultural differences, GOP executives are almost uniformly activist in governing. Thompson and Engler instituted reforms in welfare and education. Whitman called for across-the-board tax cuts. Engler and Thompson are better known as policy innovators.

Abortion. School prayer. School choice. Welfare reforms. Health care. Tax cuts. Tax increases. Spending cuts. Activism. Common sense. After the 1998 Congressional returns favoring the Democrats, social and economic challenges as argued in the Gingrich "Contract with America" appear in no little jeopardy. However, it is too soon to say if the politics of the 1990s hold any significant changes in U.S. political culture.[16]

Livingston's second illustration of federalism affecting bureaucracy is that the American political party system is *highly decentralized*. Livingston concludes that the decentralization of power within the political parties enhances the decentralization of the political decision-making process and provides strength to federalism. The character of the parties lends support to federalism, and federalism, in turn, nourishes the decentralized character of the parties. According to Livingston, American political parties are decentralized in three ways:

1. As discrete units, local parties exist to pursue control over state and local governments. Political parties are free associations of citizens who wish to influence the expenditure of taxpayers' dollars.
2. Because local parties are organized at the "grass roots," national parties exercise only periodic and ineffective control over local parties.
3. Local parties exercise considerable control over national parties. National political conventions are organized by collectives of state and local political parties. Forces of the religious right, for example, have captured many GOP local party organizations and insisted that certain social issues, such as abortion, pornography, homosexuality, and prayers in public schools become priorities. The Republican National Committee (RNC) might think these concerns are divisive, but President Bush could not ignore the right wing's call for "family values."[17] These priorities originated at the grass roots of the GOP party structure. Political parties are private affairs; only public opinion constrains them.

Today, as Democrats are "stealing" Republican ideas, Republicans are "stealing" Democratic feelings. You can't walk down a hallway on Capitol Hill without bumping into a GOP representative waxing treacly his or her compassion for the underpriviledged. Each member touts his or her collection of community groups, which, he or she says, has had unbelievable success working with drug addicts/single parents/deadbeat parents. "We've got to show a little more soul," Ohio Representative John Kasich told reporters after the Republicans lost the 1996 budget fight.

The third, and final, feature that contributes to the increased vitality of modern day federalism is the diversity of *social values* in the United States. Livingston argues that the diverse people and values within a society determine the shape and character of political and governmental institutions.

Federalism, as an arrangement of political power, responds to the changing values of society. What are the social values of American society?

Ways of behavior differ from state to state. Some states allow lotteries; others do not. Some states are restrictive in cigarette and alcohol sales; others are not. Some states maintain tough environmental standards; others do not. Some states have taken firm positions against racial and sexual discrimination; others back off from this enforcement. These illustrations indicate that public bureaucrats will have considerable difficulty enforcing laws mandated by the U.S. Congress if support for such policies does not emerge from the grass roots throughout the nation. From affirmative action to speed limits, public administrators have difficulty implementing laws that people do not support. Public bureaucrats have been described as timid and ineffectual and at the same time power-seeking and dangerous. In reality, their influence depends upon the consensus of political support for government laws and programs. Cooperative federalism, the grass roots nature of the political party system, and the diverse social values of Americans require public bureaucrats to share power and responsibilities with federal, state, and local officials. Administrative federalism is the upshot of these political compromises.

BEHAVIORS, INSTITUTIONS, PROCESSES, AND POLICIES

There is no homogeneous conception of bureaucracy, but public bureaucracies operate in the administrative worlds of behaviors, institutions, processes, and policies.[18] These "worlds" significantly affect the professional lives of public administrators. The administrator is engaged in a *behavioral* world—an incredibly complex amalgam of personal needs, interpersonal relations, and small and large social groupings. The deportment, habits, and tendencies of men and women shape the context, structure, and function of the organizations in which they toil. As college students, your behavior toward professors, administrators, and alumni will affect the functioning of your college. Interests and actions do influence the institution.

The administrator also functions in an *institutional* world. Your college environment reflects the institution in which you study, in which your professors teach, and in which administrators implement various academic programs. Educational policies and procedures are institutionalized into an academic format that provides opportunities for students to achieve. The institution is a formally defined context in which administrators labor and to which a public organization's clientele respond. An institution's context shapes its policies and procedures for selecting, monitoring, and promoting its employees and delivering its services. Police, fire fighters, schools, libraries, and universities formalize and make routine their respective employee behaviors.

As the contexts change, so will the specifics of institutions and functions. For example, the spread of AIDS in the 1980s changed the context, structure, and function of the Department of Health and Human Services; likewise, terrorism influenced the operation of the Department of Defense. Behavioral characteristics of bureaucrats depict *people without organizations.* The legal and formal features of institutions and functions portray *organizations without people.*

U.S. public administrators work in a world of major *processes* as well. Communicating with employees and clientele, coordinating people and programs, motivating employees, and controlling reporting and budgeting procedures are examples of major processes of public management. Computer and electronic data-processing techniques are common to public managerial processes. Processes are a series of changes leading to some result or a series of operations. As students, you experience processes in seeking a college degree. Penalties occur if you fail to register for classes on time, fail to pay your tuition on time, fail to arrive at class on time, fail to study effectively, or fail to meet prescribed academic deadlines. In many respects, the college experience is a process for organizing your goals and objectives.

Development, implementation, and evaluation of public *policies* constitute the fourth major world of the public administrator. Individuals, affiliated with small and large groups, can influence the policies and procedures of formal organizations, which affect the major functions of agencies. Students, as clientele, may influence the policies adopted by their college or university. Administrators and professors respond to your individual and collective behaviors as consumers of education by changing policies, then processes, and, eventually, perhaps the institution. Successful administration includes the development, implementation, and evaluation of effective public policies.

SUMMARY

- *Administration* involves people, action, and interaction. It is a process in which human beings work toward common goals.
- The breakdown of government employees is 14.8 percent federal, 24.2 percent state, and 61.0 percent local. By implication, the impacts of federal government budget cuts will be felt most acutely at state and local jurisdictions, not in Washington.
- Public administration uses artistry but is not an art. It uses science but is not a science. It is more properly thought of as a *craft*, seeking to achieve goals and to meet standards, and in doing so, often demanding all the creativity, capability, and civility that its harried practitioners can muster.
- We have *no public philosophy* by which to judge government. There are no widely shared beliefs about what all levels of U.S. governments should—or should not—do. Sooner or later we must come to terms with the welfare state. We need more rigorous standards for judging whose welfare is being advanced, and why.
- With the emergence of frequent *political dysfunction* in Washington, states, counties, cities, and special districts are political jurisdictions where U.S. governments are being revitalized, restructured, and refocused as locations for more effective solutions of problems.
- Public administration involves elements of *policy and system politics* but originates from *partisan politics.*
- Public administrators rely on, and are vulnerable to, the law.

- *Legalism* tends to limit and influence the operations of public institutions more than it limits private institutions. In private administration, laws usually tell administrators only what they *can't* do. In public administration, laws tell administrators what they *can and can't* do.
- The U.S. Constitution established a *republican form of government* and created a *federal* system. It also advocates the *separation-of-powers* concept and encourages rule of law, representative institutions, and individual liberty. Public administration is grounded in *constitutionalism*.
- *Centralization* of power in U.S. federalism is not accompanied by the *centralization of governmental function.*
- Federalism is also tempered by the diversity of *social values* in the United States.
- The "worlds" of behaviors, institutions, processes, and policies significantly affect the professional lives of public administrators. In the next chapter, we will examine the environment in which public administrators practice their craft. The following case study shows how behaviors, institutions, processes, and policies apply to the suburban-urban crisis after the Los Angeles riots. The case is analyzed in the framework of partisan, policy, and system politics and within contexts of "fend-for-yourself" federalism, legalism, and political culture.

CASE STUDY

America's Suburban-Urban Crisis and the Los Angeles Riots

Police power is the heart and soul of any society. The police are on the cutting edge of change. As economic, social, and cultural values change, the police are commissioned to enforce the evolving mores of modern society. Public school teachers, fire fighters, sanitation workers, street repair crews, and public bus drivers constitute the core of the public sector players, but the power of the police to interpret and enforce laws is preeminent among local and state government functions.

This heart and soul is a reflection of its societal context, and in this country even police power must answer to democratic principles. The credibility of local police power rests on constitutional rule of law. Majority rule and minority rights form a tenuous balance in the application of police functions. The states delegate police powers to counties, municipalities, and other special districts for implementation. The police power is centralized in each state's executive branch, but state governments delegate police functions to local governments.

The dynamics leading up to the brutal beating of African-American Rodney King in the early hours of March 3, 1991, test the political consensus of the American federal system. Police power is carried out within the social values of each state, and no police action can be isolated from its cultural environment. Political culture—the particular pattern of orientation to political action in which each state's political system is embedded—plays an important role in the use of police power. The Los

Angeles Police Department (LAPD) operated within the greater framework of the political cultures of Los Angeles, southern California, and the United States. How did the political culture of southern California contribute to the outbreak?

Racism, for both whites and blacks, is among the most troubling and dysfunctional problems confronting U.S. society. The prelude to the Los Angeles riots and its aftermath illustrate the essential elements of the art, science, and craft of public administration. What role did federalism play? How did the awkward relationship between the national government, states, counties, and cities contribute to the crisis in Los Angeles? How were partisan, policy, and systems politics manifest? How did the laws, rules, and regulations of the United States, California, and city of Los Angeles affect the outcome? How were republicanism and constitutionalism reflected in this crisis? What role did social values play? What behaviors, institutions, processes, and policies preceded the outbreak of the Los Angeles riots after the acquittal of the four police officers?

Brian Duffy captured the essence of the suburban-urban crisis in Los Angeles and the nation in the following perspective:

> *Changes in social attitudes during the past two decades, including faltering commitments to families and jobs, have had a doubly deleterious impact in many poor urban areas. No one, after all, forced individual rioters to loot—and most neighborhood residents refused to participate. In the years ahead, if demography is destiny, Los Angeles could be in for even more trouble. As in other big cities, demographic projections through the end of the decade suggest that population growth will far outstrip job growth, further inflaming racial tensions. In the ghettos, "jobs, jobs, jobs" is more than a campaign slogan.[19]*

Suburban-urban crisis: the behaviors

The 1992 riots occurred in a historical context. The cultures of racism, police brutality, white fears, high unemployment, widespread poverty, poor schools, drug peddlers, middle-class ambivalence, political indifference, and criminal mentality led to a hopelessness that erupted when LAPD officers Laurence Powell, Theodore Briseno, and Timothy Wind, supervised by Sgt. Stacey Koon, were found "not guilty" of beating citizen King.[20]

On that fateful night, motorist King was encircled by members of the LAPD after a high-speed chase, forced out of his car, and beaten by LAPD officers. Unknown to the officers, their behavior was recorded by a white citizen as he witnessed the beating from his nearby apartment. The video captured eighty-one seconds in which King was kicked by the officers, jolted by a stun gun, and struck fifty-six times with nightsticks. This incident led to a trial of the four LAPD officers in predominantly white, prosperous, and suburban Ventura County. The jury acquitted the officers on April 30, 1992, finding that no excessive force had been used.

Riots erupted in the south central area of Los Angeles immediately after the surprise verdict. Before the violence abated, more than fifty persons had died, thousands were injured and arrested, and billions of dollars of private and public infrastructure damage resulted from the fires and looting. A communications breakdown and shortage of ammunition kept the first 2,000 National Guard troops in their barracks during the initial outbreak of violence. The police were likewise tardy in responding to the widespread outbreak of violence.[21]

The suburban policy agenda was illuminated in the glare of the urban Los Angeles fire storms as well. Although Los Angeles is just one of many municipal jurisdictions in the nation's largest state, the riots brought the issues of race, employment, fairness, opportunity, and hope to the attention of all Americans.

There appeared to be little consensus among Caucasians, African-Americans, and Asian-Americans regarding the causes or solutions to the crisis in Los Angeles or the widespread urban dilemmas it exemplified. The King verdict and riots underscore the racial and ethnic divisiveness, economic stratification, and cultural decline confronting suburban and urban America. "The social consensus is breaking down in the 1990s," writes William Schneider. "Urban America is facing extreme economic pressure and the loss of political influence. The cities feel neglected, and with good reason: they are the declining sector of American life. Just as the Populists of the 1890s exalted the rural myth, urban leaders of the 1990s are trying to glorify the urban myth."[22]

A move to suburbia has permitted citizens to choose "the private" over "the public" to afford their own government. The riots in urban Los Angeles interrupted the privacy of the suburbs.

Suburban-urban crisis: the institutions

In the best sense, the United States is a "welfare state." In other words, the government promotes the "welfare" of its citizens. The government—meaning governments at all levels—promotes the health, education, safety, opportunity, and hope for a better future for Americans, regardless of sex, race, religion or national origin.[23] The institutions or government bureaucracies involved *directly* in this suburban-urban dilemma were the county police and state court system. The federal Departments of Agriculture, Health and Human Services, Housing and Urban Development, Labor, and California and Los Angeles agencies administering federal programs were more *indirectly* involved in the delivery of economic opportunities to the citizens of South Central Los Angeles. The LAPD and Ventura County court were *active* and *passive* institutional participants in the case of citizen King.

As a private citizen, the law specified only what King could *not* do. He could not drive his car at an excessive speed nor could he operate his vehicle while intoxicated. As public administrators, however, Los Angeles police officers are governed by rules and regulations grounded in laws enacted by the California state legislature and approved by its governor. The law prescribed to these officers precisely what they could do if they arrested King.

The Ventura County court system's participation in this public administration case could also be characterized as passive. The county court, a legal jurisdiction of the State of California, was a passive instrument in that no government official connected with Ventura County sought out the King-LAPD trial for its community of California citizens. The law permits such trials to be venued from the county in which the alleged violations occurred to a jurisdiction where the attorneys for the defendants believe their clients may receive a more receptive, if not fair, trial.[24] The attorneys for the four LAPD officers convinced Judge Stanley Weisberg to move the controversial court proceeding to the dry hills of Simi Valley, an overwhelmingly white, middle-class community thirty-five miles northwest of downtown Los Angeles.

In Ventura, the attorneys for the LAPD officers negotiated for a jury that was more understanding of their plight. The jury consisted of an even number of men and women, ranged in age from thirty-eight to sixty-five numbered ten whites, one Hispanic, and one Filipino (no blacks), and represented a political culture different from that of South Central Los Angeles.

South central LA and the simi valley typify the urban-suburban divide

South Central LA is overwhelmed with poverty and criminality, gangs of youths gone astray if not mad, and a growing variety of ethnic cultures that live in tense proximity. There is certainly more fear than hope for economic renewal of this blighted urban community. The Simi Valley, site of among other things, Ronald Reagan's Presidential Library, has a population of 100,000, 80 percent of which is white, 13 percent Hispanic, 5 percent Asian, and 2 percent African-American. The valley is a bedroom community for thousands of law enforcement officers where the average price of a home is $250,000. To no one's surprise, the citizens of Simi Valley vote overwhelmingly Republican and consider their community a refuge from the gangs, crime, high housing prices, and minorities of Los Angeles.

As indirect institutional participants, the federal departments of Agriculture (USDA), Health and Human Services (HHS), Housing and Urban Development (HUD), and Labor (DOL) implement policies enacted by the U.S. Congress over decades. State and local government agencies assisted these federal departments in implementing a variety of programs to benefit the citizens of South Central LA. The USDA carries out the food stamp program. HHS implements Aid to Families with Dependent Children (AFDC) and Medicaid. AFDC is a cash-assistance program for the poor; Medicaid is a means-tested medical plan for the poor and disabled. HUD administers criteria for establishing urban enterprise zones, urban homesteading, and housing subsidies. The DOL supervises employment and training prerogatives.

The "fend-for-yourself federalism" philosophy of the 1980s contributed to the political culture that resulted in police brutality as well as the LA riots. Competition, not cooperation, was the approach of "fend-for-yourself federalism." Diversity, competitiveness, and resiliency were to provide choices and stabilization by allowing state and local governments to fend for themselves. Were not local, state, and federal governmental institutions set up to work for the citizens of South Central LA?[25]

President Bush showed little interest in urban policy and said almost nothing about racial injustice or the plight of the underclass. "They are not our issues," said a senior Republican strategist. After the riots, the citizens of South Central LA had to fend for themselves. Bush, who committed the United States to fight a war in the Middle East, did not commit the country to fight a war against poverty in South Central LA. "Fend-for-yourself federalism" illustrates an institutional dilemma in federalism—the structure of politics in our state and nation. Gridlock between Congress and the president, no commitment by the richer states to assist the poorer ones, and lack of presidential leadership concerning poverty, racial tension, and economic blight shows how institutions of U.S. federalism impact the suburban-urban crisis.

Suburban-urban crisis: the processes

The rule of law is based on process. Public or government organizations, grounded in law and funded by taxpayers, must find ways to hold themselves accountable. Governments attempt to respond to the public's demands for accountability through the processes instituted in law-based rules and regulations. Legal restrictions and restraints are placed upon all activities of the LAPD that give its activities credibility and accountability to the public. The urban agenda, however it is defined, is based upon the rule of law.

The various government programs are also grounded in process. The USDA, HHS, HUD, and the DOL implement laws enacted by the U.S. Congress. Government programs are developed based upon laws and federal appropriations for financing those programs. Processes such as applying for food stamps (USDA), welfare (HHS), housing subsidies (HUD), and job training (DOL) create mechanisms for carrying out those laws and programs. In Los Angeles, looters were apprehended and prosecuted according to the criminal justice system established by the U.S. Department of Justice and attorney general of California. When looters were caught, they were processed through the criminal justice system. Rules and regulations abound in California's jury selection process. Only six African-Americans were present among 400 citizens in the array of likely candidates to serve on the King-LAPD trial jury. In the process for transferring the venue of the King case from Los Angeles to Ventura County, the attorneys for the defense realized the low likelihood of having African Americans on the jury in a county that was only 2 percent black. The prosecutor, defense attorneys, and judge were concerned about violating processes, developed based on rules and regulations, grounded in laws passed by state and federal legislatures.

Government programs, if nothing else, are a maze of "dos and don'ts" based on process. The process is governed by rules and regulations guiding the implementation of government programs. The looter is told that he or she cannot steal. Stealing is against the law. In apprehending the looter, however, law enforcement officials are required to follow processes in accomplishing their assigned duties.

Suburban-Urban Crisis: The Policies

Public policies in the United States may be traced in a large part to their roots in the Great Depression and the New Deal of the 1930s.[26] Federal government activities in antipoverty programs like the Social Security Act of 1935 date back to Franklin D. Roosevelt's New Deal. These programs still structure U.S. welfare policy. The most controversial part of welfare policy came much later however. Aid to Families with Dependent Children (AFDC) was established in 1962 and has caused contention since its inception.

AFDC is a joint national and state program. Depending on state poverty levels, the feds pay 50 percent of the administrative costs and up to 83 percent of the benefits. Cash benefits are paid to families where the parents are unemployed or disabled or if the child is without a parent in the home. Problems arose in this case as the economy of Los Angeles and the nation changed in the 1980s, and government policies were not reformed to confront the changes in the family structure of the underclass.

President Lyndon Johnson responded to the urban crisis of the 1960s by recommending a policy, grounded in the Economic Opportunity Act of 1964, to

---

CLINTON URBAN AGENDA

In President Clinton's first term (1993–1997), his most important efforts for the cities involved obscure actions that attracted almost no media attention:

- invigoration of the law requiring banks to provide credit to low-income communities;
- tougher enforcement of fair-lending statutes; and
- the funding of new subsidies to encourage businesses and nonprofit community development banks to enlarge their operations in depressed inner city neighborhoods.

Source: Ronald Brownstein, Washington Outlook; "National Perspective," *The Los Angeles Times*, 27 January 1997, p. 5.

---

develop a Job Corps program in which unemployed youths between the ages of sixteen and twenty-one would move away from home to residential centers to learn job skills and gain work experience. Another program resulting from these policies is Head Start, a pilot program to help prepare poor children for school, formalized in 1965. Head Start survived the massive cuts in federal spending for the inner cities during the 1980s.

The Reagan administration argued that the Great Society programs of the 1960s were misguided at best. The taxpayers dollars were being wasted, and the poor were not lifting themselves out of poverty. Funding for many of these programs was drastically cut or eliminated. The middle class had little patience with the lawless conditions existing in many poor neighborhoods and hardly anyone objected when the poor had their food, health, housing, and job creation subsidies curtailed or abolished. The middle-class taxpayer had little interest in the need for a solution to the urban crisis in places such as South Central LA until the looting began and the fires broke out.[27]

Jack Kemp, HUD Secretary under President George Bush, responded to the urban problems of the 1990s by shifting the direction of policy-making away from government intervention and toward solutions in the private sector. The Republicans favored tax incentives that encouraged businesses to open or relocate in impoverished areas of the nation's cities. Kemp advocated the reestablishment of Urban Enterprise Zones.

President Bush, however, vetoed a $700 million demonstration plan to create ten urban and rural enterprise zones because the Congressional Democrats failed to include a capital gains tax provision if or when a business was sold. Partisan gridlock between the President and Congress again contributed to the lack of political solution to the problems faced by those living in blighted areas of the nation's cities.

Suburban-urban crisis: behaviors, institutions, processes, policies, and political consensus in the 1990s

What do we learn about the practice and principles of public administration from the LA riots? With declining political leadership in meeting urban problems and in the face of federal and state budget cuts, local, state, and federal government officials (public administrators) must be "crafty" in the evaluation, development, and implementation of solutions for the suburban-urban crisis. Public administrators use science (technology) to better understand the challenges confronting the community. In the 1990s, however, public administration in the United States is primarily an art and craft.[28] What role did federalism play in the Los Angeles riots? The theme of federalism in the 1980s was that governments must "fend-for-themselves" and not look to Washington for either financial assistance or political leadership. Among the powers of any executive, especially the presidency, is the power to persuade. Racism is historical, and in the 1990s, the fallout from racism is dysfunctional to all Americans. Americans, like citizens of any nation, learn a great deal from their leaders. The president of the United States is perhaps our most visible teacher. If the president cannot deliver monetary rewards through government programs to poor neighborhoods, he can teach principles of justice and opportunity. Recent administrations, however, have considered the inequities of the inner cities "not our issues."[29] The power of the presidency to promote justice and equality was not used to its potential.

How did the political culture of southern California affect the King case and subsequent riots? "Culture" is defined as "that complex whole which includes knowledge, belief, art, morals, law, custom, and any other capabilities and habits acquired by man as a member of society."[30] The political culture of southern California is diverse, reflecting especially traditionalism and individualism, and less so moralism. In Los Angeles' cultural diversity of language, race, and economics, every community, neighborhood, and citizen must "fend-for-themselves." The social values of the Los Angeles metropolitan region are as diverse as any region of the country. The people, character, languages, ethnicity, institutions, economics, and governments of metropolitan LA reflect this social diversity.

The police have the power, grounded in law, to restrain citizens whom they perceive are not acting according to prescribed laws and norms using whatever means deemed reasonable in a given situation. In all probability, the LAPD officers beat King not because they hated him or his race, but because they feared him and the culture he represented. The police were protecting themselves from the unpredictability associated with the culture of poverty. The officers, however, were victims of "cultural lag." A unique application of video technology brought the official accountability of the LAPD officers into stark relief.

How did the laws, rules, and regulations of the United States, California, and city of Los Angeles affect the King case and the ensuing violence? The United States is divided into political jurisdictions, including states, counties, and cities. The law protects the rights of the accused and permits a venue change for cases involving community bias against the accused. The attorneys for the LAPD officers argued that a jury in suburban Ventura County would be more receptive to their interests than one in Los Angeles County. How were republicanism and constitutionalism reflected in this crisis? The United States is a republic, not a pure democracy. Politicians represent citizens of towns, cities, counties, states, and the nation indirectly, not directly. The idea of constitutionalism includes such notions as rule of law, representative institutions (republicanism), and guaranteed individual liberty. The awkward relationship between the national government, states, counties, and cities contributed to the fragmentation of government policies affecting the LA metropolitan area. The Los Angeles region is not governed by one political jurisdiction; it is governed by hundreds of towns, cities, counties, and the state of California.

William Bennett, former drug czar and education secretary, argued: "The broader issues raised by Los Angeles are the real substance of politics: justice, right and wrong, and how we should live together. The economy and jobs may be the engine of society, but what happened in L.A. is about its soul."[31] The King case and the LA riots illustrate partisan, policy, and systems politics. The criminal justice system is a system governed by processes and grounded in policies enacted by elected political officials. The federal domestic institutions (USDA, HHS, HUD, DOL, DOJ) implement urban policies written into legislation by elected officials over many decades, but these laws alone will not result in citizens changing their behavior.

Attitudes of citizens are influenced by partisan political leaders. Of these leaders, the president is in the best position to persuade citizens to be more responsible, realistic, and humane about justice, right and wrong, and how Americans should live together. Scholars, ministers, human rights advocates, and residents of Los Angeles' arson-scarred and riot-torn neighborhoods almost unanimously agree that the violence sparked by the acquittal of four LAPD policemen in the beating of Rodney King had been simmering for almost thirty years. If social conditions fail to change for the better they say civil unrest will happen again.[32] Let's hope that the King-LAPD case and Los Angeles riots are not the "soul" of partisan, policy, and systems politics in the United States. We cannot afford what historian Arthur Schlesinger Jr. calls "the disuniting of America."[33]

Federalism, or the structure of American politics, allows for a dual court system. In a small federal courtroom in downtown Los Angeles in April, 1993, the jury found that Powell "did willfully strike . . . and kick and stomp Rodney Glen King," violating King's constitutional right "not to be deprived of liberty without due process of law, including the right to be . . . free from the intentional use of unreasonable force" by policemen. Briseno and Wind were found "not guilty" in the federal court. The federal jury found Koon, the officers' supervisor, "guilty" of willfully permitting the savage beating of King.[34]

QUESTIONS AND INSTRUCTIONS

1. Why and how is police power or police bureaucracy the heart and soul of any society?
2. Why are social values important in the public administration of police powers?
3. In the Rodney King-LAPD case, how should we allocate responsibility for the crisis? How much is King to blame for his behavior? How should we assign responsibility for these events to partisan, policy, and system politics?
4. Federalism is the structure of politics in the United States. How should this structure be modified to alleviate future crises of this magnitude? What roles should federal, state, and regional governments play?
5. In the twenty-first century, what role(s) should governments have in the public-private interface of citizens in society? What aspects of the "welfare state" should be retained in providing the basics of life—food, health, housing, work, protection, and justice?

6. Rank order and illustrate the significance of behaviors, institutions, processes, and policies for understanding why public officials and administrators responded to the violence in Los Angeles as they did.

7. What unique role did technology play in the prosecution of the LAPD officers? Why did the jury see events differently?

8. A crisis may be defined as both danger and opportunity. How do the crises of the King trial and riots reflect clear and present danger to U.S. society? In what ways is this crisis an opportunity for citizens and elected officials to learn from the past?

9. Is political consensus for providing food, health, housing, jobs, protection, and justice feasible in large metropolitan areas like Los Angeles?

10. Do political jurisdictions—towns, cities, counties, states, and nations—have souls?

INSIGHTS-ISSUES/AMERICA'S SUBURBAN-URBAN CRISIS AND THE LOS ANGELES RIOTS

Clearly and briefly describe and illustrate the following concepts, issues, or points. Interpret the word "role" as meaning impact, application, importance, effect and/or illustration of certain facts, concerns, or issues from the case study.

1. Role of American federalism (political jurisdictions).
2. Role of institutions (local, state, and federal agencies and departments).
3. Role of federal and state court systems (passive/active forces).
4. Role of partisan, policy, and system politics.
5. Role of crisis (short-term vs. long-term solutions).

ENDNOTES

1. U.S. Department of Labor, Bureau of Labor Statistics, *Employment and Earnings,* 42, no. 6 (June 1995), 69.

2. William I. Buscemi, "Numbers? Borrrinning!!!," *PS: Political Science & Politics,* no. 4 (December 1997), 738–739.

3. Herbert A. Simon, Donald W. Smithburg, and Victor A. Thompson, *Public Administration* (New York: Alfred A. Knopf, 1950), 3.

4. Garry Wills, "Whatever Happened to Politics? Washington Is Not Where It's At," *The New York Times Magazine,* 25 January 1998, 27+.

5. Aaron Wildavsky, *The Politics of the Budgetary Process* (Boston: Little, Brown, and Co., 1979), 191–193.

6. David Bazelon, "The Impact of the Courts on Public Administration," *Indiana Law Journal,* 52, no. 1 (fall 1976), 101–110.

7. Arleen Jacobius, "Lawyers Buck Downsizing Trend, Executive Branch Workforce being Reduced as Attorneys Are Added," *ABA Journal*, 81 (November 1995), 24.

8. See Alan M. Dershowitz in *The Best Defense* (New York: Random House, 1982). However, the same theme runs through many other statements and writings of legal authorities. Oliver Wendell Holmes, for example, once said that his job as justice of the U.S. Supreme Court did not require him to "do" justice but merely to see that the rules of the game were followed.

9. John M. Pfiffner and Robert Presthus, *Public Administration*, 5th ed. (New York: Ronald Press, 1967). In regard to the subsequent sentence in the text, Donald S. Vaughn, former chair, Department of Political Science, University of Mississippi, points out that the law also tells the public administrator what he or she cannot do. Professor Vaughn cites the first eight amendments to the U.S. Constitution as a case in point.

10. See Herbert J. Spiro *Responsibility in Government: Theory and Practice* (New York: Van Nostrand Reinhold Company, 1969). The author probes responsibility as obligation, accountability, and cause.

11. C. Herman Pritchett, *The American Constitutional System* (New York: McGraw-Hill Book Co., 1981), 7–8.

12. David Hosansky, "Reshaping The Federal-State Relationship," *Congressional Quarterly Weekly Report*, 54, no. 40 (5 October 1996), 2824–26.

13. Bert Waisanen, "Demographic Federalism: Defining the New Federal-State Relationship," *Spectrum: The Journal of State Government*, 69, no. 4 (fall 1996), 53–58.

14. Rhys H. Williams, "Is America in a Culture War? Yes—no—Sort Of," *The Christian Century*, 114, no. 32 (12 November 1997), 1028–1033.

15. William S. Livingston, "Federalism in Other Countries: Canada, Australia, and the United States," in *Federalism: Infinite Variety in Theory and Practice* (Itasca, IL: F. E. Peacock Publishers, Inc., 1968), 131–141.

16. Dan Balz, "Activist GOP Governors Become Role Models for New Republican Majority, *The Washington Post*, 26 November, 1994, page A6; James A. Barnes, "Where Republicans Rule," *National Journal*, 30, no. 43, 24 October 1998, pages 2484–2488; and John Maggs, "Wrestling with Failure," *National Journal*, 30, no. 45, 7 November 1998, pages 2614–2516.

17. The term "right wing" is elusive. Almost without exception, "right wingers" are traditional thinkers on nearly every issue, value, and behavior confronting partisan, policy, and system politics. For example, they hold traditional views on abortion, religion, adultery, women in the workplace, sexual orientation, military spending, taxes, economic disparity, and foreign policy involvements. Therefore, a better description might be traditionalists, not right wing or right wingers.

18. Robert T. Golembiewski, Frank Gibson, and Geoffrey Y. Cornog, *Public Administration: Readings in Institutions, Processes, Behavior, Policy* (Chicago: Rand McNally College Publishing Co., 1976), 1–10.

19. Brian Duffy, "Days of Rage," *U.S. News & World Report*, 112, no. 18, 11 May 1992, 21–26.

20. George J. Church, "The Fire This Time," *Time*, 11 May 1992, 18–25; Richard Lacayo, "This Land is Your Land . . . This Land is My Land," *Time*, 18 May 1992, 28–33; Harrison Rainie, "Requiem for the Cities?" *U.S. News & World Report*, 18 May 1992, 20–26; and Rochelle L. Stanfield, "Black Frustration," *National Journal*, 24, no. 20 (May 1992), 1162–1168.

21. David Ellis, "L. A. Lawless," *Time*, 11 May 1992, 26–29.
22. William Schneider, "The Real Meaning of the 1992 Election: The Suburban Century Begins," *The Atlantic*, 270, no. 1 (July 1992), 34. See also: "It Takes a Crisis to Prompt a Remedy," *National Journal*, 24, no. 21 (May 1992), 1270.
23. John Leo, "A New Deal for the Underclass," *U.S. News & World Report*, 25 May 1992, 29.
24. Ted Gest with Constance Johnson, "The Justice System: Getting a Fair Trial," *U.S. News & World Report*, 25 May 1992, 36, 38.
25. John Shannon, "The Faces of Fiscal Federalism," *Intergovernmental Perspective*, 14, no. 1 (winter 1988), 15–17. See also: "The Return to Fend-for-Yourself Federalism: The Reagan Mark," *Intergovernmental Perspective*, 13, no. 3/4 (summer/fall 1987), 34–37.
26. Julie Rovner with Kitty Dumas, Susan Kellam, and Jill Zuckman, "Rhetoric, Not Radical Change, Likely Result of L.A. Riots," *Congressional Quarterly Weekly Report*, 50, no. 19 (May 1992), 1247–1255.
27. Thomas Sancton, "How to Get America off the Dole," *Time*, 25 May 1992, 44–47.
28. Walter Shapiro, "Lessons of Los Angeles," *Time*, 18 May 1992, 38–39; and Mortimer B. Zuckerman, "The New Realism," *U.S. News & World Report*, 25 May 1992, 92, 94.
29. Kenneth T. Walsh and Joseph P. Shapiro, "They Are Not our Issues," *U.S. News & World Report*, 18 May 1992, 26.
30. See Leslie A. White, "The Concept of Culture," *American Anthropologist*, 61, no. 227 (April 1959).
31. William J. Bennett, "The Moral Origins of the Urban Crisis," *The Wall Street Journal*, 8 May 1992, p. A8.
32. Don Terry, "Decades of Rage Created Crucible of Violence, *The New York Times*, 3 May 1992, p. 1.
33. Arthur Schlesinger Jr., *The Disuniting of America: Reflections on a Multicultural Society* (New York: W. W. Norton, 1992).
34. George J. Church, "Cries of Relief," *Time*, 26 April 1993, 18–19.

2

THE ECOLOGY
OF THE ADMINISTRATIVE CRAFT

Chapter HIGHLIGHTS

OUR ORGANIZED SOCIETY

EQUALITY AND EFFICIENCY

THE SYNERGISTIC ENVIRONMENT

EBBS AND FLOWS OF GOVERNMENT EXPANSIONS, CONSTRAINTS,
AND PROSPECTS

THE GROWTH OF PUBLIC BUREAUCRACY

COMPARING PUBLIC
AND PRIVATE ADMINISTRATION NUANCES

INTEREST GROUPS AND PUBLIC BUREAUCRACY

A communications satellite peacefully orbits the earth, silently catching and throwing radio signals. There are no winds or rains or hailstorms to buffet the satellite and affect its operation. The satellite may be affected by a meteor or the debris from the icy tail of a comet, but the odds against such occurrences are astronomical. Usually, the satellite will operate unmolested in the vacuum of space.

Public administrators do not operate in a vacuum. There are countless environmental factors that buffet public administrators, making their tasks remarkably complex. Public administration cannot be separated from environmental factors as can the satellite. Public administration occurs within the framework of the organized society. The principle barriers to the effective implementation of public programs are the conflicts between the political principles of democracy and the economic principle of capitalism.

Public administration is also carried out within the political cultures of states and communities. Culture, tangible and intangible, affects the environment in which public administration takes place.

Ecology is the study of the relationships between organisms and their environments, and public administrators not acutely aware of how environmental factors influence administration are doomed to failure. This chapter describes the relationship between public administrators and the environment in which they work.

OUR ORGANIZED SOCIETY

A drive down Main Street, U.S.A., will take you past banks, dry cleaning establishments, cafes, and retail stores. Keep driving and you'll pass churches, shopping malls, fast food outlets, factories, gas stations, and schools.

All are examples of organizations that affect our daily existence. Organizations must be managed or administered. We live in a complex society in which public organizations are needed if the smaller, private organizations are to thrive or operate at all. The alternative is anarchy.

Public organizations receive their lifeblood from legislative, executive, and judicial collectives in our organized society. Legislatures appropriate revenues for funding public programs. Presidents, governors, and mayors carry out the legislative will of the people. Courts adjudicate disputes between parties contesting, among other things, the delivery of government programs.

With its numerous organizations, modern America is the epitome of the organized society. The legislative, executive, and judicial branches of national and state governments are the basic units of public organization. For example, the president and Congress enacted the policy of social security for the elderly; the Social Security Administration implements the policy; and judges decide disputed claims.[1]

For our society's organization, questions still arise concerning the fairness and efficiency of public organizations—questions that contribute to these organizations' administrative entanglements.

EQUALITY AND EFFICIENCY

American society professes equal opportunities for all citizens. Professing equal opportunity does not, however, guarantee that citizens will achieve equal results for their efforts. Your productive contribution in the competitive market depends on your skills, assets, and efforts and also on the supply of and demand for what you have to offer. As free speech does not guarantee an audience, free enterprise does not guarantee a demand for one's services. Effort does not guarantee excellence. Although a student studies long and hard for an exam, an "A" is not a foregone conclusion. It is easy to see that these factors, when applied to individuals in the marketplace, can result in unequal individual incomes.

Our organized society, therefore, exists in an environment of equal rights and unequal incomes. Conflicts between these two phenomena result in tensions between the *political principles of democracy* and the *economic principles of capitalism.*

The United States is a democratic society with a capitalistic economic system. In keeping with our democratic political philosophy, we hold elections. In keeping with our economic philosophy, we let supply and demand decide who achieves financial success. Arthur Okun describes contemporary U.S. society as a "split-level institutional structure" because of the combination of democracy and capitalism.[2]

We have a "split-level institutional structure" because private institutions value efficiency, while public sector institutions favor equality. Efficiency gives the top-producers priority, and equality gives everyone priority.

So the services provided by public administrators reflect the concept of *equality.* The concept of *efficiency* comes from letting the marketplace decide what goods and services are produced and purchased. Services and programs produced by governments are afforded to all citizens. Police, fire, and sewers are usually produced and provided by government. Electricity, water, gas, garbage, and telephone services, although regulated by government, may be produced and provided for privately. Even though electricity, gas, and telephone utilities are produced privately, the government regulates their activities to assure "fairness" of delivery.

The rich and the poor have equal rights to travel on our network of interstate highways. Economic realities of the efficient marketplace may determine, however, that certain people not have cars to drive and that others are able to cruise along the turnpike in chauffeur-driven Mercedes. A public program is not maintained for the very poor or the ultra rich, but for the masses of middle-class citizens. In that respect, America's highway system serves as an example of an efficient economy—the more we drive, the more road and gasoline taxes we pay. "With the great quarrel between capitalism and socialism in mothballs," says Suzanne Garment, "critics of the free market do not attack it by offering some grand, principled alternative. Instead, they march under the banner of prudence, calling for a pragmatic mixed economy that values markets but avoids the extremism preached by excessively principled free-market ideologues."[3]

TABLE 2–1 Contrasting Equality and Efficiency

Equality	Efficiency
fairness	advantage
socialism	capitalism
public	private
community	individualism
government	business
inductive	deductive
democracy	bureaucracy
mediocrity	excellence
employees	executives
rights	responsibilities
informal	formal
chaos	order
collective bargaining	merit
access	restricted
unorthodox	conventional
common	elite
equal opportunity	affirmative action
republic	fascism
elections	courts
horizontal	vertical
egalitarianism	authoritarian
tolerant	bigoted
incompetence	expertise
open	closed
leveler	hierarchy
modernization	traditionalism
decentralization	centralization
average	superior
diversity	homogeneity
Christianity	religion
April 15th	July 4th
Democrats	Republicans
Clinton	Gingrich
female	male
bottom-up	top-down

Note: These terms are neither all inclusive nor mutually exclusive as applied to American governments and politics. They are set off as discussion points in the ecology of American public administration. The mix of these concepts is witnessed in the development, implementation, and evaluation of government programs and functions.

The tax revenues provide funds for public administrators to implement highway maintenance policies and to have new highways built. Via interest group liberalism, citizens lobby elected officials to vote expenditures that will benefit their well-being. As the president and Congress attempt to cut federal spending, segments of the great middle class will conflict on what programs should be cut.

The values of equality and efficiency are always in conflict. The pursuit of efficiency necessarily creates inequalities. Citizens make economic choices, like buying a car or riding a bus. If we all choose to commute only by car, bus drivers will be out of work, the victims of our equal freedom of choice and the workings of our efficient economy. It is often the role of the public administrator to step in if one of these values begins to supersede the other. This is where the public administrator's regulatory powers come into play. Through these powers, public administrators exercise great influence in determining the appropriate role of the marketplace. The public administrator does not, however, have unlimited regulatory power. As regulators of private interactions, public administrators are checked by limits on administrative power spelled out in laws such as the Administrative Procedure Act.[4]

In defending the state of affairs that leads to the conflict between equality and efficiency, Okun says, "The market needs a place, and the market needs to be kept in its place."[5] The market is kept in its place by the limited regulatory powers of public administrators. So equality may be sacrificed for the sake of efficiency and efficiency for the sake of equality. What provisions exist to protect the individual's equal rights in this market-driven economy? The issue of economic decision making in the late twentieth century focuses on ensuring the right degree of mix between government and the private sector participation. A purely government-led or, vice versa a market-dictated economy, will be not only ineffective in economic terms but also social and political terms. The market is usually more efficient than the public sector although the latter is needed to ensure that the allocation of resources is balanced.[6]

American society promotes equality by maintaining social and political rights allocated equally and designed to be distanced from the marketplace of supply and demand. For example, due process is a constitutionally mandated guarantee that governments in the United States will act with fairness, justice, equity, and reasonableness, irrespective of economic considerations. Accused criminals seek fairness through due process in prosecution procedures. Equal opportunity is protected in a court of law by the constitutionally mandated accessibility of due process. Due process is the legal cornerstone of the craft of public administration.

There are two types of due process, *substantive* and *procedural. Substantive due process* refers to the content or subject of a law. *Procedural due process,* the more commonly litigated of the two, refers to the procedures used in implementing a law or administrative practice. Deciding whether a law is constitutional is part of procedural due process.

The concept of equality is also demonstrated in the open admissions policies of many state universities. These policies require a university to accept students from all ethnic groups and income levels. The taxpayers subsidize public education to guarantee fairness, justice, equity, and reasonableness in the admission of students. The state university must pay careful attention to due process. On the other hand, a private college is not required to follow due process as stringently as a public university. A private college may, with some restrictions, select only those students who meet certain criteria that may not be used at a state institution. Such an adoption of standards of excellence embraces the value of efficiency.

The value of equality is embodied in guarantees grounded in basic citizen rights. The value of efficiency is embodied in productivity. Public administrators operate in this complex environment—an environment in which two fundamental values of our society often collide. The challenge of public administration must be to maximize efficiency without sacrificing equality and vice versa.

THE SYNERGISTIC ENVIRONMENT

"Synergy" describes the action two or more people carry out together to accomplish a task that cannot be accomplished by an individual working alone. According to the Roper Organization Inc., publisher of the Roper Public Opinion Poll, synergism is a dominant force shaping the public policy environment of the twenty-first century. This synergistic environment entails more cooperative action among government, business, and labor to deal with fundamental social and economic problems.

In a synergistic environment, issues of fairness become more significant. Two crucial questions for our democratic and capitalistic society are where and how the organized modern society establishes boundaries between the *domain of rights* (equality) and the *domain of the capitalistic marketplace* (efficiency). Conflicts between these domains are inevitable and pose dilemmas for our split-level, political economy.

Our democratic, capitalist society searches continuously for better ways to clearly establish boundaries between the domains. The marketplace needs equality to put some *humanity* into *efficiency;* our democracy needs efficiency to put some *rationality* into *equality.* Capitalistic and bureaucratic systems will be more effective if they are more humane. Equality will be more acceptable to those who value efficiency, and hence, less chaotic, if standards of consistency are applied to the diverse applications of this crucial democratic principle.[7]

Democracy is characterized by equality, due process, fairness, participation, suffrage, and electoral politics. Capitalism implies efficiency, productivity, hierarchy, competition, and entrepreneurship. Public administration finds its origins in democracy but owes much to the fundamental principles of capitalism.

The modern organized society can also be described as a *political economy.* Our society is political in that citizens have the opportunity to organize and express their priorities about what is important to them. The "economy" part of the phrase comes from the collective productivity of goods and services our society generates. The split-level structure of the political and economic systems affects public policy and administration. Communities cannot expect public services to be provided without an ample supply of *revenues*, raised by taxing citizens and businesses. Our organized society, therefore, depends upon the political system and the structure of the economic sector. The maintenance of the relationship between political power and economic structure is vital to the future of American democracy. Public administrators depend upon capitalism to generate economic growth to pay their salaries and to finance the delivery of their services to the American people.[8]

The thrust of democratic capitalism comes from the opposing values of political power and economic structure. Those middle-class citizens who do not possess the means of economic production agree to the private ownership of capital stock; meanwhile, wealthy citizens, who own the instruments of economic production, accept democratic political institutions that allow opposing interest groups to press claims for further allocation of material resources and the distribution of labor's output. The large middle class permits members of the economic elite to own capital and organize production (the economy). The economic elite allows the political prerogatives of the general population to affect the allocation of resources and the distribution of the material effects of economic production.[9]

By the early 1990s, employees of federal, state, and local governments outnumbered factory workers. In 1991, the U.S. Bureau of Labor Statistics reported 18,410,000 government jobs throughout the United States. Manufacturing jobs in the United States decreased from 19,391,000 in 1989 to 18,388,000 by 1992. Meanwhile, federal, state, and local government jobs increased from 17,574,000 to 18,410,000.[10]

The taxpayers, or our children through deficit federal spending, must raise revenues to pay salaries and benefits for those government employees. The economic philosophy is that manufacturing jobs, not service sector jobs, are the core of any nation's political economy. We could argue that those government employees have a vested interest in deficit federal spending. After all, the Reagan-Bush years were devastating to public employees. A decrease of 1,000 employees occurred in federal employment from 1989 to 1992. However, the number of state and local employees increased by nearly one million, to 15.4 million. Since 1982, there has been a 20 percent growth in the workforces of state and local governments and an 8 percent increase in the federal workforce. The nation's industrial base is declining while demands for public services continue.

By the early 1990s, the American economy had undergone a fundamental restructuring. In 1980, the sector of the economy with the most jobs was manufacturing (20.2 million). By 1992, the sector with the most jobs was services (29 million).[11] Americans opt for "market justice" over "political justice" as benefits are allocated by the economic marketplace, not by government programs and policies.[12] American participation in politics has declined as citizens do not perceive their economic well-being as greatly dependent on political involvement.[13] U.S. cultural emphasis is on individualism, not political participation. Citizens separate their personal lives and interests from other matters of national life. America is the country of *individualism par excellence*.[14] This culture of individualism negatively effects political participation levels of lower-income groups. An economic class bias emerges. Citizens of higher economic status are much more involved politically than those of lower economic status.

EBBS AND FLOWS OF GOVERNMENT EXPANSIONS, CONSTRAINTS, AND PROSPECTS

The New Deal gave rise to the modern mix of federal, state, and local public bureaucracies. However, there are other milestones in America's history that can shed light on current problems and prospects for the administrative state of the 1990s. The retrenchment and decentralization efforts, authored by Richard Nixon and Ronald Reagan, were in response to measures initiated by Woodrow Wilson, Franklin Roosevelt (FDR), and Lyndon Johnson. A review of the ebbs and flows of government expansion and constraints gives us a solid historical base for understanding why government is the way it is. The dynamics behind growth of bureaucracy may be understood by examining four crucial periods in the twentieth century. These particular years signify eras of political economy in support of and in restraint of public bureaucracies.

These eras, which have had a lasting impact upon American society, occurred around *1915, 1935, 1965,* and *1985.*

1915: NEW FREEDOM

The public sector achieved significance as an important player in American political and economic life during the Wilson administration (1913–1921). The excesses of the private laissez-faire political economy needed reform. Large corporations were dominating the American economy. Wilson's legislative reforms, known as the *New Freedom,* included a tariff revision that allowed foreign competition with U.S. corporate interests. Other reforms provided for the creation of a federal reserve system for administering our monetary system and adoption of a small income tax as authorized by the recently passed 16th Amendment.

Antitrust legislation was approved, and the Federal Trade Commission was established to police business practices. This progressive era revitalized democracy by making officials more directly responsive to public opinion. Congress extended the power of federal and state governments to regulate big business, to halt the exploitation of children in the labor force, to initiate federal road building plans, and to conserve natural resources. World War I marked the end of the progressive movement as a dynamic force in national affairs.[15]

How did the philosophy of the Progressive Era influence the conduct of public administration? A new realization that government could monitor the activities of the private sector emerged. Removal of protectionist tariff barriers, prohibition of child labor, passage of a federal income tax, establishment of a central banking system, and initial funding for highways bolstered the influence of the public sector in the national economy. As the progressive trend continued for another half-century, the power of public administrators also expanded.

1935: NEW DEAL

Under the New Deal, Roosevelt's emphasis (1933–1945) on relief, recovery, and reform called for more government intervention in the private lives of Americans. Temperamentally on the side of the underdog and an enemy of privilege and exploitation, FDR was guided by his personal experience rather than ideology or doctrine. The New Deal expanded the attitudes of the progressive era. After the stock market crash of 1929 and depression of the 1930s, people were questioning Herbert Hoover's beliefs in private enterprise and "rugged individualism." FDR responded to the crises with legislation and more public administration initiatives. How did the philosophy of the New Deal influence the character of public administration?

Government became a legitimate means for attempting to solve matters once considered private in American society. Government entered banking, stocks, pensions, housing, employment, public works development, management of the economy, and deficit spending. Although its enemies described the New Deal as socialistic, FDR's central purpose was to preserve the capitalist system by bringing about recovery. Government assumed the societal responsibilities that private corporations could not.

The New Deal, in expanding the role of public administration, saw the establishment of numerous government agencies commissioned to revitalize the American private sector. The Federal Deposit Insurance Corporation, established in 1933, guaranteed bank deposits and fostered renewed confidence in the national banking system. The Securities and Exchange Commission (1935) regulated stock exchanges, hoping to prevent a repetition of the events of 1929.

The postwar years saw an unprecedented growth in the size and scope of the federal government. Although the Roosevelt-era New Deal gave birth to the concept of big government, it was really World War II that provided the impetus for the expansion of government spending and bureaucracy to the extent that it became much larger and more powerful than ever before.[16]

The Social Security Administration (1935), which provides unemployment insurance, is an early illustration of intergovernmental attempts to share political, fiscal, and administrative responsibilities. The federal government collected the money; the states administered the legislation; and the private sector financed the program by payroll deduction. The expanded role of the public sector allowed considerable flexibility in experimenting with new plans for merging the talents of the public and private sectors to alleviate problems in society. One of the provisions authorizing payment of pensions to workers past the age of sixty-five applied to about half of the working population. In 1934 Congress created the Federal Housing Administration, now part of the Department of Housing and Urban Development, to administer an amortized home mortgage program that resulted in the suburbanization of America. After obtaining low interest loans for repayment over twenty to twenty-five year periods, many Americans achieved home ownership. The National Labor Relations Board was established in 1935 to supervise the right of workers to join unions and bargain collectively. By providing protection to farmers and wage earners, the New Deal fostered the build up of big agriculture and big labor as a check on big business. In establishing these agencies, the federal government had also assumed much larger responsibilities for regulating the movements of the economy, providing security, and protecting underprivileged groups.

Public investment became a permanent policy. Although revenues were appropriated in ways that enhanced the national wealth (low-cost housing, schools, hospitals, post offices, highways), budget deficits and a steady increase in the federal debt were viewed as a necessary evil.

As the economy grew and revenues increased, the need for public administrators also expanded. The public sector had achieved parity, in some respects, with the private sphere. Public works projects generated an incalculable contribution to the quality of American life through the construction of roads, streets, schools, parks, swimming pools, and playgrounds. The charisma of FDR promotes the myth of an ideal president that has proven impossible for future presidents to measure up to. The concept of a president with a vision for the United States—one that is larger than life—traces its orgins to FDR. Much of this emphasis is due not only to FDR, but to the economic and political circumstances during his twelve-year tenure.[17] The administrative state of the twenty-first century owes its origins to the government initiatives and reforms of the 1930s.[18] Leaders are often defined by their problems, challenges, and enemies and how they respond to them.

1965: GREAT SOCIETY

Lyndon Johnson (LBJ) (1963–1969) was a protégé of FDR. First elected to Congress in 1937, Johnson saw firsthand the positive role government could play in American life. He believed, as FDR had, that government could do good things for people. The most significant achievement of Lyndon Johnson's presidency was the sweeping social changes he managed to establish through legislation. However, Johnson's success belies the enormous challenges he faced to fulfill his far-reaching agenda. His initiatives, especially those dealing with civil rights, were opposed not only by Republican lawmakers but by southern Democrats as well.[19]

Among the key measures successfully championed by LBJ were voting rights for southern blacks, termination of racial discrimination in public accommodations, establishment of federal aid to education for the first time, and origination of the Medicare system to help America's hard-pressed senior citizens. Johnson's administration saw the establishment of the Office of Economic Opportunity (1964), Department of Housing and Urban Development (1965), Model Cities Program (1966), and Department of Transportation (1966). At the same time, millions of acres of new park land and wilderness were preserved. Johnson's celebrated "War on Poverty"

FORTY YEARS AND PROUD OF 'EM

Robert G. Torricelli
An unrepentant Democrat looks back.

Forty consecutive years of Democratic control of the House of Representatives ended this week. What began on Jan. 5, 1955, when Sam Rayburn took the speaker's oath, ultimately survived 20 national elections, nine presidents and the complete transformation of American life.

Today much of the talk among Democratic members consists of expressions of regret. Analysts review what went wrong, and the speeches identifying the failures get the applause. Perhaps I'll be alone, but I intend to declare success. This is a fundamentally different nation from what it was when the Democrats assumed control of the House of Representatives. It is also fundamentally better.

The United States of 1954 was a country where poll taxes separated citizens from their rights. Restaurants, motels, schools and whole neighborhoods segregated our citizens. Only 2 percent of African Americans held college degrees, and a bare 16 percent had graduated from high school.

Law schools teach that the Supreme Court reversed the American apartheid. Years, however, passed after *Brown* v. *Board of Education* without significant change. It was the Voting Rights Act of 1964 and the Civil Rights Act of 1965 that integrated and enfranchised people.

Two decades of Title I funding increased the number of African Americans with high school degrees to 70 percent, and college graduates to 17 percent. In 1965, Head Start brought 4-year olds to the classroom; it remains the single most successful program ever devised for maintaining high-risk children in school.

The Class of 1955 might have had prayer in high school, but only 63 percent of the students ever graduated. Those who remained weren't offered advanced science or math courses in a majority of school districts until the passage of the Defense Education Act of 1958. Higher education had traditionally been the province of the wealthy.

A decade after the GI Bill there were still only 430,000 annual college graduates. Following the passage of the Higher Education Act of 1965, college enrollment increased by 300 percent.

Perhaps the largest public construction project in history began with the Interstate Highway Act of 1956, which ultimately doubled the nation's highway system and provided new corridors for economic growth. Other legislation guided generations of technology into the marketplace. The Energy Policy and Conservation Act of 1975 set standards for gas mileage and forced a 100 percent improvement in efficiency. The creation of NASA was the first in a series of efforts that led to the lunar landings and ultimate commercialization of space.

Poverty and age were indistinguishable in the America of 1954. The average Social Security benefit was $59. A child was three times less likely than now to survive its first year of life. The indexing of Social Security helped lower poverty rates among seniors to the lowest in the population. Medicare brought 32 million seniors into the health care system. The Women, Infants and Children program began to

(continued)

reduce infant mortality and AFDC brought vulnerable children basic subsistence. Revelations of child hunger in 1954 gave rise to the School Lunch Program.

In 1954 the local river was the most common disposal site for waste water. Carbon monoxide was clouding our cities and was completely unregulated. Congress passed the Clean Water Act in 1973 and the Clean Air Act in 1990. Today, three-quarters of cities treat their water, and auto emissions have decreased 25 percent.

Deregulation of the airline, trucking and telecommunications industries has produced millions of jobs and lowered prices for transportation and telephone services.

Has the price of all this been an unacceptably large and expensive federal government? There are now fewer federal employees than at any time since the Eisenhower administration. The marginal tax rate is half the 1955 level, and government spending is at the lowest level of GDP since 1959. If not for the interest payments on the debt accrued during the Reagan and Bush years, there would be no budget deficit this year.

But progressive government is always a victim of its own success.

The 75-cent minimum wage of 1955 isn't even a memory. Millions of the urban poor brought their new educations to the suburban communities that grew along the miles of federal highway. Tremendous environmental progress allowed people to focus on business priorities that were once set aside in deference to family health.

Democrats need to remember that success in public life means creating your own obsolescence. It should be enough to know that when needed, the Democratic Party did the right thing. As power passes to the new Republican majority, the hundreds of members of Congress who contributed to these remarkable changes should take a moment to consider their achievement. Perhaps even a few citizens might do the same.

The writer, a Democratic Party representative from New Jersey since 1983 offers a partisan perspective on policy and system developments.

Source: Robert Torricelli, *The Washington Post*, Opinion-Editorial Page, January 5, 1995. Copyright © The Washington Post. Reprinted with permission.

focused national attention on the stubborn problem of hunger and want in the midst of plenty. Johnson, recalling the potentialities of government action he had witnessed in the New Deal era, called for a Great Society.

Under this umbrella, he advocated government support of equal employment, voting rights, air pollution control, highway safety, public broadcasting, food stamps, labor training, fair housing, Social Security increases, and civil service pay raises. Federal deficits under Johnson ranged from $1.6 billion in 1965 to $25.1 billion in 1968. However, LBJ's last budget request provided a $3.2 billion surplus in 1969. We have not had a balanced budget or surplus since that year. Although Johnson is remembered for committing the country's resources to the unpopular Vietnam War, he was mostly a pragmatic president who responded to the needs of America's middle class.[20]

How did the philosophy of the Great Society influence the conduct of public administration? Although sincere in such efforts as eliminating poverty and racism, caring for the sick, and educating the masses, Johnson became caught up in a "credibility gap" of what government—domestically and internationally—

A CRIME THAT MADE CYNICISM THE RULE

Public opinion polls show many Americans regard the federal government with cynicism, an attitude that may have begun with the 1972 Watergate break-in. Government had a positive image from the Great Depression through John F. Kennedy's presidency, with a poll in 1965 showing 76 percent of citizens felt the government was trustworthy most of the time. A poll in 1997 shows public trust in Washington, D. C. at 32 percent.

Source: William Schneider, "A Crime That Made Cynicism the Rule," *National Journal*, 29, no. 25 (21 June 1997): 1306.

---

could accomplish. Opponents charged that corruption and inefficiency were resulting from a laundry list of new federal government programs. As World War I had ended the Progressive Era and the New Freedom, and as World War II had concluded the New Deal, the Vietnam War proved to be the most disastrous and divisive armed conflict since the Civil War and a calamity for the Great Society.

Political tragedy occurred not only in foreign policy. Despite the Great Society's efforts to attend to the needs of the poor and downtrodden—especially blacks—the destructive ghetto riots of the middle and late 1960s led to widespread perceptions that government assistance was not working. Public bureaucracy and public administrators were despised and disparaged. The tendency to downgrade and malign institutions of public administration, regardless of their tasks, limits, and records, is a theme capitalized on by Ronald Reagan, the antithesis of Wilson, FDR, and LBJ.

1985: REAGAN REVOLUTION

The "body politic" of the United States is more pragmatic than ideological. Rarely have the citizens of this nation strayed from the middle of the political road. Wilson was pragmatic in responding to the causes of the Progressive Era. FDR was pragmatic in responding to the causes of the depression. And LBJ was pragmatic in responding to the human and environmental concerns of the 1960s. Then, in 1980, the public elected a president who championed the ideology of the conservative wing of the minority party. Reagan's logic was simple: Why should the national government tax the people and then send the money back to the states? Why not let the states do the taxing and administer the programs?[21]

Reagan (1981–1989) began by rejecting the moderate to liberal consensus that had come to dominate both Democratic and Republican administrations since the election of FDR in 1932. Reagan envisioned a better America, based on less government and more individual enterprise. Not since FDR had there been such a massive redirection of public goals. The essence of the "revolution" was Reagan's belief that our problems were caused by high government spending and by government intervention in the private marketplace.

On defense issues, the conservatives got their rapid defense buildup but failed to sustain it. The overall trend in the second Reagan term was a resumption of regulatory growth. On trade issues, Reagan talked a hard line. But William A. Niskanen Jr. writes that "for the first time since World War II, the United States added more trade restraints than it removed." Neither Reagan nor Bush scaled back on affirmative action programs or clean air regulations. Abortion is legal. Organized prayer is not in the schools.

Budget deficits did not dilute the influence of big government. Conservatives failed to discredit the notion that solving problems is government's responsibility. Reagan will be remembered as a better communicator than persuader. Reagan's accomplishments did not constitute a lasting conservative revolution in policy. No one knows yet the philosophical impacts of Newt Gingrich's Contract with America. Conservatives may yet achieve a revolution. But Reagan in the 1980s and Gingrich in the 1990s had to realize their failure to make converts and not just conquests.

The perspective of recent presidents had been that if something was wrong, it was the responsibility of government to attempt to correct the malfunction. In contrast, Reagan planned a full-scale retreat from the march toward a welfare state for the masses. Although Reagan's rhetoric was *revolutionary in purpose,* his actions were *evolutionary in practice.*[22] Reagan talked tough, sometimes in revolutionary tones, but governed pragmatically, or in evolutionary ways. Reagan, the person, was a "throwback" to simpler times. LBJ tried to be all things to all people. He governed in the charismatic shadows of FDR and John F. Kennedy. FDR, JFK, and Reagan had at least one thing in common. They used rhetoric to raise their agendas for subsequent policy implementation by public administrators. Under Reagan, tax cuts and the buildup of defense took precedence over balancing the budget. The budget deficits emerging from the Reagan administration made "fiscal conservatives" out of politicians from all jurisdictions and political stripes during the 1990s. Reagan budget deficits ranged from a low of $127.9 billion in 1982 to a high of $220.7 billion in 1987. The implication of these figures for future commitment to public programs, domestic or foreign, is that the budgets of the public sector must be leaner at all government levels. Public administrators will continue to attempt to do more with less, and taxpayers will demand the same level of service delivery for similar costs.

Early in the 1980s, Reagan gave the fight against inflation precedence over the previous administration's attempts to moderate the recession. Tax cuts were made, but the corresponding domestic spending cuts were not. Despite the reduction in tax revenues, defense spending was increased, and the deficit grew larger while the recession worsened.

Reagan's income tax cuts reduced revenues for domestic benefits and services. The recession reduced the business profits that were usually taxed for public programs. Public administrators were affected by deep cuts in grants to state and local governments and for programs serving the poor. However, the chief sources of federal budget growth since the 1950s—Social Security, Medicare, government employee pensions, and other middle-class programs—were too politically sensitive for the Reagan administration to cut.

U.S. PRESIDENTS—BIG IDEAS AND SMALL IDEAS

Big ideas: Wilson, FDR, Truman, and Reagan

Woodrow Wilson (1913–1921): He stirred the national government to regulate the industrial trusts, then ruined his health trying to create the League of Nations.

Franklin D. Roosevelt (1933–1945): To attack the Great Depression and fight World War II, he invented Big Government and vastly expanded Washington's role in people's lives.

Harry S. Truman (1945–1953): From the A-bomb to the Marshall Plan and NATO to desegregation of the military, the modest Missouri haberdasher wasn't shy about taking big steps.

Ronald Reagan (1981–1989): His few big ideas—smaller government, lower taxes, a stronger military—anticipated the end of the Cold War and remolded public attitudes.

Small Ideas: Hoover, Eisenhower, Carter, and Bush

Herbert Hoover (1929–1933): Faced with the gravest economic crisis in U.S. history, he tried "trickle-down" policies and left it to the states to aid the hungry and unemployed.

Dwight D. Eisenhower (1953–1961): He had one big idea—the Interstate Highway System—and otherwise was a steward in a self-satisfied period of peace and prosperity.

Jimmy Carter (1977–1981): An engineer by training and temperament, he fiddled incessantly with domestic programs but got overwhelmed by international events.

George Bush (1989–1993): His reluctance to do much in domestic policy cost him a second term. His Administration was chronicled in a book titled *Marching in Place*.

Sources: Burt Solomon, "Thinking Small," *National Journal* 30, no. 4 (24 January 1998): 157–160. See Michael Duffy, *Marching in Place* (New York: Simon & Schuster, 1992).

Another priority for the Reagan administration was economic growth, not economic fairness. Therefore, tax rates were framed to provide the greatest benefits to high-income families. Reagan focused on reducing the marginal tax rates that would enhance savings, investment, and the work ethic.

The Reagan administration's policy toward regulations valued productivity over concerns of health, safety, civil rights, and the environment. The growth of productivity in the 1970s had slowed, in part due to environmental regulations. During the Reagan years, natural resource policy focused upon production of energy resources rather than conservation. Even public lands and wilderness areas were no longer sacred.

Ironically, deficits were a means of advancing the "Reagan Revolution." President Clinton was pressured to curb federal spending and to restrain the growth of major federal entitlement programs. An increasing portion of the taxpayer's dollar was devoted to paying for interest on the federal debt. Benefits and

services was curtailed. As federal programs were reduced, state and local jurisdictions were forced to search for new ways of financing and implementing services no longer paid for by Washington. The shift of political power away from
Washington and toward state and local governments reflects Republican political
philosophies. The middle class continues its revolt against taxes and therefore
local services are reduced or kept to a minimum. Due to their lack of political
clout in the economic system, the poor feel the effect more than the middle class
and, certainly, more than the upper class.

Wilson, FDR, and LBJ advocated government intervention to provide a measure of equal opportunity in our democratic, capitalistic system. Reagan, instead
of overthrowing cardinal elements of the New Freedom, New Deal, and Great
Society, sought to redirect government's role in society toward efficiency and
productivity. Federal spending certainly did not decrease under Reagan.

Reagan, however, changed the agenda from *proportionally more* spending to proportionally less spending. The power of the federal government has furthermore
been enhanced by two World Wars and conflicts in Korea and Vietnam. However,
wars are important to the life of political bureaucracy because wars enhance federal budgets and tend to consolidate the centralization of federal power. During
World War I, World War II, Korea, and Vietnam, national defense expenditures increased considerably and enhanced the dominance of the federal government.

The benchmarks—1915, 1935, 1965, and 1985—illustrate the ebb and flow of
government response to the demands of citizens. The political, social, and
economic environment of the day has tremendous influence on public administrators. We can see that presidents, in leading and marshalling support from
public bureaucracies, respond pragmatically to the dynamics of their times.

Believing that in the 1990s, just as FDR knew in the 1930s, new conditions
were imposing new requirements on government and those who conducted it,
President Clinton set out to transform the remnants of the New Deal party into a
diverse and durable coalition capable of dominating American politics and
advancing the progressive tradition into the twenty-first century.[23]

The concept of a rhetorical presidency, as discussed by Woodrow Wilson in
his study, "Constitutional Government in the United States," reflects doubts on
executive power. The executive office of the president consists of a rigid and
formal constitution and the informal historical development of the American
party system. In a rhetorical presidency, the president sheds his traditional role
of executive officer as one type of power is exchanged for another. A form of
constitutional government is essential but with strong opinion leadership rather
than governance by an executive power. Wilson, FDR, LBJ, and Reagan used
rhetoric effectively.[24]

Bill Clinton represented the theses of Wilson, FDR, and LBJ. Newt Gingrich
carried the banner of Reagan. Clinton and Gingrich confronted the other's
perspectives on politics in an emerging set of American politics called, by E. J.
Dionne Jr., "the new radicalism." Clinton and Gingrich espoused fundamentally
different approaches to economic turbulence, moral uncertainty, and
international disorder. The new conservatives wanted to resolve the country's

political crisis by shrinking government. They denied any link between economic developments and the country's moral state. Family, church, neighborhood, workplace organizations—traditional institutions—should be in charge of solution of the moral crisis.[25]

The theses of Wilson, FDR, and LBJ—that a free market economy could not function properly in the absence of rules, workers' rights, government spending on public goods, and continuing public investments to enhance the skills and opportunities of the work force—was the political argument advocated by Clinton. Clinton did not seek absolute equality or anything like it, but he knew that rising inequality was dangerous for American democracy. The adversaries of Gingrich argued that the new conservatism reached back not to Reagan but to the Gilded Age of the 1890s. If only economic change goes on unfettered, the new conservatism argued, everyone will be better off. The language of the new conservatives was that of joyful anarchism. The new conservatives were reluctant to acknowledge that "a capitalist society depends on noncapitalist values in order to hold together and prosper."[26]

The purpose of progressivism is not to use government to destroy the free market. Government should be used to strengthen the institutions of civil society. But progressives abdicated the definition of liberty to their conservative adversaries. Progressives must confront the politics of liberty and community and assure citizens that government will not weaken the bonds of civil society.

Clinton campaigned for president, in 1992 and 1996, as a "New Democrat." As the new conservatives venture toward the extremes of political traditionalism, the New Democrats support states' rights and a less activist national government that provides citizens with mechanisms to help themselves (such as job training)—rather than a varied assembly of expensive social services.[27] The Clinton political model stressed pragmatism and moderation. According to *National Journal* columnist William Schneider, the Reagan political successes of the 1980s were not without costs. "Reagan's success in the 1980s had the effect of ideologizing the GOP: Stick to the right, and you can be another Reagan. Clinton's success in the 1990s has de-ideologized the Democrats: Stick to the mainstream, and you can be another Clinton."[28]

The successes of any president's agenda are determined largely by whether he can govern from the political center. That agenda recognizes that government is not the solution to all problems, nor the cause, but must be a tool, a conduit, a mechanism, a catalyst to provide opportunities to those willing to accept responsibility. According to Leon Panetta, at one time President Clinton's chief of staff, this government largesse—and limitation—are the essence of the "vital center" from which most Americans want the president and Congress to govern.[29]

THE GROWTH OF PUBLIC BUREAUCRACY

The organization of federal, state, and local jurisdictions is evidence of the fragmented nature of public administration in the United States. The concept of federalism, or the structure of politics in the United States, implies a system of authority apportioned constitutionally between the national and state governments.

Frederick S. Lane points out the three principal dimensions of federalism: *political, fiscal,* and *administrative.* The political dimension accounts for the ways in which local, state, and national jurisdictions participate in the decision-making processes. The fiscal dimension indicates which jurisdictions pay what amount for services. The administrative dimension tells us which level will supervise the administration of various services. Lane concludes: "Federalism is a contradiction: it tries to marry diversity and central direction."[30]

There are about 80,000 government bodies in the United States. There is one national or central government and fifty state commonwealths. The remaining jurisdictions are local governments, such as municipalities (cities), counties, townships, school districts, and special districts.

- *Counties* (about 3,000)—Counties are jurisdictions that include both the nation's largest cities and its smallest villages. Counties possess powers and offer services that may vary considerably and are created explicitly to serve the interests of the local community.
- *Townships* (about 17,000)—Townships are subdivisions of counties. Townships vary greatly in functions and governmental organization. They exist mainly in northeastern and north central states.
- *School districts* (about 15,000)—School districts are separate governments established to administer public school systems.
- *Special districts* (about 28,000)—Special districts are limited-purpose governments established to administer one or several public functions for a designated area.[31]

In 1992, change was the magic word in the presidential and congressional elections. George Bush and Bill Clinton focused on interpretations of change. Political debates concerning change centered on ways in which counties, townships, school districts, and special districts could be more effective in delivering public services. The Ronald Reagan-led Republican Party of the 1980s sought to reduce the influence of federal agencies on the lives of citizens. The Reagan policies succeeded in reducing significantly the federal government's power and influence on state and local jurisdictions. As a result, some functions of public policy are now relegated to private groups and not-for-profit organizations.

The impacts of the political agenda raised by the Reagan and Bush administrations in the 1980s must be dealt with by the presidential and Congressional wings of the national Democratic Party in the mid-1990s. The Democrats—in the White House and in Congress—are challenged to govern effectively by cutting federal spending programs and raising taxes, and thereby, stem the tide of red ink in federal deficits. The battles of partisan, policy, and system politics determine what government programs will be abolished and the ones to be retained, perhaps even bolstered. In one way or another, all 80,000 units of government in the United States will be affected.

Comparing Public and Private Administration Nuances

We now have a better idea of what administration is, so let us proceed to describe and designate the different forms it may take. In some respects these forms are as numerous as the various fields that apply them. Within the fields of health administration, welfare administration, and university administration, for example, each institution often has its own distinctive type of administration, which may differ considerably from that of another institution. In another sense, no essential differences exist from one institution to another because administration deals with the working relationship of human beings. This common denominator is often a stronger unifying bond than the disparateness of the numerators.

It is sometimes said that administration is the same everywhere, and to some degree this is true. Running a hospital or a factory presents similar problems that tend to appear whenever human beings seek to work cooperatively. It is helpful, though, in furthering our understanding of administration to distinguish the two broad areas where it is used—the public and private sectors.

The ways in which public administration differ from private business administration are worth emphasis. Public and private administration exhibits two areas of comparison and conflict: *substantive* and *procedural.*

Substantive issues of public and private administration raise questions concerning the issues of politics versus profits, the measurement of objectives, and management versus administration. These are areas of potential conflict.

Procedural issues address management as a universal process. Issues for procedural deliberation include open versus closed systems, methods of evaluation, criteria for decision making, personnel systems, planning and efficiency.[32]

Substantive issues refer to conceptual or abstract concerns such as goals, objectives, means, ends, values, results, and priorities. Nobel Prize winning author, Herbert Simon, argues that the means and ends of public administration differ significantly from those of private administration.[33] He maintains that the importance of an end or value should not be ignored and that the process, or means, of management is a value in itself and cannot be separated from other values.

The purpose of a college education, for example, is to seek learning, training, and knowledge about the significant values of life. The *end* is learning, training, and knowledge. Education is the substance and the institution is the procedure. The institution provides the procedural means for the attainment of specific substantive ends. The *means* are provided by the curricula of the respective disciplines. In other words, the *means* for achieving learning, training, and knowledge are to meet the requirements of your discipline's prescribed curricula by attending classes and successfully completing exams.

Justice and the implementation of justice, for example, illustrate *ends* and *means.* Justice, in the philosophical realm, is an *end* in itself, a commonly held value. Justice can only be found in the United States by a *means*—due process of law. Justice is an example of a substantive issue; the matters of the judicial process constitute processes, authorities, and institutions that enforce procedural concerns. By unpacking the distinctions between substantive and procedural issues in public administration, the differences between administration in the private and the public sector will become clear.

SUBSTANTIVE ISSUES

1. Politics versus Profits—One distinction between public and private administration is that the goals of public administration are grounded in politics and decision-making processes that may affect an entire community of citizens, whereas the goals of private management are founded on the maximization of profit. Decision making in public bureaucracies is achieved by meeting the objectives of compromise, consensus, and democratic participation. These objectives are different from the private sector's emphasis on the concepts of efficiency, rationality, and profit. Although the goals of public administration and private administration respond to outside clientele pressures, their concepts of bottom line accountability differ: one's god is a consensus of citizens concerned about the issues confronting an entire community and the other's god is profit. The private organization *also* suffers constraints, but these usually hinge on its need to make a profit. As long as it is advancing toward this goal, the private organization enjoys considerable latitude in the way it operates and in the specific goals it may set for itself. This profit motive accounts for another feature that many feel distinguishes the two types of administration—differences in their efficiency.

2. Measurement of Objectives—Objectives grounded in compromise, consensus, and democratic participation differ from objectives based on efficiency, rationality, and profit. The private sector ultimately makes rational decisions based upon clear, concise, and quantifiable statements found in the sales ledger. The public sector deals with social intangibles such as health, welfare, and common defense. The private sector places prime consideration on individual values and preferences, whereas the public sector allocates communal services offered to all citizens.

For example, McDonald's produces hamburgers at a market price, responding to the public's hunger for hamburgers. State universities produce college graduates, based upon their successfully meeting the requirements of the learning, training, and knowledge of a certain curriculum. You may immediately recognize if McDonald's has satisfied your demand for food. However, the success, or lack thereof, of your college professors in motivating you to think may not be fully appreciated for a much longer time.

3. Management versus Administration—In the private sector, the term "management" commonly refers to those persons in line *positions*, whereas in the public sector, the term "administration" refers to those in line *functions*. (Line personnel command, have authority, and are generalists; staff personnel possess knowledge and skills, give advice, and are specialists. Read sections of the next chapter for more explanation and illustration.)

A position implies *authority* for corporate action; a function implies *duty*, such as the function of the police to protect and assist the public. Modern technologies, rewards (profits), and penalties (defaults) enhance private sector productivity. Depending upon market trends, profits may be as likely in one year as defaults are in the following one.

However, the less systematic and less structured public sector produces intangible services difficult to measure. The term *management* is characterized by decision making in the private sector corporate model of hierarchy. The term administration suggests decision making by the public sector collegial model of consensus. One is led by a CEO; the other is guided by a committee or unspecified group of citizens.

Procedural Issues

1. Open versus Closed Systems—Procedural concerns, such as accountability, reflect the *dilemma* of the open versus closed systems, or the goldfish bowl of public administration versus the closed board room of private administration. The openness of the goldfish bowl image magnifies and broadcasts the activities of the public administrator and politician, while the closed boardroom image shows how those in the private sector can harbor corporate secrets to seek a competitive edge. Government bureaucrats and politicians operate in the glare of the public's right to know about operations financed by taxpayers. The private corporation, meanwhile, escapes such scrutiny unless the firm breaks the law or defrauds the public, for example, by polluting the air or selling harmful products. In such cases, an arm of government may demand more accountability. Failing these transgressions, private sector administration is a process to which the public is not invited.

2. Methods of Evaluation—Consensus, compromise, and democratic participation by citizens promote a natural diversity in the evaluation of government services. Community leaders seek consensus, agree to compromise, and advocate citizen participation to find support for policies. In contrast, efficiency, rationality, and concern for profit cause private sector entrepreneurs to view corporate evaluation differently. If a phase of an industry fails to produce profits, rationality dictates efficiency in cutting losses.

The public sector focuses on social good; the private sector emphasizes fiscal control. The two may, in some cases, be incompatible. For example, the social good of the Department of Defense (DOD) may be to prevent war; however, if the privately-owned Boeing Corporation does not receive enough revenue from government business with the DOD, the company may go out of business. Another illustration: If a university decides to toughen academic standards and slice the undergraduate enrollment by several thousand students, the resulting social good for the school may be a heightened academic reputation; however, private entrepreneurs operating bookstores, eateries, bars, and other businesses frequented by students may feel the pinch, lay off local employees, and even close their doors.

3. Public versus Private Decision-Making Criteria—Although the formal steps in decision making may be similar in both public and private management areas, the criteria managers use in making decisions are not. The definition of the goal or problem, the preferred consumer response, and the allocation of resources may apply similarly to both sectors: the logic, or mode of thinking, behind such decision making is distinct.

The public sector university's bookstore is, for example, under very different constraints from a privately run bookstore across the street. The public sector bookstore demands a higher standard in procedural process (the manner in which a function is carried out) and maintains certain expectations and guarantees in hiring, firing, promotions, and general conduct of bookstore business. The private sector bookstore can sell items based upon the supply and demand of the marketplace; the public sector bookstore must respond to every course, no matter how esoteric or obscure, and to every program offered by the state university.

4. Personnel Systems—Recruitment and socialization processes by both private management and public administration allow people to obtain and maintain employment and to be promoted under a system that evaluates skills, knowledge, and expertise. Unlike the private sector however, an applicant for a full-time civil service position governed by a merit system will go through a fixed process, monitored by law.

Women and minorities may also receive some preference in the recruitment process for public sector jobs, a preference not always afforded them in the private sector. The personnel systems in the public and private arenas reflect their essential differences. Public sector employees enjoy the privileges of administrative due process because laws prescribe guidelines for recruitment, selection, promotion, and retention of employees. Merit plans that evaluate skills, knowledge, and expertise are a hiring tool, but they may differ greatly from agency to agency. Private enterprise employees have no guarantees of due process; profit needs require flexibility as to the "when and how" of hiring and firing. In competitive work environments, skills dictate success.

5. Long-Term and Short-Term Planning—Planning may be considered part of the process of decision making. Some argue that planning is a means of controlling employees. The private sector manager does not need to seek consensus among employees before acting; the manager alone makes decisions, and the company's profit or loss ledger reflects success or failure. For the public sector employee, planning becomes hazardous if political leaders are continuously changing after elections regardless of their own success or failure.

Public officials need program continuity and political stability to carry out their responsibilities consistently without turmoil and change. In the private sector, planning is easier because there are no demands of due process or legally prescribed guarantees concerning hiring, firing, and promotion. The public administrator may not have this luxury. Stable political and economic conditions are essential for planning in both sectors.

For example, America's Middle East and China policies should transcend political leaders and political parties. In other words, a new policy should not be adopted, changed significantly, or abandoned because a new political leader takes office. Foreign governments—allies and enemies—will not know how to respond if policy changes occur with every new president.

Likewise, private entrepreneurs cannot plan or act decisively under economic conditions of stagnation or high interest rates and steep inflation. In the private sector, planning is easier because there are no demands of due process or legally prescribed guarantees concerning hiring, firing, and promotion. The public administrator may not have this luxury. If the political and economic environments are unstable, entrepreneurs will shy away from new investments.

6. Efficiency—The need for efficiency is paramount in both the public and private sectors. Hierarchical control, coordination, planning, meritorious performance, and authority lines are emphasized in both public and private sectors. Stockbrokers and investors in private corporations demand efficiency and productivity for their dollars. Likewise, taxpayers demand that public administrators produce more services more effectively with fewer dollars. However, the bottom line, or profit concern, of the private sector allows managers to realize success or failure immediately; the circumstances of the public sector, with its less precise methods of evaluation, may take longer to reflect the value and efficiency of a public service.

BLURRING OR BIFURCATION?

On the substantive issues we have discussed (politics versus profits, measurement of objectives, and management versus administration), a comparison of the public and private sectors reveals more blurring than bifurcation into two separate arenas. A comparison of procedural issues (open versus closed systems, methods of evaluation, public versus private decision-making criteria, personnel systems, planning, and efficiency) reveals distinctions concerning the accountability factor, but similarities in developing participative personnel systems to evaluate the expertise, knowledge, and skills of employees.

The public sector is grounded in *political equality* with consideration for everyone's opinion, seeking consensus, compromise, and democratic participation. The private sector is based upon *economic efficiency*, seeking definitive results, rationality in decision making, and maximization of profit. In practice, the realities of political equality and economic efficiency blend into what many call the "American System." To a larger degree than most people realize, Alexander Hamilton's "American System" still plays a critical role in American economic development. The government uses investment and trade policies to promote American industry, and thus American jobs. President Dwight D. Eisenhower's Interstate Highway System was a 1950s version of Hamilton's system of canals. Charlene Barshefsky, U.S. Trade Representative, followed Hamilton's lead when she signed agreements making certain U.S. companies accessed world telecommunications markets. Profits for the rich may mean jobs for the rest of us. If so, perhaps the special interests are joined with the national interests.[34]

Public administration, then, differs in significant ways from private administration. These differences hinge largely on the greater legal accountability of the former compared to the flexibility of the latter. Determining which sector is the

---

PAYING THE PIPER

Forest City Ratner, a prominent developer in New York City, spent more on lobbying the municipal government in 1996 than any other business or group. The company paid $436,382 to hire lobbyists to help insure the success of several real estate projects, from shopping centers to office buildings to parking lots.

Source: Clifford J. Levy, "Developer Ranks No. 1 in Spending on Lobbying," *New York Times*, 15 May 1997, p. B5.

---

most efficient remains a complex question, subject not only to variances in products and procedures but also to differences in purposes and processes.

Interest Groups and Public Bureaucracy

The corps of Washington lobbyists has grown steadily since the New Deal, but especially since the early 1970s. This growth parallels the growth in federal spending and the expansion of federal authority into new areas. Voters may appear to demand political reform, but government is unlikely to change except in composition. Government's unwieldly size and contradictory complexity has developed due to the cumulative inertia of entrenched lobbyists and special-interest groups. Reforms will continue but only gradually. Substantive change can come from the presidency or the electorate, but not unless individuals are willing to make personal sacrifices for widespread social welfare.[35]

Lobbyists compete vigorously to safeguard traditional spending in their areas of interest. During the Reagan administration, pressures to reduce federal spending intensified competition by interest groups for the dwindling supply of federal dollars. Industries, labor unions, ethnic groups, religious groups, professional organizations, citizen groups, and even foreign business interests all periodically—and some continuously—seek to exert pressure on national and state legislatures to attain legislative goals. *Pressure by interest groups usually has a selfish aim: their members wish to assert rights. win privileges, or benefit financially.* A group's power to influence legislation is often based less on its arguments than on the size of its membership, its financial resources, and the astuteness of its representatives. If there were any doubt about the increasing presence of special interests in American politics, within the Capital Beltway, the interstate highway that circles Washington, DC, there are 2,200 trade groups that employ more Washingtonians than any other organization except government or travel and tourism. See table 2-2 depicting the top Power 25 pressure or interest groups.

Expert articulation of particular citizen interests drives public bureaucracies in the United States. Legislatures write vague laws. Public administrators interpret those statutes with specificity in the *Federal Register*. The statutes are then codified in the *Code of Federal Regulations*. The public philosophy of the United States in the twenty-first century is no longer capitalism, but instead *interest group*

TABLE 2–2   The Power 25

1. American Association of Retired Persons
2. American Israel Public Affairs Committee
3. AFL-CIO
4. National Federation of Independent Business
5. Association of Trial Lawyers of America
6. National Rifle Association of America
7. Christian Coalition
8. American Medical Association
9. National Education Association
10. National Right to Life Committee
11. National Association of Realtors
12. American Bankers Association
13. National Association of Manufacturers
14. American Federation of State, County, and Municipal Employees
15. Chamber of Commerce of the U.S.A.
16. Veterans of Foreign Wars of the United States
17. American Farm Bureau Federation
18. Motion Picture Association of America
19. National Association of Home Builders of the U.S.
20. National Association of Broadcasters
21. American Hospital Association
22. National Governors' Association
23. American Legion
24. National Restaurant Association
25. International Brotherhood of Teamsters

Source: Reprinted from the December 8, 1987 issue of *FORTUNE* by special permission; copyright 1997, Time, Inc.

liberalism, a concept developed by Theodore J. Lowi. Lowi claims that capitalism has declined as an ideology and is dead as a public philosophy. Capitalism, the old public philosophy, has become outmoded since World War II because the elite, such as lobbyists, no longer agree about whether government should be involved in making policies for private citizens or for private sector businesses. Republicans and Democrats, as participants in interest group liberalism, fully agree that government should be a player in monitoring, if not directing, the relations among private citizens.[36] Interest groups reflect partisan bearings. Labor unions lean toward Democratic Party candidates. Many, but not all, business groups flock toward Republicans. See table 2-3 for groups loved and hated by partisan Republicans and Democrats.

TABLE 2–3   Loved and Hated by Partisans

Loved by Democrats, Hated by Republicans		
Ranking by:	D	R
*Service Employees International Union	24	101
*Union of Needletrades, Industrial, and Textile Employees	60	115
*Intl. Association of Machinists and Aerospace Workers	30	110
*Natl. Association of Letter Carriers	21	83
*Hotel Employers and Restaurant Employees International Union	53	110
*American Federation of State, County and Municipal Employees	6	38
*Handgun Control Inc.	39	96
*American Federation of Teachers	18	65
*Communications Workers of America	33	84
*Children's Defense Fund	23	70

Loved by Republicans, Hated by Democrats		
Ranking by:	D	R
*Americans for Tax Reform	115	30
*National Association of Wholesaler-Distributors	107	28
*Citizens for a Sound Economy	109	33
*National Automobile Dealers Association	74	21
*National Federation of Independent Business	7	2
*Christian Coalition	12	4
*Associated General Contractors of America	89	35
*American Farm Bureau Federation	38	10
*National Beer Wholesalers Association	65	22
*National Retail Federation	54	18

Source: Reprinted from the December 8, 1987 issue of *FORTUNE* by special permission; copyright 1997, Time, Inc.

As the Great Depression ended and World War II began, U.S. capitalism came to be called "conservatism," but Lowi argues that this description is a misnomer. He states that capitalism never became conservative, but declined because it became irrelevant and erroneous. Capitalist ideology according to Lowi, did not endure as the public philosophy because it could accept only one legitimate type of modern social control-competition. Lowi concludes that the old dialogue between liberalism and conservatism "passed into the graveyard of consensus," spelling the "decline of meaningful adversary political proceedings in favor of administrative, technical and logrolling politics. In a nutshell, politics became a

TABLE 2–4   The 10 Most Generous Interest Groups

(In Terms of Political Action Committee Donations to Congressional Candidates over the Past Decade: 1985–1995)	
Interest Group	10-Year Contributions
1. Banking and Finance	$56,096,840
2. Energy	50,494,379
3. Agriculture	48,901,280
4. Transportation Unions	45,928,239
5. Insurance	42,120,605
6. Real Estate	40,692,087
7. Media	37,994,112
8. Government Employee Unions	37,443,503
9. Doctors, Dentists, Nurses	36,831,744
10. Transportation Firms	30,148,453

Source: *Time* 146, no. 7 (14 August 1995): 20. Reprinted with permission.

question of equity rather than a question of morality. Adjustment comes first, rules of law come last, if at all."[37] As interest groups clash, the priority becomes equal opportunity for any group to put forth its unique version of how life should be conducted. The values of any particular organization are secondary.

In interest group liberalism, diverse groups check the values, or perspectives, of opposing interests by arguing for their own set of values in the great American marketplace of ideas. Milk producers, tobacco growers, billboard advertisers, movie makers, bankers, physicians, broadcasters, cable TV operators, farmers, entrepreneurs, and energy interests are a few of the more than 2,000 lobbyists who insist that their concerns should be written into law. Whether liberal or conservative, the elite want to use the power and funding of government for their personal ends. According to Lowi, the most significant difference between liberals and conservatives, Democrats and Republicans, can be found in the interest groups with which they identify. Accepted as legitimate, the values of organized interest groups guide Congress members in their votes, presidents in their programs, and bureaucrats in their administrative discretion. The only necessary guidelines for the framing of laws depend upon the validity or legitimacy of interest group demands.[38]

The philosophy of interest group liberalism is pragmatic, with government playing the role of broker, and optimistic about government's role; that which is good for government is also good for society. The liberal process of private interaction with public officials is accessible to all organized interests and offers no value judgments concerning any particular claim or set of claims. Interest

---

THE CONSTITUTION OF STATUS

Democratic ideals involve social components as well as legal and political ones, and the Constitution alone cannot change the social structures in the United States that impose a barrier to full implementation of democratic ideals. To make progress on social equality, development of a better understanding of the social factors involved with group politics and group conflicts is necessary. Moral justifications offered in support of legal arguments may in fact be veiled attempts by particular groups to maintain their superior status in the social hierarchy.

Source: J. M. Balkin, "The Constitution of Status," *Yale Law Journal* 106, no. 8 (June 1997): 2313–2374.

---

group liberalism defines the public interest as the amalgamation of claims of various interests. The principle of representation extends into public bureaucracy as administrators afford due process to all citizens. To represent such diverse political, economic, and cultural interests, legislatures make open-ended, vague laws and issue broad delegations to public administrators to regulate interests in society. Says Lowi: "It (interest group liberalism) impairs legitimacy by converting government from a moralistic to a mechanistic institution. It impairs the potential of positive law to correct itself by allowing the law to become anything that eventually bargains itself out as acceptable to the bargainer . . . . Interest group liberalism seeks pluralistic government in which there is no formal specification of means or of ends. In a pluralistic government there is, therefore, no substance. Neither is there procedure. There is only process."[39] In other words, procedures and processes are vital, and substance and values are at the mercy of the strongest interests.

In recent years, private interests have contributed ever increasing amounts of money to participants fighting to preserve the status quo of the political system, or to change it, subsequently purchasing privilege, power, and profit. It would not be an exaggeration to assert that the American government—president, executive branch, and Congress—has been bought and sold. The Madsonian faction is firmly in the saddle and rides the nation.[40] According to a *Wall Street Journal*/NBC News survey, an overwhelming 77 percent of Americans believe that political campaigns are excessively influenced by special interests and wealthy contributors and that the system needs to be changed. However, campaign finance reform as an issue requiring the federal government's attention was ranked next-to-last out of seven issues.[41] In an era when politics seems, increasingly, to be the pursuit of self-interest under the banner of some high-sounding principle, one can be excused for doubting whether the opponents of campaign finance reform are really so passionately devoted to the protection of the First Amendment. Nonetheless, the free speech argument is important enough to deserve being addressed on its merits.[42]

SUMMARY

- The *ecology* of the administrative craft deals with the relationships between public administrators and their environments. Public administrators cannot operate in a vacuum.
- With its numerous organizations, modern America is the epitome of the *organized society*. Our organized society exists in an environment of equal rights and unequal incomes. Conflicts between these two phenomena result in tensions between the *political principles of democracy* and the *economic principles of capitalism.*
- The political economy of the United States is that of *democratic capitalism.* The thrust of this ideology comes from the opposing values of political power and economic structure.
- *Democracy* is characterized by equality, due process, fairness, participation, suffrage, and electoral politics. *Capitalism* implies efficiency, productivity, hierarchy, competition, and entrepreneurship.
- Public administration finds its *origins* in democracy but owes much to the fundamental principles of capitalism.
- The dimensions of U.S. federalism are *political, fiscal,* and *administrative.* Through federalism, Americans "structure" fifty sets of partisan politics. Counties, townships, school districts, and special districts constitute the great majority of the 80,000 governments in the United States.
- Americans opt for *"market justice"* over *"political justice."* Benefits are allocated by the economic marketplace, not by government programs and policies. American participation in politics has declined as citizens do not perceive their economic well-being as greatly dependent on political involvement.
- U.S. cultural emphasis is on individualism, not political participation. Citizens separate their personal lives and interests and other matters of national life. America is the country of *individualism par excellence.*
- The American culture of individualism negatively effects political participation levels of lower-income groups. An *economic class bias* emerges. Citizens of higher economic status are much more likely to be politically involved than those of lower economic status.
- The ebbs and flows of government expansion and constraints may be understood by looking at four critical periods in the twentieth century. These eras of political economy occurred around the years *1915, 1935, 1965,* and *1985.*
- In 1992, for the first time in American history, the number of federal, state, and local jobs outdistanced the number of manufacturing jobs.
- *Substantive issues* of public and private administration raise questions concerning issues of politics versus profits, measurement of objectives, and management versus administration. Procedural issues concern open versus closed systems, methods of evaluation, decision-making criteria, personnel systems, planning, and efficiency.

- The public philosophy of the United States in the late twentieth century was *interest group liberalism.* Whether liberal or conservative elites use the power and purse of government for their personal ends. The influence of organized interest groups extends to Congress in their votes, presidents in their programs, and bureaucrats in their administrative discretion.
- The philosophy of interest group liberalism is *pragmatic,* with government exercising its role as broker. In pluralistic government, procedure and process may be as important as substance.
- The effectiveness of interest groups in the *"Iron Triangle"* of elected officials, consumers, and government bureaucrats depends, in large part, upon the group's number of members, size of its budget, and expertise of its Washington staff. Now that we have explored the ecology of the craft, we are ready to move to another important subject public administrators must be aware of— the *anatomy,* or *structure,* of organizations.

The following case study shows how the private infrastructure of citizen interests affects the interplay of partisan, policy, and system politics. Are the political principles of democracy and economic principles of capitalism realized in the politics of building and economic development of the Hubert H. Humphrey Metrodome?

CASE STUDY

Private Infrastructure: Public Influence[43]

A growing controversy in many cities is the political economy of attracting and retaining professional sports teams.

Conflicts continue between political leaders and sports team owners over the issues of franchise team retention and stadium construction. Team owners claim that a major league team offers psychological and economic benefits to the host state. However, governors and mayors balk at the idea of providing them with expensive stadia and benefits. Teams may leave or threaten to abandon their current gathering of fans for the prospective attendance figures of another set of fans in another U.S. community. If so, efficiency, rationality, and profit for players and team management may triumph over compromise, consensus, and democratic participation of a particular community of citizens.[44]

The cooperation between the public and private sectors in the building of the Hubert H. Humphrey Metrodome in Minneapolis illustrates the inner dynamic of civic planning and corporate entrepreneurship that contribute to economic growth, more revenues for public programs, and, indirectly, to a healthier community with a better quality of life. In the ecology of democratic capitalism, where a growth economy is necessary, more vibrant economies can provide more tax dollars to support more public services. If a community's tax base is declining, the number and quality of public programs will decline. The enclosed, multiuse stadium is not only a center of entertainment in the community but also a symbol of civic vitality that may be linked to sports, politics, and economics. In the twenty-first century, the dome stadium will be as much the center of civic activity as the public square with its gazebo was at the beginning of the twentieth century. The dome stadium is often the center of the metropolis, if not in geographic terms, then certainly economically. Such a building opens up opportunities for varied entertainment and adds to convention and tourism prospects. Cities retain and seek major league professional franchises as dome tenants because of the perception that professional sports teams bring dollars and good publicity to the community.

The politics of the metrodome

This case study depicts the intricate weaving of political theory and practical politics. Personalities and individual efforts are set against the broader background of how issues are contested in Minnesota's public life. The study also illustrates how the public and private sectors can work together to produce an outcome acceptable to both forces, pointing out how business incentives and efficient market techniques may be incorporated into the workings of government.

Beginning in the early 1960s, the Minnesota Twins and Minnesota Vikings played their games at Metropolitan Stadium in Bloomington, Minnesota, a Minneapolis suburb. The stadium, built for the Minneapolis Millers minor league baseball team in the mid-1950s, was expanded for major league sports in 1961 and 1965. The Minnesota teams represent two diverse communities. When the Met was built in 1955, Bloomington was a "neutral" suburb, a rustic community with a population of about 10,000, a village that carried little, if any, political or economic clout in the state.

Within five years, Bloomington's population rose to 50,000. The "Bloomington strip," a string of hotels and restaurants, developed around the nearby stadium and airport. Minneapolis witnessed the exodus of city dwellers and city businesses to Bloomington and other surrounding suburbs. Minneapolis needed the economic development a domed facility could generate with more jobs and a larger tax base, and the city wanted the national attention that professional sports teams bring. At the Met, the sight lines for football were poor. The stadium was essentially a baseball stadium that accommodated football in the fall and winter. The seating capacity was 48,700, one of the smaller pro football stadiums, but a suitable capacity for baseball. (There are only eight home NFL football games yearly, whereas there are eighty-one baseball dates.) The Vikings, therefore, needed a new home more than did the Twins. Besides the problem of viewing football from baseball angles, the field was an annual victim of Minnesota winters. Although some football purists claimed the Vikings had a psychological edge over opponents in the freezing weather, Viking management argued that stressful weather conditions kept fans away and created miserable weather conditions for those who chose to brave freezing temperatures. Regardless, the Vikings wanted out of the Met and threatened to leave Minnesota. As former Minnesota state senator, Steve Keefe, pointed out, "The Minnesota Vikings are not a Minnesota team. They're a company that plays football and happens to be located in Minnesota. They're here to make money. They're not here because they love us . . . no matter how much we love them." Why did government get involved in the sports stadium business? William Donald Schaefer, former mayor of Baltimore and former governor of Maryland, comments: "You look at the prestige, you look at the jobs, you look at the things it generates in a city. You won't be able to replace them, and once they are gone, they are gone." Local government in Minnesota was characterized as a "strong council-weak mayor" urban arrangement of political power. The local political culture, therefore, dictated an active role for business in the stadium project. The mixture of business involvement made it improbable that a Minneapolis stadium could be constructed exclusively with public money. A conservative, Scandinavian community such as Minneapolis-St. Paul is likely to be frugal with the taxpayers' dollars, refusing to invest in such a public commitment.

Partisan, policy, and system politics in the metrodome

Minneapolis was governed by a strong council-weak mayor plan, therefore, dominance by a political machine or party boss was unlikely. In recent years, neither the Democratic nor Republican parties, either in state or national politics, had been dominant for an extended length of time. Political power in Minneapolis is historically dispersed.

Minnesota state government is likewise characterized by a high degree of citizen participation. Despite such civic mindedness the citizens of Minnesota were never allowed an opportunity to express their preference in a direct vote on the stadium issue, because a tradition of citizens' referenda does not exist in Minnesota. Former governor Rudy Perpich, a populist Democrat, appointed a seven-member Stadium Commission whose functions and procedures were defined by the state legislature. Although members of the commission represented a broad base of interests in Minnesota, their decisions on the cost and location of the new stadium were by no means political in a partisan sense.

The extent of an interest group's influence depends on its resources. In this case, the resources were substantial. The Industry Square Development Company (ISDC), a private group of interested citizens, emerged as the "public service investment." John Cowles, Jr., owner of the *Minneapolis Star and Tribune,* committed $4 million in cash and $900,000 in land (the company owned three-fourths of a block of the Industry Square area), and the First National Bank and the Northwestern National Bank pledged $1 million each. The Vikings agreed to commit $972,500 until other businesses could be found to pay all or part of the remaining sum.

On November 15, 1978, Cowles announced that at least forty-two business firms, including the Minnesota Vikings football team, had pledged $14,750,000 to pay the costs of the stadium land package. Of the total, $10.7 million had come from private investors who promised to buy common stock in ISDC if Minneapolis were chosen as the stadium site. The remaining $4 million had been given in the form of tax deductible, charitable contributions.

Other interests concerned with the stadium project were the Minneapolis Chamber of Commerce and the AFL-CIO. Ad hoc groups included the Committee to Let the People Decide, a group advocating more democracy in the stadium process; Citizens Opposed to the Stadium Tax (COST); and Minnesotans Against the Downtown Dome (MADD). COST's leader was Fred Primoli, a St. Paul bar owner, who opposed the extra 2 percent tax on every drink for a Minneapolis stadium that would benefit bar owners across the Mississippi River. Two neighborhoods near the proposed stadium site, Elliot Park and Cedar Riverside, combined forces to form MADD.

Members of the Stadium Commission had four policy options. They could decide: (1) to build a multipurpose, open-air stadium in Bloomington for football, baseball, and soccer at a cost estimate of $37.5 million; (2) to remodel the Met in Bloomington and build an open-air football and soccer stadium, Bloomington's Met, at a cost estimate of $42 million; (3) to construct a multipurpose, domed stadium in

Minneapolis at a cost estimate of $55 million; (4) or to do nothing. The last option was never a popular alternative, since the Vikings had informed commission members that it would be "exceedingly difficult" for the team to sign a long-term lease for an open-air Bloomington stadium.

The commissioners' final decision was insulated from the control of democratic politics. They were accountable to no one—not the legislators, not the interest groups, not the public. (Throughout the 1970s, not one public opinion poll showed that either Minnesota, metropolitan, or Minneapolis residents favored a Minneapolis stadium over a Bloomington stadium, whether it be a new construction or a remodeled Met.)

The Metropolitan Stadium Commission was created by the Minnesota legislature, therefore the creation of the Stadium Commission was, in effect, the creation of another branch of government. According to researcher Amy Klobuchar, the transfer of authority from the legislative branch of the government to a bureaucratic one (the Commission) represents a phenomenon of American politics that commenced soon after the New Deal. "There is a certain appeal of this 'apolitical' mode of decision-making, concludes Klobuchar. "Things seem cleaner, neater. Decisions are more comprehensive and prompt. In the hands of the commissioners, the stadium issue was no longer considered a legislative beachball to be tossed to and fro by the prevailing political winds." The Commission voted by a 4-3 margin to locate the new stadium in Minneapolis. "In choosing the Minneapolis alternative, I am simply making my best judgment based on what I perceive to be in the long-term, public interest," stated commission chair, Dan J. Brutger.

The Minneapolis dome, while winning no high awards for architectural aesthetics, was built primarily with private funds, came in $8 million under the $55 million budget, and was completed on time. From a purely economic perspective, the project was quite successful.

The Metrodome provides important home field advantages for the Twins throughout the American League season in postseason championship competition and during World Series games. In 1987 and 1991, the Minnesota Twins defeated the St. Louis Cardinals and Atlanta Braves, respectively, in the World Series. During these World Series games, the noise levels created by overjoyed Minnesota fans broke noise level records, to the dismay of environmentalists. Baseball traditionalists, perhaps suffering from cultural lag, were not happy either; the World Series was played inside a building on a green rug for the first time in baseball history. During the season, the winning Twins provided entertainment for a record 2.2 million customers. Both the liquor and hotel-motel taxes, levied to pay for the Metrodome, were lifted in 1984. With the exception of the indirect state subsidy in the form of the real estate tax exemptions, the dome is self-supporting.

With no professional teams, did Bloomington's plight worsen? The land upon which the old Met stood, appraised at $5 to $7 million, was sold for more than $18 million because of highly competitive bidding. Conflicts between Minneapolis and Bloomington, city and suburb, subsided when, in 1992, the Mall of America (MOA), the nation's largest shopping and entertainment complex, opened on the old stadium site.

Where the Vikings played those "ice bowl" NFL playoff games and Harmon Killebrew hit home runs, MOA employs ten thousand people in permanent jobs and is expecting forty million customer visits annually by 1996. MOA is expected to house 270 stores, about thirty eateries, fourteen movie screens, ten nightclubs, twelve sets of restrooms and a two-level eighteen-hole miniature golf course. A seven-acre "Camp Snoopy" theme park from Buena Park's Knott's Berry Farm also draws people. MOA enticed Nordstrom, Bloomingdale's, and Macy's—big names in the shopping world—into their suburban Bloomington site. Mall operators expect 70 percent of sales to come from customers within a radius of 150 miles.

Controversies over public subsidies for private projects are part of America's social, political, and economic infrastructure. However, not everyone is pleased with Minneapolis' march into the future. "The park should be banned from baseball," stated the late Twins and Yankee manager, Billy Martin. Researcher Klobuchar, commenting on how economics has changed the sports of our youth, concludes: "The teams no longer play football or baseball, but domeball, a climate controlled, Orwellian version of sports." What can we learn from the political economy of domeball?

- A complex, sensitive relationship between public and private spheres of influence has developed in every American community; a combination of public and private forces and priorities that is unique to every American community.
- Partisan, policy, and system politics blend and are not separate modes of operation.
- The values of democracy and bureaucracy are at work simultaneously. Citizens democratically elect their civic leaders every four years, having exercised their voting rights. The public does not, however, contribute directly to every public decision made in society during the interim. At this juncture, the principles of bureaucracy or public administration come to the front. In the Minnesota case, the corporate private bureaucracies, such as the *Minneapolis Star and Tribune,* the Mott Foundation, First National Bank, Northwestern National Bank, and the Minnesota Twins and Vikings, emerged to influence public policies.
- The extent of an interest group's influence depends on its financial and human resources.
- While public administrators need revenues for implementing a variety of publicly funded programs, business interests need to be creative by introducing new projects for achieving a more vibrant local economy. Businesses realize profits; profits are taxed; these revenues pay for qualified public personnel to provide government services. In democracy and capitalism, freedom to offer new ideas in the entrepreneurial spirit is essential for achieving human potential.

QUESTIONS AND INSTRUCTIONS

1. Was the public interest of Minnesotans served by the legislature's decision to create a Stadium Commission with the power to decide this issue? Was the decision to build a new stadium in the best interests of Minnesotans?
2. To whom, if anyone, was the Stadium Commission accountable for its decision?
3. What role did Minnesota's political culture play in stimulating local economic forces to build a new stadium?
4. In what ways are partisan, policy, and system politics evident in the building of the new stadium?

5. What interest groups influenced the partisan, policy, and system decision-making processes to relocate the Twins and Vikings in downtown Minneapolis?
6. How are the political principles of democracy and the economic principles of capitalism manifest in this case?
7. Should professional sports franchises be permitted complete economic freedom to move to a more profitable economic setting without first compensating the community that supported them over the years? In other words, do the Minnesota Twins and Vikings owe compensation to the citizens of Bloomington?

INSIGHTS-ISSUES/PRIVATE INFRASTRUCTURE: PUBLIC INFLUENCE

Clearly and briefly describe and illustrate these concepts, issues, or points. Interpret the word "role" as meaning impact, application, importance, effect and/or illustration of certain facts, concerns, or issues from the case study.

1. Role of private sector (interest groups);
2. Role of public sector and/or elected officials;
3. Role of partisan, policy, and system politics (if any);
4. Role of economic growth for benefiting public sector projects;
5. Role of Stadium Commission in policy decision making.

ENDNOTES

1. Emmette S. Redford, *Democracy in the Administrative State* (New York: Oxford University Press, 1969), 3.
2. Arthur M. Okun, *Equality and Efficiency: The Big Tradeoff* (Washington, DC: The Brookings Institution, 1975), 4.
3. Suzanne Garment, "Making A Case for Regulation," *Washington Post,* 2 February 1997, p. A8.
4. Henry T. Abraham, *Freedom and the Court: Civil Rights and Liberties in the United States* (New York: Oxford University Press, 1977), 110–129.
5. Okun, *Equality and Efficiency,* op cit 119.
6. Ralph D. Christy, "Markets or Government? Balancing Imperfect and Complementary Alernatives," *American Journal of Agricultural Economics* 78, no. 5 (December 1996): 1145–1157.
7. *Ibid.,* 120.
8. Lester M. Salamon and John J. Siegfried, "Economic Power and Political Influence: The Impact of Industry Structure on Public Policy," *American Political Science Review* 71, no. 4 (December 1977): 1026–1043.
9. Adam Przeworski and Michael Wallerstein, "Democratic Capitalism at the Crossroads," *Democracy* 2, no. 3 (July 1982): 52–68.
10. Barbara Vobejda, "In Job Strength, Manufacturing Eclipsed by Public Sector," *Washington Post,* 18 August 1992, p. 11A.

11. *U.S. News & World Report,* 17 August 1992, 13. See also John Rouse, "Government-Dominated Work Force Creating Change," *Muncie Star,* 23 August 1992, p. 10A.

12. Robert E. Lane, "Market Justice, Political Justice," *American Political Science Review,* 80, no. 2 (June 1986), 383–402. See also Jennifer Nedelsky, *Private Property and the Limits of American Constitutionalism* (New York: Oxford University Press, 1990).

13. Harry Holloway with John George, *Public Opinion,* 2d ed. (New York: St. Martin's Press, 1986), 157.

14. William Watts and Lloyd A. Free, eds., *The State of the Nation* (New York: University Books, Potomac Associates, 1967), 97.

15. John D. Hicks, George E. Mowry, and Robert E. Burke, *A History of American Democracy* (Boston: Houghton Mifflin Co., 1966), 552–558; and Henry Bamford Parkes, *The United States of America: A History* (New York: Alfred A. Knopf, 1968), 560–564.

16. Larry D. Gerber, "World War II and the Expansion of Government in America," *National Forum* 75, no. 4 (fall 1995): 30–34.

17. Robert J. Samuelson, "Roosevelt Romantized: FDR Made the Modern Presidency—Dooming his Successors to Failure and Unpopularity" *Newsweek* 28, no. 17 (21 October 1996): 52.

18. Hicks, Mowry, and Burke, *A History of American Democracy,* 670–691; and Parkes, *The United States of America,* 628–645.

19. Stephen Gettinger, "Fulfilling the Great Society," *Congressional Quarterly Weekly Report* 53, no. 23 (10 June 1995): 1615–1618.

20. See Doris Kerns, *Lyndon Johnson and the American Dream* (New York: Harper & Row, 1976), 210–250; Lyndon Baines Johnson, *The Vantage Point: Perspective of the Presidency, 1963–1969* (New York: Holt, Rinehart, and Winston, 1971); John E. Schwarz, *America's Hidden Success: A Reassessment of Public Policy from Kennedy to Reagan* (New York: W. W. Norton & Co., 1988).

21. Larry Berman and Bruce Allen Murphy, *Approaching Democracy* (Upper Saddle River, N.J.: Prentice Hall, 1996), 125.

22. Jonathan Rauch, "What Revolution?," *National Journal,* (21 January 1989): 158. See also John L. Palmer and Isabel V. Sawhill, eds., *The Reagan Record* (Washington, D.C.: The Ballinger Press, 1984); "The Reagan Record," *The Urban Institute Policy and Research Report* 14, no. 1 (August 1984): 1–17; "Perspectives on the Reagan Years: Popular vs. Political Leadership," 17, no. 1 (April 1987): 1–3.

23. Al From, "Budget Deal Is the New Deal for Democrats," *Los Angeles Times,* 12 May 1997, p. B5.

24. Robert Eden, "The Rhetorical Presidency and the Eclipse of Executive Power: Woodrow Wilson's 'Constitutional Government in the United States,' " *Polity* 28, no. 3 (spring 1996): 357–379.

25. E. J. Dionne Jr. "The Era of 'Big' Government: Why You'd Miss It if It Went," *Kettering Review* (summer 1997): 32–39.

26. *Ibid.,* 36.

27. Larry Berman and Bruce Allen Murphy, *Approaching Democracy* (Upper Saddle River, N.J.: Prentice Hall, 1996), 128.

28. William Schneider, "What Democrats Have Learned," *National Journal,* 30, no. 13 (28 March 1998): 726.

29. Leon E. Panetta, "The True Balance of Power," *New York Times,* 2 February 1997, 146, no. 50691, p. 15.

30. Frederick S. Lane, *Current Issues in Public Administration* (New York: St. Martin's Press, 1982), 156.

31. Lawrence J. O'Toole, Jr., *American Intergovernmental Relations, Foundations, Perspectives, and Issues* (Washington, DC: CQ Press, 1985), 2.
32. Michael A. Murray, "Comparing Public and Private Management: An Exploratory Essay," *Public Administration Review* 35, no. 4 (July/August 1975): 364–371.
33. Herbert A. Simon, *Administrative Behavior* (New York: Macmillan, 1957).
34. Walter Russell Mead, "To Tether Big Business to the National Interest, Read Hamilton." *Los Angeles Times,* 23 February 1997, pp. M2, 6.
35. Jonathan Rauch, "The End of Government," *National Journal* 28, no. 36 (7 September 1996): 1890–1896.
36. Theodore J. Lowi, *The End of Liberalism: The Second Republic of the United States* (New York: W. W. Norton & Co., 1969).
37. *Ibid.,* 43.
38. *Ibid.,* 51.
39. *Ibid.,* 63.
40. Richard N. Goodwin, "Perspective in Politics," *Los Angeles Times,* 30 January 1997, p. A9.
41. Albert R. Hunt, "Campaign-Financing Overhaul Is Wanted but Not Passionately," *Wall Street Journal,* 19 September 1997, 130, no. 57, p. 6.
42. Andrew Bard Schmookler, "When Money Talks, Is It Free Speech? PACs Give Big Bucks to Buy Access and Influence," *The Christian Science Monitor,* 10 November 1997, 15.
43. For an authoritative account of the politics of building the Hubert H. Humphrey Metrodome, see Amy Klobuchar, *Uncovering The Dome* (Prospect Heights, Ill.: Waveland Press, Inc., 1982). The Minnesota dome case study is based on Klobuchar's research. See also Gwen Ifill, "Meet Economic Development's New Designated Hitter— the Stadium," *Washington Post,* National Weekly Edition, 6 April 1987, p. 19; and Hal Lancaster, "Stadium Projects Are Proliferating Amid Debate Over Benefit to Cities," *Wall Street Journal,* 20 March 1987, p. 37; Rod S. Shilkrot, "Minnesota's Magnificent Mall of America," *Home & Away* (May/June 1992): 38–43; and Jennifer Lowe, "Oh Beautiful, for Spacious Mall," *Muncie Star,* 16 August 1992, p. 9C.
44. Gary Boulard and Laura Loyacono, "Free Agent Franchises," *State Legislatures* 22, no. 5 (May 1996): 20–26.

3

THE ANATOMY
OF PUBLIC ORGANIZATION

CHAPTER HIGHLIGHTS

THE BASIS OF ORGANIZATION

POINTS ABOUT PYRAMIDS

LINE AND STAFF

CENTRALIZATION AND DECENTRALIZATION

THE CRAFT AND POLITICAL CULTURE

Every public administrator works within an organizational framework. The successful public administrator must have a solid understanding of the principles of organization and must realize that the structure of an organization plays a vital role that cannot be overlooked. This chapter provides an examination of the key organizational principles that have a major impact on how public administration operates. The public administrator who understands the broad implications of organization will be better prepared to meet the daily challenge of contributing to a public institution that most effectively serves its constituents.

The *anatomy* of public bureaucracy is its organizational framework or administrative structure.

THE BASIS OF ORGANIZATION

The structures of most public organizations are rather complex. These complexities can, however, be simplified by taking a look at the fundamental principles of organization outlined by Luther Gulick. Gulick, a trailblazer in U.S. administrative theory, classified organizations into four categories. These categories are based on an organization's *raison d'être*—the reason it was established. The categories are *purpose, process, place,* and *clientele.*[1] Gulick's categories should be viewed as a Navy captain views the terms "port" and "starboard"—terms that may seem so basic as to be unimportant but are essential elements of a more complex operation.

PURPOSE

Organizations established on the basis of *purpose* are oriented toward the accomplishment of specific tasks. Examples of organizations developed on the basis of purpose are school systems, fire departments, and the branches of the military. The activities that these organizations engage in are fundamentally purpose-specific and seldom extend beyond that purpose.

PROCESS

A *process* organization is oriented not so much toward accomplishing specific goals but toward performing certain functions. From our understanding of the law as process, we might guess that a good example of such an agency is a city legal department. Typically, at least in a large city, this department will consist of a group of lawyers who service other departments. One lawyer may represent the city's urban renewal authority in the use of eminent domain while another may defend the city's public works department in lawsuits. These types of organizations concern themselves almost completely in the procedural aspects of administration.

GOVERNMENT AGENCIES AND COMMISSIONS FORMED DURING THE NEW DEAL

The anatomy of U.S. public bureaucracy—its organizational framework or administrative structure—owes much of its agency development to the 1933–1945 era of the Depression, World War II, and Franklin D. Roosevelt's leadership skills during the New Deal. Led by then House Speaker Newt Gingrich (R-Ga), Republicans argue the welfare state FDR created and nurtured has gotten out of control. Much of what FDR accomplished is now under attack. Agencies in the federal bureaucracy that were created during the FDR era face privatization, rethinking, consolidation and elimination.

For Roosevelt, change was policy. "It is common sense to take a method and try it. If it fails, admit it frankly and try another. But above all try something," FDR said. In the political fashion of the New Deal, Roosevelt built dams and brought electricity to millions, created farm subsidies and unemployment insurance, regulated a stock market gone out of control, set up a social security program for the elderly, and gave unions the right to organize. While many agencies no longer exist as they were created, other federal agencies and departments absorbed many functions in a greatly expanded welfare state. Listed are the agencies created during the 1933–1945 time frame.

1933

Civilian Conservation Corps: Provided jobs for the unemployed.

Farm Credit Administration: Provided a credit system for farmers.

Federal Civil Works Administration.

Federal Deposit Insurance Corp. (FDIC): Insured bank deposits.

Federal Emergency Relief Administration: Cooperated with the states in relieving hardships caused by unemployment and drought (today, Federal Emergency Management Administration).

Immigration and Naturalization Service: Regulated immigration.

National Labor Board: Remedied unlawful labor practices.

National Recovery Administration: Promoted recovery from the Depression.

Public Works Administration: Increased employment and purchasing power through construction of useful public works, such as bridges, in various states.

Tennessee Valley Authority: Provided power to south-central states.

1934

Bureau of Air Commerce: Early incarnation of the Federal Aviation Administration.

Export-Import Bank of Washington: Regulated trade between United States and foreign countries.

Federal Communications Commission (FCC): Regulated radio, telephone, and telegraph systems.

Federal Housing Administration (FHA): Insured private lending companies against loss on home mortgage loans and on loans for improving small properties.

National Archives and Records Service: Managed U.S. government records.

Securities and Exchange Commission: Protected the public from investing in unsafe securities and regulated stock market practices.

1935

National Labor Relations Board: Administered the National Labor Relations Act.

National Youth Administration: Provided job training for unemployed youths and part-time work for needy students.

Resettlement Administration: Resettled and rehabilitated farm tenants and sharecroppers.

Rural Electrification Administration: Aided farmers in electrification of homes.

Social Security Board: Provided unemployment relief and old-age pensions.

Work Progress Administration: Provided work for the needy in public works projects.

1936

U.S. Maritime Commission: Oversaw U.S. maritime policy.

1937

Farm Security Administration: Provided resettlement and economic help for farm families.

1938

Air Safety Board: Investigated accidents (today, National Transportation Safety Board).

Civil Aeronautics Administration (today, Federal Aviation Administration).

Civil Aeronautics Authority (today, Federal Aviation Administration).

Federal Crop Insurance Corp.: Provided insurance protection against unavoidable loss of certain crops.

1939

Federal Works Agency: Administered by the WPA.

Works Project Administration (WPA): Created and administered work relief projects.

1940

Bureau of the Public Debt: Issued government securities.

Civil Aeronautics Board: Regulated airline economics and investigated accidents.

Defense Plant Corp.: Issued government-backed loans and guarantees to enlarge U.S. industrial facilities to combat Nazi threat.

National Defense Research Committee: Wartime research effort.

Selective Service System: Registered civilians for the military.

1941

Committee on Fair Employment Practices: Encouraged fair employment.

Office of Price Administration: Administered rationing programs for tires, gasoline, meat, sugar, and other commodities.

Office of Scientific Research and Development: Joint civilian-military research efforts, including development of the atomic bomb.

1942

Office of Strategic Services (today, a branch of the Central Intelligence Agency).

Office of War Information: World War II propaganda agency.

War Manpower Commission: Mobilized manpower for wartime.

War Production Board: Mobilized and allocated industrial facilities and plants for wartime.

Source: Reuters; *Washington Post*, 12 April 1995, p. A23.

POLIS ARCHITECTURE

Government buildings should project a distinct public character different from private office buildings. Public buildings should project democratic values that are untainted by consumerism. Government buildings should be characterized by classical architecture, regional distinctiveness and a delightful play of form and color. Architecture should not only evoke governance, but bureaucracy and democracy as well.

Source: Charles T. Goodsell "Bureaucracy's House in the Polis: Seeking an Appropriate Presence," *Journal of Public Administration Research and Theory* 7, no. 3 (July 1997): 393–419.

PLACE

Organizations under this heading serve particular locales. Only a few public agencies meet the strict classification standards for this category, but the idea is clear; these organizations are involved in the administration of a particular locale only. The neighborhood city halls that Boston and a few other cities have established are one example. These centers provide a variety of services to the people in a particular neighborhood.

CLIENTELE

Closely linked to *place* organizations, *clientele* organizations are not a common feature of our administrative landscape. These agencies serve particular groups of people. One notable example is the federal government's Bureau of Indian Affairs, designed to provide a variety of services to all Native Americans, regardless of the region in which they live. Another example is the federal government's Children's Bureau, which, from the time of its creation in 1912 to its dissolution in 1969, sought to furnish a variety of services to children, proudly claiming that it serviced the whole child.[2] Overlap in the categories is obvious, but there is always a dominant organizational motif. Fire departments are not only established for the purpose of putting out fires but are also organized on the basis of the area of their fire protection coverage; yet purpose, not place, is the main reason for establishing a fire department. Organizations are established not only on the basis of one of Gulick's categories but also through a combination of purpose, process, place, and clientele, regardless of which factor dominates.

POINTS ABOUT PYRAMIDS

The organizational structure of most institutions is best thought of as a pyramid. The organization must delegate its work to a number of employees. To make sure that these employees do the work delegated to them and to see to it that their efforts are coordinated, the organization establishes supervisors. These supervisors may be so numerous that they, in turn, require supervisors. As a result, one or more levels of hierarchy tend to emerge in any sizeable organization, with the numbers of persons in each level dwindling until the tip of a pyramid is reached.

Soldiers are grouped into squads under the control of sergeants. Squads are formed into platoons under the leadership of lieutenants. Platoons are collected into companies under the command of captains. The progression continues up to the apex of the divisional triangle, headed by the division's commanding general. However, and this is a point that bears continued emphasis, nearly every organization is part of an even bigger organization, and so the infantry division and its general are answerable to still others above. The pyramidal structure continues into the higher levels of the Pentagon where the secretaries of the army, navy, and air force are accountable to the secretary of defense. The latter, meanwhile, occupies one of twelve seats in the cabinet, a body presided over by the president of the United States.

Much less structurally rigid organizations than infantry divisions or police forces tend to assume, to a greater or lesser degree, a pyramidal structure. A large university, for example, will often contain many subunits and a variety of levels of authority. Yet we generally find that the professors are under the administrative leadership of their department chairpersons; the chairpersons are responsible to their deans; the deans are answerable to the heads of their respective universities; and the chancellors are accountable to the president of the university. The pyramid model brings with it the concepts of *unity of command, chain of command,* and *span of control.*

Unity of command describes the exclusive relationship of those who follow orders to those who give orders. This principle is based on the idea that no one can serve two masters. This maxim has been true for work organizations, particularly those operating under the bureaucratic norms of delegation, specialization, and accountability, and accounts for much of their success.

Requiring an individual or a group to respond to the orders of two or more superiors may produce conflict, confusion, and even chaos. If unity of command does not exist, conflict and confusion will not only characterize those being commanded but those doing the commanding. In other words, multiple superiors will not only confuse their subordinates but also each other.

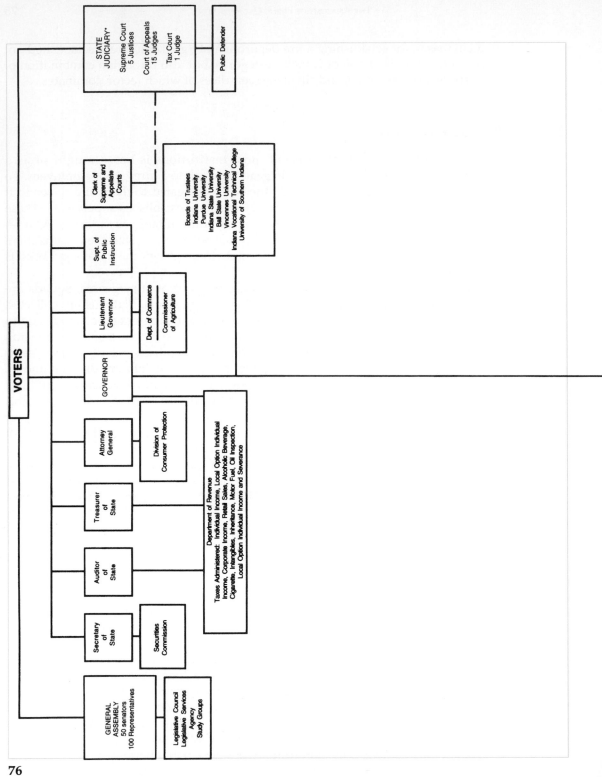

STATE BOARDS, DEPARTMENTS, COMMISSIONS AND OTHER AGENCIES*

Board of ACCOUNTS . . . ADJUTANT GENERAL . . . Department of ADMINISTRATION . . . ADMINISTRATIVE BUILDING COUNCIL . . . ADVOCACY SERVICES . . . AERONAUTICS DIVISION . . . AFFIRMATIVE ACTION OFFICE . . . AGING AND REHABILITATIVE SERVICES . . . Office of AGRICULTURE . . . AIR POLLUTION CONTROL BOARD . . . AIRPORT AUTHORITY . . . ALCOHOLIC BEVERAGE COMMISSION . . . Board of ANIMAL HEALTH . . . ARTS COMMISSION . . . BOXING COMMISSION . . . BUDGET AGENCY . . . CIVIL RIGHTS COMMISSION . . . COMMUNITY RESIDENTIAL FACILITIES COUNCIL . . . Department of CORRECTION . . . CRIMINAL JUSTICE INSTITUTE . . . Department of EDUCATION . . . EDUCATION COUNCIL . . . EDUCATION EMPLOYMENT RELATIONS BOARD . . . EDUCATIONAL SERVICES FOUNDATION . . . EGG BOARD . . . Bureau of ELEVATOR SAFETY . . . EMERGENCY MANAGEMENT AGENCY . . . Department of WORKFORCE DEVELOPMENT . . . Department of ENVIRONMENTAL MANAGEMENT . . . ETHICS COMMISSION . . . FAMILY AND SOCIAL SERVICES ADMINISTRATION . . . Department of FINANCIAL INSTITUTIONS . . . Department of FIRE AND BUILDING SERVICES . . . FIRE MARSHAL . . . Commission on FORENSIC SCIENCES . . . GOVERNOR'S VOLUNTARY ACTION COMMITTEE . . . GREAT LAKES COMMISSION . . . Department of HEALTH . . . HEALTH FACILITIES COUNCIL . . . HEALTH PROFESSIONS BUREAU . . . Commission for HIGHER EDUCATION . . . HISTORICAL BUREAU . . . HOSPITAL REGULATORY AND LICENSING COUNCIL . . . HOUSING FINANCE AUTHORITY . . . INDUSTRIAL BOARD . . . INSURANCE DEPARTMENT . . . KANKAKEE RIVER BASIN COMMISSION . . . Department of LABOR . . . LAW ENFORCEMENT TRAINING BOARD . . . LIBRARY SERVICES AUTHORITY . . . LITTLE CALUMET RIVER BASIN COMMISSION . . . MEDICAL ADVISORY COMMISSION ON DRIVER LICENSURE . . . MEDICAL AND NURSING GRANT FUND BOARD . . . MEDICAL EDUCATION BOARD . . . MENTAL HEALTH . . . MERIDIAN STREET PRESERVATION COMMISSION . . . Bureau of MINES AND MINING . . . Bureau of MOTOR VEHICLES . . . Department of NATURAL RESOURCES . . . OCCUPATIONAL SAFETY STANDARDS COMMISSION . . . OHIO RIVER VALLEY WATER SANITATION COMMISSION . . . PERSONNEL DEPARTMENT . . . PESTICIDE REVIEW BOARD . . . PORT COMMISSION . . . Commission for PROPRIETARY EDUCATION . . . PROFESSIONAL LICENSING AGENCY . . . PUBLIC EMPLOYEES' RETIREMENT FUND . . . RADIATION CONTROL ADVISORY COMMISSION . . . REDEVELOPMENT COMMISSION . . . REHABILITATION SERVICES AGENCY . . . Committee on SAFETY . . . Board of SAFETY REVIEW . . . SCHOOL PROPERTY TAX CONTROL BOARD . . . STANDARDBRED BOARD OF REGULATIONS . . . STATE EMPLOYEES' APPEAL COMMISSION . . . STATE FAIR BOARD . . . STATE LIBRARY . . . STATE OFFICE BUILDING COMMISSION . . . STATE PLANNING SERVICES AGENCY . . . STATE POLICE DEPARTMENT . . . STREAM POLLUTION CONTROL BOARD . . . STUDENT ASSISTANCE COMMISSION . . . Board of TAX COMMISSIONERS . . . TEACHERS' RETIREMENT FUND BOARD . . . TECHNOLOGY PREPARATION CURRICULUM DEVELOPMENT . . . Department of TRANSPORTATION . . . UTILITY CONSUMER COUNSELOR . . . UTILITY REGULATORY COMMISSION . . . Department of VETERANS' AFFAIRS . . . Commission on VOCATIONAL EDUCATION . . . Council on VOCATIONAL AND TECHNICAL EDUCATION . . . WAGE ADJUSTMENT BOARD . . . WAR MEMORIALS COMMISSION

BELOW: Semi-independent agencies largely ex officio in nature

CREAMERY EXAMINING BOARD . . . ELECTION BOARD . . . Board of FINANCE . . . JUDICIAL CONFERENCE . . . PROPERTY TAX REPLACEMENT FUND BOARD . . . PROSECUTING ATTORNEYS COUNCIL . . . Board for PUBLIC DEPOSITORIES . . . Commission on PUBLIC RECORDS . . . RECIPROCITY COMMISSION . . . SCHOOL BUS COMMITTEE . . . SURPLUS PROPERTY EVALUATION COMMISSION

*There are approximately 400 boards and agencies. Those listed above are only representative.

Chart by: INDIANA CHAMBER OF COMMERCE

FIGURE 3–1   Indiana State Government: A Simplified Organizational Chart.

Source: *Here is Your Indiana Government* (Indianapolis, IN: Indiana Chamber of Commerce, 1991), page 47

The unity of command principle may come into conflict with methods of boards and commissions. It is argued that such multiple-headed bodies are suitable only for semijudicial organizations (such as regulatory commissions) or for certain policy-making or advisory functions. If an organization is administering a program, if it is *doing* things, then the reins of its authority should converge eventually into one pair of hands. Responsibility can then be pinpointed, and conflicting orders, internecine warfare, and a host of other organizational ills can be avoided.

Unity of command usually requires a *chain of command,* the second concept in the pyramid model. In any large organization the person at the top cannot oversee all that is going on below. He or she needs others to help do this. Frequently, these helpers cannot supervise all those beneath them. As a result, several echelons of command may emerge through which authority is presumed to proceed downward in a neat, orderly flow. Unity of command dictates that the captain of A Company does not give orders to the soldiers of B Company. With chain of command, the battalion major does not give orders directly to soldiers from either company, but works instead through their company commanders.

Even less structured organizations observe, to some degree, the same principle. The college dean, if he or she has reason to be disturbed by the behavior of a particular professor, will usually first contact the professor's department chairperson before taking any direct action against the faculty member. In this way the chain of command at the university streamlines the administrative process.

A third concept linked to a pyramidal structure is *span of control.* Span of control refers to the number of units, whether individuals or groups, that any supervising unit, whether an individual or a group, must oversee. Unlike unity of command and chain of command, span of control does not constitute a principle of organization. Instead, it serves as a frame of reference. Span of control is not something that organizations *ought* to have but something they *do* have. Usually, a government organization develops guidelines for span of control based on an organization's mission. A challenge exists in making sure that the number of the subunits to be supervised is neither too many nor too few—to make sure that the supervisor's span of control is neither too great nor too small. Unfortunately, public administration provides no hard and fast criteria for determining such things. As with so many other questions concerning this capricious craft, the only intelligent answer is the highly unsatisfactory, "It all depends."

Public administrators in America have functioned with relatively narrow spans of control. It is rare to find a manager overseeing more than twelve subordinates or subunits, and it is not rare to find a manager overseeing as few as three.

Figures 3–1 and 3–2 illustrate how principles of unity command, chain of command, and span of control need to be, grounded in political compromise, consensus, and democratic participation.

The tighter the span of control, the more intervening levels between top and bottom, increasing paperwork and procrastination. A tight span of control also leads to decisions being made and policies being formulated too far from the scene of action. It can lead to difficulties in acquiring and retaining the services of top-notch people in vitally important, but no longer top-rated positions.

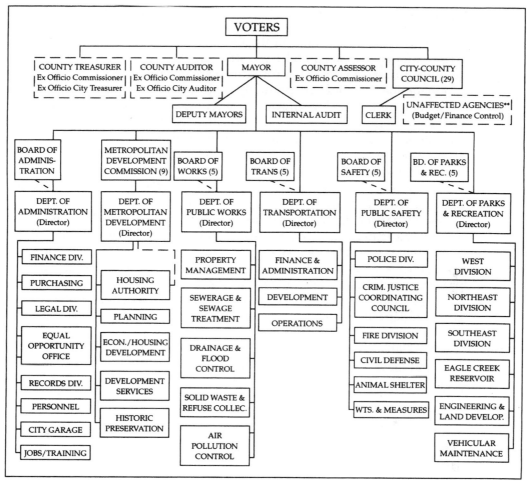

*Chart does not list certain county offices, such as sheriff, recorder, surveyor, coroner, clerk of Circuit Court or prosecuting attorney, which were not affected by consolidated city legislation.

**Council reviews budgets of municipal operating departments and corporations including otherwise unaffected bodies, such as Airport Authority and Health and Hospital Corporation.

FIGURE 3–2 Organization Chart: Consolidated Government for Indianapolis–Marion County
Source: *Here is Your Indiana Government* (Indianapolis, IN: Indiana Chamber of Commerce, 1991), page 81.

As with so much in public administration, span of control becomes a question of finding a proper balance for each situation. In finding this balance, we must assess the specific circumstances involved, keeping in mind that a gain achieved by moving in one direction may be offset by some losses. These losses do not, however, necessarily cancel the gain. If an executive has 100 agencies under his or her tutelage, some consolidation is almost always needed, even at the expense of creating more administrative levels. However, every consolidation carries a price tag that we must be willing to pay if we wish to reap the benefits.

LINE AND STAFF

The individuals working in the pyramid examples discussed earlier—U.S. Army infantry divisions and large state universities—are called *line personnel.* Another group of people to be considered are *staff personnel.*

Where line personnel are primarily concerned with implementing policy, staff personnel are the working members of an organization who do not implement policy. Line agencies and employees are directly responsible for furthering an organization's goals. Staff responsibilities are primarily concerned with assisting senior administrators in the determination of policy and the effective operation of the agency.

Line people are generalists, occupy positions of authority in the organization, and command implementation of the organization's operations.

The Departments of Agriculture, Commerce, Defense, Education, Energy, Health and Human Services, Housing and Urban Development, Interior, Justice, Labor, State, Transportation, Treasury, and Veterans Affairs constitute the major line agencies of the federal government. These organizations administer clientele programs and deal directly with the public.

The primary line officers are members of the President's cabinet. These line and staff departments and agencies were established in the following order:

1789: State; War; Treasury; Attorney General;

1798: Navy;

1829: Postmaster General;

1849: Interior;

1870: Justice;

1889: Agriculture;

1903: Commerce and Labor;

1913: Commerce; Labor (split);

1939: Office of Management and Budget;

1947: Defense (took the place of Navy and War);

1953: Health, Education, and Welfare;

1965: Housing and Urban Development;

1966: Transportation;

1971: (Postmaster General removed from cabinet);

1974: Office of the U.S. Trade Representative;

1977: Energy;

1979: Health and Human Services; Education (HEW split into HHS and Education);

1989: Veterans Affairs;

1993: Environmental Protection Agency; United Nations Ambassador;

Note: The Office of Management and Budget and the Office of U.S. Trade Representative are part of the Executive Office of the President and are not executive departments.

Source: Barbara J. Saffir, "Evolution of Cabinet," *Washington Post,* 9 February 1993, p. A15.

The expansion of the President's cabinet has occurred over time. The U.S. Constitution does not provide specifically for a cabinet, but Article II, Section 2 stipulates that a president may seek advice from heads of the executive departments. Cabinet status for an agency puts the agency on stronger footing when dealing with the Office of Management and Budget on fiscal and policy matters. In 1993, President Clinton proposed that the Environmental Protection Agency receive cabinet status. He also elevated the position of ambassador to the United Nations to cabinet level.

Staff people are specialists who provide skills, knowledge, and expertise to line personnel. For example, staff personnel draw up job classifications, program computers, or provide legal services. These are the employees who are most accurately referred to as the "staff." Staff agencies aid the chief executive and line personnel in developing, evaluating, and implementing public policies. Within the executive office of the president of the United States, for example, the main staff agencies are the White House Office, Office of Management and Budget, Council of Economic Advisors, National Security Council, Office of Policy Development, Office of the U.S. Trade Representative, Council on Environmental Quality, and Office of Science and Technology Policy.

The essence of staff work is thought, fact-finding, and planning.[3] Staff units are usually formed on the basis of process. An organization's computer center, for example, is typically comprised of people engaged in a process while serving a variety of purposes, places, and clientele within the context of the larger organization in which they operate.

In a school system, the computer center prepares figures on attendance records for principals, correlates statistics on children with learning disabilities for the director of special education, and pinpoints certain cost trends for the budgeting department. The latter chore illustrates that staff agencies may serve not only line departments but also other staff units.

The bureaucratic pyramid, in its pure form, makes no provision for staff units and their personnel. Traditionally, staff units have played only a small and shadowy role in the structure of work organizations. The place they occupied was usually at the hands or feet of the organization's leader, providing advice and assistance.

Staff services and personnel have increased tremendously. They occupy a greater place in an organization's structure, play a greater role in its activities, and consume a greater chunk of its budget. In so doing, they provide the organization with new benefits and new problems.

The problems stem from the model pyramid having no provision for staff units. It is difficult, at times almost impossible, to establish the correct niche for

**THE DEPARTMENT HEAD VERSUS YOUR P.A.
PROFESSOR-LINE VERSUS STAFF**

A student of political science need go no further than his or her university bureau-cracy to note the tensions inherent between staff and line personnel. Faculty members in the Department of Political Science are selected, retained, and promoted based upon their skills, knowledge, and expertise in a subfield or subfields of political science. Political science faculty are hired to teach a certain specialty, such as political theory, political parties, legislative studies, the presidency, constitutional law and jurisprudence, law and courts, federalism and intergovernmental relations, state politics, public policy, urban politics, comparative politics, foreign policy, and public administration. Faculty specialize in a certain subfield or subfields of political science, developing skills and expertise in that area or areas of knowledge.

As experts in particular aspects of political science, faculty are "staff" advisors in your college or university community to the chairperson of the Department of Political Science, a "line" official. Line officials are in command; they have certain authority as specified in the university's administrative guidelines; and in the case of the political science chairperson, the department head is a generalist in the discipline of political science. The dean, provost, and president of your college or university are also line officials. The tension between the chairperson, or department head, of the political science department and a certain faculty member who teaches a particular specialty in political science is almost a given. An individual political science professor might consider courses in public policy and administration to be most important in the department's academic curriculum. The department head must evaluate and balance the priorities of this and other recommendations of the political science professors under his or her supervision as he or she makes decisions as to what courses to offer students.

The faculty member, as specialist, promotes student interest in a certain subfield or subfields of political science expertise. The department head, as generalist and the administrative authority in command of the political science administrative unit, has responsibility that all subfields of political science are given appropriate emphasis in course offerings. Department heads, implementing line functions, and faculty, carrying out staff teaching assignments, have different program priorities in the Department of Political Science. It is not difficult to imagine that they, as line and staff employees of your college or university, often come into interpersonal conflicts as each person seeks to do their jobs to the best of their respective abilities.

staff within an organization's hierarchy. Staff people tend to be specialists whose expertise does not lend itself to a graded ranking except, possibly, within their own ranks. The authority of a line unit is fairly definite. Its personnel know which units are above them and which ones are below. The authority of staff units is, by contrast, much more nebulous and elusive. Such authority is determined by whatever need the line units have for the staff group at a particular time, the proficiency the staff can demonstrate in meeting this need, the administrative and political skill with which the staff handles its relationships with other units within the organization, and a variety of other factors.

Underlying the uncertainties of line-staff dilemmas is the principle that specialization tends to destroy hierarchy. The more the members of an organization are differentiated from each other in terms of specific and separate skills, the harder it becomes to position them on a hierarchical scale. As management expert Peter Drucker has pointed out, knowledge, in and of itself, knows no hierarchy. There is no higher or lower knowledge. Thus, the increasing presence of staff personnel is disturbing and disrupting bureaucracy and bureaucratic organizations as specialists, begin to dominate generalists in making agency policies. Staff people are undermining the cherished bureaucratic principles of unity of command, chain of command, and span of control.

Unity of command requires one channel of authority, but specialization creates several channels of authority. The specialists, in one form or another, start giving orders. That these orders are not labeled as such and stem not from rank but from expertise does not fundamentally alter the situation. If the organization intends to use the energies and abilities of specialists, it must respond to what they say. To the extent that the specialists' capabilities are used, the authority of line personnel, particularly those in a supervisory capacity, is undermined. The contrasting assignments of line (generalist) and staff (specialist) personnel generate a good deal of conflict and tension in organizations. At times, line people will complain or become annoyed at the staff people for not sharing enough responsibility. More often, however, line personnel resent and repel the intrusions of staff people. To line employees, the activities of staff personnel frequently seem more subversive than supportive.

To reduce the rivalry and rancor that may creep into line-staff relationships, organizations try to integrate the two as much as possible. They may make the staff people spend time familiarizing themselves with line functions and line personnel, sometimes requiring staff personnel to perform some line functions for a time. They may recruit their staff people from the ranks of the line personnel, giving them special training for their new positions.

There is no "correct" organizational arrangement of unity of command, chain of command, span of control, and line and staff, therefore the alignment of these organizational principles varies from organization to organization and is based upon the most satisfactory way to serve the needs of clientele.

CENTRALIZATION AND DECENTRALIZATION

One issue that has bewildered public managers since the beginning of public organization is centralization. Arguments have been raised on issues concerning the balance between nation and state in relation to the concept of devolution. States have undertaken policy reforms that work to their individual advantages but at the expense of national interest. Devolution is perceived to be an attempt to simplify

incentives for common interests. However, reforms should balance multiple interests within the framework of the federal government.[4] In early times their concern
focused largely on how to achieve it; for in those days, even the simplest communication between headquarters and the field often took weeks, months, or, in a few
instances, years. Egyptian pharaohs, Roman emperors, and Chinese mandarins
spent a good deal of time wondering and worrying about how to control and use
the energies and experimentation of subordinates in their distant subunits.

The emphasis has shifted. Now the number one concern often centers on how
much centralization should be achieved. Centralization is no longer viewed as an
unmixed blessing. Its opposite, decentralization, has become the watchword, if
not the battle cry, of many theorists and practitioners involved in the administrative craft. A sequence of movements throughout U.S. history has tried to downsize and decentralize government. Assaults on big government began with
Thomas Jefferson and were continued by Jacksonian Democrats, the states' rights
movement, and the antistatism movements of the twentieth century.[5] The "citizen legislator" is a quaint vestige of early American democracy that continues to
dominate state government. Forty-one states have legislators who meet part
time—some for as little as thirty days a year—and spend the rest of the time
practicing law, tilling fields, or staffing shops as ordinary citizens. However, the
federal government's desire to send power to the states is increasing these legislators' workload and making it tough to keep up.[6] Only months after Congress
turned control of welfare over to the states, legislatures around the country
began considering whether to hand off responsibility for the poor once again,
this time to county and local governments.[7]

We have seen how decentralization has characterized our country's *political*
system since its inception. While such political decentralization may facilitate
and foster *administrative* decentralization, it does not necessarily ensure it—at
least not in all instances.

Political decentralization calls for policies to be developed as much as possible
at the lower levels (the "grass roots"). Administrative decentralization requires
that those organizations charged with carrying out these policies allow their subunits a great deal of autonomy in interpreting and applying them. When a city
institutes its own health program, this an example of political decentralization at
work. If at the same time its health department refuses to set up neighborhood
centers or insists that even the centers' most minor decisions must be made at
headquarters, then we cannot say the program is administratively decentralized.

Centralization and decentralization are relative terms. Nearly every organization of any size and scope must, to some extent, decentralize, for once it sets
up subunits it must grant them some degree of discretion in carrying out their
functions. The question, therefore, becomes one of deciding how far this independent discretion should go. Many argue that it should be pushed to the
maximum limits.

Decentralization, or lack of, is no abstract concept in public organizations. An
organization's *tasks, values,* and *organizational structures* are related to unique political, administrative, and economic characteristics. Nor are the structural

---

WHO CONTROLS WELFARE?

Neither the president nor the governors have as much control over welfare as they would have us believe. Welfare recipients are affected more by cyclical economic forces than by government regulations. Perhaps more important, welfare is ultimately a local matter. Lawmakers in Washington or state capitals may pass grandiose reforms, but low-level officials have a lot of discretion in carrying them out.

Source: Bradley R. Schiller, "All Welfare Is Local," *New York Times,* 28 January 1997, p. A21.

---

arrangements of an organization value neutral. The locations of decisions affect an administrator's objectives and values. The perspectives of federal employees located in Washington are different than those implementing services in Peoria. As Miles' Law states, "Where you stand depends upon where you sit."

The willingness of congressional Republicans to shift power and responsibility from the federal government to the states will make finance research more important. States will have to respond to increased marginal expenditure costs and reduced federal aid. States may also have to overcome spending limits and short-term policy perspectives. State finance research should focus on state spending determinants, interactions with local governments, federal aid changes, discretionary tax changes, and whether budgets are structurally balanced.[8] It is believed that state governments will gain control of many social programs being run by the federal government. Legislators and other state officials will finally have the flexibility to choose which programs will work best for their situation. Experts believe that no single pattern of welfare and Medicaid reform will emerge. They also state that reforms will evolve over time as states learn from their experience and that of other states.[9]

The structure of an organization affects the delivery of services to its clientele. Public organizations must mobilize resources to perpetuate themselves and their values. Decisions cannot be imposed from the top down if those in the subunits do not ascribe to the values and methods of implementing particular services. Administrators sometimes entertain *reorganization* plans to gain more control over the structure of the organization's policies and programs. Since any reorganization is implemented by the permanent bureaucracy, or the employees in the field accomplishing the everyday tasks of the organization, any decisions to decentralize, or to recentralize, are of great consequence to the organization. These decisions should be made with sensitivity to the skills, knowledge, and expertise of field employees to operationalize the organization's values and purposes.[10]

The Reagan Administration saw centralization as the best way to put its values into action and to achieve its goals. For most of the 1980s, the administration "devised a strategy for centralizing unprecedented decision-making power in the White House."[11] The Reagan Administration centralized the budgetary process, the federal appointments process, decision making in the executive branch, and control of federal regulation.[12] A future president may take the opposite approach and opt for decentralization as a way of expressing a different set of values and achieving different goals. There are two types of decentralization: *political* and *administrative*.[13]

POLITICAL DECENTRALIZATION

Political decentralization describes the allocation of powers among territories, which, in this context, refers to states, provinces, counties, municipalities, and other local governments. According to this approach to governing, general purpose government officers residing in a specific territory coordinate public sector activities, because they are in closer contact with citizens and may alter programs according to particular territorial priorities. Political decentralization advances few real restrictions for guidelines and control, keeping them at a minimum to allow for local discretion. The territories, or subunits, possess considerable power, coordinating and reshaping resources coming into their geographic areas to meet local needs. Manifestly parochial and unable to formulate and act on national goals, politically decentralized systems experience difficulty "vertically" integrating a diverse set of governmental activities. The transfer of political power from nation to state to community constitutes a vertical pass-through of influence at each level. How is this vertical pass-through frustrated in a decentralized system?

Issues such as equal opportunity, the environment, and occupational safety illustrate the barriers to vertical pass-through posed by the parochialism of local jurisdictions. Congress may, for example, impose affirmative action criteria for implementing equal opportunity goals for every state in the union. If local groups of citizens are opposed to civil rights, however, any form of equal opportunity may be frustrated.

Likewise, when administrative specialists in the Environmental Protection Agency (EPA) interpret U.S. environmental statutes to mean that private industry must control its waste emissions, EPA field officials may be frustrated in their efforts to enforce these laws if a community values the economic status of that industry more than clean air or water. If occupational safety is a concern of federal officers but not of local government, industry, and labor leaders, then Congress and the Occupational Safety and Health Administration may be wasting their time attempting to convince local residents otherwise. Groups of citizens in every political jurisdiction must be committed to the goals of the organization, at least in some fashion, before procedures and processes are effective in implementing these goals.

ADMINISTRATIVE DECENTRALIZATION

Administrative decentralization occurs when a public organization delegates powers to subordinate levels within the same department or agency. The delegating authority may revise or retract such delegations at will. The central office in Washington transfers functions performed by the federal government to regional or state offices, for example. Where political decentralization pertains to powers allocated among geographic areas, administrative decentralization emphasizes functions, or specialties, and lines of authority for implementing agency functions. Functional and professional specialties of the central office bureaus and agencies are held in high regard in the field offices.

Politically decentralized jurisdictions grapple with "vertical" integration of governmental activities; administratively decentralized systems experience difficulties with "horizontal" integration of governmental activities. Instead of a city that relates to a vertical hierarchy of state and federal governments for policy determination, as is the case in political decentralization, federal administrators, in administrative decentralization, horizontally coordinate the activities of several agencies within the same geographic area. In such operations, problems are often addressed in a fragmented manner with specialists (staff) dominating the narrowly focused programs and generalists (line) concerned for the whole project and guidelines emanating from the central office.

For example, the issue of civil rights concerns several federal departments and agencies; specific implementation policies need horizontal coordination at the grass roots level of citizen impact. Those departments challenged to coordinate civil rights regulations based upon administrative discretion of bureaucrats include the Departments of Commerce, Education, Health and Human Services, Housing and Urban Development, Justice, Labor, and Transportation. Independent agencies also involved include the Commission on Civil Rights, the Equal Employment Opportunity Commission, and the Small Business Administration. The line officials of these departments and agencies could be in agreement on general purposes for implementing civil rights statutes; however, the more narrowly focused specialists within each bureaucracy may disagree on the specifics.

GOVERNMENTAL STRUCTURE AND AMERICAN VALUES

Decentralization has its proponents in every political camp. Suspicion of the dangers inherent in a strong, centralized government dates back beyond the American Revolution. Participation, access, and responsiveness are characteristics of decentralized systems that in principle promote flexibility and democracy within federal organizations at the grass roots. By allowing flexibility within federal guidelines, political decentralization enhances the ability of state and city officials to meet the needs of their constituents. Rigid functional categories of administratively decentralized systems restrict options of leaders representing general purpose governments. Students of political decentralization argue that governors and mayors are more able to effectively allocate available resources according to local priorities than are nonelected bureaucrats. There are cogent arguments against political decentralization as well. Local jurisdictions may be fragmented and ineffective; states sometimes refuse to grant sufficient resources for local bureaucracies to implement functions in a professional and effective manner. Accusations of unprofessional behavior and political graft undermine citizens' confidence in the legitimacy of local governments. Regional and national concerns may be overlooked, ignored, or unmanageable by smaller jurisdictions.

Conflicts between political and administrative decentralization models pit the values and priorities of geographic area (Peoria) against administrative function (Washington). Local partisans champion the political will of the former; national leaders insist upon the dominance of the latter. A balance between the extremes usually results. The vertical and horizontal mixing of political and administrative decentralization illustrates that values, tasks, and organizational structure interrelate in an effective organization. Our discussion implies that structural arrangements selected for implementing a task affect the success administrators enjoy and whether their objectives and values will be achieved. From a national perspective, 72 percent of state and local employment consists of workers in labor-intensive local activities such as street maintenance and public schools. Decentralization moves government closer to citizens, offering elected officials and voters opportunities to witness more closely programmatic and fiscal consequences of their decisions. Decentralization also permits decision makers flexibility to meet local conditions.

However, centralization of functions at the state level may promote more uniform policies, resulting in certain economies of scale and may eliminate impacts of local fiscal disparities on the quality and costs of services. The ebb and flow of centralizing and decentralizing decisions in individual states is constant. The percentage of state and local employment that is local is presented in table 3-1.

TABLE 3–1   Percentage of State and Local Employment That Is Local (December 1996)

Rank	State	Percent	Rank	State	Percent	Rank	State	Percent
1	New York	79.0%	17	Missouri	71.21%	34	Alabama	66.11%
2	California	77.8	18	Iowa	71.0	35	Washington	66.1
3	Illinois	77.0	19	Arizona	70.9	36	Oklahoma	65.9
4	Florida	76.4	20	Mississippi	70.8	37	Kentucky	65.6
5	Minnesota	75.0	21	Nevada	70.4	38	Rhode Island	65.4
6	New Jersey	74.9	22	Colorado	70.4	39	Louisiana	65.0
7	Ohio	74.7	23	Nebraska	70.1	40	Montana	64.8
8	Wyoming	74.3	24	New Hampshire	69.9	41	Arkansas	63.0
9	Texas	74.1	25	Indiana	69.8	42	Vermont	62.7
10	Wisconsin	73.1	26	Georgia	69.6	43	W. Virginia	62.7
11	Tennessee	73.1	27	Idaho	68.7	44	Alaska	62.3
12	Pennsylvania	73.0	28	Maine	68.7	45	Utah	62.2
13	Oregon	72.8	29	Maryland	68.6	46	S. Carolina	61.3
14	Massachusetts	72.4	30	N. Carolina	67.4	47	New Mexico	58.5
15	S. Dakota	72.1	31	Virginia	67.4	48	Delaware	45.8
	United States	72.0	32	Connecticut	66.9	49	Hawaii	20.2
16	Michigan	71.8	33	N. Dakota	66.6	50	Kansas	n/a

Source: *State Policy Reports* 15, no. 7-1 (April 1997):15.

Decisions to centralize or decentralize public organizations cannot, therefore, be divorced from values, tasks, and organizational structure. An appropriate organizational design facilitates an administrator's values and objectives; an inappropriate organizational structure frustrates his or her purposes and accomplishes the opposite.

A variety of political, administrative, and economic characteristics typify public program functions. As new values and technologies emerge, organizational objectives change; new technologies affect community values. Issues of governmental centralization and decentralization include political, administrative, economic, and technological factors that may point the agency in conflicting directions while attempting to integrate its values, tasks, and organizational structure into an effective organization. In a dynamic society espousing democracy and capitalism, we may ask: an effective organization for whom, what, when, where, and how?

THE CRAFT AND POLITICAL CULTURE

Many are claiming that the United States is in the midst of a "culture" war that deals with moral values and life-styles.[14] Therefore, an understanding of culture is of great value to public administrators. To recognize the expectations and guidelines for professional behavior in one's culture is to promote understanding of the organization. The culture of an organization provides guidelines for member behavior and performance. For example, taking examinations can be mastered best by those students who understand that their academic setting is influenced by culture. Class size is one feature of academic culture. The number of students in class influences the type and number of assignments professors may require. If the number of students in your class reaches into the hundreds, you may assume that your professor will emphasize short answer examinations instead of essays. However, the culture of small classes allows your professor to be more personable in his or her approach to teaching students and gives the professor more flexibility for evaluating your writing skills and critical thinking abilities. An understanding of this classroom culture can help you steer toward classes where you are likely to perform at your best.

For our purposes, "culture" is defined as "that complex whole which includes knowledge, belief, art, morals, law, custom, and any other capabilities and habits acquired by man as a member of society."[15] An awareness of culture is crucial for understanding the development, implementation, and evaluation of public administration.

Culture, or ways of life common to a society, government organization, or interest group, includes the *ideal* and the *real*. Ideal cultural patterns focus on what citizens do or say if they adhere completely to the recognized standards of the culture. Real behavioral patterns refer to actual citizen observations and behaviors. Various aspects of cultures, such as religious rituals, work habits, beliefs and ideologies, and marriage relationships, relate to and affect one another.

Culture may be divided according to:

- *Technology,* or the ways in which people create and use tools and other material artifacts;
- *Economics,* or the patterns of behaving relative to the production, distribution, and consumption of goods and services;
- *Social organization,* or characteristic relations among individuals within a society, including the division of labor and the social and political organization; and the relationship between a society and other societies;
- *Religion,* or ways of life relative to the human concern for the unknown;
- *Symbolism,* or systems of symbols (such as language, art, music, literature) used to acquire, order, and transfer knowledge.[16]

The nature of our organized society and developments in public administration history underscore the importance of political and bureaucratic culture in the environment of public administration. Partisan, policy, and system politics occur within a larger framework of political culture.

Political culture, according to Daniel Elazar, is "the particular pattern of orientation to political action in which each political system is embedded."[17]

Culture puts limits on individuals in organizational settings. An organization is a subculture. For example, your public administration class is a subculture of the Department of Political Science, a subculture of a larger academic unit—usually a college of humanities, a subculture of the university or college. An understanding of the concept of culture is vital because we must recognize that an organization's members or employees are not free agents in any society.

Any organization, whatever its limits or prospects, is part of a larger social system. At least indirectly, its employees are subject to a larger set of values. Certain cultural patterns of conduct and beliefs can be found in any organization. The culture of an organization reflects a consensus of the particular values of that organization, but no organization can be isolated from its cultural environment.[18]

An understanding of culture can also allow for an advance indication of how people will act in a situation. A keenly developed sensitivity to culture can also be a substitute for experience. If you expect to climb the ladder of managerial success, close attention to your organization's culture is important. Traditions, customs, and patterned modes of behavior run through organizations. If you understand such structuring influences, you may even be able to facilitate changes in the organization.

According to J. Steven Ott, there are three levels of organizational culture and their interaction.[19] Level 1A includes artifacts, technology, and art. Level lB entails patterns of behavior, familiar management tasks, visible and audible behavior, and norms. Level 2 focuses on values, testable in the physical environment and testable only by social consensus. Level 3 concludes with basic assumptions and their relationship to the environment; nature of reality, time, and space; nature of human nature; nature of human activity; and nature of human relationships. On your college or university campus, illustrations of artifacts, technology, and art are abundant. It could be the administration building, main library,

Levels of Organizational Culture and Their Interaction

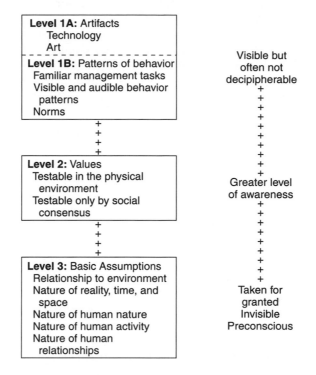

FIGURE 3–3

Source: J. Steven Ott, *The Organizational Culture Perspective,* page 62. Copyright © 1989 Harcourt Brace & Company. Reprinted with permission.

health center, basketball arena, football stadium, or parking garage. It could be the technology of the shuttle bus that circulates to and from the dorms and classroom buildings. It could be the artwork of plant life maintained by the grounds keepers. These illustrate Level 1A.

Certain norms of deportment are expected of students and faculty. Visible and audible behavior patterns include arriving at class on time. Familiar management tasks comprise daily routines for college classroom productivity and performance. These illustrate Level lB. Values, testable in the physical environment and by social consensus, provide greater levels of awareness about organizational culture levels and their interaction. The classroom limits or promotes effective exchanges between students and professor. The heating or cooling systems may malfunction, the lighting may be poor, the acoustics may be wierd, the chairs may have splinters in them, or the roof may leak. The physical environment of the classroom contributes to the culture of the academic exercise. The social consensus may well be that the class should adjourn pronto, but that's not the decision of Professor Jones, who insists that hot or cold air, lighting, acoustics, splinters, or rain should *not* interfere with the exciting revelations of public administration! The physical environment is now suspect, therefore the social consensus for continuing the class tests the culture, dictated to the students by the professor. Aspects of physical environment and social consensus illustrate Level 2.

After students sit in a cold (or hot) classroom; follow the professor's lecture in near darkness; listen to the professor's voice as it bounces off the ceiling, to the radiator, to the concrete floor, back up to the ceiling, and finally into one's brain; pull splinters from their hands and other extremities from a chair first used during the 1960s; and see a $50 public administration textbook ruined by rain pouring through a gigantic hole in the roof, students question basic assumptions about the nature of reality, time, and space concerning the culture, or ways of life common to a college classroom. The questioning of these basic assumptons, at Level 3, examines relationships of students to their cultural environment. The components of culture are *material* and *nonmaterial*. See levels of organization culture and their interaction in Figure 3–3.

Physical layout and organizational techniques are illustrations of material culture. Both contribute to the environment of public administration by focusing upon the interaction between habitat and culture and by emphasizing how and why certain actions occur. As students attend different classes in their academic experience, they move from one classroom culture to another. In chemistry, a chart showing the elements is part of the material culture. In biology, perhaps a skeleton hangs for the professor's demonstration to students. In architecture, drawing boards are a common indication of material culture.

Technology plays a key role in influencing material culture. Equipment and techniques affect the character of organizations. Personal computers are likely to be more helpful to you than typewriters when you are conducting research or writing a paper. The use of video cassette recorders in college classrooms allows an expanded teaching dimension. If technology becomes increasingly complicated, an organization may find more difficulty in entering a new field of endeavor. Not all culture is observable in the same way as material culture.

Nonmaterial culture includes beliefs, systems of communications, and modes of conduct. Rituals, taboos, and jargon are modes of conduct that influence important aspects of nonmaterial culture. All organizations follow these prescribed formulas where employees may act in ritualistic unison, observe a system of taboos, or speak in a peculiar jargon. One of the rituals of college classes is to arrive on time; cheating on examinations is taboo. Public administrators communicate in a jargon of "alphabet soup" of acronyms for departments, agencies, and programs.

Material and nonmaterial culture may conflict if organization members confuse patterns of conduct with changes occurring in the world outside the organization. In other words, your nonmaterial value system, or beliefs, may not be in line with the realities of the material world, which can result in *cultural lag*. Our organized society is constantly changing. Our values and preferences, however, tend to remain the same. The challenge is to respond appropriately to the changes in society without altering core values.

Material and nonmaterial bureaucratic cultures reflect a larger political culture. Political culture, as Elazar notes, includes perceptions held by the general public and politicians concerning the nature of politics and the perceived role of government in society. A statewide political culture provides a framework for what citizens expect from those in government and how they perceive office holders, bureaucrats, and campaign workers. Political culture outlines boundaries and practices of citizens, politicians, and public officials with respect to the art of politics and government. Elazar carves out three types of political culture in the United States and describes the relation of bureaucracy to each type. The three types of political culture are *individualistic, moralistic,* and *traditionalistic.*

Individualistic—In this type of political culture, politics is viewed as dirty. Only professionals participate in politics. Parties dole out favors and responsibility. Party cohesiveness is strong. Competition arises between parties, not over issues. New programs are not to be initiated unless demanded by public opinion. Political competition focuses on winning office to reap tangible rewards. Government is viewed as a marketplace. Economic development is favored. The appropriate spheres of activity are largely economic. Bureaucracy is viewed ambivalently. The type of merit system favored is one that is loosely implemented. Indiana, Nevada, New Jersey, and Pennsylvania are examples of states reflecting the individualistic political culture.

Moralistic—In a moralistic political culture, the practice of politics is viewed as healthy and as every citizen's responsibility. Everyone can participate. Political parties are vehicles to attain goals believed to be in the public interest. Party cohesiveness is subordinate to principles and issues. Competition is over issues, not parties. Political orientation focuses upon winning office to implement policies. Government is viewed as a commonwealth, answering directly for the general welfare and common good of the people. Appropriate spheres of activity include any area that will enhance the community through nongovernmental action. New programs are initiated without public pressure if such are believed to be in the public interest. Bureaucracy is viewed positively, bringing desirable political neutrality. A strong merit system is favored. Colorado, Michigan, Minnesota, North Dakota, Oregon, Utah, Vermont, and Wisconsin reflect the moralistic political culture.

Traditionalistic—Politics is viewed as a privilege in which only those with legitimate claim to office should participate. Participation in politics is limited to the appropriate elite. Political parties serve as vehicles to recruit people for public offices not desired by established power holders. Party cohesiveness depends upon family and social ties and is highly personal. Competition is between the elite-dominated factions within a dominant party. The orientation to politics depends upon the political values of the elite. Government is viewed as a means of maintaining the existing order. Appropriate spheres of activity are those that maintain traditional patterns. New programs are initiated if the program serves in the interest of the governing elite. Bureaucracy is viewed negatively, as it depersonalizes government. It is thought that merit should be controlled by the political elite, therefore no merit system is favored. Mississippi, South Carolina, Tennessee, and Virginia are states reflecting the traditionalistic political culture.

Some states fall into more than one type of political culture. Those states that are mainly moralistic political cultures yet also have individualistic traits are California, Iowa, Kansas, Montana, New Hampshire, South Dakota, and Washington.

THE CULTURE OF CORRUPTION

It has not just been Ulysses S. Grant, Warren G. Harding, and Richard M. Nixon—our most famously scandal-burdened presidents—who wrestled with accusations of corruption. It has also been John Adams and John Quincy Adams, two of the most incorruptible men in U.S. political history, who were harried throughout their presidency by accusations of corruption and abuses of power. Rutherford B. Hayes, a paragon of propriety, was known during his unhappy administration as "His Fraudulency" for having allegedly stolen the 1876 election from Samuel J. Tilden.

Harry S. Truman, a folk hero today for what Americans like to remember as his plain-speaking honesty, was buffeted by charges of "cronyism" and "corruption"— for creating what Nixon and many others in 1952 liked to call the "mess in Washington." Even Dwight D. Eisenhower, famously genial, enormously popular, legendarily honest, suffered from embarrassing revelations about his chief of staff, Sherman L. Adams, and other improprieties. What is happening today to Bill Clinton, and so many other political figures, is in many respects part of the ordinary pattern of U.S. political life.

In an era when charges are made—in the media and likewise in the courtrooms— against government officials on a rather frequent basis, the terms, corruption and scandal, virtually become synonymous in the minds of many Americans. But they imply different interpretations. While both signify moral unsoundness, corruption denotes legal violations, or breaking of laws, whereas scandal simply offends moral feelings.

So, as the Monica Lewinsky scandal offended notions of sexual morality (personal lies) to millions, incidences of abortions, poverty, racism, economic disparity, lowering of education standards, and social welfare policies (institutional lies) are scandals to others. Officials in the Clinton administration offended the moral feelings of many citizens, creating scandal, but not necessarily resulting in corruption, or the breaking of laws.

Source: Alan Brinkley, "The Culture of Corruption," *Los Angeles Times,* 2 November 1997, p. M1.

States that are mainly individualistic but have moralistic traits as well are Connecticut, Illinois, Massachusetts, Nebraska, New York, Ohio, and Rhode Island.

States that are individualistic yet traditional are Delaware, Hawaii, Maryland, and Missouri. Those that are traditionalistic, yet individualistic, are Alabama, Arkansas, Florida, Georgia, Kentucky, Louisiana, New Mexico, Oklahoma, Texas, and West Virginia. States that are traditionalistic, yet moralistic are Arizona and North Carolina.[20]

Political culture can then be said to encompass a state's orientation to political action. Culture includes knowledge, belief, art, morals, law, custom, capabilities, and habits institutionalized within an organization's environment. Material culture is observable, focuses upon relationships of people distributed in space, and includes tools and techniques for fulfilling organizational purposes. Nonmaterial culture is not so obvious because it incorporates belief systems and patterns of conduct. No organization can be isolated from its cultural environment. This means the bureaucratic culture of government organizations in a particular state cannot be divorced from that state's political culture.

When one examines the various aspects of public or government organizations, one must look beyond mere descriptions of facts, and seek out factors that define reality or the culture of government, including:

1. the history of government, or how it developed;
2. the role of government as perceived by members of society;
3. the structures and processes considered proper to government; and
4. the values, mores, and habits of the primary people, especially the elected and appointed officials, and the bureaucrats working beneath those officials.[21]

Culture impacts the everyday operations of a government organization. Culture resides in the ideas, values, norms, rituals, and beliefs of *socially constructed realities,* or organizations. Patterns of belief or shared meaning result in organizations adopting their own ways of perceiving problems and establishing ways to resolve them.[22] The dynamics of culture incorporate the following elements of analysis: traditions, perceptions, attitudes, assumptions, perspectives, values, behaviors.

SUMMARY

- The *anatomy* of public bureaucracy is its organizational framework or administrative structure.
- *Purpose, process, place,* and *clientele* explain why an organization was established.
- *Unity of command* shows the relationship between those who order and those who follow orders. Unity of command usually requires a *chain of command,* because in any large bureaucracy, the person at the top cannot oversee all that is going on below. *Span of control* refers to the number of units, individuals or groups, that any supervising unit must oversee.
- *Staff personnel* are specialists who provide skills, knowledge, and expertise to line personnel. The purpose of staff functions is to provide planning, fact-finding, and organizing support for line executives.
- Staff units in the executive office of the president include the White House Office, Council of Economic Advisers, Office of the U.S. Trade Representative, Office of Management and Budget, National Security Council, Council on Environmental Quality, Office of Policy Development, and Office of Science and Technology Policy.
- *Line personnel* are primarily concerned with developing, *implementing,* and evaluating policy. Line administrators are generalists. They legitimize authority and are in command. Line employees are directly responsible for furthering an organization's goals. Staff and line employees sometimes

come into conflict. This should come as no surprise because their goals and functions are inherently different.

• Line departments in the federal government include Agriculture, Commerce, Defense, Education, Energy, Health and Human Services, Housing and Urban Development, Interior, Justice, Labor, State, Transportation, Treasury, and Veterans Affairs.

• *Decentralization* occurs when an organization delegates powers to subordinate levels within the same department or agency. Political decentralization addresses the allocation of powers among states, counties, cities, and other local governments. Decisions to centralize or decentralize cannot be divorced from the values, tasks, and structure of an organization. Americans seem to agree that governmental power should be shifted to the states. However, a 10 percent increase in efficiency as a result of state control would only reduce government costs by less than 0.5 percent.[23]

• *Political culture* consists of the particular pattern of orientation to the political action of a political system. Any organization, whatever its limits or prospects, is part of a larger social system. Indirectly, an organization's employees are subject to a larger social system. Its employees are also subject, indirectly, to a larger set of values. No organization can be isolated from its cultural environment.

• The next step in understanding the craft of public administration is to examine some key theories about organizations. That is the focus of the next chapter.

This case study illustrates the potential conflicts that arise between administrative and political decentralization and ways in which these modes of operation affect the delivery of an agency's programs to its clientele. Assuming society's lack of consensus concerning matters of housing, race, and urban development, what action would you have taken if you had been HUD's secretary?

CASE STUDY

HUD Goes to the Grass Roots[24]

The history of housing and urban development policies in the United States mixes politics and economics. It is the story of a federal department attempting to respond to the changing dynamics of housing, race, and urban development. Administrative decentralization by the Department of Housing and Urban Development (HUD) in the early 1970s points out how functions, values, and organizational structure of a particular department runs up against political and economic realities. The HUD case reflects conflicts that occur when politicians who represent a geographic area disagree with the public administrators responsible for program functions in that same area.

How were HUD's functions, values, and organizational structure unique? What special economic, political, and administrative characteristics contributed to the administrative decentralization of HUD? HUD's ancestry is traced to the establishment of the Federal Housing Administration (FHA) by Franklin D. Roosevelt in 1934. FHA, responding to difficult economic times, came up with the concept of the amortized mortgage, whereby a pledge to pay for a family home is prorated over a fixed number of years.

The Public Housing Administration (PHA) in 1937, Urban Renewal Administration (URA) in 1949, and Community Facilities Administration (CFA) in 1954, followed FHA as housing, home finance, and urban development bureaucracies. The administrative umbrella for FHA, PHA, URA, and CFA was the Housing and Home Finance Administration (HHFA), established by Congress and President Truman in 1947 as the agency responsible for the principal housing programs and functions of the federal government. HHFA was only an "umbrella" for supervision and coordination of such programs, not a cabinet department with presidential prestige. The mid-1960s, however, brought citizen pressure to resolve the nation's urban problems, especially those related to discrimination and race. As in 1934, housing administrators were challenged to respond to difficult economic times. In the early 1970s, those knocking on government's door were not poor whites; they were African Americans who wanted to realize the American dream of political and economic opportunities. In 1965, HHFA and its subordinate agencies—FHA, PHA, URA, and CFA—became the Department of Housing and Urban Development (HUD).

Centralization before decentralization

President Nixon's new leader in housing policy implementation, former Michigan governor George Romney, took the helm at HUD in 1969 with a burst of enthusiasm and elan. HUD was an agency with a most challenging and timely mission. Romney was eager to see what it, and he, could do. He immediately found himself confronted with the sticky administrative challenges of how best to organize HUD and to respond to diverse housing and urban development problems, including ways for integrating blacks into better housing. In a flurry of newly-mandated programs and emerging bureau power struggles, HUD was already bogged down in paperwork and procrastination. It was attempting to administer a potpourri of programs and was not effectively administering most of them.

Romney looked to decentralization to supply part of the solution. As president of American Motors, he used this device to help bring the beleaguered automaker back to profitability. His subsequent experience as a successful governor of a large state had persuaded him that the grass roots could and should play a greater role in governmental activity. His first move toward decentralization was to obtain control of HUD's far-flung operations by centralizing all power in his office. This may seem a strange way to decentralize, but this sort of consolidation is recognized as a necessary first step in undertaking such a process. A person or an office must possess authority before it can be given away. Romney's first initiative, therefore, was to make sure his office possessed authority by restricting the authority exercised by the agency's ten regional offices and its functional units in Washington.

After consolidating HHFA operations in his Washington headquarters, Romney then delegated a considerable amount of this authority to seventy-seven HUD local field offices. "HUD employees at the area offices," Romney insisted, "are more familiar with local conditions and are in better positions to make judgments on HUD's programs and to be most effective with these programs. The local employees work closely with the local government leadership and are able to involve local officials in the decision-making process. The local HUD employees are more informed with respect to local conditions."

About half of these field offices would handle only the department's FHA mortgage-insurance program. The other half would operate the agency's other programs, such as urban renewal, public housing, community planning, and similar programs. These offices would, of necessity, be more thinly staffed than the ten larger regional offices that had previously discharged such functions, therefore they would not have the in-depth specialization that the latter had enjoyed. Area office employees would have to be generalists, with the authority and the responsibility to carry out or to oversee, as the case may be, a large and diverse number of activities. The decentralization scheme went into effect, and soon a network of local offices was handling most of HUD's ordinary business. In the process, these offices and their employees were making numerous decisions affecting the shape and fate of the department's programs in their respective areas.

How did HUD's decentralization affect the challenges confronting the nation? How did HUD's values, tasks, and organizational structure change? Political decentralization of housing prerogatives to the states and municipalities was not functioning properly, at least for African Americans. State and local jurisdictions met neither the aspirations nor the needs of African Americans. Interestingly, the civil rights leaders of the late 1960s and early 1970s called for political centralization of public accommodations, housing, and other civil rights programs by the federal government. In other words, on issues of civil rights, political leaders from grass roots jurisdictions were insensitive to local political and economic needs. State and local leaders looked to the White House, Congress, and federal departments for solutions.

The consolidation of FHA, PHA, URA, and CFA functions, first under the umbrella of HHFA and subsequently under HUD's direction, represented changes in the organizational structure of the housing department, which likewise represented a change in political values. Changes in the structural arrangements of HUD were, by no means, value neutral. The locations of decision making do affect administrators' objectives and values. As Romney decentralized, he reached for some measure of programmatic control in reality, thereby recentralizing a bureaucracy represented by employees, with quite differing values, pulled in all directions by a diverse clientele.

Although the handling of many routine, often irksome, administrative matters, such as minor budget alterations, interpretation of grant-in-aid contracts, and the overseeing of basic procedures, all improved, problems touching on fundamental program issues increased. HUD's administrative decentralization resulted in a generalist, as opposed to a specialist, emphasis in the area offices. Under the old HHFA umbrella, the FHA area offices reflected specialist application of specific skills, knowledge, and expertise. Changes in HUD's structure, as a result of numerous decentralization directives, encouraged area office employees to be knowledgeable in all of HUD's programs, not only FHA mortgage inquiries. Teetering on the edge of becoming "a jack of all trades, yet master of none," employee program effectiveness in the field suffered.

Processes versus programs

How did administrative experimentation and adaptation fare in the HUD case? The most outstanding feature of the area office concept was administrative, not programmatic. The response of area office personnel to administrative matters, in other words minor budget alterations, interpretation of grant-in-aid contracts, and general procedures for how dollars are used (as opposed to the substantive impact of dollars), was improved under decentralization. As "generalists," however, area office personnel lacked the necessary knowledge to deal with the complexities contained in HUD's various programs. As one employee put it, "HUD is now operating like the post office. If you want a ten cent stamp, you go to one window. If you want a fifty cent stamp, you go to the same window. General Motors does not operate in this manner. Different programs appeal to different user groups."

Although area office personnel responded positively to minor budget alterations, interpretation of grant-in-aid regulations and the impact of actual use of dollars caused the economy of HUD operations to be questioned. Some local officials expressed dismay over the additional cost that, in their view, decentralization entailed. More local offices consumed a greater share of HUD's budget. Paying the administrative expense involved in hiring new personnel and maintaining new and expanded offices proved expensive. This expansion made less money available for the programs. One employee maintained that HUD's clients were "getting the shaft," while another labeled the scheme the "Romney Follies."

The reduction of administrative detail work at HUD's Washington headquarters did not materialize. In an ideal decentralized pattern, line and staff officials at headquarters are freed to concentrate on policy-making. HUD's central office was so busy issuing directives; changing job descriptions; and monitoring the closing, combining, and establishing of field offices and the supervision of their staff professionals that the attention required for policy implementation increased instead of declining. HUD's private and public clientele were confused by the constant reorganizations and changes in delegation responsibilities. The creation of better public relations for HUD was probably not Romney's most immediate concern. The control of HUD's diverse program functions was. The alteration of HUD's administrative structure to respond to an emerging set of values and priorities; the control of its permanent bureaucracy consisting of former FHA, PHA, URA, and CFA personnel; and the renewal of its diverse program tasks and functions appeared crucial for Romney's survival as an administrative leader. These were the secretary's priorities.

With HUD's massive decentralization, it is not surprising to learn that there was an absence of uniform policies and inconsistent application of housing programs at the grass roots. Area office personnel's response to administrative matters appears to have been quite satisfactory under decentralization, but when these same employees were asked to resolve problems concerning program matters they usually found themselves at a loss and, more often than not, had to call senior officials in either the regional office or in the central office in Washington for consultation. HUD's administrators and clientele became confused and frustrated as national housing objectives tended to fuse the values of equality and efficiency, promoting equal housing opportunity and responding to market demands.

The absence of consensus

There is fragile, if any, consensus on housing, racial, and urban development policies in the United States. There will be no neat solutions to the issues raised by decentralization. As the history of FHA, PHA, URA, CFA, HHFA, and HUD illustrates, some combination of administrative decentralization is desirable and feasible in practice, and, as some of the material to be covered later will make clear, it may even be a necessary goal. But decentralizing national programs should be approached with caution, care, and some measure of political consensus.

In conclusion, HUD, a multipurpose department, suffered from a lack of consensus on department goals.

1. By confusing generalist and specialist roles of former FHA, PHA, URA, and CFA employees, HUD's field objectives were confounded and misunderstood; the interaction and coordination of employees and production components needed to carry out program functions was often frustrated.
2. In political decentralization among jurisdictions representing nation, states, and municipalities, there is the need for vertical integration (up and down the political hierarchy) of governmental activities.
3. In administrative decentralization, there is the necessity for horizontal integration (across departments and agencies) of governmental activities within one or more geographic jurisdictions. The complexity of coordination necessary to perform HUD tasks required careful monitoring of vertical and horizontal integration of governmental activities; such emphasis was not forthcoming.
4. The priorities of local politicians often conflicted with HUD regulations implemented in area offices, typifying conflicts between geographic area and administrative function.

QUESTIONS AND INSTRUCTIONS

1. How are the categories of purpose, process, place, and clientele represented in HUD's attempts to respond to the changing dynamics of housing, race, and urban development?
2. How are the principles of unity of command, chain of command, and span of control manifest in HUD's decentralization of program functions?
3. How are HUD's tasks, values, and organizational structures reflective of unique political, administrative, and economic characteristics?
4. Why was it necessary for HUD's secretary to centralize HUD's program functions before decentralizing them?
5. How did the structure of HUD affect the delivery of services to its clientele?
6. Why did HUD field employees become "generalists" rather than "specialists" in carrying out their tasks? Why did HUD's area office decentralization promote administrative, not programmatic, employee expertise?
7. In what ways do the premises of political decentralization by geographic area and administrative decentralization by program function come into conflict?
8. Why is there an absence of consensus on housing, race, and urban development policies in the United States?
9. Was HUD's administrative decentralization a success? Why or why not? If so, for whom? If not, for whom?

INSIGHTS-ISSUES/HUD GOES TO THE GRASS ROOTS

Clearly and briefly describe and illustrate these concepts, issues, or points. Interpret the word "role" as meaning impact, application, importance, effect and/or illustration of certain facts, concerns, or issues from the case study.

1. Role of political decentralization (geography);
2. Role of administrative decentralization (bureaucracy);
3. Role of, or lack of, political consensus on these controversies;
4. Role of the market for HUD's operations (FHA loans);
5. Role of red tape (process) vis-à-vis FHA loans (programs).

ENDNOTES

1. Luther Gulick and L. Urwick, *Papers on the Science of Administration* (New York: Institute of Public Administration, 1937), 15.
2. For a more detailed critique of the various bases of organization, see Scuyley C. Wallace, *Federal Decentralization* (New York: Columbia University Press, n.d.), 91–146.
3. John M. Pfiffner and Frank P. Sherwood, *Administrative Organization* (Englewood Cliffs, N.J.: Prentice-Hall, Inc., 1960), 170–188.
4. John D. Donahue, "The Devil in Devolution," *The American Prospect* no. 32 (May–June 1997): 42–48.
5. Mary O. Furner, "Downsizing Government: A Historical Perspective," *USA Today* 126, no. 2630 (November 1997): 56–58.
6. Dana Milbank, Wall Street Journal, 8 January 1997, p. A1.
7. Judith Havemann, "After Getting Responsibility for Welfare, States May Pass It Down," *Washington Post*, 28 January 1997, p. A1.
8. Steven D. Gold, "Issues Raised by the New Federalism," *National Tax Journal* 49, no. 2 (June 1996): 273–287.
9. Hal Hovey, "The Challenges of Flexibility," *State Legislatures* 22, no. 1 (January 1996): 14–19.
10. David O. Porter and Eugene A. Olsen, "Some Critical Issues in Government Centralization and Decentralization," *Public Administration Review* 36, no. 1 (January/-February 1976): 72–84.
11. Harold Seidman and Robert Gilmour, *Politics, Position, and Power: From the Positive to the Regulatory State,* 4th ed. (New York: Oxford University Press, 1986), 127.
12. *Ibid.*
13. Herbert Kaufman, "Administrative Decentralization and Political Power," *Public Administration Review* 29 (January/February 1969): 3–15.
14. See Rhys H. Williams, "Is America in a Culture War? Yes—No—Sort of," *The Christian Century* 114, no. 32 (12 November 1997): 1038–1043. Quotes from Tylor's Primitive Culture in Leslie A. White, "The Concept of Culture," *American Anthropologist* 61, no. 227 (April 1959). White reports that there is great divergence of view among anthropologists as to a definition of culture.
15. Thomas R. Dye, *Power & Society: An Introduction to the Social Sciences* 4th ed. (Monterey, Calif.: Brooks/Cole Publishing Co., 1987), 39.

16. *Ibid.*, 40.
17. Daniel J. Elazár, *American Federalism: A View from the States* (New York: Harper & Row, Publishers, 1984), 109.
18. John M. Pfiffner and Frank P. Sherwood, *Administrative Organization* (Englewood Cliffs, N.J.: Prentice-Hall, Inc., 1960), 249–272.
19. J. Steven Ott, *The Organization Culture Perspective* (Chicago: The Dorsey Press, 1989), 62.
20. Elazar, *American Federalism*, 136.
21. Harold F. Gortner, Julianne Mahler, and Jeanne Bell Nicholson, *Organization Theory: A Public Perspective* (Fort Worth, Tex.: Harcourt Brace & Company, 1997), 71.
22. Gareth Morgan, *Images of Organization* (Beverly Hills, Calif. Sage, 1986).
23. John D. Donahue, "The Disunited States: "Devolution"—Shifting Power From Washington to the Fifty States—Is No Cure for What Ails American Government," *The Atlantic Monthly* 279, no. 5 (May 1997): 18–21.
24. Material for this case study is drawn from John E. Rouse, Jr., "Administrative Decentralization as a Complement to Revenue Sharing A Case Study of the HUD Programs" (paper presented to the annual meeting of the American Political Science Association, Chicago, 1975). See also John E. Rouse, Jr., "The Impact of Decentralizing Program Administration: The Department of Housing and Urban Development/Case Study (Ph. D. diss., University of Maryland, 1974).

4

THE PHYSIOLOGY
OF ORGANIZATION

CHAPTER HIGHLIGHTS
DEMOCRACY IN BUREAUCRACY
BASELINE ORIGINALS IN ORGANIZATIONAL LIFE
NEOCLASSICAL THEORIES
HUMAN RELATIONS THEORIES

A young man, we'll call him "Phil," landed a job as an administrative assistant in his state's highway department. Although it was not a position of great authority, it was a chance to learn the ropes in one of the state's larger departments. Fresh out of college, Phil was fired up. He was ready to change "the system" to make it more effective, more responsive, more than what the citizens of his state had come to expect of the highway department. He was determined to serve the public in a positive, productive manner. He had good ideas on how to improve everything from snow removal to bridge inspections.

Phil was idealistic, but not naive. He had a framed political science degree on his wall and had worked in numerous local political campaigns in his home county and in the county where he went to college. But once he started work in the highway department, Phil was astonished at what he found.

His immediate supervisor had owned a business but had no prior experience or training in public administration. The supervisor was not the least bit interested in Phil's ideas on how to improve the highway department. Phil was never told as much in precise words, but the subtle message was clear: "Do as you're told, and don't make waves."

As papers crossed Phil's desk, he learned more about the highly-detailed complexity of the day-to-day functioning of the department. He understood the issues and the policies, but the complex forces driving the bureaucracy overwhelmed him. Getting simple things accomplished took a great deal of effort. The operation seemed to move painfully instead of moving smoothly to meet the needs of the public. Surprise and shock came at the realization that one administrator seemed to make decisions based not on what was best for the citizens driving on state highways but on what was best for his poker buddies who just happened to get frequent state contracts.

Phil was not prepared for the intricate, informal, and occasionally unethical pressures involved in the daily operation of a real-life bureaucracy. Pressures mounted and he became confused and disheartened. The chain of command he was forced to follow seemed to arbitrarily stifle every chance for employees to improve the organization, to feel a part of the team. The way things worked had little to do with his dreams of public service. He felt swept away by the bureaucratic current, as if he were trying to hold on to a slippery log floating swiftly down a raging river. In less than a year, he quit his job.

Phil would have been better prepared to deal with the inner workings of a bureaucracy if he had a more thorough background in the basic theories about how bureaucracies and other organizations work. If he understood what forces were sweeping him toward frustration, he would have seen "the big picture" and not felt so helpless.

Physiology is the study of life processes, activities, and functions. As a medical student must study physiology to understand how the human body works, students of public administration must be familiar with organizational theories so they will be better prepared than Phil when confronted by the realities of bureaucracy. This chapter provides a look at the most influential and helpful organizational theories and theorists.

DEMOCRACY IN BUREAUCRACY

Bureaucracy and *democracy* are the central pillars of the public and private organizations of our society. Bureaucratic hierarchy and democratic equality influence the functions and vital processes of all organizations. Despite the apparent paradox, bureaucracy and democracy are both antithetical and complementary.

In partisan politics, we periodically elect presidents, governors, and mayors. In such electoral processes, we take advantage of the fundamental principle of democracy. While in office, however, presidents, governors, and mayors depend upon principles of bureaucracy, where formalism, strict rule adherence, impersonality, unity of command, chain of command, span of control, and similar values contribute to the exercise of authority. Authority in a bureaucracy is checked by democratic voting procedures, but only on a periodic basis. As we consider the functions and vital processes of organizations therefore, an understanding of the philosophical differences between bureaucracy and democracy is crucial for understanding why public organizations exist.

The development of our organized society underscores the need for democracy in the administrative state. We, the voting public, come into contact with numerous public and private organizations each day. The functions of government are always expanding their influence on the public. Legislatures continuously allocate public functions to administrative structures. What input should employees and clientele have in internal decision making within public organizations? Can there be democracy in bureaucracy? How democratic should life in organizations be?

If you are not already employed, in a matter of years, even months, you will probably enter the American workforce. You may be employed by a business, labor, social, or public organization. You will be full of ideas and energy for expressing your solutions to your employer's challenges and problems, and you will want to be heard. How much democracy will exist in your bureaucratic workplace? The *authoritarian tenets of bureaucracy* and the *egalitarian tenets of democracy* are major forces shaping life and the pursuit of happiness in the twenty-first century. These concepts interact with other organizational philosophies, such as capitalism, nationalism, industrialism, and socialism, historical antecedents to democracy and bureaucracy.

Defining democracy is not easy. We live in a democracy. In the classical sense, though, our system of *political economy*, or politics and economics, is not a democracy, but a republic. We have a democratic *type* of government; however, we have a republican *form* of government. In our republic, elected officials represent us in our state and national legislatures. Other tenets of democracy call for "rule by the people." However, who are the "people"? How, and by what means, do they "rule"?

Democracy is not an economic, social, or ethical concept, but a political one. It points toward the realization of the values of liberty, equality, human worth, human dignity, and freedom by guaranteeing the right to secret voting. With these values comes free expression of ideas, free association of persons, representation,

---

PROTESTANT ETHIC AND CAPITALISM

Max Weber wrote *The Prostestant Ethic and the Spirit of Capitalism* in 1904–1905, with the intention of showing why a total revolution in the organization of society, or the rationalization of life, occurred only in the West and not in other parts of the world. However, Weber's intention has been obscured by much philosophizing, and mythmaking, about the so-called "Protestant Ethic."

Source: Daniel Bell, "The Protestant Ethic," *World Policy Journal* 13, no. 3(fall 1996): 35–38.

---

legislatures, due process of law, and the privilege of assuming our soap box and speaking our minds about almost anything.[1]

While democracy has a leveling, or *horizontal,* feature about its application, bureaucracy is *vertical.* Democracy implies equality and equal opportunity; however, bureaucracy also denotes hierarchy. Every four years American citizens vote for, or perhaps against, a presidential candidate because of the candidate's and the party's support of political principles as expressed in the party's platform. The party platform serves as the voters' guide to how its leaders should address the nation's challenges during the next term. Voting, which espouses equality, is a political right in a democratic society.

However, once a candidate becomes president, the direct democratic powers of voters are diluted; voters, as citizens, may encourage members of Congress to oppose the president's new programs, for example, but the rights of suffrage in our electoral democracy come only periodically. Except for those periodic elections, the premises of bureaucracy, or hierarchy, assume preeminence in our society. Public institutions—ranging from health to defense—develop, evaluate, and implement public policies.

The oft-used term, *bureaucracy,* has two meanings. In its most popular sense, the concept refers to any substantial public organization or group of organizations, as in "federal bureaucracy" or in "welfare bureaucracy." The other meaning is more specialized; it refers to a particular method or manner of administration. A bureaucracy in this sense is an organization or group of organizations that operates in a particular way.

What constitutes the bureaucratic way of doing things? The German sociologist Max Weber (1864–1920) was the first to define it. He saw bureaucracy as an impersonal system operating on the basis of "calculable rules" and staffed by full-time and professional (as opposed to political) employees. Bureaucracy presupposes hierarchy, but this hierarchy is based on organizational rank, not on social status or other considerations.

The chief characteristic of a bureaucracy in Weber's sense of the word was its uniform, nonarbitrary, and nonpersonal method of administering the public's affairs. "Bureaucracy," wrote Weber, "is like a modern judge who is a vending machine into which the pleadings are inserted along with the fee. The machine then disgorges the judgement based on reasons mechanically derived from the code."[2]

UNDERSTANDING BUREAUCRATIC CULTURE

Inattention to social systems in organizations has led researchers to underestimate the importance of culture—shaped norms, values, and assumptions—in how organizations function. Concepts for understanding culture in organizations have value only when they derive from observation of real behavior in organizations, when they make sense of organizational data, and when they are definable enough to generate further study. The attempt to explain what happened to "brainwashed" American prisoners of war in the Korean conflict points to the need to take both individual traits and culture into account to understand organizational phenomena. For example, the failure of organizational learning can be understood more readily by examining the typical responses to change by members of several broad occupational cultures in an organization. The implication is that culture needs to be observed, more than measured, if organization studies are to advance.

Source: Edgar H. Schein, "Culture: The Missing Concept in Organization Studies," *Administrative Science Quarterly* 41, no. 2 (June 1996): 229–241.

In Weber's view, bureaucracy is a bloodless mechanism devoid of the capriciousness and color we associate with human activity. Yet the positive features of such an administrative approach, characterized by impersonality and professionalism, must not be overlooked. Impersonality implies impartiality, and professionalism opens the possibility for an employee selection system based less on social status than on personal skill.

The bureaucratic way has made headway in Europe, especially in Germany. As such, it has brought more uniformity, predictability, and equality to public administration.

Bureaucratic systems rest upon a highly systematized administrative arrangement, therefore they often show resistance to change. The devotion to "calculable" rules often causes rule-conscious bureaucrats to "go by the book," regardless of the situation. Such persistence of routinized organizational behavior may, however, prove advantageous. France, with its long history of unrest and upheaval, has often been held together by its plodding, but enduring, bureaucracy.

Although the bureaucratic style has conquered the public sector in Western Europe, it has scored somewhat less decisively in this country. The dynamics of U.S. political bureaucracies, especially in state and local jurisdictions, are highly personal. It is often *who* one knows rather than *what* one knows that affects the administrative system. Just as personalities so often count for more than parties or principles in policy making, so personalities often outweigh "calculable rules" in policy execution. This is not always true, but it is verified often enough to differentiate U.S. administration from that of other economically developed democracies such as England, France, or West Germany.

Lessened concern for abiding by rules provides many rewards. Although U.S. administration has often been accused of stodginess, and rightly so, it is perhaps less guilty of such offenses than its Western European counterparts. It is much easier to bend, if not break, the rules in the United States than elsewhere in the world of modern democratic capitalism. The U.S. administrative setup, reflecting vast differences in bureaucratic cultures, can more easily accommodate individual idiosyncrasies and initiatives.

Before breaking out into cheers, the antibureaucratic enthusiast should note some of the benefits that we thereby forego. A system more open to the influence of individual personality is open to caprice and whim. As "calculable rules" become more easily manipulated it is also more vulnerable to corruption. If change can sometimes come more quickly, then such change may spring not only from public demand but from personal desire as well.

The distinctiveness of U.S. administration in this respect should not be overstated. The bureaucratic way of doing things is scarcely a stranger to our shores. The systems of other countries are certainly not incapable of capriciousness or change. Yet for both good and ill, bureaucracy in Weber's sense characterizes the U.S. public sector less than that of many other modern, developed nations.

INTERPRETATIONS OF "BUREAUCRACY"

According to Dwight Waldo, the term "bureaucracy" has two interpretations. The *popular-pejorative* interpretation is widely recognized in society: bureaucracy is bad because bureaucrats are timid, ineffectual, power-seeking, and dangerous.

A second interpretation of bureaucracy is *descriptive* and *analytical*. This interpretation says that bureaucracy fosters advanced legal and economic systems and, therefore, advances civilization. Descriptive and analytical terms used for this interpretation include form of government, formalism, rules, impersonality, hierarchy, expertise, records, large-scale, complex, efficiency, and effectiveness.

In reality, the concept of bureaucracy is neither good nor bad. Bureaucracy simply is; it exists. The concept of bureaucracy entails procedures for organizing people within a certain culture for the purpose of implementing a particular set of goals and objectives. *Bureaucracy exists for accomplishing tasks.* The tasks range from fighting dictators to fighting poverty.

How, then, are the societal values of democracy and bureaucracy antithetical, yet complementary?

According to Waldo, there are two problems in reconciling democracy and bureaucracy. One concern focuses upon the definition of the *administrative "unit."* Any organization able to respond to clientele is a unit. The function of a unit of bureaucracy may be defined by the manner in which the organization responds to its clientele. Academic departments, as administrative units at a college or university, are organized depending upon the demand from students for certain skills, knowledge, and expertise.

For example, English and math may be the largest departments on campus because most college curriculums mandate that students take courses in these subjects. Meanwhile, the departments of philosophy, anthropology, and foreign languages may be smaller because the demand for courses taught by those departments is lower than for English and math courses.

Waldo's concern is the status and weight to be accorded to *nondemocratic values.* Liberty and equality are democratic values. Examples of nondemocratic values are national security, personal safety, productivity, and efficiency. If the chairperson of an academic department is elected by members of that unit, the values of democracy have predominated. However, if the department head is selected by the dean of the college, then the values of bureaucracy—efficiency and productivity—have taken precedence.

BASELINE ORIGINALS IN ORGANIZATIONAL LIFE

Max Weber, Frederick Winslow Taylor, Elton Mayo, and Chester Barnard form an intellectual baseline of early classical thinkers concerned with the anatomy and physiology of private and public organizations. Thinking of the organization as a "rational machine" provides a useful metaphor in understanding this approach to organizational behaviors.[3]

MAX WEBER

Weber's work on the nature of bureaucracy is considered by many the most important of its kind. He was trained in law, history, and economics. He viewed action as both individual and social. Weber postulates the *"ideal-type"* of bureaucracy, not referring to goodness or "badness," but suggesting a standard or model for organizational environment. Characteristics of the ideal-type may be found in any organization.

In the following list, John M. Pfiffner and Frank P. Sherwood summarize components of Weber's ideal-type. These components contribute to our understanding of the functions and vital processes of organizations.

- *Emphasis on form.* Bureaucracy's first, most cited, and most general feature according to Weber is its emphasis on form of organization.
  In a sense the rest are examples of this.
- *The concept of hierarchy.* The organization follows the principle of hierarchy, with each lower office under the control and supervision of a higher one.
- *Specialization of task.* Incumbents are chosen on the basis of merit and ability to perform specialized aspects of a total operation.
- *A specified sphere of competence.* This flows from the previous point. It suggests that the relationships between the various specializations should be clearly known and observed in practice. In a sense, the use of job descriptions in many American organizations is a practical application of this requirement.
- *Established norms of conduct.* There should be as little as possible in the organization that is unpredictable. Policies should be enunciated and the individuals within the organization should see that these policies are implemented.
- *Records.* Administrative acts, decisions, and rules should be recorded as a means of insuring predictability of performance within the bureaucracy.[4]

SHAME VERSUS OFFICIAL CENSORSHIP

Moral censorship is a strong weapon of the culture-war propaganda that can intrude upon a person's privacy in ways that are unmatched by any kind of bureaucracy. Conservatives try to use shame as an alternative to official censorship and as a means to instill a sense of fear and self-loathing among freethinking individuals. The true meaning of shameful behavior is somewhat obliterated. It offers more to nonconformity and nonacceptance of prevalent trends than to immorality. It is, however, important to realize that shame and repentance come from within, and not from outside pressures.

Source: Carl F. Horowitz, "The Shaming Sham," *The American Prospect*, no. 31 (March–April 1997): 70–76.

Weber emphasized the universality of bureaucracy by emphasizing its rationality. His observations on bureaucracy coincided with the industrial revolution in Germany at the turn of the century. In seeking rationality in human behavior, he concluded that the ideal-type is the best means for achieving rationality at the institutional level.

Weber also assumed freedom for bureaucrats. Far from promoting a master-slave relationship, he emphasized that people were free agents, even within nineteenth century economic bureaucracies.

Finally, Weber forecast a general separation of policy-making and administration. The ideal-type organization is grounded in predictable, decision-making processes and is staffed by professionals, therefore bureaucracies should not be subverted by nonprofessionals according to Weber. In this view, professionals organize and implement expertise. Nonprofessionals, armed only with opinions about expertise and goals, do not fit Weber's game plan. Neither the monarch ruling by divine right nor the elected American president would be part of Weber's ideal-type framework.[5]

FREDERICK WINSLOW TAYLOR

Mass production suffered a long and fitful birth when it appeared in America in the mid-eighteenth century. Oliver Evans, Linus Yale, Lillian and Frank Gilbreth, and Henry Ford made huge contributions to its development. But it was Frederick Winslow Taylor who developed the underlying theory of scientific management that gave mass production its enduring form. Scientific management capitivated the American consciousness and catapulted Taylor's ideas onto center stage, where they have remained. Yet until the publication of Robert Kanigel's "The One Best Way," little was known about the man who revolutionized the workplace.[6]

Frederick Taylor (1856–1915) is often called the father of scientific management. He recognized the importance of technology, work, and organization to understanding the functions and vital processes of bureaucracies. In the opening of his classic, *The Principles of Scientific Management*, Taylor wrote:

The principal object of management should be to secure the maximum prosperity for the employer, coupled with the maximum prosperity for the employee.

"The words ` maximum prosperity' are used, in their broad sense, to mean not only large dividends for the company or owner, but the development of every branch of business to its highest state of excellence, so that prosperity may be permanent."[7]

According to Taylor, scientific management is both liberating and economically rational. Employees and employers are assumed to be rational. Through rationality in the work process, labor and management determine the proper way of completing a task.

Taylor, like Weber, assumed the importance of the individual foresaw the shift of power from both the *bourgeoisie* (economic elites) and the *proletariat* (masses) to the *expert* (possessor of skills and knowledge).

Taylor emphasized cooperation in the workplace and spoke of making life better for each employee. He represented a pre-World War II spirit that there are principles and laws that order our knowledge of the world. In seeking the scientific method, the impersonality of organizations results.

ELTON MAYO

In 1932, Harvard Business School professor, Elton Mayo (1880–1949), and a team of researchers completed five years of study outside Chicago, Illinois, at the Hawthorne plant of the Western Electric Company. Later published as *The Human Problems of an Industrial Civilization,* Mayo's research found that many problems in worker/management relations are caused not by insufficient task specialization or inadequate wages, but by social and psychological forces. The "Hawthorne Experiments," as they were subsequently known, were the first systematic research to expose the *human factor* in work situations. The study marked a major turning point in the history of administrative theory and practice.[8]

The Hawthorne experiments encouraged management people to conceptualize an organization as a *social institution.*

According to Pfiffner and Sherwood, Mayo's Hawthorne findings contributed to the ideological revolution in organization and management in two ways: by challenging the physical or engineering approach to motivation and by becoming the first real assault on the purely structural, hierarchical approach to organization. In other words, there was no scientific or best way to motivate employees to be productive. The "father knows best" authoritarian way of running an organization was seen as only one of several approaches available. The whims of scientific management were no longer accepted as gospel. The human relations movement was underway.[9]

Elton Mayo concluded from studying the "Hawthorne Experiments" that informal organization is more important in determining worker cooperation than formal organization; that output is set by social norms, not individual abilities; and that the group heavily influences the behavior of individual workers. Mayo's experiment showed how a group of young, female employees at Western Electric

Company reacted positively to every change made in their working conditions while they were working in the test room. However, another experiment conducted along the same lines produced quite different results.

Mayo and his colleagues persuaded the management of the company to put in a group of men engaged in making parts of telephone switches on a piece-rate incentive system. This new system would allow the men to increase their earnings without undue physical strain, and these were depression times when most workers seemed desperate to earn more money, therefore the researchers and the company expected a great jump in productivity. Their expectations came to naught. The output of the men remained the same.

The research group then began to investigate why the workers responded or, rather, failed to respond. Unlike the young, female relay assemblers, most of whom had expected to get married and leave their jobs before too long, the male workers had developed a work culture of their own. They had become a cohesive and compact group with their own codes, rules, and norms. Among these rules were prohibitions against doing too much or too little work. So solidly entrenched were these understandings among the male employees that they remained impervious to any blandishments from management. The men rationalized that the incentive plan was an attempt to eventually cut out some jobs or to reduce wage rates. The company assured them that such was not the case and pointed to its record, which indicated no instance of its ever having acted in such a manner. The men remained unconvinced and so productivity went on at the same level.[10]

Mayo and his associates had come up against the informal organization, grounded in large part on informal communications. This phenomenon has interested and intrigued organizational theorists since, and their research shows far-reaching ramifications.

CHESTER BARNARD

Chester Barnard (1886–1961) completes the baseline foursome. Intrigued by the experiments at the Hawthorne plant, Barnard formulated a theory of organizational life that focuses on *the organization as a system, formal and informal organizations, and the role of the executive.* In *Functions of the Executive,* Barnard distinguishes between *organizational purpose* and *individual motive.* He postulates that each person in the organization reflects a dual personality, one organizational and the other individual. As an individual leaves home and enters the workplace, he or she becomes the "organization man or woman."

An organization is a collection of actions focused toward a purpose; an equilibrium is necessary for an organization to sustain itself. A successful equilibrium must exist between the organization and its employees. The organization receives energies and productive capacities from employees, and employees receive compensation, benefits, and meaning from their work.[11]

Although the distinction between formal and informal organization is now commonplace, Barnard, in the late 1930s, introduced these concepts as new, analytic tools for examining organizational life. According to Barnard, *formal organization* is comprised of the consciously coordinated activities of people, while *informal organization* entails the unconscious group feelings, passions, and activities of the same individuals. Informal organization is essential to the maintenance of formal structures and relationships. The formal organization cannot exist without its informal counterpart. Not all activity can be structured by a chain of command because of the reality of informal organization.

Finally, Barnard addresses *executive functions* of organizations. These functions are:

- maintaining organization communication,
- securing essential services from individuals, and
- formulating the purpose and objectives of the organization.

Barnard writes that the functions of the executive are "those of the nervous system, including the brain, in relation to the rest of the body. It exists to maintain the bodily system by directing those actions which are necessary more effectively to adjust to the environment. But it can hardly be said to manage the body, a large part of whose functions are independent of it and upon which it in turn depends."[12]

The writings of Weber, Taylor, Mayo, and Barnard form an axis around which the theory and practice of public organizations revolve. Focusing upon three early organizational themes—system, hierarchy, and structure—writers who follow these "classical" thinkers assume that understanding human rationality is central to theorizing about organizational physiology.

NEOCLASSICAL THEORIES

The neoclassical perspective toward organizational theory is represented by the works of Luther Gulick and Herbert Simon. "Decision-set" organizational theory is characterized by several important themes, including: decision making as the heart and soul of administration; administrative capacity as measured by efficiency; organizational roles, not individual roles, are emphasized as they relate to decision making; and instrumental rationality as the center of operation.

LUTHER GULICK

In 1937, Luther Gulick and Lyndall Urwick edited the *Papers on the Science of Administration*, a collection of eleven papers reflecting the predominant thinking concerning organizations in Europe and the United States prior to World War II. Divided into two groups, the papers examined structural aspects and social and environmental aspects of organization.[13]

Gulick's "Notes on the Theory of Organization," in which he introduced the acronym POSDCORB, has influenced teaching and thinking about public administration for over fifty years. Consequences of Gulick's *POSDCORB* concern the Wilsonian separation of politics from administration, the need for a division of work to reach organizational objectives, and the efficiency criterion for judging governmental activities. In POSDCORB, Gulick outlines the work of the chief executive in the following manner:

Planning is working out in broad outline the things that need to be done and the methods for doing them to accomplish the purpose set for the enterprise;

Organizing is the establishment of the formal structure of authority through which work subdivisions are arranged, defined, and coordinated for the defined objective;

Staffing is the whole body of bringing in and training the staff and maintaining favorable work conditions;

Directing is the continuous task of making decisions and embodying them in specific and general orders and instructions and serving as the leaders of the enterprise;

Coordinating is the important duty of interrelating the various parts of the work;

Reporting is keeping those to whom the executive is responsible informed as to what is going on, which includes keeping himself or herself and subordinates informed through records, research, and inspection;

Budgeting with all that goes with budgeting in the form of fiscal planning, accounting, and control.[14]

HERBERT SIMON

After World War II, in 1947, Simon illustrated the decision-set perspective in "The Proverbs of Administration," incorporated later into his classic, *Administrative Behavior*. He viewed the decision as the central act of organization and instrumental rationality as the basis for decision making. By *instrumental rationality*, Simon meant that the individual is rational and responsible only within the environment of a particular organization. The organizational environment encompasses the purposes of rational behavior; autonomous individuals behave only within the confines of those organizational purposes.

In emphasizing the decision as the basis for administrative theory, Simon distinguished between *value* premises and *factual* premises of public administrators. He wrote, "The process of validating a factual proposition is quite distinct from the process of validating a value judgment. The former is validated by its agreement with the facts, the latter by human fiat."[15] In other words, the facts of any circumstance are validated by the given set of values in which those facts, or actions, occur.

Simon focuses upon the *"means-end"* sense of rationality as most significant. Administrators weigh the means, ends, and consequences of acting, therefore, Simon suggests, that decisions may prove "objectively" rational, "subjectively" rational, "deliberately" rational, "organizationally" rational, or "personally" rational. Regardless of adverb, to be rational means consideration of *only* those

---

MILES' LAW

Rufus E. Miles, Jr. proudly claims to have parented Miles' Law. The law states that, "Where you stand depends on where you sit." Miles says he discovered the law while serving as a division director of the former Bureau of the Budget. He noted that a budget examiner might be a constant critic of an agency whose budget he oversaw, yet if the examiner were to be later hired away by the agency, he would promptly do a 180° turn and become one of the agency's most adamant advocates. What position a bureaucrat takes depends on what position he is in, or, "Where you stand depends on where you sit."

Miles points out in illustration how John Gardner, as chairman of President Johnson's Task Force on Education, authored a report strongly favoring the removal of Education from the Department of Health, Education, and Welfare. Shortly thereafter, Gardner was appointed secretary of HEW. When asked whether he now planned to push for Education's removal from HEW, he firmly and flatly rejected any such nonsensical idea.

---

choices present within a prescribed system of values. Government employees are not autonomous individuals. The organizational environment of the department or agency articulates the values that incorporate the determination of rational behavior.

In other words, an employee is rational and responsible only within the environment of a particular department or agency. A government employee acts rationally only within the framework of the department's preestablished goals and purposes.

Values, on the other hand, are arbitrary, regardless of their origins. Human decree, sanction or authority, validates a certain set of organizational values. Executives, legislatures, and judges decide by fiat that a set of values, encompassed in laws and implemented by bureaucrats, are of importance to organizations and to society. Citizens of public organizations, then, respond to the rules and regulations and the boundaries imposed upon them by these values.

All decisions in organizations only satisfy and suffice, that is, they *"satisfice."* Our focus on choices and decision making and acceptance of organizational premises brings us to the limits of administrative rationality. This final Simon theme, that of "satisficing," recognizes that rationality, or human reasoning, is bounded by administrative settings. After analyzing the problem and considering the complexities of the situation, administrators "satisfice," surveying their options and selecting the first one they find at least minimally satisfactory. With prospects for "satisficing" by employees, Simon concludes that rationality is bounded. In describing *"bounded rationality,"* he concludes that an administrator's reasoning options are limited by unconscious habits and skills, values and conceptions of purpose, and degree of information and knowledge.[16]

HUMAN RELATIONS THEORIES

As we have seen in the previous passages, Max Weber speaks in *bureaucratic* terms; Frederick Taylor writes in *productivity* terms; Chester Barnard thinks in *organizational* terms; and Herbert Simon stresses *decisional* terms. Writing histories of the increasing bureaucratization of society, each of these authors emphasizes *efficiency* in some form as a potent force in any organization, but also concludes that organizations embody social purposes. In other words, they believe that if there is conflict within the organization, individuals must subordinate their interests to those of the organization.

For example: If students are not learning, the professor is not at fault. Instead, the onus usually is placed upon the students to change their behavior or study habits to respond to the professor's demands. Likewise, if the college's basketball team is losing, the assumption is that the players are lousy, lazy, and do not respond to their coach's leadership. Student athletes must subordinate their ways of acting to those of the administrator in charge. Human relations theories question such assumptions, placing responsibility on the professor to change his or her teaching methods and on the coach to change his or her leadership style and set up a new strategy for winning games. This shift in responsibility makes for several new ways of envisioning organizational structure and function.

MARY PARKER FOLLETT

An early prophet of human relations thinking was Mary Parker Follett (1868–1933). While the classical and neoclassical writers were attempting to construct a field of public administration along systematic and somewhat mechanical lines, Follett was marching to the beat of a different drummer.

She had become impressed with the psychological factors she had seen at work in her active life as an organizer of evening schools, recreation agencies, and employment bureaus and as a member of statutory wage boards. Already the author of two books on political science, *The New State* and *Creative Experience*, she embarked on a series of speculations in the 1920s concerning the functions and vital processes of organizations. Her work signaled the advent of a new era in administrative theory.[17]

In various papers and articles, Follett depicted administration as essentially involved with reconciling the agendas of both individuals and social groups. An organization's principal problems, in her view, were not only determining what it wanted its employees to do, but guiding and controlling the employees' conduct in such a way as to get them to do it. This, she indicated, was a much more complex task than previous writers had suggested.

Follett not only anticipated what was to become the human relations school of administration, she also foreshadowed the humanistic school that was to grow out of it. She urged organizations to stop trying to suppress the differences that may arise within their boundaries and seek to integrate those differences, thereby allowing them to contribute to the organization's growth and development. She advocated replacing the "law of authority" with the "law of the situation," admonishing organizations to exercise "power *with*" rather than "power *over*" their members.

A philosophical analysis of Mary Parker Follett's writings on democratic and organizational theories reveal similarities with the current feminist theory. These similarities include the notion that human relations supercede individual rights, the theory that knowledge is context specific, her sensitivity to the role of power as an obstacle in the development of knowledge claims, and her method of conflict resolution through the integration of opposing interests. Her writings provide important insights into modern organization and management principles.[18]

While Follett's writings did not go unnoticed, they failed to score the impact that similar ideas would later achieve. This was perhaps due partly to the fact that she was a woman writing in a society not yet willing to take women thinkers seriously. A more serious obstacle, however, may have been that she was an iconoclast, challenging the sacred credos of her time. She died during the same year Elton Mayo wrote on the Hawthorne experiments. Mayo's work was the first systematic research to expose the "human factor" in work situations. Mayo's study, as we have seen, marked a major turning point in the history of administrative theory and practice.

MASLOW, MCGREGOR, AND LIKERT

Like Follett, organizational psychologists Abraham Maslow, Douglas McGregor, and Rensis Likert wrote from a progressive, humanistic viewpoint. They have profoundly influenced the teaching and practice of public administration concerning the role of democracy in bureaucracy, advocating expanded scope and encouragement for individual initiative and enterprise by allowing employees to make many of their own decisions on the job. These authors call for *less hierarchy and more humanity in organizational life* and emphasize *the integration of individuals in organization.*

Writing in *Motivation and Personality* (1954), Maslow identifies a hierarchy of personal needs that the organization must contend with to successfully integrate the individual. He writes that food and shelter demands are the first needs humans meet. Then freedom from physical harm and deprivation is sought. Next, the desire for affectionate and supportive relationships with family, friends, and associates becomes a priority. Then comes recognition of worth by peers. Finally, there is the need to actualize one's inherent potential, to release one's creative abilities, to achieve everything that one hopes for in life.[19]

Like Maslow, McGregor's thinking is essentially optimistic concerning individuals' capacity for self-realization. McGregor examines possibilities for merging individual and organizational demands in ways that would prove satisfactory to both. In *The Human Side of Enterprise* (1960), McGregor outlines management's conventional view of harnessing human energy to organizational requirements he calls "Theory X," and then boldly steps forward with a new theory of administration he calls "Theory Y."

Theory X is based on these assumptions:

- The average person is by nature lazy. He or she will work as little as possible. Such an individual lacks ambition, dislikes responsibility, and prefers to be led.
- By nature resistant to change, he or she is gullible, not very bright, and the ready dupe of the charlatan and the demagogue. Such a person is furthermore inherently self-centered and indifferent to organizational needs.

Theory Y, or McGregor's new way of merging individual and organizational demands, takes a more humanistic approach:

- People are not naturally passive, lazy, and dumb. They are, on the contrary, eager for opportunities to show initiative and to bear responsibility.
- Work is a natural activity and people by nature want to perform it.
- People work best in an environment that treats them with respect and encourages them to develop and use their abilities.
- There is no inherent and intrinsic conflict between the goals of the organization and the goals of the individual member. Meeting the goals of the individual will only result in the organization becoming more productive.[20]

Rensis Likert, writing in *The Human Organization* (1967), develops four systems that positively or negatively influence the integration of individuals into organizations.

- System 1 is *punitive authoritarian* and closely resembles Theory X mentioned previously. System 1 administrative leaders have no confidence or trust in subordinates.
- System 2 is *benevolent authoritarian* and is more generous and humanitarian toward the employee. While System 1 takes everything from the individual and gives little in return, System 2 rewards employee behavior only as prescribed employer directives are followed. If the employee does his or her tasks as prescribed, he or she is dutifully rewarded. System 2 leaders are condescending in bestowing their confidence and trust, engaging in something resembling a master/servant relationship with subordinates.
- System 3 is *consultative* and allows still more participation by employees. Administrative leaders in such an organization may be democratic, allowing free discussion regarding policy-making, but still assuming final responsibility for all decisions. System 3 illustrates substantial, but not complete confidence and trust in subordinates.
- System 4 is a *participative group model* and closely resembles Theory Y mentioned previously. Senior bureaucrats promote complete confidence and trust in employees in all matters. Employees are used for guidance and for coordinated problem solving. Employees are not treated punitively.

NETWORKING DEMOCRATIC BUREAUCRACY?

Public administration has evolved into a less hierarchical, less insular, and more networked field of interest. This evolution has important effects on democracy, including obligations for the public interest, meeting public preferences and enhancement of political deliberation, civility, and trust. The values and actions of public administrators can affect the outcome of networked public administration such that the latter can either threaten or strengthen democratic governance.

Source: Laurence J. O'Toole Jr., "The Implications for Democracy in a Networked Bureaucratic World," *Journal of Public Administration Research and Theory* 7, no. 3 (July 1997): 443–450.

According to Likert, administrative leaders adopting the participative style achieve from 10 to 40 percent greater productivity, experience much higher levels of employee satisfaction and much better employee health, enjoy much better labor relations, suffer less absence and less turnover, obtain better product quality, and, finally, record better customer satisfaction as a result of better products and services than managers operating with System 1, 2, or 3 styles.[21]

SUMMARY

- The *physiology* of organization deals with the functions and vital processes of public bureaucracies and their subunits.
- Bureaucracy and democracy are at the center of what occurs in the public and private organizations of our society.
- In a classical sense, our system of *political economy,* or politics and economics, is not a democracy but a republic. We have a democratic *type* of government; however, we have a republican *form* of government.
- *Democracy implies equality while bureaucracy* implies hierarchy. Bureaucracy exists for accomplishing tasks ranging from fighting dictators to fighting poverty.
- Max Weber's *"ideal-type"* of bureaucratic organization entails an emphasis on form, hierarchy, specialization of tasks, specified spheres of competence, established norms of conduct, and record keeping.
- The advent of large scale bureaucracy has seen the shift of power from both the *bourgeoisie* (economic elites) and the *proletariat* (masses) to the *expert* (possessor of skills and knowledge).
- The acronym *POSDCORB* outlines the work of the chief executive in terms of planning, organizing, staffing, directing, coordinating, reporting, and budgeting.
- *Formal organization* is only part of the study of bureaucracy. Every organization has its informal counterpart—its unconscious group feelings, passions, and activities.
- *Informal organization* is essential to the maintenance of formal structures and relationships.

- Weber stresses bureaucratic terms, Taylor productivity terms, Barnard organizational terms, and Simon decisional terms. All emphasize *efficiency*.
- The human relations theorists, Maslow, McGregor, and Likert, emphasize principles of *equality*. They call for less hierarchy and more humanity in organizational life.
- While the study of theories related to the craft of a public administration is vital, it is also valuable to look at a concrete example. While you're reading the following case study, see if you can spot where previously discussed theories come into play in the real world of public administration.

CASE STUDY

An Authoritarian Approach to Management[22]

Richard Patton had grown up in a small town in a largely rural midwestern state where the economy was based on agriculture. His parents were hardworking and devout and had subjected their children to severe discipline. As a boy, Patton had done odd jobs to pay for his own clothes and school supplies. He was a typical product of a society that valued the work ethic: disciplined, conservative, industrious, and respectful of authority.

At the university, where he studied public administration, Patton was mainly interested in those aspects of courses he considered down-to-earth. He found theoretical and philosophical propositions boring because he had difficulty in applying the abstract to practical matters. Upon graduation Patton got his first job in his own state as an assistant to the director of the Social Welfare Department in Jefferson County, a rural county of about 40,000 people who were neither wealthy nor poor. Demand for social welfare services was not great, and the problems facing the department staff of ten were readily taken care of. Patton won the respect of his director and coworkers by his conscientious work and reliability. When the director moved on after a year, Patton succeeded him in the post.

A year later Patton accepted an offer to direct a department in a large county with more industry, a more varied economy, and a more diverse population than Jefferson County. Patton became head of a department with forty staff members governed by the Polk County Board of Commissioners and the county Social Service Commission. Although the county had a mixed population that included Native Americans, Hispanics and African Americans, no members of these groups worked at the department.

It was a typical public welfare agency, administered by the county; supervised by the state; and funded by the county, state, and federal governments. Its programs included Aid for Families with Dependent Children (AFDC), Work Incentive (WIN), Supplemental Security Income (SSI), and Medicaid, all administered under guidelines set by the state and federal governments. The staff members, Patton soon discovered, frequently failed to follow guidelines and even appeared unfamiliar with them, applied rules inconsistently, and were sometimes indifferent to their clients' needs.

Employees often arrived late at the office, took time off without permission to take care of personal matters, left clients waiting while getting coffee or chatting with fellow employees, and were inefficient and lackadaisical. Patton found few of them had the education and training for their work and quickly discovered the reason: qualified people were hard to obtain because of the low pay scale, the minimum acceptable by state requirements. The county commissioners, politically and economically conservative, held budgets to the lowest possible level. Salary levels in all county offices were not competitive with those in the private sector. Patton's initial review of the agency revealed that three persons appeared potentially useful in establishing an organizational structure to replace the present slipshod operation. They were the assistant director and two other employees who had ill-defined supervisory powers.

The course of action necessary to reform the agency appeared clear to Patton. What was needed was a highly structured and disciplined organization. He envisioned himself as keeping close tabs on the programs administered by the agency. Supervisors would be selected from within the organization. Authority would be delegated to the supervisors, and line workers would be classified according to a strict hierarchy. Jobs would be highly specialized and all employees would be trained to do their jobs in a prescribed manner. Weekly staff meetings would be used to review and modify work styles and to inculcate respect for authority.

In putting his plans into effect, Patton rejected suggestions of the workers. He felt that their ideas on pay, job design, and office procedures had no place in a well-run operation. "If they don't like the way the office is run, they can work some other place," he said. Despite Patton's authoritarian approach to management, some improvement was made. The office was brightened by fresh paint, and the furniture was rearranged so that counselors had more privacy in discussing problems with their clients. Responsibility for certain tasks was assigned to specific people, files were kept up-to-date, and clients problems were handled more quickly. Patton and his supervisors, carefully chosen from among the staff, seemed to receive proper respect from other employees.

Dissatisfaction and dissent soon boiled over, however. Line workers challenged Patton's edicts at staff meetings, complained about many of the imposed rules and regulations, wrangled over policies and goals, and threatened to appeal to the governing boards. Patton's supervisors periodically approached him with suggestions for changes. He had been upset at first and had felt they were interfering with his prerogatives as an administrator, but he was now willing to listen to their opinions, especially since he was beginning to fear losing his job if the extent of the objections among the staff reached the agency's governing boards.

The supervisors explained to him that, although many improvements had been made in the department, they believed the administrative structure had to be made more responsive to staff personnel. They suggested that staff input in salary plans, office-procedural policies, and staff meetings be increased and that a program of upgrading jobs and pay be introduced. They thought that the administrative system was too strict. The department under the former director had not been tightly controlled, but the work had gotten done, and the public had seemed satisfied as to the level of service delivery. It was hard for Patton to believe he had been wrong in thinking the welfare department needed the imposition of a more rigid system, but he now recognized that his reforms had failed and that there were aspects of management to which he had been blind. Copyright c 11/88. From: *Practicing Public Management*, 2E. By: Meyer et al.

QUESTIONS AND INSTRUCTIONS

1. Analyze Patton's conception of leadership.
2. If we grant that the welfare department needed to be made more efficient, what course could Patton have followed to make his reforms more acceptable to his staff?
3. What needed changes in the department did Patton overlook?
4. What courses of action would you recommend for Patton to correct his mistakes?
5. Would another organizational theory and management practice have been more appropriate for the welfare department than that followed by Patton? Explain.
6. What are some of the organizational factors that can impede change? What are some factors that can facilitate change? How can resistance to change be overcome?

INSIGHTS-ISSUES / AN AUTHORITARIAN APPROACH TO MANAGEMENT

Clearly and briefly describe and illustrate these concepts, issues, or points. Interpret the word "role" as meaning impact, application, importance, effect and/or illustration of certain facts, concerns, or issues from the case study.

1. Role of Mr. Patton's work ethic (values) as line official;
2. Role of applying general (literature) to particular (case study);
3. Role of democracy (or lack thereof) in bureaucracy;
4. Role of informal group dynamics' impact upon formal organization;
5. Role of Weber's "ideal type" model in Mr. Patton's department.

ENDNOTES

1. Dwight Waldo, *The Enterprise of Public Administration* (Novato, Calif.: Chandler & Sharp Publishers, Inc., 1980), 33–47.
2. H. H. Gerth and C. Wright Mills, eds. *From Max Weber: Essays in Sociology* (New York: Oxford University Press, 1946), 197.
3. Michael M. Harmon and Richard T. Mayer outline the most important contributions to conceptual theories of public organizations. The authors create a general framework for examining the world confronting the public administrator. They describe six perspectives that bridge the theoretical with actual practice in public organizations. These perspectives, as analyzed by various authors, focus upon three

organizational themes—system, hierarchy, and structure. See Harmon and Mayer, *Organization Theory for Public Administration* (Boston: Little, Brown, and Co., 1986).

4. John M. Pfiffner and Frank P. Sherwood, *Administrative Organization* (Englewood Cliffs, N.J.: Prentice-Hall, Inc., 1960), 56–57.

5. *Ibid.,* 217.

6. Wellford W. Wilms, "Father Time, THE ONE BEST WAY," *Los Angeles Times,* 1 June 1997, p. 6.

7. Frederick Winslow Taylor, *The Principles of Scientific Management* (New York: W. W. Norton & Co., Inc., 1947), 9.

8. Elton Mayo, *The Human Problems of an Industrial Civilization* (New York: Macmillan, 1933). Also see F. J. Roethisberger and William J. Dickson, *Management and the Worker* (Cambridge, Mass.: Harvard University Press, 1946).

9. F. J. Roethsberger and William J. Dickson, *Management and Worker* (Cambridge, Mass.: Harvard University Press, 1946), 552.

10. Pfiffner and Sherwood, *Administrative Organization,* 102.

11. Chester Barnard, *Functions of the Executive* (Cambridge, Mass.: Harvard University Press, 1968).

12. *Ibid.,* 217.

13. Luther Gulick and Lyndall Urwick, eds. *Papers on the Science of Administration* (New York: Institute of Public Administration, 1937).

14. Gulick, "Notes on the Theory of Organization," in Gulick and Urwick, *Science of Administration,* 13.

15. Herbert A. Simon, "The Proverbs of Administration," *Public Administration Review* 6 (winter 1946): 53–67.

16. Herbert A. Simon, *Administrative Behavior: A Study of Decision-Making Processes in Administrative Organization,* 3rd ed. (New York: The Free Press, 1976).

17. Mary Parker Follett, *The New State: Group Organization—The Solution to Popular Government* (New York: Longmans, Green, 1918); *Creative Experience* (New York: Longmans, Green, 1924); and *Dynamic Administration* Henry C. Metcalf and L. Urwick, eds.

18. Noel O'R. Morton and Stefanie A. Lindquist, "Revealing the Feminist in Mary Parker Follett," *Administration & Society* 29, no. 3 (July 1997): 348–372.

19. Abraham Maslow, *Motivation and Personality* (New York: Harper and Brothers, 1954).

20. Douglas McGregor, *The Human Side of Enterprise* (New York: McGraw-Hill, 1960).

21. Rensis Likert, *The Human Organization: Its Management and Value* (New York: McGraw-Hill, 1967).

22. C. Kenneth Meyer and Charles H. Brown, "An Authoritarian Approach to Management," *Practicing Public Management: A Casebook,* 2d ed., 90–92. Reprinted with permission of Bedford/St. Martin's Press, Inc.

5

PEOPLE AND PERSONNEL

Chapter Highlights

CONFLICTING DOCTRINES
IN AMERICAN PUBLIC ADMINISTRATION

PROCEDURES AND POLICIES

EMPLOYEE RECRUITMENT

THE POSTRECRUITMENT PHASE

PROMOTION

THE CHALLENGES OF PUBLIC PERSONNEL ADMINISTRATION

THE CHANGING DEMOGRAPHICS
OF THE FEDERAL WORK FORCE

EQUAL OPPORTUNITY AND AFFIRMATIVE ACTION

PERFORMANCE RATINGS

POSITION CLASSIFICATIONS

"Let me control personnel," George Kennan has said, "and I will ultimately control policy. For the part of the machine that recruits and hires and fires and promotes people can soon control the entire shape of the institution."[1]

Few administrative theorists or practitioners would dispute this statement, and in the course of history, few able administrators have thought or acted otherwise. Their attitudes and approaches to the subject have, however, often differed.

Thomas Jefferson, for example, believed that civil servants should be provided with "drudgery and subsistence only" so that they would not want to stay too long in office.[2] This would enable the country to escape the establishment and growth of an administrative class, a development that Jefferson greatly feared. His fears were echoed by a U.S. business journal in the 1920s, which published an editorial stressing "the urgency of keeping this country's civil service ineffective lest it become dangerous."[3]

Most public administrators have taken a different tack, and through the years increasing effort has gone toward improving the capabilities and stature of those toiling in the public sector. Today, with the increased importance of the public sector in private lives, increased emphasis should be placed upon strengthening the competency of civil servants.

CONFLICTING DOCTRINES IN AMERICAN PUBLIC ADMINISTRATION

Herbert Kaufman provided a foundation for describing conflicts in the doctrines of public administration—a foundation that remains solid in the twenty-first century. He notes that different values are reflected in different periods in American history. The quests for representativeness, for neutral competence, and for executive leadership reflect norms of public personnel administration.[4]

The quest for *representativeness* has its roots in the colonial period. In our republican system, government bureaucrats are accountable to policies initiated by representatives of the voters. The quest for *neutral competence* originated in the 1880s with abuses of legislative supremacy, the long ballot, and the spoils system. The goal of this quest was "taking administration out of politics."

The quest for *executive leadership* was an effort to deal with such governmental issues as budgeting, reorganization, fragmentation, and the size of the bureaucracy. The personnel function is an essential part of these issues.

In addition to these "quests," it is helpful to examine Donald E. Klingner's and John Nalbandian's description of factors affecting public personnel practices that may contribute to the conflicting values in public administration. These factors are:

- *Value Influences.* These considerations especially concern rights of the individual, administrative efficiency, responsiveness, and social equity.
- *Mediating Activities.* These interventions include affirmative action, human resource planning, productivity, and labor relations.
- *Core Functions.* These essentials focus on procurement, allocation, development, and sanction of human resources.[5]

PROCEDURES AND POLICIES

Public organizations in this country use essentially one of two different methods of establishing and operating personnel systems. One method stresses *political appointment and election* while the other emphasizes an *objective determination of merit.*

Political appointment and election has a long history in the United States. Units of the Revolutionary army frequently elected their own officers, and once the hostilities ended, states and their communities elected most of the administrators they would need. This practice has continued in many places. Many cities and towns, particularly older ones, follow the same practice. Some New England communities elect as many as fifty officials. Newer areas of the country, such as the Far West, disdain such practices, but even they maintain county organizations with many elective posts. No other major country in the world elects so many of its administrators as does the United States. Most state governments elect some officials whose tasks would be regarded in Europe or Canada as purely administrative.

The selection of civil servants grounded in both merit and political patronage is not mutually exclusive, argues James E. Leidlein. Fears that any relaxation of a merit-based system will lead to the returned dominance of political patronage are not warranted.[6]

Although election is supposed to give the people a deciding voice in determining who will administer their government, it can lead to abuses, such as confusing and misleading promises and campaign funding from special interests. Underlying such problems is that most of the electorate finds it impossible to know all the candidates for whom they must vote.

The political appointment of officials is a practice that also dates back to colonial times. Even John Adams, who considered himself something of a paragon of political propriety, felt constrained to provide his ne'er-do-well son-in-law with a government job. Such practices gained increased favor with the arrival of Andrew Jackson at the White House. Jackson strongly adhered to Jefferson's views on rotating public servants in office. At the same time, Jackson did not believe that this would entail any loss of public confidence. As he put it, "The duties of all public servants are, or at least admit of being made, so plain and simple that men of intelligence may readily qualify themselves for their performance."[7] Old Hickory's espousal of this philosophy was fortified in that he had a virtual army of job seekers at his back clamoring loudly for the plums of patronage.

From Jackson's time on, U.S. presidents frequently found themselves besieged by persons seeking positions on the public payroll. One aggressive appointment seeker jumped into Abraham Lincoln's carriage to ask for a job while the president was riding through Washington. Lincoln started to listen to him but then drove him away, saying, more in despair than in anger, "No I will not do business in the street."

When a disappointed job seeker assassinated President James Garfield in 1881, the nation's appetite for such administrative practices began to change. Political appointment continues to play a prominent role in U.S. administrative life, however. Our presidents, for example, have nearly one hundred times more appointments to fill than do British prime ministers.

The assassination of President Garfield did have its effect. It gave rise to an alternative method of recruitment, namely the *merit system.* Two years after the president's violent death, Congress passed the Pendleton Act, setting up a systematized procedure for hiring and employing vast numbers of federal civil servants in nearly every category. The merit system principle has continued to grow. It not only encompasses over 90 percent of positions in the federal government but includes increasing numbers of employees in state and local governments. About two-thirds of our states have comprehensive merit systems that cover the vast majority of their job holders. Even those remaining states without comprehensive merit systems make some provisions for merit-style appointments. The federal government has helped prod states and municipalities to move in this direction, for federal grants-in-aid frequently require the recipient agency to operate a merit system of some sort.

The Pendleton Act, passed in 1883, provided the substance of modern merit principles. First, administrative reform focused upon *nonpolitical appointments* in attempting to neutralize the civil service. Such nonpartisanship in selecting, promoting, and regulating public bureaucrats was a reaction against the evils of the spoils system. Second, the Pendleton Act embraced *egalitarianism,* the most important legacy of Jacksonian democracy. Congress, in adopting civil service reform, refused to pattern the U.S. career system after the British. The American merit system would be open to all applicants of appropriate aptitude and skills. Theoretically, at least, all classes of citizens may contest for government employment. Third, *competence,* as determined by competitive examinations, constituted a theme of the Pendleton Act's provisions. The emphasis was the requirement that exams be practical, related to the duties to be performed, and not grounded in theoretical or scholarly essays based on academic achievement.[8]

More recently, the Civic Service Reform Act of 1978 established the merit system principles that the government employs today. The act states, in addition to many other merit principles, that:

> *Recruitment should be from qualified individuals from appropriate sources in an endeavor to achieve a workforce from all segments of society, and selection and advancement should be determined solely on the basis of relative ability, knowledge, and skills, after fair and open competition which assures that all receive equal opportunity.*

Another key part of the 1978 law states:

> *Employees should be retained on the basis of the adequacy of their performance, inadequate performance should be corrected, and employees should be separated who cannot or will not improve their performance to meet required standards.*

TABLE 5–1 Expansion of Merit System and Public Service During Presidential Terms

President	Term	Events
Chester Arthur	1881–1885	Through the Pendleton Act of 1883, created U.S. Civil Service Commission and the merit system.
Grover Cleveland	1885–1889	Extended the competitive civil service in 1888 by 5,320 positions through blanketing in the Railway Mail Service. Congress creates the Interstate Commerce Commission, the first federal regulatory commission. Woodrow Wilson's "The Study of Administration" is published in *Political Science Quarterly.*
Benjamin Harrison	1889–1893	Extended the competitive civil service by blanketing in the Indian Service, Fish Commission, and Weather Bureau.
Grover Cleveland	1893–1897	Increased the size of the competitive civil service by 32,000 positions with one order in 1896.
William McKinley	1897–1902	Revised the civil service rules in 1899, which excepted over 5,000 positions from the competitive civil service. In 1901, Galveston (TX) is first city to install commission form of government, and Oregon becomes the first state to adopt initiative and referendum.
Theodore Roosevelt	1902–1909	Showed strong support for the civil service reform movement after serving as Civil Service Commissioner from 1889 to 1895. In 1906, Bureau of Municipal Research founded in New York City to further the management movement in government. In 1908, Staunton (VA) appoints first city manager.
William Taft	1909–1913	Extended the competitive civil service by 39,000 positions by blanketing in fourth-class post-masterships and assistant post-masters and clerks. Frederick W. Taylor publishes *The Principles of Scientific Management.* In 1912, Taft Commission calls for a national executive budget, position classification first adopted at the municipal level in the City of Chicago. Sumter (SC) is first to install council-manager form of city government, and Congress approves eight-hour day for federal employees.
Woodrow Wilson	1913–1921	Almost doubled the federal workforce to a total of nearly 1,000,000 during World War I. In 1913, the sixteenth Amendment to the Constitution creates the first permanent federal income tax, the Federal Reserve Act creates a central bank responsible for monetary policy. In 1914, Dayton (OH) is the first major city to have a city manager. In 1920, the Retirement Act creates the first federal civil service pension system, the nineteenth Amendment gives women the right to vote.
Warren Harding	1921–1923	Saw the comprehensive civil service hold, during the postwar reductions, the ground it had previously gained. In 1921, the Budget and Accounting Act establishes (1) the Bureau of the Budget in the Department of the Treasury and (2) the General Accounting Office as an agency of Congress. In 1923, the Classification Act brings position classification to Washington—based federal employees and establishes the principle of equal pay for equal work.

continued

TABLE 5–1 Expansion of Merit System and Public Service During Presidential Terms, *continued*

President	Term	Events
Calvin Coolidge	1923–1929	Extended the competitive civil service in 1927 by blanketing in the Bureau of Prohibition. In 1926, Leonard D. White's *Introduction to the Study of Public Administration* is the first text in public administration.
Herbert Hoover	1929–1933	Placed 13,000 previously excepted positions in the competitive civil service.
Franklin Roosevelt	1933–1945	Established new temporary emergency agencies, with the majority excepted from the competitive civil service during the Great Depression, saw the Ramspeck Act of 1940 extend the competitive civil service to more than 182,000 permanent positions, increased the number of federal employees during World War II to 3,816,300 in 1945. In 1933, New Deal begins, Tennessee Valley Authority (TVA) established by Congress as independent public corporation. In 1935, Social Security program created. In 1937, the Brownlow Committee's report says that the "President needs help" and calls for the reorganization of the executive branch. In 1939 the Hatch Act passed to inhibit political activities by federal employees, the federal government first requires states to have merit systems for employees in programs aided by federal funds.
Harry Truman	1945–1953	Alternately expanded and contracted the federal workforce, which challenged personnel management. In 1945, the Manhattan Project marks the federal government's first major involvement with science in a policymaking role. In 1946, the Employment Act creates the Council of Economic Advisors and asserts that the policy of the federal government is to maintain full employment. In 1949, the National Security Act creates the Department of Defense.
Dwight Eisenhower	1953–1961	Through an executive order in 1953, a Schedule C class of positions were excepted from the competitive civil service. In 1955, Second Hoover Commission recommends the curtailment and abolition of federal government activities that are competitive with private enterprise; the Department of Health, Education and Welfare (HEW) created. In 1958, National Aeronautics and Space Administration(NASA) created. In 1959, New York City is first major city to allow collective bargaining with its employees, Wisconsin is first state to enact a comprehensive law governing public sector labor relations, the Advisory Commission on Intergovernmental Relations (ACIR) is established.
John Kennedy	1961–1963	Signed Executive Order (EO) 10925 requiring "affirmative action" be used in employment, EO 10988 encouraging the unionization of federal workers.

continued

Table 5–1 Expansion of Merit System and Public Service During Presidential Terms, *continued*

President	Term	Events
Lyndon Johnson	1963–1969	In 1965, the Department of Housing and Urban Development (HUD) is established, Medicare is created through amendments to the Social Security Act. In 1966, the Freedom of Information Act allows greater access to federal agency files. In 1967, Age Discrimination in Employment Act is passed.
Richard Nixon	1969–1974	In 1969, Executive Order 11491 granted federal employees rights to join or not to join labor organizations, created the Federal Labor Relations Council (FLRC) to supervise the creation of bargaining units and elections. In 1970, the Bureau of the Budget (BOB) is given more responsibility for managerial oversight and renamed the Office of Management and Budget (OMB), the Postal Reorganization Act creates the U.S. Postal Service as a public corporation, Hawaii becomes the first state to allow state and local government employees to strike, the Environmental Protection Agency (EPA) is established. In 1974, the Congressional Budget and Impoundment Control Act revises the congressional budget process and creates the Congressional Budget Office (CBO).
Jimmy Carter	1977–1981	Guidelines holding sexual harassment prohibited by Title VII of the Civil Rights Act (1964) posted. Zero-based budgeting required of federal agencies. The Presidential Management Intern Program is established. In 1977, the Department of Energy is created. In 1978, the Civil Service Reform Act abolishes the U.S. Civil Service Commission and replaces it with (1) the Office of Personnel Management (OPM), (2) the Merit Systems Protection Board (MSPB), and (3) the Federal Labor Relations Authority (FLRA).
Ronald Reagan	1981–1989	The "Reagan revolution" was an attack on the quality and size of government. It reflected widespread citizen dissatisfactions—real and perceived—with government programs. Reagan: government "not the solution to the problem. Government *is* the problem." The Civil Service Reform Act was not used to rebuild a merit system in serious disrepair. The roles of government bureaucratic authority and power in a democratic system questioned. Without funding and leadership, career civil servants, regardless of their acclaimed merit, were caught in a Catch-22.
George Bush	1989–1993	Urged government officials to uphold the highest ethical standards and called government service an opportunity for public service, not private gain. In 1989, the National Commission on the Public Service, the Volcker Commission, called for a revitalization of the public service.

continued

TABLE 5–1 Expansion of Merit System and Public Service During Presidential Terms, *continued*

President	Term	Events
Bill Clinton	1993–	Emphasized reinventing government themes, performance review, and a revitalized bureaucracy. In 1993, Executive Order 12871 created the National Partnership Council calling for a new framework in labor-management relations. Reforms in position classification, pay and promotion opportunities advocated. Downsizing of the federal government initiated.

Sources: Data from U.S. Civil Service Commission, *Biography of an Ideal: The Diamond Anniversary History of the Federal Civil Service* (Washington: U.S. Government Printing Office, 1958); Patricia Wallace Ingraham, *The Foundation of Merit: Public Service in American Democracy* (Baltimore: The Johns Hopkins Press, 1995); Jay M. Shafritz and E. W. Russell, *Introducing Public Administration* (New York: Addison Wesley Longman, Inc., 1997), adapted from Jay M. Shafritz and Albert C. Hyde, *Classics of Public Administration*, 4th ed. (Fort Worth, Tex.: Harcourt Brace, 1997).

THE PLUM BOOK

The government pamphlet *Policy and Supporting Positions,* also known as the Plum Book, lists 8,000 of the choicest jobs available in the federal government. These political appointment positions pay from $86,160–$148,400 annually, making the book a hot topic when it comes out every four years.

Source: Andrew Ferguson, "The Political Hacks' Ultimate Fantasy Book," *Fortune* 135, no. 4 (3 March 1997): 46–47.

To summarize, key *merit system principles* are: recruiting, selecting, and advancing employees on the basis of their abilities, knowledge, and skills; providing equitable and adequate compensation; training employees to assure high-quality performance; guaranteeing fairness for applicants and employees; and protecting against coercion for political purposes.

Despite the law, the merit system has its detractors who say such a system eventually leads to a triumph of *mediocrity*, with initiative and enterprise sacrificed to the pressures of security and the forces of stagnation. Even when a merit system encourages merit, the argument continues, it may lead only to a *"meritocracy"* that shuts out otherwise capable people who cannot pass its tests or meet its formal and sometimes fatuous requirements.

Although the merit system may have lost some of its luster, it retains a good deal of support from both theorists and practitioners. If it leads to a "meritocracy" then, they say, this is still likely to be more egalitarian and democratic than a system built on political contacts and allegiances. When operated properly, it attracts the better people and encourages them to stay and develop their capabilities.

In a 1990 decision, the United States Supreme Court ruled that the U.S. Constitution prohibits partisan political considerations for hiring, promoting, or transferring most public employees. The ruling clearly prevents a mayor or local chief executive from reserving nonpolicy-making jobs such as road equipment operations, prison security, highway repair, and parks department for the party faithful. Although the practical impacts of the ruling are difficult to assess, the Supreme Court dealt a sharp blow to political patronage at all levels.

In conclusion, the federal government labor force is enlisted on the basis of merit, though, in the early 20th century, employees were hired on the basis of patronage. While enlistment on the basis of merit forbids involvement in politics, patronage enlistment actively encouraged political involvement. According to Ronald N. Johnson and Gary D. Libecap, the inherent corruption and inefficiency in the patronage system led to its demise. The adoption of the merit system of recruitment imposes effective control over the performance and actions of the labor force.[9]

EMPLOYEE RECRUITMENT

If the merit principle has become the most widely accepted basis for personnel operation in U.S. administration, it nevertheless continues to catalyze controversies and pose problems. In terms of recruitment, there is first the task of making sure that the system truly rewards merit. Most civil service systems make extensive use of comparative examinations to bring this about. While such exams may more impartially weigh the merits of the various candidates than would a system built on favoritism, they offer difficulties of their own.

For one thing, the exams must be *predictive*. In other words, high scores on the examinations should correlate with high performance on the job and vice versa. This is not necessarily the case. The issue of the validity of tests (whether test results are accurate or appropriate) and other recruitment criteria has come to the fore, thanks to the increased efforts to recruit members of minority groups into government service. Civil rights supporters claim that many of these criteria serve to exclude blacks, Puerto Ricans, Chicanos, and others. In so doing, these tests fail to determine the true capability of a job applicant. A study in Chicago found that a black police recruit would perform as well as a white recruit who scored 10 percent higher on the entrance exam.[10] In other words, the entrance test failed to measure the true ability for police work of black applicants in comparison with white applicants.

The federal government encourages test validation as a means of ensuring and expanding equal opportunity. The move to include more members of minority groups in public administration is part of a larger movement aimed at making government agencies more representative of the public they serve. This brings us to another issue in administration. Government agencies have at times become "captured" by one or more sector of society. The "captive" agency, a term used by public administration scholar Brian Chapman, tends to recruit heavily from one particular ethnic, religious, social, or geographical group.

TABLE 5–2: December 31, 1991* Full-Time Permanent White-Collar College Graduate Federal Civilian Employment in the Executive Branch by Academic Discipline a Group.

Academic Discipline Group	Degree Holders	% of Total
Agriculture and Natural Resources	44,541	6.7%
Architecture and Environmental Design	4,581	0.7
Area Studies	1,581	0.3
Biological Sciences	29,492	4.4
Business and Management	139,696	20.9
Communications	8,074	1.2
Computer and Information Science	12,500	1.9
Education	40,487	6.0
Engineering	109,705	16.4
Fine and Applied Arts	6,224	0.9
Foreign Languages	5,130	0.8
Health Professions	45,668	6.8
Home Economics	3,964	0.6
Interdisciplinary Studies	13,385	2.0
Law	28,267	4.2
Letters	12,658	1.9
Library Science	2,533	0.4
Mathematics	14,186	2.1
Military Science	713	0.1
Physical Sciences	31,214	4.6
Psychology	17,984	2.7
Public Affairs and Services	19,270	2.9
Social Sciences	72,344	10.8
Theology	1,831	0.3
Unspecified Academic Discipline	2,354	0.4
Total	668,754	100.0

Data Source: Records for 1,582,384 federal civilian employees in executive branch agencies with full-time work schedules, permanent tenure, and white-collar occupations were extracted from the Central Personnel Data File (CPDF).

Of the total (668,754) of full-time permanent white-collar college graduate federal civilian employment in the executive branch by academic discipline group, 496,742, or 74.3 percent, held bachelor's degrees, 141,947, or 21.2 percent, held master's degrees, and 30,065, or 4.5 percent, held doctorate degrees. The 668,754 degree holders in white-collar federal civilian employment represent 42.3 percent of the full-time employees.

* According to May Eng, Office of Workforce Information, Statistical Analysis and Services Division, U.S. Office of Personnel Management, the 1991 academic group distributions would remain unchanged if they were updated.

THE POSTRECRUITMENT PHASE

After the recruit qualifies for and receives an employment appointment, he or she still has obstacles to overcome before claiming full-fledged membership in the organization. The rigors of the *probationary period* measure the skills, knowledge, expertise, and responsiveness of every employee. During this time the recruit can be dismissed without the safeguards that protect those who have successfully completed such a phase. Probationary periods vary in length from six to twelve months, three years, or even seven years. The lesser term lengths are common in state and local governments, while the federal government and some other subnational jurisdictions require longer probations. The time frames may vary depending upon the nature of the position. While a fledgling sanitation person may acquire permanent status in six months, an officer of the police force may have to wait the entire year. A teacher, on the other hand, may not be awarded tenure after three years. The largest probation periods are usually found at colleges and universities where new faculty members may be scrutinized for seven years before achieving tenure. Some positions, such as political appointments to high-level posts, confer no privileges or permanency.

Training is also an aspect of the postrecruitment phase. Some agencies do nearly all their own recruit training. These include police departments, fire departments, and the like. Other public bodies, such as school systems and public health agencies, expect the newcomer to have acquired the needed basic skills. Usually, the higher the professional level of the position, the more likely it is that the recruit for that position will have obtained the essential training prior to appointment.

Training of all types is receiving increasing attention in public administration. A fast-moving and fast-changing society exhibits a high need for, and must place increasing emphasis on, wide-ranging and high-level skills. Not so long ago a police officer's training consisted of some on-the-job supervision. Today an officer is likely to receive many weeks or months of schooling at a police academy. The same holds true for many other public positions. Street cleaners are now apt to operate fairly complicated equipment where previously they may have pushed brooms, and so they, too, must receive a certain level of instruction to cope with their once simple tasks.

A survey by the Public Agenda Foundation conducted among eight focus groups nationwide and a national, random telephone survey of 1,000 American adults on welfare reform indicated that 77 percent of the respondents—black, white, and welfare recipients—believed that enrollment in job training and education programs is absolutely essential. Only a minority (19 percent) of the respondents believed that reducing the benefits of most welfare recipients would be effective welfare reform.[11]

The fastest growing area of attention in recent years may be *in-service training*. The upsurge of interest in this training method arises from the growing realization that in a modern society scarcely anyone is ever fully trained for the rest of his or her career. Not only must skills be continually upgraded, but new skills

PROFILE OF FEDERAL CIVILIAN NON-POSTAL EMPLOYEES
MARCH 31, 1997

Introduction

The **"typical Federal civilian employee"** is a topic of frequent interest for the news media, businesses, private citizens and organizations. This factsheet lists the summary statistics often requested for speeches, letters and reports. **(Data are for total on-board employment (i.e., all work schedules) unless otherwise indicated and may differ from other releases due to coverage—e.g., agency, work schedule, tenure—and as-of dates.)** If you have any questions, please call the Office of Communications at 202-606-1800.

Demographic characteristics

Age	44.9 years average for full-time permanent employees
Length of Service	16.0 years average for full-time permanent employees
Retirement Eligibility	11.2% of full-time permanents covered under Civil Service Retirement (excluding hires since January 1984)
Education Level	39.4% have Bachelor's Degree or higher degree
Gender	55.4% men and 44.6% women
Race and National Origin	29.4% minority group members: 16.8% Black, 6.2% Hispanic, 4.4% Asian/Pacific Islander, 2.0% Native American
Disability Status	7.3% have disabilities
Veterans Preference	25.4% have veterans preference (14.8% are Vietnam Era veterans)
Retired Military	4.3% of total: 0.5% officers and 3.8% enlisted personnel

Job characteristics

Average Annual Base Salary (adjusted to include locality pay)

for Total	$42,904 worldwide; $55,407 in Washington, DC-MD-VA-WV Metropolitan Area
for Full-Time Permanents	$44,294 worldwide; $56,191 in Washington, DC-MD-VA-WV Metropolitan Area
Special Rates	9.5% paid higher rates for retention in shortage occupations
General Schedule Grade	9.3 average grade; 11.1 in Washington, DC-MD-VA-WV Metropolitan Area
Pay System	73.0% General Schedule, 13.8% wage systems, and 13.2% others
Work Schedule	92.6% full-time, 3.7% part-time and 3.7% intermittent
Tenure	91.1% permanent appointments; 88.3% full-time permanent appointments
Occupation and PATCO	86.1% White-Collar (24.2% Professional, 28.0% Administrative, 19.0% Technical, 12.5% Clerical, 2.4% Other), 13.9% Blue-Collar
Supervisory Status	11.2% Supervisors and Managers
Union Representation	74.4% eligible and 59% represented

Service (Position Occupied)	77.8% Competitive, 21.8% Excepted, and 0.4% Senior Executive Service
Agency	40.6% Department of Defense and 13.4% Department of Veterans Affairs
Geographic Location	96.6% USA and 15.0% Washington, DC-MD-VA-WV Metropolitan Area
Retirement Plan	40.1% Civil Service Retirement (including 1.5% in special plan for law enforcement and firefighter personnel)
	2.7% Civil Service Retirement <u>and</u> Social Security,
	50.7% Federal Employees Retirement System <u>and</u> Social Security,
	5.3% Social Security only,
	0.7% Foreign Service Retirement or other system, 0.5% none.
Life Insurance	93.6% eligible for Federal Employees' Group Life Insurance: 14.1% waived, 25.3% have basic coverage and 54.2% have more than basic coverage
Employment in This Profile	1,855,824 Total; 1,638,821 Full-Time Permanent

Data Sources: U.S. Office of Personnel Management's Central Personnel Data File covers Federal civilian employees except Members and employees of Congress, Architect of the Capitol, Botanic Garden, General Accounting Office, Library of Congress, Congressional Budget Office, Judicial Branch, White House Office, Office of the Vice President, Federal Reserve Board, U.S. Postal Service, Postal Rate Commission, Tennessee Valley Authority, Central Intelligence Agency, National Security Agency, Defense Intelligence Agency, National Imagery and Mapping Agency, Public Health Service's Commissioned Corps, and foreign nationals employed overseas.

must be acquired if the employee and the organization are to meet the shifting demands and the changing work patterns characteristic of our time. Administrators are progressively accepting the notion that education is a lifelong process and that the organizations they manage must plan to provide training on a nearly nonstop basis throughout an employee's career.

PROMOTION

Once an employee achieves tenure as a member of the organization, the promotion possibilities emerge. Advancement may come in the form of a pay increase; an increase in grade at the present level; or a move up to a new level, usually involving at least some new duties and responsibilities.

Merit systems customarily provide two basic criteria for promotion: *seniority* and *merit*. In the majority of instances, both factors enter into consideration. The question to be answered in evaluating this system is, "Which of these, seniority or merit, is the most conducive to effective administration?"

The answer at first seems obvious. Merit is usually deemed the most effective method for determining who shall rise and who shall not. *Who determines what is meritorious?* Seniority presents obvious drawbacks. It rewards the incompetent along with the competent. James E. Brennan argues that it is far better to raise the salaries of those low-paid employees who have proved worthy to competitive averages, while decelerating salary increases among the more highly paid. Once inequities are resolved, Brennan emphasizes, merit increases should be based on job values, rather than human values.[12]

THE CHALLENGES OF PUBLIC PERSONNEL ADMINISTRATION

There are 19,521,000 government employees. Of that number, 61.0 percent, or 11,906,000 jobs, are in local government; 24.2 percent, or 4,719,000, are in state government, and 14.8 percent, or 2,895,000 are federal employees (1995 figures). Almost all government employees are paid with tax dollars. Given the cost of managing them, the public has a real interest in governments that are efficient, effective, and economical. To serve that interest, local, state, and federal governments must:

- Attract high-quality job applicants;
- Hire a reasonable share of the high-quality applicants;
- Train and develop employees;
- Motivate employees to perform at their best; and
- Retain good performers and remove poor ones.

Any employing organization's ability to achieve these goals is closely linked to its personnel policies, systems, and procedures. For the federal civil service, those policies, systems, and procedures are inextricably bound to the concept of merit, defined through various laws and regulations. Today the U.S. civil service is experiencing a "quiet crisis" in its inability to meet the goals listed previously. There is a body of evidence suggesting that "the Government is not perceived as an 'employer of choice' by many graduates of the country's most highly rated academic institutions."[13] Ironically, "since the Federal Government employs relatively more managers, professionals, and technicians than other U.S. employers, the skills required of Federal workers are greater, on average, than those employees in the nation as a whole."[14] This attitude toward federal employment is therefore damaging. Results of one survey said that less than half of senior-level federal managers and executives would work for the government again if they had a choice.[15]

THE CHANGING DEMOGRAPHICS OF THE FEDERAL WORK FORCE

Federal civilian employment reached a peak of nearly 3.4 million persons during World War II, receded to 2.0 million in 1947, and subsequently rose to 2.5 million in 1951. After nearly fifteen years of only minor fluctuation, federal government civilian employment reached almost 3.0 million in 1967 and fluctuated in the range of 2.8 to 3.0 million between 1968 and 1984. Beginning in 1985,

U.S. OFFICE OF PERSONNEL MANAGEMENT FACT SHEET
TOTAL FEDERAL CIVILIAN EMPLOYMENT (ALL AREAS)

AGENCY	As of September 1997*	As of January 1993	Change	% Change
TOTAL	2,783,704	3,038,041	(254,337)	–8.4
LEGISLATIVE BRANCH	31,355	38,303	(6,948)	–18.1
JUDICIAL BRANCH	30,641	28,111	2,530	9.0
US POSTAL SERVICE & POST RT COMM	853,350	782,980	70,370	9.0
EXECUTIVE BRANCH				
(Excl USPS & Postal Rate Comm)	1,868,358	2,188,647	(320,289)	–14.6
STATE	24,108	25,982	(1,874)	–7.2
TREASURY	140,369	165,904	(25,535)	–15.4
DEFENSE, TOTAL	749,461	966,087	(216,626)	–22.4
DEFENSE, MILITARY TOTAL	723,032	936,731	(213,699)	–22.8
ARMY, MILITARY FUNCTIONS	223,489	288,866	(65,377)	–22.6
DEPT OF THE NAVY	204,930	293,510	(88,580)	–30.2
DEPT OF THE AIR FORCE	172,342	204,150	(31,808)	–15.6
DEFENSE LOGISTICS AGENCY	46,080	64,501	(18,421)	–28.6
OTHER DEFENSE ACTIVITIES	76,191	85,704	(9,513)	–11.1
DEFENSE, CIVIL TOTAL	26,429	29,356	(2,927)	–10.0
JUSTICE	117,261	97,652	19,609	20.1
INTERIOR	67,865	77,313	(9,448)	–12.2
AGRICULTURE	106,539	113,687	(7,148)	–6.3
COMMERCE	34,792	37,608	(2,816)	–7.5
LABOR	15,787	17,719	(1,932)	–10.9
HEALTH & HUMAN SERVICES (incl. SSA)	126,523	131,066	(4,543)	–3.5
HOUSING & URBAN DEVELOPMENT	10,908	13,292	(2,384)	–17.9
TRANSPORTATION	64,179	70,086	(5,907)	–8.4
ENERGY	17,078	20,706	(3,628)	–17.5
EDUCATION	4,640	4,995	(355)	–7.1
VETERANS AFFAIRS	243,311	260,349	(17,038)	–6.5
ENVIRONMNTL PROTECTION AGCY	18,045	18,351	(306)	–1.7
EQUAL EMPLOY OPP COMM	2,631	2,927	(296)	–10.1
FEDERAL DEPOSIT INS CORP (incl. RTC)	8,265	22,360	(14,095)	–63.0
FEDERAL EMERGENCY MGMT AGCY	4,888	4,554	334	7.3
GENERAL SERVICES ADMIN	14,309	20,690	(6,381)	–30.8
NATIONAL AERO & SPACE ADMIN	19,844	25,191	(5,347)	–21.2
NATL LABOR RELATIONS BD	1,992	2,132	(140)	–6.6
NUCLEAR REGULATORY COMM	3,081	3,539	(458)	–12.9
OFFICE OF PERSONNEL MGMT	3,603	6,861	(3,258)	–47.5
PANAMA CANAL COMMISSION	9,777	8,573	1,204	14.0
SMALL BUSINESS ADMIN	4,380	5,768	(1,388)	–24.1
SMITHSONIAN, SUMMARY	5,188	5,512	(324)	–5.9
TENNESSEE VALLEY AUTHORITY	14,510	19,129	(4,619)	–24.1
U.S. INFORMATION AGENCY	6,534	8,283	(1,749)	–21.1
AGENCY FOR INTERNATL DEVEL	2,783	4,218	(1,435)	–34.0
ALL OTHER AGENCIES	25,707	28,113	(2,406)	–8.6

* Preliminary; subject to agency revisions.

Note: As of October 1, 1996, the Defense Mapping Agency no longer reports 113 A data. The above statistics reflect a drop of about 7,000 employees as of that date.

Source: *U.S. Office of Personnel Management Office of Workforce Information Monthly Report of Federal Civilian Employment (SF 113-A)*. 11/20/97

Table 5–3 Employment of Women by General Schedule (GS) and Related Grades
1986–1996

	1986	1990	1994	1995	1996	% change '86–'96
Total GS and Related	**785,069**	**831,662**	**786,343**	**758,772**	**729,392**	**–7.1%**
GS 1	4,236	3,513	2,057	2,245	1,974	–53.4%
GS 2	13,440	8,123	4,853	4,207	3,999	–70.2%
GS 3	64,409	41,522	25,883	23,026	19,747	–69.3%
GS 4	134,786	118,284	81,305	71,438	59,924	–55.5%
GS 1–4	**216,871**	**171,442**	**114,098**	**100,916**	**85,644**	**–60.5%**
GS 5	151,844	152,559	128,264	118,424	109,623	–27.8%
GS 6	75,152	83,545	83,923	80,924	76,855	2.3%
GS 7	88,580	99,042	98,348	96,152	94,375	6.5%
GS 8	18,948	21,034	28,515	28,607	28,299	49.4%
GS 5–8	**334,524**	**356,180**	**339,050**	**324,107**	**309,152**	**–7.6%**
GS 9	75,420	81,507	74,392	72,367	70,540	–6.5%
GS 10	14,321	16,235	7,374	7,518	7,872	–45.0%
GS 11	69,939	90,093	95,000	91,433	89,528	28.0%
GS 12	43,828	65,125	82,565	84,435	85,722	95.6%
GS 9–12	**203,508**	**252,960**	**259,331**	**255,753**	**253,662**	**24.6%**
GS 13	18,712	31,804	44,709	47,575	49,480	164.4%
GS 14	7,611	13,228	19,836	20,393	20,904	174.7%
GS 15	3,843	6,048	9,319	10,028	10,550	174.5%
GS 13–15	**30,166**	**51,080**	**73,864**	**77,996**	**80,934**	**168.3%**

Source: Affirmative Employment Statistics: Office of Workforce Information. (202) 606-1990 OWI@OPM.GOV

federal government civilian employment again exceeded 3.0 million and increased to 3.1 million by 1987. A downward trend began in 1990 and continued through 1995.

The demographic composition of the labor force has changed and will continue to change. The Office of Personnel Management and U.S. Bureau of Labor Statistics data indicate that many workforce changes and conditions are more prevalent in the federal work force than in the nonfederal sector of government employment. The nonfederal work force includes private sector employees and state and local government employees.

Adjusting to changes in the number of women, minorities, and older workers in the federal government can be accomplished through a variety of human

TABLE 5–4　Minority Employment by General Schedule (GS) and Related Grades 1986–1996

	1986	1990	1994	1995	1996	% change '86–'96
Total GS and Related	**356,092**	**437,374**	**440,079**	**432,116**	**421,781**	**18.4%**
GS 1	3,046	2,625	1,611	1,863	1,721	–43.5%
GS 2	8,209	5,830	3,647	3,114	2,903	–64.6%
GS 3	32,883	25,567	17,553	15,359	13,130	–60.1%
GS 4	58,997	62,079	48,598	43,980	37,649	–36.2%
GS 1–4	**103,135**	**96,101**	**71,409**	**64,316**	**55,403**	**–46.3%**
GS 5	61,316	72,906	67,127	64,793	62,014	1.1%
GS 6	27,888	37,474	40,532	39,966	38,766	39.0%
GS 7	35,843	47,361	50,574	50,293	50,383	40.6%
GS 8	7,948	10,939	15,229	15,642	15,741	98.0%
GS 5–8	**132,995**	**168,680**	**173,462**	**170,694**	**166,904**	**25.5%**
GS 9	34,353	42,544	41,045	40,662	40,553	18.0%
GS 10	5,767	6,998	3,834	4,113	4,372	–24.2%
GS 11	32,376	48,403	51,777	50,184	49,642	53.3%
GS 12	25,468	40,001	51,410	52,702	53,593	110.4%
GS 9–12	**97,964**	**137,946**	**148,066**	**147,661**	**148,160**	**51.2%**
GS 13	12,682	20,720	28,342	30,015	31,311	146.9%
GS 14	5,839	8,954	12,122	12,365	12,719	117.8%
GS 15	3,477	4,973	6,678	7,065	7,284	109.5%
GS 13–15	**21,998**	**34,647**	**47,142**	**49,445**	**51,314**	**133.3%**

"Minorities" include Blacks, Hispanics, Asian/Pacific Islanders, and American Indians/Alaska Natives

Source: Affirmative Employment Statistics: Office of Workforce Information. (202) 606-1990 OWI@OPM.GOV

resource policies and programs such as child care, flexible work schedules, diversity training, and reemployment incentives. Demographic differences in the federal work force indicate that different policies and programs may be needed in different agencies and regions. Work force planners should consider specific needs of the workforce and the organization.[16]

Each sector's changes in minority composition between 1976 and 1996 varied considerably by racial and ethnic group.

In addition to the differences between the federal and nonfederal work forces in terms of their gender, minority, and age characteristics, there were also differences in these characteristics within the federal government by agency and

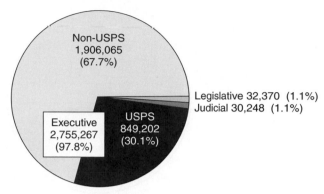

Total Employment: 2,817,885

FIGURE 5–1   Distribution of Federal Civilian Employment by Branch, July 1997.

Source: U.S. Office of Personal Management, *Federal Civilian Workforce Statistics: Employment and Trends* (Washington, DC: U.S. Government Printing Office, July, 1997)

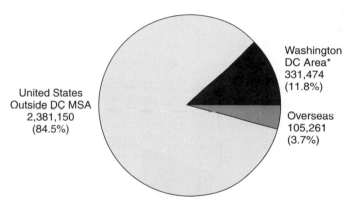

Total Employment: 2,817,885

*Washington, DC–MD–VA–WV MSA includes the District of Columbia; Calvert, Charles, Frederick, Montgomery, and Prince George's Counties in Maryland; Arlington, Clarke, Culpeper, Fairfax, Fauquier, King George, Loudoun, Prince William, Spotsylvania, Stafford, and Warren Counties, and the Cities of Alexandria, Fairfax, Falls Church, Fredericksburg, Manassas, and Manassas Park in Virginia; and Berkeley and Jefferson Counties in West Virginia.

FIGURE 5–2   Distribution of Federal Civilian Employment by Major Geographical Area, July 1997.

Source: U.S. Office of Personal Management, *Federal Civilian Workforce Statistics: Employment and Trends* (Washington, DC: U.S. Government Printing Office, July, 1997)

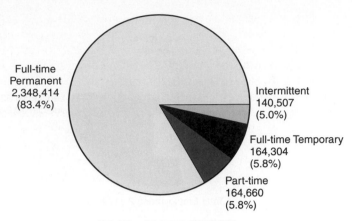

Total Employment: 2,817,885

FIGURE 5–3 Distribution of Federal Civilian Employment by Work Schedule/Appointment , July 1997.

Source: U.S. Office of Personal Management, *Federal Civilian Workforce Statistics: Employment and Trends* (Washington, DC: U.S. Government Printing Office, July, 1997)

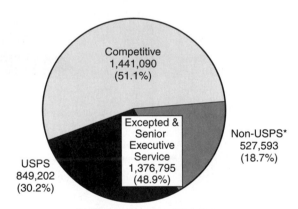

Total Employment: 2,817,885

*Includes: Congress, Judiciary, Schedules A,B,C, foreign nationals overseas, National Guard, Veterans Readjustments, TVA, FBI, Foreign Service, Veterans Affairs physicians and nurses.

FIGURE 5–4 Distribution of Federal Civilian Employment by Service, July 1997.

Source: U.S. Office of Personal Management, *Federal Civilian Workforce Statistics: Employment and Trends* (Washington, DC: U.S. Government Printing Office, July, 1997)

geographic region. There were differences as well among agencies and regions in the degree to which they changed between 1976 and 1996. While the proportion of an agency's work force that is female or belonging to a minority group provides a good indication of the degree of workforce diversity in the agency, that statistic only tells part of the story. Of at least equal relevance is the degree of change in those demographic characteristics over time.

Tables 5-3 and 5-4 show changes between 1986 and 1996 in the percentage of female and minority employees in the federal agencies examined. The nonfederal work force includes private sector employees (about 88 million workers in 1990) and state and local government employees (about 14 million workers in 1990). There are some differences in the demographic composition of private sector and state and local government workers.

As a result of downsizing of the federal government, total employment declined by 7.5 percent or 153,043 workers from 2,043,449 as of September 30, 1994, to 1,890,406 as of September 30, 1996. Major reductions by agency were:

- the Department of Defense—down about 81,000 workers to 781,224;
- the Department of Agriculture—down nearly 16,000 workers to 112,472;
- the Department of Treasury—down almost 10,900 to 146,275; and
- the Department of Interior—down 10,000 workers to 70,922.

Work force changes reflect downsizing initiatives implemented by the Clinton Administration. As of September 1996, the federal civilian work force employed 267,201 blue-collar workers or 14.1 percent, and 1,623,205 white-collar workers or 85.9 percent. The white-collar work force was distributed among the following occupational categories:

- professional—459,121 or 28.3 percent;
- administrative—528,238 or 32.5 percent;
- technical—365,449 or 22.5 percent;
- clerical—224,040 or 13.8 percent; and
- other—46,357 or 2.9 percent.

The 153,000 jobs eliminated from the work force since 1994 removed 27 percent or 41,000 blue-collar workers, and 73 percent or 111,500 white-collar workers. While most of the demographic components of the federal work force declined between September 30, 1994, and September 30, 1996, the relative magnitude of the decline varied among designated categories and/or groups. The net change by occupational category during the 1986–1996 period were as follows:

- clerical jobs declined by 191,000;
- professional jobs increased by 18,000;
- administrative jobs increased by 55,000;
- technical jobs rose by 6,000; and
- other jobs increased by 6,000.[17]

Table 5–5   Major Federal Civilian White-Collar Pay Schedules Effective January 1998

	General Schedule									
	1	2	3	4	5	6	7	8	9	10
GS-1	$12,960	$13,392	$13,823	$14,252	$14,685	$14,938	$15,362	$15,791	$15,809	$16,214
2	14,571	14,918	15,401	15,809	15,985	16,455	16,925	17,395	17,865	18,335
3	15,899	16,429	16,959	17,489	18,019	18,549	19,079	19,609	20,139	20,669
4	17,848	18,443	19,038	19,633	20,228	20,823	21,418	22,013	22,608	23,203
5	19,969	20,635	21,301	21,967	22,633	23,299	23,965	24,631	25,297	25,963
6	22,258	23,000	23,742	24,484	25,226	25,968	26,710	27,452	28,194	28,936
7	24,734	25,558	26,382	27,206	28,030	28,854	29,678	30,502	31,326	32,150
8	27,393	28,306	29,219	30,132	31,045	31,958	32,871	33,784	34,697	35,610
9	30,257	31,266	32,275	33,284	34,293	35,302	36,311	37,320	38,329	39,338
10	33,320	34,431	35,542	36,653	37,764	38,875	39,986	41,097	42,208	43,319
11	36,609	37,829	39,049	40,269	41,489	42,709	43,929	45,149	46,369	47,589
12	43,876	45,339	46,802	48,265	49,728	51,191	52,654	54,117	55,580	57,043
13	52,176	53,915	55,654	57,393	59,132	60,871	62,610	64,349	66,088	67,827
14	61,656	63,711	65,766	67,821	69,876	71,931	73,986	76,041	78,096	80,151
15	72,525	74,943	77,361	79,779	82,197	84,615	87,033	89,451	91,869	94,287

Senior Executive Service

ES-1 $102,300

ES-2   107,100

ES-3   112,000

ES-4   118,000

ES-5   118,400

ES-6   118,400

Executive Schedule (EX)

I $151,800

II   136,700

III   125,900

IV   118,400

V   110,700

Administrative Law Judges

AL-3/A $76,980

AL-3/B   82,880

AL-3/C   88,800

AL-3/D   94,720

AL-3/E   100,640

AL-3/F   106,560

AL-2   112,480

AL-1   118,400

Senior Level (SL & ST)

Minimum $89,728

Maximum   118,400

Contract Appeals Boards (CA)

Chairman $118,400

Vice Chairman   114,848

Other Members   111,296

Source: U.S. Office of Personnel Management, http://www.opm.gov/oca/payrates/index.htm

TABLE 5–6   Some Federal Agencies' Gender and Minority Composition Changed More Than Other
Agencies' Between 1976 and 1996

	Percentage of Workforce					
	Female			Minority		
Agency	1976	1996	Change	1976	1996	Change
Agriculture	26.7	41.7	+15.0	13.9	19.9	+6.0
Air Force	27.1	33.2	+6.1	17.9	24.2	+6.3
Army	30.5	37.8	+7.3	16.7	25.9	+9.2
Commerce	39.2	45.7	+6.5	21.1	25.2	+4.1
Defense	35.1	37.5	+2.4	22.7	26.7	+4.0
Education	a	60.3	a	a	44.5	a
Energy	a	38.4	a	a	21.7	a
EPA	35.9	49.1	+13.2	11.8	26.8	+15.0
FDIC	30.2	48.8	+18.6	11.8	22.9	+11.1
GSA	33.6	42.2	+8.6b	40.0	36.9	−3.1b
HHS	60.7	59.9	−0.8	31.4	41.4	+10.0
HUD	44.5	59.6	+15.1	26.9	43.6	+16.7
Interior	28.8	37.6	+8.8	26.7	26.3	−0.4
Justice	31.4	39.0	+7.6	20.9	31.5	+10.6
Labor	46.3	48.5	+2.2	30.6	32.9	+2.3
NASA	19.1	32.7	+13.6	8.4	20.1	+11.7
Navy	23.5	32.2	+8.7	20.5	28.3	+7.8
State	43.7	44.5	+0.8	26.4	22.8	−3.6
Transportation	17.7	27.3	+9.6	13.3	20.2	+6.9
Treasury	45.6	54.9	+9.3	21.0	33.0	+12.0
VAc	49.7	54.1	+4.4	28.7	34.4	+5.7
All agencies	34.9	44.0	+9.1	21.5	29.1	+7.6

a The Departments of Education and Energy did not exist in 1976. HHS was the Department of Health, Education, and Welfare in 1976, from which the Department of Education was created.

b Some of the differences between 1976 and 1996 at GSA may be due to transfers of National Archives and Records Administration employees in 1985 and building operations employees at various times during this period.

c The Department of Veterans Affairs was the Veterans Administration in 1976.

Sources: *The Changing Workforce: Demographic Issues Facing the Federal Government* (Washington DC: U.S. General Accounting Office, 1992): 58; and United States office of Personnel Management, *Federal Civilian Workforce Statistic Demographic Profile of the Federal Workforce: As of September 30, 1996* (Washington, DC: U.S. Government Printing Office, 1997): 25–37. Chris Holdgreve, Graduate Assistant, Department of Political Science, Ball State University, Muncie, Indiana, compiled these figures.

Of the 153,000 employees reduced from the work force since September 30, 1994, over 88,700 or 58 percent were men and about 64,300 or 42 percent were women. As of September 30, 1996, men (1,058,566) represented 56 percent and women (831,840) represented 44 percent of the total federal work force. The shift to a predominate professional and administrative work force is benefiting women. The percentage of women holding these jobs rose from 38.6 percent in 1994 to 39.8 percent in 1996. Despite downsizing, women gained higher levels of responsibilities with comparable increased pay. Since 1994, women gained some 7,900 jobs in the General Schedule and related 12–13 grades. Women increased by 2,300 jobs in the General Schedule and related 14–15 grades. Women secured 541 additional jobs in the highest paying executive grades and levels. During the 1986–1996 time frame, women gained 59,000 professinal jobs, 54,000 administrative jobs, and 40,000 technical jobs. Since September 30, 1994, the average age increased for women from 41.6 to 42.5 years, for men from 44.0 to 44.6 years, and for minorities from 41.4 to 42.2 years.

Since 1986, minorities gained over 98,000 professional, administrative, and technical jobs in the federal work force. Some 64,000 of these gains were at the GS 9–15 grades. There were 1,341,157 nonminorities (70.9 percent) and 549,249 minorities (29.1 percent) in the work force in 1996. Over 121,000 nonminority and 32,000 minority employees were reduced from the work force since September 30, 1994. Each minority group had a net loss of employees since 1994. However, Hispanics and Asians percentage representation in the work force increased while non-minorities, blacks, and Native Americans percentage representation in the work force declined. Hispanics and Asians employment rose in higher paying professional and administrative jobs while blacks and nonminorities employment declined in these occupational categories. Native Americans gained in professional jobs but declined slightly in administrative jobs.

Employees with veterans status or preference (505,519) declined by approximately 53,000. However, the percentage of veterans holding federal jobs rose from 28.0 percent to 29.5 percent of the work force as of September 30, 1996. In this period, the Department of Defense (DOD) veterans work force (280,480) declined by slightly over 33,000 jobs. As of September 30, 1994, DOD still employed 55.5 percent of veteran workers. Between September 30, 1994, and September 30, 1996, the number of Vietnam Era Veterans (VEV) declined by nearly 25,900 jobs to 315,582 workers. However the percentage of VEVs in the total federal workforce increased from 61.1 percent to 62.4 percent because of government downsizing.[18]

Table 5-6 indicates some Federal agencies' gender and minority composition changed more than other agency compositions between 1976 and 1996.[19]

EQUAL OPPORTUNITY AND AFFIRMATIVE ACTION

Equal employment opportunity refers to "the idea that no person should be denied the opportunity for employment because of discrimination based on race,

AMERICANS WITH DISABILITIES ACT

The purposes of the Americans with Disabilities Act (ADA) are to provide a clear and comprehensive national mandate for the elimination of discrimination against individuals with disabilities. Access to employment, housing, public accommodations, education, transportation, communication, recreation, institutionalization, health services, voting, and public services is afforded to more than 43 million Americans with one or more physical or mental disabilities. ADA defines "qualified individual with a disability" as a person with a disability who, with or without reasonable accommodation, can perform the essential functions of the job that such individual holds or desires.

ADA prohibits discrimination on the basis of disability in employment, public services, and public accommodations. New buses and trains must be accessible to the disabled. Telecommunications companies must operate relay systems that allow hearing- and speech-impaired Americans to use telephone service. The Equal Employment Opportunity Commission (EEOC) issues regulations to carry out requirements of the act.

Since September 30, 1994, total disability employment declined in the federal work force by nearly 12,761 jobs (8.8 percent) to 132,344 workers. The percentage representation of persons in the work force declined slightly from 7.4 to 7.3 percent between September 30, 1994, and September 30, 1996. Those workers identifying themselves as severely disabled (severe disability categories designated by the Equal Employment Opportunity Commission) declined by 9.3 percent or about 2,300 jobs to 22,272. Since 1986, employees with disabilities increased by 4,221 workers from 128,123 to 132,344.[22]

color, religion, sex, national origin, or physical disability."[20] While *equal opportunity* is essentially a passive concept, *affirmative action* is an active one.

In some ways, equal employment opportunity redefines the merit system to emphasize that the merit philosophy not only recruits, selects, and advances employees on the basis of their relative abilities, but also calls for a workforce representative of all the people. Equal opportunity is principal among the ideas that fuel the American way of life. *Affirmative action implements equal opportunity for minorities and women.* Honest people often agree on the lofty goals of equal opportunity but disagree on the manner in which such a sometimes vague philosophy is carried out.

As a passive strategy, equal opportunity implies nondiscrimination. Equal opportunity and nondiscrimination are passive instruments of public policy because they rely on families, schools, and pertinent forces in U.S. society to abolish stereotypes and prejudices that prohibit creation of a balanced workforce. Affirmative action is an active strategy, intended to ensure equal opportunity.

With the possible exception of trade unionism, which we shall examine in a subsequent chapter, no issue in the post-World War II era has engaged public

---

COMPARING SEXUAL HARASSMENT IN SWEDEN AND USA

While the American state formally recognizes the existence of sexual harassment and has taken steps against it, the Swedish state has been reluctant to provide legal remedy. According to R. Amy Elman, this difference can be attributed to Sweden's centralized state and the strength of labor, which has the organizational capacity to effectively dismiss issues pertaining to women's sexual inequality. By contrast, Elman concludes, American women benefitted from an autonomous feminist movement and a decentralized state proved more permeable to feminist demands.

Sweden's lack of legislative recognition of sexual harassment provides one of the most compelling challenges to the conventional characterization of the Swedish state as interventionist, innovative, and egalitarian. While Sweden prides itself on the adoption of its most recently revised Equal Opportunities Act(1994), intended to promote equal rights for women with respect to employment, it has failed to mitigate effectively a central condition at work that is highly disadvantageous to women, sexual harassment.

Source: R. Amy Elman, "Feminism and Legislative Redress: Sexual Harassment in Sweden and the United States," *Women & Politics* 16, no. 3 (summer 1996): 1–27.

---

personnel administration as has the quest for equal opportunity. Public administration is an integral part of modern society and, as such, is not impervious to society's pressures and concerns. As the campaigns for the rights of women and minorities emerge and accumulate legitimacy and recognition, they shake and buffet public personnel administration along with the rest of American life. There is no question that personnel administration needed the shake-up. The federal government has a somewhat questionable record in equal opportunity.

The controversy over affirmative action follows from the noble aspiration of providing equal employment opportunity for all Americans. As noted earlier, in private administration the law tells administrators only what they *cannot do*, and in public administration the law tells administrators what they *can do*. The implementation of equal employment opportunity and affirmative action is, therefore, grounded upon a host of federal, state, and even local laws.

The following items have been crucial in the attempt to achieve *social equity* through proportional representation in the nation's workforce: the Civil Rights Act of 1964, Executive Order 11246 of 1965, and the 1972 Equal Employment Opportunity Act.

The development of the affirmative action concept began in the mid-1960s with the passage of the most far-reaching civil rights law since Reconstruction. The Civil Rights Act of 1964 prohibits job discrimination on the basis of race, sex, religion, national origin, age, and physical disability, and the Equal Employment Opportunity Commission was simultaneously created for the purpose of administering the law. The law gives operational meaning to the 1954 Supreme Court desegregation case of *Brown v. Board of Education,* which holds that the previous doctrine of "separate but equal" facilities for the races will no longer satisfy

Constitutional requirements and specifically that blacks everywhere are permitted to attend the same public schools as whites.

President Lyndon Johnson signed Executive Order 11246 in 1965. It repeated nondiscrimination and affirmative action language used earlier, requiring government contracts to prohibit discrimination by the contractor and to use "affirmative action" to ensure that workers are employed without regard to race, creed, or color. The 1972 legislation also requires state and local governments to develop affirmative action plans.

Other legislation of significance for affirmative action includes the Equal Pay Act of 1963, amendments to the Fair Labor Standards Act of 1938, the Age Discrimination in Employment Act of 1967 as amended in 1978, Title VI of the Vocational Rehabilitation Act of 1973, and the Vietnam Veteran's Readjustment Assistance Act of 1974.[21]

In the government workplace of the twenty-first century, the modernist feminist agenda squarely confronts conservative traditionalism. Tradition calls for women to focus and commit their energies to "kitchen, children, and school," expecting women to find satisfaction in feeding the family, comforting their husbands, raising children, praying and obeying, and teaching youngsters about God and country. This traditional view runs against the new and increasingly important presence of women in the marketplace or work force.

The Clarence Thomas/Anita Hill sexual harassment hearings before the U.S. Senate Judiciary Committee and Paula Jones' sexual harassment charges against President Clinton brought sex out of the proverbial closet and placed them on the political agenda—thrusting them into the *marketplace of ideas.* The broader issues raised include a woman's evolution and/or liberation from the more restrictive roles of children, church, and schools. A woman's right to choose abortion and economic opportunities and protections in the workforce (including freedom from sexual harassment and other forms of discrimination) constitute the *new moral values.* The sexual harassment controversies featuring Thomas, Hill, Jones, and Clinton are symbolic of greater, more significant economic changes in U.S. society. Women exert more power than ever before in America's political economy.

Social conservatives call for government to put the "father knows best" genie back into the bottle of traditional values. But attempts by either the right or left to "legislate morality" confronts a pragmatic political culture and economic realities. Economically and politically, women—as their economic power in society grows—will cast aside the arbitrary nature of certain male authority, if not its domination. The issues of sexual harassment and affirmative action plans in the workplace divide males and females of all races. Women do not want to be exposed, patronized, fondled, or harassed. They seek respect for their professionalism, and, sooner if not later, they will demand it. The sexual harassment arguments of Hill and Jones reverberate in American politics and are realized in government workplaces.

REVERSE DISCRIMINATION

The problem of reverse discrimination emerged in the Supreme Court cases of *Regents of the University of California v. Allan Bakke* (1978) and *Weber v. Kaiser*

Aluminum and Steel Corporation and United Steelworkers Union (1979). *The Bakke case was a public sector concern. The Weber case was a private sector matter.* The distinction is crucial, because legalism in general and laws in particular circumscribe and influence the operation of a public institution more than a private one.

Bakke was a white male suing the medical school of the University of California at Davis for admission, claiming that the medical school rejected his application in favor of less qualified minority students. In a voluntary attempt to correct years of minority discrimination, the medical school established a quota for minority students for each entering class. The Supreme Court's ruling agreed that Bakke had been unfairly denied admission, but the scope of the decision was carefully narrowed.

First, the medical school is a public institution, supported by taxpayers. Second, the case was one of admission to a public university, not a public sector employment matter. Third, although the court outlawed the quota system, it "played" a different kind of judicial politics as well. If public sector bureaucracies avoided an inflexible quota system, affirmative action programs would remain constitutional. In this way the court allowed for consideration of racial and sexual differences in accepting students. In other words, quotas were made *illegal* for the public sector; however, race and sex remain acceptable for consideration in entrance requirements. The Bakke decision confused employers, bureaucrats, lawyers, and court watchers.

If the Bakke case left the constitutionality of affirmative action in doubt, the Weber Supreme Court decision made some headway in settling the issue, at least in part. Because the Kaiser/Weber was a private concern, no public sector monies were involved. As free agents in a democratic society, the Kaiser Aluminum Company and United Steelworkers Union cooperated in establishing an affirmative action program for minority employees.

Brian Weber, a white lab technician with more seniority than two black applicants, filed suit, claiming reverse discrimination against the company and the union. By placing minorities in 50 percent of the openings in a training program, and thereby establishing a quota system, management and labor created a voluntary program that afforded special preferences to blacks. The Louisiana plant was located in a region where 39 percent of the local workforce was black. Fifteen percent of the employees of the plant were black, but only 2 percent of the skilled craft workers were black. Therefore, the Weber case raised not only the issue of equal employment opportunity, but also a concern for a representative workforce.

The Supreme Court decided in favor of the affirmative action program sponsored by a joint effort of management and labor, concluding that Title VII of the Civil Rights Act of 1964 was passed for the particular purpose of improving the economic plight of black Americans. In other words, private sector employers could voluntarily establish a hiring and promotion program grounded upon improving the employment skills of blacks. To repeat an earlier distinction, the law tells the manager only what he cannot do in the private sector, such as the Kaiser case; however, the law tells the administrator what he can do in the public sector.

Technically court cases address only the particular set of facts of any court case. To a large degree, the courts in the United States are passive units of fragmented and decentralized federal and state judicial bureaucracies. Courts consider only cases that merit jurisdiction before particular tribunals. Plaintiffs must take their particular set of grievances into court. To do so, plaintiffs need the skills of talented lawyers, money to finance such actions, and the patience and ego strength to see things through, win or lose.

Affirmative action issues concern *quotas, layoffs, work environment,* and *compensation.* The most controversial issue posed by affirmative action focuses upon the establishment of quotas for making employment decisions. Quotas, of course, specify that a precise percentage of appointments have to be minorities, women, and/or handicapped persons.

DECLINING IMPORTANCE OF AFFIRMATIVE ACTION

David H. Rosenbloom maintains that the importance of affirmative action began declining in the 1980s because:

1. there is *no strong consensus* favoring affirmative action, which reduces the organizational coherence and political integrity of affirmative action programs;
2. there is a *continuing constitutional stalemate* as shown by the nonlinear direction of various Supreme Court cases over a fifteen-year period; and
3. there are *priority internal demands* such as executive leadership, retrenchment, and productivity.[23]

Considering the pros and cons, what is the significance of affirmative action in our society? Affirmative action choices challenge public sector managers and some employees but promotes representativeness in government bureaucracies. Affirmative action raises issues of potential and real discrimination confronting women, minorities, and handicapped employees. The visibility of affirmative action issues heightens the awareness of discrimination in workplaces.

Perceptions about affirmative action produce a great deal of political and administrative rhetoric. However, the definitive impacts, in terms of concrete results, for the purported beneficiaries are questionable. Until the affected groups attain more education and experience, changes will come slowly and progress likely incremental. To its credit, however, affirmative action forces government departments and agencies to broaden and intensify their recruiting efforts, to examine the validity of their examinations, and to question the value of recruitment and promotion criteria. It stimulates innovation and opens governmental organizations. The administrative branch becomes, as a result, more representative of the population it serves. Affirmative action, referred to as equal opportunity under the Civil Rights Act of 1964, means to many Americans in the twenty-first century the use of practices such as making quotas and giving preferential treatment. Many argue that affirmative action should be based on criteria of *class* instead of considerations of *race or sex.*[24] To others, affirmative action is a policy aimed at eliminating discrimination in employment based on race, color, religion, sex, or national origin. It does not encourage the hiring or promotion of unqualified people because they are minorities or women, nor does it impose quotas. It is not reverse discrimination, because it promotes equal opportunity.[25]

President Clinton argues that affirmative action must be reformed rather than eliminated. Despite its flaws, affirmative action has been effective in providing equal opportunity to women and minorities. It must be eliminated only when discrimination is finally abolished.[26] Critics of affirmative action are often silent about the veterans' preference program, which benefits mostly males. Since 1944, federal agencies have provided preferential hiring consideration to veterans as a means of rewarding them for service to their country. Many argue that women are especially disadvantaged by veterans' preference.[27] Opponents of affirmative action may have an easier time removing affirmative action from government offices and institutions than from American culture. In the following instance, even conservatives accept the merits of an affirmative action candidate.

The curtailment of affirmative action may mean less than is generally expected. . . . Affirmative action is now a firmly established institutional practice, indeed virtually a reflex of many university, corporate and political decision makers. (As Mr. Bush's appointment of Clarence Thomas illustrates, even conservatives need the legitimacy of multiracial representation.) Just as discrimination did not end with formal rulings against it, neither will affirmative action end with formal rulings.[28]

The bottom line is that affirmative action has contributed to the process of public administration, if not to its substantive contents. Affirmative action forces governments to hire, promote, and fire employees under the auspices of procedures and administrative due process.

EFFORTS TO REMAKE FEDERAL PERSONNEL SYSTEM

The Clinton administration, according to *Washington Post* writer Stephen Barr, inaugurated plans to reorganize the way the bureaucracy recruits, hires, classifies, promotes, and fires federal workers as part of its "reinventing government" initiative.[29] After twelve years of Republican indifference to the federal personnel system, the Clinton administration described the system as broken. "Hiring is complex and rule bound; managers can't explain to applicants how to get federal jobs. The [job] classification and pay system are inflexible." The report was written by Vice President Al Gore's National Performance Review.

Once hired by the government, most employees are placed in one of 450 job categories and ranked on the General Schedule, which outlines fifteen pay ranges that correspond with fifteen work grades. The draft report, "Reinventing Human Resources Management," also calls for improvements in the awards and bonus system, employee training, the Senior Executive Service, and labor-management relations.

The report proposes extending probationary periods from one to a maximum of three years and eliminating "time-in-grade" requirements, which propel people through the personnel ranks. The draft report ignores what has been a problem

State and Local Government Employment and Payroll

No. 506. Governmental Employment and Payrolls: 1980 to 1995

[For **October**. Covers both full-time and part-time employees. Local government data are estimates subject to sampling variation; see Appendix III and source]

TYPE OF GOVERNMENT	1980	1985	1988	1989	1990	1991	1992	1993	1994	1995
EMPLOYEES (1,000)										
Total	**16,213**	**16,690**	**17,588**	**17,879**	**18,369**	**18,554**	**18,745**	**18,823**	**19,420**	**19,521**
Federal (civilian) [1]	2,898	3,021	3,112	3,114	3,105	3,103	3,047	2,999	2,952	2,895
State and local	13,315	13,669	14,476	14,765	15,263	15,452	15,698	15,824	16,468	16,626
Percent of total	82	82	82	83	83	83	84	84	85	85
State	3,753	3,984	4,236	4,365	4,503	4,521	4,595	4,673	4,694	4,719
Local	9,562	9,685	10,240	10,400	10,760	10,930	11,103	11,151	11,775	11,906
Counties	1,853	1,891	2,024	2,085	2,167	2,196	2,253	2,270	(NA)	(NA)
Municipalities	2,561	2,467	2,570	2,569	2,642	2,662	2,665	2,644	(NA)	(NA)
School districts	4,270	4,416	4,679	4,774	4,950	5,045	5,134	(NA)	(NA)	(NA)
Townships	394	392	415	405	418	415	424	(NA)	(NA)	(NA)
Special districts	484	519	552	568	585	612	627	(NA)	(NA)	(NA)
OCTOBER PAYROLLS (mil. dol.)										
Total	**19,935**	**28,945**	**34,203**	**36,763**	**39,228**	**41,237**	**43,120**	**(NA)**	**(NA)**	**(NA)**
Federal (civilian) [1]	5,205	7,580	7,976	8,636	8,999	9,687	9,937	(NA)	(NA)	(NA)
State and local	14,730	21,365	26,227	28,127	30,229	31,551	33,183	34,540	36,545	37,714
Percent of total	74	74	77	77	77	77	77	(NA)	(NA)	(NA)
State	4,285	6,329	7,842	8,443	9,083	9,437	9,828	10,288	10,666	10,927
Local	10,445	15,036	18,385	19,684	21,146	22,113	23,355	24,252	25,878	26,787
Counties	1,936	2,819	3,532	3,855	4,192	4,404	4,698	4,839	(NA)	(NA)
Municipalities	2,951	4,191	4,979	5,274	5,564	5,784	6,207	6,328	(NA)	(NA)
School districts	4,683	6,746	8,298	8,852	9,551	9,975	10,394	(NA)	(NA)	(NA)
Townships	330	446	556	599	642	664	685	(NA)	(NA)	(NA)
Special districts	546	834	1,020	1,104	1,197	1,287	1,370	(NA)	(NA)	(NA)

NA Not available. [1] Includes employees outside the United States.

Source: U.S. Bureau of the Census, *Historical Statistics on Governmental Finances and Employment,* and *Public Employment,* series GE, No. 1, annual; <http://www.census.gov/pub/govs/www/apes.html>; (released August 1997).

No. 507. All Governments—Employment and Payroll, by Function: 1995

[For **October**. Covers both full-time and part-time employees. Local government amounts are estimates subject to sampling variation; see Appendix III and source]

FUNCTION	EMPLOYEES (1,000)					OCTOBER PAYROLLS (mil. dol.)				
	Total	Federal (civilian) [1]	State and local			Total	Federal (civilian) [1]	State and local		
			Total	State	Local			Total	State	Local
Total	**19,521**	**2,895**	**16,626**	**4,719**	**11,906**	**(NA)**	**(NA)**	**37,714**	**10,927**	**26,787**
National defense [2]	831	831	(X)	(X)	(X)	(NA)	(NA)	(X)	(X)	(X)
Postal Service	849	849	(X)	(X)	(X)	(NA)	(NA)	(X)	(X)	(X)
Space research and technology	22	22	(X)	(X)	(X)	(NA)	(NA)	(X)	(X)	(X)
Elem and secondary educ	6,252	(X)	6,252	50	6,202	13,939	(NA)	13,939	119	13,820
Higher education	2,414	(X)	2,414	1,954	461	4,591	(NA)	4,591	3,794	797
Other education	129	12	117	117	(X)	260	(NA)	260	260	(X)
Health	544	141	403	166	238	(NA)	(NA)	977	431	546
Hospitals	1,303	174	1,129	522	608	(NA)	(NA)	2,658	1,258	1,399
Public welfare	526	10	516	230	286	(NA)	(NA)	1,145	549	597
Social insurance administration	167	68	98	98	-	(NA)	(NA)	254	254	(X)
Police protection	926	86	840	91	749	(NA)	(NA)	2,477	287	2,190
Fire protection	360	(X)	360	(X)	360	950	(NA)	950	(X)	950
Correction	655	28	627	413	213	(NA)	(NA)	1,620	1,062	559
Streets & highways	564	4	560	257	303	(NA)	(NA)	1,357	667	690
Air transportation	86	49	37	3	35	(NA)	(NA)	104	8	96
Water transport/Terminals	27	15	12	5	7	(NA)	(NA)	37	14	23
Solid waste management	115	(X)	115	2	114	263	(NA)	263	6	258
Sewerage	130	(X)	130	1	128	345	(NA)	345	4	341
Parks & recreation	387	26	361	47	314	(NA)	(NA)	502	81	421
Natural resources	421	210	211	168	43	(NA)	(NA)	475	395	80
Housing & community dev	151	20	131	(X)	131	(NA)	(NA)	315	(X)	315
Water supply	165	(X)	165	1	164	410	(NA)	410	3	407
Electric power	82	(X)	82	6	76	296	(NA)	296	26	270
Gas supply	11	(X)	11	(X)	11	28	(NA)	28	(X)	28
Transit	210	(X)	210	20	190	676	(NA)	676	80	595
Libraries	152	5	147	1	147	(NA)	(NA)	207	1	206
State liquor stores	10	(X)	10	10	(X)	18	(NA)	18	18	(X)
Financial administration	520	131	388	168	220	(NA)	(NA)	916	444	472
Other government administration	436	24	413	53	359	(NA)	(NA)	644	137	507
Judicial and legal	401	53	349	130	219	(NA)	(NA)	994	428	565
Other & unallocable	673	138	535	206	329	(NA)	(NA)	1,256	603	653

X Not applicable.   NA Not available.   [1] Includes employees outside the United States.   [2] Includes international relations.

Source: U.S. Bureau of the Census; <http://www.census.gov/pub/govs/www/apes.html>; (released August 1997).

State and Local Government Finances and Employment

No. 512. State and Local Government Full-Time Equivalent Employment, by Selected Function and State: 1995

[In **thousands**, for **October**. Local government amounts are estimates subject to sampling variation; see Appendix III and source]

STATE	EDUCATION Total State	EDUCATION Total Local	Elem. & secondary State	Elem. & secondary Local	Higher education State	Higher education Local	PUBLIC WELFARE State	PUBLIC WELFARE Local	HEALTH State	HEALTH Local	HOSPITALS State	HOSPITALS Local
United States..	1,468.7	5,619.2	41.4	5,341.2	1,330.8	278.0	226.8	265.1	160.1	208.6	496.2	551.4
Alabama.........	34.2	86.7	-	86.7	30.3	-	4.3	1.1	6.8	3.9	12.2	20.1
Alaska..........	7.3	11.4	2.9	11.4	3.9	-	1.8	0.1	0.5	0.6	0.3	0.2
Arizona.........	24.8	90.8	-	83.6	22.4	7.2	5.3	4.0	2.1	2.7	0.7	4.6
Arkansas	18.6	58.2	-	58.2	15.3	-	3.7	0.2	4.0	0.3	4.9	3.8
California	117.2	553.1	-	490.9	112.6	62.1	3.7	52.0	10.1	33.3	34.5	75.4
Colorado........	32.7	77.4	-	76.0	31.5	1.4	1.0	4.4	1.2	2.4	4.6	7.9
Connecticut......	18.0	67.0	-	67.0	15.2	-	4.8	1.8	2.6	1.4	12.3	-
Delaware	6.8	13.7	-	13.7	6.5	-	2.0	-	1.8	0.2	2.3	-
District of Columbia .	(X)	10.0	(X)	8.8	(X)	1.1	(X)	1.8	(X)	2.1	(X)	3.8
Florida	42.2	274.4	-	253.0	39.6	21.4	11.2	5.8	14.7	5.8	16.4	36.8
Georgia	40.7	181.4	-	180.7	35.0	0.7	7.7	1.4	4.4	8.2	14.4	42.0
Hawaii	30.4	-	23.2	-	7.1	-	1.1	0.1	2.8	0.2	3.2	-
Idaho	7.6	27.1	-	26.2	7.1	0.9	1.8	0.2	1.2	0.9	1.0	4.3
Illinois	55.3	232.1	-	212.6	52.4	19.5	13.4	7.1	3.2	6.7	15.2	15.2
Indiana.........	46.6	123.0	-	123.0	41.8	-	5.2	1.6	1.7	2.7	11.1	23.0
Iowa	25.9	72.8	-	66.6	24.7	6.2	2.7	1.5	0.3	2.0	8.1	8.9
Kansas.........	21.0	70.6	-	64.9	20.3	5.7	1.7	0.8	0.9	3.2	6.6	7.3
Kentucky	30.3	90.7	-	90.7	26.2	-	4.6	0.5	2.0	4.5	5.5	3.2
Louisiana	34.1	102.0	-	102.0	30.2	-	6.0	0.7	5.3	0.9	18.7	13.3
Maine..........	6.8	31.1	-	31.1	5.6	-	1.9	0.2	1.1	0.2	1.5	1.1
Maryland	19.7	104.9	-	96.0	17.7	8.9	7.9	2.3	6.0	3.6	6.9	-
Massachusetts.....	23.7	129.5	-	129.5	23.0	-	6.6	2.7	3.9	2.1	11.8	6.1
Michigan........	63.4	196.2	-	184.2	62.8	12.0	14.6	2.6	2.1	9.7	15.6	13.2
Minnesota........	38.7	109.8	-	106.1	37.2	3.7	2.2	11.0	2.1	3.7	7.2	13.3
Mississippi	16.8	69.5	-	63.9	15.3	5.7	3.4	0.3	3.3	0.3	9.0	18.0
Missouri	26.3	118.1	-	113.0	24.4	5.1	7.5	2.1	3.3	3.5	12.4	7.8
Montana........	7.1	26.7	-	26.5	6.4	0.1	1.3	0.9	0.4	0.6	1.3	0.8
Nebraska	10.8	43.7	-	41.2	10.1	2.5	2.9	1.1	0.7	0.4	4.4	4.3
Nevada	6.1	27.3	-	27.3	6.0	-	1.0	0.4	0.7	0.8	1.7	3.6
New Hampshire....	5.7	24.7	-	24.7	5.3	-	1.3	2.5	0.8	0.1	1.0	-
New Jersey......	45.8	178.9	14.8	169.2	27.6	9.8	5.4	11.5	2.5	4.0	17.1	6.4
New Mexico	16.9	43.3	-	40.9	15.9	2.4	1.4	0.5	2.9	0.4	5.4	2.6
New York	49.0	400.8	-	375.3	43.9	25.5	7.5	51.8	8.9	17.2	55.6	61.4
North Carolina.....	45.6	162.5	-	149.0	42.6	13.5	1.3	13.4	2.0	13.9	15.6	17.8
North Dakota......	7.8	13.6	-	13.6	7.3	-	0.3	0.9	1.3	0.3	1.4	-
Ohio	68.0	212.7	-	207.5	65.6	5.2	2.2	22.3	3.8	17.5	17.7	15.1
Oklahoma........	25.5	80.0	-	79.6	23.5	0.4	5.8	0.4	3.8	1.0	6.1	9.5
Oregon.........	16.2	68.2	-	61.0	15.2	7.2	4.6	0.8	1.5	3.5	7.3	2.3
Pennsylvania......	50.6	208.4	-	200.1	47.6	8.3	11.6	21.7	1.7	5.2	21.0	2.8
Rhode Island......	7.0	18.1	0.4	18.1	5.8	-	1.8	0.1	1.3	0.1	1.5	-
South Carolina.....	27.2	80.4	-	80.4	24.3	-	4.9	0.2	8.1	2.0	9.8	14.3
South Dakota	5.6	16.8	-	16.8	5.1	-	1.0	0.2	0.6	0.2	1.4	0.4
Tennessee	38.6	100.7	-	100.7	36.5	-	4.6	3.7	3.6	3.3	10.6	12.3
Texas..........	91.5	547.9	-	517.3	86.8	30.7	24.0	3.7	10.4	16.1	40.3	43.7
Utah	22.0	39.0	-	39.0	21.1	-	3.0	0.4	1.4	1.1	3.9	1.0
Vermont	4.6	16.6	-	16.6	4.2	-	1.1	-	0.5	-	0.3	-
Virginia.........	44.9	149.2	-	149.2	42.2	-	2.3	7.5	5.8	5.3	18.0	3.5
Washington........	36.8	87.0	-	87.0	36.1	-	7.3	1.2	7.0	4.1	8.1	8.9
West Virginia......	13.6	41.0	-	41.0	12.1	-	2.6	-	0.7	1.5	1.5	3.3
Wisconsin........	29.8	114.1	-	105.2	28.5	8.9	1.2	13.3	1.7	4.7	7.6	3.9
Wyoming........	3.3	16.1	-	14.4	3.2	1.7	0.3	-	0.5	0.2	1.4	4.1

See footnote at end of table.

State and Local Government Employment

No. 512. State and Local Government Full-Time Equivalent Employment, by Selected Function and State: 1995—Continued

[In thousands, for October. Local government amounts are estimates subject to sampling variation; see Appendix III and source]

STATE	HIGHWAYS		POLICE PROTECTION		FIRE PROTECTION		CORRECTION		PARKS AND RECREATION		GOVERNMENT ADMINISTRA-TION[1]	
	State	Local	State	Local	State	Local	State	Local	State	Local	State	Local
United States. .	**253.3**	**289.9**	**89.6**	**689.2**	**(X)**	**274.3**	**409.2**	**205.8**	**38.6**	**207.3**	**339.6**	**586.1**
Alabama.	4.3	6.6	1.0	9.9	(X)	4.5	4.3	2.4	0.8	2.9	5.4	6.8
Alaska	2.8	0.9	0.4	1.4	(X)	0.7	1.3	-	0.1	0.6	2.5	1.9
Arizona.	2.9	4.0	1.7	11.1	(X)	3.9	7.6	4.8	0.7	3.5	5.5	13.0
Arkansas	3.6	3.6	0.9	5.4	(X)	2.3	3.4	1.2	0.8	0.8	2.6	5.8
California	17.3	21.6	11.0	79.5	(X)	30.0	43.1	27.8	3.7	32.2	23.6	78.4
Colorado.	3.1	5.3	1.1	9.5	(X)	3.7	4.2	2.9	0.3	5.8	5.3	9.4
Connecticut.	4.0	3.8	1.6	8.0	(X)	4.1	7.4	-	0.4	2.2	7.0	4.4
Delaware	1.5	0.7	0.8	1.2	(X)	0.3	1.8	-	0.3	0.3	2.3	0.9
District of Columbia .	(X)	0.8	(X)	4.5	(X)	1.6	-	4.2	(X)	0.4	(X)	3.3
Florida.	10.6	13.6	3.8	44.9	(X)	18.2	31.1	13.3	1.1	15.6	21.2	35.6
Georgia	6.1	7.8	2.3	18.8	(X)	12.2	19.1	6.2	2.9	4.3	5.0	16.4
Hawaii	0.8	1.0	-	3.3	(X)	1.6	2.1	-	0.3	1.9	3.6	2.2
Idaho	1.8	1.6	0.4	2.9	(X)	0.9	1.5	0.8	0.2	0.7	1.8	3.4
Illinois	8.4	11.5	3.7	39.4	(X)	14.6	13.6	8.1	0.8	17.5	11.8	29.0
Indiana.	4.6	6.4	2.0	12.5	(X)	5.8	6.3	3.8	0.1	3.9	4.1	14.3
Iowa	2.7	5.5	0.9	5.7	(X)	1.7	2.3	0.9	0.2	2.2	4.0	5.4
Kansas.	3.8	5.6	1.0	6.6	(X)	2.5	3.6	1.9	0.5	2.4	4.6	6.7
Kentucky	5.4	3.0	1.7	6.0	(X)	2.8	5.3	2.2	2.2	1.5	8.1	4.8
Louisiana	5.7	4.9	1.1	12.4	(X)	4.1	6.8	2.6	0.9	2.8	5.3	10.6
Maine.	2.8	1.5	0.5	2.4	(X)	1.6	1.2	0.6	0.2	0.6	2.0	2.3
Maryland	5.0	4.6	2.3	13.4	(X)	6.1	10.6	2.5	0.7	6.4	8.2	7.5
Massachusetts.	4.6	5.9	1.9	16.4	(X)	12.8	6.1	5.0	1.1	2.1	12.6	9.1
Michigan.	3.8	10.1	3.0	20.3	(X)	7.7	16.5	4.8	0.8	5.8	7.1	21.1
Minnesota.	4.9	7.5	0.9	9.0	(X)	2.3	3.4	3.8	0.6	4.3	5.3	12.5
Mississippi	3.4	5.3	1.0	6.6	(X)	2.6	3.7	1.0	0.4	0.8	2.0	6.5
Missouri	6.7	5.3	2.2	14.1	(X)	5.0	6.7	2.3	0.7	3.5	5.9	9.5
Montana.	1.8	1.3	0.4	1.7	(X)	0.5	0.8	0.3	0.1	0.4	1.4	2.1
Nebraska	2.4	3.1	0.7	3.5	(X)	1.1	2.0	0.8	0.4	1.1	1.6	4.0
Nevada	1.5	1.3	0.6	4.1	(X)	1.6	2.9	1.3	0.2	2.2	1.9	4.8
New Hampshire	2.0	1.3	0.4	2.6	(X)	1.4	1.0	0.5	0.2	0.3	1.5	1.7
New Jersey.	8.0	10.7	3.7	28.5	(X)	7.7	9.0	7.1	2.4	5.6	18.0	20.9
New Mexico	2.7	1.6	0.6	4.4	(X)	1.6	3.9	1.3	0.7	1.6	4.2	4.0
New York	14.1	30.1	5.4	71.1	(X)	19.7	33.9	24.2	2.6	10.7	40.5	39.6
North Carolina	12.6	3.3	3.3	16.5	(X)	5.4	12.4	3.6	0.7	4.0	10.0	10.4
North Dakota.	1.0	1.1	0.2	1.1	(X)	0.3	0.5	0.2	0.1	0.7	1.1	1.5
Ohio	8.6	13.3	2.5	27.2	(X)	18.5	14.7	7.5	0.9	7.8	11.7	30.6
Oklahoma.	4.1	5.6	1.7	7.9	(X)	3.9	7.8	1.1	1.8	2.2	5.1	6.1
Oregon.	3.4	4.0	1.2	6.2	(X)	3.2	2.9	2.8	0.5	2.2	6.5	6.1
Pennsylvania.	13.7	10.6	6.4	25.1	(X)	5.7	12.8	10.7	1.0	4.2	13.6	26.6
Rhode Island.	0.9	1.0	0.3	2.6	(X)	2.0	1.7	-	0.1	0.8	2.5	1.6
South Carolina.	5.1	2.4	2.3	8.5	(X)	3.2	8.1	2.0	0.6	2.3	4.3	7.6
South Dakota	1.2	1.6	0.3	1.3	(X)	0.4	0.7	0.3	0.1	0.7	1.4	1.7
Tennessee	4.7	6.7	1.6	12.0	(X)	5.9	7.0	4.3	1.1	3.7	4.9	9.8
Texas.	14.0	18.9	3.4	53.4	(X)	18.5	43.0	20.9	1.2	13.4	16.3	39.4
Utah	1.8	1.5	0.7	4.0	(X)	1.6	2.5	0.7	0.3	2.3	2.9	3.4
Vermont	1.1	1.0	0.5	0.8	(X)	0.3	0.9	-	0.2	0.2	1.3	1.0
Virginia.	12.0	3.9	2.5	14.2	(X)	7.0	12.7	6.2	0.9	6.0	7.4	13.2
Washington.	6.2	6.7	1.8	10.6	(X)	5.4	7.4	3.5	0.5	4.9	5.2	13.9
West Virginia.	6.1	0.8	0.9	2.4	(X)	0.9	0.8	0.4	1.0	0.9	3.0	3.2
Wisconsin	2.0	9.1	0.9	13.3	(X)	4.8	6.5	2.4	0.3	3.8	5.5	10.7
Wyoming	1.7	0.7	0.2	1.4	(X)	0.3	0.5	0.3	0.1	0.6	0.9	1.5

- Represents or rounds to zero.   X Not applicable.
[1] Includes Financial Administration, Central Administration, and Judicial and Legal.

Source: U.S. Bureau of the Census; <http://www.census.gov/ftp/pub/govs/www/apes/95html>; (released June 97).

State and Local Government Finances and Employment

No. 513. State and Local Government Employment and Average Earnings, by State: 1990 and 1995

[For October]

STATE	FULL-TIME EQUIVALENT EMPLOYMENT (1,000)				FULL-TIME EQUIVALENT EMPLOYMENT PER 10,000 POPULATION [2]				AVERAGE OCTOBER EARNINGS [3] (dol.)			
	State		Local [1]		State		Local [1]		State		Local [1]	
	1990	1995	1990	1995	1990	1995	1990	1995	1990	1995	1990	1995
United States	3,840	3,971	9,239	10,119	154	151	371	385	2,472	2,854	2,364	2,763
Alabama	79	81	148	165	196	191	367	389	2,196	2,421	1,749	2,017
Alaska	22	22	21	24	401	366	385	391	3,543	3,727	3,491	4,051
Arizona	50	58	136	161	137	135	370	373	2,334	2,570	2,540	2,689
Arkansas	43	48	78	90	182	192	330	364	1,922	2,353	1,545	1,823
California	325	338	1,091	1,141	109	107	367	362	3,209	3,664	3,073	3,523
Colorado	54	57	130	148	165	153	395	394	2,765	3,234	2,292	2,612
Connecticut	58	63	98	102	178	193	299	311	3,018	3,321	2,854	3,491
Delaware	21	22	17	19	314	307	250	269	2,245	2,743	2,458	2,755
District of Columbia	(X)	(X)	57	47	(X)	(X)	939	927	(X)	(X)	3,024	3,425
Florida	160	175	497	534	123	123	384	377	2,095	2,488	2,247	2,485
Georgia	112	115	270	333	173	159	418	462	2,037	2,456	1,872	2,164
Hawaii	49	51	13	14	445	436	120	119	2,317	2,624	2,536	3,013
Idaho	19	21	37	46	186	179	372	396	2,100	2,476	1,772	2,165
Illinois	145	141	416	444	127	119	364	377	2,520	3,027	2,463	2,985
Indiana	89	89	196	217	161	153	354	375	2,496	2,583	2,036	2,375
Iowa	57	53	107	116	207	187	387	408	2,936	3,126	2,024	2,367
Kansas	50	48	104	118	200	187	421	461	2,077	2,325	1,979	2,315
Kentucky	75	73	114	133	204	190	310	344	2,141	2,488	1,823	2,523
Louisiana	85	93	155	171	200	214	368	394	2,047	2,359	1,713	1,860
Maine	22	21	42	45	179	172	345	364	2,352	2,618	1,978	2,349
Maryland	89	81	159	172	186	161	333	341	2,609	2,835	2,776	3,159
Massachusetts	93	82	196	220	155	135	325	362	2,541	3,068	2,554	2,961
Michigan	144	141	316	324	155	148	340	339	2,858	3,342	2,646	3,255
Minnesota	70	73	163	196	160	157	374	425	2,936	3,266	2,552	2,830
Mississippi	47	50	105	122	183	186	407	453	1,824	2,394	1,543	1,798
Missouri	74	79	171	192	145	149	334	361	1,965	2,232	2,052	2,297
Montana	17	18	35	38	211	208	434	439	2,072	2,534	1,959	2,347
Nebraska	29	30	68	76	186	181	430	465	2,075	2,290	2,089	2,413
Nevada	19	21	42	53	160	134	348	345	2,502	2,864	2,574	3,085
New Hampshire	16	17	33	38	145	147	301	335	2,352	2,669	2,215	2,641
New Jersey	112	125	304	312	145	157	393	393	2,859	3,563	2,698	3,553
New Mexico	40	42	57	68	262	251	379	404	2,100	2,390	1,783	2,119
New York	285	257	866	856	158	142	482	471	2,997	3,423	2,795	3,479
North Carolina	107	115	244	281	161	159	368	389	2,372	2,570	2,065	2,287
North Dakota	15	16	20	22	234	257	314	340	2,057	2,440	2,138	2,450
Ohio	139	143	385	425	128	128	355	381	2,510	3,083	2,236	2,696
Oklahoma	65	68	116	129	208	206	369	393	1,975	2,018	1,761	2,113
Oregon	52	52	100	114	184	166	353	362	2,302	2,848	2,322	2,896
Pennsylvania	127	152	361	369	107	126	304	306	2,437	3,025	2,403	2,911
Rhode Island	21	20	27	29	205	203	266	288	2,586	3,240	2,656	3,169
South Carolina	79	78	116	136	227	213	333	370	1,956	2,318	1,848	2,141
South Dakota	13	14	24	27	192	194	349	364	1,979	2,355	1,733	2,004
Tennessee	79	84	175	188	163	161	358	359	2,055	2,389	1,883	2,196
Texas	223	268	706	858	131	143	415	456	2,192	2,492	1,952	2,229
Utah	37	42	51	63	216	214	294	321	2,000	2,524	2,092	2,460
Vermont	13	13	18	21	233	216	312	363	2,302	2,471	2,090	2,455
Virginia	117	116	221	247	188	175	356	373	2,267	2,553	2,248	2,505
Washington	91	96	164	188	187	175	336	344	2,459	3,094	2,515	3,338
West Virginia	34	35	59	60	188	189	326	327	1,919	2,212	1,862	2,203
Wisconsin	67	64	183	201	136	126	375	393	2,503	3,153	2,372	2,900
Wyoming	11	11	24	27	239	227	539	565	2,045	2,203	2,110	2,309

X Not applicable.   [1] Estimates subject to sampling variation; see Appendix III and source.   [2] Based on estimated resident population as of July 1.   [3] For full-time employees.

Source: U.S. Bureau of the Census, *Public Employment*, series GE-90-1, No.1, and <http://www.census.gov/pub/govs/www/apes.html>; (released August 1997).

for the bureaucracy: the role of political appointees, their increasingly short tenures in the executive branch, and how they relate to senior career managers.

Gore's efforts aim to eliminate federal programs, shift them to the states, or offer them to the private sector. However, according to Barr, some officials inside the Clinton administration are concerned that the themes of the first round of reinvention—customer service, performance measurement, and improved labor-management relations—are being deemphasized by political appointees as they focus on ways to save money through privatization, program elimination, or devolution to the states.[30]

PERFORMANCE RATINGS

If an organization is going to use merit rather than seniority as a standard for promotion or demotion, how does one determine job performance? The most common device used is for a superior to give a subordinate a *performance rating*. The system seems simple, but in practice it generates complications and controversies.

The essence of the performance rating problem is grounded in the absence of objective data and procedures for making these systems work effectively. Even when a supervisor attempts to be fair and impartial, neutral criteria may often prove scarce. Administrative decision makers give into personal whims if they are capricious in their actions.

However difficult these ratings systems are to administer, they are universally part of the government workplace and culture. (*Table 5-7* is a typical *performance rating form*.) This evaluation sheet is used to appraise the performance of managers in the Massachusetts state government. It includes provisions for comments by the reviewing supervisor and the person being evaluated.

Workforce morale and *government performance* are closely related. The ability of governments to function effectively and efficiently is related directly to the quality, competency, and motivation of its work force. Despite positive attitudes toward their jobs and the work they do, only about half of the respondents would recommend the federal government as an employer, while over one-fourth say they definitely would not. Several factors traditionally viewed as reasons to remain in federal employment lost strength as retention factors in one three-year period according to surveys conducted for the Merit Systems Protection Board. These include: the intrinsic value of the work; salary; current health insurance benefits; and opportunity to have an impact on public affairs.

Many employees argue that the federal government's performance management program does not create an atmosphere that strongly encourages quality performance. Large percentages of employees believe their work units can increase the quantity and quality of the work they perform with the same people.[31]

POSITION CLASSIFICATIONS

Public sector personnel organizations have systems of *position classification*. The federal government, for example, allocates positions by fifteen basic grade

Table 5-7 Personnel Evaluation for Managers Form DPA 57, The Commonwealth of Massachusetts

Name of Person Evaluated	Position Title and Grade	Organizational Unit	Period Covered by this Evaluation Month Day Year
Name of Evaluator	Position Title and Grade	Organizational Unit	From: _____ To: _____

Instructions: At the beginning of each evaluation period, the manager to be rated should review this form and be informed of the factors on which his or her performance will be evaluated. All ratings must be done by persons who have supervised the manager for at least 90 days. This rating will represent your evaluation of the manager's actual performance on his or her present job.

Suggestions: Consider only one factor at a time. Don't let your rating in one influence your rating of another. Base your judgement on the requirements of the job and the manager's performance in it as compared with others doing similar work. Carefully read the description of each factor before making each entry, and assign the rating which most nearly describes your opinion.

Grading: Performance will be evaluated by the immediate supervisor (*) and, when necessary, the reviewing supervisor (**) by placing a check mark (√) in the appropriate box in the numerical scale from 1 to 10, based on the following standards:

If the manager's performance demonstrates ability that is—

—outstanding and far exceeds job standards, check the box numbered 10

—above average, exceeds job standards, check box 7, 8 or 9

—average, meets job standards, check box 4, 5 or 6

—below average, does not meet job standards, check box 1, 2 or 3

Evaluation

Factor	Below Average	Average	Above Average	Outstanding
Job Knowledge Adequacy of professional skills, experience and knowledge to do the job	1* | ** |2* | ** |3* | ** Lacks the understanding, skill and experience to perform the job. Requires constant supervision.	4* | ** |5* | ** |6* | ** Has sufficient knowledge, skills and experience to perform tasks with a minimum of guidance.	7* | ** |8* | ** |9* | ** Has a good knowledge of the work to be performed. Above average understanding of procedures.	10* | ** Has a thorough understanding of the job and all related procedures, laws, regulations and technical tasks. Extensive professional skill and experience.

Category	1 2 3	4 5 6	7 8 9	10
Productivity Meeting established standards of quality and quantity of work production.	Fails to meet established deadlines. Production does not meet established standards. Requires a high degree of assistance.	Work is generally accurate and complete. Meets established standards and deadlines.	Completes assignments on time with above average results. Accepts additional tasks when requested.	Consistently completes complex assignments quickly and accurately. Regularly does more than required with exceptional competence.
Communication: Oral Oral facility with language which expidites results while maintaining relationships; maintain channels.	Frequently fails to achieve understanding from listeners. Speaks in poorly organized fashion. Has difficulty articulating thoughts.	Has adequate ability in making an oral presentation. Occasionally is required to repeat or amend position to achieve desired response.	Presents ideas and material in an effective manner. Has above average ability to obtain agreement and support for desired goals.	Outstanding ability to present ideas and articulate thoughts to diverse audiences and organizations. Expedites results through ability to command positive responses.
Communication: Written; Presenting and explaining ideas clearly and effectively in writing; developing written work in a logical and comprehensive manner.	Lacks the ability to provide written communications in a logical, understandable and timely manner. Requires constant rewrite and editing.	Written communications are readable and understandable with only occasional need for editing and rewriting. Usually completes written assignments within prescribed time limits.	Effectively presents thoughts in writing in a very understandable style with very little need for interpretation or repetition.	Consistently writes complex directives, letters, reports, etc. in a clear, concise, highly understandable style. Writing is convincing and timely, and achieves desired results.
Leadership Inspiring teamwork and productivity; maintenance of discipline; stimulating suggestions; checking the work of subordinates.	Is unable to motivate staff to meet organization goals in an efficient and effective manner.	Maintains effective work output by utilization of available personnel resources.	Effectively utilizes the skill of available staff to obtain a high degree of productivity. Maintains good level of morale; promotes teamwork.	Obtains outstanding productivity and quality of work while maintaining excellent morale. Maintains positive relationships with other agencies.

continued

159

Table 5-7 Personnel Evaluation for Managers Form DPA 57, The Commonwealth of Massachusetts, *continued*

Factor	Below Average	Average	Above Average	Outstanding
Management Skills Efficient use of staff and budget to achieve agency goals; establishing and shifting priorities as necessary; effective delegation of authority; implementing policies and procedures.	1 | 2 | 3 | Has difficulty utilizing staff and resources efficiently. Overlooks priorities of goals and objectives. Lacks understanding of management skills required.	4 | 5 | 6 | Accepts established priorities and utilizes resources to meet them. Plans activities and directs subordinates while achieving average results.	7 | 8 | 9 | Uses staff and budgetary resources efficiently. Implements policies and procedures and has above average ability to adjust priorities to meet goals and objectives.	10 | Achieves agency goals and objectives through superior management skills. Outstanding use of human and budgetary resources to meet priorities. Delegates authority effectively.
Problem Solving and Decision Making Logical and practical thinking; objectivity and deliberation in decision making; application of knowledge and skills to new situations; foreseeing consequences or recommendations.	1*|** 2*|** 3*|** Is unable to adapt to problems of above average difficulty. Does not analyze all facts of problem. Will not make decisions, or makes them hastily or too slowly.	4*|** 5*|** 6*|** Recognizes problems as they occur and contributes to their resolution. Makes suggestions for improvement. Usually coordinates decisions to achieve desired objectives.	7*|** 8*|** 9*|** Applies a highly logical approach to problems presented. Makes suggestions for improvement and carries them through promptly. Suggests conclusions that are accepted. Provides alternate approaches when necessary.	10*|** Anticipates and analyzes difficult situations before they become problems. Logically and quickly applies corrective action with superior results. Generates new and innovative ideas.
Affirmative Action Demonstrating active support of AA goals; knowledge and communication of AA information; monitoring and evaluating activities and progress.	1 | 2 | 3 | Fails to implement AA goals, activities monitoring and evaluation.	4 | 5 | 6 | Accepts responsibility for achieving goals. Informs staff. Works to resolve problems and implement policy.	7 | 8 | 9 | Analyzes situations and provides solutions to achieve goals with above average results.	10 | Outstanding ability to achieve agency goals. Initiate action, expedite results.

	1	2	3		4	5	6		7	8	9		10	

Initiative & Responsibility
Self-starting action; willingness to take the lead and be responsible for decisions, enthusiasm for improvement; working independently with success; open-mindedness toward opposing views.

1	2	3		4	5	6		7	8	9		10	
Is reluctant to accept more than what is perceived to be the required job. Displays little or no initiative. Objects to suggestions for improvement.				Will accept responsibility for work assigned. Displays initiative on selected projects. Seldom seeks out additional work.				Works independently with success. Obtains above average results with self-initiated projects. Is open minded to opposing views.				Develop new and original programs with constant success. Takes responsibility for all actions and results. Exceptional ability to adapt to relevant objections or suggested improvements.	

Staff Development and Training
Development and training of new employees through instruction and by example. Setting and measuring standards of performance; conducting instructive performance appraisal discussions.

1	2	3		4	5	6		7	8	9		10	
Does not set standards for agency tasks nor evaluate employees' performance. Fails to train or develop staff for job improvement and upward mobility.				Periodically measures workers performance against set standards. Routinely instructs staff and assists in improvement of work habits.				Sets standards and measures degree of achievement with individual workers in a cooperative manner. Implements training to improve performance. Sets above average example.				Exceptional ability to develop staff through participative management and regular performance review. Supports upward mobility through the efficient utilization of training programs.	

Evaluator's comments (to include recommended areas and methods for improvements):

Total numerical rating _____

_____
Signature

Reviewing Supervisor's comments (Reviewing supervisor must evaluate the employee when the evaluator's rating totals more than 95 or less than 40):

Total numerical rating _____

_____
Signature and Title

Comment of person evaluated:

I have reviewed this rating and it has been discussed with me.

Signature _____ Date _____

161

PERSONNEL BUREAUCRACIES

The Civil Service Reform Act of 1978 (CSRA) constitutes a major restructuring of federal civil service in the United States, and the Civil Service Commission (CSC), in particular. The functions once administered by the CSC (1883) are allocated to three separate personnel bureaucracies. The Office of Personnel Management (OPM), as the central personnel agency directly answerable to the president, aids the president in establishing rules for administering civilian employment; advises the president on employment matters; executes, administers, and enforces civil service laws, rules, and regulations; coordinates research to enhance public personnel administration; and maintains and upgrades existing personnel practices such as examinations, executive development, and performance evaluations.

OPM has no authority over employee appeals. The appellate and quasi-judicial responsibilities previously implemented by the CSC are vested in the Merit Systems Protection Board (MSPB). The MSPB decides most appeals and complaints, issues regulations regarding the nature and scope of its review, establishes time limits in which appeals must be settled, and orders corrective and disciplinary actions against employees or departments and agencies if appropriate. As an independent federal agency, the MSPB is constituted as a bipartisan organization, consisting of three board members appointed by the president and confirmed by the Senate.

The CSRA's final structural change created the Federal Labor Relations Authority (FLRA). The FLRA determines appropriate units of representation, supervises labor organization elections, decides unfair labor practice cases, rules on negotiability issues, rules on exceptions to arbitration awards, mediates disputes, settles impasses, and prosecutes unfair labor practices.

---

levels, ranging from GS (General Schedule) 1 to GS 15. Each level is paid more and, ostensibly, requires more in terms of ability and output than the level below it. Within each grade level there are ten steps, each paying more than the preceding one. The higher steps of any grade pay more than the lower steps of the grade just above it. Consequently, an employee working at the tenth step of grade 12 will be earning more than an employee at the first step of grade 13. Advancement from one step to another takes place chiefly on the basis of seniority.

Advancement from one grade to another is based in theory on merit, although in practice seniority enjoys consideration too. *The premise for adopting classification schemes is that different positions require varying degrees of ability and require varying amounts of responsibility.* The adoption of a classification plan has long been considered essential for the effective operation of a merit system, for it is designed to place the emphasis on *what* rather than *who* a person knows. An effective position classification program provides a basis for a fair and workable personnel operation that, without fear or favor, may reward good performance and penalize poor. In principle, such a position classification framework is "open" and objective. One crucial question is, "How many classifications should there be?" Should the various jobs be distributed throughout a large number of separate grades and levels, or should they be compressed into a comparatively few broad categories? If the federal government's personnel system features fifteen grades with ten steps each, is this too many, too few, or about right?

The problem is relative and one to which there can be no precise answer. There are no precise criteria defining narrow and broad classifications. To some, the federal government's fifteen grade levels may seem too numerous. To others they may seem too few. We do know, however, that moving in either direction will yield various advantages and disadvantages.

A personnel system employing numerous narrow classifications organizes its job structures more precisely to each level. If there are two classifications for typists rather than one, better typists can be placed in the upper class and less-capable typists can be put in the lower one. In principle, if typist A does better work than typist B, then A can be given a higher rating than B. It is further assumed that A will be given not only more money and more status, but also more difficult and more responsible assignments. In this sense, using many relatively narrow categories can be fairer to all concerned. Narrow categories also permit more extensive use of promotion as an incentive. More levels mean more possibilities for moving up, and at the same time, such promotional opportunities can be used as a sanction against those who fail to perform adequately.

Many public organizations have relatively few classification levels, particularly in the lower range of jobs. Postal workers, police officers, fire fighters, and others can usually move up only to a position of command. There are relatively few such positions in most organizations. Opportunities for promotion are limited.

Narrow and, therefore, numerous job classifications present distinct difficulties, however. The more classifications there are, the more personnel work the organization must do. Each classification must be carefully described and demarcated, and each job must be carefully plugged into the right classification. This results in a system that is not only costly but also cumbersome and complicated.

Use of numerous and narrow classifications may alleviate because those performing somewhat more demanding tasks can then more easily receive recognition for doing so. This pattern can, for the same reasons, create tensions and prompt questions such as: "Why should he be classified higher than I am when my job requires as much or more responsibility as his?" Arguments frequently emerge over whether a position should be put in one class or another. For example, in a regional office of one federal agency, a personnel officer balked at classifying a job at grade level 14, despite pleas and exhortations from the agency's other top officials that he do so. By coincidence, the personnel officer himself held only a grade 13 position, and he could not bring himself to categorize the new post at a higher level than his own.

SUMMARY

- The quests for *representativeness, neutral competence,* and *executive leadership* are norms of public personnel administration. Value, mediation, and core functions are factors affecting public personnel practices.

- Public organizations in the United States use two methods of establishing and operating personnel systems: (1) *political appointment* and *election* and (2) an objective determination of *merit.*
- The Pendleton Act of 1883 questioned the practice of *nonpolitical appointments,* embraced *egalitarianism,* and recognized *competence,* as determined by competitive examinations, related to duties performed.
- The expansion of the merit system and development of public service are closely associated with passage of legislation and presidential leadership.
- Key *merit system principles* are: recruiting, selecting, and advancing employees on the basis of their abilities, knowledge, and skills; providing equitable and adequate compensation; training employees to assure high-quality performance; guaranteeing fairness for applicants and employees; and protecting against coercion for political purposes.
- *Test validity* for predicting on-the-job performance and other selection criteria pose problems for public agencies grounded in merit principles.
- Two basic criteria for promotion are: *seniority* and *merit.*
- Federal, state, and local governments must: attract high-quality job applicants; hire a reasonable share of the high-quality applicants; train and develop employees; motivate employees to perform at their best; and retain good performers and remove poor ones.
- There are 19,521,000 government employees. Of that number, 61.0 percent, or 11,521,000 jobs, are in local government; 24.2 percent, or 4,719,000, are in state government; and 14.8 percent, or 2,895,000 are federal employees (1995 figures).
- Representative bureaucracy is a basic policy goal pursued by public personnel managers. A separate but related policy choice is whether to pursue that goal *passively* or *actively.* A passive strategy is *equal opportunity.* An active strategy is *affirmative action.*
- The *declining importance* of affirmative action is because: (1) no strong consensus favoring affirmative action exists; (2) U.S. Supreme Court decisions regarding affirmative action are nonlinear; and (3) executive leadership, retrenchment, and productivity take priority over affirmative action programs in government agencies.
- Despite huge federal deficits and inefficiency in the federal bureaucracy, state employees' numbers have increased more than five times faster than federal workers.
- The average age of federal civilian nonpostal employees is 44.9 years; length of service is 16.0 years; 39.4 percent have bachelor's or higher degrees; 55.4 percent are men and 44.6 percent are women; and 29.4 percent are minority group members.
- The *demographics* of the federal work force are changing. The percentage of the work force that was female increased from 34.9 percent in 1976 to 44.0 percent in 1996. The percentage of the workforce that were minorities increased from 21.5 percent in 1976 to 29.1 percent in 1996.

- The premise underlying *position classification* schemes is that different positions require varying degrees of ability and impose varying amounts of responsibility.
- Public personnel administration, more than anything else, is a process encompassing *procedures, rules,* and *regulations.*
- The recruitment, selection, and promotion phases are grounded in *legislation* and *law,* reflecting the values of accountability and responsiveness to the public.

The following case study illustrates how complex a personnel matter can get. How does the issue of merit come into play in this situation?

CASE STUDY

Personnel Dilemma: Terminate or Retain[32]

In a reorganization of the State Department of Education, a planning commission was established to coordinate activities and programs of its more than fifty sections and divisions and to institute and carry out comprehensive programs for the public schools and institutions of higher learning. Commission members were the superintendent of Public Instruction, the secretary of the state board of education, and the directors of the Federal Program, Finance, and Instruction divisions of the department. Staffing of the commission was provided by the state board of education, headed by Dr. Frank Jordan.

In July, Dr. Jordan received funds to hire an additional secretary to perform secretarial and clerical services for the planning commission. The board at one time had only one secretary for six professional staff persons, and this secretary could not handle that work load and take on additional duties for the commission.

Jordan's administrative assistant, Barbara White, who served as personnel officer and supervisor of the clerical staff, began working with the Department of Personnel to classify the new position and announce the opening. She consulted with the board's office planner, Pamela Goldsmith, and the facilities coordinator, John Rodriguez, to determine the classification for the new position. No one was sure what duties would be assigned to the person hired other than that he or she would act as secretary to the Planning Commission. The job would include making arrangements for meetings, preparing agendas, recording and transcribing minutes, and providing data and materials requested by Commission members. It was thought that the person would also serve as secretary to Goldsmith and perhaps do some work for Rodriguez.

After reviewing the anticipated duties with Dr. Jordan, White submitted a job summary to the Department of Personnel requesting a Secretary Grade I classification. The qualifications for this position were graduation from high school, one year of secretarial experience, and the ability to type 45 wpm and take dictation at 80 wpm. The classification was approved and the opening was announced.

The Department of Personnel submitted a list of four eligible applicants to the board and, after interviewing them, Dr. Jordan and Barbara White decided to employ Edith Reichel. Her experience was not entirely what was wanted—she had held only one secretarial position and had worked the past three years as a clerk in the state auditor's office—but she was enthusiastic about getting the job and expressed a willingness to improve her skills and take on new responsibilities. In addition, she won Dr. Jordan's sympathy because she was divorced and had two small children to support.

After Reichel began working, it soon became apparent to Barbara White that employing her had been a mistake. Reichel was a heavy smoker and cigarette ash covered her desk and papers. She was restless and disrupted office work by visiting with other staff members, and she was inattentive when receiving instructions, often making mistakes that resulted in her work having to be redone. Moreover, the position required abilities Reichel did not have. Goldsmith was working on a comprehensive plan for reorganizing the filing system of the department and needed assistance in her studies that she could not entrust to Reichel.

Antagonism also quickly arose between the board's regular secretary, Hazel Holmberg, and Edith Reichel. Instead of lightening Holmberg's onerous work load, Reichel added to the burden. Because of Reichel's inefficiency, Holmberg had to assist her in collecting material for the Commission meetings and, because Reichel's shorthand was poor, Holmberg had to take the minutes as well. As a consequence, Holmberg complained to White and threatened to seek a transfer unless something was done.

White consulted Pamela Goldsmith about Reichel's performance and found that she, too, considered it unsatisfactory. They held a counseling session with Reichel, who, apologetic, blamed her deficiencies on problems with her two children and promised to improve. For some weeks her work was almost satisfactory, and it looked as though the problem was resolved. But Reichel soon slipped back into her old habits, and Rodriguez discussed getting rid of Reichel while she was still on probation. None of the three supervisors, however, was willing to assume the responsibility for taking action.

The question of whether to start proceedings to release or retain Reichel remained in limbo until near the end of the fifth month of her employment when she failed to report for work one morning. The Planning Commission was to meet at ten o'clock, and telephone calls made to Reichel at her home to find out where she had placed the data and papers required for the members went unanswered.

Fortunately these items were discovered by Holmberg just before the meeting began. Reichel called the office at 11 o'clock to say that she had taken a bus to visit friends in a neighboring town the night before and had missed the bus back. She did not return to work until the next morning.

White reported the difficulties encountered with Reichel to Dr. Jordan, informing Dr. Jordan that only a few more weeks remained on her probationary period. If no action were taken, Reichel would become a permanent employee and it would be hard to remove her, even if her work continued to be unsatisfactory. Although Jordan was busy trying to meet a deadline for completing the department budget, he promised to talk the situation over with Reichel. When she appeared in his office, he was so preoccupied with budgetary matters that he merely told her there had been some complaints about her work and urged her to try to improve it, which he felt sure she could.

After leaving Dr. Jordan's office, Reichel related to White what had occurred, saying that he had been "very nice" and reassuring about the quality of her work and her future in the department. Later, discussing the matter with Goldsmith,

White said that apparently Dr. Jordan, rushed in getting the budget together, would not take the time to deal with such a minor matter as a Grade I secretary's deficiencies. To this end, White arranged for Reichel to attend a week-long secretarial training workshop to brush up on her typing and shorthand. At the end of the probationary period, Reichel became a permanent employee.

Reichel's good intentions did not last long and she lapsed again into her old ways. Other staff members, believing her poor performance placed an extra burden on them, complained of her slipshod work to employees in other offices at the capitol. Through friends, word of this got back to Reichel. She exclaimed that she wished she had never taken the job in the first place and that there had never been any fault found with her work in the state auditor's office. Dr. Jordan and White, she said, had not been honest with her.

Repeated complaints of staff members to Jordan finally persuaded him that to restore staff morale he would have to get rid of her and arrange for someone else to do the secretarial work for the Planning Commission. There was no strong basis for firing Reichel, so he decided to reclassify her position to a Secretary Grade II and reassign her to work in one of the auxiliary programs attached to the department.

QUESTIONS AND INSTRUCTIONS

1. How would you allocate the blame in permitting Reichel to complete her probation and become a permanent staff member?
2. Would an orientation and training program and closer supervision have prevented the situation from developing?
3. What do you think of the manner in which the problem was finally resolved?
4. Do you think that Reichel was correct in her belief that her superiors had not dealt honestly with her?
5. Is it fair to the state for administrators to keep an employee who performs poorly out of sympathy for his or her personal problems or because they find reprimanding or firing a person too painful an experience? How tough must administrators be?

INSIGHTS-ISSUES / PERSONNEL DILEMMA: TERMINATE OR RETAIN

Clearly and briefly describe and illustrate these concepts, issues, or points. Interpret the word "role" as meaning impact, application, importance, effect and/or illustration of certain facts, concerns, or issues from the case study.

1. Role of classification plan for separating function/ position from personality.
2. Role of morality/pragmatism of affirmative action in public sector employment.
3. Role of procedure/s in public sector employment practices.

4. Role of probationary period for seeking permanent public sector employment.
5. Role of public sector planning commission for coordinating government agency activities and programs (as contrasted with private sector emphasis on efficiency "bottom-line" priorities).

ENDNOTES

1. Quoted in John Franklin Campbell, *The Foreign Affairs Fudge Factory* (New York: Basic Books, 1971), 139–140.
2. Ibid., 47.
3. Quoted in George E. Berkley, *The Administrative Revolution: Notes on the Passing of Organization Man* (Englewood Cliffs, N.J.: Prentice-Hall, 1971), 141.
4. Herbert Kaufman, "Emerging Conflicts in the Doctrines of Public Administration," *The American Political Science Review* 50 (December 1956): 1057–1073.
5. Donald E. Klingner and John Nalbandian, *Public Personnel Management: Contexts and Strategies* (Englewood Cliffs, N.J.: Prentice-Hall, Inc., 1985).
6. James E. Leidlein, "In Search of Merit, A Practitioner's Comments on 'The Staffing Function in Illinois State Government after Rutan' and "Curbing Patronage without Paperasserie," *Public Administration Review* 53, no. 4 (July–August 1993), 391–392.
7. Quoted in Paul Van Riper, *History of the United States Civil Service* (New York: Harper & Row, 1958), 36.
8. Steven W. Hays and T. Zane Reeves, *Personnel Management in the Public Sector* (Boston: Allyn and Bacon, Inc., 1984), 16.
9. Ronald N. Johnson and Gary D. Libecap, "Patronage to Merit and Control of the Federal Government Labor Force," *Explorations in Economic History* 31, no. 1 (January 1994): 91–120.
10. Cited in Patrick V. Murphy, *The Criminal Justice System in Crisis* (Syracuse, N.Y.: Maxwell School of Citizenship and Affairs, 1972).
11. "The Values We Live By: What Americans Want from Welfare Reform," *Spectrum:The Journal of State Government* 70, no. 3 (summer 1997): 5–6.
12. James E. Brennan, "Merit Pay: Balance the Old Rich and the New Poor," *Personnel Journal* 64, no. 5 (May 1985): 82–85.
13. U.S. Merit Systems Protection Board, *Attracting Quality Graduates to the Federal Government: A View of College Recruiting* (June 1988), vii.
14. The Hudson Institute, *Civil Service 2000,* A Report Prepared for the U.S. Office of Personnel Management (June 1988), 10.
15. *Washington Times,* 25 May 1989, p. B5.
16. *The Changing Workforce: Demographic Issues Facing the Federal Government* (Washington, DC: U.S. General Accounting Office, 1992), 3.
17. United States Office of Personnel Management, *Federal Civilian Workforce Statistic: Demographic Profile of the Federal Workforce, As of September 30, 1996* (Washington, DC: U.S. Government Printing Office, 1997), 5–7.
18. Ibid.
19. *The Changing Workforce: Demographic Issues Facing the Federal Government* (Washington, DC: U.S. General Accounting Office, 1992), 76.

20. Ralph C. Chandler and Jack C. Plano, *The Public Administration Dictionary* (New York: John Wiley & Sons, 1982), 246.
21. Klingner and Nalbandian, *Public Personnel Management*, 62–69.
22. United States Office of Personnel Management, *Federal Civilian Workforce Statistic: Demographic Profile of the Federal Workforce, As of September 30, 1996* (Washington, DC: U.S. Government Printing Office, 1997), 6.
23. David H. Rosenbloom, "The Declining Salience of Affirmative Action in Federal Personnel Management," *Review of Public Personnel Administration* 4 (summer 1984): 202–205, 248–249.
24. Raymond W. Mack, "Whose Affirmative Action?" *Society* 33, no. 3 (March–April 1996): 41–44.
25. Nancy Stein, "Questions and Answers about Affirmative Action," *Social Justice* 22, no. 3 (fall 1995), 45–53.
26. "The Future of Affirmative Action: President Clinton's Remarks," *Congressional Digest* 75, nos. 6–7 (June–July 1996): 166–169.
27. Ann Crittenden, "Quotas for Good Old Boys," *Wall Street Journal*, 14 June 1995, p. A18.
28. Paul Starr, "Civil Reconstruction: What to Do Without Affirmative Action," *The American Prospect*, no. 8 (winter 1992), 7–14.
29. Stephen Barr, "Administration Drafts Plan to Remake Personnel System," *Washington Post*, 16 December 1993, p. A23.
30. Barr, "Shaving the Fat, Sparing the Meat: Agencies Grapple with Reinvention's Phase II, *Washington Post*, 30 January 1995, p. A13.
31. *Working for America: A Federal Employee Survey* (Washington, DC: U.S. merit Systems Protection Board, 1990).
32. C. Kenneth Meyer and Charles H. Brown, *Practicing Public Management: A Casebook*, 2nd ed., pp. 178-181. Copyright © 1989 by St. Martin's Press, Inc. Reprinted with permission of Bedford/St. Martin's Press, Inc.

6

PUBLIC SECTOR LABOR-MANAGEMENT RELATIONS

CHAPTER HIGHLIGHTS

DECLINE, TRANSFORMATION, OR REFORMATION?

MAJOR ISSUES IN STATE AND LOCAL
GOVERNMENT LABOR RELATIONS

WHEN COLLECTIVE BARGAINING FAILS

COLLECTIVE BARGAINING FOR FEDERAL EMPLOYEES

CONFLICTS IN STATE CIVIL SERVICE AND COLLECTIVE BARGAINING
SYSTEMS

IMPACTS OF LABOR LAWS ON PUBLIC SECTOR LABOR RELATIONS

FUTURE OF PUBLIC SECTOR UNIONS: STAGNATION OR GROWTH?

On August 3, 1981, air traffic controllers in the United States went on strike. Federal law prohibits such a strike. Then-president Ronald Reagan fired the strikers. The controllers belonged to the union PATCO—the Professional Air Traffic Controllers Organization. The 17,500 member union accounted for only 1 percent of the federal civilian workforce.

During its twenty-year existence, PATCO had a stormy labor-management relationship with the federal government. There were work slowdowns and "sick-outs" staged by the union. There were court battles between PATCO and the Federal Aviation Administration (FAA). The issues involved in the disputes included wages, working conditions, FAA policies, and even the number of "orientation" rides the controllers received from the airlines. An orientation ride was a free plane trip.

A year before the strike, in the presidential election year of 1980, the controllers announced a "withdrawal of enthusiasm," a work slowdown that managed to delay flights until the FAA secured a restraining order against the union. That year, PATCO's leadership decided to back the candidacy of Reagan. With their candidate later winning the White House, the union readied a new list of demands.

The controllers, who worked in the extremely high pressure atmosphere of airport control towers, were earning at that time a base salary of about $30,000, which, with overtime, brought their average earnings to about $34,000. They could retire from their demanding jobs at age fifty with a minimum of twenty years of service. The union's first demand on the Reagan Administration was for a $73,000 salary and a thirty-two-hour workweek. PATCO soon scaled back the salary demand to $60,000.

The Reagan Administration offered PATCO an 11.4 percent pay hike, far below the union demand, but far more than the new Republican administration was prepared to offer any other federal union. PATCO leaders approved the offer, but the rank and file rejected it and the leaders quickly sided with the members. On August 3, 1981, more than two-thirds of the nation's 17,500 air traffic controllers walked off their jobs.

The Reagan Administration threatened to dismiss the strikers if they did not return to work within forty-eight hours. Only 1,000 went back to work, leaving 11,000 on the picket lines and out of work. From his California ranch, Reagan said, "There is a law that federal unions cannot strike against their employers, the people of the United States. What they did was terminate their own employment by quitting."

The dispute between PATCO and the federal government is a vivid example of the conflict that can emerge when public sector labor and management don't agree. This chapter explores the delicate relationship between public employee unions and public administrators.

DECLINE, TRANSFORMATION, OR REFORMATION?

The decline, transformation, or perhaps reformation of public sector unionism occurs within the context of our changing political culture. With the decline of the middle classes, lack of real wage increases, and a growing number of high-income families and those below the poverty line, the U.S. political economy is increasingly becoming more segregated into the wealthy and the poor. The decline of trade unions, the greater numbers of women in the work force, the loss of manufacturing jobs to overseas workers, and the growing immigration are blamed for our country's variety of woes. Higher wages, lower taxes, job-training, barriers to foreign trade, and recruitment of the poor by businesses are suggested ways to end trends toward economic disparity.[1]

Unions in the United States originally arose to combat the terrible work and wage conditions of the early *Industrial Revolution.* After the Great Depression of the 1930s, organized labor, which then existed only in the private sector, was thriving and calling for macroeconomic policies advocating high employment and high wages. Since then, membership in public sector unions such as teachers' and fire fighters' unions has grown, while unionism in general is declining.

Public opinion surveys that span fifty years show a major transformation in labor union membership demographics and politics. A mere 33 percent of union members had average or above average incomes in the mid-1930s, compared to 52 percent of nonunion households. In 1993, 53 percent of union members had average or above average incomes, compared with 40 percent of nonunionists. Only 32 percent of union members had at least attended college in the mid-1930s, with 6 percent being college graduates. The figures have increased in 1993, with 42 percent having at least attended college and 19 percent being college graduates.[2]

The Bureau of Labor Statistics reports that membership in labor unions increased to 16.6 million in 1993 from 16.4 million in 1992. The increase in union membership followed fourteen consecutive years of decline. The increase matched the overall increase in the labor force and labor union share remained steady at almost 16 percent.

The largest gain in union membership was in government employees, the most unionized sector, which increased from 37 percent to 38 percent. The demographic group most likely to be unionized are working men aged forty-five to sixty-four, 27 percent of whom are unionized.[3] Public sector unionism is a product of the Great Society of the 1960s and has changed the overall labor movement emphasis from high employment and high wages to an emphasis on redistribution of society's economic resources. Today, public sector unions represent a larger percentage of the U.S. labor movement than ever before.

Table 6-1 shows that in a dramatic forty-three-year period, 1953 to 1996, private union membership ebbed while public unions experienced meteoric membership increases. This enhanced importance of public sector unionism as a component of the overall U.S. labor movement is leading to increased demands for more government intervention in the economic arena.

Leo Troy, in describing the rise and fall of American trade unions from Franklin Roosevelt to Ronald Reagan, argues that organized labor has changed its philosophy of "more" for its clients to a philosophy of "more government intervention" in America's political economy.[4] Troy claims a philosophical division between America's private sector and public sector unions concerning the definition and implementation of "more government intervention" in our economy and society. Private sector unions wish to enhance their clients' incomes. Public sector unions, says Troy, argue for raising taxes so that client salaries may be increased.

TABLE 6–1 Private and Public Sector Membership and Density in the U.S., 1953–1996

Membership (000's)			Density (percent)	
Year	Private	Public	Private	Public
1953	15,540.2	789.8	35.7 (a)	11.6
1962	14,731.2	2,161.9	31.6	24.3
1970	16,978.3 (a)	4,012.0	29.1	32.0
1973	16,803.5	5,077.8	26.6	37.0
1976	16,166.8	5,980.3	25.1	40.2 (a)
1983	13,142.6	5,410.7	17.8	34.4
1989	10,520.0	6,422.0	12.4	36.7
1991	9,909.0	6,627.0	11.9	36.9
1994	9,620.0	7,094.0(a)	10.9	38.7
1996	9,410.0	7,829.7	10.0	37.6

(a) denotes historic peak.

See *Unions in Transition: Entering the Second Century* (1986), edited by Seymour Martin Lipset, page 82.

Sources: Leo Troy and Neil Sheflin, *Union Sourcebook* (West Orange, N.J.: IRDIS, 1985); Bureau of the Census, U.S. Department of Commerce *Statistical Abstract of the United States* 1991 (Washington, DC: 1991), 425; Bureau of Labor Statistics, U.S. Department of Labor, *Employment and Earnings* (Washington, DC: January, 1995), 216; *Statistical Abstract of the United States* 1997 (Washington, DC: 1997), 440. Reprinted by permission of Leo Troy.

Troy claims that public sector unions and private sector unions are on a collision course. "On one hand, private sector unions want government to vigorously apply macroeconomic policies to stimulate economic growth and avoid depression; on the other hand, public sector unions want a redistribution of the national income from the private to the public sector in the form of social services and transfer payments."[5]

Despite being larger than private sector unionism, public sector unionism is most likely in *transformation*. The rise of public sector organized labor activities in the 1960s and 1970s was followed by a leveling, or maturation, of such activities through the 1980s and into the 1990s.

With the growth of unionism in the 1970s, the challenges began to overshadow the benefits. Public employee organizations began to arouse increasing anxiety and alarm. The power of public sector unionism proved most powerful at the state and local levels. The significant and growing number of collective bargaining rights had not occurred simply through political pressures. Union leaders had become proficient in using more bargaining strategies.

One strategy was the "whipsaw." This stratagem calls for the union to make a breakthrough by scoring a special success in negotiating with a particular community or with a particular agency. Once the "breakthrough" is established, labor efforts to broaden the political front by seeking comparable concessions from other agencies and/or communities becomes easier.

The case of the professional air traffic controllers illustrates the potential for such developments. Not only did President Reagan stress his duty to ensure that the laws declaring public sector strikes illegal were enforced, but he also set a tone for labor management relations in general by establishing higher ground for the administration's "philosophical warfare" against labor. PATCO represented only 17,500 employees. The postal unions represented a work force of more than 500,000 persons. In taking a definitive position against the air controllers, Reagan sent organized labor a clear message. The postal unions subsequently settled their contract differences with management.[6]

A negative reaction against growing union power arose. It was catalyzed, if not caused, by the increasing financial strain that governments of all types, but especially those of the larger cities, were undergoing. Even before California's Proposition 13 signaled the start of taxpayer rebellion, Cleveland, Baltimore, Detroit, and other major cities had started to trim their work forces, despite strong resistance from municipal unions. Public and private unions may be in some decline and are not as strong as they once were, but neither show signs of extinction.

The United States is not unique in the decline of private sector unionism. Contrary to assertions of the "unique school," unionism in the private sectors of Canada and Western Europe has also declined and for the the same reason—structural changes in the labor market.[7] From a global perspective, unionism is not in a period of maturation; it is in decline throughout the world. Data from England, France, Italy, Japan, and West Germany imply similar trends toward maturation or decline.

A survey of union membership shows that about 15 percent of the active labor force in the United States were union members and while 38 percent of government workers were in unions, just a little over 10 percent of private sector workers were unionized. Blacks have the highest rate of unionization, as do workers aged thirty-five to sixty-four. Transportation, public utilities, and construction have the highest rates of union labor among industries.[8]

According to Troy, the development, and perhaps decline, of unionism in the United States is rather decisive and absolute, but Dwight Waldo provides a more comprehensive perspective for understanding the importance of public sector labor relations.

The concepts of public and private are very central in the conceptual and emotional structuring of the Western world. A great deal of our thought and action concerning government, law, morals and social institutions relates one way or another to this distinction, a distinction which the modern experience has taught us to make. But we need to appreciate public and private are not categories of nature; they are categories of history and culture, of law and custom. They are contextual and subject to change and redefinition.[9]

The U.S. peak year for the labor movement, measured in terms of "union density," came in 1953. Union density refers to the extent of union membership in the total work force. That year, trade union membership accounted for 25.9 percent of the labor force and 32.5 percent of nonfarm employment. By 1983, the density had decreased to 16.6 percent and 20.7 percent, respectively. Total union membership reached its zenith in 1975, but over a dozen years or so, from the mid-1970s to the mid-1980s, overall union membership declined by almost 4 million members.

David Lewin cites key factors for the rise in public unionism during the decline of overall unionism.[10] Among those factors at work from 1960 to 1975 were the passing of state laws permitting collective bargaining by state employees and the rapid growth in public employment.

During the late 1970s and throughout the 1980s, however, political and economic factors changed. From a political and economic environment that promoted employee unionism and collective bargaining rights, the current attitude emphasizes imposing penalties for illegal strikes by pubic employees. According to 1997 statistics, the share of workers who were union members continued to decline. Union members accounted for 14.1 percent of wage and salary employment in 1997, down from 14.6 percent in 1996. The union membership rate has fallen steadily from 20.1 percent in 1983, the first year for which comparable data are available. About three-fifths of the 16.1 million union members in 1997 were in private nonagricultural industries, where they constituted 9.8 percent of wage and salary employees. About 6.7 million union members worked in government (federal, state, and local), accounting for 37.2 percent of government employment. Among the private nonagricultural industries, transportation and public utilities had the highest unionization rate (26.0 percent), followed by construction (18.6 percent). Manufacturing and mining also had above-average unionization rates, at 16.3 and 13.9 percent, respectively. Among the occupational groups, the unionization was highest among those working in protective service jobs (39.9 percent). This group includes many government workers such as police officers and firefighters.[11]

Troy, Distinguished Professor of Economics at Rutgers University, Newark, calls private sector unionism *"Old Unionism"* and public, or government, sector unionism the *"New Unionism."* The Old Unionism shares about 7 percent of the nonfarm labor market, the percentage it had at the start of the twentieth century. While the Old Unionism is in decline, the New Unionism continues to expand. In the first year of the Clinton presidency, New Unionism rose nearly 5.5 percent, or 370,000, to in excess of 7 million members. The New Unionism is more widely distributed across the country than the Old Unionism ever was.

According to Troy, public, or government, sector unionism constitutes attempts to "organize the organized." The most organized of full-time public employees are fire protection (65 percent), teachers (58 percent), police (54 percent), and sanitation (50 percent). Why is Old Unionism in a permanent state of decline? Markets produce structural changes in labor arrangements. The shift from a goods-dominated to a service-dominated labor market assists the transformation. Increasing substitution of "high tech" for traditional manufacturing accompanies the decline of Old Unionism.

Competition abhors monopoly. State and local governments account for the bulk of public employees. As these governments extend their encouragement of unionization and bargaining, the disparities in the strength of the New and Old Unionism will grow. Troy states that a great potential exists for the unionization of state and local government employees.

PUBLIC SECTOR UNIONS

Teacher Unions:

American Federation of Teachers/National Education Association
American Association of University Professors (AAUP)

Protective Services Unions:

International Association of Fire Fighters (IAFF)
Fraternal Order of Police (FOP)
Police Benevolent Association
Service Employees International Union (SEIU)

Local Transit Employee Unions:

Amalgamated Transit Union (ATU)
Transport Workers Union (TWU)
United Transportation Union (UTU)

State and Local Government Employee Unions:

American Federation of State, County, and Municipal Employees (AFSCME)

Assembly of Government Employees (AGE)

Source: Michael Ballot with contributions from Laurie Lichter-Heath, Thomas Kail, and Ruth Wang, *Labor-Management Relations in a Changing Environment* 2d ed. (New York: John Wiley & Sons, Inc., 1996), 474–478.

A state of permanent decline of Old Unionism (private sector model) is attributed to market competition, fundamental structural changes, and market "repeal" of the National Labor Relations Act. The NLRA states and defines the rights of employees to organize and to bargain collectively with their employees through representatives of their choosing. Union leadership and its supporters were late in recognizing the new environment confronting the Old Unionism.[12] The reform of labor relations and the steady increase in the number of labor unions show that Old Unionism is in a continuous decline and that New Unionism is rapidly taking over. Aside from profound changes in the structure of the labor market, New (public sector) Unionism, will also increase the strength of organized labor.[13]

MAJOR ISSUES IN STATE AND LOCAL GOVERNMENT LABOR RELATIONS

Collective bargaining has been used by state and local government employees since the 1960s. Arguments questioning collective bargaining for government employees include the following:

- *Sovereign power and public accountability.* Many believe that public sector collective bargaining infringes on the sovereign power of the state. Unions directly affect the sovereign power of the state to determine service levels of different programs (police, fire, library, sanitation, for example) and rules and regulations (production, benefits, vacation days, for example). The government unions, as private interest groups, would unduly influence public, or communitywide, decisions. The union seeks to increase the pay and benefits of its members. Unionized municipal departments are likely to have higher expenditures (budgets) than nonunionized departments. Also, private interest groups, in this case government unions, are not accountable to the public or community. Elected officials are accountable to the electorate or the populace that elects them. The electorate may vote the government officials out of office, but not government workers.

- *Fiscal responsibility and public budgeting.* But public sector unions soon encountered fiscal realities. In the 1960s and 1970s, union demands caused state, county, and municipal budgets to inflate, raising taxes, especially property taxes. States began to impose tax and/or spending limits. Elected officials operated with fixed budgets and small reserves. Union monetary demands were curtailed. These fiscal constraints slowed the growth of public sector unionism. Funds were reallocated, employment was cut, and citizens faced lower levels of public services.

- *Public goods and monopoly.* Government as a monopoly supplier is of concern to the citizenry. Government is the only supplier of certain public goods (police and fire protection, for example). In elementary and secondary education, public schools significantly outnumber private schools and maintain "near-monopoly" powers. Therefore, a strike or work stoppage would completely interrupt the provision of these services to customer citizens. However, citizens are not without redress. They may flee the city, county, or state if they are not pleased with the level of government services provided and/or the taxes charged to support that level of services. This flight reduces the community's tax base, causing reductions in the level of services provided by government.

- *The right to strike.* If government is monopolist and, therefore, supplier of essential services, strikes by government employees may endanger the health and safety of the population. The tasks of police, fire, and sanitation workers are perhaps more paramount than the functions of school teachers and transit workers. In the public sector, the costs are primarily on the users of the service. However, with government employees, the users, or citizens, are also the employers. Strikes are legal for some government workers in twelve states: Alaska, California, Hawaii, Idaho, Illinois, Minnesota, Montana, Ohio, Oregon, Pennsylvania, Vermont, and Wisconsin. In 24 states, strikes are either not covered by public sector labor relations laws or are prohibited. But no sanctions or penalties are specified for striking in violation of antistrike laws. Fifteen states penalize striking workers severely, including their employee association or union.[14]

(Near-monopolies, however, occur in the private sector as well. If employees of private airline companies went on strike, such actions would not only inconvenience millions of travelers but could cost the U.S. economy billions of dollars. When UPS [United Parcel Service] employees walked out, the USPS [United States Postal Service] could not adequately handle the overflow of packages. If employees of private sector utilities agreed on a work stoppage, telephone, gas, electricity, and cable television services might come to a sudden halt.)

When Collective Bargaining Fails

In those cases where a stalemate is reached and the bargaining process breaks down, alternatives are available for avoiding a strike.

A device that is sometimes used when labor-management negotiations flounder is *mediation*. The mediator, or in some cases mediators, help carry out negotiations between the disputing parties. They may group both sides around a table and try to find ways to open previously entrenched positions or to point out possibilities for conciliation. When conflicts among the parties push disputes beyond negotiated solutions, the mediator may even put the two sides in separate rooms and run from room to room in a continuing effort to break the deadlock. Some jurisdictions authorize fact-finders to shift to mediation when their recommendations have failed to dissolve the differences separating the parties involved.

Mediation is an art. According to one experienced practitioner, a good mediator should:

- have a good sense of timing, knowing when to advise each side on when to make each move;
- avoid relieving the parties themselves of responsibility to solve the dispute;
- be able to distinguish the power contest between the negotiating parties from internal power struggles (such as union leaders fearful of losing face with their members); and
- avoid passing on the merits of the respective positions.[15]

Another alternative is *fact-finding*. Under this process, an individual or, more frequently, a mutually acceptable panel is set up to review the disputed issues and make recommendations. These recommendations are not binding, but if the fact-finding machinery has been properly constituted, and if its analysis of the facts is accurate, both sides will be under a good deal of pressure to accept its suggestions.

Neither mediation nor fact-finding assures a peaceful settlement to a labor dispute. For that type of guarantee we must turn to a third alternative, *interest arbitration*. This device differs from the other two in one crucial respect: it produces a definite decision and usually one that is binding on both sides. When binding arbitration has been agreed upon, the arbitrator's word is final and there is no further appeal.

BARGAINING HOMILIES

Be sure that you have set clear objectives on every bargaining item and that you understand on what ground the objectives were established.

Do not hurry.

When in doubt, caucus.

Be well prepared with firm data support for clearly identified objectives.

Always strive to keep some flexibility in your position; don't get yourself out on a limb.

Do not concern yourself with only what the other party says and does; find out why. Remember that economic motivation is not the only explanation for the other party's conduct and actions.

Respect the importance of face saving for the other party.

Constantly be alert to the real intents of the other party, with respect not only to goals, but also to priorities.

Be a good listener.

Build a reputation for being fair but firm.

Learn to control your emotions; don't panic. Use emotions as a tool, not an obstacle.

Be sure as you make each bargaining move that you know its relationship to all other moves.

Measure each move against your objectives.

Pay close attention to the wording of every clause negotiated; words and phrases are often the source of grievances.

Remember that collective bargaining negotiations are by their nature part of a comprehensive process.

There is no such thing as having all the pie.

Learn to understand people and their personalities; it may mean a payoff during negotiations.

Consider the impact of present negotiations on negotiations in future years.

Source: *Collective Bargaining by Objectives: A Positive Approach* (Englewood Cliffs, NJ: Prentice-Hall, Inc., 1977), p. 150. Reprinted by permission of Reed C. Richardson.

If arbitration is not accepted by either party at the outset, it does not guarantee a peaceful resolution, but it is rarely used without such prior agreement. One typical way of going about setting up arbitration is for each side to choose a representative and for the two representatives to choose a third member of what then becomes an arbitration panel.

Administrators tend to view third-party proceedings such as fact-finding, mediation, and arbitration with some suspicion. While they recognize that such devices help considerably to avoid strikes, they often feel that they result in decisions injurious from a management perspective. Third parties have nothing at stake except their own future arbitration or mediation business. They show a tendency, it is felt, to split the issue down the middle, with perhaps some leaning toward the labor side. Some administrators question not only the leaning toward labor but also whether most disputes should automatically be split down the middle in any case. They feel many issues do not lend themselves to that type of decision. In any case, management loses control in such proceedings, and decisions are made by those who cannot be fully aware of all their implications, and who, in any case, do not have to live with them.

Unionists have tended to look more favorably on third-party intervention. They have particularly favored arbitration. As a fire fighters' union official once expressed it, without compulsory arbitration in the background, collective bargaining for employees becomes collective begging.[16]

COLLECTIVE BARGAINING FOR FEDERAL EMPLOYEES

The Federal Service Labor-Management Relations Statute, Title VII of the Civil Service Reform Act of 1978, allows nonpostal federal employees to bargain collectively through labor organizations of their choice and thereby participate with agency management in the development of personnel policies and practices and other decisions that affect their working lives.[17] The 1970s–1990s saw the federal labor-management relations program evolve from a simple executive order that provided for consultation between agency management and employee organizations to a formal collective bargaining program established by law.

The program is enforced by an independent administrative agency, the Federal Labor Relations Authority (FLRA), as well as by the federal courts. The latest available data from the Office of Personnel Management (OPM) shows that about 1.3 million federal employees, or 60 percent of the total nonpostal federal work force, were represented by unions. They were represented by 101 labor organizations in 2,266 bargaining units.

The Lloyd-LaFollette Act of 1912 established the right of federal employees to belong to labor organizations as long as the organizations did not impose a duty on employees to engage in or assist in a strike against the government, but it was not until 1962, when President Kennedy issued *Executive Order 10988*, that a federal labor-management relations program was officially established.

The order was the result of a presidential task force study that found that 33 percent of federal employees, mostly in the postal service and among blue-collar workers, belong to employee organizations. Since they lacked guidance, the various agencies of the government had proceeded on widely varying courses in dealing with these organizations. Some, such as the Tennessee Valley Authority and various units of the Department of Interior, had engaged in close to full-scale collective bargaining with the trade unions that represented their employees, but most had done little or nothing.

Among other provisions, Executive Order 10988 recognized the right of federal employees to join, or refrain from joining, employee organizations and established procedures for granting recognition to federal employee organizations. These organizations were given the right to consult or negotiate with agencies on matters that concerned working conditions and personnel policies within the limits of applicable federal laws and regulations.

Certain other matters, including the agency's mission, its budget, its organization and assignment of personnel, and the technology of performing its work were deemed "management's rights" and, therefore, nonnegotiable. The order also allowed individual agencies to establish procedures to deal with grievances, appeals, and negotiation impasses, but it specifically precluded strikes or binding arbitration as means of resolving such disputes. Arbitration hearings by private arbitrators were permitted for employee grievances so long as the arbitrators' decisions were advisory and not binding on agencies.

Executive Order 10988 provided for a variety of union recognition policies. The percentage of employees supporting the union in the bargaining unit determined the type of recognition.

- *Exclusive recognition.* A union had to show that it represented at least 10 percent of the employees in the respective unit. The union then had to be chosen by a majority of the employees of the unit to be their representative.
- *Formal recognition.* A union had to show it represented 10 to 50 percent of the unit employees. If the union could show that 10 to 50 percent of the unit employees belonged to the union, a union had to be consulted by the employer-agency on personnel matters.
- *Informal recognition.* This status was granted if less than 10 percent of the unit employees were members of the union. However, the employer-agency had no duty or obligation to meet, consult, or negotiate with the union.[18]

In 1969, a review of the program by an interagency study committee indicated that the policies of Executive Order 10988 had brought about more democratic management of the work force and better employee-management cooperation, and that negotiation and consultation had produced improvement in a number of personnel policies and working conditions. The review also found that union representation of employees in exclusive bargaining units had expanded greatly to include 52 percent of the total federal work force subject to the order.

As a result of the study committee's recommendations, *Executive Order 11491* was issued on October 29, 1969. The new order retained the basic principles and objectives underlying Executive Order 10988 and added a number of fundamental changes in the overall labor-management relations structure. A Federal Labor Relations Council (FLRC), composed of the chairman of the Civil Service Commission, the director of the Office of Management and Budget, and the secretary of Labor, was established as a central body to administer the program and make final decisions on policy questions and adjudicate three types of labor management disputes:

1. negotiability appeals;
2. exceptions to arbitration awards; and

3. appeals of decisions by the assistant secretary of Labor for Labor-Management Relations on unfair labor practice and representation cases. Although the Federal Service Labor Management Relations Statute was modeled after the National Labor Relations Act applied to the private sector, it also carried over many policies and approaches of the executive order program. As a result, federal labor relations bargaining is different from labor-management relations programs in the private sector in several ways:

- *"Bread and butter" issues,* such as wages, fringe benefits, and many other issues relating to hiring, firing, promoting, and retaining employees, which are the focus of private sector bargaining, usually cannot be negotiated in federal contracts. Since the first executive order, federal sector bargaining has been limited to the way personnel policies, practices, and procedures are implemented.
- *Traditional bargaining incentives* (i.e., strikes and lockouts) are prohibited.
- *"Agency shop"* or *"fair share" representation fees* are prohibited. Under the federal program, employees are entitled to select a union to represent them, but they cannot be compelled to join or pay a fee for the representation that the union is required to provide.

In 1991, the U.S. General Accounting Office conducted a large-scale survey of those involved in public sector labor relations concerning the effectiveness of the federal labor-management relations program. Among those surveyed were officials responsible for program operations in federal agencies, leaders of federal employee unions, and neutral parties, including current and former officials of the Federal Labor Relations Authority (FLRA), and other third-party agencies, arbitrators, and academics.[19]

Agency officials represented the Departments of Defense, Air Force, Navy, Health and Human Services, Labor, Transportation, Veterans Affairs, the General Services Administration, Government Printing Office, Internal Revenue Service, and Immigration and Naturalization Service. Union officials included presidents of the three largest federal unions—the American Federation of Government Employees, the National Treasury Employees Union, and the National Federation of Federal Employees. Neutrals included six incumbent and former FLRA officials, including the chairperson, general counsel, a regional director, and three former chairpersons.

GAO's work was accomplished in two parts. First, GAO interviewed thirty experts in federal labor relations to get their views on the state of the program. Next, using the information gathered in these interviews, GAO developed a questionnaire to survey union and agency representatives involved in day-to-day program operations at federal facilities throughout the country to obtain their perspectives on the federal labor-management relations program. GAO asked union and agency representatives to evaluate various components of the program, such as collective bargaining, dispute resolution procedures, and labor management cooperative efforts. The questionnaire sample consisted of 510 agency representatives and 664 union representatives.

In the end, the GAO report called for a major overhaul of policies and processes governing federal labor-management relations, providing a new framework that

- motivates labor and management to form productive relationships to improve the public service;
- makes collective bargaining meaningful;
- improves the dispute resolution processes; and
- is compatible with innovative human resource management practices that emphasize employee involvement, teambuilding, and labor-management cooperation.

Under a draft plan for "reinventing government," President Clinton issued *Executive Order 12871* on October 1, 1993, which created the National Partnership Council establishing a framework for a new era in labor-management relations. Under the leadership of Vice President Al Gore, the federal government changed its thirty-year history of tense, sometimes bitter, labor-management relations by treating unions as a partner.

According to the report, the council proposes statutory changes required to make labor-management partnership a reality. The council stresses joint problem-solving approaches for managers, supervisors, and union officials.

Robert M. Tobias, president of the National Treasury Employees Union, stated: "In my mind, it's the first time an administration has accepted the fact that unions have a role to play in the creation of personnel policies and practices and in helping to create a more efficient and effective government."

As part of its recommendations for changing the workplace, the Gore proposal advocates cutting back on the number of managers in government. The council report stated, without specifying how many positions will be eliminated, "We no longer will need 285,000 separate supervisory staff and 585,000 systems control staff. Some employees may view such pruning as threatening—to their jobs or their chances for promotion. But we do not seek to throw people out of work." the council's report noted. The report referred to separate administration proposals to downsize the federal government by attrition and offer "buyouts" of up to $25,000 for workers who will voluntarily depart.

Bruce Moyer, executive director of the Federal Managers Association, concluded that "downsizing throughout the government work force is inevitable, including the management and supervisory ranks. If agencies are to succeed," Moyer added, "they will need to bring managers and supervisors into the reengineering process that rethinks what the work of the agency is and how it must get done. This cannot be accomplished by executive fiat; it will require the special talents and commitment of all managers and supervisors throughout the government."

The number of managers in the federal government will be reduced from a ratio of 1 to 7 to 1 to 15.

THE "WHO, WHAT, WHERE, AND HOW" OF UNFAIR LABOR PRACTICES

If either labor or management fail to perform their obligations to each other, an unfair labor practice (ULP) charge may be filed. A ULP charge may also be filed if either labor or management interferes with the rights each has been given under labor laws. Employees may also protect their rights under labor laws by filing ULP charges against labor or managment.

For example, it is illegal for agency management to threaten or retaliate against employees for seeking union representation or refuse to provide union information necessary for the union to fulfill its representational responsibilities. Similarly, unions may not try to influence management to discipline employees who did not join the union or refuse to represent employees because they are not a union member. Neither an agency nor a union may refuse to bargain with the other in good faith.

Although individuals and agencies may file ULP charges, the vast majority of charges in the federal sector are filed by unions. Historically, approximately 95 percent of ULP charges are filed by unions and less than 5 percent are filed by employees and management. Once a charge has been filed, the Federal Labor Relations Authority (FLRA)'s Office of General Council (OGC)—in the FLRA's Regional Offices—investigates charges of ULP. The OGC employs a variety of innovative alternative dispute resolution techniques to resolve the charges—without litigation. During the 1990s, approximately 89 percent of all ULP charges filed were either withdrawn, dismissed, or settled at this stage.

For those charges that are meritorious and have not been resolved at the preliminary stages of the process, the OGC issues a ULP complaint. The case is then prosecuted by the OGC in a trial before the FLRA's Office of Administrative Law Judges (ALJ), appointed by the Authority. On an annual basis, an average of 88 percent of cases for which a ULP complaint was issued result in settlement without a hearing.

After the trial, the ALJ decides whether a ULP was committed and issues a written Decision and Recommended Order. An ALJ decision may be appealed to the Authority by any party. If an appeal is not filed with the Authority, the ALJ's decision becomes final. On appeal, the Authority may affirm, modify, or reverse the ALJ's Decision and Recommended Order in whole or in part. The Authority's decision may be appealed to the appropriate federal court of appeals.

Source: See unfair labor practices. Federal Labor Relations Authority, 607 14th Street, NW, Washington, DC 20424. Telephone 202-482-6540. Web site: www.flra.gov.

The proposals offered by the National Partnership Council expand the role of unions in the federal workplace but alter some of the rules that affect individual workers. Employees would have more of a voice in how work is performed and would help determine what performance expectations should be set for their jobs. Workers would participate in shaping bonus and award programs. Management would be able to offer nonmonetary awards, such as a day off.

The council proposals would lead to significant changes in how jobs are classified, influencing the pattern of pay and promotion opportunities afforded workers. In many cases under the proposals, employees would be able to move up and transfer jobs faster than they currently can.

The system for hiring employees was changed, with greater control placed in the hands of agencies rather than the Office of Personnel Management. New hires would probably spend more time on probation and a streamlined process for firing workers may be introduced. In their discussion of the report, several council members stressed the importance of a "good government standard" proposed for labor-management bargaining.

In the report, the council endorsed what it calls "a workable conceptual framework" that would phase in over four years an increased number of topics—including the right to hire, assign, demote, or lay off employees—that would be subject to bargaining. Council member Alice Rivlin, director of the Office of Management and Budget, stated that the standard "emphasizes that it is not the relation between labor and management that matters so much. It is how we jointly serve the citizens of the country and the taxpayers."[20]

CONFLICTS IN STATE CIVIL SERVICE
AND COLLECTIVE BARGAINING SYSTEMS

Joel Douglas, professor of public administration at City University of New York, and arbitrator of government employee relations, explores the impacts of the emergence of public-sector labor relation systems on the legal structure and design of state civil service systems. According to Douglas, many jurisdictions have developed "dual personnel systems" with civil service and collective bargaining provisions existing side by side.

Collective bargaining and state civil service merit systems often contradict each other. As of 1990, twenty-eight states had enacted public sector collective bargaining legislation covering state employees. Under collective bargaining, twenty-eight statutes allow state employees new forms of governance where bilateral negotiations regulate the terms and conditions of their employment. Collective bargaining is used by 6.3 million public employees, accounting for 37 percent of the public sector work force, in these states. Public sector unions were largely responsible for passage of collective bargaining legislation. Public sector collective bargaining includes: (1) mandatory subjects that must be negotiated, (2) prohibited subjects that may not be negotiated, and (3) permissive subjects that may be negotiated.

In the twenty-eight states where collective bargaining is allowed, there are four categories of statutory relationship between collective bargaining legislation and civil service systems. In the first category, legislation guarantees the continuation of, and adherence to, merit systems. Protection of merit system principles and systems varies from broad-scale philosophical encouragement to requirements for civil service commissioners to be politically neutral. Alaska, California, Maine, New Hampshire, New Jersey, Vermont, and Washington have civil service merit systems protected, in some form, by legislation. In the second type of statutory relationship civil service merit systems may not be within the scope of bargaining, but they are statutorily protected by designating certain topics as under their exclusive domain. Negotiation is limited and appointments, conduct of exams, grading of examinations, grievances, hiring and selection, performance rating, position classification, promotion, and retirement are identified in one or more states as legislatively excluded from the bargaining process. These subjects are placed under the exclusive jurisdiction of civil service merit systems. Connecticut, Iowa, Kansas, New Hampshire, New York, Ohio, and Wisconsin enacted legislation reserving specific subjects to civil service merit systems and restricting the scope of bargaining.

Still other states have statutorily selected a third approach: protecting collective bargaining agreements that supersede existing civil service merit systems. The labor contract is presumed superior and preempts existing civil service law. Civil service is deemed inferior to the strength of public sector union politics. Several states, such as Florida, Hawaii, and Illinois, limit contract supremacy to certain subjects.

Finally, eleven states are management-rights states where topics are removed from the scope of bargaining and are declared to be a management right that is not subject to the collective bargaining process. This method attempts to statutorily protect civil service and limit subjects negotiable by collective bargaining. Kansas, Minnesota, Montana, and Nebraska follow this approach.

Labor relations systems supersede but do not replace existing civil service merit systems. State legislatures fail to terminate procedures for civil service merit systems, yet they have not successfully integrated labor relations systems with civil service merit systems, resulting in numerous problems. Dual personnel systems develop in many jurisdictions. Douglas reveals that dual personnel systems are commonplace, but they are not recommended. Collective bargaining and civil service merit systems do not blend well. Civil service merit systems flourish where there is a statutory commitment to merit, subjects have been removed from bargaining and reserved to merit systems, and management rights are designated and are not subject to bargaining.[21]

The structure of civil service and labor relations legislation is consistent, in as far as civil service statutes predate collective bargaining laws in every state. The silence of legislatures enhances the scope of negotiations and allows issues to be litigated. Confusion exists, however, over primary and concurrent jurisdiction, scope of bargaining, and election of forum as bilateralism replaces unilateralism in public sector workplace decision making. *Table 6-2* depicts the status of labor relations legislation in all fifty states.

TABLE 6–2 Labor Relations Legislation for State Employees

State	Statute	Date
Alabama	No comprehensive statute	N/A
Alaska	Collective Bargaining in Public Employment Act	1972
Arizona	State Employees: Payroll Deductions Act	1983
Arkansas	State Employees: Payroll Deductions Act	1983
California	Collective Bargaining: State Employee Organizations Act	1971
Colorado	State Employees' Grievance Procedure Act	1973
Connecticut	State Employee Relations Act	1965
Delaware	Public Employees' Right to Bargain and Organize Collectively Act	1965
Florida	Public Employee Relations Act	1974
Georgia	Strikes by State Employees Act	1982
Hawaii	Collective Bargaining in Public Employment Act	1970
Idaho	No comprehensive statute	N/A
Illinois	Public Labor Relations Act	1983
Indiana	No comprehensive statute	N/A
Iowa	Public Employment Relations Act	1974
Kansas	Public Employee Labor Relations Act	1971
Kentucky	No comprehensive statute	N/A
Louisiana	Public Employees: Dues Checkoff	1966
Maine	State Employees Labor Relations Act	1969
Maryland	No comprehensive statute	N/A
	State Employees' Grievance Procedure	1977
Massachusetts	Collective Bargaining by Public Employees Act	1973
	State Employee Grievance Procedures	1965
Michigan	Public Employment Relations Act	1978
Minnesota	Public Employment Labor Relations Act	1971
Mississippi	No comprehensive statute	N/A
Missouri	Collective Bargaining by Public Employees Act	1967
Montana	Collective Bargaining for Public Employees Act	1973
Nebraska	Public Employees Bargaining Act	1967
Nevada	State Employees: Checkoff	1981
New Hampshire	Public Employee Labor Relations Act	1975
New Jersey	Employer-Employee Relations Act	1968
	Public Employees: Dues Deduction	1981

TABLE 6-2 Labor Relations Legislation for State Employees *(continued)*

State	Statute	Date
New Mexico	Labor Management Relations in the Classified Service Act	1978
New York	Public Employees' Fair Employment Act	1967
North Carolina	Public Employee Membership in Labor Unions Act	1981
	State Employees: Checkoff	1981
North Dakota	No comprehensive statute	N/A
	Public Employee Dispute Mediation Act	1969
Ohio	Public Employee Bargaining Act	1983
Oklahoma	No comprehensive statute	N/A
Oregon	Collective Bargaining Public Employment Act	1975
Pennsylvania	Public Employee Relations Act	1970
Rhode Island	Collective Bargaining by State Employees Act	1958
South Carolina	State Employees' Grievance Procedure	1982
South Dakota	Public Employees' Unions Act	1969
Tennessee	No comprehensive statute	N/A
	State Employees' Dues Deductions	1980
Texas	Public Employee Collective Bargaining Ban Act	1947
	Public Employees: Checkoff	1967
Utah	No comprehensive statute	N/A
	State Employees' Grievance Procedure	1979
	Public Employees: Checkoff	1969
Vermont	State Employee Labor Relations Act	1969
Virginia	Strikes by State Employees Act	1970
	State Employees' Grievance Procedure	1982
Washington	Public Employees' Collective Bargaining Act	1967
	Union Security Agreements-State Employees Act	1977
West Virginia	State Employees: Checkoff	1982
Wisconsin	State Employment Labor Relations Act	1966
Wyoming	No comprehensive statute	N/A

IMPACTS OF LABOR LAWS ON PUBLIC SECTOR LABOR RELATIONS

The impacts of law in public sector unionization are hotly debated. Richard B. Freeman and Casey Ichniowski offer five broad conclusions about the role of labor law in the rise of collective bargaining in the public sector.[22]

1. *The legal environment is critical in determining whether public sector employees bargain collectively with their workers.*

   The probability that a municipal department is governed by a collective contract is enhanced by favorable state public sector labor laws. According to Freeman and Robert G. Valletta, "state public sector laws are a prime determinant of the likelihood that municipal workers are covered by collective bargaining and have a moderate impact on wages and employment of public sector workers."[23] The enactment of laws mandating arbitration results in nearly all police departments bargaining contractually for their workers.[24] Favorable public sector laws likely bring substantial growth in the extent of bargaining coverage.[25]

2. *Economic benefits and costs do not readily explain the timing of public sector labor laws.*

   Public sector labor laws call for legalization of union activities, requiring managers to "meet and confer" with unions, require managers to bargain with unions, and mandate arbitration or certain final closure mechanisms to provide a contract.[26] A review of comparative state literature does not explain why certain states enact laws earlier rather than later.[27]

   By the mid-1980s, eight states had no legislative policy for laws governing collective bargaining rights for state employees; eight states prohibited bargaining; six states permitted but did not obligate the employer to negotiate with the union; four states granted the union the right to present proposals and/or meet with the employer; and in twenty-four states, the employer had the duty to bargain with the union. Alabama, Georgia, Kentucky, Nevada, North Carolina, Tennessee, Texas, and Virginia prohibited state employees from collective bargaining.

   By the mid-1980s, eight states had no legislative policy governing collective bargaining rights for police; four states prohibited bargaining; nine states permitted but did not obligate the employer to negotiate with the union; two states allowed the union the right to present proposals and/or meet with the employer; and twenty-seven states mandated that the employer had the duty to bargain with the union. Alabama, North Carolina, Tennessee, and Virginia prohibited police from collective bargaining.

   By the mid-1980s, three states had no legislative policy governing collective bargaining rights by teachers; four states prohibited bargaining; twelve states permitted but did not obligate the employer to negotiate with the union; one state allowed the union the right to present proposals and/or meet with the employer; and thirty states mandated that the employer had the duty to bargain with the union. Alabama, Georgia, North Carolina, and Virginia prohibited teachers from collective bargaining.[28]

3. *Public sector laws favorable to collective bargaining raise wages in nonunion as well as union departments but have substantial adverse employment consequences only for nonunion departments.*

Laws enhance the bargaining power of unions and affect economic outcomes and alter management decision making in both union and nonunion departments. Public sector union members in states favoring collective bargaining receive 6 percent higher salaries than those workers in municipal departments in states with unfavorable laws. Salaries of nonunion municipal workers are approximately 3 percent higher in states with comprehensive public sector labor laws than in other states, implying that nonunion municipal employers pay better salaries because of concerns that their employees too may organize.[29]

4. *Among states that obligate employers to bargain, wages are no higher with compulsory arbitration than with other dispute resolution mechanisms, whereas wages are noticeably higher with strike-permitted laws.*

Potential arbitration creates an environment in which municipalities accept high negotiated settlements as public sector officials fear arbitration processes will result in even higher wages. Everything else being equal, municipalities in states with compulsory arbitration would pay more for comparable labor than municipalities in states requiring state employers to bargain with unions. Compulsory arbitration states would pay more for labor than duty-to-bargain states.

Arbitration impacts wages little in states that encourage bargaining, however. Evidence indicates that arbitration laws reduce strike rates. Although compulsory arbitration states do not differ noticeably from duty-to-bargain states, states that permit strikes pay between 2 and 9 percent higher salaries than states prohibiting strikes. In other words, strike-permitted state's laws raise pay; arbitration-permitted states' laws have effectively no impact on pay.[30]

5. *Arbitrators do not favor one side or the other nor respond greatly to the facts of a case when labor and management make "reasonable" proposals; rather, they tend to "split the difference."*

Arbitration occurs in a wide range of settings. Most involve a third party arbitrator or panel of arbitrators hearing and deciding how a dispute is to be resolved. Laws usually bind disputants to arbitration awards. "Conventional arbitrators tend to split the difference between the parties' final offers with little additional systematic reference to the facts of the case," states David Bloom.[31] Arbitrators weigh facts but do so differently, and because offers and facts are often unrelated, arbitrators "split the difference" when employers and employees propose alternatives that reflect diverse sets of facts. *Table 6-3* outlines the legal environment for state, local, police, fire fighters, and teachers in the fifty states.

The secret to handling all or most of the labor troubles that occur in the public sector is good management. Nearly all sides consider this the sine qua non of good labor relations, and mediocre management probably causes more labor trouble than militant union leadership. Many management people agree

TABLE 6–3 State Bargaining Legislation, 1992*

State	State	Local	Police	Fire Fighters	K–12 Teachers
Alabama	-	-	-	Y	-
Alaska	X	X	X	X	X
Arizona	-	-	-	-	-
Arkansas	-	-	-	-	-
California	Y	Yb	Yb	Yb	X
Colorado	-	-	-	-	-
Connecticut	X	X	X	X	X
Delaware	X	Xb	X	X	X
Florida	X	Xb	X	X	X
Georgia	-	-	-	Y	-
Hawaii	X	X	X	X	X
Idaho	-	-	-	X	X
Illinois	X	X	X	X	X
Indiana	-	-	-	-	X/Y
Iowa	X	X	X	X	X
Kansas	Y	Yb	Yb	Yb	X
Kentucky	-	-	X	X	-
Louisiana	-		-	-	-
Maine	X	X	X	X	X
Maryland	-	Xb	-	-	X
Massachusetts	X	X	X	X	X
Michigan	Ya	X	X	X	X
Minnesota	X/Y	X/Y	X/Y	X/Y	X/Y
Mississippi	-	-	-	-	-
Missouri	Y	Y	-	Y	-
Montana	X	X	X	X	X/Y
Nebraska	X	X	X	X	Y
Nevada	-	X	X	X	X
New Hampshire	X	X	X	X	X
New Jersey	X	X	X	X	X
New Mexico	X	X	X	X	X
New York	X	Xb	X	X	X
North Carolina	-	-	-	-	-
North Dakota	Yc	Xc	Yc	Yc	X
Ohio	X	X	X	X	X
Oklahoma	-	X	X	X	X

TABLE 6-3   State Bargaining Legislation, 1992* *(continued)*

State	State	Local	Police	Fire Fighters	K–12 Teachers
Oregon	X	Xb	X	X	X
Pennsylvania	X/Y	X/Y	X	X	X/Y
Rhode Island	X	X	X	X	X
South Carolina	-	-	-	-	-
South Dakota	X	X	X	X	X
Tennessee	-	-	-	-	X
Texas	-	-	Xb	Xb	-
Utah	-	-	-	-	-
Vermont	X	X	X	X	X
Virginia	-	-	-	-	-
Washington	X	X	X	X	X
West Virginia	Yd	Yd	Yd	Yd	Yd
Wisconsin	X	X	X	X	X
Wyoming	-	-	-	X	-

X: collective bargaining provisions;

Y: meet and confer provisions;

X/Y: collective bargaining on some issues; meet and confer on other issues.

a: Negotiations may be established under civil service regulations.

b: Local option permitted.

c: Meet and confer established by attorney general opinion.

*Most recent data available at publication date of this text.

Source: Richard C. Kearney, *Labor Relations in the Public Sector* 2d ed. (New York: Marcel Dekker, Inc., 1992), 70–71. Reprinted by permission of Marcel Dekker, Inc., New York, NY.

with this statement as well. Union excesses, say some, spring perhaps most often from managerial misdeeds and mistakes. The real key to achieving peace on the public labor front may lie in developing better policies and better administrators.

FUTURE OF PUBLIC SECTOR UNIONS: STAGNATION OR GROWTH?

The reasons for union prominence in the public sector include: (1) changes in the legal environment, (2) changes in public attitudes, and (3) changes in economic conditions. Recent changes in each of these areas will certainly affect the future of public sector unionism, as they have affected their course for the last thirty years.

The changes in the legal environment brought about the striking expansion in public sector union participation between 1960 and 1976. From 1976 through 1986 there was little or no growth in union expansion in the public sector. The proportion of government workers affiliated with unions or union-like organizations hovers unchanged at around 36 percent.

Changes in public attitudes toward unions paralleled the expansion of public sector union expansion between 1960 and 1976. By allowing public employees to bargain collectively, legislatures recognized that the sovereignty of state government was not threatened by union activities. The 1976–1986 period witnessed a consolidation of public unions. Public attitudes toward public sector unions became less favorable during this period.

Unlike private unions, the political power of public sector unions affects demand for government services, budgets, and outcomes of local elections. Growth in government employees and budgets results directly from citizen demands for increases in government services. Since 1986, the growth in citizen demand for public services has declined. The slowdown in the growth of income and urbanization and the aging of the baby-boom population are two reasons for the decline in demand.

Changes in economic conditions affected growth in public sector employees, programs, and budgets. In the 1960–1976 period, the gross national product averaged an annual rate increase of 8.1 percent, state and local government expenditures expanded at 10.7 percent, and state and local employment moved from 11.2 to 15.3 percent of total nonagricultural employment. When the economy slowed over the next decade and a half, the demand for public services naturally did likewise.

The future of public sector unionism rests on these same three factors. Changes in the legal environment, changes in public attitudes, and changes in economic conditions will shape the future of public sector unionism. Legislation and executive rulings will again be crucial. Union supporters advocate a uniform national law permitting government employees to join unions and requiring public sector employees to bargain collectively, but public support for unions has not grown. Women and part-time workers change the composition of the work force. Demographic trends may again influence the demand for public services, leading to more schools, teachers, and related public services. An increase in the number of school teachers will enhance the leverage of government workers. An increase in the number of elderly will proportionally increase the demand for government services. The demand for public services may be met through more privatization of government functions, but not all public services are suitable for private sector implementation[32]

In summary, the argument is made that unions are still needed to protect the worker. Evidence shows that as unions decline, the gap between executive and worker pay is growing. Instead of freeing the worker, automation has made it possible for management to expect even more from employees. Employee participation in management is still controlled by management or administration.[33]

SUMMARY

- Public sector unionism is a product of the Great Society of the 1960s and changed the overall labor movement emphasis from high employment and high wages to redistribution of society's economic resources.
- The decline, transformation, or perhaps reformation of public sector unionism occurs within the context of our changing political culture. Despite being larger than private sector unionism, public unionism is in *transition.* About 37 percent of government workers engage in collective bargaining. Future government unionization depends upon organized labor's ability to organize the unorganized.
- Unions [the positives] usually prevent strikes or shorten those that do occur. Union leaders much prefer to resolve disputes by negotiation. Public employee unions bring public sector problems before the public.
- Trade unionism [the negatives], according to its detractors, erodes the concept of government work as a public service. Unions perpetuate some of the worst features of personnel systems. Unions diffuse responsibility and make accountability more difficult to pinpoint. Unionization greatly increases the political involvement of public employees.
- In the public and private sectors, the fundamental role of unions is not merely to secure economic benefits. They are a means by which employees seek to avoid manipulation.
- Major issues in state and local government labor relations focus on the sovereign power of the state and public accountability of government-based unions, perceived pressures of public sector unions on fiscal and budgeting issues, government as the monopoly supplier of certain public goods, and the right of public sector employees to strike.
- When collective bargaining fails, alternatives for avoiding strikes include *mediation, fact-finding,* and *arbitration.*
- The increasing financial strain experienced by all levels of government in the 1980s brought on a reaction against growing union influence. While the rate of public employee union growth is leveling off or is perhaps in decline, government workers now constitute more than 37 percent of union members. As private sector union membership decreases, this proportion will increase.
- AFL-CIO private sector unions lost 165,000 members in 1990, while government unions, representing 37 percent of public employees, gained 150,000 members.
- "Bread and butter" issues usually cannot be negotiated in federal government contracts. Strikes, lockouts, and "agency shop" practices are prohibited in the public sector.
- Civil service statutes predate collective bargaining laws in every state. To determine the relationship between the potentially conflicting merit and collective bargaining systems, states have enacted statutes to specify the role of collective bargaining. Public sector collective bargaining includes:

(1) mandatory subjects that must be negotiated, (2) prohibited subjects that may not be bargained, and (3) permissive subjects that may be bargained.
- The percentage of organized full-time employees varies by type of government. Of all public sector employees, 37 percent are part of labor organizations.
- The legal environment, economic benefits and costs, favorable collective bargaining laws, compulsory arbitration, strike-permitted laws, and labor-management arbitrators account for many developments in the emergence of collective bargaining in the public sector.
- Explanations for union growth in the public sector include: (1) changes in the legal environment, (2) changes in public attitudes, and (3) changes in economic conditions.
- The major federal employee unions are: American Federation of Government Employees, National Air Traffic Controllers Association, National Association of Agriculture Employees, National Association of Government Employees, National Federation of Federal Employees, National Treasury Employees Union, National Weather Service Employees Organization, and United Power Trades Organization.
- Approximately thirty-five states, the District of Columbia, and the federal government permit some form of collective bargaining law for selected public sector workers. Prospects appear dim for public employee union leaders enhancing the power of collective bargaining laws in the remaining state legislatures and in the U.S. Congress.
- State legislatures have enacted employee organizations for fire fighters in thirty-eight states, for teachers in thirty-five states, for police officers and certain local workers in thirty-three states, and for state workers in twenty-eight states.
- The absolute prerequisite for good labor relations is good management.

The following story offers an interesting glimpse at the nuts and bolts of public sector union negotiations. While you're reading, try to see the situation from the viewpoints of both the union and the city.

CASE STUDY

Union Contract Negotiations in Springfield[34]

The city of Springfield began negotiations in June with the American Federation of State, County, and Municipal Employees local for a three-year contract. The city's negotiations were conducted by City Manager Adam Arbuthnot under guidelines recommended by the Labor Negotiations Committee of the City Council and approved by the full council. The union demanded an across-the-board wage hike of 10 percent and increased fringe benefits.

Progress in the negotiations and the positions of the union local were reported regularly to the committee and council over the next several months, and the council held three special meetings, each lasting more than two hours, to hear from department heads and to discuss wages and benefits. The council reviewed data on wage increases for the past five years and compared these rises to the cost-of-living index. The data revealed that nearly all employees had received pay hikes equal to, and in many instances exceeding, the rise in the cost of living during the period. Springfield's employees, according to statistics, had fared better than workers nationally, and the council considered that its past wage actions had been reasonable.

In determining the wage increase for employees in relation to the cost of living, the council decided that increases in benefits mandated by the federal government during the year should be considered. These included the city's share in the Social Security tax increase and unemployment compensation insurance premiums. The council also decided to take into consideration the employer's share of insurance premiums. It concluded that a wage increase for the next year should not exceed 4.59 percent for all employees.

The council was largely composed of small business managers who hired only a few employees. These managers believed they were familiar with pay and working conditions in the community and felt that city employees were adequately compensated in comparison with employees in the private sector. They were bolstered in this belief since turnover was small in nontechnical and semitechnical positions in city employment.

The city, however, was forced to modify its 4.59 percent limit on wage increases because of the union's firmness in its demands and continued rises in the monthly cost-of-living index. It increased the rate to 5.95 percent in August, to 6.3 percent in September, and, finally, to 6.5 percent in October. Council members believed 6.5 percent was a very reasonable offer in that fringe benefits (retirement, Social Security, workers' compensation, and unemployment compensation) would raise the de facto pay and benefits increases to 7.2 percent.

Council members acknowledged that the average cost-of-living index would exceed 7.5 percent but maintained that their offer was fair because last year the city had given a cost-of-living increase that exceeded the actual cost-of-living rise by 0.5 percent. In further justification, they maintained that the increases in the federally mandated Social Security tax and unemployment compensation tax plus health insurance cost increases raised benefits another 1 percent. The overall increase offered by the city (taking into consideration the proposed wage and benefits increase of 7.2 percent, the previous year's increase of 0.5 percent, and benefits increase of 1 percent) amounted to 8.7 percent.

By late October all issues between the city and union were tentatively resolved, except for the union's insistence on a 7.5 percent rather than the city's 6.5 percent wage increase. An impasse having been reached, the union filed a request for conciliation and fact-finding with the state labor commissioner. Upon his recommendation, a three-year agreement calling for a 7.0 percent increase for the next year and additional increases the next two years at the rate of increase in the cost of living was accepted by both parties and signed on December 19.

Meanwhile, a dispute began to develop over what seemed to be a minor matter— filling a vacancy in the Municipal Light Department—that was to upset the agreement. Two electric line workers (one the union steward and the other the secretary of the local) approached Mayor Thomas Wentwaller and asked to appear before the City Council to express employee concerns about employing an additional line worker. The line workers suggested that money could be made available for hiring better qualified workers by charging for services that the city had been previously providing at no cost to electricity users. The council approved their suggestion and imposed a new service charge that permitted a pay increase for line workers.

The council believed that the increase was made with the full knowledge of the union, since the two line workers were members and officers and the president was also a line worker. In the past the union had also left decisions on merit increases and individual wage adjustments to the city. The council thought this situation was no different from others in which adjustments had been made and no complaints had been filed.

Although there was some grumbling about this action among the rank and file of the union, it took no formal action until April when it filed a complaint with the state labor commissioner. It accused the city of violating collective bargaining procedures and interfering with the union's affairs. The union contended that the city was required to hold to the 7 percent salary increase, that it had improperly given raises above that figure to a selected occupational classification (electric line workers), and that it had made special provisions for rates of pay and wages for specific individuals in the bargaining unit without inclusion of the union representative.

The union recognized the need for the city to award the pay increase to the line workers in order to compete with the private sector, especially the Southern Public Utility Corporation, but felt that competitive salary and wage problems existed in every department and that the same considerations and adjustments should be given to all employees. The union further believed that the city's unfair labor practice was creating a serious morale problem among employees that could have an effect on the amount and the quality of work performed. The union asked that the city be ordered to return to the bargaining table and renegotiate rates of pay and wages for all employees covered by the bargaining unit.

The city itself saw the need for a higher percentage across-the-board increase than the 7.0 percent in the contract because of continued rises in the cost of living but decided to hold the increase because of the complaint of engaging in improper practices filed with the labor commissioner. The city's defense filed with the commissioner made the following points:

1. The city's wage scales were competitive overall, but a salary raise was necessary to fill the vacant line worker position.
2. The city had used benefits paid its employees as part of the percentage raise offered the union.
3. Union members had bypassed their official representatives in requesting the increase for the line workers.
4. Merit raises had never before been the subject of grievances against the city.
5. The unlawful labor practice suit was not filed until five months after the contract was signed.

QUESTIONS AND INSTRUCTIONS

1. If you were the labor commissioner, how would you rule in the case?
2. As a student learning about public personnel administration, how would you react to the following observations:

a. The line worker should not have been recognized for purposes of salary and wage negotiation by the city council.
b. The basis for the wage increase should have been that it was a merit increase rather than an adjustment to the salary schedule.
c. The city manager was the official negotiator for the city and, therefore, should have been the party who conducted negotiations with the union.
d. Street Department employees are not as skilled as line workers and, therefore, should not expect the same salary schedule.
e. Regional competition for obtaining line workers is greater than for obtaining help in such departments as Street Repair, Sanitation, Water, and Police; the latter jobs are competitive only locally.

3. Do you think that public employees should have the right to form unions for the purpose of collective bargaining? Why?
4. Do you think public employees have the right to strike?
5. In the area of labor-management relations, what functions should the mayor perform? the city manager? the city council?

INSIGHTS-ISSUES/UNION CONTRACT NEGOTIATION IN SPRINGFIELD

Clearly and briefly describe and illustrate these concepts, issues, or points. Interpret the word "role" as meaning impact, application, importance, effect and/or illustration of certain facts, concerns, or issues from the case study.

1. Role of cost of living data (as contrasted with market supply and demand pressures) for granting government employees wage and salary increases.
2. Role of business executives for making political decisions effecting public sector, or government, operations.
3. Role of laws and procedures (unlawful labor practices) in administering public sector labor/management relations.
4. Role of public sector (Municipal Light Department as contrasted with private sector Southern Public Utility Corporation) for providing public utilities to citizens.
5. Role and potential of public sector unions for speaking up for employee morale and promoting employee productivity.

ENDNOTES

1. Richard B. Freeman, Robert B. Reich, Josh S. Weston, John Sweeney, William J. McDonough, and John Mueller, "Toward a Apartheid Economy? *Harvard Business Review* 74, no. 5 (September–October 1996): 114–127.
2. "Union Members: Demographic Change, Differences," *Campaigns & Elections* 15, no. 9 (September 1994): 55–56.
3. Diane Crispell, "Have the Unions Stopped Shrinking?" *American Demographics* 16, no. 6 (June 1994): 14.

4. Leo Troy, "The Rise and Fall of American Trade Unions: The Labor Movement from FDR to RR," in *Unions in Transition: Entering the Second Century,* ed. Seymour Martin Lipset (San Francisco: ICS Press, Institute for Contemporary Studies, 1986), 75–109. See also: Troy, "Is Unionism in Permanent Decline?," *Chicago Tribune,* 1 September 1986, section 1, page 11.

5. *Troy,* "The Rise and Fall," 106.

6. William J. Lanouette, "Sending Labor a Message," *National Journal* 34 (22 August 1981): 1516.

7. Troy, "Is the U.S. Unique in the Decline of Private Sector Unionism?" *Journal of Labor Research* 11, no. 1 (spring 1990): 111–114.

8. "Union Members: Who They Are, Where They Work, and What They Earn," *Monthly Labor Review* 119, no. 5 (May 1996): 42–43.

9. Dwight Waldo, *The Enterprise of Public Administration: A Summary View* (Novato, Calif.: Chandler & Sharp Publishers, Inc., 1980), 164.

10. David Lewin, "Public Employee Unionism in the 1980s: An Analysis of Transformation," in *Unions in Transition: Entering the Second Century,* ed. Seymour Martin Lipset (San Francisco: ICS Press, Institute for Contemporary Studies, 1986), 241–264; see also: Chimezie A. B. Osigweh, "Collective Bargaining and Public Sector Union Power," *Public Personnel Management* 14 (spring 1985): 75–84; Douglas M. McCabe, "Labor Relations, Collective Bargaining, and Performance Appraisal in the Federal Government Under the Civil Service Reform Act of 1978," *Public Personnel Management,* 13 (summer 1984): 133–146; and R. Douglas Collins, "Agency Shop in Public Employment," *Public Personnel Management* 15 (summer 1986): 171–179.

11. U.S. Department of Labor. Bureau of Labor Statistics. "Union Members in 1997," *News.* Washington, DC, (January 30, 1998), 1–2. Internet address: http://stats.bls.gov/newsrels.htm.

12. Troy, *The End of Unionism: A Reappraisal* (St. Louis, Mo.: Center for the Study of American Business, 1994); *The New Unionism in the New Society: Public Sector Unions in the Redistributive State* (Fairfax, Va.: George Mason University Press, 1994).

13. Troy, "The End of Unionism: A Reappraisal," *Current,* no. 373 (June 1995): 26–33.

14. Michael Ballot with contributions from Laurie Lichter-Heath, Thomas Kail, and Ruth Wang, *Labor-Management Relations in a Changing Environment* 2d ed. (New York: John Wiley & Sons, Inc., 1996), 478–482.

15. George Bennet, "Tools to Resolve Labor Disputes in the Public Sector," *Personnel* 50, no. 2 (March–April 1973).

16. *Boston Herald-American,* 28 March 1973.

17. *Federal Labor Relations: A Program in Need of Reform* (Washington, DC: U.S. General Accounting Office, 1991). GAO Publication GAO/GGD-91-101.

18. Ballot, *Labor-management Relations,* 429.

19. *Federal Labor Relations: A Program in Need of Reform.*

20. Stephen Barr, "Gore Group to Recommend Partnership with Unions: New Era of Labor-Management Relations Envisioned; Proposal Comes as Budget Restrains Outlays," *Washington Post,* 2 September 1995, p. A25. "Major Changes Urged in Labor Relations," *Washington Post,* 1 February 1994, p. A19. Bill McAllister and Kenneth J. Cooper, "Unions Applaud Personnel Plan, but Greeting on Hill Is Mixed," *Washington Post,* 8 September 1993, p. A9.

21. Joel M. Douglas, "State Civil Service and Collective Bargaining Systems in Conflict," *Public Administration Review* 52, no. 1 (January/February 1992): 162–172.

22. Richard B. Freeman and Casey Ichniowski, "Introduction: The Public Sector Look of American Unionism," in *When Public Sector Workers Unionize,* ed. Richard B. Freeman and Casey Ichniowski (Chicago: University of Chicago Press, 1988), 1–15.

23. Freeman and Robert G. Valletta, "The Effects of Public Sector Labor Laws on Labor Market Institutions and Outcomes," in *When Public Sector Workers Unionize,* eds. Freeman and Ichniowski (Chicago: University of Chicago Press, 1988), 81–103. See also Dale Belman, John S. Haywood, and John Lund, "Public Sector Earnings and the Extent of Unionization," *Industrial and Labor Relations Review* 50, no. 4 (July 1997): 610–627. "The extent of public sector unionization appears positively correlated with earnings for both state and local government workers and for those covered and not covered by collective agreements." (610)

24. Ichniowski, "Public Sector Union Growth and Bargaining Laws: A Proportional Hazards Approach with Time-Varying Treatments," in *When Public Sector Workers Unionize,* eds. Freeman and Ichniowski (Chicago: University of Chicago Press, 1988), 19–38.

25. Gregory M. Saltzman, "Public Sector Bargaining Laws Really Matter: Evidence from Ohio and Illinois," in *When Public Sector Workers Unionize,* eds. Freeman and Ichniowski (Chicago: University of Chicago Press, 1988), 41–78.

26. Freeman and Valletta, "The Effects of Public Sector Labor Laws."

27. Henry S. Farber, "The Evolution of Public Sector Bargaining Laws," in *When Public Sector Workers Unionize,* eds. Freeman and Ichniowski (Chicago: University of Chicago Press, 1988), 129–166.

28. Valletta and Freeman, "Appendix B: The NBER Public Sector Collective Bargaining Law Data Set," in *When Public Sector Workers Unionize,* eds. Freeman and Ichniowski (Chicago: University of Chicago Press, 1988), 404–405.

29. Freeman and Valletta, "The Effects of Public Sector Labor Laws."

30. Freeman and Valletta, "The Effects of Public Sector Labor Laws," 97–99.

31. David E. Bloom, "Arbitrator Behavior in Public Sector Wage Disputes," in *When Public Sector Workers Unionize,* eds. Freeman and Ichniowski (Chicago: University of Chicago Press, 1988), 122.

32. Linda N. Edwards, "The Future of Public Sector Unions: Stagnation or Growth?" *AEA Papers and Proceedings* 79, no. 2 (May 1989): 161–165.

33. John Buell, "The Future of Unions," *The Humanist* 57, no. 5 (September–October 1997): 41–42.

34. "Union Contract Negotiations at Springfield," in *Practicing Public Management: A Casebook,* 2d ed., by C. Kenneth Meyer and Charles H. Brown. 196–199. Copyright © 1989 by St. Martin's Press, Inc. Reprinted with permission of Bedford/St. Martin's Press, Inc.

For this chapter, see also: Gerald W. McEntee, "Political Action '86—Why It Matters," *Public Employee* 51 (October 1986): 4–5. See also McEntee, "Rebuilding Labor's Strength," *Public Employee,* 51 (November/December 1986): 4–5; and Steven W. Hays and T. Zane Reeves, *Personnel Management in the Public Sector* (Newton, Mass.: Allyn and Bacon, Inc., 1984), 317–347.

The opening section of this chapter on the Professional Air Traffic Controllers Organization PATCO is based largely on news reports published at the relevant times. Of special interest are accounts published in *Time,* 24 August 1981; an editorial in the *New York Times,* 9 August 1991; and an Associated Press dispatch of 17 March 1992. See also David Nagy, "How Safe Are Our Airways?," *U.S. News & World Report* XCI (24 August 1981): 14–17; Jeffery L. Sheler, "A Hard Line Against State, Local

Unions Too," *U.S. News & World Report* XCI (24 August 1981): 20–21; Marvin Stone, "Strikes Against the People," *U.S. News & World Report* XCI (24 August 1981): 76; Jonathan Alter, "Featherbedding in the Tower: How the Controllers Let the Cat Out of the Bag," *Washington Monthly* 13 (October 1981): 22–27; Bill Keller, "Most Pro-Reagan Unions Rewarded," *Congressional Quarterly Weekly* 40 (28 August 1982): 2116; Kevin P. Jones, "Are the Only Good Air Controllers. . . . The Union Workers Fired?" *National Journal* 43 (26 October 1985): 2436–2437; Stephen Gettinger, "Congress Wrestles With Air Safety Concerns," *Congressional Quarterly Weekly* 43 (9 November 1985): 2293–2297.

7

LEADERSHIP

During the late 1930s, J. Robert Oppenheimer seemed to have found happiness teaching theoretical physics at the University of California at Berkeley. A shy and nervous man, he was pleased that he seldom had to venture into the laboratory, let alone the workday world outside the campus. Instead, he could spend much of his time working out equations on his blackboard and indulging in his favorite hobby, reading mystical Hindu poetry in the original Sanskrit. True, he contributed money to political causes that seemed to meet his ideals, and he did enjoy a reasonable social life, but he was largely occupied with theoretical physics and esoteric poetry when World War II broke out.

The war wrought great changes in Oppenheimer's peaceful and sheltered existence. In a few short years, he found himself assembling and directing a task force of over 1,000 scientists and technicians in developing the atomic bomb. This involved, among other things, running an entire community, because the scientists and their families were forced to live in seclusion in an isolated area in New Mexico. As everyone now knows, the Los Alamos community stayed together, the scientists accomplished their work, and the bomb was built. Afterward, many of the physicists involved agreed that no one but Oppenheimer could have done it.[1]

AN OVERVIEW OF LEADERSHIP

Oppenheimer made a rapid transformation from a shy, nervous professor into a forceful and effective administrator. His experience is an extreme example of one of the most fascinating phenomena in administration—the mystery of leadership. Leadership and the qualities it demands have puzzled and perplexed many an administrative theorist. Peter Drucker, noted writer and organization consultant, reports, "Among the effective executives I have known and worked with, there are extroverts and aloof, retiring men, some even morbidly shy. Some are eccentrics, others are painfully correct conformists. Some are fat and some are thin. Some are worriers and some are relaxed. Some drink quite heavily and others are total abstainers. Some are men of great charm and warmth; some have no more personality than a frozen mackerel."[2]

As most of us encounter it, history is the story of the great people of our past—the Ceasars, Lincolns, and Gandhis who have led us to war, revolution, or greater freedom. But as times passes, the great names fade. A century from now, even the most famous of today's leaders will be reduced to a sentence or two in a high school history textbook. A millennium on, Bill Clinton or Newt Gingrich may not even merit a footnote.[3]

Anyone who hopes to spell out the qualities of a leader is engaged in a perilous and problematic mission. One helpful observation, however, can be made at the outset. *Leadership is, to a great extent, determined by the needs of the situation.* "It is more fruitful to consider leadership as a relationship between the leader and the situation than as a universal pattern of characteristics possessed by certain people," Douglas McGregor notes.[4] In a similar vein, William J. Reddin, after surveying the research on management style, concludes that "no single style is naturally more effective than others. Effectiveness depends on a style's appropriateness to the situation in which it is used."[5] There is, in short, no ideal leadership style and most probably no ideal leader.

Leaders can be endangered by limiting their analysis of a situation in terms of previous successes, by failing to integrate new data, and by losing their sense of humility. The most effective leaders view their positions as opportunities to constantly learn, accept each situation on its own terms, and remain open to new ideas. According to Karlene Kerfoot, a humble attitude will lead to the greatest learning.[6]

If some leaders can lead only when no one is above them, others can only lead successfully when the reverse is true. There are people who would do well in the second highest position of a large organization but who would flounder if placed in overall command of a small one. In other words, they are natural seconds-in-command. Arthur Schlesinger puts Dean Rusk, who served as secretary of state during the Kennedy and Johnson administrations, into this category. Writes Schlesinger of Rusk:

> He was a superb technician: this was his power and his problem. He had trained himself all his life to be the ideal chief of staff, the perfect number-two man. The inscrutability which made him a good aide and a gifted negotiator made him also a baffling leader. When assistant secretaries brought him problems, he listened courteously, thanked them, and let them go; they would depart little wiser than they came. Since his subordinates did not know what he thought, they could not do what he wanted. In consequence, he failed to imbue the Department with positive direction and purpose. He had authority but not command.[7]

Situational differences requiring different leadership styles do not only concern matters of hierarchical position. Different types of organizations may also demand different types of leaders. Many a successful business executive has failed miserably after attempting to transfer with all his or her administrative prowess to the public sector. Few public-sector executives test their leadership skills directing a business firm. If so, they would probably frequently fail. Furthermore, an organization may need different leaders at different stages of its existence.

The relationship of leadership ability to the particular situation that calls the leader into being makes the task of defining and detailing a list of general leadership qualities elusive and difficult. Certain qualities do, however, seem to characterize most leaders in most situations. Although this list does not constitute a formula, one could possess all the qualities on the list and still be unable to lead, it does provide something of a basis from which the student may gain a perspective on one of the most intriguing and enigmatic aspects of the administrative craft.

OPTIMISM, CONVICTION, CIVILITY, HUMOR, AND NOSTALGIA

As president, Ronald Reagan projected optimism, conviction, and nostalgia for a simpler time in America. His memory poignantly beckons Americans once again to recall a political past when Presidential leadership seemed more simple and open than it is today. President Reagan opposed Communism and opined of "the magic of the marketplace," as he unself-consciously put it, stood for irreducible verities in American government and politics. Conservative scholars ridicule mainstream academics who conclude Reagan was a mediocre leader. They praise his unwavering devotion to conservatism, his strong leadership, his civility, and humor.

Sources: *New York Times*, 24 February 1998, page 20A; see also Stephen Goode, "The Reagan Legacy," *Insight on the News* 13, no. 39 (27 October 1997): 10–14.

LEADERSHIP QUALITIES

Probably no quality is more pertinent and pervasive among successful leaders than the quality of *optimism*. To lead successfully, one must believe that his or her leadership will make a difference. No matter how dismal a journey, the leader must be able to see positive results.

Harlan Cleveland stresses this quality of leadership. "Prophecies of doom," he reminds us, "do not in fact move people in action."[8] Indeed, they are more likely to have the reverse effect. To be happy, one must believe in the possibility of happiness, the great Russian writer Tolstoy once suggested. The same holds true for leadership. To exercise leadership, one must believe in its possibilities.

That *energy* and *enterprise* must accompany such optimism should be reasonably obvious. This does not mean that every luminary in the ranks of leadership has been a whirlwind of activity, but one cannot hope to meet leadership's obligations without some deliberate and diligent application of one's talents. Leaders often do not seem to be working hard at their jobs, but such appearances can be deceptive. A leader may be relaxed and easygoing, but laziness and indolence will usually lead to failure.

What about *intelligence?* Certainly, it is rare to find a leader who is both dumb and successful, and some have been extraordinarily brilliant. Take Napoleon and William Pitt, those young titans who confronted each other across the English Channel at the beginning of the nineteenth century. Each was at home in a variety of disciplines, including mathematics, languages, and the law. In this country, and during the same period, a president (Thomas Jefferson) had come to power who was accomplished in architecture, science, agriculture, law, political theory, and many other fields of study. Nevertheless, when it comes to correlating intellectual ability with leadership, some qualities seem more crucial than others.

According to Albert C. Yates, good leaders must be virtuous people who can be trusted to make the right choices to restore optimism and spirit to the society. Intelligent leaders, without virtue, can lead society toward selfishness and cynicism. *Virtue* embodies all that is good and right in human life and is a combination of values such as commitment, integrity, compassion, truth, and competence. A dynamic relationship between leadership and values sustains a good democratic society.[9]

One vital intellectual skill is *verbal ability*. Communication skills usually accompany leadership ability, no matter what the particular situation. A ditch digger who becomes the foreman of the work gang will probably be able to communicate better than all, or at least most, of the other members of the gang.

An interesting study on this point was done years ago. Researchers tested people from various occupations as to their vocabularies. It was a multiple-choice test that presented the subjects with numerous words, ranging from the commonplace to the obscure. Each word was followed by four others, one of which was a synonym. The object was to pick the synonym. The group that placed highest on the test consisted of business executives who outscored all the professional groups, including college professors. The test was given at a time when relatively few businesspeople had a college education. Yet, as a group, they demonstrated the greatest facility at word recognition.

An ability to communicate was crucial in Dean Rusk's rise to administrative prominence. Although sharing Arthur Schlesinger's view that Rusk was more suited for a number-two than a number-one position, journalist David Halberstam writes, "A brilliant expositor, he had a genius for putting down brief, cogent, and forceful prose on paper—a rare and much needed quality in government."[10] It was this ability, reflected in the cables that he sent back while serving with the army in India during World War II, that led to Rusk being "discovered" by his superior and being slotted for the wider opportunities that came his way when the war ended.

Much more complex is the question of *creativity* and *judgment*. The problem is that these two qualities are not always compatible. Good idea people, as Daniel Katz and Robert L. Kahn point out, tend to be enthusiastic and somewhat impulsive and may fail to subject their ideas to searching criticism. They frequently have a hard time translating ideas into action, and when they do, they may fail to follow through because they soon sprout another idea that they want to work on.

Katz and Kahn maintain that leadership puts more of a priority on reasoned judgment than creativity, and if a leader can have only one of these qualities, he or she is better off with the former. One can always make up for lack of creativity by surrounding oneself with people who are creative.[11] This, to a great extent, was true of Oppenheimer. Although a brilliant physicist, he was not considered a particularly creative one. His talents lay in being able to analyze the work of others and, in so doing, to spur them on to greater efforts.

Good leaders rarely lose their heads or give in to their emotions. Instead, they deal with situations and the people involved in a disinterested manner best designed to achieve the results they have in mind. This observation is confirmed by research. Burleigh Gardner cites one study of several hundred executives, which showed that they maintained a detached, objective view of their subordinates. Other studies, says Gardner, tend to corroborate this finding.[12] This does not mean that a good leader should be a cool and clammy individual, lacking warmth and empathy. Rather, it indicates that he or she should be able to keep personal feelings in check and to appraise objectively the needs of the situation.

The Swiss psychologist, Jean Piaget, well-known for his pioneering work with children, offers an observation that may aid in summing up this rather illusive leadership quality. Piaget points out that when a child stands in front of another person, the child will tend to identify the other person's left arm as the right and vice versa. This is because the arm of the person the child is facing is on the same side as his or her own. The child is unable to put himself or herself in the other person's shoes.

As people grow older, they usually manage to make this change, at least to the point of distinguishing between the right and left sides of a person they are facing. But everyone still retains some degree of difficulty in seeing situations from the other person's position, particularly when more than physical position is concerned. The good leader will be able to do this better than most. By objectively assessing situations from the various points of view and acting accordingly, he or she exercises the influence that leadership betokens.

QUALITIES IN QUESTION

The preceding list of leadership qualities is admittedly a short one and may seem more notable for what it omits than for what it includes. Left out are at least three characteristics that are usually associated with leadership—technical competency, decisiveness, and charisma. Let us examine the first two qualities, then take an in-depth look at charisma.

Technical Competency   Government in the United States has traditionally placed a great emphasis on technical competency in selecting leaders for its various administrative agencies. Americans usually insist that school superintendents be educators, public health commissioners be doctors, and public works commissioners be engineers, or at least persons with some engineering background. Appointing technically trained people to administrative positions is often equated with progressive government and is considered a repudiation of administration by political hacks. A city-manager-run city will more likely appoint a professional law enforcement specialist as its police commissioner than will a city dominated by political bosses, although the latter also seems to be bending to this trend.

Many European countries, however, view the matter differently. They stress administrative skills and background rather than demonstrated technical expertise. When France consolidated its two major police forces in 1968, the government appointed as its new policy head a man who had previously been the chief of staff in Ministry of Education. He was neither an educator nor a police officer, but a professional administrator.

Which is the correct approach? Certainly technical expertise has much to recommend it. People who understand the work of their subordinates will possess tangible advantages when it comes to directing them. At a minimum, a supervisor who is technically expert can gain the respect of his or her subordinates in a way that a nontechnician would be unable to do.

Administrative theorists even in this country have long looked askance at the "specialist syndrome," however. The leader of an organization or an organizational unit must be able to relate the unit to its external environment. This, so the claim goes, is best done by a professional administrator. He or she is much more likely to possess the expanded frame of reference that the leader needs to manage the organization in a productive manner. Failure to assess the external environment can be, and often has been, disastrous to many organizations.

The technically trained and experienced leader has assembled a network of prior associations and preferences as well. The leader's background makes him or her more prone to favor some activities over others and to listen to some people more than others. He or she may lack the overall and objective perspective that the generalist administrator can provide.

These considerations take on heightened importance the more one engages the organizational hierarchy. As many writers have pointed out, the higher the administrative level, the more time the administrator spends on "external" in contrast to "internal" matters. As Katz and Kahn note, the larger and more complex an organization becomes, "the greater will be the commonality of their management substructures."[13] This indicates that because organizations are becoming larger and more complex, their administrative positions are becoming more alike and are therefore demanding fewer specialist skills.

Other factors also lend support to the oft-heard administrative adage that "the technician should be on tap and not on top." As David E. Lilienthal has said, the technician's work usually has a terminal point. There is the bridge to be built, the vaccine to be discovered, the patient to be cured and discharged. The administrator has to think in different terms. His or her task is never done, because in administration there is never any real completion.[14]

Some of these problems were evident in the administration of the Vietnam War. According to former Undersecretary of the Air Force Townsend Hoopes, the military leaders could think only in terms of winning the war. They avoided the question of whether some means of achieving victory might produce more problems than they solved or whether it would even be in the United States' interest to win the war. Theirs was a "can do" policy, which, while productive and useful in some situations, can prove disastrous in others.[15] Instead of questioning the usefulness of air power to begin with, for example, military officials during the Vietnam War devoted their efforts to trying to make it more efficient. The failure to evaluate the means used in achieving limited goals had devastating results.

One thing is certain—the abilities that make a person a proficient specialist in his or her field do not automatically equip him or her for administrative leadership in that field. The first-rate teacher too often turns into the third-rate principal. In writing about scientists and administration, C. P. Snow observed that "to be any good, in his youth at least, a scientist has to think of one thing, deeply and obsessively, for a long time. An administrator has to think of a great many things widely, in their interconnections, for a short time."[16] There are exceptions, such as Oppenheimer, or, for that matter, Snow himself, but more often than not the qualities that make for excellence in a specialty do not coincide and frequently conflict with the qualities that make for excellence in administering organizations devoted to that specialty. We may posit then that technical competence in the field is an advantage to an administrator, presuming that everything else is equal. The problem is that everything else is usually not equal. While such competence may be useful, particularly at the first level of supervision, it tends to pose increasing disadvantages as one moves to the higher reaches of organizational life. It is, consequently, omitted here as a necessary quality for administrative success.

Decisiveness   A quality that is often imputed to successful administrators is the ability to make quick decisions. To be sure, decision making is what administration is about. George C. Marshall maintained that the capacity to make decisions was the rarest gift that the gods could give a person. When one scrutinizes the record of many notable government executives, however, one frequently finds not a chronicle of speedy decision making, but almost its opposite. Historians have constantly commented on Franklin Roosevelt's penchant for procrastination. Some claim it was his most characteristic trait. Winston Churchill was also not keen on making decisions that did not demand immediate action. Unless it was imperative to make a major decision at once, Churchill would approach it by calling a meeting and asking for various views. Then he would request memoranda on the subject and hold another meeting. John F. Kennedy is another example. While he sought to present himself as a firm and decisive leader, his favorite book was a biography of a British prime minister named Melbourne. Lord Melbourne was a leader who ardently espoused and acted on the belief that "when in doubt what should be done, do nothing."[17]

Successful leaders prefer peace and quiet over agenda raisers and program controversy. Decisions often interrupt the peace and quiet of office politics. The complexities and implications of decision making may cause changes in agency programs, budgets, and careers. When decision makers make decisions, they must take sides. Careers of administrators and employees may be affected. In governments, there are many interests—personnel wise and programatic—with which to contend. A decision by a governmental administrator may cause reverberations throughout the staff, other governmental agencies, the legislative branches, clientele groups, the press, and the public—all of which must be taken into account. A good decision maker must be like a good billiard player: every time he or she goes to hit the ball, the decision maker must figure out what will happen when that ball hits another ball, which in turn will hit another. Any decision of consequence is likely to set off a chain of events where the ultimate impact may prove difficult to anticipate.

For reasons such as these, speedy decision making does not always make for good decision making, and good decision makers have usually taken cognizance of this fact. While there is little disputing that any administrator has to be able to make decisions before time runs out, many of the best executives have persistently preferred to stretch the time limit to the near maximum. As society and the apparatus that governs it become increasingly complicated, we may find that

---

PERSONALITY AND CHARISMA DO MAKE A DIFFERENCE

In an age of complexity, change, large enterprises, and nation-states, leaders are more important than ever. Leader effectiveness depends on his or her personality and charisma and not solely on his or her control over bureaucratic structures. In a model of leader effectiveness, age of U.S. presidents accounts for approximately 20 percent of the change in presidential needs for power, achievement, and affiliation. Needs of the president and leader self-restraint in using power, the president's age, and crises account for 24 percent of diversity of presidential charisma. A combination of the president's age, crises, needs, and charisma predict from 25 percent to 66 percent of changes in presidential performance.

Source: Robert J. House, William D. Spranger, and James Woycke. "Personality and Charisma in the U.S. Presidency: A Psychological Theory of Leader Effectiveness," *Administrative Science Quarterly* 36, no. 3 (September 1991): 364–397.

---

quick decision making, although it occasionally will be necessary, will become less and less characteristic of success in administration.

Charisma   The capacity to be colorful and heroic, to stir the emotions of people and capture their hearts and minds, has long been regarded as a powerful leadership tool. Many of those we regard as outstanding leaders have possessed these traits. They include not only political leaders such as Franklin Roosevelt, Winston Churchill, John F. Kennedy, and Ronald Reagan, but also some more purely administrative leaders such as Robert Moses, New York City's famous builder of bridges, highways, and parks, and Harry Hopkins, FDR's dynamic aide. While a charismatic leader has the ability to inspire and convince followers, reliance on charisma alone is certainly problematic, perhaps dangerous.

LEADERSHIP AND CHARISMA

The relationship between leadership and charisma is also important in understanding charisma. Katz and Kahn argue that charisma originates from people's needs and from dramatic events in association with leadership. Most persons are in no position to evaluate suggestions for organizational change, therefore charismatic leadership is most appropriate for formulating policies and altering organizational structures. In that followers are not knowledgeable concerning specific programs for attaining organizational goals, subordinates allow leaders much flexibility for such decisions.

However, Katz and Kahn emphasize:

charisma is not the objective assessment by followers of the leader's ability to meet their specific needs. It is a means by which people abdicate responsibility for any consistent, tough-minded evaluation of the outcome of specific policies. They put their trust in their leader, who will somehow take care of things. Charisma requires some psychological distance between leader and follower. Immediate superiors exist in the work-a-day world of constant objective feedback and evaluation. They are very human and very fallible, and immediate subordinates cannot build an aura of magic about them. Day-to-day intimacy destroys illusion. But the leader in the top eschelons of an organization is sufficiently distant from the membership to make a simplified and magical image possible.[18]

To operationalize charisma, Katz and Kahn emphasize the use of two particular measures. The degree of emotional arousal among followers and the global character of the leader's power as perceived by followers are crucial for charismatic success. Adherents and opponents react emotionally to charismatic personalities. The leader's portrait is global and not discriminating. Specific weaknesses are neglected in the great leader.

Katz delineates three types of interpersonal relations between charismatic personalities and followers.

- One type of charismatic leader may symbolize the followers' *wishful solutions to internal conflicts.* Instead of searching for deeper meanings and motives, followers seek release from their internal conflicts. They project their fears, aggression, and aspirations upon social measures that facilitate symbolic solution. In his or her personality and program, the charismatic leader offers symbolic solution.
- A second type of charismatic leader entails an *aggressor,* or father figure, who possesses overwhelming power; the follower is unable to escape the exercise of such power. In this type of interpersonal relation between leader and followers, there is no new ideology; but the followers identify with the aggressor, or father figure.
- A third type of charismatic leader/followers *interpersonal relationship* is void of internal conflict. In assuming that their charismatic leader may advance their interests, followers magnify the power of their leader.[19]

The concepts of power and leadership enjoy common properties; however, they are not the same. Leaders do exercise power. A leadership act is a choice of power instruments. Leadership is the point at which power is activated. Leadership entails attempts on the part of a leader, or influencer, to affect, or influence, the behavior of a follower or followers.

When the Iran-Contra scandal stymied the Reagan administration in the later years of his presidency, many blamed the charismatic president's "distant" leadership style for the fiasco. George Bush, the prototype "organization man," was unable to escape more immediate implications in the scandal. Reagan positioned himself as "victim" while Bush's role appeared to be more complicated in efforts to cover up the scheme.

A charismatic leader may fail to fully develop the abilities of subordinates, as they become overly dependent upon the leader. When the leader is absent, the organization will tend to flounder, and when he or she departs for good, it may fall to pieces.

Charismatic leadership also may inhibit communication. Subordinates become reluctant to give the leader unpleasant information or advise against policies that may be unwise. Often they lose the ability to discriminate between wise and unwise policies, for they have surrendered much of their capacity for independent judgment. This can be crucial, because a charismatic leader may not only be forceful but also foolish.

History provides numerous examples of charismatic leaders who vigorously led their nations down the road to ruin. Adolf Hitler and Benito Mussolini are two examples, but we do not have to use such extreme examples to find instances of how charismatic leadership can malfunction. Robert Moses may have built more bridges, tunnels, and highways than any man in recent history, but many New Yorkers today are questioning the wisdom of his activity. His final masterpiece, the New York City World's Fair of 1965, turned out to be a startling economic disaster.

The case of University of California physicist Ernest Lawrence offers another illustration of how charisma can lead to catastrophe. Lawrence, a charismatic leader, became head of an important laboratory at the university and persuaded many younger scientists to work with him in building two highly expensive devices, both of which turned out to be unworkable. Physicists elsewhere had branded both projects silly and impractical from the start, but the charismatic Lawrence had wrangled sufficient funds, and his star-struck subordinates gave him enthusiastic support.

While charisma is positive in many ways, its main danger in public administration is the possibility that a charismatic leader's personality may negate important advice and challenges from subordinates and citizens.

MAX WEBER'S CHARISMA TYPES AND POWER CENTERS

Max Weber's three "pure types" of authority are: *rational; traditional;* and *charismatic* grounds. In his rational emphasis, Weber believed in the "legality" of patterns of normative rules. He insisted upon the right of those elevated to authority under these rules to issue commands. This focus constituted legal authority. In his traditional emphasis, Weber believed in the sanctity of immemorial traditions. He recognized the legitimacy of the status of those exercising authority under such traditions. This focus constituted traditional authority. In Weber's charismatic emphasis, the German scholar espoused devotion to the specific and exceptional sanctity, heroism, or exemplary character of an individual person. This focus constituted charismatic authority.[20]

In Romans 12, the New English Bible translation, Paul contrasts the "enthusiastic" display of charisma with its institutional dynamics: "The gifts we possess differ as they are allotted to us by God's grace, and must be exercised accordingly: the gift of administration, in administration."[21]

Verses six, seven, and eight specifically include administration and point out how *"charisma"* in this application could become the focus of ecclesiastical organization and offices.[22]

In 1 Corinthians 12, there is a long passage about "gifts of the spirit." Verse four of this chapter refers to such "gifts" as including wisdom, knowledge, faith, healing, miracles, prophecy, delineation of true and false spirits, and ecstatic utterances and interpretation of ecstatic utterances.[23]

MAJOR CONCEPTS IN LEADERSHIP

A *leader* is a person who has the authority to decide, direct, and represent the objectives and functions of an organization.

A *manager* is a person who has the authority to direct specific organizational resources in order to accomplish objectives.

Authority is the license by an organization that grants an individual the rights to use its powers and resources.

Credibility is the recognition by an organization that one is competent to use its powers.

Source: Portnoy, Robert A., *Leadership: What Every Leader Should Know About People,* (c) 1986, page 2. Reprinted by permission of Prentice-Hall, Upper Saddle River, New Jersey.

Weber focused on the function and exercise of power in society. He concluded that there are three major points of influence for examining charismatic leaders and their impacts. They are:

1. The *law and the traditional taboos* of the particular culture or society. These might include laws, rules, regulations, customs, mores, taboos, routines, and certain ascribed standards. These properties are thought to be rational, grounded in prescribed ways of acting and behaving.

2. *Individual leadership,* largely emotional, which Weber labeled *"charisma."* Also referred to as the *cult of personality.* These personalities might include the president, governor, mayor, coach, pastor, priest, rabbi, or other community leaders. This property is thought to be often irrational, as it goes against the grain of how issues confronting the organization have been handled, dealt with, brokered, and accepted.

3. The *mass of administrators* who carry out the laws and policies of the organization, or government. In short, the "bureaucracy." Also referred to as the followers. In a governmental office, it's the employees. In U.S. society, it's the citizens. In a religious organization, it's the parishioners. On the state university's athletic teams, it's the players. These properties emphasize a rational response, grounded in prescribed ways of responding to the dictates of leaders, manager, and other authorities.

Charisma, then, is not merely the appearance of a dynamic, excited, motivated, committed, passion-filled person. Charismatic persons persuade followers to change their old ways of responding to the organizations challenges and problems and act in creative, determined, and new ways, to accomplish the tasks assigned to the government bureaucracy. In the history of organizations, there are occasions when the great man or woman arrives on the scene or otherwise comes from the ranks of the organization. The immense personal magnetism of the charismatic leader causes followers to rid themselves of their old, dysfunctional ways, and become more productive than ever for the new leader and the organization. The charismatic leader dominates decision making regardless of the logic of his or her positions. The followers abandon rational thinking and follow the new leader, perhaps a pied piper, into the unknown future of the organization. Charismatic leaders encounter challenges in democratic societies. Their followers are often educated and not easily seduced, for long periods of time, by leaders often turned pied pipers.[24]

CHARISMATIC LEADER BEHAVIORS

Perspectives on charismatic leadership in times of cultural and technological change are pertinent to understanding the dynamics of charisma. What common behaviors do charismatic leaders activate?

Robert J. House offers six categories of charismatic leader behaviors:

1. *role modeling.* The role model espouses a set of values and beliefs in which followers should believe. The model's emotional responses to rewards or punishments elicit similar emotional reactions from followers.
2. *image building.* In the cult of personality, charismatic leaders portray an image or images to followers. In the institutionalization of charisma, perceptions are as important as realities. Therefore, the creation and maintenance of an image or images are crucial considerations.
3. *goal articulation.* In organizational leadership, the development of institutional mission and goals is an ongoing process. The creation and maintenance of developing institutional mission and goals constitute leadership skills whereby the leader merges his personality characteristics with the organization's social structure. The leader provides the organization a special identity. In pointing out organization goals, the leader specifies, via articulation, goals that transcend the movement or cause. Such goals are ideological rather than pragmatic. Moral overtones abound everywhere.
4. *exhibiting high expectations and showing confidence.* Charismatic leaders communicate high performance expectations for followers. Such leadership behavior enhances subordinates's self-esteem and affects the goals followers accept for themselves. In that the charismatic leader spells out to his followers that they are competent and personally responsible, subordinates perceive themselves as competent. Leaders seek to enhance motivation, performance, and satisfaction in corresponding behavior of followers.
5. *effect on followers' goals.* Followers may evaluate their own performance according to standards articulated in specific and high leader expectations. Leader's expectations function to allow followers to derive feedback on their personal behaviors.

6. *motive arousal leader behavior.* The degree of emotional arousal among followers entails House's final category of charismatic leader behaviors. Adherents and opponents react emotionally to charismatic leaders. The enthusiasm of one group's responses is matched by mistrust of others. The organizational maintenance of emotional arousal is pertinent for the long term success of the charismatic leader.[25]

House describes four personal characteristics of charismatic leaders. Charismatic leaders exercise *dominance,* personify *self-confidence,* exhibit *influence,* and maintain *strong convictions* in the moral righteousness of his or her beliefs.[26]

Why does charismatic leadership emerge in the environment of movements for change? What historical circumstances explain such emotional arousals among followers? Weber indicates that charisma and personality blend most readily "in time of psychic, physical, economic, ethical, religious, political distress".[27]

HISTORICAL CONDITIONS FAVORING CHARISMA

Erik H. Erikson suggests that large numbers of people become "charisma hungry" under historical conditions in which religion wanes. Charismatic leaders minister well during three kinds of distress.

- One distress condition is *"fear."*
- A second, and related, condition is *"anxiety."* The condition of people not knowing who they are creates an "identity vacuum" and "anxiety."
- A third historical condition, in Erikson's terms, is *"existential dread."* Erikson's last dimension, "existential dread," needs explanation. In this type of distress, people experience circumstances in which rituals of their human existence become dysfunctional. The leader, under such conditions, who may offer meaning and provide followers a greater sense of community may emerge charismatic. In offering salvation from "fear," "anxiety," and "existential dread," the charismatic leader creates new forms of safety, or identity, or rituals.[28]

Crisis, therefore, is important to the emergence of charismatic leadership. Crises foster the emergence of charismatic leaders judged as more effective than group leaders who emerge in noncrisis situations.[29]

Therefore, charismatic movements develop and multiply during times of widespread distress in society. The charismatic leader, by virtue of unusual, personal qualities, promises the hope of salvation. Perceived by followers as specifically salvationist or messianic in nature, the charismatic leader offers himself or herself to those persons in distress as peculiarly qualified to lead them from their distressful predicament.

INSTITUTIONALIZING THE AMERICAN PRESIDENCY

The institutionalization of the American presidency and its charismatic leaders over two centuries point out the historical maturing of one U.S. public sector—government organization. Some charismatic presidents might include Washington, Jefferson, Jackson, Lincoln, Teddy Roosevelt, Wilson, Franklin Roosevelt, Truman, Eisenhower, Kennedy, Lyndon Johnson, Reagan, and perhaps even Clinton. The tests of these charismatic personalities is not their individual dynamism, but did they influence the American masses to change their old dysfunctional, perhaps destructive, ways and implement bold changes?

According to Lyn Ragsdale and John J. Thesis, III, the presidency becomes institutionalized when it attains high levels of:[30]

- *autonomy* (the independence of the presidency from other units). The growth of the organization's budget is an indicator of autonomy. The $1.7 trillion budget shapes the stability and value of the U.S. government. As the presidency becomes more institutionalized, administrations offer policy proposals independent of Congress. Since the Great Society of the 1960s, autonomous presidents acted contrary to the wishes of Congress because of executive access to budgets.
- *adaptability* (the longevity of units in the presidency). Flexibility permits presidents to create, modify, and eliminate administrative units. Adaptability is the safety valve of organization institutionalization. Units may be added to the Executive Office of the President (EOP) by executive order, public law, and presidential reorganization plans.
- *complexity* (the differentation of subunits and staff in the office). Complexity is an internal aspect of institutionalization. It points out the division of labor and specialization. The unit's differentiation improves its stability and makes it more difficult to dismantle. Complexity also promotes the unit's intricate internal identity. An indicator of complexity is the organization's total number of units, compartments, divisions, and the like.
- *coherence* (the managable volume of work). Coherence addresses abilities of the organization to manage its work load. If tasks are erratic or excessive, coherence is low. Work load follows more predicatable patterns as criteria are developed. Clearance procedures for budgets, legislation, and executive orders enhance coherence. The strongest determinants of changing levels of institutionalization are measures of national government activities. Commitments to social security, medical care, unemployment, and education, for example, are illustrated by an ever-expanding social welfare budget. The challenges, problems, and enemies define presidents. Teddy Roosevelt fought the special interests. Wilson fought World War II and child labor. Franklin Roosevelt fought the Great Depression, World War II, and the wealthy. Truman dropped the bomb. Kennedy adapted to television and confronted the Soviets in Cuba. Reagan, confident yet simplistic in a complex era, cut the federal budget. And Clinton, despite the foibles of his personal life, withstood criticisms of his presidency from a zealous prosecutor and an out-of-control media.

Ragsdale and Thesis explore institution and institutionalization. According to these researchers, to institutionalize, or institutionalization, occurs as an organization acquires value and stability as an end itself. Ragsdale and Thesis write:

> *As an organization achieves stability and value, it becomes an institution. Stability denotes that the organization is no longer a mechanistic entity, easily altered or eliminated. Instead, as an organization institutionalizes, it survives various internal and environmental challenges and achieves self-maintenance—it exists in the future because it has existed in the past. . . . As an organization institutionalizes, it acquires a distinctive identity, a way of acting, and tasks it acts upon, which are all deemed to be important in and of themselves.[31]*

In processes of organization institutionalization, stability and values merge. The longer the organization exists, prospects for developing distinguishing structures, capabilities, and liabilities grow greater. Personal interests within the organization and the dynamics of the outside environment interact to result in institutionalization.

Themes of instutionalization are illustrated in public—and private—organizations. Leaders, or managers, differ. In all organizations, personalities, leaders, and decision-making methods vary. The features of autonomy, adaptability, complexity, and coherence indicate how your college or university has continued through the many years and achieved importance despite changes in individual or outside environmental constraints.

WAYS OF ENHANCING THE EFFECTIVENESS OF MANAGERS

Good administrators exert every effort to obtain the best possible subordinates. They put aside any fears that their subordinates might appear smarter, perhaps more capable than their superiors. They know that the better the subordinates' performance the more the organization will achieve. The more the organization achieves, the more successful they, as leaders, will be. Outstanding, capable employees stimulate leaders to perform more effectively.

Many administrators, to be sure, do not take this approach. In this way they signal their own shortcomings. Princeton mathematician, Andrew Weil, has promulgated what he calls *Weil's Rule*. According to Weil's Rule, a first-rate person will surround himself or herself with equals or betters; a second-rate person will surround himself or herself with third-rate people, and a third-rate person will be able to tolerate only fifth-rate subordinates and coworkers.

C. Northcote Parkinson notes: "If the head of an organization is second-rate, he will see to it that his subordinates are all third-rate; and they will, in turn, see to it that their subordinates are fourth-rate. There will soon be an actual competition in stupidity. . . ."[32]

In short, the capable administrator will appreciate the lines that steel magnate Andrew Carnegie chose for his tombstone: "Here lies a man who knew how to bring into his service men better than he was himself."

DELEGATION

When Moses assembled his people for the Exodus, he picked the ablest among them and put them in charge of groups of varying numbers. Those selected were given the authority to settle all lesser matters and make all lesser decisions themselves, passing to the prophet only the most important issues. Delegation has played a crucial role in administration since. No administrator can hope to do everything himself or herself. He or she must delegate. This is even more urgent if the administrator is wise enough to pick the best possible people for subordinates, for they will insist on substantial chunks of authority to exercise and hone their capabilities.

According to rabbinic interpretation of biblical accounts, there were three main qualities that made Moses God's chosen leader. The first was his sense of justice, which he practiced no matter what the consequence. The second was his ability to see the needs of others and his willingness to set aside his own needs for theirs. Finally, Moses' ability to lead worked not only under adverse conditions, but also positively, as a shepherd who leads a flock.[33] The value of delegation has also been substantiated by more systematic research. According to Katz and Kahn, "The extent of delegation has proved to be one of the predictors of productivity of many kinds."[34]

Avoiding the perils and pitfalls of delegation requires adherence to a few guidelines. The leader should not delegate trivia. He or she should, rather, delegate substantial assignments and the authority to carry them out. Sending a subordinate on a mere errand is delegation of a sort, but it is not the sort that makes for wise and effective administration. The administrator should remember that when it comes to delegating an important assignment, the subordinate, perhaps less knowledgeable and experienced than the delegator, will likely be able to devote more time, effort, and zeal to the task than will the superior. Some things cannot be delegated. These include ultimate responsibility for:

- creating the climate of the organization,
- representing the organization,
- establishing the basic policy of the organization, and
- the overall performance of the organization.

PARTICIPATION

In a sense, participation in decision making is merely delegation writ large. In another sense, delegation of authority is participation writ large. In any sense, both are interwoven strands of the same tapestry.

Participation differs from delegation in that it can take in many more people and many more aspects than are commonly included in the notion of delegation. Essentially, it means allowing as many people as possible to make as many decisions as possible and to share to the maximum extent possible in making other decisions. It means giving subordinates a "piece of the action."

Participation can take many forms. Employees can be allowed to determine many of their work conditions, such as hours. They can be asked to contribute their ideas to overall organization policy. They can even play a role in selecting their superiors.

The advantages of participatory decision making are many. It usually leads to more informed and better decisions, because more minds and more varieties of experience have gone into making them. It also leads to better executed decisions, for those who are to carry them out have had some say in their formulation. It may stimulate employee development as well.

Participatory decision making does have drawbacks. For one thing, it delays, sometimes extensively, taking action. It does not always lead to a better decision and occasionally may produce a worse one. It can be terribly time-consuming to all involved and can lead to increased bickering.

EDUCATION AND ROTATION

If participation can improve the employee's knowledge and skills, then it is only one of many devices for doing so. The perceptive public manager will make use of a variety of techniques for encouraging employee growth. These may include formal education and training and rotation.

In rotation, employees enlarge their work experience and increase their abilities and knowledge. They also acquire a broader and deeper understanding of the organization and how its various parts interrelate. Even if their main job is comparatively limited, they will be able to perform it better if they see how it fits in the overall scheme. Rotation also helps to keep people from becoming bored or growing stale, as well as preparing the better ones for more responsible roles.

Corrections departments in California and South Carolina have developed innovative training programs to train a new generation of correctional institutional leaders. California's training program prepares wardens and administrators for the twenty-first century and focuses on humane treatment, initiative, integrity, vision, and judgment. South Carolina emphasizes improving leadership skills of staff members.[35]

SPEAKING UP FOR SUBORDINATES

The administrative leader must be willing, and must be able, to represent subordinates to superiors. The leader must have influence higher up and must use it to protect the rights of his or her subordinates.[36]

"The conclusion urged on us," say Katz and Kahn, "is that the most effective leader in a pivotal organizational role is not the perfect bureaucrat (rational, role-actuated, heedless of primary bonds) but rather the successful integrator of primary and secondary relationships in the organizational situation."[37]

PRAISE, CENSURE, AND SANCTIONS

People have ego needs, and any organization would do well to acknowledge them. The same holds true for the organization's leaders. They should make adequate provision to recognize the ego needs of their subordinates. The easiest and cheapest way of doing this is by praise.

THE FUNCTIONS OF INSTITUTIONAL LEADERSHIP

The relationship between leadership and organizational character is more transparent when examined in the context of the leader's key tasks.

1. *The definition of institutional mission and role.* The setting of goals is a creative task that entails self-assessment and discovery of the true commitments of the organization, as determined by effective internal and external demands. The failure to set aims in the light of these commitments is a major source of irresponsibility in leadership.

2. *The institutional embodiment of purpose.* The task of leadership is not only to make policy but to build policy decisions into the organization's social structure. This too is a creative task. It means shaping the "character" of the organization, sensitizing the organization to the complex dynamic of thinking and responding, so that increased reliability in the execution and elaboration of policies will be achieved according to their spirit as well as their letter.

3. *The defense of institutional integrity.* The leadership of any policy fails when it concentrates on sheer survival; institutional survival, properly understood, is a matter of maintaining values and distinctive identity.

4. *The ordering of internal conflict.* Internal interest-groups form naturally in large-scale organizations, because the total enterprise is, in one sense, a polity composed of a number of suborganizations. The struggle between competing interests always has a high claim on the attention of leadership. This is so because the direction of the enterprise as a whole may be seriously influenced by changes in the internal balance of power.

Source: Selznick, Phillip, *Leadership in Administration* (University of California Press, 1984), 61–63.

Public managers may also find some guidelines helpful:

- Praise at the appropriate time. A compliment loses its value the longer it is delayed.
- Praise the deed, not the person. It is not who the person is but what tasks he or she does that is important. Praising the person can lead to all sorts of problems including, oddly enough, an increase in the individual's insecurity. He may become too fearful of falling from favor.
- Praise in descriptive terms, not qualitative terms. Do not say simply, "That was a good report." Say, rather, "That report covered all the matters I needed to know about."

What holds true for praise also, to a great extent, holds true for censure. Some helpful pointers in this regard are:

- Stress the positive aspect, encouraging the employee to build skills and proficiency in the area in which he or she has proven weak.
- Concentrate on performance and those aspects of personal behavior that are distinctly job-related.
- When possible, be indirect, but make sure that the employee gets the message. One device is for the manager to talk about his or her own past mistakes.

- Pick the right time. A good occasion for giving criticism is when the manager is also conferring praise. Calling attention to weaknesses while singling out strengths makes the censure more acceptable.[38]

Criticism, to be effective, must be directed toward a correctable fault that is substantially detracting from a person's performance. It does little good to criticize someone for something that does not bear on the job, and it may do harm to criticize the employee for something he or she cannot change.

The best of administrators will come across employees who seem unable or unwilling to make any positive contribution to organizational goals. Invoking sanctions, such as suspension or transfer, may help in some cases but not all. The manager will then be faced with the question of dismissal.

Firing an employee is often the most difficult job an administrator has. For the public manager, it poses particular problems, because he or she often has to deal with civil service regulations that make dismissal difficult. Usually, the superior can only take such action when he or she is prepared to go before an appeals board and offer solid grounds for the dismissal, backed by reasonably hard evidence.

MANAGING THE MANAGER

Managers should be administrators. Administrators must practice the ideals they preach. Superiors do not "run" the unit. They must "lead" it. Employees respect administrators who practice consistency and who constantly are improving their own professional skills. Public sector managers must be as concerned with their own professional development as with the enhancement of unit employees.

THE LIMITS OF LEADERSHIP

One real, yet often overlooked, or at least underestimated, aspect of leadership is that it's diverse literature applies to as many situations as there are government organizations.

"In a bureaucracy that contains people with brains and consciences," wrote Charles Frankel following his tour of duty in Washington, "an unspoken bargain binds the man at the top to his subordinates. If they are to be the instruments of his will, he must, to some extent, be an instrument of theirs."[39] Most writers on administration would agree. "A manager is often described as someone who gets things done through other people," notes the British organizational theorist, Rosemary Stewart. "We tend to forget that this means he is dependent upon them."[40]

In a complex bureaucracy the problem intensifies. Tsar Nicholas II was one of the few truly autocratic rulers of his time. Yet he experienced constant frustration in getting his smallest orders carried out. "I do not rule Russia," the weary monarch once sighed. "Ten thousand clerks do."[41]

American presidents have consistently discovered their office to provide far less power than they had thought. Franklin Roosevelt depicted Lincoln as "a sad man because he couldn't get it all at once, and nobody can." Roosevelt's own battles with his bureaucracy are almost legendary. He once wearily described his efforts to balance the special interests of diverse government agencies as akin to boxing a featherbed.

Truman and Eisenhower suffered from the same problem. John F. Kennedy took office with the idea of changing Washington bureaucracy. But he found that when he wanted a simple sign taken down, it did not come down, even after he had given the order for its removal three times.

To many students, the president of the university may appear out-of-touch with the immediate concerns of the students. College presidents confront external and internal demands—more conflicting than not—of legislators, trustees, faculty, service staff, and community leaders.

David Lilienthal, who held such posts as the chairmanships of the Tennessee Valley Authority and the Atomic Energy Commission, once defined leadership as a humanistic art. It requires, he said, "a humanistic outlook on life rather than mere mastery of technique. It is based on the capacity for understanding of individuals and their motivations, their fears, their hopes, what they love and what they hate, the ugly and the good side of human nature. It is an ability to move these individuals, to help them define their wants, to help them discover, step by step, how to achieve them."[42]

The challenge of leadership is thus the challenge of humanism. Its successful exercise lies less and less in giving orders and more and more in developing the innate capacities of human beings. But to this must be joined a sense of mission, bolstered and buttressed by some degree of vision. The story is sometimes told of three stonecutters asked what they were doing. The first replied, "I am making a living." The second, busily at work, answered, "I am doing the best job of stonecutting in the whole country." The third, looking up with a gleam in his eye, said, "I am building a cathedral."[43]

The conclusion is obvious. Only the third person can become an effective manager, or better yet, leader.

SUMMARY

- Anyone who hopes to spell out the qualities of a leader is engaged in a perilous and problematic mission. One helpful observation can be made at the outset: *Leadership is, to a great extent, determined by the needs of the situation.*
- *Leadership qualities* include optimism, conviction, humor, civility, energy, enterprise, virtue, intelligence, verbal ability, creativity, and judgment.
- Technical proficiency, decisiveness, and charisma pose special challenges for leaders, employees, and clientele in public organizations.
- *Leadership and management are not the same.* Leadership incorporates the functions of management, that is, directing the organization's resources to accomplish objectives.
- In an age of complexity, change, large enterprises, and nation states, leaders are more important than ever. *Personality and charisma do make a difference.*

- Max Weber's "pure types" of authority are: *rational; traditional;* and *charismatic* grounds. Weber believed in the "legality" of patterns of normative rules. He believed in the sanctity of immemorial traditions. Weber espoused devotion to the specific and exceptional sanctity, heroism, or exemplary character of an individual person, or charisma.
- Weber focused on the function and exercise of power in society. He develops three major points of influence for examining charismatic leaders and their impacts. They are: (1). The *law and the traditional taboos* of the particular culture or society. (2). *Individual leadership,* largely emotional, which Weber labeled *charisma.* (3). The *bureaucrats,* or *mass of administrators,* who carry out the laws and policies of the organization, or government.
- Erik Erikson suggests that large numbers of people become *"charisma hungry"* under historical conditions in which religion wanes. Particular conditions of distress, namely fear, anxiety, identity vacuum, and existential dread, bring on the dynamics of charismatic leaders.
- Charisma is not the *objective assessment* by followers of the leader's ability to meet their specific needs. It is a means by which people abdicate responsibility for any consistent, tough-minded evaluation of the outcome of specific policies. They trust their leader who will somehow take care of things.
- The concepts of power and leadership enjoy common properties. They are not the same. Leaders do exercise power. A leadership act is a choice of power instruments. *Leadership is the point at which power is activated.* Leadership entails attempts on the part of a leader, or influencer, to affect, or influence, the behavior of a follower or followers.
- A *leader* is a person who has the authority to decide, direct, and represent the objectives and functions of an organization.
- A *manager* is a person who has the authority to direct specific organizational resources to accomplish objectives.
- *Authority* is the license by an organization that grants an individual the rights to use its powers and resources.
- *Credibility* is the recognition by an organization that one is competent to use its powers.
- The presidency becomes institutionalized when it attains high levels of four features: *autonomy, adaptability, complexity,* and *coherence.*
- As an organization achieves stability and value, it becomes an institution. In processes of organization institutionalization, *stability and values merge.* The longer the organization exists, prospects for developing distinguishing structures, capabilities, and liabilities grow greater.
- The *functions* of institutional leadership are (1) definition of institutional mission and role, (2) institutional embodiment of purpose, (3) the defense of institutional integrity, and (4) the ordering of internal conflict.
- *Ways of enhancing the effectiveness* of managers are delegation, participation, education, rotation, speaking up for subordinates, praise, censure, sanctions, and managerial accountability.
- *Some things cannot be delegated.* These items include ultimate responsibility for: (1) creating the climate of the organization; (2) representing the organization;

(3) establishing the basic policy of the organization; and (4) the overall performance of the organization.

- Leaders must be willing, and must have interpersonal skills, to *represent subordinates to superiors.* Leaders must have influence with higher ups and must protect the rights and prerogatives of his or her own subordinates.
- In times of *budgetary decrementalism,* the challenges of leaders are more demanding. Partisan, policy, and system leaders must convince employees and clientele to work smarter while doing more with less. And that isn't easy!

Our discussion of leadership can be enhanced by outlining the qualities of a person recognized as one of the greatest leaders of the twentieth century. While reading the following case study, keep in mind the situational aspects of leadership.

CASE STUDY

The Supreme Allied Commander[44]

When the *New York Times* polled a group of historians in 1961 as to how they ranked America's presidents, Dwight D. Eisenhower scored a rating of 22. This placed him in the low-average category, rated even below Herbert Hoover. Eisenhower's place in history fortunately does not rest on his presidential record alone. Ten years prior to entering the White House, he assumed command of what has been called "the most extensive and cooperative military alliance in history." His conduct of this command provides an excellent example of administrative leadership and assures Eisenhower an undeniable place in the history of democratic leadership.

When World War II broke out, Eisenhower was only fifty years old and held only the rank of lieutenant colonel, but, he had already given signs of the promise that was soon to be fulfilled. As a cadet at West Point, he had always remained in the upper third of his class and would undoubtedly have finished near the top if he had not been something of a minor hell-raiser. (He rated in the bottom third of his class in conduct.) Later, he attended the Army War College at Fort Leavenworth and graduated from its one-year course as valedictorian of his class.

His military career has also supplied indications that he was no ordinary soldier. Early in his career he saw the value of tanks, and while George Patton was writing articles promoting the tank in the *Cavalry Journal,* Eisenhower was doing the same in the *Infantry Journal.* Both men, of course, saw their pleas go largely disregarded. (In France at this time, a colonel named Charles de Gaulle was making the rounds of Parisian publishers with a book urging a greater role for tanks. His superiors had already turned down his outlandish suggestions.) Eisenhower showed equal prescience and even more enterprise when it came to airplanes. Seeing in them another major weapon of the future, he took flying lessons at the age of forty-six and earned a pilot's license. He was not a man to let himself go stale.

Eisenhower also showed that he understood something about the behavioral side of management. "Morale," he once wrote, "is at one and the same time the strongest and the most delicate of growths. It withstands shocks, even disasters, on the battlefield, but can be destroyed utterly by favoritism, neglect, or injustice." He also committed himself to the goal of maintaining a mature objectivity in his working life. Among the principles he had written down for himself were "Remember that belligerence is the hallmark of insecurity," and, "Forget yourself and personal fortunes."

Finally, Eisenhower also demonstrated a capacity for verbal communication. This will come as a surprise to those old enough to recall the stumbling syntax that so often characterized his press conferences as president, but, as an aide to General MacArthur in the 1930s, Eisenhower drafted most of the eloquent general's speeches. During his mission as commander of the Allied forces in World War II, he drafted delicate orders that were considered models of tact and understanding, wrote more than one hundred letters to his own commander, George C. Marshall, and managed to carry on a fairly lively personal correspondence as well. In one letter to a former West Point classmate, he wrote, "I think sometimes that I am a cross between a onetime soldier, a pseudo statesman, a jack-legged politician and a crooked diplomat. I walk a soapy tightrope in a rainstorm with a blazing furnace on one side and a pack of ravenous tigers on the other. . . . In spite of this, I must admit that the whole thing is interesting and intriguing."

This description not only indicates an ability to put ideas into words but also provides a fairly accurate description of just what his job entailed. Heading up the Allied forces turned out to be one of the most challenging administrative tasks in history.

Eisenhower was picked for this difficult assignment by George C. Marshall, who had spotted Eisenhower's abilities and had started grooming him for higher responsibilities once he, Marshall, had become chief of staff. When Marshall found that he could not take on the commander's role himself, because Roosevelt wanted him to stay in Washington, he sent Eisenhower in his place. It proved to be a fortunate choice.

The difficulties confronting Eisenhower stemmed not so much from the military as from the political situation. There were all types of people, parties, and pressures that had to be skillfully managed. They included the various British armed forces and their leaders, British public opinion, British political leaders, many different and often conflicting French interests, other Allied forces and their governments (including the exile governments in London), and then of course, his own troops and their commanders, his military and political superiors in Washington, and the American press and public opinion. All these, plus the persistent pressure to bring the European war to as speedy an end as possible with a minimum of Allied bloodshed, required masterly managerial skills. Eisenhower approached this Herculean task with modesty and geniality. He would share his thoughts with his subalterns as if they were his coequals, and he framed his commands as if they were advice. In the view of one of his biographers, the British Brigadier General Sixsmith, he was a superb delegator of authority, and yet he was able "to keep his finger on all that was going on. His subordinates were able to see that they were expected to act, they were told what was in Eisenhower's mind, and they knew he would not shrink from responsibility."

Regarding this latter point, Eisenhower issued a directive early in the campaign that newspaper stories criticizing him should not under any circumstances be censored. When it came time for the cross-channel invasion of France, he prepared a statement for use in the event that the invasion misfired in which he accepted full blame for its failure. During the campaign across Europe that followed, he shrugged off persistent attempts in the British press to give the credit for Allied successes to the British generals, Montgomery and Alexander.

One good illustration of Eisenhower's managerial skill was his handling of General George C. Patton. Eisenhower recognized that Patton was in many ways an excellent combat commander, particularly when it came to tank warfare. He further realized that the Germans had a high estimation of Patton and feared him as they feared no other Allied combat general. Eisenhower was also painfully aware of Patton's many weaknesses, such as his egoism, his officiousness, and his reactionary cast of mind.

When Patton set off an uproar in the United States slapping American soldiers who had been hospitalized with bad nerves or battle fatigue, Eisenhower refused to take the easy course and relieve him of command. Instead, he ordered Patton to make personal apologies to the slapped men, the medical personnel, and all others concerned. Patton, desperate to continue in command, complied. Two years later when the savage Nazi counterattack almost upset the Allies in the historic Battle of the Bulge, Patton's adept rescue of the besieged U.S. forces vindicated Eisenhower's action.

He tolerated Patton as long as he could, but after the war ended and Patton insisted on employing ex-Nazis in his zone of occupation, Eisenhower moved to replace him. Even at this point he tried to ease the aging general's humiliation by asking Patton whom he would like as a replacement. When Patton named someone who was acceptable to Eisenhower, the American commander appointed him.

His tact and concern were in evidence not only in handling his commanders. He also regularly toured the ranks, talking with the soldiers, and looking after their well-being. He sharply reproved any base commander who used his best facilities for administrative quarters instead of giving them up for the rest and relaxation of the men doing the fighting.

Behind his modest geniality lay a great singleness of purpose. He realized that the alliance would falter and flounder unless there was a single overall commander, and he made sure that this was accepted and acknowledged. He also took steps to see that throughout the Allied forces all issues would be discussed and decided on considerations other than national pride. His creation of an integrated command—integrated not only in combining the forces of several nations but also in combining the army and navy of these nations—is considered his greatest accomplishment.

He also knew how to put first things first. In North Africa he deferred his integration scheme, important though it was, to capture Tunis before the bad weather set in and when Roosevelt urged him to lead the troops into Rome, glorifying his own and the U.S. role in the city's liberation, he refused to get to England more quickly and have more time to work on the coming invasion of France.

Eisenhower had originally wanted to have an invasion of southern France accompany the cross-channel attack. Owing to a shortage of landing craft and other factors, he continually had to scale down his plan, but he did not scuttle the idea until the end. In Sixsmith's view, this decision "was typical of the man," for "he liked to keep his options open."

As a military strategist, Eisenhower did make his share of mistakes. He allowed the German military divisions in Sicily to escape, he balked at sending his airborne division to capture Rome, and he opened a hole in his front that permitted Hitler to launch the perilous and costly Battle of the Bulge. It took the Allied forces, despite their complete domination of the air and their vast superiority on the ground, nearly a year after the time they crossed the channel to bring Germany to defeat.

He was, according to Sixsmith, by no means a poor strategist either, constantly beset as he was by conflicting pressures. In the north, Montgomery was insisting that the full Allied thrust be put into his hands. He was supported by feverish public opinion in England, not only because he was their general but also because they feared the German rockets that were being launched from the area that Montgomery was trying to capture. Farther south, there was Patton, chomping at the bit, demanding more gasoline and other scarce supplies as well as men, and because American public opinion needed a hero of its own, Patton could not be completely restricted. Meanwhile, the French were clamoring for the liberation of Paris, a move that would not only detract from the route of advance but could hinder further advances, because supplies and the trucks to carry them would have to be siphoned off to maintain the city afterward.

On balance, Eisenhower handled his strategist role adequately and his administrative and political role superbly. This is Sixsmith's view, and it seems to reflect the consensus of others in a position to know. When Germany finally surrendered, General Marshall, not, as we have seen, overly given to effusive praise, sent Eisenhower a long and effusive letter of congratulations: "You have commanded with outstanding success . . . you have met and successfully disposed of every conceivable difficulty . . . you have triumphed over inconceivable logistical problems and military obstacles . . . you have made history, great history for the good of mankind. . . ."

Churchill shared much the same view. Shortly before Roosevelt died, the British prime minister wrote the president, expressing "admiration of the great and shining qualities of character and personality which he [Eisenhower] has proved himself to possess. . . ." But most important of all was the judgment of British Field Marshal Montgomery, the petulant prima donna who chafed and complained at the way Eisenhower had restricted him during the war. Said Montgomery afterward, in words reminiscent of those used by the Los Alamos physicists to describe Oppenheimer, "No one but Ike could have done it."

But if Eisenhower performed so well in the highly sensitive and highly political role of supreme allied commander, why was he such an undistinguished president? There are many possible answers to this question, and all of them may contain some element of truth. For one thing, he may not have been such a poor president as historians have believed. Eisenhower thought that his greatest contribution was to keep the United States out of war, and in view of the actions of his successors, that accomplishment may not have received its due. Eisenhower, like Kennedy and Johnson, also came under pressure to invade Vietnam, but when such a course was urged on him by his secretary of state and his military chief of staff in 1954, he asked that Congress and other nations be sounded out first. When reaction from both quarters was negative, he scuttled the idea.

Another answer may be found in his age. He was ten years older when he entered the White House than when he took over the supreme Allied command, and while sixty-two is not an unusually advanced age for high political office—Churchill was in his late sixties during World War II and Clemenceau was in his late seventies when he headed France during World War I—the years take their toll on some people more than others. That for more than three years during the war he worked day and night, smoking four full packs of cigarettes a day and getting no exercise, certainly did not contribute toward his later lack of vigor.

But most of all, the answer lies in the point raised at the start of this chapter, and that is the situational nature of leadership. Leaders create their situations, to be sure, but situations also create their leaders. Such was the case with Dwight D. Eisenhower.

Questions and Instructions

1. Can leadership be learned? Explain.
2. The ability to make good decisions is crucial if a leader is to be successful. What does this case study say about President Eisenhower's penchant for making decisions?
3. Leaders create their situations, but situations also create their leaders. In Eisenhower's case, which premise are we to believe? Why?
4. Why is Eisenhower considered a more effective war administrator than presidential administrator?
5. How did Eisenhower's network of prior associations and preferences contribute to his success as war administrator, yet detract from his record as presidential administrator? Explain.
6. How did the leadership styles of Eisenhower and General Patton differ?
7. What role, if any, did charisma play in Eisenhower's approach to leadership?
8. Why do leaders place more emphasis upon reasoned judgment than creativity? In roles as war and presidential administrators, did Eisenhower exude creativity, or did he exercise good judgment? Or did he demonstrate both?
9. To lead successfully, a person must believe that his or her leadership will make a difference. In roles as war and presidential administrators, did Eisenhower make a difference? Explain.

Insights-Issues / The Supreme Allied Commander

Clearly and briefly describe and illustrate these concepts, issues, or points. Interpret the word "role" as meaning impact, application, importance, effect and/or illustration of certain facts, concerns, or issues from the case study.

1. Eisenhower's roles as leader and manager. What circumstances afforded Ike opportunities, as supreme allied commander, to emerge as a leader and when did he act as a manager? Explain.
2. As supreme allied commander and as president, what role/s did the "political situation" have on Eisenhower's leadership? Explain.
3. How did Eisenhower define the institutional mission and role/s as supreme allied commander? Explain.
4. How did Eisenhower "order" internal conflicts as supreme allied commander? Explain.

5. Leadership qualities include optimism, energy, enterprise, intelligence, verbal ability, creativity, and judgment. In what ways, did Eisenhower deploy some or all of these characteristics? Explain.

ENDNOTES

1. The material on Oppenheimer in this chapter is drawn mainly from Nuel Pharr Davis, *Lawrence and Oppenheimer* (New York: Simon & Schuster, 1968).
2. Peter F. Drucker, *The Effective Executive* (New York: Harper & Row, 1967), 22.
3. John Yemma, "Fragments of History: A Lot Can Be Learned about Boston's Past from the Artifacts of Daily Life Buried in the Earth," *Boston Globe,* 2 March 1997, p. 18.
4. Douglas McGregor, *Leadership and Motivation* (Cambridge, MA: MIT Press, 1966), 73.
5. William J. Reddin, *Managerial Effectiveness* (New York: McGraw-Hill, 1970), 35.
6. Karlene Kerfoot, "Leadership: When Success Leads to Failure," *Nursing Economics* 15, no. 5 (September–October, 1997): 275–277.
7. Arthur M. Schlesinger, Jr., *A Thousand Days* (New York: Fawcett World Library, 1967), 403.
8. Harlan Cleveland, "A Philosophy for the Public Executive," in *Perspectives on Public Management,* ed. Robert T. Golembiewski (Itasca, Ill.: F. E. Peacock, 1968).
9. "Good Leaders Must First Be Good People," *Black Issues in Higher Education* 13, no. 9 (27 June 1996): 64.
10. David Halberstam, *The Best and the Brightest* (New York: Random House, 1969), 318–319.
11. Daniel Katz and Robert L. Kahn, *The Social Psychology of Organizations* (New York: John Wiley, 1966), 293–294.
12. Burleigh Gardner, "Successful and Unsuccessful Executives," *Advanced Management* (September 1948):.
13. Ibid., 115.
14. David E. Lilienthal, *Management: A Humanist Art* (New York: Columbia University Press, 1967), 17.
15. Townsend Hoopes, *The Limits of Intervention* (New York: David McKay, 1969), 79–80.
16. C. P. Snow, *Science and Government* (New York: New American Library, 1962), 79–80.
17. Anyone who believes that dynamic dictators are immune to such a tendency may find the following quotation from Adolph Hitler of interest. "Unless I have the incorruptible conviction: This is the Solution, I do nothing—not even if the whole party tried to drive me to action. I will not act. I will wait no matter what happens." Quoted in Walter C. Lanager, *The Mind of Adolf Hitler* (New York: Basic Books, 1972), 81.
18. Katz and Kahn, *The Social Psychology,* 545–546.
19. Daniel Katz, "Patterns of Leadership," *Handbook of Political Psychology* (San Francisco: Jossey-Bass Publishers, 1973), 216–217.
20. A. M. Henderson and Talcott Parsons, eds, *Max Weber: The Theory Of Social and Economic Organization* (New York: Oxford University Press, 1947), 328.
21. Rom. 12 New English Bible With Apocrypha.
22. Michael Hill, *A Sociology of Religion* (London: Heinmann Educational Books, 1973), 147.
23. 1 Cor. 12:4 New English Bible With Apocrypha.

24. John M. Pfiffner and Frank P. Sherwood, *Administrative Organization* (Englewood Cliffs, N.J.: Prentice-Hall, Inc., 1960), 55–56.

25. Robert J. House, "A 1976 Theory of Charismatic Leadership," in *Leadership: The Cutting Edge,* eds. James G. Hunt and Lars L. Larson (Carbondale, Ill.: Southern Illinois University Press, 1977), 193–204.

26. Ibid., 204.

27. Reinhard Bendix, *Max Weber: An Intellectual Portrait* (Garden City, N.Y.: Doubleday & Co., Inc., 1947), 245.

28. Robert C. Tucker, "The Theory of Charismatic Leaderhip," *Daedalus* 97, no. 3 (summer 1968): 745.

29. Rajnandini Pillai, "Crisis and the Emergence of Charismatic Leadership in Groups: An Experimental Investigation," *Journal of Applied Social Psychology* 26, no. 6 (16 March 1996): 543–563.

30. Lyn Ragsdale and John J. Thesis, III, "The Institutionalization of the American Presidency, 1924–92," *American Journal of Political Science* 41, no. 4 (October 1997): 1280–1318.

31. Ibid., 1282.

32. C. Northcote Parkinson, *Parkinson's Law and Other Studies of Administration* (New York: Ballantine Books, 1964), 103.

33. Ari Z. Zivotofsky, "The Leadership Qualities of Moses," *Judaism: A Quarterly Journal of Jewish Life and Thought* 43, no. 3 (summer 1994): 258–270.

34. Katz and Kahn, *The Social Psychology,* 332.

35. William Gengler and Connie Riley, "Two States' Training Programs Lead the Way into the 21st Century," *Corrections Today.* 57, no. 3 (June 1995): 104–107.

36. Douglas McGregor, *The Theory of Human Enterprise* (New York: McGraw-Hill, 1960).

37. Katz, Daniel and Kahn, Robert L. *The Social Psychology,* 321.

38. Martin R. Smith, *I Hate to See a Manager Cry* (Reading, Mass.: Addison-Wesley, 1973), 108.

39. Charles Frankel, *High on Foggy Bottom* (New York: Harper and Row, 1968), 56.

40. Rosemary Stewart, *The Reality of Organizations* (New York: Anchor Books, 1972), 48.

41. For an interesting and informative view of some of the Tsar's leadership problems, see the earlier chapters of Robert K. Massie, *Nicholas and Alexandra* (New York: Atheneum, 1969).

42. David E. Lilienthal, *Management: A Humanist Art* (New York: Columbia University Press, 1967), 16–17.

43. Drucker, *The Practice of Management* (New York: Harper & Row, 1954), 122.

44. The principal source of material for this case study is E. K. G. Sixsmith, *Eisenhower as Military Commander* (New York: Stein & Day, 1973). Another source is Ladislas Fargo, *Patton: Ordeal and Triumph* (New York: Dell Publishing, 1970).

8

COMMUNICATION

Communication and public administration, or organizational structure, are crucial factors for achieving integration and coordination of agency goals, rules, and human resources. Structures, processes, and cultures of government bureaus must be defined and communicated. Organizational structure sways communication direction and substance. Formal communication and the formal authority structure merge. Vertical communication is transmitted between government executives and agency employees. Horizontal communication probes roles of tasks, work units, and divisions.

Human communication is ongoing and interactive. Communication is dynamic, ongoing, ever-changing, and continuous. The message is sent. The receiver perceives the message and accepts the message. Communication models find their origins in Greek antiquity. Aristotle recognized the speaker, speech, and audience as communication components. Five hundred years before Christ, Greek philosopher Heraclitus, observed that "a man (or woman) can never step into the river twice. The man (or woman) is different and so is the river."[1] Change and continuity are interwined—as men or women step into the river—in a process of actions which flow through the ages. Communication is a process and flows like a stream through time.

BACKGROUND ON ADMINISTRATIVE COMMUNICATION

The study of political communication should involve an understanding of both political messages and the national political structure. The American founders in the 1790s were opposed to political organizations, parties, and campaigns. Public communications were distilled through government officials who believed themselves capable of deciding on matters of public good. According to Michael Schudson, the framers of the Constitution recognized this approach as the wrong way to run a democratic government. The 1790s offer a lesson concerning the construct of the public sphere and public participation as political communication.[2]

Through the years, administrators and administrative theorists have placed increasing emphasis on communication. In the 1930s, Chester Barnard called attention to the fact that "a common purpose must be commonly known, and to be known must in some way be communicated. With some exceptions, verbal communication between men is the method by which this is accomplished."[3]

In the 1950s, Simon stressed communication. "It is obvious," he noted, "that without communication there can be no organization, for there is no possibility then of the group influencing the behavior of the individual. Not only is communication absolutely essential to organization, but the availability of particular techniques of communication will and should be distributed through the organization. . . . " Simon went on to conclude that "only in the case where the man who is to carry out a decision is also the best man fitted to make the decision is there no problem of communication—and in this exceptional case there is, of course, no reason for organization."[4]

THE POLITICS OF GREETING

Male primates have elaborate greeting rituals that include touching the genitals of one another. Human males greet one another and interact in a far different casual manner than do women. Women put a great deal of effort into putting others at ease.

Source: Michael Segell, "The Politics of Greeting," *Esquire* 128, no. 1 (July 1997): 84–86.

More recent writers have assigned communication an equal, if not more important, role. They consider such organizational ingredients as solidarity and support, along with command and control, to be closely related to organizational communication. Some even view organizations as essentially systems of communication and regard all or nearly all organizational problems as communication problems. Such an approach may go too far, but it can prove helpful.

Communication presents as many problems as any other aspect of administration, if not more. There are, first, the *technical* problems.

Parties involved in a communications network may not only withhold information but may also intentionally distort it. The distortions that come about through maliciousness, however, are exceeded by those that occur through mischance.

Communications problems arise not only from information that is too slow, incomplete, or distorted, but also from information that is overabundant. This is the problem of *communication overload*. Occasionally, this communication problem also arises by intent. For example, school superintendents sometimes purposely flood their school board members with reports and other documents, which, although completely accurate, are so voluminous it is impossible for the board members to know what is happening. As the board members struggle in vain to keep abreast of the swelling tide of information, the superintendent calmly proceeds to do pretty much whatever he or she wants to do.

Most overload problems, however, arise from sheer force of circumstances, and the circumstances that make for too much communication are increasing all the time. The growing complexity, specialization, and interdependence of today's organizational world are adding to the rising flood of information—a process being aided and abetted by the exponential growth of *communications technology*. An organization may take great care and achieve great success in developing excellent lines and flows of communication, only to sink under the profusion of information that may develop as a result.

FORMAL AND INFORMAL COMMUNICATION

Communication falls into two basic categories, formal and informal. They are easily defined. *Formal communication is written communication; informal is oral.* Of course, not all informal communication is verbal. Attitudes and even ideas can be transmitted by means of inflection, gesture, and body language, but although nonverbal communication has a place in organizational life, its role is usually not great and, in any case, it is hard to analyze and define. Consequently, our discussion of informal communication will be directed toward verbal communication. What factors govern the use of one form of communication over the other? Under what conditions does formal communication take precedence over informal and vice versa?

Usually, two factors foster the use of formal communication. One of these is *organizational size*. As organizations grow, they tend to make increasing use of formal communication and, correspondingly, diminishing use of its opposite. The other factor is *public character*. Public organizations tend to rely more heavily on formal communication than do private ones. A brief examination of the merits of formal communication will show why this is true.

Bureaucratic establishments are inclined to depend on written official documents that keep, process, and update images of reality. Organizations harbor and manage distrust so they rely on the papers or the written word. Images must be shared and binding and the way these are updated should be regulated. Organizations make and maintain what is called "papereality," a world of symbols or written representations that take precedence over things and events portrayed.[5]

THE ADVANTAGES OF FORMAL COMMUNICATION

Formal communication fosters *accountability*. This makes it indispensable for governmental affairs, particularly in a democracy. Unless the public and those who serve its information needs, such as the press and legislators, can find out what orders were given and who gave them, it cannot make the judgments needed to ensure truly democratic government.

By facilitating accountability, formal communication places natural restraints on arbitrariness, capriciousness, favoritism, and discrimination. By proceeding on formal instructions and keeping records of their transactions, public officials find it much more difficult, although certainly not impossible, to depart from acceptable standards of impartiality and fairness. Of course, the rules and standards may be unfair, but if so, this is at least a matter of public record and can be easily determined. An administrator with integrity will welcome the opportunity to document his or her actions.

Many of the scandals and sensational political events of recent decades that have shed valuable light on governmental operations illustrate this advantage of formal communication.

Formal communication in this way curbs the disparities and discrepancies that can occur even without express design. With all the good will in the world, distortions can and will creep in when formal communication is absent. Written communication allows everyone concerned to receive the same message and to check back on it if he or she is at any time uncertain as to what it says.

This brings us to still another asset of formal communication. It saves time. In any large organization, it would be difficult to issue all instructions orally. Not only would distortions occur as the message was relayed from person to person

---

MISCOMMUNICATION ABOUT INCORRECT ASSUMPTIONS

Many government services are underused because the paperwork is complex and was designed without the appropriate audience in mind. Moreover, most people do not adequately read instructions. Government form compilers make incorrect assumptions concerning the respondents' attitudes, ability, and knowledge. Compilers expect that respondents will read the whole form and have a higher reading level than most possess, while assuming an unavailable background knowledge. To make government programs more effective, reductions in the forms' complexity are necessary as well as changing the respondents attitudes toward reading instructions.

Source: Carel Jansen and Michael Steelhouder, *Journal of Technical Writing and Communication* 22, no. 2 (spring 1992): 179–195.

---

or group, but time would be needlessly consumed. Written communication allows an almost infinite number of people to receive the same message at the same time, and if these people forget any portions of it, they do not have to check back to the sender of the message, for they have it in front of them.

Written communication can also save time when it travels from the bottom to the top. It would be nearly impossible for any large and complex organization to orally receive all the information that it may need to obtain from its far-flung operations. Its phones would be constantly busy and its office personnel continually relaying what they think headquarters needs and wants to know. As a superior receives information from subordinates, he or she may save time by insisting the data be in writing. He or she can usually read memoranda from several different people in the time it takes to talk to one person. This also allows the supervisor to schedule more efficiently and to allocate periods of the day or week for reviewing such messages.

Written communication also allows information to be more fully developed with all of its ramifications discussed. Issues of any importance usually require such treatment. The document that results can then be circulated to others for still further analysis, until all possible points of view have been solicited and all aspects have been explored.

Finally, written communication not only helps to inform the recipient but may also do the same for the sender. Francis Bacon said that an index is chiefly useful for the person who makes it and the same can be said for many of the memoranda, reports, and so on that flow through the corridors of bureaucracy. By accumulating data in writing, the administrator encounters items that may have been overlooked. Expressing ideas in written form usually helps the person doing the writing to ferret out details previously disregarded and to see relationships and implications previously missed. Many a bureaucrat will frequently testify that he or she did not fully understand an issue until after writing a memo about it.

There are many good reasons the written word looms so large in the operations of government. We should bear them in mind when we discuss some of the less attractive aspects of written communication.

THE DISADVANTAGES OF FORMAL COMMUNICATION

Shortly after he was appointed secretary of Housing and Urban Development, George Romney held a press conference and displayed a stack of paper that stood two and a half feet high and weighed fifty-six pounds. This, he said, represented the paper generated by an application for a single, urban-renewal project.[6]

Although the problem, as Romney explained it, was caused more by faulty organization than by a sheer obsession with formal documents, it does illustrate that one of the ways in which organizational pathologies work is by generating a profusion of paper. The use of the written word tends to encourage its further use, and many a governmental and private organization have found themselves swamped in a *sea of documentation.*

Romney's display is only one of many incidents that have shed light on this startling problem.

Few organizations have managed to escape the ravages of the paper revolution. The late Federal Bureau of Investigation (FBI) director, J. Edgar Hoover, consistently boasted that the FBI was not a bureaucratic agency, and considering the highly personalized manner in which he ran the agency, he was, to some extent, right. Yet the FBI did not manage to avoid the maze and craze of documentation. Its agent's manual encompassed 32,000 rules and regulations, and its files would have filled an area equal to twelve football fields. When an agent in Philadelphia was scheduled to speak at a dinner, his office sent out a report on the event to headquarters and thirty-seven other field bureaus and then filed the report under eleven different categories in its files.[7]

In a desperate effort to stem the ever-swelling flow, Congress enacted the Paperwork Reduction Act of 1980. This legislation gives the Office of Management and Budget near absolute authority to approve activities, such as requests for information, that would generate more paper. Sponsors of the act claimed that a mere 1 percent reduction in bureaucratic paperwork would save the nation a billion dollars. The act also established the Federal Information Locator System to provide an index to information sources within the federal government. Such a system would, it was hoped, encourage federal agencies to share information and keep them from collecting data other agencies had already compiled.[8]

The main goal of the 1980 paperwork legislation was to reduce the public's paperwork burden by 25 percent. For example, paperwork for federal employment guidelines, defense procurement contracts, and even individual income tax forms was to be reduced. The result of the legislation, however, has been to enhance the power of the White House, especially the Office of Management and Budget (OMB), at the expense of the Congress. In the struggle for control of the regulatory process, the executive won this battle over the form and content of regulations issued by federal departments and agencies. Members of Congress argue that they are empowered to oversee departments and agencies. Congressional committees use appropriations power to control decisions of executive agencies. OMB insists that the responsibility to determine if regulations are an unnecessary burden on

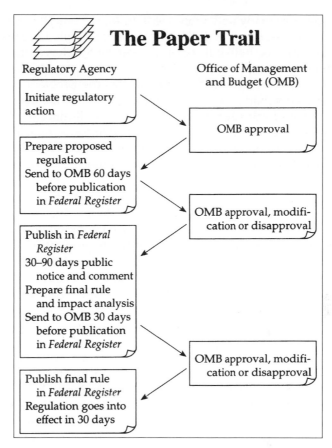

The Paper Trail

Regulatory Agency

Office of Management and Budget (OMB)

Initiate regulatory action

OMB approval

Prepare proposed regulation
Send to OMB 60 days before publication in *Federal Register*

OMB approval, modification or disapproval

Publish in *Federal Register*
30–90 days public notice and comment
Prepare final rule and impact analysis
Send to OMB 30 days before publication in *Federal Register*

OMB approval, modification or disapproval

Publish final rule in *Federal Register*
Regulation goes into effect in 30 days

Source: Kitty Dumas, "Congress or the White House: Who Controls the Agencies?" *Congressional Quarterly Weekly Report.*

the public belongs to the president. However, more than fifty years ago Congress ceded statutory authority to the executive branch on what and how information was collected by the federal departments and agencies. The struggle between the two branches of government over the content and process of the regulatory paperwork continues. The formal communication process in this balance-of-powers debate creates a massive paper trail as outlined in the figure "The Paper Trail."

The states, too, have been moving ahead to abridge the rising tide of paperwork. Kentucky, Minnesota, Ohio, and Washington are only a few of those states that have launched paperwork reform measures. When an inventory in Indiana showed that the state had 68,300 different forms, officials managed to eliminate 20,000 of them within the following two years.

Praiseworthy and productive as such steps may be, one must not forget that the growing crush of paper is in many respects a symptom of other organizational problems, not only a problem in itself. One frequent cause of excess paperwork is an insufficiency of delegation. A superior who insists on making all decisions personally and who needs to know everything that is going on, down to the smallest detail, will find his or her desk piled high with memoranda, reports, and requests. In like manner, an agency that has split duties among several sub-units when the tasks could be handled by one will also add to its paper problems. This, according to Romney, was the problem at HUD. An urban-renewal application had to travel through the hands of too many assistant secretaries.

Some of the advantages of written communication lead to its abuse. If it promotes accountability, then it also fosters self-protection. People may put something in writing so that they cannot be accused of having done something improperly or so that they can point to the record later on and show where they were right.

Whatever the causes of paper profusion, its cost can be immense. We have already seen some estimates of the cost involved in printing, storing, and circulating forms, but other costs may also be included. A memo may save the superior's time but may consume inordinate amounts of the subordinate's time; this also bears a price tag. It is not uncommon for a public employee to spend a day or more drafting a memorandum on an issue that could have been settled in a ten-minute conversation with the superior. When this occurs, the time involved in formal communication is usually working against the organization instead of for it.

Each piece of paper, we should remember, tends to spawn offspring of its own. One person's contribution evokes a similar or even greater contribution from others. If Ralph sends a memo to Ed, then Ed must often send a memo back. Ed may at the same time send a memo to Mary asking her for comments. Mary may not even have waited for Ed to act. If Mary has heard about Ralph's memo, then she may feel inclined to do some memo writing on personal initiative. To make the memo better, Mary may send a memo to Jane seeking some additional information, which, in return, produces a memo from Jane. And so it goes.

Meanwhile, the ever-bulging files start to produce problems other than the costs of storage. Completeness of information, carried too far, can lead to less information, or at least information that can be used less easily.

These problems have an impact on the organization's employees. Formal communication by virtue of being formal is less humane. It may have a dispiriting and even deadening effect on human relations. Indeed, people start to "turn off" when too many formal communications pour in on them and the messages end up in wastepaper baskets unread.

Finally, while formal communication is usually clearer and less liable to be misunderstood than its opposite, this is not always the case. The story is told of how J. Edgar Hoover became irked at the sender of a memo because the sender had not left wide enough margins for the FBI chief to scribble his comments. Wide margins were a bureau policy, so he wrote in it, "Watch the borders" and sent it back. For the next week FBI agents fanned out on the Mexican and Canadian borders in the bewildering belief that their boss wanted them to keep a vigil.

The Information Highway

Technology impacts modes of communication, formal and informal. In an era of faxes, computers, and photostat machines, communication challenges will emerge that are even more complex, demanding, and technical. Computer electronic mail and telephone answering machines contribute to the narrowing of the gulf between formal and informal communication distinctions.

Technology is crucial in the development of the information highway that would link every home to a fiber-optic network over which voice, data, television, and other services would be transmitted. The Internet's architecture is determined by an informal group of U.S. based software and computer engineers. The Internet's global scope and electronic commerce's growth make its management an international policy issue. Analysts and government believe a hands-off approach is best.[9]

People and organizations determine the course of the future, not computers. As a form of communication, the Internet can be used by individuals, private corporations, and government agencies for good or bad, but it cannot influence the direction our society chooses to take. The Internet only reflects the society that created it. The development and use of the telegraph and telephone provide a definitive pattern for how the newest form of networked communication, the Internet, will be used in the future.[10]

The lack of accountability and civility have increased as the anonymity in U.S. society has increased, states newspaper columnist Ellen Goodman. She cites the anonymous zones of talk radio and cyberspace among the fox holes for people who want to say anything and everything with impunity.[11]

Despite the downside of the information highway, Internet access has made communication between local government and citizens much easier nationwide. Public records access, personnel postings, permitting, and legislative updates are available online in dozens of cities and counties.[12] For example, former Massachusetts Governor Weld launched his renewed government cutting effort with a toll-free number and an Internet address to take taxpayer suggestions and offers of cash prizes of up to $5,000 for state workers' top bureaucracy-busting ideas.[13]

Informal communication is used heavily in Japanese industry and interoffice memoranda. Superiors spend considerable time "walking the floor" and talking with their employees. Conferences are common at all levels and are often conducted in an informal and relaxed atmosphere. Judging from Japan's growth rates and productivity levels, it does not seem to have hurt their administrative processes.

Informal Communication

Oral communication offers a solution to many of the problems encountered in written communication. It does not flood the office worker's desk or clog the files. It can evoke immediate feedback, which, in turn, can lead to a resolution of

---

CENSUS BUREAU ANNOUNCES MAJOR EXPANSION OF DATA DISSEMINATION ON INTERNET

The Commerce Department's Census Bureau offers a new Internet data delivery system that significantly expands user access to the agency's vast data resources as part of the Clinton Administration's initiative to make government more efficient and accessible to the public.

"This new system will complement the Census Bureau's existing Internet site by giving the public online access for the first time to our largest data collection programs," said James F. Holmes, acting Census Bureau director.

The new system, referred to as "American FactFinder," is being built under a privatized contract with the Census Bureau by IBM Global Services Corporation, principal contractor responsible for systems integration and user-interface design. The Oracle Corporation and Environmental Systems Research Institute Incorporated are privately subcontracted for relational database design, data warehousing, and mapping applications.

The first data released by the new system will be preliminary reports from the 1997 Economic Census, 1990 Census of Population and Housing files, American Community Survey test and demonstration data, and results of the Census 2000 Dress Rehearsal. The full range of Census 2000 data products are available via the American FactFinder system beginning in January 2001, with the release of the state population totals for reapportionment and the detailed population totals to the census block level for redistricting.

The American FactFinder permits users to define custom tabulations, contingent on meeting strict confidentially protections. The Census Bureau guarantees the confidentially of individual responses for seventy-two years.

A detailed description of the new system is available at the Census Bureau's public Internet site *<http://www.census.gov/dads/www>* or on the Census Bureau Home Page click on "Subjects A-Z" and American FactFinder. The Census Bureau is the preeminent collector and provider of timely, relevant, and quality data about the people and economy of the United States. In more than one hundred surveys annually and twenty censuses a decade, evolving from the first census in 1790, the Census Bureau provides official information about America's people, businesses, industries, and institutions.

Source: CB98-188, Public Information Office, Department of Commerce, Bureau of the Census, October 6, 1998. For further information, contact Sandra Rowland, telephone 301-457-3584, or contact the Public Information Office at email: pio@census.gov, or telephone 301-457-3030 or fax 301-457-3670.

---

any issues and clarification of any points that may be involved. In so doing, the one communicating can be assured that his or her information has been received. Speaking and listening permit the use of shading, emphasis, and gesture. Conversation is also significantly more human and often more humane. People are dealing together directly.

Efforts are also under way to substitute oral for written communication. President Johnson's task force on cutting red tape, for example, urged federal officials

---

EMPLOYERS AND E-MAIL

Most people are introduced to e-mail and Internet access in the workplace. It's in the workplace that they discover, too often, a lesser-known aspect of this exceptionally fluid and informal form of communication: *It has no guarantee of privacy.* For reasons that have occasioned much armchair psychological speculation, most of those new to e-mail seem to act as if they had a high expectation of privacy— indeed, as if they are talking to intimate friends. E-mailers also frequently blurt out things electronically that would never be said face-to-face.

Source: "Employers and E-mail," *Washington Post*, 18 April 1998, p. 18A.

---

to make more extensive use of the telephone and less use of "time-consuming written communications."[14] It is possible that the use of oral communication will grow apace in governmental agencies, although it will most likely never replace formal communication. For reasons noted earlier, the written word and the printed document will probably continue to serve as the mainstay of the communications process in any developed democracy.

GRAPEVINES

Any agency that has an informal organization will also have an informal communications system, often referred to as the "grapevine." Informal organizations are found in almost all organizations, therefore grapevines are ubiquitous.

The "grapevine," or informal communication network in government organizations, can have negative effects such as resentment, embarrassment for upper-level administrators, distorted messages, rumor diffusion, and subversion of administrative decision-making. Grapevines develop when employees share common hobbies, lunch schedules, families ties, common hometowns, and social relationships. These informal networks operate quickly, often accurately, and with resilience. It is suggested that management should use the network for its own purposes to complement formal networks. Administrators should also be candid about information if possible.[15]

Grapevines can also be terribly efficient. "With the rapidity of a burning powder train," says Keith Davis, a professor of management who has studied grapevines for years, "information flows out of the woodwork, past the manager's door and the janitor's mop closet, through steel walls or construction-glass partitions."[16] What is more, Davis claims, over three-fourths of this information is accurate.

Even when it is not accurate, says Davis, it may convey a psychological truth, for many rumors that run rampant through an organization are "symbolic expressions of feelings." If the rumor is that a certain employee is planning to quit, it may reflect the wish on the part of fellow employees that he or she would quit. Or it may reflect the employee's own desire to leave.

Davis advises managers to pay careful attention to the grapevine's information, for it may tell them more than they know about what is going on within their organization. He also urges them to disseminate whatever information they have to counter whatever errors the grapevine may be spreading. Beyond that, there is little that the administrator can do, because the grapevine, he says, "cannot be abolished, rubbed out, hidden under a basket, chopped down, tied up, or stopped." Managers might just as well accept it, for it "is as hard to kill as the mythical glass snake, which, when struck, broke into fragments and grew a new snake out of each piece."

THE OTHER ORGANIZATION

Organizational charts and manuals of procedure rarely provide us with an accurate picture of an organization. What is not official or even readily visible may often be the most important. Even the most formal organizations, which pride themselves on going strictly "by the book," rarely do so. An informal system of authority, which supersedes, at least to some extent, the formal one, may arise. In the army, for example, the lieutenant clearly outranks the sergeant. But when the sergeant has had twenty years of army service and the lieutenant is fresh from a college Reserve Officers Training Program (ROTC), the sergeant, rather than the lieutenant, may end up running the platoon.

Communication also flows frequently through informal channels. The office grapevine is usually faster and more complete than the office memo. Aboard a ship, for example, the real communications center is often not the captain's office but the kitchen or galley, and navy cooks are usually better sources of news than commanding officers. This is how the term "scuttlebutt" came to have its current meaning. The informal organization may spawn a network of relationships for which the organization chart and the manual of procedure provide few clues. All employees in the office may hold the same grade, but Jones, the oldest, gets the seat nearest the window, while Smith, the youngest, fetches the coffee for the 10:30 A.M. break. All the employees are assigned the same work, but because Black does better at processing form A while Brown performs better in processing form B, the A forms end up on Black's desk and the B forms on Brown's.

One of the most extreme examples of how the informal organization can overwhelm the formal organization is the U.S. prison system. Ostensibly, prisons are run by wardens and correction officers according to prescribed rules and regulations. In practice, this has rarely been the case. Sociologists and criminologists who have studied prisons have found out that most prisons have traditionally been run by the prisoners. This does not mean that prisons are democratic institutions; they are far from it. Rather, the supervisory personnel, faced with the enormous difficulties involved in everyday prison operation, eventually surrender basic control to what are often the toughest inmates in the institution.[17]

There is much brutality and ugliness in the typical prison, but those who have studied prisons feel that more often it results from too little, rather than too much, application of official authority. There are some exceptions to this, particularly at smaller institutions. In recent years prison officials have been asserting more control over penal facilities, but prisons have traditionally produced a whole subculture of beatings, homosexual gang rapes, and other grim and gruesome rituals, while the prison officials avert their eyes and try to get through the day with a minimum of trouble.

In most cases, the informal organization does not loom so large on the administrative scene, and its role should not be overstressed. It usually colors the formal organization but does not radically alter it. No matter how expert and experienced a sergeant may be, and no matter how naive and nervous the lieutenant may be, it is the lieutenant and not the sergeant who bears the final responsibility for the platoon. There is a limit as to how much authority the sergeant can acquire and how much the lieutenant may abdicate. Nevertheless, informal elements influence the operation of nearly all organizations, and the administrator must be alert as to what they are and what they do.

There are two aspects of informal organization that merit special attention. One concerns the role of *informal rules;* the other concerns the role of *small groups.*

WHOSE RULES?

Employees of organizations, like citizens of nations, tend to obey only those rules they believe in. Workers will accept a rule only if they regard it as legitimate in terms of their values. They will not accept it just because those who issued it had a legal right to do so.

Employees have also become adept at evading rules or bending them to suit their needs and desires, and the more rules the organization tends to set down, the more dexterity its members may show. "Any complex maze of rules," write Katz and Kahn, "will be utilized by the guardhouse lawyers in the system to their own advantage."[18] In this fashion the employees may use rules they dislike to defeat, rather than to serve the organization's purposes. Employees do this in some cases by enforcing the organization's rules to the letter, thereby creating pandemonium. Traffic police have driven their departments to despair by merely giving out a ticket to every motorist who deserved one, flooding the police department with a sharply increased workload and a sharply increased number of complaints from the community's more substantial citizens. In 1970, French customs inspectors, irate over the failure of the government to meet their demands, staged a "strike" by thoroughly inspecting every piece of baggage visitors brought into France. In doing so, they nearly paralyzed operations at France's international airports and disrupted travel in Europe.

The informal organization not only achieves frequent and sometimes spectacular success in sabotaging the formal organization's rules, but it also manages to establish and enforce rules of its own. Many of these rules concern work output. Those who exceed the informal quota may be branded as "ratebusters," while those who fail to carry their fair share of the load may earn the title of "chiseler." Seniority is another rule that governs many procedures of many informal organizations. Those with job seniority get the better assignments and the more congenial conditions. The most junior members may not only get the less desirable assignments but may also experience various petty harassments, like being sent to fetch the "left-handed monkey wrench." Sometimes the harassment is not so petty. College fraternities' hazing rituals have resulted in frequent injury and occasional death to their initiates.

Probably no informal rule is more widespread than the ban on *"squealing."* This prohibition is instilled in most Americans during their school years and tends to stay with them the rest of their lives. The taboo against *"tattling"* is so widely and deeply ingrained that even those who would stand to benefit from it tend to dislike it. The *"informer"* or *"spotter,"* no matter how useful he or she may be, rarely wins esteem in the eyes of management, and though the informer may increase his or her earnings, "squealing" seldom enhances chances for promotion.

While the formal organization often encounters difficulty in enforcing its rules, the informal organization usually succeeds in securing support and adherence to its own codes of behavior. Sanctions against offenders can take many forms, not excluding violence. Prisoners who depart from the informal rules can meet injury and even death at the hands of their fellow inmates, and when a New York City policeman named Frank Serpico decided to inform on corruption within the police force, he received several death threats from irate colleagues.[19]

Many informal rules are benign. While the *golden rule* remains an unattainable goal, it has become a nearly universal governing principle and, as such, governs a good deal of organization behavior. If people do not naturally love their neighbors as themselves, they do tend to help others who have helped them or at least try to refrain from injuring them. Gouldner claims that this norm is as ubiquitous and as important as the incest taboo in modern society.[20] As such, it counteracts the harshness that other rules, both formal and informal, may produce in organizational operations.

THE SMALL GROUP

The basic unit for the formal organization may be the division, the department, the section, or all three, plus others. The primary basis for the informal organization is usually the small group. Although many informal norms and rules are organization wide, many others are promulgated and enforced by small work groups. The small group consists of no set number of individuals. Rather, it designates any group whose members are in continual, face-to-face contact with each other. Such groups often follow the structural lines of the formal organization. The small group in the army infantry is typically the squad. In the university it is usually the department. Whether it conforms to any formally recognized structure, forces from within customarily dictate a good deal of its behavior.

The importance of the small group springs chiefly from the importance of primary relationships over secondary relationships in human behavior. Those people we work with every day invariably become more important to us than those whom we see infrequently or with whom we conduct relations at a distance. Out of such primary relationships come norms, codes, procedures, and the means for their enforcement. The famed "silent treatment" is most powerfully exercised on those with whom we are in daily contact.

An interesting example of how the small group develops and enforces its own rules is found in Peter Blau's *The Dynamics of Bureaucracy.* Blau reports on an office of a federal agency that had certain law-enforcement powers over business. Many times businessmen caught violating the law by agents would make implicit if not explicit offers of a bribe. The agents uniformly rejected such offers, for it was not only against organizational policy but against their own code to accept them. However, the agents had also learned to make use of these suborning attempts to prod the businessmen, making them settle the case on the agents' own terms. "Being offered a bribe constituted a special tactical advantage for an agent," writes Blau. "An employer who had violated one law was caught in the act of compounding his guilt by violating another one. Agents exploited this situation to strengthen their positions in negotiations."[21]

In refusing to accept bribe offers, the agents were abiding by the organization rules. These rules also called for agents to report such attempted bribes to their superiors, however. Here the agents departed from the formal rules, for to them reporting bribe offers constituted "squealing" and "squealing" constituted a cardinal sin. Blau could find only two cases in the recollection of the current agents when one of their number had reported the offer of a bribe. The agent in one case left the office. In the second, the agent concerned remained at work but was still undergoing the punishment of ostracism. This agent stoutly maintained his "innocence," claiming he had turned in the businessman only after the latter had pressed his bribe offer vigorously and in the presence of other parties. The agent's protestations were to no avail. None of his colleagues would have any dealings with him that were not absolutely necessary for the conduct of office affairs. Such are the workings of small groups and informal organizations.

THE INFORMAL BALANCE SHEET

The informal organization and the small groups that make it up can do a great deal of damage. They may, and often do, subvert the purposes of the organization, because they show a persistent tendency to do what is most congenial to their members and reject organizational endeavors that may conflict with their own basic goals. The British sociologist, Michael Banton, in his study of a U.S. police organization, was told that "first the front office decides and then the locker room decides."[22] He was left with the distinct impression that it was the locker room's decision that mattered most.

The informal organization can not only make things difficult for the formal organization, but it can also make things difficult for its members. Not only are the ratebusters or the chiselers usually punished, but sanctions may also be invoked against the member who dresses differently, who espouses radical views, or who in any way speaks or acts in a manner that marks him or her as "different."

Sometimes the informal organization acts in an entirely opposite way, but this can prove even more counterproductive to organizational goals. It may cover up for one or more of its members who fail to do what is expected. The alcoholic who arrives back from lunch in a stupefied state may be allowed to sleep it off in an unobtrusive place while the rest of the group tells the supervisor that he or she is gone on an official errand. Such practices harm not only the organization but also the individual, because it permits him or her to avoid confronting his or her problem and trying to resolve it.

The sense of team loyalty, which the informal organization fosters, can generate a variety of evils.

The informal organization also has a positive role to play, and organizational theorists are coming to accept and avow this. Note the following quotations:[23]

> *The incompleteness of the formal plan provides a vacuum which like other vacuums, proves abhorrent to nature. (Simon, Smithburg, and Thompson)*
>
> *No organization chart and no book of policies and procedures can specify every act and prescribe for every contingency encountered in a complex organization. To attempt such specification merely produces an array of instructions so ponderous that they are ignored for the sake of transacting the business of the organization. Moreover, even if such specifications could be provided, they would soon be out of date. . . . (Katz and Kahn)*
>
> *It would not, in any sense, be an exaggeration to assert that any large organization would come to a grinding halt within a month if all its members began behaving strictly in accordance with the structure of responsibility and authority defined by the formal organization chart, the position description, and formal controls. (McGregor) Reduced to its formal power, to the theoretical pact which constitutes it, every organization, every human enterprise is incapable of adapting itself to its environment. (Crozier)*

What these writers are saying is: *The formal organization cannot exist without its informal counterpart.* All organizational design is inevitably incomplete and imperfect, for there is too much complexity and variability in the interaction of human beings ever to be compressed into a formal system. As employees come and go, as new technologies develop and new problems arise, the formal plans and procedures, no matter how well designed, become increasingly outmoded. Periodic revamping can help but can never hope to keep pace with the rate and sweep of the changes taking place that affect organizational operations. Consequently, the facts of organizational life frequently become the unofficial rules and procedures.

FOREIGN LANGUAGE STUDY

Some employees of the Food and Drug Administration once decided to compile a dictionary to help people learn "bureaucratese." Here are some sample definitions from the new dictionary:

Infrastructure—(a) the structure within an infra; (b) the structure outside an infra; (c) a building with built-in infras. Meaningful—(a) opposite of meaningless; (b) the same as full of meaning; (c) when used as "meaningful relationship," it is what used to be called being in love (archaic).

In depth—(a) opposite of shallow; (b) opposite of out of depth; (c) should always be used before words such as study, research, analysis, and review so that readers will think that you didn't do a quick and dirty job.

If Ms. Green tends to wield the authority that belongs to Ms. White, then more often than not, Green possesses some competence that White lacks. If the seasoned sergeant exercises more authority than does the neophyte lieutenant, then undoubtedly many a soldier's life has been saved because of it. Young ROTC lieutenants used to be told, "Be good to your sergeant lest he carry out every order you give." If small groups tend to call the shots as they see them, then often they see them much better than does top management.

This brings us to the question of how the informal organization affects organizational productivity. You have read several ways in which it can sabotage and subvert organizational goals. However it can also do the reverse. Elton Mayo and his colleagues found in their Western Electric studies that informal, work-group norms could affect productivity in a positive way. More recently, Katz and Kahn have stated that the correlation between the informal group norms and productivity is likely to go in the way the organization would like to go.[24]

The small group has an important role in the informal organization. Research indicates that the larger the work unit, the greater the absenteeism and accidents. Small groups meet social and emotional needs, and whether they are the "highest" needs, such needs remain important for organizational purposes. In another of his books, *Bureaucracy in Modern Society*, Peter Blau writes that "the effective enforcement of unofficial standards of conduct in cohesive work groups has important implications for official operations. . . . Many studies have found that the existence of cohesive bonds between co-workers is a prerequisite for high morale and optimum performance of duty. . . . "[25]

The ultimate aim is to make the formal and the informal organization merge. Can this be achieved? According to Chris Argyris, informal organization results from the desires of organization members to satisfy needs that the formal organization neglects or even thwarts. He reports on studies he has done of two departments of a business corporation. One department did not attempt to meet such needs, and consequently its members developed informal ways of satisfying them. The other department made ample provision to meet these needs, through job security, personal recognition, variety, and challenge in work assignment. As a result, says Argyris, morale was high, personal relationships were warm, and the need for informal organization was hardly felt.[26]

Up, Down, and Across

Information in government agencies moves in three basic directions:

- upward from subordinate to superior,
- downward from superior to subordinate, and
- horizontally from one organizational unit to another.

No matter which way it flows, however, it runs into problems.

According to Katz and Kahn, communication up the line may occur in many forms, but such information may be reduced to what the person says:

1. about himself, his performance, and his problems;
2. about others and their problems;
3. about organizational practices and policies; and
4. about what needs to be done and how it can be done.[27]

The basic problem of upward communication is the nature of the hierarchical administrative structure because the first role requirement of executives and supervisors is to direct, coordinate, and control the activities of persons below them. Therefore, employees fear that information passed along the hierarchical chain of command may be used for control purposes. The employees are unlikely to pass along information that may affect them adversely. This concern makes the upward route the most difficult.

Upward communication networks are an important way for government employees to relay information to line officials. A functioning network can:

- facilitate quick and efficient upper-level administrative feedback;
- use government employee skills, knowledge, and expertise;
- communicate unique, yet valuable, information;
- improve public sector employee morale.

Employees have personal reasons for withholding or manipulating information. They may fear that the action such information would produce would prove disadvantageous to their interests. Or, if others stand a chance of being adversely affected, they may be fearful of being cast in the role of the informer. This particular problem in upward communication reflects problems inherent in hierarchy. As the French writer, Albert Camus, once noted, "There is nothing in common, in effect, between a master and a slave. One cannot speak or communicate with a subjugated human being. In place of that natural and free dialogue by which we acknowledge our resemblance and consecrate our destiny, servitude causes to reign the most terrible of silences."[28] Of course, bureaucratic relationships are rarely those of a master and slave, but wherever hierarchy is introduced, it will tend to act in this fashion. Chester Barnard once noted that information received from a low-status person will often receive scant attention, while information received from a high-status person may set off a reaction well beyond what was intended.[29]

Katz and Kahn point out that a superior is supposed to give orders and a subordinate is supposed to receive them. This means that upward communication goes against the organizational grain, for the subordinate is not used to telling things to the superior and the superior is not used to listening to things from the subordinate.[30] History supplies numerous examples of leaders who succumbed to this weakness and suffered severe setbacks as a result. Among them were such presidents as Woodrow Wilson, Lyndon Johnson, and Richard Nixon.

Unplugging the Upward Flow

Perhaps the most important step that an administrator can take in resolving or at least reducing these impediments to the upward passage of information lies in his or her own conduct. If he or she acts on the belief that information should move swiftly and surely upward, then the information is much more likely to do so. If he or she shows subordinates that the bad news should be told along with the good, and in as fresh and pure a form as possible, the subordinates will not only be more inclined to do so but will also be more likely to deal with their own subordinates in the same way.

In an organization of any size and complexity, however, this will not be enough. Fortunately, there are other ways and means of seeing to it that those above are kept adequately informed by those below. One such device is the trade union. Informing those on top of what is happening beneath them is one of the major contributions that unions can make to the administrative process. Many an executive shielded by middle management from much of what is going on at the rank-and-file level finds the unions a valuable supplier of needed information. The executive need not worry that the union's representatives will omit any unpleasant news.

Other means for improving the upward information flow are formal devices for hearing complaints. These may include grievance committees, appeals boards, and various clientele service units. For example, a mayor who sets up little city halls throughout the city to receive and process complaints may find that these complaints will give some excellent clues as to where problems may exist in his or her administration.

Investigatory units can also prove helpful in this regard. Many large police departments have a special unit to investigate police officers. The heads of the "shoefly squad," as it is usually called, can often provide the police commissioner with information that he or she might not hear from other subordinates.

Sometimes executives make their own field inspections, talking directly with rank-and-file personnel. This does not always have to be a formal inspection.

An executive can also disregard the chain of command on occasion and call someone several levels below for some direct conversation. An executive may

---

ELECTRONIC ACCESS TO LOCAL GOVERNMENT INFORMATION

In Santa Monica, California, municipal government installed a city-wide Public Electronic Network (PEN) of microcomputers and terminals to provide its residents with twenty-four-hour access to local government information. PEN bridges the gap between citizens and the bureaucracy of local government by giving users access to city council meetings, community center events, bus line schedules, and other city information. Users can send electronic mail to officials, city departments, or to each other. City officials are dedicated to a twenty-four-hour turnaround in response to questions or concerns. On-going discussions on topics such as crime or schools are read and commented on.

Source: Michael Artonoff, "Communication: Fighting City Hall at 2400 Baud," *Personal Computing* 13, no. 10 (October 1989): 170–174.

---

also stipulate a period each week or month when the office door will be open to anyone within the organization who has a matter to discuss. Surveys and polls of the organization's members and of its clients may also provide valuable information in addition to indications as to how the upward communications process is working.

There are, in short, many means available to ensure an upward flow of communication. Any public manager who wants an undistorted picture of what is going on in the organization should experience no trouble in obtaining it.

COMMUNICATING DOWNWARD

According to Katz and Kahn, there are five varieties of communications down the line, from superior to subordinate:

1. Specific task directives: job instructions.
2. Information designed to produce understanding of the task and its relationship to other organizational tasks: job rationale.
3. Information about organizational procedures and practices.
4. Feedback to the subordinate about his performance.
5. Information of an ideological character to inculcate a sense of mission: indoctrination of goals.[31]

While downward communication is less problematic than upward, communication down the line nevertheless encounters numerous obstacles and impediments. When it is oral, downward communication is subject to almost all the alterations that can creep in when it moves the other way. The captain tells the lieutenant to have the soldiers ready at 0800. The lieutenant, for protection, tells the sergeant to have them ready at 0700. And the sergeant, in a further manifestation of the same fear, makes sure the men are ready at 0600. As a result, the captain finds the soldiers sleepy and disgruntled when they are ordered into action.

When downward communication is written, difficulties may develop. The message may not be complete or the recipient may not be willing to accept it. The biggest problem, however, is probably the inability or the refusal of the recipient to absorb the information that seems to be cascading downward. As we have already seen, memoranda senders encounter persistent problems in this respect.

Organizations have tried to get around this in many ways. In some organizations, important messages are sent to the recipient's home, occasionally by special messenger, as an insurance that he or she will read it. And at least one school system makes a practice of following up the written messages that it distributes to its teachers in the school by broadcasting the same message through a loudspeaker.

There are other, and usually better, ways of surmounting this communication difficulty. People will often read material on bulletin boards that they might ignore if placed in their agency mail slots. This is particularly true if the bulletin board also carries other information besides that which emanates from the "front office." Consequently, a notice placed on a bulletin board can score a greater impact than if it were sent individually to each organization member.

Another useful device is the organization publication or house organ. Such publications usually depend for their appeal on the reporting of a wide range of personal items within the organization. The adroit administrator will also seek to sandwich in useful information regarding announcements, company policy, and so forth. Some private organizations have begun using in-house TV. They broadcast interviews with employees, both managerial and nonmanagerial, along with news of what the company is doing. Some also televise the company's annual stockholders' meeting.

Whatever the means used, the astute public administrator will develop techniques for making sure that the information he or she has sent has gotten through to those for whom it is intended, and the manager will check for feedback from employees. Not infrequently, the way in which a decision has been communicated will have a greater effect on agency operations than the substance of the decision.

CROSS-COMMUNICATION

A generation or so ago, lateral or horizontal communication received relatively little attention from administrative thinkers. Now it is becoming as important, and in some cases more important, than communication up and down. The growth of specialization and interdependency is making it increasingly vital for information to flow through the organization as well as to move up and down its ranks.

According to Katz and Kahn, communication among peers, in addition to providing task coordination, also furnishes emotional and social support to the individual. The mutual understanding of colleagues is one reason for the power of the peer group. Psychological forces always push people toward communication with peers; people in the same boat share the same problems. On the other hand if there are no problems of task coordination left to a group of peers, the content of their communication can take forms irrelevant to or destructive of organization functioning.[32] The communication channels become dysfunctional if line officials in the organizational hierarchy are charged with initiating all communications. The agency softball team or annual picnic, for examples, should be informal arrangements where someone other than the line officials communicate their directions.

Staff meetings can be particularly helpful in stimulating cross-communication. This assumes of course, that they are genuine interchanges of ideas and data and not just monologues by the person who presides. Within a broader context, interdepartmental committees may also aid the lateral communications process. And house organs, bulletin boards, and many of the other devices already cited can, and usually do, aid in spreading information from one section of the organization to another.

Physical arrangements can also play an important role in either helping or hampering cross-communication. It is more likely that units placed along the same corridor may experience more functional communication flows than units located on separate floors. Spreading units along the same corridor will usually encourage more communication than placing them on separate floors. And removing partitions that divide offices and work places from one another may greatly assist the cross-communication flow. Organizational practices designed to resolve other problems may foster cross-communication as well. In-service training, for example, may bring people from various parts of the organization together and result in a good deal of cross-communication. Organization-wide activities, such as bowling teams or hobby clubs, and an organizationally run cafeteria or dining room will also bring employees together and may lead to an interchange of information. Many of the tough problems that arise in Israeli kibbutzes, for example, are solved over the dining room tables in the evening.

Rotation of employees is also useful in improving cross-communication. The rotated employee can give new coworkers a better understanding of how things operate "over there." More importantly, former relationships can be used to maintain some communication flow with his or her former work unit. In any case, the rotated employee is likely to meet ex-colleagues from time to time and fill them in on what is happening at the new assignment.

As our technological society advances, and as organizations become more complex, cross-communication will become increasingly important. It is a subject that administrators will have to devote more attention to in the future than they have in the past.

SUMMARY

- Administrators and administrative theorists place increasing emphasis on communication.
- Communication problems arise not only from information that is too slow, incomplete, or distorted, but also from information that is too abundant. This is a problem of communication overload.
- Communication falls into two basic categories—formal and informal. Formal communication is written. Informal communication is oral. Formal communication fosters accountability, while informal communication does not produce mounds of paperwork.
- Formal communication restrains arbitrariness, capriciousness, favoritism, and discrimination.
- Organizational size and public character are factors affecting the use of formal communication.
- Among the symptoms of organizational pathology is the generation of a profusion of paper—a set of documentation.
- The paper trail includes the regulatory department or agency, the office of Management and Budget (OMB), public notice and comment, and codification of the rule in first the *Federal Register* and finally the *Code of Federal Regulations*.
- The informal communications system is often referred to as the "grapevine."
- Upward communication focuses on the employee, his or her performance, and problems; others and their problems; organizational practices and policies; and what needs to be done and how it can be done.
- Information moves in three basic directions: upward from subordinate to superior, downward from superior to subordinate, and horizontally from one organizational unit to another.
- Downward communication includes job instructions, job rationale, information about organizational procedures and practices, feedback to the subordinate about his or her performance, and indoctrination of goals.
- The growth of specialization and interdependency is making it increasingly vital for information to flow through the organization as well as to move up and down its ranks.
- Informal organization is more important in determining worker cooperation than formal organization. In this "other organization," output is set by social norms, not individual abilities, and the group greatly influences the behavior of individual workers.
- Employees of organizations, like citizens of nations, tend to obey those rules they believe in.
- The importance of the small group focuses upon the centrality of primary relationships over secondary relationships in human behavior.

This chapter began with an example of Winston Churchill's communication style. The following case study offers more details on one of history's greatest communicators.

CASE STUDY

Action This Day[33]

Words always came easily to Winston Churchill. As a young man, he engaged in many daring exploits while serving as a lieutenant with the British forces in India and later in South Africa. It was not so much the exploits themselves, however, but his skill in writing about them that gained him the prominence that was to win him a seat in Parliament and launch his political career.

His bitter denunciations of Britain's appeasement policies during the 1930s acquired sharpness and thrust through the pungent language he so often employed. "These are the years when the locust has eaten" was one of the phrases he used to describe that sorry period. When he served as prime minister during the war that ensued, he managed to warm the hearts and rally the spirits of his people with the stirring speeches he delivered in what he called "England's darkest hour."

Churchill's abilities as a communicator also characterized his administration, and they offer an interesting illustration of how a particular administrator sought to handle his many communication problems at a crucial time.

From the outset of his administration, Churchill placed a heavy emphasis on the written word. "Let it be very clearly understood," he informed his war cabinet, "that all directions emanating from me are made in writing, or should be immediately afterwards confirmed in writing, and that I do not accept any responsibility for matters relating to national defense on which I am alleged to have given decisions unless they are recorded in writing."

The message indicates one of the main reasons he adopted such a policy. War administration is crisis administration and as such can lead to considerable confusion. Orders given in a hurry and quickly passed down can easily be misunderstood, with dire results. Other orders that are vital may go unheeded or become lost in the far-flung and fast-moving governmental machinery. Churchill wanted none of that, and because he had no problem in handling the written word, he used this facility to keep intermediaries at a minimum and to stay in direct touch with a vast number of people.

Through the timesaving device of formal communication Churchill was able to personally direct much of Britain's governmental activity. He retained for himself the cabinet post of minister of defense, and there is no indication that wearing two hats in the cabinet impeded Britain's effort in any way. Most accounts of Britain's history during this time indicate that the country was better off with the prime minister playing a dual role.

His extended use of personal memoranda, all of which carried the imprint of his personal style and bore his signature or initials, also had an invigorating impact on the government. An official several ranks below him might find on his desk a message from the prime minister directing him to do such and such. In the words of Cabinet Secretary Lord Normanbrook, such messages often have a "startling effect."

There was yet another reason for Churchill's heavy reliance on written communication—the discipline it imposed on him. He was less likely to get carried away by a whim if he made it a point never to give orders that were not confirmed in writing afterward.

Although the profuse stream of memoranda that issued from his office bore his distinct personal style, usually opening with the phrase "Pray tell me . . . " they were by no means literary extravaganzas. He could be remarkably concise, as when he once ordered the mass production of a controversial new weapon. His memo read, "Sticky bombs—make one million—WSC." As he once noted, "It is sheer laziness not compressing information in a reasonable space."

Churchill also insisted that subordinates follow the same policy in dealing with him. He spent little time in interviewing people; instead, they were to address him in writing. Such correspondence were put in a box, and he would work on them at the beginning or the end of the day or at odd moments through the day. When a crisis erupted, he never had to cancel a lot of personal appointments.

He demanded that those who addressed him adhere to the rules of brevity as closely as he did himself. In 1941, he sent the following memo to the first lord of the admiralty: "Pray state this day, on one side of a sheet of paper, how the Royal Navy is being adapted to meet the conditions of modern warfare." (Emphasis added) He was particularly hard on the needless use of banalities and truisms. He once replied to an official's memo by pointing out to the hapless fellow that his memo had employed every cliché in the English language except the British men's room admonition, "Please adjust your dress before leaving."

None of this is meant to imply that Churchill disdained the use of the spoken word, rather that he reserved it for those times and occasions when it could be used most effectively. When Eisenhower was in London, Churchill made it a part of his regular schedule to lunch with him every Tuesday. As he said later, nothing but shop was ever discussed on these occasions. He encouraged spirited discussion in meetings, at least at the beginning of his administration, and urged anyone having a dissenting viewpoint to "Fight your corner." When one attendee remarked, "I have tried to present my case fairly," Churchill growled at him, "That's a very dangerous thing to do."

Churchill made sure that he did not spend all his time talking to higher-ups. He kept his lines of communication continually open to those below. As Robin Maugham writes, "Throughout the war, Churchill was always more interested in talking to junior officers than to the top brass—partly from pure kindness, partly from his knowledge that it was from the men in the field that he could discover what was really going on." Maugham, who served as a lieutenant in the tank corps during the war, mentions how Churchill asked him after the fall of France if he and his fellows were ready to repel a German invasion. When Maugham replied that many of their tanks could not move for want of a spring in their trackpins, Churchill exploded in fury and immediately set the whole British government into action. By nightfall, the springs had been delivered and were in place.

Despite the personal manner in which he conducted his administration, Churchill did not neglect the use of that traditional British device, the committee. He would frequently set up one group to give him information on a subject and then establish another group to supply him with advice on what to do with the information. On a more informal level, he would often set up dinner parties or after-dinner gatherings with some of the best minds both within and without the government for stimulating, if sometimes rambling, conversation. This institution, which became known as the "Midnight Follies" because of Churchill's predilection for staying up into the wee hours of the morning, was the source of many of the ideas that marked his administration.

His communications style did present drawbacks, however. He would frequently try to handle too much and consequently many matters would go neglected. Things that did not interest him would tend to pile up, and the stack of paper in his box would rise remorselessly until his secretaries could cajole him into spending more time trying to whittle it down. His personality was such that it too easily dominated any meeting at which he presided, and toward the end of the war, when fatigue and possibly age were setting in, he showed himself less receptive to ideas from others within the coalition cabinet. The Labour Party ministers protested that his cabinet meetings were becoming monologues.

Although he continued to remain more open to advice on the scientific and technical level, even here he became somewhat more remote as war weariness set in and, perhaps, as he became too infatuated with his own way of doing things. He listened too exclusively to his own science adviser, F. A. Lindeman (later Lord Cherwell), and failed to consult other scientists. He ordered, on the basis of Lindeman's faulty statistics, the rather fruitless and possibly even counter-productive saturation bombing raids on Germany. Churchill's communications policy reflected his leadership policy and both reflected the man. As such, the question becomes one of judging whether his communications style suited the role he had to play at the time and in the circumstances in which he had to play it. On balance, the judgment of history seems to be that it did.

QUESTIONS AND INSTRUCTIONS

1. How are communication modes reflective of a leader's personal style? What did Prime Minister Churchill's communication style say about his approach to communicating effectively? Explain.
2. Why did Churchill place so much emphasis upon formal communication?
3. How and when did Churchill employ informal communication as Minister of Defense?
4. How did Churchill avoid communication overload?
5. Were Churchill's communications mostly downward, across, or upward? Explain.
6. How did Churchill handle downward communication?
7. Why did Churchill shy away from most modes of informal communication during his war administration?
8. Was Churchill a less humane person because of his penchant for formal, written communications? Explain.

INSIGHTS-ISSUES / ACTION THIS DAY

Clearly and briefly describe and illustrate these concepts, issues, or points. Interpret the word "role" as meaning impact, application, importance, effect and/or illustration of certain facts, concerns, or issues from the case study.

1. Role of formal communication for enhancing administrative effectiveness.

2. Role of informal communication for enhancing administrative effectiveness.
3. Role of personality or personal style in developing communication approaches.
4. Role of "communication overload" and/or "sea of documentation" for effecting communication.

ENDNOTES

1. David K. Berlo, *The Process of Communication: An Introduction to Theory and Practice* (New York: Holt, Rinehart, & Winston, 1960), 23–24; Harold F. Gortner, Julianne Mahler, and Jeanne Bell Nicholson, *Organization Theory: A Public Perspective* (Fort Worth, TX: Harcourt Brace College Publishers, 2nd ed., 1997), 135–141.
2. Michael Schudson, "Sending a Political Message: Lessons from the American 1790s," *Media, Culture, & Society* 19, no. 3 (July 1997): 311–331.
3. Chester I. Barnard, *The Functions of the Executive* (Cambridge, Mass.: Harvard University Press, 1968), 89.
4. Herbert A. Simon, *Administrative Behavior* (New York: Free Press, 1957), 154.
5. David Dery, " ` Paperreality' and Learning in Bureaucratic Organizations," *Administration & Society* 29, no. 6 (January 1998): 677–690.
6. Frederick V. Malek, "Executive in Washington," *Harvard Business Review* (September–October 1972), 63-68.
7. *Newsweek,* 10 May 1971, 30. 50, no. 5, pp.
8. *Public Administration Times,* 15 January 1981.
9. Kenneth Cukier, "Who Runs the Internet?" *World Press Review* 45, no. 5 (May 1998): 39–41.
10. David E. Nye, "Shaping Communication Networks: Telegraph, Telephone, Computer," *Social Research* 64, no. 3 (fall 1997): 1067–1092.
11. Ellen Goodman, "Anonymity Breeds Incivility," *Boston Globe* 5 September 1996, 17A.
12. Brandi Bowser, "Opening the Window to On-line Democracy: www.localgovernment.com," *American City & County* 113, no. 1 (January 1998): 36–38.
13. Peter J. Howe, "Weld Seeks Input of Citizens, State Workers on Downsizing," *Boston Globe,* 5 August 1995, p. 12.
14. *Detroit Free Press,* 28 September 1967.
15. Alan Zaremba, "Working with the Organizational Grapevine," *Personnel Journal* 67, no. 7 (July 1988): 38–41.
16. *Time,* 18 June 1973, 67.
17. Vincent O'Leary and David Duffy, "Managerial Behavior and Correctional Policy," *Public Administration Review* (November–December 1971).
18. Daniel Katz and Robert L. Kahn, *The Social Psychology of Organizations* (New York: John Wiley, 1966), 350.
19. Peter Maas, *Serpico* (New York: Viking Press, 1973).
20. Alvin W. Gouldner, *Patterns of Industrial Democracy* (Glencoe, Ill.: Free Press, 1954).
21. Peter Blau, *The Dynamics of Bureaucracy* (Chicago: University of Chicago Press, 1955), 152.
22. Michael Banton, *The Policeman in the Community* (London: Tavistock Publications, 1964), 117.
23. Herbert A. Simon, Donald W. Smithburg, and Victor A. Thompson, *Public Administration* (New York: Alfred A. Knopf, 1950); Katz and Kahn, *The Social*

Psychology of Organizations. Douglas McGregor's statement is from his posthumously published book, *The Professional Manager* (New York: McGraw-Hill, 1967). The quote from Crozier is from *La Societ Bloque* (Paris: Editions du Seuil, 1970).

24. Katz and Kahn, *The Social Psychology of Organizations*, 379.
25. Peter M. Blau, *Bureauracy in Modern Society* (New York: Random House, 1956), 56.
26. Chris Argyris, *Personality and Organization* (New York: Harper & Row, 1957).
27. Katz and Kahn, *The Social Psychology of Organizations*, 245.
28. Albert Camus, *L'homme Revolt* (Paris: Editions Gallimard, 1951), 340.
29. Chester I. Barnard, *Organization and Management* (Cambridge, Mass.: Harvard University Press, 1948), see chapter 9, especially footnote on page 231.
30. Katz and Kahn, *The Social Psychology of Organizations*, 245–246.
31. Katz and Kahn, *The Social Psychology of Organizations*, 239.
32. Ibid.
33. Material for this case was largely drawn from Sir John Wheeler-Bennett, ed., *Action This Day: Working with Churchill, Memoirs of Lord Normanbrook and Others* (New York: St. Martin's Press, 1969). The quotation of Robin Maugham is from his *Escape from the Shadows* (New York: McGraw-Hill, 1973), 108–109.

9

Taxing, Budgeting, and Spending

Many students of public administration shudder when the course turns to the subject of taxing, budgeting, and government spending. They regard the budget as a ponderous tome of dreary figures and the process of budgeting as a tedious and humdrum chore that lacks the human interaction that makes things like personnel and leadership so much more palatable. They could not be more wrong.

This chapter places budgeting in the context of American political economy, outlining traditional, decrementalist, and reformist approaches that administrators take to deal with budgets; describing the functions of budgeting; reviewing the cycles of budgeting and stages of budget cycles; explaining how political strategies effect budgeting; and examining how economic growth, deficits, taxes, and savings interface budgets and budgeting. With every new administration at every level of government, detailed approaches to budgeting will vary, but these budgeting concepts provide a foundation on which public administrators may establish their budgeting skills. These skills are crucial, because revenues, budgets, and fiscal appropriations are at the center of most issues confronted by administrators.

INTRODUCTION TO PUBLIC BUDGETING

Most of the issues and conflicts that spring from the administrative process take the form of contests over monetary allocations. If politics is sometimes defined as the process of deciding who gets what, administrative politics often becomes the process of deciding *who gets what amount of money.* Consequently, whether one department or individual is favored over another or whether one program or policy is supported over another usually translates into a budgetary decision. In this sense, budgets are political documents.

If budgets are essentially political documents, the politics involved is often thickly veiled. To the untrained eye, a budget often conceals much more than it reveals. Expertise in cloaking some of the political aspects of a budget has advanced more than one administrator's career, while skill in figuring out what was being done has boosted more than one politician's status. It is not enough, however, to call attention to the political aspects of budgeting to define what budgeting is. Budgets are also instruments of *coordination, control,* and *planning.* They govern nearly all aspects of administration and confer a great deal of power on those who prepare them.

CONTEXT OF AMERICAN BUDGETING

Budgeting practices in the United States are the result of American ideology, federalism, and decision-making models. The political environment of budgeting is defined by our democratic ideology, which involves varying concepts of representative government. Democratic ideology is, in turn, defined by the idea of

TABLE 9–1 U.S. Government Budget. Total Receipts and Outlays, 1960–1997 (In millions of dollars)

Year	Total Receipts	Outlays	Surplus or Deficit (-)
1960	92,492	92,191	301
1961	94,388	97,723	−3,335
1962	99,676	106,821	−7,145
1963	106,560	111,316	−4,756
1964	112,613	118,528	−5,915
1965	116,817	118,228	−1,411
1966	130,835	134,532	−3,697
1967	148,822	157,464	−8,642
1968	152,973	178,134	−25,161
1969	186,882	183,640	3,242
1970	192,807	195,649	−2,842
1971	187,139	210,172	−23,033
1972	207,309	230,681	−23,372
1973	230,799	245,707	−14,908
1974	263,224	269,359	−6,135
1975	279,090	332,332	−53,242
1976	298,060	371,779	−73,719
TQ	81,232	95,973	−14,741
1977	355,559	409,203	−53,644
1978	399,561	458,729	−59,168
1979	463,302	503,464	−40,162
1980	517,112	590,920	−73,808
1981	599,272	678,249	−78,977
1982	617,766	745,755	−127,989
1983	600,562	808,380	−207,818
1984	666,457	851,846	−185,389
1985	734,057	946,391	−212,334
1986	769,091	990,336	−221,245
1987	854,143	1,003,911	−149,768
1988	980,954	1,064,140	−155,186
1989	990,691	1,143,172	−152,481
1990	1,031,308	1,252,691	−221,383
1991	1,054,264	1,323,785	−269,521

(Continued)

TABLE 9-1 U.S. Government Budget. Total Receipts and Outlays, 1960–1997 (In millions of dollars) *(Continued)*

Year	Total		
	Receipts	Outlays	Surplus or Deficit (-)
1992	1,091,631	1,381,791	−290,160
1993	1,154,401	1,409,414	−255,013
1994	1,258,627	1,461,731	−203,104
1995	1,351,830	1,515,729	−163,899
1996	1,453,062	1,560,512	-107,450
1997	1,579,292	1,601,235	−21,943
1998 estimate	1,657,858	1,667,815	−9,957
1999 estimate	1,742,736	1,733,217	9,519
2000 estimate	1,793,576	1,785,046	8,530
2001 estimate	1,862,582	1,834,392	28,190
2002 estimate	1,949,299	1,859,554	89,745
2003 estimate	2,028,157	1,945,374	82,783

capitalism, a system that assumes that a growth-directed economy supports government's ability to appropriate sufficient funds for public services.

Public sector monies are raised from taxes on *individuals* and *businesses.* It's tough to maintain viable public services if revenues supporting such activities are low or nonexistent. Whether citizen taxpayers are providing education, unemployment compensation, or national defense, they need a growth economy to finance these citizen benefits. From a capitalistic economy we are, therefore, able to afford programs that benefit all citizens. The appropriate mix of capitalism and socialism affects the size and scope of government and budgeting policies.

Deciding which level of government should provide a certain service is a matter of *federalism,* with its ever-changing division of power. The American system of federalism helps determine the scope, size, and nature of national, state, and local budget priorities. If state law conflicts with federal law, state law gives way. If local legislation conflicts with state or federal provisions, local ordinances are overruled. State boundaries, overlapping jurisdictions, economic decline of certain states and cities, and suburban growth patterns contribute to the dilemmas of budgeting in a federal system.

CYCLES IN CONGRESSIONAL BUDGETING

A historical review of five distinct congressional budget cycles affords readers opportunities to comprehend current budgetary conflicts. The ebb and flow of

---

THE WORST TAX AND THE LEAST TAX FOR THE MONEY

The local property tax (25 percent) and the federal income tax (24.5 percent) are in a dead heat as the least fair tax. The sales tax was rated least fair by 15.6 percent, the social security tax by 10.4 percent, and the state income tax by 9.1 percent. Asked from which level of government they get the least for their money, 49 percent of citizens said the federal government gave them the least, followed by 18 percent for local government, and 16 percent for the state.

Source: *Changing Public Attitudes on Governments and Taxes: 1992* (Washington, DC: United States Advisory Commission on Intergovernmental Relations, 1992).

---

power between the president and Congress, between the House and Senate, between committees, and even between subcommittees explains to readers how the president and Congress experienced cycles of interactions.

Cycle 1: Dominance of the Appropriations and Tax Committees until 1965.

The appropriations committees and the tax committees dominated congressional budgeting from the 1920s until the mid-1960s. The appropriations committees embodied the congressional power of the purse. Due in part to the constitutional requirement that tax and appropriation bills originate in the House, the House appropriations committee overshadowed its counterpart in the Senate. The roles of the committees evolved. The House committee became the guardian of the purse, saving money by cutting budgets. The Senate appropriations committee became the committee for appeals, frequently restoring funds for programs and projects deleted by the House committee.[1]

Members of the appropriations committee focused on the president's budget. Strong committee chairs and ranking minority members dominated deliberations. Thirteen subcommittees monitored thirteen appropriation bills covering programs of departments and agencies. Members became the most knowledgeable legislators in Congress on the details of the executive budget. Basically conservative, members of the appropriations committees valued economy and efficiency in an arena of spenders. They focused on weak spots in departmental requests for funds. They were not especially program oriented. Agencies had to justify any increases. Budget cutting built member reputations and earned respect. The tax committees rarely agreed with the Appropriations Committees on expenditure and revenue analyses. Happenstance produced fiscal policy, not explicit planning.

Cycle 2: The Budget Wars of 1965 to 1974.

During these years, the authorizing committees took power from the fiscal committees, the president from Congress. Great Society programs, the Vietnam War, inflation, and recurring recessions contributed to these changes. Selection of priorities, allocation of funds, and methods of financing the budget were hammered out in the budget process. The powers of the relatively conservative fiscal committees declined. The influence of more liberal program advocates in the au-

MAJOR FUNCTIONS OF BUDGETING

Budgeting has functional purposes. These functions affect every segment of the budget process from budget formulation to legislative authorization of funds.

1. **Allocating Resources to Achieve Governmental Priorities, Goals, and Policies.** The budget is a supremely political document. The budget tells who won, lost, or stayed even in the contest for available resources. Budgets incorporate thousands of decisions of what will be done and at what costs.

2. **Raising Funds Through Taxes and Loans to Finance the Budget.** Who should bear the tax burden? What proportion of personal and corporate income should taxes consume? Should the tax system be progressive, regressive, or a combination? These questions identify a divisive and controversial budgetary agenda.

3. **Stabilizing the Economy Through Fiscal Policy and Monetary Policy.** Recessions result in lower personal income and corporate profits. Revenues decline. Expenditures for unemployment insurance and other welfare programs rise. Deficits also rise. The central bank in the United States is the Federal Reserve Board (FED); the FED determines monetary policy. During recessions, the FED reduces interest rates. Fiscal policy addresses how budgets are raised and allocated to citizens.

4. **Holding Operating Agencies Accountable for the Use of Budgeted Resources.** Departments and agencies must account through the budget system for the efficiency and cost effectiveness of their programs. The budget process should enforce accountability. To control the bureaucracy, budgeting and systems of accountability have been institutionalized.

5. **Controlling Expenditures.** Controlling expenditures is the core function of budgeting. This is a traditional and fundamental function. Most government operations do not permit monies to flow automatically to departments and agencies after Congress or the legislature approves appropriations. Money is apportioned or allotted monthly, quarterly, or at other intervals by the central budget office.

6. **Transferring Funds from One Level of Government to Another.** State and local governments rely on a tax base inadequate to finance their own programs. They petition for a larger share of national revenue (grounded in the 1913 federal income tax). Intergovernmental financing calls for federal, state, and local governments to share in the costs of major domestic programs, including welfare, education, health, and transportation.

7. **Serving as a Mechanism for Achieving Planned Social and Economic Development.** To many Americans, planning implies some version of socialism, even communism. Despite these misgivings, the United States has had a mixed economy (capitalism with government stimulus and support) for approximately sixty years. Planning implies consistency in government budgeting plans grounded in reasoned expectations for revenues.

8. **Providing Leverage to Improve Management in Operating Agencies.** Public administrators, in the budget process, realize opportunities to examine efficiency, productivity, and effectiveness of programs and projects funded by the taxpayers. Budgeting is essentially resource management. Improving management may or may not be in demand, but it is where merit, pragmatism, and partisan politics meet.

Source: Donald Axelrod, *Budgeting for Modern Government* , 2nd ed., pp. 7-13. Copyright © 1995 by St. Martin's Press, Inc. Reprinted with permission of Bedford/St. Martin's Press, Inc.

**THE FEDERAL GOVERNMENT DOLLAR
FISCAL YEAR 2000 ESTIMATES**

WHERE IT COMES FROM...

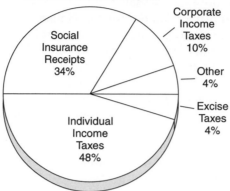

WHERE IT GOES...

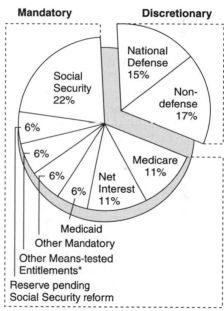

*Includes earned income tax credits, food
stamps and veterans' pensions*

FIGURE. 9–1 The Federal Government Dollar Fiscal Year 2000 estimates.

thorizing committees grew. The insulation of entitlement expenditures from the appropriations process gained leverage. Congress increasingly intervened in budget implementation, once an executive prerogative. Legislative staffs expanded and became more professional.

The enlargement and liberalization of the House Appropriations Committee occurred in the early 1970s. The seniority system broke down. Advocates of program expansion and greater expenditures now controlled appropriation committees in both houses. The appropriations committees became spenders, like the authorizing committees. These changes resulted in the increase of the president's budget rather than its decrease. In the 1960s, the Congressional appropriations were usually lower than the president's budget requests. By the early 1970s, the reverse secenario was true.

The appropriations committees and revenue committees no longer controlled spending over social security, income maintenance programs, and health delivery systems financed by the federal government (Medicare). The authorizing committees now controlled expenditures. Congressional budgeting was distributed among the appropriations, tax, and authorizing committees. The legislative process was more fragmented. The president orchestrated his priorities through the Office of Management and Budget. Congress had no congressional budget to consider the budget as a whole. No comprehensive development of program priorities occurred. No coordination of fiscal and economic policies emerged. Congressional actions took place gradually. Decisions appeared isolated and sometimes unrelated. Consensus on fiscal policy between the president and Congress became increasingly difficult. Uncontrollable expenditures soared. Deficits grew larger. Inflation worsened. President Nixon impounded $18 billion of water pollution control, transportation, housing, education, rural development, and other domestic programs. In 1973 the impoundments were unprecedented in size, scope, and severity. The confrontational Nixon sought to dismantle the Great Society of the 1960s with an ideological fervor. In 1974, Congress, on a bipartisan basis approved the Budget and Impoundment Control Act. Nixon acquiesced.

Cycle 3: The Congressional Budget Act of 1974.

The Congressional Budget Act of 1974 rivals the Budget and Accounting Act of 1921—in significance, scope, and potential impact. The 1921 legislation created the executive budget system in the federal government. The 1974 legislation provided a broad framework for:

- simultaneously considering expenditures, revenue, deficits, and debt;
- formulating fiscal and economic policy;
- controlling expenditures;
- developing independent sources of information to evaluate the president's budget; and
- controlling the president's implementation of the budget.

Two new standing committees, the budget committees, played a central role in the reorganization. The four fiscal committees, appropriations and revenue, remained. The budget committees recommended overall fiscal policy and broad national priorities. They would guide other committees in their spending and tax decisions.

The framework for congressional budgeting were the first and second concurrent resolutions. No later than April 15, or approximately two and one-half months after submission of the executive budget, the budget committees were required to include in the first concurrent resolution recommendations for the following:

- total budget authority (appropriations) in the aggregate and for each of the twenty functions;
- total budget outlays (expenditures based on new and old budget authority) in the aggregate and for each of the twenty functions;
- the level of revenue with recommended increases or decreases;
- the proposed budget surplus or deficit based on the difference between outlays and revenues;
- the level of debt with recommended increases or decreases; and
- the level of loan obligations and loan guarantees was added in 1985 and 1990 to control the credit activities of the federal government.

The budget committees relied heavily on analyses and estimates by the Congressional Budget Office (CBO) and other standing committees. Action by both houses on the first resolution was to occur by May 15.

Congress was required to adopt a second concurrent resolution by September 15. The first resolution was tentative. However, the second resolution was to be firm and binding. Once Congress had adopted the second resolution, no bills raising expenditures or lowering revenues could be approved without special congressional action. The second concurrent resolution was intended to synthesize Congress's final decisions on fiscal policy and program priorities.

The Budget and Impoundment Control Act of 1974 did not usher in a revolution in congressional budgeting. It did focus attention on major problems. It forced legislators to examine problems closely. It spelled out the consequences of alternative actions. It provided vastly improved and authoritative data for debate and decision making. The CBO provided independent economic analysis, policy analysis, and program evaluation. The act expanded the dialogue on fiscal issues between legislators and their constituents.

The new timetable and fiscal ceilings proved useful. The control of impoundments materialized. The reconciliation process indirectly contributed to controlling entitlements. However, no budget process can convince members of Congress to overcome ideological, partisan, and economic differences. Building a coalition on fiscal policy and national priorities requires political will. A brilliantly contrived budget process is no substitute for political consensus.

Cycle 4: The Balanced Budget and Emergency Deficit Control Act of 1985.

The 1974 budget legislation did not reduce deficits. The act's timetable was not adhered to. Committee squabbles became common. The act could not overcome a government controlled by two parties and a divided and paralyzed Congress. The president and Congress could not ignore uncontrollable deficits and debt. With no political consensus on priorities and policies, the legislators could only focus on process. The Balanced Budget and Emergency Deficit Control Act, better known as Gramm-Rudman-Hollings (GRH), became law late in 1985. GRH set a maximum deficit amount for federal spending for each of the fiscal years 1986 through 1991. By the latter date, the deficit would be progressively reduced to zero. The 1985 budget legislation called for across-the-board cuts in federal spending to reach the targeted deficit level if the budget deficit exceeded the prescribed maxiumum by a specified sum in any given fiscal year. This last provision was as if the complicated, political decision-making for balancing federal budgets of $1.7 trillion could be put on auto pilot. Like the 1974 act, the 1985 act turned out to be a paper tiger. Deficits continued to grow. No auto pilot system would get this budget plane safely back on the the ground. A system of automatic cuts pleased no one. GRH needed a good boost. But no party or political faction could muster the strength to give it a boost.

Cycle 5: The Budget Enforcement Act of 1990 (BEA).

President Bush and Democratic congressional leaders could not meet the GRH target of $64 billion for fiscal year 1991. The deficit was at least $110 billion greater than that figure. If the targets of GRH were to be followed, deep across-the-board cuts, known as sequestrations, in domestic and defense programs would be forthcoming. Bush and legislative leaders held a summit meeting. They decided to abandon the GRH deficit-reduction targets. They substituted expenditure limits on discretionary programs (excluding social security and deposit insurance) over five years. But there were no annual deficit targets. No priorities were changed. Political priorities were frozen. Entitlements, representing 60 percent of the expenditures, were protected. Budgeting control emphasized only on discretionary programs—about 40 percent of federal spending. Many argued that the BEA was the first serious attempt to slice expenditures. Deficits were smaller than they otherwise would have been.

The Democratic Party, at least in numbers, controlled both houses of Congress and the executive in 1993. Despite these majorities political consensus on expenditures, taxes, deficits, and debt remained fleeting. The 1993 Omnibus Budget-Reconciliation Act was passed by a bare majority in both chambers and without a single Republican vote. The bill provided $504.8 billion in deficit reduction according to the White House but only $433 billion according to the Congressional Budget Office. Tax increases were primarily on the wealthy and defense cuts were the majority of spending reductions.[2]

The perception of raising taxes resulted in political defeats for President Bush after supporting the BEA. The more traditional economic thinkers in the Republican Party skewered Bush in the 1992 presidential primaries, mocking his promise that he would not raise taxes. A similar perception of raising taxes occurred again in 1993—this time with the Democratic Party majorities in Congress. Although the 1993 economic package proved to be the beginning of economic

TABLE 9–2 Milestones in Federal Budgeting, 1979–1997

Year	Event	Significance
1789	Constitution	Gives Congress the power to levy taxes and requires appropriations by Congress before funds are distributed.
1802–1867	Committee structure	House Ways and Means Committee established as standing committee in 1802. House Appropriations Committee established in 1865. Senate Finance established in 1816. Senate Appropriations Committee established in 1867.
1837, 1850	House and Senate Rules	House and Senate bar unauthorized appropriations.
1870, 1905–1906	Antideficiency Act	Requires apportionment of funds to prevent over-exposure.
1921	Budget and Accounting Act	Provides for an executive budget. Establishes the Bureau of the Budget and the General Accounting Office.
1939	Reorganization Plan No. 1	Transfers Bureau of the Budget to the new Executive Office of the President and expands the bureau's role.
1967	President's Commission on Budget Concepts	Adoption of the unified budget, including trust funds.
1974	Congressional Budget and Impoundment Control Act	Establishes the congressional budget process. House and Senate budget committees, and the Congressional Budget Office. Also estabishes procedures for legislative review of impoundments.
1980	Reconciliation process	Reconciliation used for the first time at start of congressional budget process.
1985, 1987	Gramm-Rudman-Hollings Acts	Set deficit reduction targets and sequestration procedures.
1990	Budget Enforcement Act	Shifts from fixed to adjustable deficit targets, caps discretionary spending, establishes pay-as-you-go rules for revenues and direct spending, and directs and establishes new budgeting rules for direct and guaranteed loans.

TABLE 9–2 Milestones in Federal Budgeting, 1979–1997 *(continued)*

Year	Event	Significance
1990	Chief Financial Officers Act	Provides for a chief financial officer in major agencies to oversee financial management and integrate accounting and budgeting.
1993	Omnibus Budget-Reconciliation Act	Establishes a new deficit-reduction target of $514 billion over a five-year period, maintains discretionary spending caps at or below fiscal year 1993 levels for five years, and sets in motion the largest tax increase in peacetime.
1997	Balanced Budget Act	Bipartisan efforts create deficit reduction legislation with political advantages without offering substantive reform. Compromise promises a balanced budget by 2002, but no provisions to reduce government size, cut corporate subsidies, or restructure Medicare.

Sources: Allen Schick, *The Federal Budget: Politics, Policy, Process* (Washington, DC: The Brookings Institution, 1994), 36; Donald Axelrod, *Budgeting for Modern Government* (New York: St. Martin's Press, 1994), 205; Jonathan Rauch and Eliza Newlin Carney, "The Easy Way Out," *National Journal* 29, no. 19 (10 May 1997): 928–931.

recovery that included a balanced budget in 1997, the Republicans used the issue to skewer the Democrats in the 1994 off-year elections.

Voters appear to demand political reform, observes Jonathan Rauch, but government is unlikely to change except in political composition. The unwieldly size and contradictory complexity developed due to the cumulative inertia of entrenched lobbyists and special interest groups. Reforms will continue, Rauch emphasizes, but they will be gradual. Substantive change can come from the presidency and the electorate, but not unless citizens make personal sacrifices for widespread social welfare.[3]

Prospects for balanced budget agreements obscure the urgent need for entitlement reforms. According to Rauch, deficits—less than 2 percent of the nation's gross domestic product in 1996—are a minor concern. Entitlements, growing by more than 10 percent a year after 2030, constitute the federal government's biggest long-term financial problems.[4] Republicans and Democrats, claim Rauch and Eliza Newlin Carney, created deficit reduction legislation in 1997 that had political advantages without offering substantive reform. The compromise appears to promise a balanced budget by 2002, but there are no provisions to reduce government size, cut corporate subsidies, or restructure Medicare.[5]

Phases of the Budget Cycle

Federal budgeting can be understood in four phases: executive preparation, legislative consideration, implementation and control of the enacted budget, and audit and evaluation. According to Douglas Lee, a "budget, after all, is only an accounting of the financial cost of many political and social decisions.[6] The term budget originates from the Middle English word for pouch or purse.[7] Federal budgeting is a continuous and overlapping process. Stages of the budget cycle are linked. The findings of audit/evaluation are important data for preparation of future budgets. The federal fiscal year begins in October. Many local governments start their fiscal years in January. Excepting Alabama, Michigan, New York, and Texas, state governments begin their fiscal years in July. The fiscal year in Alabama and Michigan begins in October. New York starts in April, and Texas begins in September. Fiscal years are named after the year in which they end. The federal fiscal year that began on October 1, 1999, was the 2000 fiscal year.

Executive Preparation. The president (or governor, mayor, or chief executive on the state and local levels) transmits general directions for department and agency request preparation. The department or agency reviews current operations, program objectives, issues, and future plans as they relate to the upcoming annual budget. Cabinet secretaries and agency heads submit projections for requirements reflecting current operations and future plans. Supporting memoranda and related analytic studies identify major issues, alternatives for resolving issues, and comparisons of costs and effectiveness.

The Office of Management and Budget (OMB) develops economic assumptions, obtains forecasts of international and domestic situations, and prepares fiscal projections. The OMB compiles total outlay estimates for comparison with revenue estimates. It develops recommendations for the president on fiscal policy, program issues, and budget levels.

As appropriate, the president discusses budgetary outlook and policies with the director of the OMB and with cabinet secretaries and agency heads. He reviews budget recommendations and decides on department and agency budget estimates, grounding his decisions on overall budget assumptions and policies. He may often revise his budget message. He transmits recommended budget estimates to Congress within fifteen days after Congress convenes.[8]

Legislative Consideration. The predominant legislative power in the Western world is the power of the purse.[9] Congress acts on requests for budget authority and does not vote directly on outlays of taxpayer dollars. Congress grants budget authority to departments and agencies. Budget authority permits them to incur obligations and to spend federal monies. This is accomplished through passage of appropriation bills.

The budget committees hold hearings as they prepare for the drafting of the first concurrent resolution on the budget. The appropriations committees hold special hearings on the budget overview with the director of the OMB, secretary of the treasury, and chair of the Council of Economic Advisors. Subcommittees of

---

CONGRESSIONAL BUDGET TIMETABLE

November 10	Current services budget submitted
15 days after Congress convenes	President's budget submitted
March 15	Committees submit budget reports to budget committees
April 1	Congressional Budget Office sends report to budget committees
April 15	Budget committees report first budget resolution to House and Senate
May 15	All authorization bills reported
May 15	Final action on first budget resolution
7 days after Labor Day	Final action on appropriations bills
September 15	Final action on second budget resolution
September 25	Final action on budget reconciliation measure
October 1	Fiscal year begins

Source: Marshall E. Dimock, Gladys Ogden Dimock, and Douglas M. Fox, *Public Administration* (New York: Holt, Rinehart and Winston, 1983), 369.

---

the appropriation committees also hold hearings and review justifications from each department and agency. The House appropriations subcommittees draft appropriation bills and reports. The budget committees receive the views and budget estimates of all committees and draft the first concurrent resolution.

Congress receives the president's budget within fifteen days after Congress convenes. It adopts the first concurrent resolution on the budget on May 15. The House of Representatives debates and passes appropriation bills, with or without amendments. The Senate receives the House-passed versions of appropriation bills and refers them to the Senate Appropriations Committee. The Senate debates and passes appropriation bills with or without amendments. If Senate bills differ from House versions, bills are sent to conference. Conference committees consider items of disagreement between the two Houses and makes recommendations for resolving differences in conference reports. These reports are submitted to each body for action. Congress adopts the second concurrent resolution of the budget on September 15.

Authorizing legislation is substantive legislation enacted by Congress that sets up or continues the legal operation of a federal program or agency either indefinitely or for a specific period or sanctions a particular type of obligation or expenditure within a program. Authorizing legislation is usually a prerequisite for appropriations. An appropriation act is a statute, under the jurisdiction of the House and Senate Committees on Appropriations, that provides authorization for federal agencies to incur obligations and to make payments out of the treasury for specified purposes. There are thirteen regular appropriation acts enacted annually.

Implementation and Control of the Enacted Budget. Spending of federal taxpayer dollars must proceed in a manner consistent with appropriation laws. Once the appropriation bill is approved, the Treasury Department draws an appropriation warrant, countersigned by the General Accounting Office (GAO) and forwarded to the department or agency. The departments and agencies revise operating budgets in view of approved appropriations and program developments. The director of the OMB distributes budget authority to each department and agency by time periods, usually every three months, or by activities over the duration of the appropriation. The departments and agencies allot apportioned funds to various programs or activities. The budgetary term for allotments is apportionment. Central budget-office discretion to curtail allotments is often limited. The term for withholding of federal appropriations by the president is impounding. Since 1974, presidents have been able to continue to impound funds. Congress, however, can veto these impoundments.

Audit and Evaluation. An audit is an "examination of records, facilities, systems, and other evidence to discover or verify desired information. Internal audits are those performed by professionals employed by the entity being audited; external audits are performed by outside professionals who are independent of the entity.[10] Different forms of audits include:

- financial audit, or a review of financial records to determine whether the funds were spent legally, if receipts were properly recorded and controlled, and if financial records and statements are complete and reliable;
- management or operations audit, or focus on efficiency of operations, on waste of government resources, and on use and control of resources;
- program audit, or examination of the extent to which desired results are being achieved, on objectives of the program being met, and whether there might be lower cost alternatives to reach the desired results; and
- performance audit, part of sunset legislation, which establishes "a set schedule for legislative review of programs and agencies unless affirmative legislative action is taken to reauthorize them. Thus, the `sun sets' on agencies and programs,"[11] or assessment of the total operations of a department or agency, including compliance, management, and program audits.

To illustrate the focus of each audit, consider a state highway department appropriation to purchase road salt for snow and ice removal. A financial audit considers if the department purchased the salt, if the salt was actually delivered, if competitive practices were used in selecting a supplier, and if the department spent the correct amount on salt. A management audit considers if the salt inventory is adequately protected from the environment, if the inventory is adequate or excessive, and if other methods of selecting a supplier would result in lower costs. A program audit considers if the prevailing level of winter highway clearing is an appropriate use of community resources and if alternatives to deployment of salt would be less costly to the community. Finally, a performance audit examines all operations of the highway department.[12]

The GAO conducts an independent audit of financial records, transactions, and financial management and makes reports to Congress. The departments and agencies review compliance with established policies, procedures, and requirements. They evaluate accomplishments of program plans and effectiveness of management and operations. The OMB reviews department and agency operations and evaluates programs and performance. The OMB conducts and guides departments and agencies in organization and management studies and assists the president in improving management and organization of the executive branch.

The Budget and Accounting Act of 1921 set the start of the fiscal year at July 1. It created the Bureau of the Budget (changed in 1970 to the Office of Management and Budget) and the General Accounting Office. This legislation authorizes the president's budget message to Congress. The Congressional Budget and Impoundment Control Act of 1974 set the start of the fiscal year at October 1. It created the Congressional Budget Office and House and Senate Budget Committees. It requires the current services budget and congressional budget resolutions.

BUDGETS AND POLITICAL STRATEGIES

The incrementalism perspective of budgeting is that it is primarily, if not exclusively, a process of political strategy.[13] This approach is heavily favored over public service delivery orientation models, originating from public finance economics, and budgeting techniques models, attempting to make budgeting more rational. Budgeting, appropriating, and spending focus on strategies and role playing.

Budgeting, then, is incremental, says Aaron Wildavsky. "The largest determining factor of the size and content of this year's budget is last year's budget. Most of the budget is a product of previous decisions. . . . The budget may be conceived of as an iceberg with by far the largest part below the surface, outside the control of anyone. Many items in the budget are standard and are simply reenacted every year unless there is a special reason to challenge them."[14]

Budgets are grounded in percentage increments to the historic budget base according to some notion of fairness for continuing funding of each department and agency. The annual focus is on percentage monetary adjustments to existing programs, grounded on the respective budget bases of departments and agencies.

1. Roles. Operating departments and agencies, chief executives, and legislators participate in the budget process to provide government services to the public without waste.

Operating departments and agencies are units of government bureaucracies that spend taxpayer monies for the delivery of services. They focus on the clientele they serve. They are not concerned with the services or priorities of other departments and agencies. They are not particularly interested in comparisons of the costs of those services relative to the value of services. They recognize the value of their services and will try to increase the availability of those services, regardless of the overall budget conditions of the government. Their purpose is to expand service opportunities.

The office of the chief executive (president, governor, mayor) employs budget specialists to argue on behalf of government departments, agencies, and their programs. At the federal level, the budget specialists are located in the OMB. In the states, various titles designate the units of executive office budget specialists. For example, in Mississippi, it's the Budget Office. In Arizona, it's the Finance Division. In Iowa, it's the State Controller's Office. In Kentucky, it's the Office of Policy and Management. In Washington state, it's the Office of Planning and Fiscal Management.

Budget analysts are guided by the priorities of the chief executive. The chief executive must balance the priorities and interests of the population. Departments and agencies have a clientele orientation. Priorities of a single department or agency should not be expected to coincide with that of the chief executive, selected by the population of the municipality, state, or nation. The interests of farmers, or even college professors, for examples, are not the same as the general population. All programs do not have equal weight. Those with the strongest support in the legislature will do better than others.

Elected members of the national, state, and municipal *legislatures* champion the priorities of their constituencies. They advocate programs and projects that benefit the people who elect them. They do not champion the overall perspectives of particular departments and agencies or their programs. They focus on a subset of the population (states, legislative districts). The department or agency focuses on clientele across states and districts. The legislator focuses on state or regional geographical assembly of citizens. Electoral regions (states, legislative districts) include diverse clientele groups. Legislators may have scarce interest in government programs and spending beyond their states and districts.

But legislators often cannot compete with the expertise of chief executives, departments, and agencies. Most state legislators are part-time legislators. They are likely paid minimum wage salaries and have minimum support staff to research the development, implementation, and evaluation of government programs and services. The circumstances may be worse for city council members. They may have no salary and no support staff. Members of local school boards (special districts) experience similar scarcities. Members of the national legislature are paid good salaries, enjoy large budgets for their Washington offices, and access both the varied, and extensive, skills and expertise of the Congressional Budget Office, Legislative Reference Service at the Library of Congress, and General Accounting Office. Therefore, the role, and institutional history, of the national legislatuture is more developed than those at the state, local government, and special district levels.

2. Strategies. Strategies entail planning, directing, maneuvering, and managing tangible and intangible forces, personnel, programs developing and maintaining

BUDGET TERMS

Authorizations: Involves determination of maximum spending levels for each program approved by the legislative branch; it is the responsibility of subject matter standing committees of the U.S. House of Representatives and U.S. Senate.

Appropriations: One of the most crucial to budget making; entails the power to spend or to incur financial obligations; "spending" committees in the U.S. House of Representatives and U.S. Senate exercise major roles in this stage/phase of budgetary process.

Authorizing Legislation: Legislation enacted by Congress to permit the establishment or continuation of a Federal program or agency. Authorizing legislation is normally required before the enactment of budget authority, and such authority is usually provided in separate legislation.

Budget Authority (BA): Authority provided by law to enter into obligations that will result in immediate or future outlays. It may be classified by the period of availability, by the timing of congressional action, or by the manner of determining the amount available.

Budget: The President's request to Congress for new programs, allocation of resources to serve national objectives, embodiment of fiscal policy for programs, and information about the national economy essential for the private sector.

Budget Cycle: Executive formulation and transmittal, legislative authorization and appropriation, budget execution and control, review and audit.

Continuing Resolution: Legislation that provides budget authority for specific ongoing activities when a regular appropriation for those activities has not been enacted by the beginning of the fiscal year. Some continuing resolutions provide interim funding for part of the fiscal year until the regular appropriations bill is enacted. Others provide funding for the full fiscal year.

Fiscal Year: The Federal Government's yearly accounting period, which begins on October 1 and ends on the following September 30.

Outlays: Government spending. Outlays are payments, normally in the form of checks issued, cash disbursed, and electronic fund transfers, net of refunds, reimbursements, and offsetting collections. Outlays include interest accrued on public issues of the public debt.

Receipts: Government income. All income, net of refunds, collected from the public by the Federal Government in its sovereign capacity, primarily through the exercise of its power to tax.

Sequestration: Reduction of new budget authority of other budgetary resources, as defined in the Balanced Budget and Emergency Deficit Control Act of 1985, as amended.

favorable and advantageous operational environments, and seeking sufficient monies to implement omnipresent and contingent strategies.

Executives, department and agency heads, legislators, and numerous clientele use budgetary strategies for maintaining or increasing the amount of monies available to them. As they develop strategies, budgetary participants relate their requirements and powers to the needs and powers of each other. Political systems impose restraints and create opportunities for participants. Strategies link intentions and perceptions of budget officials and political systems.[15] Strategies emphasize *cultivating clientele* and *developing confidence.*

Departments and agencies cultivate active clientele for lobbying the legislature and chief executive. Most departments and agencies experience little difficulty in locating clientele. Interest groups find ways to petition government decision making and spend funds. Departments and agencies accessing and servicing large and strategically placed clientele are less likely to have their budgets reduced. They not only concentrate on individual constituencies but seek to expand their clientele. They proactively secure feedback on their programs and their effectiveness. They want constituents to offer suggestions for improving services.

The development of confidence, or deploying actions of personnel and programs to match or fit in with the expectations of others playing the power game, is a vital part of group strategies. Budget officials are guardians of the department or agency treasury. Presentations are geared to that end. As guardians, budgeteers espouse the effectiveness of programs and promise efficiency for spending taxpayer dollars. Preparation is important as administrative leaders develop and maintain confidence. Public hearings afford officials opportunities to exude confidence in their department or agency missions and programs. Requests for information must be met promptly and in appropriate details.

Contingent strategies depend on budget circumstances.

In defending its base for budget cuts, officials might suggest that a politically popular program be eliminated. In Indiana, for example, where the political culture nurtures high school basketball programs, budget officials call for reduction of athletic budgets when school districts confront fiscal problems. Officials argue that the community's high school basketball program faces an all or nothing choice. Any budgetary reduction would make the program impossible. It might as well be eliminated. In the Hoosier state, high school basketball has a jurisdictional, or statewide, clientele base. Strong clientele may prevent across-the-board reductions. Therefore, Indiana school districts and their elected school boards may decide to cut art, music, or history programs, rather than basketball appropriations.

In an effort to increase the budgetary base and current scope of existing programs, the department or agency may argue that this year's budget proposal is merely a continuation of existing efforts, that it is nothing new. However, legislators and taxpayers, and even school board members, have come to question every line expenditure, and this approach might bring the confidence of the department or agency into scrutiny. Efforts to expand the budget base of the department or agency necessitate the deployment of different tactics. But, in times of close scrutiny of the personalities and arguments of government executives, legislators and taxpayers do not like being "suffered fools." The "foot in the door finance" approach may start small, yet seek to expand its base. Administrators

---

TAXING MATTERS

Most Americans think they do not get much value for their federal income tax dollars, asserts Tibbet L. Speer. Most citizens suggest increasing taxes on another demographic or economic group as the solution to U.S. tax problems. Although U.S. taxes are lower than many other countries, only 42 percent of U.S. taxpayers think they get their money's worth. Opinions about local property taxes, state taxes, and other taxes are similar. The U.S. tax structure is neither progressive nor regressive, but fairly proportional, writes Elia Kacapyr. Three-fourths of the tax revenue burden falls on individuals instead of corporations. However, the top 1 percent of wealthy households paid nearly a third of taxes collected in 1995. Tax revenues have averaged about 19 percent of the Gross Domestic Product since 1959.

Sources: Tibbet L. Speer, "Taxing Time," *American Demographics* 19, no. 4 (April 1997): 40–45, and Elia Kacapyr, "Taxing Considerations," *American Demographics* 20, no. 3 (March 1998): 28–30.

---

often set up a program on a "temporary" basis with hopes that interim extensions will make it permanent. The program may be advertised as "paying for itself." The budgetary allotment sought may be grounded in emergency or crisis.

The Uses of Incrementalism. Developments in society do not often occur without warning. Departments and agencies prepare their budgets incrementally. The most rational guide for next year's budget is based on the development, implementation, and evaluation of this year's appropriations. Even sophisticated forecasting models are grounded in the events of recent unit and program histories. Departments and agencies must not strive to be "too successful," for they may "win" their "program war," and next year's budget may not be necessary.[16]

ECONOMIC GROWTH, TAXES, AND SAVINGS

Economic growth, central to many of the country's concerns as a society, requires investment, which, over the longer term, depends on savings. The nation's saving consists of the private saving of households and businesses and the saving or dissaving of all levels of government. In general, government budget deficits represent dissaving; they subtract from national saving by absorbing funds that otherwise could be used for investment. Conversely, government surpluses add to saving.

American hostilities toward taxes are well-documented. However, the per capita tax level in the United States is not considered high. The people of the United States are not overtaxed. Taxation as a percentage of national income is lower in the United States than in any other major industrialized country. The opposition to taxes clearly cannot be traced to a heavy tax burden. Citizens rebel against paying higher taxes because they believe that governments are inefficient, even wasteful, in spending assessed revenues for their various operations.[17]

Since the 1970s, private saving has declined while federal budget deficits have consumed a large share of these increasingly scarce savings. The result has been to decrease the amount of national saving potentially available for investment. The depressing effect of deficits on growth might have been mitigated had they financed higher levels of public investment. However, as a share of Gross Domestic Product (GDP), federal investment spending has declined over the past two decades. Therefore, private saving remains low. Federal budget deficits declined significantly from the levels of the 1980s and early 1990s, making available some additional funds for investment. (See table 9-3.)

Nevertheless, total national saving and investment remain significantly below the levels experienced in the 1960s and 1970s. Economists note that these low levels of saving and investment raise concerns for the nation's future productive capacity and future generations' standard of living. The most certain way to increase the resources available for investment is to increase national saving, and the most direct way for the federal government to increase national saving is to achieve and maintain a balanced federal budget. Budget surpluses increase saving and allow the government to reduce the level of federal debt held by the public.

Growing deficits and the resulting lower savings lead to dwindling investment, slower growth, and finally a decline in real Gross Domestic Product. Living standards, in turn, stagnate and fall. Therefore actions on the deficit might be postponed, but they could not be avoided. Since 1995, robust economic growth and policy action combined to sharply reduce the deficit and are projected by the Congressional Budget Office to result in budget surpluses.

Major progress was made on deficit reduction, culminating in the passage of the Balanced Budget Act of 1997. The balanced budget or surpluses that are projected represent an enormous improvement in the federal government's fiscal position throughout the next decade. The improvements in national saving and reduced debt and interest costs can be expected to produce tangible gains in economic growth and budgetary flexibility over the longer term. The emergence of unsustainable deficits is substantially delayed under recently enacted fiscal policy.

In recent years, the federal deficit has declined substantially from $290 billion in fiscal year 1992, 4.7 percent of Gross Domestic Product, to a Congressional Budget Office projected level of $23 billion in fiscal year 1997, .03 percent of GDP, which would be the lowest since 1974. This improvement is due, in part, to deficit reduction initiatives enacted in 1990 and 1993 as well as to subsequent spending restraint. Recent legislation attempting to control the deficit included the Omnibus Budget Reconciliation Act of 1990, the Budget Enforcement Act of 1990, and the Omnibus Budget Reconciliation Act of 1993. The Balanced Budget Act of 1997, along with the strong recent performance of the economy, is expected to extend this recent progress by achieving a balanced budget by 2002 followed by several years of budget surpluses on a unified budget basis.

Policy action accounted for about 25 percent of the recent improvement in the CBO's budget estimates. The remainder of the improvement was due primarily to economic factors. The unified budget includes annual Social Security trust fund surpluses. These surpluses are expected to be temporary, peaking at $140 billion (including interest) in 2009 before declining and eventually turning to deficits in the following decade.[18] The decline in the deficit significantly slowed growth in the federal debt held by the public.

These recent fiscal improvements represent substanial progress in the near term toward a more sustainable fiscal policy. However, longer term problems remain. While the federal budget would be in surplus in the first decade of the 21st century, deficits would reemerge in 2012, soon after the baby boom generation begins to retire. These deficits would then escalate, exceeding 6 percent of GDP before 2030 and exceeding 20 percent of GDP by 2050. A comparison of federal debt to the size of the economy tells a simlar story—near-term improvement followed by potentially unsustainable growth as the baby boomers retire. Such levels of deficits and debt imply a substantial reduction in national saving, private investment, and the capital stock. Given the nation's labor force and productivity growth assumptions, GDP would inevitably begin to decline.

These negative effects of rapidly increasing deficits and debt on the economy would force policymakers to act before facing probable consequences such as rising inflation, higher interest rates, and the unwillingness of foreign investors to invest in a weakening American economy. The aging of the U.S. population, which corresponds to slower growth in the labor force and faster growth in entitlement program spending, and the rising costs of providing federal health care benefits are primary causes of large deficits. In 2008, the first baby boomers are eligible for early retirement benefits. As the baby boomers retire, labor force growth is expected to slow considerably and, eventually, stop.

These demographic changes mean fewer workers to support each retiree. Between 1997 and 2025, the number of workers per Social Security beneficiary is projected to decline by 33 percent. Without a major increase in productivity, low labor force growth will inevitably lead to slower growth in the economy and in federal revenue. As slow growth in the labor force constrains revenue growth, the large retired population places major expenditure demands on Social Security, Medicare, and Medicaid. In fifteen years, the Social Security trustees estimate that the program's tax revenue is expected to be insufficient to cover current benefits.

The economic benefits of a sustainable budget policy include increased saving and investment levels and faster economic growth, which results in higher living standards. The future implications of current policy decisions are usually not captured in the budget process. The budget is a short-term, cash-based spending plan focusing on the short- to medium-term cash implications of government obligations and fiscal decisions. While the sustainability of the government's fiscal policy is driven primarily by future spending for social security and health care commitments, the federal government's commitments and responsibilities extend far beyond these programs.

The main influence of budget policy on long-term economic performance is through the effect of the federal deficit on national savings. Conversely, the rate of economic growth helps determine the overall deficit or surplus through its effect on revenues and spending. Federal deficits reduce national savings while federal surpluses increase national savings. The level of savings affects investment and, in turn, GDP growth.[19]

ROOTS OF THE DEFICIT PROBLEM

The budget deficit was not of major concern to policymakers from the end of World War II through the mid-1970s. From 1947 until 1974, deficits averaged less than 1 percent of the (GDP). As a result of World War II and the Great Depression, the public debt reached 114 percent of the GDP in 1946. But the budget situation became significantly worse after the mid-1970s. Deficits averaged 2.9 percent of GDP during the last half of the 1970s, 4.0 percent during the 1980s, and during the first three years of the 1990s, 4.4 percent. The public debt increased faster than the economy. The ratio of public debt to GDP more than doubled. In 1992, the federal government had revenues of $1.076 trillion and outlays of $1.475 trillion. The budget deficit equaled 37 percent of revenues.

The deterioration of the country's fiscal circumstances was caused by the interaction of several factors. There were systemic policy mistakes. Unanticipated and unpredictable changes in the fiscal environment occurred. The policymakers had little or no direct control over changes beyond their control.

First, an unexpected economic slowdown began in the mid-1970s. The slowdown baffled economists. The rate of economic growth slowed by approximately 1 percent after 1973. From the late 1940s through 1973, real per capita GDP expanded at an average annual rate of 2.5 percent and real output per hour of labor expanded at an average rate of 2.1 percent. From 1973 through 1995, real per capita GDP expanded at only 1.5 percent a year and output per hour of labor expanded at only 0.8 percent a year. Federal revenues expand as the economy increases. This economic slowdown had a significant impact on federal budgets.[20]

Second, the domestic entitlements the federal government committed to during the 1962–1972 period contributed significantly to growing deficits. Congress and three presidents enacted laws establishing Medicare, Medicaid, food stamps, guaranteed student loans, Title XX social services, and supplemental security income programs. The slowdown in the economy resulted in a decline in income growth. Increasing numbers of people became eligible for means-tested domestic programs. Unexpected demographic developments made more persons eligible for domestic entitlements. The divorce rate doubled. The fraction of births to unwed mothers more than tripled. The poverty rate declined from 22.4 percent in 1959 to 11.1 percent in 1973. The poverty rate increased an average of over 14 percent from 1980 through 1995. Health care costs, new entitlement commitments, were unexpectedly expensive. With the enactment of Medicare and Medicaid in 1965, the federal government assumed more responsibility for the country's health care provisions.

Third, the Reagan administration began the 1980s with large increases in defense spending. The Republican president made an ambitious effort to increase defense capabilities. Defense outlays increased from 4.9 percent of GDP in 1980 to 6.3 percent in 1986. Reagan called for cutbacks on the domestic side of government. Wage increases had elevated many Americans into higher tax brackets. Reagan promoted reductions in tax burdens. The administration's efforts made the deficit problems worse. The nondefense domestic discretionary budget declined from 5.2 percent of GDP in 1980 to 3.8 percent in 1986. However, the Reagan administration could not convince the Democratic Congress to significantly slow the increase in domestic entitlement spending programs.

Finally, the weak cyclical performance of the economy after 1974 contributed to growing deficits. Between fiscal years 1955 and 1974, the economy operated at or above its capacity in twelve of the twenty fiscal years. Between fiscal years 1964 and 1974, the economy operated at or above its capacity in nine of eleven fiscal years. Between fiscal years 1975 and 1996, the economy operated at or above capacity in only four fiscal years. The 1964–1974 period economic indicators were misleading.

The economic practice of sustaining over the long run increasing domestic entitlements, without appropriate tax increases, was sliding into deficit spending. Rising interest rates contributed to economic downturns. The growing size of the structural deficit caused federal expenditures on net interest to rise. Between 1951 and 1977, federal expenditures on net interest amounted to no more than 1.5 percent of GDP. After 1984, it expanded to 3 percent or more. Profound changes occurred in the composition of federal spending and taxes. Entitlements, other mandatory expenditures, and interest payments had lawmakers thinking benefit levels and eligibility criteria.[21]

In summary, factors contributing to growing federal deficits over the last thirty years were:

- the unexpected economic slowdown of the mid-1970s;
- domestic entitlement commitments the federal government enacted between 1962 and 1972;
- Reagan administration policies for increasing national defense capabilities and appropriations, decreasing nondefense discretionary budget spending, and reducing tax burdens; and
- a weak cyclical performance of the economy since 1974.

According to John Steele Gordon, five trends have increasingly affected government fiscal policies over the last sixty years.

First, a powerful but fundamentally flawed concept in the discipline of economics has completely changed the way both economists and politicians view the national economy and their responsibilities toward it.

FISCAL AND MONETARY POLICIES

Fiscal policy entails federal government policies with respect to taxes and spending and debt management, intended to promote the nation's macroeconomic goals, particularly with respect to employment, gross domestic product, price level stability, and equilibrium in balance of payments. The budget process is a major vehicle for determining and implementing federal fiscal policy.

The other major component of federal macroeconomic policy is monetary policy. Monetary policy entails policies, which affect the money supply, interest rates, and credit availability, intended to promote national macroeconomic goals, particularly with respect to employment, gross domestic product, price level stability, and equilibrium in balance of payments. Monetary policy is directed primarily by the Board of Governors of the Federal Reserve System and the Federal Open Market Committee. Monetary policy works by influencing the cost and availability of bank reserves.

Source: *A Glossary of Terms Used in the Federal Budget Process* (Washington, DC General Accounting Office, March, 1981), 59, 97.

Second, the responsibilities of government in general and the federal government in particular, as viewed by the public, have greatly increased.

Third, a shift in power from the Executive to Congress has balkanized the budget process by sharply limiting the influence of the one politician in Washington whose constituency is national in scope, the President.

Fourth, the decay of party discipline and the seniority system within Congress itself has further balkanized the budget process, dividing it among innumerable committees and subcommittees. This has made logrolling (you vote for my program and I'll vote for yours) the order of the day on Capitol Hill.

Finally, the political-action-committee system of financing congressional elections has given greatly increased influence to spending constituencies (often called special interests, especially when they are funding someone else's campaign) while sharply reducing that of the electorate as a whole, which picks up the tab.[22]

DECREMENTALISM AND CUTBACK BUDGETING

On coming to power in 1981 the Reagan administration did not offer reforms to solve the problem of government spending and federal deficits. Reagan argued that big government in Washington destroyed economic prosperity produced by free markets. Reagan's OMB leader, David Stockman, instead adopted strategies of top-down budgeting and budgeting for legislative advantage.[27]

Top-down budgeting, as implemented by Stockman, focused upon several changes in the traditional budgeting process. By the spring of 1981, Stockman

---

BUDGET COMPONENTS AND REFORM TECHNIQUES

- **The Capital Budget.** A budget that deals with large expenditures for capital items normally financed by borrowing. Capital projects calls for long range returns and life spans, are relatively expensive, have physical presence, and involves investments in community facilities. Examples include buildings, roads, sewage systems.[23]
- **The Operating or Expense Budget.** Annual projection of revenues and expenditures for regular and recurring operations of governments which serves as a primary instrument of planning and financial control. Examples include wages, salaries, personnel costs, supplies, materials, and travel costs.
- **Performance Budgets.** Performance budgets focus upon departmental objectives and accomplishments. They do not emphasize the purchase of resources utilized by the department. This technique accounts for the cost of performing measured accomplishment units during the fiscal year. A performance budget includes sections on demand, workload, productivity, and effectiveness.[24]
- **Program Budgets.** In a program budget, the focus is on output. The concept rests not on what governments purchase, nor on the tasks in which government is involved, but upon the outputs of government, as nearly as may be defined. This technique delineates the goals of a department and categorizes tasks contributing to each goal. The focus is on product, not input. Planning Programming Budgeting Systems, or PPBS, focuses on accountability.[25]
- **Zero-Based Budgets (ZBB).** ZBB requires its practitioners to adopt two words of basic terminology and three procedures for implementation. ZBB terms **decision units** and **decision packages;** ZBB steps: **identification, formation,** and **ranking.**[26]

---

was convinced that deficit spending must be addressed because a large structural deficit in the Reagan program was emerging. In top-down budgeting, Stockman dealt with the total budget, not particular programs.

Budgeting for legislative advantage became his second strategy for attempting to master the budget process and the increasing deficits. The former Michigan congressman ran OMB more like a congressional office than an executive institution. The aims of budgeting for legislative advantage were to hammer home the perception that the Reagan mandate for tax and spending cuts had not eroded and to use the ponderous budget procedures of Congress against itself.

George Bush, part of the Reagan administration as vice president, inherited Reagan's budgetary legacy of huge deficits. More federal spending was added to the national debt during Reagan's presidential tenure than was added during all previous administrations combined. Perhaps Reagan's chief contribution to budgetary politics, on the other hand, was calling attention to excessive middle-class entitlements and in moving from incremental budgeting to decremental estimates. From domestic to defense spending, the representatives of the American

---

ADMINISTRATIVE AUDIENCES

Thomas J. Anton points out that an administrator must try to appease three audiences:

1. The administrator's own *employees,* who look to the administrator to preserve and, if possible, enhance their working conditions and their status. Such considerations can be met by increasing the organization's appropriation.
2. The agency's *clientele group.* The people from this group also desire increased funds for the agency, because they are usually the most direct beneficiaries of the agency's expenditures. These first two pressures for budgeting increases would probably exist under any form of budgeting.
3. Finally, there are the *review officials,* including superiors, budget bureau officials, and legislators. All of these, but particularly the latter, have an interest in being able to cut the budget. In making cuts, they achieve a sense of fulfillment and importance.

Source: Thomas J. Anton, "Roles and Symbols in the Determination of State Expenditures," *Midwest Journal of Political Science* 11, no. 1 (February 1967): 29.

---

people have yet to find the line-items for equal sacrifice in implementing federal budgetary policies.

Incremental budgeting demands little inquiry because the increment, not the base, is considered. Incremental decision making entails routine, requires negotiations and accommodation grounded upon mutual respect, is delegated to specialists, and is almost invisible. It seems merely distributive, historical, annual, repetitive, predictable, and automatic. It is rewarding and can create stable coalitions.

Incremental budgeting distributes only the increment, but takes nothing away from anyone; decremental budgeting, meanwhile, redistributes resources from people who absorb cuts in appropriations. Incremental budgeting rewards increments to everyone, as credit for such enhancement is to be shared; decremental budgeting engenders blame for the pain of losing accustomed funding.

The incremental model minimizes the intellectual task of creating a new budget every year, facilitates the political task of adopting a budget, and appears ethical. Such a model, accepting the base as a given, eliminates the necessity for rethinking everything. The political task of building a coalition to support this year's new budget allows a majority of political interests with economic stakes to form and take hold. No one appears hurt; everyone gains a little in incremental budgeting. Even if the balance struck a decade ago has little or no ethical or political relevance today, the overall equity is never examined. Numerous interests may be unhappy with the process and results, but everyone knows what would be received under incrementalism. No one knows with certainty what new assumptions decrementalism would bring.

Decremental budgeting is chaotic and conflict-laden. It may result in coercion, involve confrontation, and generate mistrust. It is clearly redistributive, breaks precedents, is multiyear, erratic, unpredictable, painful, can foster unstable coalitions, and requires active leadership for overcoming such obstacles.

Decremental budgeting received considerable political support in the 1980s. The Omnibus Budget Reconciliation Act of 1981 reduced the 1982 federal budget by $35.1 billion. It was passed by voice vote in the House of Representatives; an eighty to fourteen Senate vote approved the measure. The Social Security Act Amendments of 1983 also entailed significant benefit reductions; the House passed the Amendments by 243 to 102; the Senate approved the decrements by fifty-eight to fourteen. What unique set of politics was required to support decrementalism?

The overarching consideration was the definition of the political issue.

Cutback management strategy saw the dominant issue as something more important than the consequences of individual cuts. The president did not emphasize the individual cuts; he spoke only of the larger picture. In the case of the 1983 Social Security cuts, the overriding issue focused upon was preventing the economic collapse of the Social Security system. The redefinition of the issue provided a reason for voting for the cutback legislation.

A second consideration bringing together such a decremental coalition concerned *parliamentary procedures*. David Stockman, former director of the OMB, developed a reconciliation strategy whereby members of Congress voted only on the entire package and *not* on individual programmatic cuts. Your congressperson voted to save the national economy, or Social Security, not to cut back your widowed mother's pension.

Equity constituted a third consideration. Everyone—the self-employed, beneficiaries, workers, new government employees, and the better-off among the retired—assumed some of the economic hardship. The philosophy of equal sacrifice boosted the prospects for decrementalism.

Definition of the political issue, voting procedures, and equity, however, are often not enough. Leadership may emerge from the speaker of the House, the majority leader of the Senate or the chairs of the budget committees; however, the president occupies the best position to define the issues and exert political pressure. The president (or governor or mayor) defines the overarching issue, focuses public attention on the problem, and persuades legislators to form blocks of support behind decrementalism efforts.[28]

Decrementalism suggests a centralized political system dominated by top-down budgeting. Incrementalism explains budgeting as a bottom-up process. What's the difference? The budgeting process includes the countervailing forces of centralization and decentralization, autonomy and interdependence, micropolitics and macropolitics. The president and his key advisors dominate the top-down process. A limited number of people are involved in such an approach; the developments are less visible to the public. Top-down strategy confronts the mixture of defense and domestic components of the budget, the budget's size, the impact of the budget upon fiscal policies, and the executive's policy initiatives to force cutbacks. As suggested in our discussion of decrementalism, routine is not a common feature of the top-down process.

There have been top-down characteristics of the budgetary process since the passage of the Budget and Accounting Act of 1921. Top-down elements are more difficult to document as the process is less routine, involves fewer people, and receives less publicity, and as such have garnered less attention than the bottom-up developments. Researchers find it difficult to observe, conceptualize, and explain the top-down process. According to budget theorists Barry Bozeman and Jeffrey D. Straussman, such features are often ignored or relegated to historical "disturbances."[29]

Incrementalism reflects the bottom-up budgeting process. The late budget theorist Aaron Wildavsky reported that incrementalism focuses on the significance of adjusting the margins from last year's budgetary base with little, if any, examination of the baseline so assumed.

Why the emphasis upon the bottom-up process? First, incrementalism is explainable. Budget variations may be explained by using simple projections. Second, incrementalism gives an adequate account of the bottom-up process. Third, incrementalism is emphasized extensively in the administration and budgeting literature. Finally, incrementalism dominates policy makers' perceptions of how budgeting actually occurs and portrays the actual experience of policy makers themselves.

Top-down and bottom-up processes are operative in every budget cycle. As the demands of the budget cycle change with developments in fiscal policy, presidential leadership, economic growth, foreign conflict, congressional assertiveness, and other factors, the use of the respective processes changes. Although the top-down process of federal budgeting grew more important in the Ford and Carter administrations, the Reagan administration implemented perhaps the most important shift in budget policy, determining that the "controllable" portion of the budget includes entitlements offering social services to the middle class.

The baseline federal outlay projections for entitlements consist of social insurance programs such as Social Security, Medicare, unemployment insurance, and railroad retirement; means-tested programs such as Medicaid, food stamps, assistance payments, supplemental security income, veterans' pensions, guaranteed student loans, and child nutrition; civilian and military employee retirement and disability; and programs offering veterans' benefits, farm price supports, general revenue sharing, and other social services.[30]

The desire to curb the development of middle-class entitlement spending, promote economic changes, and alter public perception of economic issues and economic thinking encouraged Reagan administration policy makers to adopt top-down strategies. Bozeman and Straussman state that conventional budgeting wisdom did not keep pace with events. Concluding that budget theory should be reformulated, these theorists argue that the political and economic environments changed and led to a perceived demand for reductions in the rate and level of spending. Such cutback management, they argue, may be achieved only through coordinated fiscal management with top-down strategies. Under such conditions, incrementalism becomes a less satisfactory explanation of federal budgeting.[31]

The Reagan Administration left a budgetary legacy for future presidents that is best described by John Shannon: "The creation of a fiscal environment that forces state and local officials to become more self-reliant stands out as the primary impact the Reagan Administration has had on our federal system."[32]

While he orchestrated budget cuts in federal domestic spending, however, Reagan led ambitious efforts to secure increased defense spending and military capabilities. He reduced tax burdens, but that action brought on higher deficits and greater national debt. Reagan never proposed a federal budget less than the estimates of the Democratic Party controlled Congress. Reagan's agenda was as important, if not more so, than his accomplishments. Five years after Reagan left the presidency, Newt Gingrich led Republican takeovers of the U.S. House and Senate as followers of Reagan's political ideas and antigovernment spending agenda won power.

FEDERAL SPENDING IN THE STATES

The key to economic development of any state is the money it can bring into its economy from out-of-state. If a state cannot attract outside investments, no state policies will produce economic growth. Economic activities developing from without determines whether total personal income will grow and how fast. Rapid growth in outside money inevitably increases activities developing from within the state. Inside activities such as state and local government (schools, roads, safety, prisons, sanitation), retailing, banking and finance, real estate, health care, and services benefit from investments of outside revenues.

The development and expansion of manufacturing and promotion of tourism depend on private sector out-of-state monies. The federal government is a major outside factor in state economies. In fiscal year 1996, total federal spending amounted to $1.4 trillion. This spending included direct payments, such as Social Security, to individuals within states; grants to state and local governments; procurement of goods and services, such as weapons for the Department of Defense; and wages and salaries for federal employees. Federal spending impacts jobs and personal income for state residents.

The manner in which federal assistance is distributed significantly affects the finances of state and local governments. Federal assistance is not distributed on an equal per capita basis. Changes in federal assistance have had immense and unequal impacts on state budgets. Future changes, increases or decreases, will affect states differently. The distribution of federal spending comes in four major categories.[33] Tables 9-3 and 9-4 offer data and analyses for understanding why elected leaders and government officials want to increase certain types of federal spending in their state.

TABLE 9–3 Categories of Federal Spending

Distribution of Federal Spending Traceable by State, FY 1997 ($ Billion)		
Category	Amount	Percent of Total
Direct Payments For Individuals	$781.9	54.7%
Grants To State and Local Governments	229.8	16.1
Procurement	193.1	13.5
Salaries and Wages	166.1	11.6
Other Programs	57.9	4.1
Total	$1,428.8	100.0

TABLE 9–4 Per Capita Federal Spending (FY 1997)

Rank	State	Amount	Rank	State	Amount	Rank	State	Amount
1	Virginia	$7,857	18	South Dakota	$5,463	34	Iowa	$4,753
2	Alaska	7,715	19	Kentucky	5,440	35	Delaware	4,719
3	Maryland	7,683	20	Penn	5,434	36	Nebraska	4,713
4	New Mexico	7,192	21	Washington	5,404	37	Idaho	4,696
5	Hawaii	6,966	22	Louisiana	5,321	38	N Carolina	4,677
6	N Dakota	6,758	23	Tennessee	5,320	39	Vermont	4,632
7	Mass	6,110	24	New York	5,272	40	Texas	4,544
8	Rhode Is	5,954	25	Oklahoma	5,221	41	Ohio	4,533
9	Missouri	5,868		United States	5,133	42	Oregon	4,512
10	Montana	5,840	26	Colorado	5,061	43	Illinois	4,440
11	Maine	5,784	27	Arkansas	5,021	44	N Hampshire	4,299
12	W Virginia	5,733	28	S Carolina	5,004	45	Minnesota	4,287
13	Alabama	5,687	29	California	4,986	46	Indiana	4,283
14	S Dakota	5,622	30	New Jersey	4,910	47	Nevada	4,225
15	Florida	5,600	31	New Jersey	4,910	48	Michigan	4,159
16	Wyoming	5,509	32	Kansas	4,820	49	Utah	4,097
17	Miss	5,503	33	Georgia	4,779	50	Wisconsin	4,024

Source: *State Policy Reports* 16, no. 10-2 (May 1998): 3.

CHANGES IN STATE BUDGETING SINCE 1970S

The recession of the early 1990s hit the states especially hard. The governors and state legislatures felt the fallout as 50 percent of the states could not fund their fiscal 1992 budgets despite the more than $16 billion increase in state taxes in fiscal 1991. Personal income and business income tax collections fall during an economic slowdown. In turn, state revenues decrease, but the economic distress causes citizens to pressure state governments for relief. Service costs in education, health care, welfare, and corrections are made worse by budget shortfalls. Compared with fiscal 1981, state governments in fiscal 1990 appropriated less for education and highways and more for corrections, debt service, and human services.[34]

Two events of the 1970s contributed to the state budget shortfalls of the 1990s. First, the tax revolt movement swept the country. The trend was symbolized by Proposition 13, the California property tax revolt in 1978. Second, the decline of federal assistance in real, per capita terms to state governments resulted in "fend-for-yourself," or "go-it-alone" federalism. The Reagan and Bush administrations promoted the pull-out of federal grants to state and local governments.

The structural budget deficits confronting state governments in the 1990s originated in the 1980s. From fiscal year 1981 through fiscal year 1990, trends in state government spending, revenues, and employment indicate that some state governments acted responsibly to replace lost federal aid, some were forced by federal or state court orders to spend more on schools and prisons, some assumed higher state employees' health and pension costs, and some were victimized by ambitious politicians who promised more public services to their constituents. The states have more government than citizens are inclined to pay for. Cutbacks in state spending necessitated by these shortfalls especially affect programs for the poor. Despite efforts to reduce state government spending, twenty-eight state legislatures, trapped between services and deficits, passed tax increases in fiscal 1992.

Our examination of the fiscal policies of the 1980s illuminates the changes in state budgetary processes during the 1970–1990 period. As a result of fiscal policies of the past, functions relatively uncommon in 1970 but common in 1990 were:

- dollar-level ceilings and policy ceilings issued by the executive to agencies for preparing budget requests;
- guidance in preparing budget requests based upon current levels of service;
- instructions for agencies ranking requests by priority;
- overall policy guidance—written and otherwise;
- program effectiveness and productivity information required for requesting new and revised programs;
- computer use in agency budget preparation, analysis of agency requests by the budget office, and preparation of the governor's budget;
- inclusion of effectiveness and productivity measures in budget documents;

- conduct of effectiveness and productivity analysis by the central budget office and the legislature;
- use of analysis in decision making by the executive and legislative branches;
- accounting systems that collect information by appropriation, department, organizational unit, program, and levels within a program;
- master's degree education of professional budget office personnel; and
- academic disciplines other than business and accounting constituting a majority of budget office personnel.[35]

SUMMARY

- If politics is sometimes defined as the process of deciding who gets what, administrative politics often becomes the process of deciding who gets *what amount of money.* If budgets are essentially political documents, the politics involved are often veiled.
- It is not enough to call attention to the political aspects of budgeting to define budgeting. Budgets are also instruments of *coordination, control,* and *planning.* They govern nearly all aspects of administration and confer a great deal of power on those who prepare them.
- Public sector budgets are raised from taxes on individuals and businesses. It's tough to maintain effective public services if revenues supporting such activities are low or nonexistent. Whether we are providing national defense or unemployment compensation, we need a *growth economy* to finance government benefits.
- Budgeting occurs in the realm of certain *myths* about American policy making. Myths concern living standards, the middle class, isolationism, free market expectations, power of elected executives, corruption, and effectiveness of local governments.
- *Functions of budgeting* include allocating resources to achieve governmental priorities, goals, and policies; raising funds through taxes and loans to finance the budget; stabilizing the economy through fiscal and monetary policies; holding operating agencies accountable for the use of budgeted resources; controlling expenditures; tranferring funds from one level of government to another; achieving planned social and economic development; and improving management in operating departments and agencies.
- *Budget cycles* feature the dominance of the appropriations and tax committees; the rise of power of the authorizing committees; the enactment of the Budget and Impoundment Control Act of 1974 and introduction of the budget committees; the paper tiger affect of the Balanced Budget and Emergency Deficit Control Act of 1985; and the Budget Enforcement Act of 1990, followed by Budget Acts of 1993 and 1997.
- *Stages of the budget cycle* are executive preparation, legislative consideration, implementation and control of the enacted budget, and audit and evaluation.

- Operating departments and agencies, chief executives, and legislatures play roles in the budget process and offer *strategies* for cultivating clientele and developing confidence in their ideas, priorities, and programs.
- Growing deficits and the resulting lower savings lead to dwindling investments, slower economic growth, and finally decline in real Gross Domestic Product. *Living standards,* in turn, stagnate and fall.
- Major progress was made on deficit reduction in the past several years, culminating in the passage of the *Balanced Budget Act of 1997.* Policy action accounted for about *25 percent* of the improvement in the Congressional Budget Office's budget estimates. The remainder of the improvement was due primarily to economic factors.
- The *roots* of federal deficits are grounded in the unexpected economic slowdown in the mid-1970s, the domestic entitlements the federal government committed to during the 1962–1972 period, the Reagan administration's commitment to increased defense spending in the 1980s, and the weak cyclical performance of the American economy after 1974.
- *Fiscal policy* entails federal government policies with respect to taxes and spending and debt management, intended to promote the nation's macroeconomic goals, particularly employment, gross domestic product, price level stability, and equilibrium in balance of payments.
- *Monetary policy* entails policies, which affect the money supply, interest rates, and credit availability, intended to promote national macroeconomic goals— particularly employment, gross domestic product, price level stability, and equilibrium in balance of payments.
- The key to economic development of any state is the money it can bring into its economy from *out-of-state.* The per capita distribution of total federal spending varies from a high of $7,857 in Virginia, to $4,024 in Wisconsin. Thirteen states exceed the national average by more than 10 percent while eleven fall below the average by more than 10 percent. In fiscal year 1997, total federal spending in the states amounted to $1,428.8 billion.
- Most of America's approximately 80,000 governments divide their budgets into two sections, one for *capital* projects, the other for *expenses.*
- The status-quo reinforcing effect of traditional line-item budgeting, often referred to as incremental budgeting because it concerns itself with increments of change rather than program change, can influence whole governments.
- *Line-item budgets* usually include categories for personnel, equipment, and maintenance, among others.
- As governments grew in size and complexity, citizens and administrators became dissatisfied with traditional budgeting. Line-item budgets failed to show the impact of expenditures on programs, future costs and effects, and relationships between capital and operating costs.

- Performance budgets, program budgets, and zero-based budgets constitute *budgetary reforms.*
- *Incremental budgeting* demands little inquiry because the increment, not the base, is considered. Incremental decision making entails routine, requires negotiations and accommodation grounded upon mutual respect, is delegated to specialists, and is almost invisible. Incrementalism explains budgeting as a bottom-up process.
- *Decremental budgeting* is chaotic and conflict-laden. Decrementalism suggests a centralized political system dominated by top-down budgeting.
- The Reagan administration significantly effected budgeting allocations and processes in the states and the nation. Reagan created a fiscal environment in which state and local officials had to become more *self-reliant,* shifting financing responsibility from the national treasury to the states and localities. Large federal deficits, increased defense spending, and high levels of federal spending for Social Security and Medicare forced public sector administrators to *do more with less.*
- Each year's *budget deficit* is the difference between revenues and outlays in that year. Continuing large federal deficits absorb savings otherwise available to finance investment. A new fiscal policy is essential to the economic well-being of the United States.
- The federal debt is the accumulation of all past deficits. As President Reagan entered office in 1981, the federal debt was $709 billion. The estimated debt for the year 2000 is nearly $7 trillion.
- The *tax-and-spend policies* of the 1960s and 1970s resulted in the *tax-and-spend-and-borrow fiscal policies* of the 1980s. There was little fiscal and political accountability in the 1980s.
- In the 1980s, the Republican Party's commitment to balanced federal budgets were sacrificed in favor of *political pragmatism.*
- Political consensus grounded in the *decrementalism* of cutting back government programs is more difficult than the *incrementalism* of adding programs.
- The *per capita tax level* in the United States is not high with respect to America's economic competitors. The people of the United States are not overtaxed. Taxation as a percentage of national income is lower in the United States than in any other major industrialized country.
- The American philosophy of taxation is: "Don't tax me. Don't tax thee. Tax the fellow behind the tree."
- Two events of the 1970s contributed to the state budget shortfalls of the 1990s: the *tax revolt* and the *decline of federal assistance.* The structural budget deficits confronting state governments in the 1990s originated in the 1980s.

Public administrators realize that difficult decisions are made when the details of budget-decisions are known. This case study illustrates some of the tough budget decisions a typical town faces each year.

CASE STUDY

Cutting Back at City Hall[36]

The Smithville City Council meeting of June 23 had aroused more public interest than its usual weekly sessions because it was the time set for presenting the completed operating budget for the fiscal year starting July 1. The budget specified the estimated revenues and expenditures for personnel services and the maintenance and operation of the city. On the table before each council member was a copy of the proposed budget over which department heads, the controller's staff, the city manager, and the council had been struggling for months—a neatly bound book with a light blue cover containing 163 pages of tables and charts. A public hearing would be held on the proposed budget before it was presented to the council for final approval at its last regular meeting in June.

In presenting the budget, City Manager James Harmsworth said the fact that it was a balanced one was due to the hard work put into it by city employees and council members. Failing revenues and higher operating costs made it seem early in the year as if there would be a shortfall, ranging from a "best-case scenario" of $1,739,495 to a "worst-case scenario" of $5,139,000. State law prohibited deficit spending by municipalities, and so figuring out a budget that would meet this requirement was not an easy task. Earlier Harmsworth had presented to the council the capital budget, down about $2 million, or 39 percent, from last year. He believed the completed operations budget was equally successful.

The grim situation that Smithville, population 65,000, faced early in the year was due in part to a general business slump in the state that had affected the city's revenue. The city's income from services was down, sales tax receipts had dropped, and there was a loss in federal revenue sharing.

Early in the year Harmsworth had told the council: "This is one of the most critical times in my ten years as city manager. But the problem is a manageable one if the council will respond to it. During the year we must try to alleviate the situation. A year from now, if something isn't done, it will no longer be a manageable problem."

Recognizing that Draconian measures were needed, city negotiators had resisted demands for pay increases by the three employees' unions, the Fraternal Order of Police (FOP), the International Association of Fire Fighters (IAF), and the American Federation of State, County, and Municipal Employees (AFSCME). FOP members had asked for pay raises of 7 percent, then lowered their demand to 4 percent, and finally accepted, by a 55 percent vote of the membership, no increase at all in the face of the bleak prospects presented to them. Similarly, the fire fighters had dropped their first request of an 8.5 percent increase to a 6.5 percent one and then were forced to settle for none at all; AFSCME members had abandoned their more reasonable request of a cost-of-living increase of 3 percent.

Union leaders had objected strongly to what they considered "taking the brunt" of retrenchment, arguing that instead of lowering salaries and cutting down on personnel, the city's revenue could have been raised if officials had taken proper prevention measures to offset declines in the sales tax and utilities income.

John J. Patrick, FOP president, had told a council budget study session: "It's up to City Council to determine whether they want a cut in the quality and efficiency of police services. It has known for months that sales taxes have not been up to budgeted estimates, and it could have acted to avert the present crisis by changing the city charter." He pointed out that a charter provision required that 70 percent of the one cent sales tax be used to fund capital improvements. "Other cities can cut capital improvements and give their employees a little raise," Patrick had said. "Smithville has made the wrong choice between capital improvements and its employees."

Judith Weintraub, president of the employees' federation, had been critical of officials for meeting rising utility costs by taking money from the general fund. "I realize that the city charter requires residents to vote approval of increases in the water, sewage, and trash-removal rates," Weintraub had said, "but officials have allowed the present inadequate rates to go on for years."

To these criticisms officials had replied that it was difficult to persuade the public to approve increased rates for services and higher taxes in a period of business decline. A vote on such matters at a time like this would undoubtedly reject the needed increases, and it could be several years before the time was right for seeking a second vote.

Harmsworth briefed the council on the proposed budget and presented enlarged tables and charts on a screen. He first displayed a budget summary showing estimated revenues for all funds—general, capital, cable television, room tax (on hotels and motels), street and alley, revenue sharing, Smithville Municipal Authority, Smithville Utilities Authority, and the sinking fund. The budget summary revealed a total income of $35,018,179 and total expenditures of $34,710,324, well under the anticipated income.

Harmsworth presented a table comparing the projected expenditures for the new fiscal year with those for the past year that illustrated dramatically the budgetary task facing the city. The city had planned to spend $49,507,154 for the past year. Fortunately, it had been possible to reduce this amount by almost $12 million using carryover funds from previous years, placing a moratorium on buying supplies, dropping training programs, eliminating travel expenses and automobile use reimbursement, postponing the filling of vacant positions, and employing other money saving devices.

When pressed by council members to discuss the fiscal year 1988 operations and maintenance budget of the General Fund, Harmsworth indicated that $1,343,310 was spent for electricity, natural gas, and telephone service; $1,248,520 for landfill fees; $763,470 for gasoline, oil, tires, and vehicle and equipment repair parts; $238,800 for insurance; $376,460 for membership in the Lake Region Master Water Conservancy District; and $205,090 for water treatment chemicals. Harmsworth, as a seasoned and politically astute city manager, was quick to add that the "O & M portion of the budget would be decreased by 11.7 percent for FY '89 and that no part of the budget would remain unaffected by the sharp knife of Smithville's retrenchment plan."

Harmsworth said the worst aspect of cutting down on costs was the impact it would have on personnel—lowering the already inadequate pay of the men and women who protect the people from criminals and maintain order, who save people and buildings during fires, who collect trash and garbage, who provide a clean and adequate water supply, and who keep up the streets, parks, and public buildings. They were the human element in government budgeting, he said, and a significant proportion of the general fund went for their services. Such personnel services in the new fiscal year, Harmsworth explained, were estimated to be $17,772,324 out of a total expenditure budget of $23,725,446.

The council budget committee and officials, Harmsworth continued, had worked out a plan that would save the jobs of employees—a plan calling for a reduction in force of only forty persons. Last year there had been 683 persons on the city's payrolls, the most ever employed, and the projection for the new fiscal year was 643 persons. The reduction in force, however, would not substantially affect the essential services of the fire, police, emergency medical, and sanitation departments, whose combined work force numbered 361 persons. Instead, the forty proposed layoffs would occur in the areas of professional and management level employees, clerical staff, and so forth. To minimize the salary cutback of employees, $400,000 would be transferred from the capital improvement budget and $175,000 would be saved by reducing street lighting to every other street. Additional salary funds would also be obtained from reduced health care and insurance premiums and by deletion of a separation and retirement budget. Thus, personnel would be penalized only by a 5 percent salary reduction and a freeze on merit pay and furloughs once a month for all employees. These changes would result in net savings for the following categories: salary reduction, $820,000; merit raise freeze, $343,000; and furloughs, $750,000.

QUESTIONS AND INSTRUCTIONS

1. In developing the Smithville budget, officials endeavored to make reductions easy on employees. From this standpoint, how do you evaluate their success in the following: hiring freeze, cost-of-living pay freeze, merit pay freeze, furloughs, reduction by attrition, cutting back on force, elimination of training programs, and freeze on travel?

2. Other methods of cutting back include putting ceilings on positions, load-shedding, demotions, personnel transfers, and reclassifying positions. Do you believe Smithville officials should have done more in these areas?

3. Officials could have quickly solved most of the budget-cutting problems by a 10 percent reduction in the work force. Do you think they were wiser to choose instead the complex program they did?

4. Is the criticism of union leaders valid who faulted officials for failing to attempt to alter the city charter permitting increases in utility rates or reducing the 70 percent of the sales tax going to capital improvements, when city officials knew long before that revenue would be substantially lowered?

5. Do you agree with the president of the Fraternal Order of Police that in the Smithville budget capital improvements were allowed at the cost of "a little" raise for employees?

6. Do you think it fair not to make reductions in force for essential services such as fire and police protection and to place the burden of retrenchment almost wholly on employees providing other services?

7. Do you think it is possible that efficiency and productivity might be increased after a retrenchment program has been effected?
8. Researchers have reported what they consider negative results in retrenchment in government: (a) an increase in polarization-management vs. labor, whites vs. blacks, political appointees vs. career officials, and veterans vs. nonveterans; (b) increases in waste, fraud, and failure to maintain standards; (c) an increase in the age of the work force; (d) a higher level of organizational chaos—disruption of programs and processes; (e) a decline in morale; and (f) an increase in decision-making uncertainty. How serious are these findings?

INSIGHTS-ISSUES / CUTTING BACK AT CITY HALL

Clearly and briefly describe and illustrate these concepts, issues, or points. Interpret the word "role" as meaning impact, application, importance, effect and/or illustration of certain facts, concerns, or issues from the case study.

1. The role of the public's right to know (public document), or the public nature of budgets and budgeting (public hearing).
2. The role of law; deficit spending by municipalities prohibited.
3. The role of economic and business trends; impacts upon city's revenues; subsequent implications for government budget cuts?
4. What was the role of budget reductions on personnel? What interests offered advice to city council persons on cutbacks and reductions?
5. The role of budget cuts on essential services: what services were reduced because of cutbacks?

ENDNOTES

1. Donald Axelrod, *Budgeting for Modern Government* (New York: St. Martin's Press, Inc., 1995).
2. "1993 Budget-Reconciliation Act," *Congressional Quarterly Weekly Report* 51, no. 37 (18 September 1993): 2482–2498.
3. Jonathan Rauch, "The End of Government," *National Journal* 28, no. 36 (7 September 1996): 1890–1896.
4. Rauch, "Ducking the Challenge," *National Journal* 29, no. 6 (8 February 1997): 260–265.
5. Rauch and Eliza Newlin Carney, "The Easy Way Out," *National Journal* 29, no. 19 (10 May 1997): 928–931.
6. L. Douglas Lee, "How Congress Handles the Budget," *The Wharton Magazine* 4 (winter 1980): 29.
7. Marshall E. Dimock, Gladys Ogden Dimock, and Douglas M. Fox, *Public Administration* (New York: Holt, Rinehart and Winston, 1983), 359.
8. Mikesell, John L. *Fiscal Administration*, "Analysis and Applications for the Public Sector," (Chicago, IL: The Dorsey Press, 2ed, 1986) 75–85.

9. Dimock, Dimock, and Fox, *Public Administration,* 367.

10. Peter F. Rousmaniere, *Local Governments Auditing—A Manual for Public Officials* (New York: Council on Muncipal Performance, 1980), 83.

11. Advisory Commission on Intergovernmental Relations, "Sunset Legislation and Zero-Based Budgeting," *Information Bulletin* 76, no. 5 (December 1976): 1.

12. Mikesell, *Fiscal Administration,* 48.

13. Mikesell, *Fiscal Administration,* 56–60.

14. Aaron Wildavsky, *The Politics of the Budgetary Process* (Boston: Little, Brown and Co., 1984), 63–126.

15. Mikesell, *Fiscal Administration,* 56–60.

16. Mikesell, *Fiscal Administration,* 56–60.

17. For more detailed explanations of comparatively low U.S. tax burdens, see Louis Ferleger and Jay R. Mantle, "America's Hostility Toward Taxes," *Challenge* 14, no. 4 (July-August 1991): 54; "No Pain, No Gain: Taxes, Productivity, and Economic Growth," Challenge 36, no. 3 (May–June 1993): 11–20; and *A New Mandate: Democratic Choices for a Prosperous Economy* (Columbia, Mo: University of Missouri Press, 1994).

18. See *Federal Debt and Interest Costs,* Congressional Budget Office, May 1993, and *Federal Debt: Answers to Frequently Asked Questions* (27 November 1996).

19. *Budget Issues: Analysis of Long-Term Fiscal Outlook,* Congressional Budget Office, October 1997 (GAO/AIMD/OCE-98-19).

20. Robert D. Reischauer, "The Budget: Crucible for the Policy Agenda," in *Setting National Priorities: Budget Choices for the Next Century,* ed. Robert D. Reischauer (Washington: The Brookings Institution Press, 1997), 4–11.

21. Reischauer, "The Budget," 4–11.

22. John Steele Gordon, "The Federal Debt," *American Heritage* 47, no. 7 (November 1995): 82–92.

23. Rauch, "A Capital Idea for the Budget," *National Journal* 18, no. 49 (6 December 1986): 2948–2949.

24. Mikesell, *Fiscal Administration,* 135–155.

25. Samuel M. Greenhouse, "The Planning-Programming-Budgeting System: Rationale, Language, and Idea-Relationships," *Public Administration Review* 26, no. 6 (December 1966): 271–277.

26. See Peter A. Pyhrr, "The Zero-Base Approach to Government Budgeting," *Public Administration Review* 37, no. 1 (January–February 1977): 1–8; see also Allen Schick, "The Road from ZBB," *Public Administration Review* 38, no. 2 (March–April 1978): 177–180.

27. Hugh Heclo, "Executive Budget Making," in *Federal Budget Policy in the 1980s,* ed. Gregory B. Mills and John L. Palmer (Washington, DC: The Urban Institute Press, 1984), 255–291.

28. Robert D. Behn, "Cutback Budgeting," *Journal of Policy Analysis and Management* 4, no. 2 (1985): 155–177.

29. Barry Bozeman and Jeffrey D. Straussman, "Shrinking Budgets and the Shrinkage of Budget Theory," *Public Administration Review* 42, no. 6 (November-December 1982): 509–515. Lance T. LeLoup. *Budgetary Politics* (Brunswick, OH: King's Court Communications, 1986), 16–21; Greenhouse, "The Planning-Programming-Budgeting System," see also Robert D. Behn, "Cutback Budgeting," 155–177.

30. Murray L. Weidenbaum, "Budget Dilemma and Its Solution," in Control of Federal Spending, ed. C. Lowell Harris (New York: The Academy of Political Science, 1985), 47–58.

31. Bozeman and Straussman, "Shrinking Budgets," 511.

32. John Shannon, "The Return to Fend-for-Yourself Federalism: The Reagan Mark," *Intergovernmental Perspective* 13, no. 3/4 (summer-fall 1987): 34–37.

33. *State Policy Reports,* 16, no. 10 (May 1998), 2–7.

34. Henry J. Raimondo, "State Budgeting in the Nineties," in *The State of the States* (Washington, DC: Congressional Quarterly, Inc., 1993), 31–49.

35. Robert D. Lee, "Developments in State Budgeting: Trends of Two Decades," *Public Administration Review* 51, no. 3 (May-June 1991): 254–262.

36. C. Kenneth Meyer and Charles H. Brown, *Practicing Public Management: A Casebook,* 2nd ed., pp. 166–169. Copyright © 1989 by St. Martin's Press, Inc. Reprinted with permission of Bedford/St. Martin's Press, Inc.

10

THE PRODUCTIVITY CHALLENGE: WORKING SMARTER WHILE DOING MORE WITH LESS

Productivity in the public sector refers to excellence in individual and collective performance—especially in times when public employees are expected to do more with less. The employees could be public school teachers, occupational safety inspectors, highway patrol officers, fire fighters, air traffic controllers, maintenance crews removing snow from the streets, or sanitation workers removing waste and technological excess from communities.

In these areas of worker expertise, there are widely divergent views as to what excellence is. *Excellence,* in its various forms, is based on the cultural context of a particular function. Therefore, measuring excellence and employee productivity in government funded organizations is a problematic assignment. The public sector usually deals in services, which, because they are intangible and often widely variable, almost always present problems in productivity measurement. Many government experts concede that some public sector functions are not measurable with the mechanisms currently available.

Despite these difficulties, an organization should adapt excellence as its main component. The system should enable an organization to achieve high-performance levels from their employees. Outstanding performance not only benefits the organization but also improves the delivery of services to the citizens.[1] Most citizens care about the performance of their public institutions. Parents worry about the quality of their children's schools. City dwellers anxiously scan the latest crime statistics. Drivers pray for better roads, transit riders for dependable buses and subways, air travelers for effective air traffic control.[2]

Posing particular difficulties for analyses are numerous staff operations, such as personnel work and social casework. As for the latter, one has only to think of the complexities involved in trying to measure the productivity of a caseworker in a public welfare office. Should the caseworker be rated on how many cases he or she clears from the welfare rolls or on how many people he or she adds to the welfare rolls? Using either standard can produce distortions.

EFFICIENCY AND EFFECTIVENESS

Related to these problems is the central task of distinguishing between efficiency and effectiveness. Efficiency means doing *things well,* while effectiveness means doing the *right things well. Efficiency,* essentially, is the input or contribution of labor, capital, and other resources into an effort matched against the output of product produced or measured, regardless of the mechanism selected to gauge output. *Effectiveness,* meanwhile, calls for a preestablished standard of comparison; a focus upon a certain quality of production; an ability to mobilize, organize, and direct resources for specified purposes, taken within a certain cultural context.

As one commentator noted, a man might be efficient in driving nails into a table. Effectiveness enters the picture when we question whether he should be driving nails into a table at all. Questions regarding quality make the public productivity measurer's task still more of a hazard and a hassle. A fiddler isn't necessarily producing more by fiddling faster. Nor can a pianist be hailed as especially

---

PERFORMANCE OF PUBLIC WORKS

Asked to grade the performance of key public works services on a 4.0 scale (A=4–F=0), Americans rated roads and bridges at 2.14; water supply, 2.70; and solid waste disposal, 2.32. How would Americans prefer to raise needed additional revenues to improve public works? Dedicated taxes are the choice of 35 percent, followed by 29 percent for user fees, 12 percent for general taxes, and 13 percent for no increase in spending or revenues (volunteered).

Source: *Changing Public Attitudes on Governments and Taxes: 1992* (Washington, DC: United States Advisory Commission on Intergovernmental Relations, 1992).

---

productive for playing Chopin's Minute Waltz in fifty seconds. On a more mundane and realistic level, a narcotics squad that makes a lot of arrest quotas for their narcotic divisions had to change them when they realized that such productivity measures were not producing "quality" arrests, in other words, arrests of major dealers.[3]

GOVERNMENT PERFORMANCE PERCEPTIONS

Before a public administrator confronts productivity issues, he or she should have a good idea about public perceptions of government performance. Those perceptions are not always as negative as is commonly believed. The following section is a brief overview of perceptions and should be kept in mind when exploring productivity issues in this chapter.

There are understandable reasons for the sometimes unfavorable perceptions we have of the way government performs. In a series of interviews with business and government leaders, Mark Abramson found four explanations for the public's dissatisfaction with government performance. The reasons are:

- Democracy is messy.
- Government takes a bum rap.
- Government must shape up.
- The country must shape up.[3]

*DEMOCRACY IS MESSY

Democracy is not cost effective. Democratic governments are designed to promote equity and fairness. Pluralism is central to the way our society is organized, therefore the inherent nature of our government admits of inefficiency and ineffectiveness. Americans, on the other hand, expect only satisfactory performance from the variety of government jurisdictions and their respective functionaries, not optimum performance. We accept that the democratic values of equity, due process, equal opportunity, and openness take prominence over bureaucratic values of efficiency and effectiveness. Human nature dictates, however, that what is wrong with society gets more attention than what's right about how the system is working.

The need for improvements receives more press coverage than the task performed without fanfare. Perceptions of performance are crucial. Despite cost effectiveness dilemmas, there is a need for communicating to citizens the impacts of equity, due process, equal opportunity, and other democratic values concerning government's performance. Administrators and employees must develop more valid methods for judging the performance of public programs to prevent outsiders from doing so. The costs of democracy must be communicated to the taxpayers who will elect politicians; the politicians, in turn, appropriate monies.

In a society where advertisements, music, and sports receive priority over civic education via the nation's radio and television media, citizens must realize the importance of public policies and their corresponding impacts upon their lives. If there is to be political consensus concerning government functions, elected leaders must convince citizens of the necessity for maintaining solid infrastructures of schools, libraries, highways, hospitals, sanitary facilities, prisons, and public safety functions. Governments cannot be all things to all people. Although sometimes messy, the functions of government must be understood and appreciated by its citizenry.

*GOVERNMENT TAKES A BUM RAP

This assertion, that government takes a bum rap, assumes that government's performance is better than its critics suggest. The media, politicians, academics, and government oversight agencies accentuate what's wrong with public sector bureaucracies. According to Charles Goodsell, public bureaucracy as stereotype, discriminator, and bungler is not a factual reality. (See the following section of this chapter for more explanation.) Surveys and nationwide public opinion polls reveal approximately 75 percent of citizen experiences with municipal, state, and federal departments and agencies are positive. These organizations compete satisfactorily with private companies for service deliveries. According to Goodsell, American bureaucratic performance is superior.[4]

Public service, writes Herbert Simon, is often vaguely characterized as "bureaucracy" and is unfairly blamed for inefficiency in government. Opponents of government organizations argue that human behavior is driven by self-interest and must be linked through economic markers to social goals, requiring privatization. However, organizations are effective means to meet human needs and may be improved by commitment to social good.[5]

The bum-rap criticisms suggest that elected representatives, who supervise public managers, need to be more proactive in advocacy for government performance. According to Abramson, public managers also need to be proactive in explaining the role of the press in covering government activities. There is, likewise, a need for training public managers in public relations, marketing, and communications.[6]

*Government Must Shape Up

This perspective maintains that, individually and collectively, as employees and as a system, government needs to improve performance and images. The disincentives for innovation need to be overcome. The role of management needs continued emphasis. Managers must assume responsibility for improving the performance of their programs, for providing continuity and leadership, and for effectively recruiting, retaining, and developing personnel.

If the public is to assume that public managers are members of a "profession" responsible for the performance of their colleagues and programs, better incentives are needed to promote such a vision. Support systems of government should encourage and reward public administrators rather than penalize them for taking risks. There is no public philosophy by which to judge the effectiveness of government programs. No popular consensus emerges for reducing spending programs not deemed worthy of government support and raising taxes to provide a sufficient "safety net" of societal benefits for all citizens.

Some states, however, are redefining public service, and in a manner of speaking, are "shaping up." Several states are employing information technology to disperse social services to citizens. For example, Maryland implemented an electronic benefits transfer system that distributes benefits. Food stamps and welfare checks are processed through automated teller machines and grocery-store terminals. This innovation is estimated to save the state $1.2 million each year.

In other experimentations with technology, states are using multimedia kiosks in libraries and shopping malls to provide twenty-four-hour government information and services. These touch-screen kiosks permit citizens to register their vehicles, order birth certificates, learn about job opportunities, and obtain access to information referrals. Such efforts reflect government's attempts "to shape up," reducing bureaucratic waste and offering citizen-customers better services more effectively.[7]

The Country Must Shape Up

The special problems of productivity are not unique to the public sector. The performance of the nation as a whole, not only the public sector, is important for a national common purpose. The federal deficits may be traced back to a society grounded in short-term consumerism with little, if any, long-term commitment to values that promote savings and investments for the future.

New creative mechanisms must be established to cause the business community and government to develop more innovative solutions to national problems. Everyone is responsible for maintaining a healthy relationship between productive public sector employees and clientele interfacing government. The country must become more disciplined in its political economy.

In the 1990s, the United States emerged as the Michael Jordan of worldwide economic competition. But even a great basketball star needs good teammates

---

GOVERNMENT, MORALITY, AND FAMILY

The government has a role to play in restoring morality to public life, argues William R. Marty. Marty says that government should not reflect the views held by religious fanatics or libertarian lunatics, but strive to guarantee that government institutions that support moral growth remain strong. This government role involves support for the traditional family structure, guarantee some degree of moral education in the schools, and gives parents flexible choices in the education of their children.

Source: William R. Marty, "Government, Morality, and the Family," *Journal of Interdisciplinary Studies 7*, nos. 1–2 (Annual 1995): 1–25.

---

and competitive opposition! A strong economy and improvements in federal budget discipline help generate a positive outlook for the nation, emphasizes Alan Greenspan, chairman, Board of Governors of the Federal Reserve System (FED). But the FED chair stresses that fiscal policy must remain opposed to deficit spending, that achieving a budget surplus is not at all certain, and that legislators should take this uncertainty into account as they prepare for future federal budgets. Social Security and Medicare are country or systemwide priorities and demand primary focus for "shaping up" the country.[8]

A CASE FOR PUBLIC BUREAUCRACY

Someone making a case for government bureaucracy? Preposterous, you say? Absurd? Charles T. Goodsell, who refers to bureaucracy as American public administration, has done just that. Supported by "hard facts" (or empirical data in the academic world), Goodsell concludes that most citizens view definitive experiences with public bureaucracies in a favorable perspective. Citing national opinion surveys, Goodsell points out that the vast majority of clients of public bureaucracy are pleased with their bureaucratic encounters and transactions. The charge that bureaucracy is dysfunctional cannot be substantiated, argues Goodsell.

The theme of Goodsell's analysis is that Americans tend to downgrade and malign public institutions without considering their tasks, limitations, and records of service. Depictions in popular culture of heartless, asinine, and stupid bureaucrats originate from unusual, even eccentric, cases. The atypical case reinforces stereotypes, striking responsive chords of those traumatized by occasional bureaucratic horror stories. Individuals and enterprises exploit this pejorative view of public bureaucracy without having to fear being held accountable for their accusations. This spurious thinking does not take into account national opinion surveys and other data that indicate that most citizens perceive their experiences with public bureaucracies in a favorable light.

BUREAUCRACY AS STEREOTYPE

Goodsell debunks false notions and highlights overlooked features of public bureaucracy on four fronts: stereotype, discriminator, bungler, and comparitive. First, there is no homogeneous conception of public bureaucracy. In other words, the equality of public bureaucratic life does not mirror a single, unified, and capitalized opponent. Behaviors, institutions, functions, and processes are common features of bureaucracies; however, they manifest themselves in different ways in every bureaucracy.[9] To illustrate, Goodsell visited twenty-eight welfare waiting rooms in fourteen cities and towns throughout the United States. Located from coast to coast and in the frostbelt and sunbelt, these offices administered Social Security, Aid to Families with Dependent Children, food stamps, and unemployment compensation.

The author entered the waiting rooms as if he were a first-time client, taking notes and categorizing the twenty-eight sites into five distinct types. The *Dog Kennel* waiting rooms were characterized by a labyrinthine layout of rooms and hallways, a sense of crowdedness, and a coercive and suppressive atmosphere with armed guards and threatening signs. The *Pool Hall* featured a large, open space; empty drabness; and a disinterested rather than coercive atmosphere. Instead of being threatened, clients were ignored. The *Business Office* manifested blandness of color and an air of efficiency, similar to a commercial establishment. The *Bank Lobby* exhibited a grandiose exterior facade and interior ornaments, displaying a mood of physical security. The *Circus Tent* demonstrated color, commotion, and animated conversation. In summary, one makes a mistake in viewing bureaucracy as a monolithic stereotype.

BUREAUCRACY AS DISCRIMINATOR

Second, the view that governmental organizations systematically discriminate against underprivileged subgroups of the population is not supported by empirical data. To simplify decisions, public administrators may stereotype clientele based on their own racial and class biases. On encountering particular stresses in the poorer sections of urban cities, public school teachers, police, fire fighters, welfare workers, building inspectors may systematically, yet unconsciously, discriminate against certain underprivileged groups in the population.

Goodsell reveals that empirical studies do not substantiate significant levels of antiminority, antipoor discrimination in urban delivery of bureaucratic services. While not denying the practice of discrimination in our society, he refused to blame public bureaucrats for the sins of the society and the legacy of a long history of discrimination.

BUREAUCRACY AS BUNGLER

Third, Goodsell considers that public bureaucracies are inefficient, inflexible, and noninnovative in comparison to private businesses. The prevailing values of an essentially capitalist society and an ideological dislike of big government, taxation, and regulatory limits on business may contribute to these allegations.

The absence of clear, consistent, and quantifiable goals, as spelled out in legislative statutes, complicates assurance of high levels of agency performance. In other words, citizens perceive public bureaucracies as wasteful, unresponsive, inflexible, incompetent, regressive regarding change, and a bungler. On the contrary, available comparative data on the efficiency, costs, and quality of services in refuse collection, hospitals, transportation, utilities, and insurance reveal that on some occasions privately-owned business performs better and, at other times, government functions more satisfactorily.

According to the Federal Productivity Measurement Program, annual output per year per employee rose at an average annual rate of 1.1 percent from 1967 through 1994. Using the same general concepts used to measure private sector productivity, a variety of factors, ranging from management action to external forces such as legislation and natural disasters, shaped government productivity as measured by the indexes of annual output, employment, and output per employee.[10]

Academic debates over the successes of capitalism versus socialism do not mirror organizational realities. Of all public organizations, the U.S. Postal Service (USPS) takes the most abuse. The private sector stereotype argues that private delivery modes, such as United Parcel Service (UPS), are far superior. However, the thirty-three cent first-class letter finances a lot more than the cost of mailing an envelope weighing one-half ounce.

First-class mail fees subsidize weekly religious publications; thousands of news, sports, and special magazines and newspapers; corporate advertising for mail order companies; political candidate and party flyers; and other mailings supporting free enterprise activities. Business corporations are organized bureaucracies as well. Private companies provide public services such as electricity, natural gas, telephone, water, and other utilities in certain states. Instead of responding to market demands, they respond as private monopolies. Therefore, comparisons between the two sectors reflect the inevitable apples versus oranges dilemma. If public organizations are bunglers, they are not alone.

COMPARATIVE BUREAUCRACIES

Finally, Goodsell affirms that American bureaucracy surpasses the overall performance of most other national bureaucracies. In offering comparisons, he concludes that systematic data available indicate that American bureaucracies perform better than the great majority of the 150 or so other national bureaucracies. These data include public opinion polls that offer favorable comparisons to Western European bureaucracies and favorable comparisons with those bureaucracies in the Third World. Patronage, overcentralization, nonenforcement of rules, inequitable treatment of clients, political dominance, corruption, waste, and inefficiency characterize bureaucracies in less-developed countries. As an example, Goodsell offers comparative postal data showing that the U.S. Postal Service, in terms of productivity, speed, and courtesy, is one of the best, if not the best, in the entire world.

In summary, *public bureaucracy as stereotype, discriminator, and bungler is not a factual reality.* U.S. public organizations are not homogeneous, antipoor, and antiminority. Goodsell's research, based upon client polls, public opinion surveys, exit interviews, and mailed questionnaires, finds that the considerable majority of public bureaucracy encounters are viewed satisfactorily. Surveys and nationwide public opinion polls reveal positive citizen experiences with municipal, state, and federal departments and agencies. These organizations compete satisfactorily with private companies for service deliveries. The U.S. Postal Service, as proto-type of government service criticism, is one of the best in the world. In making his case for bureaucracy, Goodsell argues that the realities of U.S. public bureaucracy are not to be found in the Sunday newspaper supplement diatribes.

PRIVATIZATION OF THE PUBLIC SECTOR

Privatization, in other words, means that a service previously produced by a government agency is now produced by a nongovernmental organization. The government may sell to private buyers or a private concern may sell to govern-ment. *Contracting out,* as it is often called, is thought to be more efficient because:

- It harnesses competitive forces and brings the pressure of the marketplace to bear on inefficient workers.
- It permits better management, free of most of the distractions characteristic of overtly political organizations.
- It places the costs and benefits of managerial decisions more directly on the decision maker, whose own rewards are directly at stake.[11]

As government at all levels has come under attack, the conclusion that the private sector performs and produces more effectively has received considerable credibility. If privatization is the answer in general, however, no one seems to agree on the particulars, such as what products will be produced privately or what provisions for private entrepreneurship will follow.

Conflicting definitions of privatization center around provisions, or provid-ing, and production, or producing [12] Executives, legislators, and judges make and interpret policies that provide a service or services. Government carries out functions as buyer and seller. A good example of services that are privatized to varying degrees is security. A four-part scheme of possible overlap of sectors, government and nongovernment, providing and producing security services follows. Of the four possibilities, there are two admixtures of responsibility and two possibilities where one sector or the other takes full responsibility for provi-sion and production of security.

- *Case 1* Government does both—The legislature writes the law and provides the money; the Department of Corrections runs the prison. Neither function is private.
- *Case 2* Production is private—The City of Bloomington decides to provide security when the high school hockey teams play at the city arena and it contracts with Pinkertons for the guards.

- *Case 3* Provision is private—Government sells to a market of private buyers. The North Stars hockey team wants security at Metropolitan Sports Center, and it contracts with the Bloomington city police.
- *Case 4* Both activities are private—A department store decides that it wants uniformed security and employs (or contracts privately for) its own guards. Government performs neither activity.[13]

The policy decision in Case 1, the pure-case public sector, shows government as a public bureau producing the service. Case 2 entails the controversial system of governments contracting out. Case 3 illustrates government as selling services to a private buyer. Case 4 portrays a pure case of a private agency selling to a private buyer. Of the two words, *provision* is the more complicated to explain. The word "providing" can be confusing. For example, society (or government) provides medical care to the elderly; however, medical doctors are the providers. To provide in this context means to make policy, to decide, to buy, to regulate, to franchise, to finance, to subsidize.

A publicly provided service is described in this manner:

1. where the decision whether to have it (and the decisions about who shall have it and how much of it) is a political decision;
2. when government arranges for the recipients not to have to pay directly for the service themselves; and
3. when the government selects the producer that will serve them.

A privately provided service is one

1. where the individuals and nongovernmental organizations make their own decisions whether or not to have it;
2. where, if they choose to have it, they pay for it in full out of their own resources, whatever these may be; and
3. where they select the producer themselves.[14]

There are mixed cases of public and private provisions as well. Government may provide a service and allow citizens to decide whether to use it. The financing of such provisions may be divided between public and private sectors as users finance a portion and the government pays part of the costs. Some citizens (the wealthy) may pay the full cost of provisions while government picks up the complete tab for others (the poor). Government may finance the complete cost but permit the user to choose the vendor. The provision of schools is financed, publicly, via taxes.

Nontax devices, such as regulations and franchising, are used as well. Government regulations require restaurant owners to clean the premises themselves at their own expense; in franchising provisions of water, gas, or electricity, government allows a monopoly to develop, which, in turn, permits an average price, overcharging some customers while subsidizing still others. In privatizing the provision of services, government withdraws or reduces its role as buyer, regulator, standard setter, or decision maker.

Now let us examine the concept of *production*, as it applies to activities of government. Government officials decide to produce services they determine should be provided. In other words, government operates, delivers, runs, performs, sells, and administers services. As emphasized, service production is less complicated than service provision. Production may be divided into line services and support, or staff, services; production may be divided into labor intensive functions, equipment and facilities; production may focus upon the substance of the work itself or the management, or administration, of work. For example, a municipality may divide refuse collection among several garbage collection companies or the management of worker pension funds among several financial institutions.

In privatizing public sector production, the question of competition is an important one. If the shift is merely from a public sector provider to a single private sector one, a monopoly supplier still exists. The deregulation of railroads, aviation, trucking, banking, health care, and telecommunications has taken place in the private sphere to encourage competition. Despite such efforts, questions concerning competitiveness still remain.

The neat distinctions between government's primary policy decision providing a service and the secondary decision producing a service are not, in reality, easily discerned. The Federal Aviation Administration administers air safety for public and private good. The Department of Defense contracts with private providers for base support and maintenance. Pinkerton and Wells Fargo, private security firms, have a long history of public service. Public day-care centers allow young mothers economic opportunities in the private sphere.

Privatization of some government services, notably Social Security and the Postal Service, is being considered to decrease costs and increase efficiency. Proponents think that the competition created by contracting out will improve federal government programs. So far, many state and local governments are experimenting with privatization, but the federal government resists. Unions oppose the practice because they fear the adverse effects on employee salaries and benefits.[15]

Contract compliance programs help companies comply with numerous laws governing contracts and subcontracts with the federal government, avoid criminal prosecution, and reduce violation fines. Contract compliance programs include:

- codes of ethics to be adhered to by private sector employees;
- strategies for effective delegation of responsibilities;
- procedures for reporting violations, corrective measures for noncompliance, and constant evaluation of the compliance program; and
- a records management system for keeping records for the contract duration as specified by law.[16]

Privatization, therefore, is an effective way of providing necessary services, usually provided by the government, and overcoming the problem of shrinking federal, state, and local government budgets and ailing infrastructure. The government plays the role of prudent purchaser and manager of services offered by

---

PUBLIC VERSUS PRIVATE POSTAL PRODUCTIVITY

Perhaps the most maligned public agency is the U.S. Postal Service (USPS). The cost of a first-class stamp has risen in the past and will certainly rise steadily in the future. Statutes prohibit private firms from competition with the U.S. Postal Service for first-class service. It is possible that private entrepreneurs could find cheaper, more effective ways to deliver a huge volume of first-class mail, but the U.S. Postal Service is more than a national post office. USPS is a conduit, a catalyst for undergirding capitalism by facilitating consumer advertising through the mails, for bolstering the free press, disseminating information through newspapers and magazines, and for promoting commerce in general.

By comparison, United Parcel Service (UPS) delivers twice the number of parcels as the U.S. Postal Service, with lower rates, faster deliveries, and an 80 percent lower damage rate, and still makes a profit. But will UPS deliver your favorite fashion catalog, news magazine, or church bulletin for mere pennies? The point is that the U.S. Postal Service subsidizes at a reasonable cost many and varied cultural, economic, and even political activities in the United States.

---

private sector contractors. Privatization aims at creating a market-driven partnership for the betterment of taxpayers, but it faces resistance from citizens as they fear elimination of services.[17] Privatizing government functions, then, is seen as a way of increasing efficiency and producing significant savings.

Empirical evidence *usually* shows private enterprises to be more efficient than public enterprises. Public sector productivity is lower than private sector productivity, labor costs are higher in the public sector than in the private sphere, and public utilities are less cost effective than private utilities.[18] On the other hand, no one promised that democratic government was cost effective, at least when measuring efficiency. *Fairness* is a more accurate standard for ascertaining the effectiveness of government services.

FEDERAL PRODUCTIVITY IMPROVEMENT PROGRESS

Productivity improvements need institutionalization; that is, the structural and environmental barriers, if they are to be eliminated, require the commitment and political leadership of executives at all government levels. To this end, the General Accounting Office (GAO) suggested that the Office of Management and Budget (OMB) assume a more active role in eradicating barriers to enhanced federal productivity.[19]

The OMB has called attention to the issue, outlining goals for productivity improvements for targeted government functions; short-term improvements required for immediate deficit reduction; and a long-term focus, using an institutionalized productivity program that alters the behavior of managers and efficiency

---

SEVEN ELEMENTS OF AN EFFECTIVE PRODUCTIVITY MANAGEMENT REPORT

1. A manager serving as a focal point for productivity in the organization.
2. Top-level support and commitment.
3. Written productivity objectives and goals and an organizationwide productivity plan.
4. Productivity measures meaningful to the organization.
5. Use of the productivity plan and measurement system to hold managers accountable.
6. Awareness of productivity's importance throughout the organization and involvement of employees in the productivity effort.
7. An ongoing activity to regularly identify productivity problems and opportunities for improvement throughout the organization.

Source: "Increased Use of Productivity Management Can Help Control Government Costs," *GAO Report*, 10 November 1983, p. 36.

---

of government functions. To realize productivity gains, however, legislation is needed to overcome constraints to improving productivity. Working with Congress, the OMB intends to identify and eliminate barriers and disincentives to productivity improvements.[20]

WAYS OF MEASURING GOVERNMENT OPERATIONS

Despite the difficulties and dilemmas they engender, productivity measures are assuming increasing importance in public administration. Progress has been neither smooth nor swift, but it has occurred. In some instances remarkable successes have been achieved.

One of the first federal agencies to use efficiency measurements was the Division of Social Security. In the mid-1950s, it began its work-sampling program, where an employee in every office periodically measures the amount of work being done by various employees. These samples are not taken in an attempt to judge the employees' efficiency but to determine how long it takes to handle the various operations that the office is performing. This information from all Social Security offices is then compiled into averages, and each office is subsequently rated as to how it performs in respect to the overall averages for its region and for the nation.

The averages provide a useful yardstick for measuring how any one office is operating. Of course, numerous factors may make any particular office rate above or below its regional or national average. An office may be so small, for example, that maintenance functions, as opposed to line operations, consume too large a proportion of its work-hours. Nevertheless, once such factors have been taken into account, the averages provide a tool that indicates which regions, which offices, or even which individuals are performing well and which are not.

In the early 1960s, the Bureau of the Budget (now known as the Office of Management and Budget) decided to see if other federal functions could use productivity measures. It attempted to develop such measures for five federal agencies, and two years later announced that it had succeeded. In 1971, the Bureau of the Budget, General Accounting Office, and the Civil Service Commission (now called the Office of Personnel Management) coordinated efforts to improve government employee productivity. This joint effort soon produced productivity measures covering 56 percent of the federal civilian work force. Pleased with this success, the OMB issued formal instructions to each federal agency with 200 or more employees to report annually on what progress it was making to promote productivity.

As public discontent with public sector performance mounted during the 1970s, many states and municipalities began following the federal government's lead. One of the more noteworthy efforts occurred in New Jersey, which in 1978 appointed a productivity coordinator for each department of the state government. Using a modified carrot-and-stick approach, New Jersey ordered its departments to file quarterly reports on what they were doing to improve productivity, while at the same time, the state offered the opportunity to tap a newly established Productivity Investment Fund to finance such initiatives.

The program soon began to realize its productive capacity. By early 1980 the fund had financed sixteen proposals among the 100 submitted. Many involved such simple steps as installing food freezers at a mental hospital, thereby enabling the institution to serve prepackaged frozen foods and save $70,000 by reducing personnel costs. More ambitious endeavors included new equipment in the Division of Motor Vehicles, which produced annual savings of a quarter million dollars; a revised recycling program for obsolete paper records, which turned an expense into a financial benefit; and conversion of the state's Vital Statistics and Registration program to microfilm, which cut retrieval time by 50 percent.[21]

It is usually felt that productivity measures lend themselves most easily to certain types of operations. In other words, particular functions rather than whole programs may provide the productivity analyst with challenging opportunities to enhance employee productivity. It is also possible, at least in many cases, to determine the productivity of a particular facility. Harry P. Hatry and Diana R. Dunn offer some ways of measuring the effectiveness of a recreation facility including accessibility, use, safety, attractiveness, and overall satisfaction.[22]

First, one can measure the number of people within so many miles or so many minutes of the facility to determine its *accessibility*. If it is a specialized facility, such as a playground, then the measure could be limited to the number of children in the appropriate age group. Census maps, police listings, and other data can be used to discover whether the facility is conveniently located. The proximity to public transportation can also be taken into account.

From there we can go on to measure *use*, taking into account how many persons use the facility, how often they use it, and for how long. This can be estimated by visiting the facility at representative times and taking random samples of the participants, asking them how often they come, what services they use, how long they stay, and so on. Some estimate of crowdedness can also be made by examining sign-up sheets or by observation of waiting times. The evaluator can also ask users if they feel crowded.

Safety is another factor that should enter into the evaluation. What is the rate of injury? What about crime? These data can be supplemented by asking users if they felt the facility was dangerous. The accidents and the crime that may occur in the facility must be balanced, however, with the accidents and crime that it may have averted elsewhere. Unsupervised swimming and playing on public streets also lead to accidents. Lack of recreational outlets can be linked to increased crime. Has the facility had any impact on crime and accidents in the neighborhoods it serves?

Attractiveness is another, although perhaps lesser, criterion that can be used in weighing the productivity of a recreational facility. Does it contribute to the neighborhood's physical design? Does it upgrade the neighborhood? Here, in addition to the opinion of residents, one can check the effect, if any, on property valuations and possibly on the amount of business done by nearby commercial establishments.

Then there is the final and determining factor of *overall satisfaction*. People in the area served by the facility can be asked such questions as, "Would you say that the recreational opportunities in this community are excellent, good, fair, or poor?" Doing this on a yearly basis will provide some idea of trends.

Much of the evaluation will be achieved through polling. This, however, need not be extensive or expensive, for only a reasonably representative sample is required. The results can be matched against other data. If, for example, the community served by the facility had a population of 100,000 and attendance at the facility came to 50,000, and if a random sample of 100 users showed that they used the facility 2.5 times a year, it can be estimated that about 20,000 people, or one-fifth of the community, are being served.

Hatry and Dunn claim that evaluations of recreational programs can be done at a cost of no more than 1 or 2 percent of the recreation budget. It is an expenditure that might be well worth making.

It is also possible to develop productivity measures for entire programs. The Institute of Traffic Management at Northwestern University, for example, has worked out what it calls a law enforcement index for evaluating the effectiveness of a police department in enforcing traffic laws. It is based on a simple equation in long division, the number of citations divided by the number of fatal and personal injury accidents.

The institute says that the *Enforcement Index*, or *EI*, should equal twenty. In other words, a police department should give out penalty citations equal to twenty times the number of fatalities and personal-injury accidents caused by motorists.

The approach differs considerably from the quota system used by many police departments. Under the latter system, traffic officers are instructed to hand out a fixed number of citations every day or week. The Enforcement Index established a relationship between enforcement and accidents, and, because evidence indicates that accident rates do respond positively to traffic enforcement, the number of citations is allowed to fall as the number of such accidents declines. If a department could reduce the number of such accidents occurring in its jurisdiction to one a year, it would need to give out only twenty citations to meet the standard set by the index.

REINVENTING GOVERNMENTS

Reinventing governments is the most recent effort to reform public organizations and management. Reinvention is a cornerstone of the Clinton administration's agenda for change in government operations. Reinvention is proceeding on several levels.

- One is that of *political symbolism* and *rhetoric:* reduce waste, eliminate unnecessary programs, and improve efficiency.
- A second level is found in the *reinvention laboratories* created throughout the federal government. The focus is on quality, customer service, streamlining processes and procedures, and eliminating unnecessary rules and regulations.
- A third level is found in *policy* and *system changes.* The emphasis is on examining broad functions, decentralizing major activities, and providing legislative support for necessary changes.[23]

The reinventing government campaign is aimed at transforming the government into a less bureaucratic, low-cost but high-quality service entity. The Clinton administration strives to decentralize power to the states, localities, and private enterprises. The huge federal deficits and transition of the country from the traditional industrial economy to a global economy spur efforts at reinventing governments.[24]

Advocates of reinventing government contend that administrative institutions were established based on the model of command-and-control. They suggest that the bureaucratic model remained the same throughout the twentieth century, but the command-and-control form became obsolete with the advent of the modern information age. According to Patrick J. Wolf, political autonomy is essential for bureaucratic effectiveness. Public managers should be encouraged to act, not only as "administrative entrepreneurs," but also as "political entrepreneurs."[25]

The U.S. Office of Personnel Management (OPM) plays a major role in reinventing government. Since the 1993 signing of *Executive Order 12862* by the President Clinton mandating a reform in government, the OPM has led efforts to reduce the federal work force to its smallest size in thirty years, resulting in the reduction of the national debt by 60 percent. According to Brenda Paik Sunoo, the approach embraced by the OPM serves as a model for the humane downsizing of government and the outplacement of employees.[26]

PRINCIPLES OF ENTREPRENEURIAL GOVERNMENT

1. Entrepreneurial public organizations act as catalysts. The old-model government used bureaucracies, but entrepreneurial governments increasingly find other ways to get the job done.
2. Entrepreneurial governments are competitive. The old-model governments were monopolies and viewed competition in the public sector as waste and duplication.
3. Entrepreneurial governments are mission driven. Bureaucratic public organizations are driven by rules and by budgets.
4. Entrepreneurial governments shift accountability to outcomes, producing results-oriented government.
5. Entrepreneurial governments are customer driven.
6. Anticipatory government, the idea of prevention rather than cure, addresses the rapidly changing world in which we live.
7. Community-owned government reflects the idea of pushing control of services and public programs into the hands of communities. Enterprising government captures the idea of earning money rather than spending it.
8. Entrepreneurial government must be decentralized to preserve its flexibility.
9. Entrepreneurial government is market-oriented and does not always create programs to attack problems.

Source: Ted Gaebler and David Osborne, "Reinventing Government: An Agenda for the 1990s," *Public Management* 74, no. 3 (March 1992): 4–8. See also: *Reinventing Government: How the Entrepreneurial Spirit Is Transforming the Public Sector* (New York: Addison-Wesley Publishing Co., 1992).

PROGRAM EVALUATION

When Planning Programming Budgeting Systems (PPBS) began to diminish in the federal bureaucracy, many found a replacement in another analytical device—program evaluation. Some state and municipal governments have warmly welcomed this technique and have set up offices to evaluate their program performance.

According to Ralph C. Chandler and Jack C. Plano, program evaluation is "an assessment of the effectiveness of a program through the application of a research design aimed at obtaining valid and verifiable information on the structure, processes, outputs, and impacts of the program. Program evaluation is an effort to help decision makers determine whether to maintain, modify, or discontinue a specified program. Program evaluation is concerned with whether program activities have been successful in resolving the public problem identified, and the extent to which other factors may have contributed to the problem's resolution."[27] There are three phases in program evaluation:

1. selection and identification of goals and objectives of the program,
2. execution of the evaluation according to scientific guidelines, and
3. feedback of results and recommendations.

The overall goals of program evaluation, or PE as it is sometimes called, can be simply stated. PE increases our understanding of government activities, leads to governmental improvements, and produces financial savings. The tools it uses also seem familiar—for the most part, they greatly resemble the types of analytical devices developed for PPBS, Zero-Based Budgets (ZBB), and Management By Objectives (MBO).

Legislative backing and buttressing have played a major role in the flourishing of program evaluation at all government levels.

POLICY DEVELOPMENT

The taxing, budgeting, and government spending priorities place program evaluation *at the center, not at the periphery,* of policy making in the public sector. To improve the effectiveness of program evaluation, such priorities need to assume their rightful place at the center of the policy making and budget making processes. Program evaluation needs consideration alongside financial and political sources of information.

For example, the National Institute of Corrections is promoting the use of policy-driven responses in the development of intermediate sanctions. The policy-driven approach enhances the participation of local and state officials from the executive, legislative, and judicial government branches. This policy-driven method is unlike the program-centered method, which only involves one state agency. Policy-driven responses also target specific offenders for correctional programs and ensures program evaluation and information exchange between concerned parties.[28]

According to Larry Polivka and Laurey T. Stryker, the principal purposes of the program review unit are to bring rigorous analytical perspective to influence agency budget requests, to assess agency effectiveness for meeting program objectives as set forth by the legislature and executive, and to develop program performance measures for agency implementation.[29]

The effectiveness of the evaluation unit depends upon the location of the evaluation, the selection process, the implementation of recommendations, and the evaluation strategies. Implementation of recommendations occurs as incorporation of evaluation results are part of the governor's high priority statement, agency policy guidelines, budget development process, performance agreement monitoring, process (or efficiency) and outcome (or effectiveness) of program budget measures, and annual legislation.

PPBS, ZBB, MBO, and similar policy planning and budgeting innovations contribute to the history of the development of public policy. However, evaluation focuses on fundamental value choices that contribute to initiating or terminating a policy or increasing or reducing program appropriations. Polivka and Stryker, formerly analysts for the Office of Governor, State of Florida, spell out certain conditions for maintaining a consistently influential role for program evaluation in the policy and budget development processes of state government.

- Evaluations are done by a unit organizationally close to key decision makers, rather than one buried in the bureaucracy;
- Key decision makers are actively involved in the selection of evaluation topics and the formulation of research designs;
- The policy budget development processes have a formal structure with relatively rational decision-making procedures heavily dependent on information, including evaluation data;
- Evaluations are clearly designed to address a significant policy issue(s) and are neither more nor less methodologically sophisticated than is required to make a reasonably valid, relevant, and timely contribution to the resolution of the policy issue;
- The evaluator is prepared to play an assertive role in the policy and budgeting processes by clearly articulating and actively defending policy positions most compatible with the findings of his/her study;
- Evaluators are not demoralized that decision makers will frequently make policy choices responsive to factors other than evaluation findings. Political and fiscal conditions change and evaluation findings and recommendations initially rejected may later be used in the generation of new or amended policies.[30]

The productivity challenge in the public sector is hampered by structural and environmental barriers, therefore the need for evaluation of productivity is always present. In the private sphere, technology becomes an intervening factor between monetary rewards and corporate failures. However, productivity indices in the public sector are grounded in politics with merit principles sometimes receiving less prominence. As citizens, elected officials, and administrators consider the effectiveness of the bottom-line delivery of public services, there will be enhanced interest in proactive, rather than reactive, program evaluations and employee performance evaluations.

SUMMARY

- Most citizens care about the *performance* of their public institutions. Parents worry about the quality of their children's schools. City dwellers anxiously scan the latest crime statistics. Drivers pay, and pray, for better roads, transit riders for dependable buses and subways, air travelers for effective and safe air traffic control operations.
- Measuring productivity has long been an accepted, almost routine, practice in business. This, however, has not been the case in government. Productivity in the public sector refers to *excellence in individual and collective performance*. There are widely divergent views as to what excellence is.
- Government organizations should strive for *excellence*. The political system should enable organizations to achieve high-performance levels from their employees. Outstanding performance not only benefits the organization but also improves the delivery of services to the citizens.

- Reasons explaining citizen complaints with government performance are: *Democracy is messy. Government takes a bum rap. Government must shape up. The country must shape up.*
- Public bureaucracy as stereotype, discriminator, and bungler is *not* a factual or an empirical reality. U.S. public organizations are not homogeneous, antipoor, and antiminority.
- Definitions of the privatization of public responsibilities center around *provisions*, or providing, and *production*, or producing, of goods and services. *Privatization*, often called contracting out, means that a service previously produced by a government agency is now produced by a nongovernmental organization.
- The *reinventing government campaign* aims at transforming governments into a less bureaucratic, low-cost, but high-quality service organizations. The Clinton administration seeks to decentralize power to the states, localities, and private enterprises. The huge federal deficits and transition of the country from the traditional industrial economy to a global economy spur efforts at reinventing governments.
- Reinvention is proceeding on several levels. One is that of *political symbolism* and *rhetoric:* reduce waste, eliminate unnecessary programs, and improve efficiency. A second level is found in the *reinvention laboratories* created throughout the federal government. The focus is on quality, customer service, streamlining processes and procedures, and eliminating unnecessary rules and regulations. A third level is found in *policy* and *system changes.* The emphasis is on examining broad functions, decentralizing major activities, and providing legislative support for necessary changes.
- Political autonomy is essential for bureaucratic effectiveness. Public managers should be encouraged to act, not only as *"administrative entrepreneurs,"* but also as *"political entrepreneurs."*
- Barriers to productivity measurement are numerous. The *budget process* is a significant structural barrier to federal productivity improvement. *Personnel systems* may restrict, delay, or prevent the hiring of qualified personnel and the discharge of nonproductive personnel. *Structural barriers* may cause problems with centralized decision making. Regional and field offices may duplicate and fragment lines of authority. *Lack of accountability* is an obstacle to productivity improvement, as are low morale, inadequate pay structure, managerial inexperience, senior administrator turnover, and misplaced priorities for policy making and direction.
- *Efficiency* means doing things well, while effectiveness means doing the right things well. Efficiency is essentially the input or contribution of labor, capital, and other resources into an effort matched against the output of product produced or measured, regardless of the mechanism selected to gauge output.
- *Effectiveness,* meanwhile, calls for a preestablished standard of comparison, a focus upon a certain quality of production, an ability to mobilize, organize, and direct resources for specified purposes, all taken within a certain cultural context.

- Accessibility, use, safety, attractiveness, and overall satisfaction constitute preset *ways of measuring effectiveness of public services.* The *Enforcement Index,* a mechanism for gauging the effectiveness of enforcing traffic laws, is an example of a preset evaluation tools. Assuming that productivity measures can be developed and implemented, the benefits to public administration and the public in general are immense.
- Measuring productivity may also provide a basis for *deemphasizing rules, regulations,* and *supervision.* Working with a good set of productivity measures, the employee can often become his or her own boss, at least to a substantial extent. Objective criteria, rather than a supervisor, guide an employee's labors and determine his or her achievements.
- Entrepreneurial public organizations act as *catalysts* to innovation, are competitive and mission driven; produce results-oriented government; are customer driven, anticipatory, community-owned, decentralized, flexible, and market-oriented.
- *Program evaluation,* which may increase our understanding of government activities and lead to improved productivity and financial savings, is firmly entrenched in government. PPBS, ZBB, and MBO are illustrations of attempts to evaluate public programs. The principal purposes of program evaluation are to bring rigorous analytical perspective to influence agency budget requests, assess agency effectiveness for meeting program objectives established by elected leaders, and develop program performance measures for agency implementation.

When discussing the area of productivity, it's easy to get wrapped up in theories and forget the human element. This case study is a reminder that people and their feelings are key in productivity.

CASE STUDY

A Problem of Motivation.[31]

As part of a work-force program to make mothers who were recipients of Aid to Families with Dependent Children (AFDC) self-supporting, the State Tourism and Recreation Department employed six women and assigned them to various divisions. Under the plan, the federal and state governments jointly paid the women's salaries while they underwent a six-month training program. At the end of this period, each division had the option of hiring or releasing the women—a decision based on performance and the recommendations of supervisors.

Julie Davis was one of the three trainees chosen for regular employment, assigned to the Tourist Information Office. The mother of two girls, ages six and eight, Davis had received aid from AFDC since her husband was killed in an auto accident five years before. On her marrying she had given up her job as a receptionist and typist in a wholesale grocery firm. Davis had naturally reentered the workforce with some trepidation, given her 10-year hiatus from the workforce. Initially she displayed enthusiasm and performed her duties efficiently. After about six weeks, however, Jeff Baker, her supervisor, noticed she was developing poor working habits such as long coffee breaks, tardiness, and absenteeism.

Baker felt Davis's low performance had resulted from her association with two employees in the Conventions unit of the department. Baker arranged a meeting with her and advised her of the unacceptability of her work behavior. He had received complaints from other employees that she was not carrying her share of the load. "Julie," he said, "generally your work has been very good but lately your job performance has not lived up to expectations. Although our standards are higher than other sections of this department, the chances for promotion and career advancement are a lot better for the hardworking employee. You can do a lot better than you have been doing!" After the session with Baker, Davis's work and behavior immediately improved. She volunteered to assist others whenever her own work was completed and quickly acquired the necessary skills for several other positions in the section. She often worked as a substitute in the absence of other employees.

At the end of the training period, Baker recommended that the agency hire Davis at the level of Grade 5. The quality of her work remained consistently high and she continued to assist others willingly. Six months later, when she had completed a year with the agency, she was promoted to Grade 6 and assigned additional responsibilities. Indeed, a bright future seemed on the horizon.

About two months later, one of the employees Davis had been assisting resigned because of a death in the family. The announcement for the newly opened position emphasized it was limited to employees of the department. Since Davis was familiar with many aspects of the position, she discussed applying for it with Baker, who advised her that even though she was the only staff member familiar with the job, her chance of being on the list of applicants supplied by the Bureau of Personnel was small because she had only fourteen months' experience instead of the required two years. He said she would make the list only if there were no applicants with the required experience. This was possible, though unlikely. Davis decided to apply and hope for the best. There were several applicants with the required experience and she did not make the list.

Davis's attitude changed immediately. She became irritable and her relationship with other staff members deteriorated. She developed intense feelings of insecurity. Each time a new employee was hired she felt as though she might be replaced. As a result of this constant fear she developed an ulcer. In another meeting with her, Baker reassured her of her abilities, explained the steps involved in employee termination, and outlined the grievance procedures available to employees should termination occur. Initially, Davis seemed to gain confidence and her work improved, although not to the level of her previous performance. She had become confused and felt angry toward Baker for what she considered to be unwarranted encouragement.

Since Baker felt he could no longer adequately motivate Davis, he recommended that she be transferred to another supervisor, Malcolm Tate. After a few weeks, her work performance and attitude improved considerably, and Tate soon considered her among the best employees he had ever supervised.

The problem in the department appeared to be resolved, but Tate was to encounter the same problem as Baker. In the next four months, two employees under Tate's supervision were to retire. Both positions were at the Grade 7 level.

Davis was now qualified for both, but there were others in the agency better qualified. Even if she made the list, there was a good possibility she would not be selected for the position.

QUESTIONS AND INSTRUCTIONS

1. Was transferring Davis the best course of action Baker could have taken? What other choices did he have?
2. Do rules stating that a person must have two years' experience bear any relationship to the realities of an employee's efficiency and the needs of an organization? Should the rules be reviewed?
3. Do you feel that the manner in which Davis was hired through the workforce program affected her job performance?
4. Do you feel that Davis's home situation may have been the cause of her attitudes toward her job?
5. Should Tate have encouraged Davis to apply for a new position when the possibility of not being selected existed?
6. What could Tate have done to prevent the recurrence of the previous situation if Davis was not selected for one of the Grade 7 positions?
7. Davis seemed to be experiencing stress. What do you think could have been the main cause of the stress? Was the stress-risk behavior related to the actions of others or was it related to her own expectations? What could Baker have done to reduce the level of personal stress that Davis was experiencing? What could Davis have done about her own situation?
8. Did Davis appear to be internally or externally motivated? What are the implications associated with both of these motivations?
9. What follow-up program should the state adopt for graduates of workforce programs now holding jobs?

INSIGHTS-ISSUES / A PROBLEM OF MOTIVATION

Clearly and briefly describe and illustrate these concepts, issues, or points. Interpret the word "role" as meaning impact, application, importance, effect and/or illustration of certain facts, concerns, or issues from the case study.

1. The role of education and a training program as contributor to motivation and productivity.
2. The role of measuring productivity in the public sector; difficulty for gauging impacts of nonproductive working habits. The role of consistency in job performance.

3. The role of position classifications, required experience, and employee competition for new job classifications.
4. The role procedures regarding employee status in job classification scheme.
5. The role of culture or the cultural context (or expectations of high standards and high-employee productivity) in the workplace.

ENDNOTES

1. G. Chris Hartung, "Institutionalized Excellence: Not Just More Pop Government Jargon?" *Public Management* 78, no. 7 (July 1996): 25–29.
2. David Osborne, "Grading Governments, *Washington Post,* 13 April 1997, p. A8.
3. Mark A. Abramson, "The Public Manager and Excellence," *The Bureaucrat* 14, no. 3 (fall 1985): 9–13.
4. Charles T. Goodsell, *The Case for Bureaucracy: A Public Administration Polemic* (Chatham, N.J.: Chatham House Publishers, 1983), 55–60.
5. Herbert A. Simon, "Why Public Administration?" *Public Administration Review* 58, no. 1 (January–February 1998): II.
6. Abramson, "The Public Manager and Excellence," 11.
7. Mitch Betts, "States Redefining Public Service," *Computerworld*
8. Alan Greenspan, "Statement by Alan Greenspan, Chairman, Board of Governors of the Federal Reserve System, before the Committee on the Budget, U.S. Senate, January 29, 1998," *Federal Reserve Bulletin* 84, no. 3 (March 1998): 183–185. 27, no. 16 (19 April 1993): 1–2.
9. Goodsell, *The Case for Bureaucracy*, 38–60.
10. Donald Fisk and Darlene Forte, "The Federal Productivity Measurement Program: Final Results," *Monthly Labor Review* 120, no. 5 (May 1997): 19–29.
11. E. S. Savas, *Privatizing the Public Sector* (Chatham, N.J.: Chatham House, 1982), 89.
12. Ted Kolderie, "The Two Different Concepts of Privatization," *Public Administration Review* 46, no. 4 (July-August 1986): 285–291.
13. Kolderie, "The Two Different Concepts," 285.
14. Kolderie, "The Two Different Concepts," 286.
15. Richard L. Worsnop, "Privatizing Government Services: Can For-Profit Businesses Do a Better Job?" *CO Researcher* 6, no. 30 (9 August 1996): 699–717.
16. Richard D. Lieberman, "The 'Criminalization' of Government Procurement," *Civil Engineering* 63, no. 3 (March 1993): 68–70.
17. Charles R. Rendall, "Privatization: A Cure for Our Ailing Infrastructure?" *Civil Engineering* 66, No. 12 (December 1996): 6.
18. Steve H. Hanke, "Privatization: Theory, Evidence, and Implementation," in *Control of Spending,* ed. C. Lowell Harris, *Proceedings of the Academy of Political Science* 35, no. 4 (New York: 1985), 101–113.
19. U.S. General Accounting Office, *Increased Use of Productivity Management Can Help Control Government Costs,* November 10, 1983.
20. Executive Office of the President, Office of Management and Budget, *Management of the United States Government: Fiscal Year 1986* (Washington, DC: Government Printing Office, 1986), 67.

21. Richard F. Keevey, "State Productivity Improvements: Building on Existing Strengths," *Public Administration Review* 40, no. 5 (September–October 1980): 451–458.

22. Harry P. Hatry and Diana R. Dunn, *Measuring the Effectiveness of Local Government Services: Recreation* (Washington, DC: Urban Institute, 1971).

23. Patricia W. Ingraham, "Reinventing the American Federal Government: Reform Redux or Real Change?" *Public Administration* 74, no. 3 (autumn 1996): 453–476.

24. Bill Clinton. "Remarks on the National Performance Review," *Weekly Compilation of Presidential Documents* 31, no. 36 (11 September 1995): 1511–1516.

25. Patrick J. Wolf, "Why Must We Reinvent the Federal Government? Putting Historical Developmental Claims to the Test," *Journal of Public Administration Research and Theory* 7, no. 3 (July 1997): 353–389.

26. Brenda Paik Sunoo, "Reinventing Government," *Workforce* 77, no. 2 (February 1998): 60–64.

27. Ralph C. Chandler and Jack C. Plano, *The Public Administration Dictionary* (New York: John Wiley & Sons, 1982), 91

28. Phyllis D. Modeley, "Taking a Policy-Driven Approach to Developing Intermediate Sanctions," *Corrections Today* 57, no. 1 (February 1995): 74–76.

29. Larry Polivka and Laurey T. Stryker, "Program Evaluation and the Policy Process in State Government: An Effective Linkage," *Public Administration Review* 43, no. 3 (May-June 1983): 255–259.

30. Polivka and Stryker, "Program Evaluation," 259.

31. C. Kenneth Meyer and Charles H. Brown, *Practicing Public Management: A Casebook,* 2nd ed., pp. 103–105. Copyright © 1989 by St. Martin's Press, Inc. Reprinted with permission of Bedford/St. Martin's Press, Inc.

11

ADMINISTRATIVE LAW
AND CONTROL

During the first 100 years of U.S. history, several factors conspired to keep the administrative sector of our many governments comparatively small and weak. Fragmentation and personalism, for example, deterred the growth of large and formalized bureaucracies like those starting to emerge in Europe. The antigovernmental attitudes of the American people probably acted as an even greater deterrent. In the end, our legalistic approach to governmental problems may have served as the greatest deterrent. The ways in which U.S. legalism imposed limits on, and even substituted for, administrative power were noticed by Lord James Bryce, the perceptive British observer who began visiting our shores late in the nineteenth century. In his 1888 book, *The American Commonwealth*, Bryce wrote:

> *It is a great merit of American government that it relies very little on officials [administrators] and arms them with little power of arbitrary interference. . . . [The government] has taken the direction of acting through the law rather than through the officials. That is to say, when it prescribes to the citizen a particular course of action it has relied upon the ordinary legal sanctions, instead of investing the administrative officers with inquisitional duties or powers that might prove oppressive.*[1]

As the quotation suggests, Bryce wholly approved of this approach. Had he been more legalistically trained or oriented himself, he might have pointed to a particular legalistic feature of our system that served as the main roadblock to a greater assumption of power and responsibility by U.S. administrators. This feature is our constitutionally enshrined principle of separation of powers.

The Constitution stipulates that the legislative branch enact the laws and the executive branch execute and enforce them. Through the first century of our existence, the courts—the judicial branch—took a particularly rigorous attitude toward this demarcation of authority. They ruled that Congress could not give away its power, even if it voted in such a manner. Consequently, efforts to bestow substantial discretion on any administrator or administrative agency drew the Supreme Court's prompt disapproval. Congress, said the Court, could not delegate its fundamental powers. Rules and regulations that would have the force of law would have to be passed by the body charged with passing laws.

As Bryce was writing his 1888 book, however, the Court was readying to alter the course of U.S. administrative history. Congress, confronted with the pressing need to regulate the country's expanding railroad industry, realized that it could not possibly devote the continuous time and effort that such a task demanded and passed the Interstate Commerce Act of 1887. This act set up a new agency, the Interstate Commerce Commission (ICC), to carry out this regulatory function. In a landmark decision, the Supreme Court ruled the Interstate Commerce Act, along with the agency it established, to be constitutional.

The newly created Surface Transportation Board was scarcely given carte blanche discretion. Congress set down specific standards regarding its jurisdiction and prescribed rather detailed criteria for use of its discretionary power in policing the railroads. Congress even spelled out the various forms of misbehavior that the Surface Transportation Board was to police, such as rebating, rate discrimination, and pooling. The new regulatory commission was, in the words of Theodore Lowi, "relatively well shackled by clear standards of public policy, as stated in the statute and as understood in common law."[2]

From this time on, Congress, along with most state legislatures, began delegating more and more legislative power to administrative agencies, and the Supreme Court became increasingly cooperative in permitting them to do so. When Congress amplified the ICC's powers, for instance, by passing the Transportation Act of 1920, the Court let the Act stand, even though the increased powers were accompanied by far fewer specific criteria to guide and control their application.

Although the court modified its once hard line stand on delegation, it was still not ready to capitulate completely. The Court, for example, invalidated order after order of the Federal Trade Commission on grounds that its "unfair method of competition," standard was too vague. In the regulatory agency's first two decades, or from 1915 until the mid-1930s, the Court judged that the FTC's congressionally imposed standard gave the agency too much discretionary power.[3]

The New Deal brought the issue to a head when President Roosevelt, trying to wield broad executive power to pull the country out of the depression, found himself on a collision course with the nation's highest tribunal, leading to a series of hostile Court decisions which culminated in the famous Schechter case of 1934.[4] In this case, a majority of the justices struck down the National Recovery Act and with it the elaborate planning machinery and the wide blanket of administrative power that the act had promulgated. The Reagan administration approached things differently. According to Harold Seidman and Robert Gilmour, Roosevelt's "New Deal" marked the birth of the positive state, and the Reagan "revolution" was geared to end it.[5] "The evolution from the positive to the regulatory state commenced in the 1960s, but President Reagan was the first to redefine the federal government's role as limited, wherever possible, to providing services without producing them."[6] Reagan worked to privatize government services in an effort to minimize the negative aspects of big government.

During the last fifty years of the twentieth century, the administrative sector surged forward, spurred on by what might be called the permissive attitude the Court took toward the delegation issue. Administrative agencies acquired increasing functions along with more powers to carry them out. They may prescribe rules and issue orders that have the force of law and may impose penalties on those who disobey. Some agencies have even acquired the subpoena power and/or the contempt power. What were once the closely guarded prerogatives of elected officials increasingly have been placed into the hands of nonelected functionaries.

The Congress, state legislatures, and city councils bear the responsibility for administering and enforcing legislation. The president, state governors, and mayors—and their executive branches—bear the responsibility for administering and enforcing legislation. However, "upon reflection the Congress is institutionally incapable of providing in legislation itself a detailed answer for every issue that may arise under it. The same is true for state legislatures."[7] Therefore, the United States, a country espousing democratic capitalism, exists in the *era of the administrative state.*

DEFINING ADMINISTRATIVE LAW

Administrative law is an amorphous body of law. . . . Administrative law is created or affected by the activities of government agencies. The term 'administrative law' is akin to many other conceptual terms and is hard to define.
-Joseph J. Simeone

Administrative law controls a system: a system which, in the simplest terms, has only one goal: to deliver government services to its citizens.
-Charles Koch, Jr.

1. That branch of law concerned with the procedures by which administrative agencies make rules and adjudicate cases; the conditions under which these actions can be reviewed by courts. 2. The legislation that creates administrative agencies. 3. The rules and regulations promulgated by administrative agencies. 4. The law government judicial review of administrative actions.
-Jay M. Shafritz

Broadly speaking, administrative law deals with (1) the ways in which power is transferred from legislative bodies to administrative agencies; (2) how administrative agencies use power; and (3) how the actions taken by administrative agencies are reviewed by the courts. More specifically, administrative law is concerned with the legal developments which have so dramatically increased the powers and scope of the administrative branch.
-Kenneth F. Warren

Sources: Joseph J. Simeone, "The Function, Flexibility, and Future of United States Judges of the Executive Branch," *Administrative Law Review* 44, no. 1 (winter 1992): 159–161; Charles Koch Jr., *Administrative Law and Practice* (New York: West Publishing Co., 1985); Jay M. Shafritz, *The Dorsey Dictionary of American Government and Politics* (Chicago: The Dorsey Press, 1988); Kenneth F. Warren, *Administrative Law in the Political System* 3d ed. (Upper Saddle River, N.J.: Prentice Hall, 1997), 23.

The Impact of Administrative Growth on Democratic Ideals and Administrative Law

The administrative presidency, with corresponding implications for state governors, county executives, and municipal mayors, finds philosophical origins in George Washington's first cabinet. Thomas Jefferson, the original "outsider" advocating state's rights and decentralization of power, called for the pluralist model of presidential leadership. Alexander Hamilton—called our first accountant of the nation's purse—called for a strong chief administrator with direct, accountable lines of program authority.

Jefferson represented values of equality of uniform participation, or democratic ideals, while Hamilton called for efficient administration, articulated in hierarchy and bureaucracy. How has the emergence of the modern administrative state redefined basic democratic principles of our 1787 U.S. Constitution? Tenets of administrative law are grounded in constitutionalism, shared governmental powers, popular government, individualism, and political equality.[8]

Constitutionalism. A constitutional governmental system regards the people, not the government, as sovereign. Rule of law emphasizes supremacy of the law and the notion of limited government. A constitutional government is politically legitimate if it rests securely upon popular consent.

Many Americans believe that the growth of administrative expertise challenges the primacy of democratic constitutionalism. According to this argument, administrative discretion permits public administrators to "govern" the United States, and governmental regulations are threats to democratic constitutionalism. The undemocratic character of administrative experts compromises constitutional democracy. The new cadre of governmental experts forms an administrative elite that evolves into a democratically irresponsible oligarchy.

Shared Powers. The division of powers among the chief executive, administrative, legislative, and judicial branches and among different levels of government permits each political entity a limited check over the powers of other authorities in the governmental system. Decision-making powers in this system are not monopolized by a single governmental branch. Presidents, legislators, and judges tend to delegate more of their prescribed powers to government bureaucrats as the weight of increasing governmental regulation increases.

The expansion of administrative policy-making powers is enhanced as other branches of government become increasingly bogged-down with peripheral concerns. Public administrators, for example, absorb more power as constitutionally elected politicians agonize over the role of government in the resolution of moral dilemmas. Many citizens perceive the public administration system as a closed, political system that circumvents the open decision-making structure authored by the constitutional framers. Political bureaucracy emerges with a less than well-defined philosophy of the public interest.

Popular Government. Democratic government implies that the ultimate determination of public policy resides with the people. Stressing majority will, individual rights, and liberty, popular government is the opposite of absolutism. The shift of power from political institutions to administrative agencies raises questions about the democratic functioning of popular government.[9]

If public policy making is "farmed out" to government bureaucrats, how "popular" can government be? The administrative state, grounded in structures, functions, and rationality, may not be suited to the flexibility required to meet the public's demands. A system based on knowledge, skills, and expertise conflicts with a system based on partisan politics and spoils. All government officials, elected and appointed, are servants of the people and should be held accountable for their performance in the public's interest. It can be difficult to ensure that a nonelected official can be that accountable.

Individualism. Freedom, personal well-being, and capabilities of individuals may conflict with the regulation of society by public bureaucracies. According to some, bureaucracy stymies the will of citizens, expressing the powers of the system and not the individual.

The tug of war between societal rights and individual rights challenges the political consensus of democratic governments. Regulatory agencies prescribe rules

---

WHY ADMINISTRATIVE LAW MATTERS

1. The growth of government by public administrators is the most important political innovation in modern times.
2. In the present day, the effects of administrative government influence us literally every moment of our lives.
3. Bureaucratic government has provided no utopian cure for the shortcomings of free enterprise.
4. Administrative law seeks to reduce the tendencies toward arbitrariness and unfairness in bureaucratic government.
5. Administrative law, a relatively new and open-ended field of law, has not yet succeeded in playing its assigned role effectively.

Source: Lief H. Carter, *Administrative Law and Politics: Cases and Comments* (Boston: Little, Brown and Company, 1983), 4.

---

that may destroy the freedom of individuals, with new structures of apolitical power over individuals emerging in their place.

In balancing societal and individual rights, government regulators are called upon to implement guidelines of federal, state, and local laws in a "fair" manner. Issues of administrative law ultimately involve questions of due process of law. The question is: due process or fair treatment for whom? Liberty is sacrificed and our way of life is altered when an administrative agency or a court makes a decision that benefits a larger group at the expense of the individual. The rights of the individual—bolstered by the Fourth Amendment to the U.S. Constitution, which monitors unreasonable searches and seizures, and the Fifth Amendment, which guards against self-incrimination—can be undermined by the exercise of excessive regulatory control.

Political Equality. Grounded in democratic philosophies of equality under the law and equal opportunity for all persons, government is to treat and represent all persons equally. Laws forbid arbitrary treatment of citizens by government officials, but in practice U.S. administrative agencies do not afford complete equality to all persons or groups. The reality of U.S. political bureaucracy is that preferential treatment is given to special interests.

Sexual and racial discrimination are well-known and publicized aspects of our society. Since the Great Society of the 1960s, citizen groups have been organized to represent the interests of women and minorities. Affirmative action programs call for special compensatory measures from government to rectify past discriminatory practices by society. In theory, at least, the rule of law principle demands that government bureaucrats treat all individuals equally. Public bureaucracy, as prescribed by Max Weber's "ideal-type," rests upon knowledge, skills, and expertise, and not upon equality or political influence.

Constitutionalism, shared powers, popular government, individualism, and political equality are the political philosophies upon which administrative laws

Table 11–1 James Q. Wilson's Four Periods of Bureaucratic Growth

Period	Focus	Key Acts Passed
1887–1890	Control monopolies and rates	Interstate CommerceAct Sherman Act
1906–1915	Regulate product quality	Pure Food and Drug Act Meat Inspection Act Federal Trade Commission Clayton Act
1930–1940	Extend regulation to cover various socioeconomic areas, especially new technologies	Food, Drug, and Cosmetic Public Utility Holding Company Act National Labor Relations Act Securities and Exchange Act Natural Gas Act
1960–1979	Expand regulation to make America a cleaner, healthier, safer, and fairer place to live and work	Economic Opportunity Act Civil Rights Acts of 1960, 1964, and 1968 National Environmental Policy Act Clean Air Act Occupational Safety and Health Act
1978–1993	Deregulation movement as a reaction to bureaucratic overexpansion	Paperwork Reduction Act Air Deregulation Act Radio and TV Deregulation Banking Deregulation

Sources: James Q. Wilson, "The Rise of the Bureaucratic State," *Policy Making,* ed. Francis E. Rourke, 4th ed. (Boston: Little, Brown, 1986), 125–148; and Kenneth F. Warren, *Administrative Law in the Political System* 3d ed. (Upper Saddle River, N.J.:Prentice-Hall, 1997), 45.

find implementation in modern American society. The individual needs the assurance of protection in law from the potential misuse of regulatory power. The conflicts between individual citizens and their governments and the resolution of these conflicts by the law allow understanding of how these philosophies are played out in American life.

Traditional and Contemporary Cornerstones of American Administrative Law

The traditional cornerstones of administrative law are the independent regulatory agency, a uniform administrative procedure law (Administrative Procedure Act, 1946, as amended), substantial evidence judicial review, and notice and comment ruling.[10]

The *independent regulatory agency,* as a descriptive concept, is a misnomer. All agencies are directly dependent in unique ways upon executive and legislative branches of government and indirectly upon the judicial branch. The independent agencies, as they are called, emerged from the American constitutional provision of separation of powers.

There are three types of regulation. The best known is the old-style economic regulation. The second type, the new social regulation, is a product of the 1970s. A third type of regulation is subsidiary regulation.[11] Economic regulation emerged from the social and economic challenges of the 1930s. From the devastating consequences of the depression, the New Deal created the Federal Deposit Insurance Corporation (FDIC), Tennessee Valley Authority (TVA), Federal Communications Commission (FCC), Securities and Exchange Commission (SEC), National Labor Relations Board (NLRB), and Civil Aeronautics Board (CAB). These regulatory bodies were established from 1933 through 1938.

After World War II, other agencies were created to monitor and confront emerging national problems. The Atomic Energy Commission (AEC), Selective Service System (SSS), National Aeronautics and Space Administration (NASA), Federal Maritime Commission (FMC), Equal Employment Opportunity Commission (EEOC), Environmental Protection Agency (EPA), Occupational Safety and Health Administration (OSHA), and Consumer Product Safety Commission (CPSC) were created to administer and regulate, respectively, programs concerning atomic energy, military conscription, space exploration, shipping, employment discrimination, environmental protection, occupational safety, and consumer product safety. In addition, there is a need to regulate the activities of agencies implementing Social Security, medical care, welfare, food stamps, veterans' benefits, and internal revenue programs.

The development and enactment of a uniform *administrative procedure law* is the *second* traditional cornerstone of administrative law. The Administrative Procedure Act, enacted in 1946, brings a degree of standardization to administrative practices and procedures and public access to those procedures. Before the enactment of APA, administrative practice and procedure questions were decided on a constitutional basis. The APA brought order from chaos. Unless they can find justifiable exception, agencies must follow the fundamental outlines of APA's broad and general statute. Such legislation was an advance of immeasurable proportions in administrative law and the protection of citizen rights.

Judicial review is the *third* traditional cornerstone of administrative law. Substantial evidence review is a dominant feature of administrative practice and procedure. The courts may rule on the merits of agency action if things go askew. Derived from statutory and nonstatutory sources, judicial review permits judges to scrutinize allegedly illegal administrative actions. Judicial review, as a basic right, rests on the congressional grant of general jurisdiction under Article 3 of the U.S. Constitution.

The *rule-making procedure* constitutes the *fourth,* and final traditional cornerstone of administrative law. Rule-making guides subsequent application of policy, and, it is argued, clear rules promote fairness. Rule-making is also a forceful, efficient, yet democratic way for agencies to implement their mandates. Prior to the advent of rule-making, agencies resorted to policy interpretation on a case by case, ad hoc basis. Rule-making is a more rational means of policy-making than adjudication, because adjudication is reactive and potentially disjointed. Rule-making is more comprehensive, facilitating planning and coordination.

Contemporary pressing demands call attention to new cornerstones of administrative law. These are public participation in the administrative process, administrative process in informal and discretionary governmental activity, and the evolving definition of the mission of administrative agencies and development of effective oversight of their activities.[12]

The courts have held that *public participation* is pertinent to sound and equitable decision making in administrative processes. Until the mid-1960s, the prevailing perspective was that the agency was representative of the public interest. The courts insisted upon citizen rights to participate in the administrative process; Congress and the agencies soon recognized the validity of public participation as well.

The *administrative process* in formal and discretionary governmental activity is a *second* contemporary cornerstone. The development of procedural law to cover persons in public institutions, aliens, and the governance of educational institutions emphasizes the broadening development for protecting the rights of citizens in previously neglected areas. Aspects of administration once thought purely discretionary are subject to regulation as well.

A *third,* and final, contemporary cornerstone of administrative law is the *continuing definition of the mission of administrative agencies and development of effective oversight of their activities.* Each new administration advocates regulatory reform, but each administration fails to redefine the mission with sweeping regulatory reform. Congress may strengthen its oversight functions by demanding better analyses of the potential effects of proposed legislation, stronger program evaluation requirements in legislation, greater oversight of program design and development of regulations, and more use of program evaluation information. The final cornerstone, then, is the continuing development and fulfillment of mission and likewise improvement in oversight.

WHAT IS ADMINISTRATIVE LAW?

There is no commonly agreed upon subject matter of administrative law. There are, however, certain "parameters" wherein the application of administrative law is appropriate. Bernard Schwartz argues that administrative law does not relate to public administration in the same manner that commercial law relates to commerce and land law relates to land. Rather the definition of administrative law centers around powers and remedies to answer the following inquiries: (1) What powers may be vested in administrative agencies? (2) What are the limits of those powers? (3) What are the ways in which agencies are kept within these limits?[13]

All law may be generally categorized as either procedural or substantive. For example, the Environmental Protection Agency establishes New Source Performance Standards that prohibit emissions from industrial, stoker-fired boilers in excess of 0.10 pounds of fly ash per million BTU of heat input. The Administrative Procedure Act specifies that such a rule be published in *The Federal Register* so that interested persons may comment before the ruling becomes final. The requirement for publishing the rule in *The Federal Register* is procedural; the rule for limiting emissions from stoker-fired boilers is substantive.[14]

Administrative law originates primarily from interpretations of legal statements that describe procedures agencies follow. Such judicial interpretations emanate primarily but not exclusively from due process clauses as detailed in constitutions, from applicable administrative procedure statutes, and sometimes from clauses within statutes establishing an agency and also prescribing a procedure to follow.

Administrative law is not regulatory law. The differences between regulatory and administrative law are the subject of the next chapter. Numerous government agencies and departments, cooperating with legislatures, create regulatory laws that affect even the most trivial of activities. Several of the more recognizable regulatory agencies include the Federal Communications Commission (FCC), which regulates broadcasting and interstate telephone rates; the Occupational Safety and Health Administration (OSHA), which regulates the safety of the workplace; and the Food and Drug Administration (FDA), which tests drugs for marketing and monitors the contents of the food we eat. The laws, consent decrees, rules, and regulations made and enforced by these agencies are not administrative law. Instead, "regulatory law governs the citizenry; administrative law governs the government. We might say that administrative law governs the bureaucracy as other constitutional provisions govern the judicial, legislative, and presidential powers in government."[15]

Administrative law applies legal principles originating from statutes, common law, constitutions, and regulatory laws to the government agencies affected.

ADMINISTRATIVE DISCRETION AND ITS LIMITS

The exercise of discretion occurs in context of the informal administrative process. The difficulty lies in ascertaining ways to restrict discretion without unduly limiting the flexibility of the administrator. Administrators need some discretion for implementing their functions in a reasonable and efficient manner; excessive discretion may result, however, in the violation of the rights of private citizens. To find the proper balance, author Kenneth Culp Davis suggests that greater use of administrative rule-making curbs unreasonable discretion. The tremendous rise in use of rule-making has helped make this dilemma less of a problem.

Although administrators find themselves blessed with powers their predecessors little dreamed of possessing, they also find themselves subjected to numerous restraints as well. The legislative and judicial branches of government have not been content to stand aside and let administrators run the country, subject only to broad policy prescriptions and rather vague standards regarding the public interest. These two branches have acted to limit administrative discretion by, among other things, imposing increasingly strict standards on how administrators may use their new prerogatives.

Congress first took action in 1946 through passage of the Administrative Procedure Act (APA). This detailed piece of legislation set down specific rules on the ways in which administrative agencies are to proceed. The courts have since taken up the task, and, based on broadened interpretations of the "due process" clauses in the Fifth and Fourteenth Amendments to the Constitution and the Administrative Procedure Act itself, they have subjected administrative actions to progressively stricter review.

Judicial review since the Schechter case has focused not so much on matters of substance as on matters of procedure. In other words, the courts have concerned themselves less with what the administrative sector is doing and more with how it is doing it. The judges have, in effect, admitted that they do not have the expertise to determine whether a drug is safe, a welfare payment is adequate, or a highway route is well designed. As long as the administrative agency can show that its decisions in such matters are not arbitrary but are based on some legitimate rationale, the judges will not be inclined to interfere. They have become increasingly disposed to speak out, however, when they find that the agency is proceeding in a manner contrary to administrative due process.

"Administrative due process," writes Lewis Mainzer, "is that procedure which will normally be accepted by the courts as reasonable under the circumstances, whether or not the judge thinks the substantive decision was correct."[16] Davis puts it this way: "The dominant tendency in both state courts and federal courts is toward the middle position known as the substantial-evidence rule . . . the court decides questions of law but limits itself to the test of reasonableness in reviewing findings of fact."[17]

Due process, however, is not fully encapsulated by the criterion of "reasonableness" alone. It also implies what the Supreme Court has referred to as the criterion of "fundamental fairness." In attempting to set up standards for administrative due process, the courts, basing their findings on the federal government's Administrative Procedure Act and similar state acts and on their new interpretations of the Constitution, have worked out a fairly strict set of rules that administrators must follow to meet due process requirements. The following set of rules has developed as case law on administrative due process accumulates.

1. **Adequate Notice.** Before administrators or agencies can take any action that would directly affect one or more persons or institutions, they must usually give such affected parties adequate notice. How much notice is adequate? This depends on the circumstances and often becomes a matter of litigation before the courts. Rarely is a period of less than thirty days deemed to be adequate, and frequently a much longer interval is required.

The adequacy of the notice, the timeliness of the information, and the proper distribution of the notice are of particular importance. Concerning adequacy, the APA states that: "Persons entitled to notice of an agency shall be timely informed of—(1) the time, place, and nature of the hearing; (2) the legal authority and jurisdiction under which the hearing is to be held; and (3) the matters of fact and law asserted."[18]

However, in some situations, administrative agencies are empowered to act with scarcely any notice. If a building inspector finds a structure so unsafe it is in danger of collapse at any moment, for example, or a health inspector finds a restaurant serving contaminated food, they can usually order the situation remedied immediately. Unless it can be shown that the public safety demands precipitate action, however, the rule of adequate notice must govern.

2. **Disclosure of Reasons.** In addition to giving adequate notice, administrative agencies are usually required to state their reasons for taking their intended action. In most instances, the affected party may demand that the agency put these reasons in writing. This tends to deter agencies from acting in an arbitrary and capricious manner and at least gives the affected party written evidence to use in seeking subsequent redress in the courts.

3. **The Right to a Hearing.** Beginning in the late 1960s, the courts began to broaden dramatically the right of aggrieved parties to have a hearing. Motorists deprived of their licenses, welfare clients deprived of their benefits, public-housing tenants faced with eviction, and prisoners sentenced to solitary confinement sued for the right to be heard with favorable results in the courts.[19] Even the private sector found itself affected by the dictum in certain cases as students faced with expulsion were also granted the right to be heard.

   The expansion that has taken place in requiring hearings also affects rule-making. Agencies that seek to promulgate new rules must usually schedule hearings and allow those who think differently to state their case. Even those who may not be directly affected by the new rule can have their voices heard.[20]

4. **The Right to Further Appeal.** If, after a hearing, the protesting party is still not satisfied, he or she may appeal to a higher echelon within the agency and, as a last step, to the courts. Available figures suggest that increasing numbers of citizens are taking this final step.

The aggrieved party may seek judicial redress on the grounds that he or she was not given adequate notice, that the agency's procedures are not clear, that the agency is not abiding by administrative due process or its own procedures, that it has behaved in an arbitrary or discriminatory manner, or that the agency lacks jurisdiction in doing what it did or plans to do. As Mainzer points out, "Despite the Administrative Procedure Act and mountains of court opinion, the standards of administrative due process are extraordinarily indefinite."[21] Thus, numerous possibilities exist for carrying administrative issues into the courtroom.

There are, at the same time, numerous limitations on using the courts to reverse or mitigate administrative actions. First, the courts will not entertain the case until the petitioner has exhausted all recourse within the administrative agency. The courts will likewise not intervene in cases where there is no remedy.

Finally, as previously noted, the courts balk at deciding questions of fact or weighing the validity of one expert opinion against another. They prefer to confine themselves to questions of law and procedure.

OPENING UP THE GOVERNMENT

Citizen access and participation in the administrative process gained support during the late 1960s and 1970s. The presumption is in favor of public access whenever possible. There are circumstances where information and participation are denied under the law, but in general, the department or agency searches for an appropriate balance between citizen interests and governmental needs for secrecy. The federal Freedom of Information Act (1966), the Privacy Act (1974), the "government in sunshine" laws, and provisions for increased citizen participation in governmental policy-making and decision-making processes have made important contributions to opening the government.

The Freedom of Information Act, or FOIA, is part of the Administrative Procedure Act (1946). Prior to its adoption, governmental information and records could be revealed only to "persons properly and directly concerned." Such records could be subject to secrecy if a policy was "in the public interest" or if said data pertained "solely to the internal management of an agency." The FOIA reversed such practices, guaranteeing openness to "any person." If information is withheld, the burden of proof for the necessity of secrecy is placed upon the agency. The agency has ten days to respond; if the decision goes against the petitioner, he or she may appeal to a higher level in the agency. Certain items such as "trade secrets and commercial or financial information obtained from a person," deemed "privileged and confidential," and "personal and medical files or similar files the disclosure of which would constitute a clearly unwarranted invasion of personal privacy" are not subject to disclosure.

Agencies with significant numbers of requests from businesses brought in the largest fees. Fee leaders included DOD, HHS, EPA, Treasury, Transportation, Agriculture, and Labor. Almost 75 percent of the FOIA requests originate from business and law firms. An estimated 91 percent of requests are honored. A research assistant at a college in California and a newspaper reporter in Oregon asked the Department of Energy for details on the Nuclear Emergency Search Team (NEST). A consulting firm in Maryland asked the Department of the Navy for copies of procurement contracts. An inmate at a prison in the midwest asked the Department of the Army for instructions on how to make a bomb and where to detonate the mechanism in Denver. A hospital in Massachusetts asked for a Quality Assurance Profile from the FDA.[22]

The Privacy Act is a part of the Administrative Procedure Act and addresses what information is collected on citizens and how that information is used, requiring agencies to publicly report the existence of systems of records maintained on individuals; requiring that the information contained in these record systems be accurate, complete, relevant, and up-to-date; providing procedures

Table 11–2   How to Make an FOIA Request

General information regarding the FOIA (Freedom of Information Act) law can be found at the U.S. Department of Justice (DOJ) web site (www.usdoj.gov). This site includes most of the Office of Information and Privacy documents related to policies regulating the government-wide FOIA programs.

Federal Aviation Administration (FAA) publications and much regulatory information and data are publicly available, and an FOIA request may not be necessary to obtain it. If you have questions about the need for an FOIA request, please contact the headquarters FOIA office. An FOIA request must be written and must be for FAA records; it is not appropriate to ask questions under the FOIA law. You may make a request by indicating that you are seeking records under the Freedom of Information Act.

Each request should describe the particular record to the fullest extent. The request should describe the subject matter of the record, and, if known, indicate the date of the record, the place where it originated, and the name of the originating person or office.

A processing fee may be assessed for search, review, and duplication activities associated with an FOIA request. Fees are assessed depending on the category of the requester. The four categories of requesters are: commercial; educational or noncommerical scientific institutions; news media; and all other requesters. More information on FOIA fees may be found in the DOJ Freedom of Information Act Guide, pages 413–415; or Department of Transportation 49 *Code of Federal Regulations*, Part 7, "Public Availability of Information" (7.43).

Requesters should indicate their willingness to pay applicable fees in their FOIA requests.

The envelope in which the request is sent should be marked "FOIA" and mailed to:

Freedom of Information Act Program, AAD-40
Headquarters Office
Federal Aviation Administration
800 Independence Avenue, SW
Washington, DC 20591
Main Number (202) 267-9165
Email: 9.ahr.foia@faa.dot.gov

Source: Federal Aviation Administration, web site, www.faa.gov

whereby individuals can inspect and correct inaccuracies in almost all federal files about themselves; specifying that information about an individual gathered for one purpose not be used for another without the individual's consent; and requiring agencies to keep an accurate accounting of the disclosure of records and, with certain exceptions, making these disclosures available to the subject of the record. The potential conflict with the FOIA is avoided with the disclaimer

OPEN THE DOORS: FAMILY PLANNING DISPUTE

A controversy over distribution of federal family planning funds has the potential for disrupting traditional programs and closing some clinics in areas of East Central Indiana.

If so, that could make it difficult for patients and others who have come to depend on the services. Whether it would border on tragedy might depend on whether alternative services of similar quality become available. Full understanding of that point has been hard to come by, and that is part of the controversy.

Planned Parenthood of East Central Indiana (PPECI) is at the center of the funding debate. It stands to lose significantly when final approval is given to federal funding proposals.

Currently, the organization's annual subsidy under the federal Title 10 family planning program is $743,484. That would drop to $271,218 next year, according to a proposal from the Indiana Family Health Council, a state agency that funnels federal dollars to local organizations.

Planned Parenthood has said some of its clinics could simply disappear—Winchester being one of the examples. And services at its main Muncie clinic, 424 West Main Street, could be affected. Presumably, some of those services would be transferred to Open Door BMH Health Center, which was encouraged to apply for family planning dollars by the state health council. Open Door is slated to receive $200,000 in 1998 for services at its clinic on South Walnut Street. Family planning grants fund a number of reproductive health services, including testing and treatment of sexually transmitted diseases, pregnancy testing and counseling, and several informational and educational programs aimed at lower-income populations.

It could be possible that Planned Parenthood, for years a nationally militant organization on the issue of abortion freedom for women, is now paying a price for that advocacy. If so, the cost is reflected in its inability to tap conventional funding sources as easily as in the past.

Locally, the organization has been critical of the health council's decision to award funds to Open Door, which it says is a family-practice clinic not solely focused on reproductive health care. Whether that would prevent Open Door from doing an equally good job in the family planning area is debatable. Competition between agency programs could be healthy.

Also, some who are more attuned to philosophical differences on the abortion issue would welcome Open Door's announced intention of providing no abortion procedures, counseling or referals. That could be considered as a needed counterpoint to Planned Parenthood's traditional policy on abortion counseling.

Nevertheless, there is a troublesome aspect to the switch of some funds from Planned Parenthood to Open Door. That is the Family Health Council's totally inadequate job of explaining the change. The council apparently handled the competitive bidding process behind close doors. This has resulted in the state Planned Parenthood organization filing an Open Door lawsuit claiming the council violated public access laws by closing its meetings. Since its funding decision, the council's staff has declined to give specifics that might explain the basis for its decisions to award money to some agencies but not to others.

(Continued)

These are public monies involved, and the council would appear to have no legal right to prevent the public from observing its decision-making process.

If the council won't open its meetings, how can the public inform itself on whether the new funding decisions are in its best interests? How does the public know that the new providers, here and elsewhere in Indiana, will be able to offer the same level of service as Planned Parenthood? And how does the council rationalize the much higher cost-per-patient aspect of the Open Door grant compared to the Planned Parenthood grant?

There might be reasonable answers to these questions, but they won't be forthcoming unless the Indiana Family Health Council lifts its veil of secrecy.

Source: "Family Planning Dispute: Open the Doors," *The Muncie Star Press*, Larry L. Shores, Editorial Page Editor, Larry S. Lough, Editor, November 13, 1997, page 4A. Reprinted with the permission.

dictating disclosure as required under Section 552, or the FOIA section of the Administrative Procedure Act. The common law right of access to information is an important source for legal development in the states. Nearly all states include statutory counterparts of the FOIA and Privacy Act.

Like the FOIA and the Privacy Act, the Federal Sunshine Act, passed by Congress in 1976, is also part of the Administrative Procedure Act. Enhancing access to government operations is the purpose of sunshine laws. The degree of openness varies from statute to statute. Most statutes permit exceptions to guarantees of openness, most notably, in labor negotiations and personnel matters. In some states, and on the federal level, a governmental body may enter executive session, and then, by majority vote, close the meeting to the public. In other states, even informal meetings are subject to sunshine statutes.

Citizen participation also opens government to the public. Citizen-initiated activities, or the citizen action movement, and government-initiated activities, or the citizen involvement movement, illustrate attempts to involve citizens. The second approach is relevant to the practice of administrative law. Hundreds of provisions require or permit some form of citizen participation in administrative policy-making or decision-making because of congressional mandates. Such legislatively induced participation ranges from creation of citizen advisory committees to requirements that public hearings be conducted prior to adoption of a policy.

THE EXPANDING ROLE OF ADMINISTRATIVE LAW JUDGES

The Administrative Procedure Act of 1946 ruled out any evidence that would be "irrelevant, immaterial or unduly repetitious," but did not go so far as to outlaw hearsay evidence as such. In 1971, the Supreme Court held that uncorroborated hearsay evidence can constitute "substantial evidence," sufficient to support an administrative ruling.[23] This did not mean that all such evidence was to be

ADMINISTRATIVE LAW JUDGES AT OSHA: E-Z TRIAL PROCESS

The Review Commission:	The Occupational Safety and Health Review Commission is an independent agency of the U.S. Government. The Commission's only function is to resolve disputes that result from inspections carried out under the Occupational Safety and Health Act of 1970, which we refer to as the Act. The Commission is completely independent of the Department of Labor and the Department's Occupational Safety and Health Administration (OSHA). It is composed of three Commission Members appointed by the president of the United States for six-year terms, and it employs administrative law judges to hear cases.
What Is an E-Z Trial?:	E-Z Trial is a method for hearing less complex cases before the Review Commission judges. It is quicker, less costly, and involves fewer legal formalities than the conventional method of hearing cases.
Rules of Procedure:	The Commission's Rules of Procedure are published in part 2200 of Title 29, *Code of Federal Regulations* (C.F.R.); Subpart M (Rules 2200.200-2200.211) covers E-Z trial. These regulations may be available in a local library and can also be obtained by writing or calling:

> Office of Public Information
> U.S. Occupational Safety and Health Review Commission
> 1120 20th Street, N.W., 9th Floor
> Washington, D.C. 20036-3419
> Telephone: (202) 606-5398

Time Is of the Essence:	Many of the document's parties are required to file such as those needed to disagree with an OSHA citation or proposed penalty must be filed within a specific period. This means that failure to file documents as required could result in a citation becoming a final order without an opportunity to appeal. Therefore, you must respond promptly to communications you receive from either the judge, the Commission, or any of the parties to the dispute.

(Continued)

Major Features of E-Z
under E-Z Trial Procedures:

1. Early discussions among the parties and
   the administrative law judge are required to
   narrow and define the disputes between
   the parties.
2. Motions, requests asking the judge to order
   some act to be done, such as having a party
   produce a document, are discouraged unless
   the parties try first to resolve the matter
   among themselves.
3. Disclosure. The secretary is required to
   provide the employer with inspection details
   early in the proceeding. In some cases, the
   employer will also be required to provide
   certain documents, such as evidence of their
   safety program, to the secretary.
4. Discovery, the written exchange of information,
   documents, and questionnaires between the
   parties before a hearing, is discouraged and
   permitted only when ordered by the judge.
5. Appeals of actions taken by the judge before
   the trial and decision, such as asking the
   commission to rule on the judge's refusal to
   allow the introduction of a piece of evidence,
   called interlocutory appeals, are not permitted.
6. Hearings are less formal. The Federal Judge of
   Evidence, which govern other trials, do not
   apply. Instead of submitting briefs (written
   arguments explaining your position in the
   case) the parties argue their case orally before
   the judge at the conclusion of the hearing. In
   many instances, the judge renders his or her
   decision "from the bench," which means the
   judge states at the end of the hearing whether
   the evidence and testimony proved the alleged
   violations and states the amount of the penalty
   the employer must pay, if a violation is found.

Cases Eligible for E-Z Trial:
[Rules 202 and 203(a)]

This is an experimental program, so it is likely
that not all relatively simple cases eligible for E-Z
Trial will be selected. The chief judge assigns
cases for E-Z Trial or, if your case is not selected,
you may request that it be chosen.

Cases appropriate for E-Z Trial are those with one or more of the following characteristics:

- relatively simple issues of law or fact with relatively few citation items,
- total proposed penalty of not more than $10,000,
- no allegation of willfulness;
- a hearing that is expected to take less than two days, or
- a small employer whether appearing with or without an attorney.

Source: Occupational Safety and Health Administration, www.osha.gov, November 1, 1995.

indiscriminately accepted. It would have to be relevant, reliable, and supportive of the point for which it was being used. Material "without a basis in evidence having rationality and probative force" would not meet the Court's standard.

Such a ruling does not close the door on the issue but only opens it wider. Hotly contested disputes can erupt at any time on whether a particular piece of hearsay evidence meets the criteria for relevance and probative value. Many, meanwhile, still question whether any hearsay evidence should be allowed to influence administrative action. The consequences of administrative decision-making can frequently exceed those of a court trial, therefore it is only right and proper, so the argument goes, that those who would have to bear these consequences should benefit from the safeguards enjoyed by those subject to a court trial. Others contend, however, that there is nothing inherently evil about hearsay evidence. Such evidence is admissible in even criminal trials in most countries in the world, including most democratic countries. To bar it from the hearing room, they contend, would only hinder administrative tribunals from making informed and judicious decisions.

The dilemma of hearsay evidence is not the only controversy confronting administrative law judges. The prospect that the administrative law judges prosecute and adjudicate cases brought before him or her is a very serious concern. When an agency discharges or demotes an employee or deprives an individual or a group of some benefit or right, the agency first brings the charges and then, during the hearing, sits in judgment on these charges. In effect, it seems to be sitting in judgment on itself. To many lawyers, this is inherently unfair and contrary to both the spirit and intent of due process. They claim the affected party should possess the right to have the charges decided by a completely external body.

While most administrative agencies adjudicate their own charges and complaints, they usually use special employees to do so. These officials are customarily called hearing examiners in most local and some state bureaucracies, but in a few states as well as at the federal level they bear the more prestigious title of administrative law judges. Formerly referred to as "Washington's hybrids," "the hidden judiciary," "trial examiner," or a "hearing officer," they adjudicate cases for federal agencies.[24]

The administrative law judge exercises his or her prerogatives when a corporation or a private citizen disputes the decision of a federal department or agency. For example, if your grandfather is denied a disability pension from the Social Security Administration or if a state university is charged with unfair labor practices by the faculty union, the administrative law judge decides the case. Until 1978, the 1,100 administrative law judges were called "hearing officers." They, according to the United States Supreme Court, are "functionally comparable" to federal court judges. An administrative law judge must have at least seven years of trial experience and pass an examination of general legal knowledge. The Office of Personnel Management certifies the administrative law judge and maintains a central registry from which agencies select judges. The position is a lifetime job in which pay ranges from $72,865 to $112,100 per year.

Administrative law judges interpret federal regulations enforced by a particular department or agency to which they are assigned. "There's a perception that people are not getting a fair shake from us because we're Department of Labor ALJs," said Nahum Litt, the Labor Department's chief administrative law judge. Some administrative law judges are former staff attorneys for particular agencies and are, on occasion, perceived as officials for those federal bureaucracies instead of independent judges.

More than 800 administrative law judges are employed by the Social Security Administration, eighty in the Department of Labor, and eighty-four in the National Labor Relations Board. The remaining number are divided among twenty-six other departments and agencies around the country. Administrative law judges in the Social Security Administration alone hear 300,000 appeals a year.[25]

Although federal ALJs are employees of the agency whose cases they adjudicate, their qualifications and civil service status have given them virtual immunity from normal agency pressures. They frequently counteract and contradict the policies of their agencies. When the Social Security Administration attempted to use the Reagan administration's stricter guidelines to pare nearly a quarter million people from the rolls of its recipients, it found itself on a collision course with its ALJs. The ALJs, using the more liberal standards of the Supreme Court, reinstated approximately three-fifths of those who appealed their loss of benefits. Their actions infuriated the heads of Social Security, who overruled many of the reinstatements. This, in turn, riled the ALJs, who felt they had acted as they should, in other words, as independent judicial officers and not as "mere bureaucrats."

Despite the independence and integrity that ALJs have usually shown, some observers continue to express doubts as to whether an agency employee should preside over a case in which the agency itself is a party of interest.

Suggestions have been made to divorce ALJs completely from any particular agency, setting up, in effect, a new administrative unit in the federal bureaucracy that would assign them to different agencies as cases arose. This would give them more independence, but would reduce their expertise in the matters under dispute, for they would no longer be specialized in the work of one agency.

Critical examination of the formal agency adjudicative process and the role of the ALJ reveals two trends. First, there is growing dissatisfaction with formal, trial procedures for resolving licensing, merger, and related economic regulation policy issues. Second, the number of benefits and enforcement cases have increased dramatically. Social Security Administration (SSA) ALJs decide 300,000 cases annually; Department of Labor ALJs resolve thousands of cases concerning black-lung benefits claims and longshoremen's compensation. Enforcement is another growth area. ALJs discipline license holders, revoke licenses, issue cease-and-desist orders, or issue civil money penalties.

ALJs license and route certification of transportation by air, rail, motor vehicle, or ship; regulate radio and television broadcasting; establish rates for gas, electrical, communication, and transportation services; monitor compliance with federal standards relating to interstate trade, labor-management relations, advertising, communications, consumer products, food and drugs, corporate mergers, and antitrust; regulate health and safety in mining, transportation, and industry; regulate trading in securities, commodities, and futures; and adjudicate claims relating to Social Security benefits, worker's compensation, international trade, and mining. The brief history of ALJs reflects tension between the need for fact-finder independence and the need for policy and management control.

INTERNAL AND EXTERNAL ADMINISTRATIVE CONTROLS

In the fifty-first of their famous *Federalist Papers,* James Madison and Alexander Hamilton pointed out,

> *If men were angels, no government would be necessary. If angels were to govern men, neither external nor internal controls on government would be necessary. In framing a government which is to be administered by men over men, the great difficulty lies in this: you must first enable the government to control the governed; and in the next place oblige it to control itself. A dependence on the people is, no doubt, the primary control of the government; but experience has taught mankind the necessity of auxiliary precaution.*[26]

As the writers of *The Federalist Papers* perceptively noted, there are two aspects of administrative control.

Internal Controls: One is the control that agencies must exercise over their own constituent elements, be they subunits or individuals. Staff units and their personnel frequently perform a controlling function even when they have no authority or mandate to do so. This is what frequently makes them suspect by line employees. Staff services provide internal control, even when they are not expressly designed to do so. Many staff services are, however, expressly designed with a control function in mind.

Internal control mechanisms include the *personnel department*. If it enjoys appropriate authority, the personnel department influences how line departments and line officials confront personnel problems. The *budget office* of any agency or any government obviously exercises a high degree of control, for it may decide who gets what amount of money for what purpose. Another staff department that exercises financial control is the *purchasing office*. Perhaps the most important financial control unit is the *auditing branch*. *Field inspections* support internal controls.

External Controls: The instrumentality that is most expressly charged with controlling administration is the *legislative branch of government.* Legislatures *control expenditures* and *confirm appointments.* The most well-known power legislative bodies exercise over administrative ones is the *power to investigate and expose*. The authority of the "independent" prosecutor in the Watergate and Monica Lewinsky controversies orignates with legislative prerogatives to investigate the professional—and personal—activities of the President. The General Accounting Office is the investigative arm of Congress and is charged with examining all matters relating to the receipt and disbursement of public funds.

THE EMERGENCE OF THE WHISTLE BLOWER

A form of government employee control at times controversial, yet often effective, is that of *whistle-blower*. The term "whistle blower" was originated by Ralph Nader to categorize those public employees who, in effect, blow the whistle on acts by their own agencies when they deem such acts to be improper.[27] Some of the more famous whistle-blowers during the early 1970s were Gordon Rule, the Navy's director of procurement, who challenged extravagant cost overruns and claims for extra compensation by Navy suppliers; A. Ernest Fitzgerald, the Pentagon cost analyst who called attention to similar cost overruns in conjunction with the Air Force's C-5A transport jet; Frank Serpico, the New York City patrolman whose reports on corruption in his department touched off a wide-ranging investigation that culminated in numerous indictments and shake-ups in the city's constabulary; and Linda Tripp, secretary in the Clinton White House who secretly recorded telephone conversations with Monica Lewinsky, intern with whom President Clinton had "inappropriate intimate contact."

A typical whistle-blower is about fifty years old, never demonstrated in the 1960s, has been at the same job for many years, and is conservative in personal style and political outlook.[28] Despite the Whistleblower Protection Act, many government employees are afraid to expose corruption for fear of reprisals. The Office of Special Counsel (OSC), charged with protecting whistle-blowers, has never won a case restoring a whistle-blower's job.[29] Wrongdoing in government and business has increasingly been exposed by persons who "blow the whistle" on illegal or improper practices. Sometimes whistle-blowers are regarded as heroes, but they are often given poor performance reviews, dismissed, and regarded as traitors.[30]

Tripp learned about the political power of knowledge in her secretarial jobs while employed at the White House.[31] Many theories exist regarding why Tripp, age forty-eight, secretly recorded the "girl talk" of Lewinsky, age twenty-four, and the latter's sexual proclivities with the president. The upbringing and background of Tripp, plus her distaste for the Clinton White House, motivated Tripp to become a whistle-blower.[32]

Many factors account for the growing prominence of whistle-blowers as agents of administrative control. One of them is the development of *administrative law* and the safeguards it extends to public employees. When the Nixon administration attempted to discharge Fitzgerald, for example, by eliminating his job, he fought back through the courts and won.[33] A midwestern high school teacher fired after he sent a letter to a local newspaper criticizing his school board won similar reinstatement. In general, the courts have become increasingly protective of whistle-blowing employees.

A second factor that has encouraged whistle blowing has been the development of the *news media.* In this connection, the press has long played an active and aggressive role in controlling administrative actions. "I fear three newspapers more than I fear 3,000 bayonettes," Napoleon once remarked, while an English contemporary, philosopher Jeremy Bentham, observed that "Without publicity, all checks are inefficient; in comparison to publicity, all checks are of small account."[34]

The development of broadcast journalism, particularly television news, and the growth of public awareness and interest in government have made the news media a form of control that rivals, if it does not exceed, that exerted by legislative bodies. This is particularly true in the United States, which does not have a government-owned television and radio network and has a long muckraking tradition. The media is not only important for what it does on its own but for the help it provides other forms of control. It has encouraged and strengthened whistle-blowing by providing considerable publicity to the whistle-blowers. It also has stimulated legislative control by providing headlines and coverage for legislative exposés. Furthermore, many newspapers and radio and TV stations act as ombudspersons, soliciting citizen complaints against the bureaucracy and then checking them out.

A third instrument of control over an administrative agency is its *clientele.* For reasons that will be more fully discussed in the next chapter, administrators, particularly in the United States, need considerable cooperation from their clientele, and the clientele often seize upon this to exercise some countervailing influence over administrators. Sometimes this takes dramatic and violent forms, such as the client takeovers of welfare offices, the student rebellions of the 1960s, and the prison riots of the early 1970s. More often, however, clients exercise control by refusing to comply with policies they do not like.

**ETHICS: PUBLIC ADMINISTRATION'S CHALLENGE
OF THE TWENTY-FIRST CENTURY**

Honesty, fairness, and productivity are characteristics of American patriotism and must be practiced consistently by every government employee. Even from the point of view of effectiveness it is smart for public administrators to be moral in carrying out government functions. The credibility of government is at stake. Laws, rules, and regulations of government should be grounded in ethics, integrity, and organization commitments.

Government employee performance and policy leadership should reflect emphasis on the following themes:

- Make ethics a part of employee orientation and training programs.
- Include ethics in the performance evaluations and regular feedback provided to employees.
- Publicize ethical dilemmas and the organization's perception of them.
- Review management practices in different parts of the organization to help identify existing or potential ethics problems.
- Develop a code of ethics.
- The actions of top government officials must be consistent with their expectations for employee conduct. Leadership by example is an effective tool to establish an ethical perspective among members of the federal, state, or local government organization.

Source: Stephan J. Bonczek, "Ethics: Challenge of the 1990s: A Local Government Perspective," *Public Management* 72, no. 8 (July 1990): 17–19.

Finally, a form of control that often receives little attention but that plays an important role in constraining many administrative agencies is the control exercised by *competing agencies.* Agencies are frequently locked in combat over jurisdiction, funding, and so on. In their continual jousting for power and position, agencies tend to control each other. James Madison saw this as one of the most effective forms of control. In a well-known passage in *The Federalist* he noted, "Ambition must be made to counteract ambition . . . the constant aim is to divide and arrange the several offices in such a manner that each may be a check on the other—that the private interest of every individual may be a sentinel over the public rights."[35]

LAW AND CONTROL: HOW MUCH IS ENOUGH?

Democratic government rests on such principles as accountability and responsibility. We have seen that the realization of such principles requires a comprehensive system of administrative control. The public has a right to demand and administrators have a need to accept a widespread network of restraints and restrictions on administrative activity. *Democratic government is controlled government.*

Of course, administrators often find such controls irksome and irritating. They are, by nature, active men and women who wish to "get on with the job." It would be strange if they did not frequently chafe at curbs placed upon their actions. In the long run, however, they, too, benefit from a suitable system of control. Control, or at least extensive control, can be counterproductive. Carried too far, it can render government ineffectual and even inert, leaving the way clear for less savory and less responsible forces to operate. As we saw in our examination of administrative law, the judicialization of the administrative process has proved to be a bonanza to various business interests that use the safeguards imposed on administrative agents to perpetuate or prolong questionable activities.

Too much control also breeds a climate of conflict and distrust that can result in a great deal of dysfunctional behavior. If it refuses to resign itself to relative immobility, an agency straitjacketed with a strict system of controls may dissipate so much of its energy trying to overcome obstacles to action that it may have little energy left to serve the public. Furthermore, it may respond to the distrust that extensive control suggests by meriting such distrust.

The American statesman, Henry L. Stimson, who served in many high government positions before and during World War II, once observed that one way to make a man trustworthy is to trust him.[36] The reverse may also be true. Certainly, the distrust that pervasive control fosters does little to encourage candor and cooperation. Control, whether exercised through legalistic or other means, has its limits if the ends of democratic society are to be served. Fortunately some of the changes now buffeting administration may help alleviate some of the problems it poses. Programmed budgeting, productivity measures, management by objectives, and other techniques may increase responsibility and accountability while replacing or reducing the role of negative control, that is, control for its own sake. Some systems of control will continue to be needed and the problems they present will doubtless persist, but the increasing professionalism also starting to characterize public administration may make extensive and elaborate control systems somewhat less necessary.

SUMMARY

- The principles of *administrative law* are grounded in constitutionalism, shared powers, popular government, individualism, and political equality.
- Independent regulatory agencies, uniform administrative procedure law, judicial review, and rule-making are *traditional cornerstones* of administrative law. Public participation in the administrative process, the administrative process in formal and informal governmental activity, and the evolving definition of the mission of administrative agencies and development of oversight of their activities are *contemporary cornerstones* of U.S. administrative law.

- Honesty, fairness, and productivity are characteristics of American patriotism and must be practiced by every government employee. Even from the standpoint of effectiveness, it is smart for public administrators to be *moral* in carrying out government functions. The credibility of government is at stake. Laws, rules, and government regulations should be grounded in ethics, integrity, and organizational commitments.

- The United States has entered the era of the *administrative state.* During the past fifty years, the administrative sector has surged forward, spurred on by what might be called the permissive attitude that the courts have taken on the delegation of power issue. Administrative agencies have acquired increasing functions, along with more powers to carry them out.

- Franklin Roosevelt's "New Deal" gave birth to the idea of the *positive,* or welfare, state, whereby government provided a "safety net" of programs to enhance the "quality of life." Ronald Reagan's "revolution," that of redefining the federal government's role as limited, or privatizing government services whenever possible, responded to the regulatory, or *negative,* aspects of big government.

- Administrative law and regulatory law act in *tandem,* but they are not the same. Agencies and departments, cooperating with legislatures, create regulatory law. *Regulatory law* governs the private activities of citizens; *administrative law* governs the regulators, applying principles originating from statutes, common law, constitutions, and regulatory laws. The provisions of adequate notice, disclosure of reasons, the right to a hearing, and right to further appeal entail a set of rules that administrators must follow to meet due process requirements.

- After a century of intense litigation and adjudication, the field of administrative law is still alive with issues. *Hearsay evidence* and the *double role* of judge and prosecutor are key controversies of administrative law, affecting public administrators and clientele. The majority of administrative law judges function as hearing examiners in the Social Security Administration.

- The major aspects of the *administrative process* include delegation of power, judicial review, the investigatory power, the rule-making process, the right to be heard and adjudicatory policy-making, informal activity and the exercise of discretion, remedies against improper administrative acts, and opening up the government. The Freedom of Information Act (1967) and Privacy Act (1974) are amendments to the Administrative Procedure Act (1946), all of which concern due process guarantees.

- The question of administrative control has two distinct aspects—*internal* and *external* controls.

- Democratic government rests on principles such as *accountability* and *responsibility;* the realization of such principles requires a comprehensive system of administrative control. The public has a right to demand, and administrators have a need to accept, a widespread network of restraints and restrictions on administrative activity. Democratic government is *controlled* government.

The following case shows the ramifications a single administrative law can have. While reading, look for issues discussed in the chapter, especially administrative due process discretion and concerns.

CASE STUDY

Administrative Discretion at the State Health Services Administration.[37]

Heidi Heitzler was excited about what she had heard at the conference she was attending on aging. As the director of the not-for-profit St. Hillary's Nursing Home and Convalescent Center, she knew exactly how difficult it was to keep the books balanced during a time when the cost of medical and health care was skyrocketing. She also knew that the clients at St. Hillary's were interested in a therapeutic milieu that provided good, nutritionally balanced meals, clean and safe rooms, and caring health care providers-nursing aides, licensed practical and registered nurses, and doctors. The future for geriatric care facilities was destined to be a good one, insofar as the proportion of the aging population that would require care was projected to continue growing. The demographics presented at the conference showed that the percent of the age group sixty-five and older was growing at twice the national population rate and expected to comprise 20 percent of the total population by 2030.

Although Heitzler's participation in the conference produced what she called a "booked and shooked" frame of mind, she realized that she would have to return to St. Hillary's and face the routine problems associated with day-to-day administration: a nurse with a drug abuse problem; a client who had brought a negligence suit against her chief physician; a client injured when she slipped and fell on a freshly-waxed floor; a leaky roof that required immediate repair; a high turnover rate among the center's nursing assistants; and all the planning that was required for the celebration of Thanksgiving. The prospects of successfully resolving these dilemmas seemed remote; but she was a dedicated administrator who had faced what appeared to be insurmountable obstacles before. She knew the value of perseverance and was certainly no stranger to adversity.

Earlier in the year, the state assembly had responded to the pressures that had been placed on it by enacting additional laws on the regulation of nursing homes for the aged. In fact, the law had given the State Human Services Agency (SHSA) wide authority and discretion to oversee the operations of nursing homes in the state. The reported cases of abuse against nursing home residents had received front page priority in the press, and the article showed the disparities associated with the quality of nursing care across the state, coupled with vast disparities between nursing home facilities. These factors had helped develop a mood among the state legislators that something should be done to alleviate the problem and do something that would benefit the aged.

Delegation by legislature

The further empowerment of the SHSA by the legislature in its regulatory function came as no surprise for Mr. Henry Ortega. As the director of SHSA, he had long been concerned about the quality of health care provided in the state's nursing homes. On another occasion, he had joined forces with the American Association of Retired Persons (AARP) and the State Mental Health Association (SMHA) in successfully getting the legislature to pass a patients' rights advocacy law. Now, at the request of the Association of Registered Recreational Therapists (ARRT), he formulated a set of rules that required each nursing home to employ at least one recreational therapist. The president of ARRT was Joliene Eggenberger, a cousin of Ortega and the wife of Senator Oscar "Big Spender" Eggenberger, a veteran chair of the state senate's powerful Appropriations Committee.

Although Ortega did not hold any hearings on his newly promulgated agency rule, he met privately with the Health Care Advisory Board, a group generally supportive of his proposals. The board, after hearing the arguments Ortega presented in support of the need for an agency regulation requiring recreational therapists, issued a formal recommendation broadly supportive of Ortega. Delighted by their response, Ortega complimented the board for its caring concern for the elderly and issued a statement on the board's action. He further stated that ". . . no formal hearing was required on the rule since such a hearing would be unnecessary and unduly time consuming, especially since there was a need to take immediate action to ensure the protection of the public interest and the welfare and safety of all nursing home residents."

Heidi Heitzler, upon learning of the new rule regarding recreational therapists, did not question the value that access to this type of therapy meant for her patients. Nevertheless, she felt that this regulation represented another "mindless act" by the bureaucrats in the state capitol. She knew she would not be able to comply easily with the regulation because Great Falls was a small, rural community.

To comply or not to comply

After examining her options, Heitzler complained to SHSA about the new rule and cited that St. Hillary's could "not afford to hire a therapist" and that the only one she was able to locate lived nearly fifty miles away and would be available only two days a week. The chief of compliance, B. J. Smith, an experienced administrator who went, as he was fond of saying, to the "College of Hard Knocks," replied to Heitzler's complaint by sending an SHSA inspection team to St. Hillary's.

The inspectors reported that St. Hillary's ". . . met or exceeded all standards," except for the lack of a recreational therapist on its staff. Based on this information, Smith ordered that decertification proceedings be initiated against St. Hillary's. St. Hillary's, at the initial hearing before James Westin, the SHSA's Hearing Examiner and General Counsel, argued that being a small nursing home in a poor rural area made it difficult to identify and hire a recreational therapist. St. Hillary's also suggested that the seriousness of the problem was mitigated because their staff were all hometown people who cared for the well-being of their elderly residents. In fact, a time-keeping log was produced that indicated that nurses frequently stayed after work to play games, supervise hobby activities, and help with other forms of patient recreation.

Westin was sympathetic to St. Hillary's dilemma, but felt that the law was clear. He found the nursing home to be out-of-compliance and issued a "recommended decertification" to the reviewing officer, Mr. Ortega. While in the process of reviewing the case, a citizen group from Great Falls visited Ortega and lobbied on behalf of St. Hillary's. Ortega ruled that St. Hillary's was in "substantial compliance" and he cancelled the decertification order.

Heitzler was happy with the decision, but Joliene and Oscar Eggenberger and SARRT were not. Senator Eggenberger informed Ortega at an Appropriation Committee meeting in which they were reviewing SHSA's biannual budgetary request, that "If I were you, I wouldn't grant any more exceptions to the recreational therapist rule." Ortega responded that he was the expert on nursing homes and that he felt Eggenberger had been intrusive in the affairs of SHSA.

Several weeks later, Hillside Nursing Home, a long-term care facility located in Carter City, requested a waiver exempting it from complying with the recreational therapist rule. The director of Hillside presented a scenario and set of facts he thought would justify the granting of a ". . . hardship exemption to the rule." That is, Hillside was located in a poor part of town and residents were disproportionately drawn from a sector that found it difficult to meet the present costs of extended nursing care for the elderly. Requiring the employment of a recreational therapist would also cause the home serious financial difficulties, and, after all, the regulations of the SHSA permitted waivers to be issued by the chief of policy, the chief of compliance, or the director. Upon reviewing the case, Shirley Jones, without seeking additional counsel, issued a waiver to Hillside.

Mr. Smith, however, had not been informed of the waiver granted to Hillside. Upon learning that Hillside did not have a recreational therapist, he called in his inspectors and inquired about the overall operation of the home. He was told that Hillside had not always measured up to either the letter or spirit of the state codes and that the facility was poorly managed. Prompted by this information, Smith ordered a surprise inspection. The subsequent inspection report showed that Hillside was in minimal compliance on most standards, deficient in some, and clearly in need of a recreational program. Smith issued an emergency decertification notice on Hillside. The notice also included a cease-and-desist order that instructed the home that it would be closed within thirty days unless it came into complete compliance on all reported deficiencies.

As expected, Hillside went to court and sought a restraining order against the SHSA. At the hearing, the lawyer for Hillside argued the following:

1. The legislature had improperly delegated too much authority and discretion to the SHSA.
2. The rule on recreation therapists was not properly related to the issue of good health care; the rule was arbitrary and unnecessary; it was established without a proper hearing; and it came about as a result of a conflict of interest.
3. The emergency decertification was arbitrary, excessive, and not authorized by law.
4. Hillside was being denied equal treatment under the law, whereas St. Hillary's was given an exemption under similar circumstances.
5. The surprise inspection violated the Fourth Amendment.
6. The waiver issued by Jones bound the agency and Smith could not legally overturn the waiver; collectively their actions violated due process of law.
7. The internal structure of the SHSA violated the separation of powers concept. The home could not, therefore, receive a fair hearing from Westin, who authorized the decertification.
8. Hillside could not receive fair treatment from Ortega, because he had a conflict of interest and was politically controlled by Senator Oscar Eggenberger.

In the final analysis, Hillside's attorney asked the court to restrain the SHSA from enforcing its orders and asked it to grant the home a permanent waiver on the rule requiring the employment of a recreational therapist.

The response of the SHSA addressed the legal arguments raised by Hillside's attorney in the following ways:

1. The legislature's broad grant of power to SHSA was valid.
2. The recreational therapist rule was related to the proper care of the aged. The rule was formulated with the advice of a statutorily established group of experts that also included input from the State Nursing Home Association. Under these circumstances, no formal rule-making procedures were required.
3. The emergency decertification process was a necessary part of the agency's statutory power to protect public health and safety.
4. Hillside was not entitled to the same treatment as St. Hillary's because Hillside's operation was deficient. Also, Hillside had a past record on poor compliance.
5. Surprise inspections were properly used in license cases and where public health was involved.
6. Mrs. Jones had not followed proper procedure in regard to the waiver granted to Hillside, therefore, the agency was not bound by her decision. Moreover, the waiver did not preclude action to be taken against the home on other grounds, as revealed in the on-site inspection.
7. Mr. Ortega was not Senator Eggenberger's prisoner. Ortega's own response at the committee hearing indicated his sense of independence. Furthermore, no conflict of interest existed because he was not a member of any of the associations interested in the outcome of the implementation or adjudication of the rule.

In closing statements, the attorney for the state argued that while it was true that the court possessed the power to restrain the agency, the court should have deferred to the expertise and primary jurisdiction of the agency. "Finally," the state's attorney opined, "the court did not have the power to waive the therapist rule—that power clearly resided within the discretionary authority of the SHSA."

EXHIBIT 1

Relevant State Statutes, Regulations and Laws Pertaining to Nursing Homes.

Statutes

Section 101—The Human Services Agency is empowered to promulgate all appropriate rules and regulations for the operations of nursing homes for the aged including procedures for granting and terminating the licenses of such homes as the director may prescribe.

Section 110—The director of the Human Services Agency shall be authorized to waive any portion of these laws or regulations of the agency if he/she deems that a home, while technically deficient in some standards, has made a good faith effort to reach substantial compliance.

Section 115—The Human Services Agency is empowered to take any appropriate actions necessary to protect the health, safety, and welfare of persons residing or working in nursing homes and to take the necessary measures to protect the public interest.

Section 120—There is hereby established a Health Care Advisory Board. This board shall have the authority to investigate and make recommendations to state agencies on matters related to health care in hospitals, clinics, nursing homes, and other health care facilities licensed to operate in the state. The board shall be composed of one representative from each of the State Medical Association, State Dental Association, State Osteopathic Association, State Hospital Association, State Nursing Home Association, State Mental Health Association, State Association of Registered Recreational Therapists, and two members of the general public to be chosen by the governor.

Civil procedure code

Section 201—The Federal Administrative Procedures Act shall apply to all state administrative agencies except as may be provided otherwise by acts of the legislature and, further provided that agencies may deviate from the APA in those instances wherein the agency has adopted or is statutorily subject to procedures substantially equivalent to those procedures contained in the APA.

Health services agency regulations

Regulation C—The director hereby authorizes the general counsel, the chief of policy, and the chief of compliance to issue waivers and exemptions to the laws and regulations of the agency, according to policy guidelines as established by the director.

Regulation M—The chiefs of the policy and compliance divisions shall be attorneys and shall serve as assistant legal counsels to the general counsel. On all matters that involve the legal interpretation of the laws and regulations of this agency, the chiefs of the previously named divisions will consult with the general counsel before taking final action on such a matter. On all other matters within the scope of their duties, the chiefs of the named divisions shall report to the director.

Regulation Q—Before any emergency or summary actions may be instituted, the chief of the compliance division must obtain the authorization of the general counsel.

QUESTIONS AND INSTRUCTIONS

1. Do administrators such as Ortega need to be concerned about the appearance of being influenced by "interest group" politics? In what ways?
2. If you were the chief inspector, would you have taken action to begin the decertification for St. Hillary's based on its noncompliance with the recreational therapist standard? Justify your response.
3. If St. Hillary's was owned and operated by a municipality, would you see any difference in the way that the SHSA dealt with the rule requiring nursing homes to hire a recreational therapist?
4. How does the study of public and administrative law pertain to the basic activities associated with day-to-day administration?
5. Do you believe that Ortega's action to mandate recreational therapy in nursing homes constitutes a conflict of interest, given his involvement and support of the SARRT Association? Why?

6. Assume the role of a trial judge and write an opinion in which you deal with the arguments presented by Hillside and the SHSA in court. As you know, you may rule on one point in favor of the agency and on another for Hillside. In the final analysis, who should win the case and why?

INSIGHTS-ISSUES / ADMINISTRATIVE DISCRETION AT THE STATE HEALTH SERVICES ADMINISTRATION

Clearly and briefly describe and illustrate these concepts, issues, or points. Interpret the word "role" as meaning impact, application, importance, effect and/or illustration of certain facts, concerns, or issues from the case study.

1. The role of concerns and problems at St. Hillary's calling for implementing internal administrative controls.
2. The role of external controls (courts) exercising administrative discretion (waving therapist rule) at St. Hillary's.
3. The role of delegation power by state legislature to State Human Services Agency (SHSA) to not-for-profit agency.
4. The role of rules and rule-making by SHSA for operating not-for-profit nursing homes.
5. The role of interest groups in determining internal administrative decision-making at St. Hillary's.

ENDNOTES

1. James Bryce, *The American Commonwealth* (1888), from the chapter, "The Strength of American Democracy," quoted in Theodore J. Lowi, *The End of Liberalism* (New York: W. W. Norton, 1979), 94.
2. Lowi, *The End of Liberalism*, 131.
3. Lowi, *The End of Liberalism*, 132.
4. *A. L. A. Schechter Poultry Corporation v. United States*, 295 US 495 (1935).
5. Harold Seidman and Robert Gilmour, *Politics, Position, and Power: From the Positive to the Regulatory State* (New York: Oxford University Press, 1986), 119.
6. Seidman and Gilmour, *Politics, Position, and Power*, 119.
7. Daniel J. Gifford, *Administrative Law: Cases and Materials* (Cincinnati: Anderson Publishing Co., 1992), 1.
8. Jerre S. Williams, "Cornerstone of American Administrative Law," *Administrative Law Review* 28 (1976): v–xii.
9. Florence Heffron and Neil McFeeley, *The Administrative Regulatory Process* (New York: Longman, 1883), 347–371.
10. Williams, "Cornerstone," v–xii.
11. Kenneth F. Warren, *Administrative Law In The American System* (St. Paul, Minn.: West Publishing Co., 1982): 111–122.
12. Dwight Waldo, *The Enterprise of Public Administration: A Summary View* (Novato, Calif.: Chandler & Sharp Publishers, Inc., 1980). See especially "Chapter 6: Bureaucracy and Democracy: Reconciling the Irreconcilable," 81–98.
13. Bernard Schwartz, *Administrative Law* (Boston: Little, Brown, 1976), 2.

14. Stanley A. Reigel and P. John Owen, *Administrative Law: The Law of Government Agencies* (Ann Arbor, Mich.: Ann Arbor Science, The Butterworth Group, 1982), 4–5.

15. Lief H. Carter, *Administrative Law and Politics: Cases and Comments* (Boston: Little, Brown and Company, 1983), 60.

16. Lewis C. Mainzer, *Political Bureaucracy* (Glenview, Ill.: Scott, Foresman, 1973), 62.

17. Kenneth Culp Davis, *Administrative Law and Government* (St. Paul, Minn.: West Publishing, 1960), 463, quoted in Mainzer, *Political Bureaucracy,* 50.

18. See Administrative Procedure Act, P.L. 404, 60 Stat. 237 (1946), as amended. 5 U.S.C., 554(b), Adjudications.

19. For an interesting, although scarcely disinterested account of a leading decision regarding prisoners' rights, see editorial, Tom Wicker, "In the Nation: Due Process for Prisoners," *The New York Times,* June 18, 1970, page 44.

20. For a more readable, but less profound account of the explanation of this right, see "Toward Greater Fairness for All," *Time,* Vol. 101, No. 9 (February 26, 1973), 95–96.

21. Mainzer, *Political Bureaucracy,* 37.

22. For analysis of the history and management of the FOIA, consult Lotte E. Feinberg, "Managing the Freedom of Information Act and Federal Information Policy," *Public Administration Review* 46, no. 6 (November/December, 1986): 615–621. See also Donald D. Barry and Howard R. Whitcomb, *The Legal Foundation of Public Administration* (St. Paul, Minn.: West Publishing Company, 1981), 331–332.

23. *Richardson v. Perales,* 402 US 389 (1971).

24. "The ' Hidden Judiciary' and What It Does," *U.S. News & World Report,* 1 November 1982.

25. Martin Tolchin, "Are Judge and Agency Too Close for Justice?" *New York Times,* 5 February 1989, p. E3; Joseph J. Simeone, "The Function, Flexibility, and Future of United States Judges of the Executive Department," *Administrative Law Review* 44, no. 1 (winter 1992): 159–188.

26. Alexander Hamilton, John Jay, and James Madison, *The Federalist Papers* (New York: Modern Library, n.d.), 337.

27. Ralph Nader, Peter Petkas, and Kate Blackwell, ed, *Whistle Blowing* (New York: Bantam Books, 1972).

28. Robert A. Rosenblatt, "Whistle-blowers," *Los Angeles Times,* 5 October 1997, page D4.

29. Timothy W. Maier, "Entrapping the Whistle-blowers," *Insight on the News* 14, no. 4 (2 February 1998): 8–12.

30. Charles S. Clark, "Whistleblowers: Are they Heroes or Disloyal Publicity Hounds? *CO Researcher* 7, no. 45 (5 December 1997): 1059–1074.

31. John Cloud, "Hot Off the Wiretap: Knowledge—especially if It's on Tape—Can Be Powerful and Scary in Washington. Just ask Linda Tripp," *Time* 151, no. 4 (2 February 1998): 42–45.

32. Jane Mayer, "Portrait of a Whistle Blower: The Family History Behind Linda Tripp's Anger," *The New Yorker* 74, no. 5 (23 March 1998): 34–39.

33. Nader, Petkas, and Blackwell, *Whistle Blowing,* 39–55.

34. Quoted in George E. Berkley, *The Democratic Policeman* (Boston: Beacon Press, 1969), 159–160.

35. Hamilton, Jay, and Madison, *The Federalist Papers,* 337.

36. McGeorge Bundy, *The Strength of Government* (Cambridge, Mass.: Harvard University Press, 1968), 56.

37. By C. Kenneth Meyer, professor and chair, Department of Public Administration, Drake University, Des Moines, IA, and Paul A. Tharp, Jr., Programs in Public Administration, University of Oklahoma, Norman, OK 73019, written for *The Craft of Public Administration,* 8th edition. The authors retain all copyright privileges.

12

Government Regulations and Regulatory Behaviors

REGULATION AND DEREGULATION

Regulations take force because the market or markets fail or otherwise do not work effectively. U.S. regulations commenced with the establishment of the Interstate Commerce Commission in 1887. Information is a scarce commodity. Decision makers cannot collect all relevant information. They act in a state of partial ignorance and uncertainty. They use the best source of information available: *what just has happened.* Government oversight and information occur in this perspective. Railroads, motor carriers, and airlines were deregulated. Public choice may be defined as "the economic study of non-market decision-making, or simply as the application of economics to political science."[1] Public choice assumes that rational individuals pursue their own interests.

Market failure. The normal operations of the marketplace fail to protect the public from actual or potential abuses of power by business firms. Utilities, for illustration, are widely regulated on the premise that particular services can be effectively provided by a single firm. That firm, by definition, is a monopoly supplier. Governments regulate the suppliers of local telephone, electricity, natural gas, and water services. Regulatory functions protect the public from monopoly power.

The Occupational Safety and Health Act and other statutes regulate working conditions, grounded in the premise that the market does not operate effectively to produce safe working conditions. The Federal Trade Commission regulates methods of competition, helping the markets to operate more effectively. The Clean Air Act and other statutes are necessary because the market would not discourage air and other pollution. In these cases, regulation is justified on a theory of market failure.[2]

Transportation regulation. The Interstate Commerce Act of 1887 established the Interstate Commerce Commisson (ICC). Federal regulation over transportation followed. Federal supervision focused on interstate commerce while states supervised intrastate commerce. The emergence of the ICC came as many believed the railroads exploited their monopoly positions and discriminated in their rate structures between long and short distance shippers. Regulation was imposed to fight the prerogatives of monopolies yet was introduced to protect competition where it worked.

The Civil Aeronautics Act commenced airline regulation in 1938. This enactment encouraged a fledgling aviation industry. This regulation was enacted to protect the airline industry from excessive or cutthroat competition. A freely operating motor carrier industry would threaten government regulation of railroad rates. The regulation of motor transport commenced in 1935.

Governmental oversight and information. A regulatory agency focuses its attention on a particular industry or upon a narrow area of human behaviors. The agency develops an "expertise" in its area of regulation. However, governmental oversight addresses the boundaries of the expertise function, asking if the function of regulation is the economic well-being of an industry. If this approach is so, government decision making becomes more important than individual business

INTRODUCTION TO LAWS AND REGULATIONS

Laws and regulations are a major tool in protecting the environment. Congress passes laws that govern the United States. To put those laws into effect, Congress authorizes certain government agencies, including the Environmental Protection Agency (EPA), to create and enforce regulations. The following is a basic description of how laws and regulations come to be, what they are, and where to find them, with an emphasis on environmental laws and regulations.

1. Creating a law.

Step 1: A member of Congress proposes a bill. A bill is a document that, if approved, will become a law.

Step 2: If both houses of Congress approve a bill, it goes to the president who has the option to either approve it or veto it. If approved, the new law is called an act, and the text of the act is known as a public statute. Some of the better-known laws related to the environment are the Clean Air Act, the Clean Water Act, and the Safe Drinking Water Act.

Step 3: Once an act is passed, the House of Representatives standardizes the text of the law and publishes it in the *United States Code.* The *U.S. Code* is the official record of federal laws.

2. Putting the Law to Work.

Now that the law is official, how is it put into practice? Laws often do not include all the details. The *U.S. Code* would not tell you, for example, what the speed limit is in front of your house. To make the laws work on a day-to-day level, Congress authorizes certain government agencies, including the EPA, to create regulations. Regulations set specific rules about what is legal and what isn't. For example, a regulation issued by EPA to implement the Clean Air Act might state what levels of a pollutant—such as sulfur dioxide—are safe. It would tell industries how much sulfur dioxide they can legally emit into the air and what the penalty will be if they emit too much. Once the regulation is in effect, EPA then works to help Americans comply with the law and to enforce it.

3. Creating a Regulation.

First, an authorized agency, such as the EPA, decides that a regulation may be needed. The agency researches it and, if necessary, proposes a regulation. The proposal is listed in *The Federal Register* so that members of the public can consider it and send their comments to the agency. The agency considers the comments, revises the regulation accordingly, and issues a final rule. At each stage in the process, the agency publishes a notice in *The Federal Register.* These notices include the original proposal, requests for public comment, notices about meetings where the proposal will be discussed (open to the public), and the text of the final regulation. (*The Federal Register* includes other types of notices, too.)

- *The Federal Register* notices related to the environment are available on the EPA's Web site (www.epa.gov).
- A complete record of *The Federal Register* notices issued by the entire federal government is available from the Government Printing Office (Web site: www.gpo.gov).

4. Carrying Out the Law.

Among the environmental laws enacted by Congress through which EPA carries out its efforts are:

1938 Federal Food, Drug, and Cosmetic Act;
1947 Federal Insecticide, Fungicide, and Rodenticide Act;
1948 Federal Water Pollution Control Act (also known as the Clean Water Act);
1955 Clean Air Act;
1965 Shoreline Erosion Protection Act;
1965 Solid Waste Disposal Act;
1970 National Environmental Policy Act;
1970 Pollution Prevention Packaging Act;
1970 Resource Recovery Act;
1971 Lead-Based Paint Poisoning Prevention Act;
1972 Marine Protection, Research, and Sanctuaries Act;
1972 Ocean Dumping Act;
1973 Endangered Species Act;
1974 Safe Drinking Water Act;
1974 Shoreline Erosion Control Demonstration Act;
1975 Hazardous Materials Transportation Act;
1976 Resource Conservation and Recovery Act;
1976 Toxic Substances Control Act;
1977 Surface Mining Control and Reclamation Act;
1978 Uranium Mill-Tailings Radiation Control Act;
1980 Asbestos School Hazard Detection and Control Act;
1980 Comprehensive Environmental Response, Compensation, and Liability Act;
1982 Nuclear Waste Policy Act;
1984 Asbestos School Hazard Abatement Act;
1986 Asbestos Hazard Emergency Response Act;
1986 Emergency Planning and Community Right to Know Act;
1988 Indoor Radon Abatement Act;
1988 Lead Contamination Control Act;
1988 Medical Waste Tracking Act;
1988 Ocean Dumping Ban Act;
1988 Shore Protection Act;
1990 National Environmental Education Act.

Source: Environmental Protection Agency, Web site: www.epa.gov. See Carol Browner, "Creating a Healthier Environment: How EPA Works for You," *EPA Journal* 21, no. 1 (winter 1995): 33–49.

decision making. Public attention is now focused on political elements inherent in governmental decision making. If the U.S. government adopts an industrial policy, or policies, government decision makers select particular industries for special forms of government support. Is the future of economic regulation grounded in subsidizing sunset industries?

Deregulation. By the late 1970s, airline regulation—by the CAB's control of airline rates and routes—was not working well. The removal of regulation, it was argued, would encourage airline competition for filling flights. Airplanes are easily transferable from city to city. Existing carriers would allocate their equipment according to supply and demand. New carriers would enter the market to meet the demands of the market. Deregulation permits flights to respond to passenger demand, producing ticket prices geared to filling flights and reduced passenger costs. Airline deregulation produced lower per passenger costs, lower fares, and allocation of flights to routes according to demand. But will airline mergers result in a less responsive industry? Will a more concentrated and oligopolistic airline industry continue producing in the postregulation competitive era?

Under deregulation, profitable routes no longer subsidize the unprofitable routes. No longer is a carrier obligated to serve an unremunerative market. Resources are allocated in a way that produces maximum consumer benefits. However, arguments favoring deregulation of the transportation industries usually do not apply to all regulation. Transportation deregulation has worked because it produces more social benefits than those produced under regulation.

Public choice. In the 1980s, critics argued that elected officials acted not to further the overall social good, but to bolster chances of their reelection to public office. This pattern, if realized, meant that government decision makers may capitulate to interest group pressures rather than acting in the good of the entire community. Elected officials try not to offend powerful interest groups. Legislators, seeking compromises, may avoid making difficult policy choices and legislate in generalities. They delegate to administrators the tasks of interpreting intentionally vague or ambiguous statutory terms. Legislators may blame administrators when one interest group of citizens complain about regulatory actions, yet take credit for the same decision if a different constituent interest group approves.[3]

EVOLUTION OF ADMINISTRATIVE REGULATIONS

In 1789, Congress granted the president the prerogative to select an administrator to "estimate the duties payable on imports." Since then, Congress continues to delegate rule-making power to administrative agencies. The full scope of regulatory power, in addition to the power to formulate rules, includes the authority for interpreting laws and regulations, enforcing rules and regulations, trying cases concerning violations of those rules, holding hearings investigating and adjudicating such circumstances, and imposing sanctions on violators. In a single agency, administrative regulatory power combines legislative, executive, and judicial powers.[4]

Administrative power expands as the power and responsibilities of government in our society expand. An industrialized, urbanized, interdependent society requires a more active role for government. The protection of individual rights, mediation of disputes, provision of benefits, and stabilization of the economy reflect accepted activities of modern U.S. government. As the 1980s began, at least fifty-eight federal agencies exercised rule-making authority and issued approximately 7,000 rules and policy statements each year.[5]

Administrative regulatory powers are vested in state and local government agencies as well. State regulatory powers and responsibilities include licensing of physicians, barbers, lawyers, architects, cosmeticians, liquor dealers, and funeral directors. States regulate commerce within their boundaries and supervise the governance of all public educational institutions. Local government agencies enforce building codes, fire, health, and safety regulations and standards. Agencies of state or local governments may also be charged with implementation of national programs via functional federalism.

Murray Weidenbaum, Mallinckrodt Distinguished University Professor and chair of the Center for the Study of American Business at Washington University in St. Louis, argues that the process of regulation is not widely understood. Regulation is the way in which a national priority or concern is translated into a specific rule. Regulation does not commence when a government department or agency issues a ruling. Regulation has it origins in Congress, when the national legislature passes a law establishing a regulatory agency, providing a mandate to issue rules governing a particular activity. The writing of a particular statute is usually the most important action of an extended rule-making process. The regulatory department or agency cannot cure basic defects in the enabling legislation. Congress perceives "market failure" or private sector inability to achieve a social goal. Departments or agencies promulgate regulations in response to laws passed by Congress to correct that "market failure." Regulatory proceedings are not, Weidenbaum says, mere matters of procedure and conformance. Regulations originate from demands for clean air, safe drinking water, safe workplaces, reliable financial markets, improved medicines, and competitive industries. The regulatory process, Weidenbaum concludes, is fundamentally bureaucratic— with all the powers and defects of government institutions—and at best is a blunt and imperfect mechanism for attempting to create a better society.[6] As argued in the previous chapter, the *United States is a regulatory state.* The vast majority of direct contacts for most citizens is likely to be with federal, state, or local administrative agencies. We are a society where nearly every activity of organizations and individuals is included in the scope of administrative regulation and control. The responsibilities and powers of administrative agencies include the following partial listing:

1. The rates that consumers pay for telephone service and electricity are determined by administrative agencies, as are the interest rates that savings and loan institutions may pay depositors.
2. Administrative agencies protect individuals from racial, sexual, and age discrimination in the major aspects of their lives: employment, education, and housing.

3. Administrative agencies determine who does and does not get radio and television licenses.
4. Administrative agencies ensure that the food we eat is pure, wholesome, and free from harmful additives and that the drugs that we purchase are safe and effective.
5. The right to join a labor union and to be protected from unfair labor practices is safeguarded by administrative regulatory power.
6. Administrative agencies are responsible for ensuring the safety of our workplaces; our methods of transportation; and the countless products that we purchase as consumers, from toys to clothing to automobiles.
7. Administrative agencies are responsible for protecting us against monopolies, false advertising, air and water pollution, incompetent health care professionals, subminimum wages and working conditions, unfair and misleading credit transactions, and fraud in securities purchases.
8. Administrative agencies determine who is eligible for welfare, food stamps, veterans benefits, Medicaid, Medicare, and Social Security.
9. Administrative agencies determine how much of our income we get to keep and whether a person may be admitted to or remain in this country.[7]

Overhead operations, independent regulatory commissions, cabinet departments, independent agencies, government corporations, the Executive Office of the President (EOP), and a variety of assorted federal agencies of more and lesser consequence issue administrative regulations daily in *The Federal Register* and annually in the *The Code of Federal Regulations*.

Overhead units carry out functions for the entire federal government. The General Accounting Office (GAO), Government Printing Office (GPO), Congressional Budget Office (CBO), Office of Management and Budget (OMB), General Services Administration (GSA), and Office of Personnel Management (OPM) issue regulations and administer support functions for most of the federal bureaucracy.

Since the creation of the Interstate Commerce Commission more than 100 years ago, **independent regulatory commissions** have been prominent in the government regulation of business. Such commissions are multiheaded, bipartisan in composition, organizationally separated from other departments and agencies, and not directly in the president's chain of command. They provide nonpartisan flexibility, continuity, and expertise in the regulatory process; assign commissioners with terms longer than the president; protect commissioners from presidential dismissal; and allow lengthy tenure for maximizing commissioner expertise and independence. These characteristics and aspirations may not be realized in each commission on every day of every year; however, these commissions possess widespread responsibilities for regulating specific industries and for protecting consumers and workers.

Examples of prominent, independent regulatory commissions are the Federal Communications Commission (FCC), Surface Transportation Board, Nuclear Regulatory Commission (NRC), Postal Rate Commission, Securities and Exchange Commission (SEC), Federal Maritime Commission (FMC), Federal Reserve System (FED), Consumer Product Safety Commission (CPSC), and Equal Employment Opportunity Commission (EEOC).

Cabinet departments enjoy similar scope, type, and impact of regulatory power as independent regulatory commissions. Major distinctions between the two types of agencies include administrative form and operations within executive departments or agencies. Cabinet agencies are led by a single administrator; cabinet secretaries are directly responsible to the president for programming. For example, the Food and Drug Administration (FDA), within the Department of Health and Human Services (HHS), is responsible for ensuring purity and safety of food, drugs, and cosmetics; the Internal Revenue Service (IRS), within the Department of Treasury, implements tax laws; the Immigration and Naturalization Service (INS), within the Department of Justice, regulates the entry, residence, and exit by aliens; and the Occupational Safety and Health Administration (OSHA), within the Department of Labor, attempts to ensure that places of work are free from hazards affecting the health and safety of workers.

Independent agencies, such as the Federal Emergency Management Agency (FEMA), Selective Service System, the National Foundation on the Arts and Humanities, and Small Business Administration (SBA), share characteristics in common with independent regulatory commissions and cabinet departments. Independent agencies are accountable to the president for direction and control; they have a single, administrative leader, and they are not positioned within a cabinet department.

The **government corporations,** such as AMTRAK, a passenger railroad; Federal Deposit Insurance Corporation (FDIC), an insurance company; Tennessee Valley Authority (TVA), an electric power generating facility; or the U.S. Postal Service, a post office, issue regulations as well. Such public corporations are multiheaded (with a board of directors), however, the president may dismiss corporation board members.

Distrust and dislike of the chief executive encouraged establishment of independent regulatory commissions. A powerful clientele group, such as the environmental lobby, called for the promotion and protection of a particular concern or interest within a single-headed independent agency. An agency within a department may seek refuge there from hostile or corrupt influences.

The total administrative regulatory process includes ten procedures, or steps. Most regulatory activities do not include touching all ten bases, either because the rule is obeyed without discussion or controversy or the agency does not actively enforce the regulation. The procedures or steps of the administrative regulatory process are identified in table 12-1.

TABLE **12–1** Steps of Administrative Regulatory Process

Step 1:	Authorizing Legislation
Step 2:	Agency Interpretation-Enforcement (rule-making)
Step 3:	Complaint
Step 4:	Investigation
Step 5:	Informal Proceedings
Step 6:	Prosecution
Step 7:	Formal Hearing (adjudication)
Step 8:	Agency Review
Step 9:	Judicial Review
Step 10:	Agency Enforcement

Source: Florence Heffron and Neil McFeeley, *The Administrative Regulatory Process,* 1983, 17. Reprinted by permission of Addison-Wesley Educational Publications.

ECONOMIC, SOCIAL, AND SUBSIDIARY REGULATIONS

The regulatory establishment expanded dramatically between 1970 and 1975. Between 1975 and 1980, regulatory expenditures increased 27 percent. From 1980 to 1985 costs decreased by 3 percent. Reagan's attempts to shut down the regulatory establishment came to a halt in 1984. Growth in the regulatory establishment resumed between 1985 and 1990, rising by 18 percent, making up lost time for the previous period.

Priorities for the broad, regulatory categories changed significantly in the 1970–1990 period. Spending for job safety and other working conditions increased by 217 percent between 1970 and 1980 and decreased by 13 percent between 1980 and 1990. Between 1970 and 1980 spending for industry-specific regulation increased by 66 percent but decreased by 23 percent from 1980 until 1990, reflecting Reagan's attempts to halt regulatory activities. Consumer safety and health regulatory expenditures decreased between 1980 and 1990, but less dramatically.

The 1970–1990 period saw a 46 percent increase in the number of regulatory personnel, with all but 3 percent of this rise coming between 1970 and 1975. Between 1970 and 1975, staffing for social regulatory activities jumped 50 percent. As the number of personnel employed by the regulatory bureaucracy grew greatly, so did its intrusion into the everyday decision-making processes of the private sector. Regulatory staffing patterns declined during the 1980–1985 period however, as there were 15 percent fewer personnel in 1985 than in 1980.[8]

In 1970, less than 70,000 employees staffed regulatory agencies for the federal government. In 1999, 127,927 employees were expected to act on regulatory matters. There are nearly 5,000 regulations in effect. About 65,000 new and modified regulations are published each year in *The Federal Register.*

TABLE 12–2 Percentage Distribution of Regulatory Costs

Federal Requirements	1977	1995
Environmental and Risk Reduction	12%	33%
Price and Entry Controls	67	34
Paperwork	21	33

Source: Thomas D. Hopkins, *Regulatory Costs in Profile* (St. Louis: Center for the Study of American Business, Policy Study Number 132, August, 1996), page 12.

The regulatory costs and federal requirements have shifted over the decades. See Table 12–2 for a profile of regulatory costs over an 18-year period.

According to Thomas Hopkins, costs of compliance with federal regulation cost $677 billion (or over $3,000 per capita) in 1996 and is estimated to cost $721 billion in the year 2000.[9] Hopkins identifies three groups of federal regulation compliance requirements.

- **Environmental and risk reduction regulations** attempt to lessen pollution and other societal risks. These include air emission and water pollution, solid waste disposal regulation, handling and labeling of hazardous materials, noise regulations, superfund compliance, and nuclear power safety.
- **Price and entry control regulations** restrict rates on business entry and include government controls on labor markets and on product prices and availability. Components include price and entry control regulations on international trade regulations, wage and hour standards (overtime, minimum wage, Davis-Bacon wages), regulations on pricing and marketing of agricultural products and services, energy rate and conservation regulations, and transporation price and entry restrictions.
- **Paperwork regulations** entail tax compliance procedures and related paperwork requirements, the latter of which do not have a direct social or economic function. Taxpayers spend time complying with the intricacies of the tax code.[10]

Tables 12–3 and 12–4 illustrate spending and staffing priorities for the federal government's regulatory agencies. Costs of staffing for private sector compliance with regulations notwithstanding, estimates for the 1999 federal budget call for sixty-one federal economic and social regulatory agencies to spend $17.9 billion in compliance regulatory activities. Public sector expenditures are a small proportion of the total cost of regulation by society. Regulatory behaviors fall into three categories—economic, social, and subsidiary regulations.

ECONOMIC REGULATIONS

What we will call *Regulation I,* or *economic regulation,* per Warren and Chilton (1989), focuses upon market aspects of industrial behavior, including rates, quality, and quantity of service, and competitive practices within a specific industry, or segment of the economy. Categories of economic regulation include finance and banking, industry-specific regulation, and general business regulation. The Comptroller of the Currency, Farm Credit Administration, Federal Deposit Insurance Corporation, Federal Reserve Banks, and National Credit Union Administration are regulators for finance and banking activities. The Commodity Futures Trading Commission, Federal Communications Commission, Federal Energy Regulatory Commission, Federal Maritime Commission, and Interstate Commerce Commission deal with industry-specific regulations. The Patent and Trademark Office in the Department of Commerce, Antitrust Division in the Department of Justice, Federal Election Commission, Federal Trade Commission, and Securities and Exchange Commission are general business regulators, dealing with agencies not directly related to finance and banking nor industry specific. Economic regulation is usually industry specific and focuses on market structure and firm conduct, regulating entry, exit, merger, and rates within markets.[11] For example, the ICC regulates railroads and trucking and the FCC regulates communications. The ICC and FCC each concentrate on a specific industry and each agency has no other responsibilities. Regulation I also concerns enforcement of congressionally mandated antitrust policies. The Justice Department and FTC regulate the frequency of mergers and combinations within particular industries. The goal of antitrust policies is maintaining and restoring competition within the market system. Competition and economic efficiency are objectives of Regulation I.

One of the most criticized forms of economic regulation is the effort of the FTC to demand that businesses tell consumers the truth, the whole truth, and nothing but the truth. The disclosure of full and accurate information by business, however, should prove compatible for desired outcomes of sellers and buyers in the market system. The most active economic regulatory agencies for spending remained relatively stable over the 1970–1990 period. Federal spending on economic regulation is expected to climb to nearly $3.6 billion in 1999, or an increase of 1.1 percent over 1998.

In finance and banking, the agency expected to enhance its funding in 1999 is the National Credit Union Administration. This regulatory agency, an independent agency expected to grow its budget by two percent from 1998 to 1999, regulates and insures federal credit unions and insures state-chartered credit unions that apply and qualify for share insurance. The Farm Credit Administration, responsible for ensuring safe and sound operation of banks, associations, affiliated service organizations, and other entities that collectively comprise the Farm Credit System, suffered a *13.1 percent decrease in its* spending authority. The Federal Deposit Insurance Corporation (FDIC), an independent agency established in 1933 to promote and preserve public confidence in banks and to protect the money supply through provision of insurance coverage for bank deposits, confronted an 11.6 percent spending reduction. The comptroller of the currency—the administrator of national banks that encountered a 1 percent cutback in spending —executes laws relating to national banks and promulgates rules and regulations governing the operations of approximately 4,000 national banks and District of Columbia banks.

TABLE 12–3 Summary of Spending on Federal Regulatory Activity (Fiscal Years, Millions of Dollars in "Obligations") Constant 1992 Dollars

Social Regulation	1960	1970	1980	1990	1995
Consumer Safety and Health	$1,073	$2,320	$3,889	$4,054	$4,826
Job Safety and Other Working Conditions	150	418	1,247	1,071	1,116
Environment	90	699	2,733	4,449	4,809
Energy	52	209	911	494	541
Total Social Regulation	$1,365	$3,646	$8,780	$10,068	$11,292
Economic Regulation					
Finance and Banking	$ 129	$ 281	$ 599	$1,154	$1,286
Industry-Specific Regulation	210	297	462	342	449
General Business	202	376	588	794	1,148
Total Economic Regulation	$ 541	$ 954	$1,649	$2,290	$2,883
GRAND TOTAL	$1,906	$4,600	$10,429	$12,358	$14,175
Annualized Percentage Change		9.2%	8.5%	1.7%	1.4%

	(Estimate)				%Change	
Social Regulation	1996	1997	1998	1999	1997–98	1998–99
Consumer Safety and Health	$4,982	$5,081	$5,387	$5,447	6.0%	1.1%
Job Safety and Other Working Conditions	1,066	1,098	1,105	1,175	0.6%	6.3%
Environment	4,136	4,484	5,367	5,228	19.7%	–2.6%
Energy	490	462	440	441	–4.8%	0.2%
Total Social Regulation	$10,674	$11,125	$12,299	$12,291	10.6%	–0.1%
Economic Regulation						
Finance and Banking	$1,309	$1,360	$1,363	$1,294	0.2%	–5.1%
Industry-Specific Regulation	396	396	418	421	5.6%	0.6%
General Business	1,223	1,244	1,226	1,327	–1.4%	8.2%
Total Economic Regulation	$2,928	$3,000	$3,007	$3,042	0.2%	1.2%
GRAND TOTAL	$13,602	$14,125	$15,306	$15,333	8.4%	0.2%
Annualized Percentage Change	–4.0%	3.8%	8.4%	0.2%		

Source: Melinda Warren and William F. Lauber, *Regulatory Changes and Trends: An Analysis of the 1999 Federal Budget* (St. Louis: Washington University, Center for the Study of American Business, St. Louis, Mo: October 1998) p. 2. Reprinted with permission.

TABLE 12–4 Summary of Staffing of Federal Regulatory Activity (Fiscal Years, Full-time Equivalent Employment)

Social Regulation	1970	1980	1990	1995	1996
Consumer Safety and Health	41,270	53,095	49,293	58,703	59,253
Job Safety and Other Working Conditions	6,486	17,894	13,610	12,592	11,956
Environment	4,525	14,958	17,646	22,110	20,747
Energy	219	5,433	3,441	3,349	3,213
Total Social Regulation	52,500	91,380	83,990	96,754	95,169
Economic Regulation					
Finance and Banking	4,969	9,524	13,049	15,830	14,171
Industry-Specific Regulation	5,675	7,483	4,629	4,788	4,206
General Business	6,609	9,251	9,611	11,246	11,318
Total Economic Regulation	17,253	26,258	27,289	31,864	29,727
GRAND TOTAL	69,753	117,638	111,279	128,618	124,896
Annualized Percentage Change					–2.9%

	(Estimate)			% Change	
Social Regulation	1997	1998	1999	1997–98	1998–99
Consumer Safety and Health	58,138	60,196	59,899	3.5%	–0.5%
Job Safety and Other Working Conditions	11,963	12,322	12,686	3.0%	3.0%
Environment	20,540	21,613	22,455	5.2%	3.9%
Energy	3,145	3,079	3,051	–2.1%	–0.9%
Total Social Regulation	93,786	97,210	98,091	3.7%	0.9%
Economic Regulation					
Finance and Banking	13,589	13,363	12,664	–1.7%	–5.2%
Industry-Specific Regulation	4,063	4,202	4,223	3.4%	0.5%
General Business	11,318	11,898	12,949	5.1%	8.8%
Total Economic Regulation	28,970	29,463	29,836	1.7%	1.3%
GRAND TOTAL	122,756	126,673	127,927	3.2%	1.0%
Annualized Percentage Change	–1.7%	3.2%	1.0%		

Source: Melinda Warren and William F. Lauber, *Regulatory Changes and Trends: An Analysis of the 1999 Federal Budget* (St. Louis: Washington University, Center for the Study of American Business, St. Louis, Mo: October 1998) p. 2. Reprinted with permission.

In industry-specific regulation, the Commodity Futures Trading Commission (CFTC) received an 11.8 percent budget increase for promoting healthy economic growth, protecting the rights of customers, and ensuring fairness and integrity in the marketplace through regulation of futures trading. Congress voted the Federal Energy Regulatory Commission a slight increase in spending to set rates and charges for the transportation and sale of natural gas and for the transmission and sale of electricity and the licensing of hydroelectric power projects. The Federal Maritime Commission, regulator of waterborne foreign and domestic offshore commerce of the United States, and the Federal Communications Commission, regulator of interstate and foreign communications by radio, television, wire, satellite, and cable, suffered slight spending declines.

In general business, the Securities and Exchange Commission (8.2 percent), the Patent and Trademark Office (9.3 percent), the International Trade Commission (11 percent), and Federal Election Commission (FEC) (18.1 percent) were in line to receive budget increases over the 1998–1999 period. The growth of the FEC budget focuses on salaries for workers investigating campaign finance laws.[12] (See Tables 12-3 and 12-4 for economic regulatory spending and staffing patterns for the 1999 federal budget.)

SOCIAL REGULATIONS

Regulation II, or *social regulation,* controls the nature and types of goods and services and production processes.

Social regulations entail consumer safety and health, job safety and working conditions, environment, and energy. Consumer safety and health regulators include the Consumer Product Safety Commission; Departments of Agriculture, Health and Human Services, Housing and Urban Development, Justice, Transportation, Treasury; and the National Transportation Safety Board. Job safety and working conditions regulators include the Employment Standards Administration and Occupational Safety and Health Administration in the Department of Labor, Equal Employment Opportunity Commission, and National Labor Relations Board. Environmental regulators include Army Corps of Engineers in the Department of Defense, Fish and Wildlife Service, Office of Surface Mining Reclamation and the Enforcement in the Department of Interior, and the Environmental Protection Agency. Energy regulators include the Economic Regulatory Administration in the Department of Energy and Nuclear Regulatory Commission.[13]

Social regulation usually cuts across industries, regulating issues such as employment opportunity, environmental protection, and occupational safety.[14] Social regulation assumes control or elimination of socially harmful impacts occurring as by-products of the production process and protection of consumers and the public from unsafe or unhealthy products. If conservatives find Regulation I unpopular, they believe Regulation II an anathema. Regulation II focuses upon the subtle regulation of clean air, occupational safety, poison prevention, boat safety, lead-based paint elimination, product safety, political

THE FTC AS THE FOURTH BRANCH OF GOVERNMENT

The Federal Trade Commission develops, evaluates, and implements consumer protection policies as the following Regulation I (economic) and Regulation II (social) decisions illustrate:

Toys Limited International Inc., and its principals, have agreed to settle Federal Trade Commission charges that they violated the Commission's Franchise Rule. This case was brought as one of the eighteen enforcement actions initiated under "Operation Trade Name Games," a cooperative law enforcement effort between the FTC and several state attorneys general. Operation Trade Name Games targeted scam artists who used the allure of selling trademarked products of well-known manufacturers—such as The Walt Disney Company, Warner Bros., The Coca-Cola Company, Pepsi-Cola Company—to hook would-be entrepreneurs. August 26, 1998.

Gateway 2000 has agreed to pay $290,000 as part of a settlement with the Federal Trade Commission. The FTC alleges that Gateway made numerous false statements in advertising its refund policy and its on-site warranty service. According to the FTC, Gateway's ads stated that it would provide free "on-site service" to consumers upon request, when such was not the case. Under the proposed settlement, in addition to paying $290,000, Gateway would be prohibited from, among other things, misrepresenting its money-back guarantee policy and its on-site service provision. July 22, 1998.

Students planning vacation getaways over *spring break* could be taken for a ride if they aren't careful consumers, according to the Federal Trade Commission. A new FTC Fact Sheet, "Avoid A Spring Break Bust," warns that flights for many spring break trips are by public charters, which have different rules than commerical flights. Lots of students don't get the trip they planned because they don't take the time to evaluate the promotion and make sure it's not run by a fly-by-night company. February 24, 1998.

The Federal Trade Commission has agreed to a final stipulated judgment and permanent injunction that brings to a close its pending lawsuit against *Pantron I Corporation* and its owner, Hal Z. Lederman. According to the FTC, Pantron and Lederman were pioneers of the program-length commercial or "infomercial." Between 1985 and 1990, they sold $100 million worth of a purported baldness cure, the "Helsinki Formula," through the widely disseminated "Discover with Robert Vaughan" infomercial. The proposed settlement prohibits the defendants from representing that the "Helsinki Formula" products will cure or prevent baldness. February 27, 1997.

The Federal Trade Commission has obtained a settlement agreement from *Jenny Craig, Inc.* to resolve deceptive advertising charges in connection with the diet program's claims about weight loss, weight loss maintenance, price and safety, as well as its use of consumer testimonials and endorsements. May 29, 1997.

The operators of the nationwide *Pizzeria Uno* restaurant chain have agreed to settle Federal Trade Commission allegations that advertising touting a line of thin crust pizzas as "low fat" was false and misleading. To settle the charges, the chain has agreed not to misrepresent the existence or amount of fat or any other nutrient or substance in pizzas or other food products containing a baked crust. January 22, 1997.

Bonlar Loan Co., Inc., a Chicago-based finance company that makes small loans to low-income consumers who often have poor credit histories, has agreed to settle Federal Trade Commission charges that it systematically violated requirements of the Equal Credit Opportunity Act (ECOA) and its implementing Regulation B and the Fair Credit Reporting Act (FCRA) when taking the processing consumer loan applications. The settlement prohibits Bonlar from violating the ECOA and FCRA in the future and requires payment of a $40,000 civil penalty. October 20, 1997.

The Federal Trade Commission is seeking comments from the public on whether to repeal its *Dry Cell Battery Rule,* which prohibits representations that dry cell batteries will not leak. The FTC promulgated the Dry Cell Battery Rule in 1964, based on its finding that, despite efforts by manufacturers to eliminate electrolyte leakage, dry cell batteries continued to leak and cause damage in ordinary use. The FTC is conducting a review of the rule as part of an overall effort to update its regulations and guides and eliminate those that are no longer necessary or useful. March 25, 1997.

The FTC approves sale of Dewar's Scotch, Bombay Gin, and Bombay Sapphire gin brands to *Bacardi & Company Limited* for $1.9 billion. Diageo is the new company formed as a result of the merger of Guinness plc and Grand Metropolitan plc. The sale was required by the FTC as part of the agency's approval of the Guinness and Grand Met merger. The merger of Guinness and Grand Met, the Commission alleged, raised significant competitive concerns in the United States market for premium Scotch and premium gin. June 11, 1998.

The *Internet* is quickly becoming the marketplace of choice for deceitful telemarketers and a new generation of fraud that uses increasingly sophisticated technology. The Internet allows fraud promoters to mimic legitimate businesses more convincingly and reaches potential victims more efficiently than ever. The FTC report, "Fighting Consumer Fraud: New Tools of the Trade," highlights the FTC's recent experience with fraud in cyberspace: how it occurs and how the agency has refashioned the "tools" of its trade to fight it. April 17, 1998.

The Federal Trade Commission issued an administrative challenge to the $40 million proposed merger of *Lucy Lee Hospital,* owned by Tenet Healthcare Corporation (Tenet), and *Doctors Regional Medical Center* (DRMC), the only two general hospitals in Popular Bluff, Missouri. According to the FTC's complaint, the acquisition would eliminate price, cost, and quality competition that now exists between these two hospitals and put consumers at risk of paying more for health care. August 20, 1998.

The Federal Trade Commission announced results of inspections of *New Jersey funeral homes* for compliance with Consumer Protection Law. The FTC used test shoppers from the American Association of Retired Persons (AARP), who visited thirty-six funeral homes to determine whether the homes provide consumers with a copy of an itemized general price list, a key requirement of the FTC's Funeral Rule. Five funeral homes were in violation of the FTC's Funeral Rule. All five agreed to enroll in the new Funeral Rule Offenders Program (FROP). July 17, 1997.

Source: Federal Trade Commission web site, www.ftc.gov.

campaigns, pesticide control, water pollution, noise control, flood disaster, energy, commodity futures trading, hazardous materials transportation, and similar potential abuses.

Regulation II covers more industries and directly affects more consumers than Regulation I. For example, OSHA's regulations govern the activities of every employer whose business affects commerce. In other words, government is involved with detailed, sometimes minute, facets of the production process.

Two concerns are raised by Regulation II. First, the apparatus of the presidency concentrates significant power and influence regulating health, safety, and environmental activities. Second, the accretion of new regulatory powers and controls could undermine citizens' faith in government, a negative reaction to overstrengthening of government and regulatory excesses of the mid-1970s.

Social regulation may be costly because certain regulatory decisions are grounded in grossly inadequate information. Even if information is forthcoming, regulatory decisions may reflect the most extreme and unrealistic assumptions about the problem's potential social interference. There could be strong resistance to alternative and innovative problem solutions. The ranking of the top ten social regulatory agencies during the 1970s and 1980s illustrates interesting changes in federal regulatory priorities.

The federal government was to spend $14.3 billion on social regulations in 1999, or a 0.1 percent decrease from the previous year. Staffing at social regulatory agencies was projected to increase by 0.9 percent, to 98,091, in fiscal year 1999.[15]

In consumer safety and health, Congress funded spending increases for Federal Highway Administration, Federal Aviation Administration (FAA), Food Safety and Inspection Service, and Agricultural Marketing Service during the 1999 fiscal year. The FAA spending increases, 19.2 percent in 1998 and 6.3 percent in 1999, provides for net increases of 185 air traffic controllers, 150 maintenance technicians, and 45 aviation safety inspectors and overall certification personnel.

In job safety and related working conditions, Congress increased the regulatory spending of the Equal Employment Opportunity Commission (EEOC) by 14.1 percent, Employment Standards Administration by almost 7 percent, and Occupational Safety and Health Administration (OSHA) by 4.6 percent. The EEOC budget increases provided for an additional 253 positions to reduce the backlog of some 65,000 individual complaints and an expanded mediation program.

In environment, the Environmental Protection Agency (EPA) was expected to add 936 staff personnel, or nearly a 6 percent enhancement over fiscal 1997. EPA's personnel number, 18,121, is the largest of any regulatory agency. The agency, with a budget of $5.2 billion, spends about 85 percent of environmental regulatory funds and 29 percent of the total regulatory dollars in 1999. (See tables 12-3 and 12-4 for spending and staffing priorities for social regulatory agencies.)[16]

SUBSIDIARY REGULATIONS

Regulation III, or *subsidiary regulation,* entails all regulatory activities accompanying Social Security, Medicare, Medicaid, Aid to Families with Dependent Children (AFDC), food stamps, veterans' benefits programs, Internal Revenue Service regulatory concerns, and categorical grant program regulations. Clientele of subsidiary regulations include individuals or state and local governments.

The general public has mixed feelings toward Regulation III. Americans would like to believe that there is no such thing as a free lunch. Freeloaders, welfare cheats, and food stamp chiselers bring on citizen suspicion, mistrust, and hostility. Most Americans do, however, consider Social Security, unemployment compensation, or veterans' benefits as legitimate. Unless there are clear and specific regulations for such benefit programs, the opportunities for cheating are almost limitless, making the costs and benefits of Regulation III difficult to quantify. Programs range from deciding eligibility for benefit programs to providing equal sports opportunities for women in college and equal educational opportunities for the handicapped. Costs are largely intangible; the market value is not readily apparent.

Economic, social, and subsidiary regulations are diverse, contradictory, and value laden. The growth of administrative regulatory power changes responsibilities and relationships among branches and levels of government. Regulations control or restrict one's choices and/or behavior, and are blamed for all sorts of societal ills, including inflation, recession, the demise of the family, individual initiative, and the federal system. Despite criticisms, the societal conditions demanding counterbalance to the vast power that private corporations and industry exercise over the lives, health, safety, and happiness of Americans are still evident. In addition, nationwide polls indicate that the American public supports, generally, the concept of regulations.[17]

When the Reagan administration came to power in 1981, one of its goals was to trim down the federal regulatory agencies. Attempts to "rein in the regulatory establishment," however, "virtually ceased in fiscal 1983.[18]In the first two years of the administration, budgets and staffing were reduced across the board. But in the last six years of the Reagan administration, expenditures for regulatory agencies (especially the Environmental Protection Agency) increased at a pace similar to the growth that took place under the Carter administration. Staffing increased as well, but "has not yet returned to the previous growth rate.[19]

ADMINISTRATIVE RULES AND RULE-MAKING

Rule-making and adjudication are not the same process. Rule-making, in general, focuses on the future and is broad in scope. Adjudication is particular, focusing upon an instance in the present or the past. Prior to the adjudication

FTC ALLEGES RAMSES CONDOM AD CLAIMS WERE DECEPTIVE

The second-largest condom manufacturer in the United States, London International, has agreed to settle Federal Trade Commission charges that its ads claiming that Ramses brand condoms are 30 percent stronger than the leading brand of condom and break 30 percent less often are unsubstantiated and deceptive.

The agreement to settle the charges will prohibit comparative claims about the strength, efficacy, or risk of breakage of any condom in the future unless London possesses and relies upon competent and reliable scientific evidence to back up the claims.

"It is vital to substantiate claims like these because they affect the health and safety of millions of Americans," said Jodie Bernstein, director of the FTC's Bureau of Consumer Protection, "Consumers need reliable information about this product to make informed personal choices."

Public health organizations believe that latex condoms are usually efficacious when used properly. According to the Centers for Disease Control, "Condoms are classified as medical devices and are regulated by the Food and Drug Administration. Every latex condom manufactured in the United States is tested for defects before it is packaged."

London International Group, Inc., based in Norcross, Georgia, advertises Ramses condoms in major magazines, including *Rolling Stone, Ebony Man,* and *People.*

According to the complaint detailing the charges, ads that claimed Ramses had " . . . 30% more strength than the leading brand," and were " . . . 30% stronger than the leading brand," suggest that Ramses brand condoms are 30 percent stronger and break 30 percent less often than the leading brand. According to the complaint, London did not possess adequate substantiation to support the claims.

The agreement to settle the charges would prohibit London from making any comparative claims about the strength, the risk of breakage, or the efficacy of any condom unless it relies on competent and reliable scientific evidence that substantiates the claim. The Commission vote to accept the proposed settlement was 4–0. A summary of the proposed consent agreement was published in the *The Federal Register.* The FCC decision was subject to public comment for sixty days, after which the commission made its decision final. Comments on similar FTC decisions may be addressed to Office of Secretary, FTC, 6th Street and Pennsylvania Avenue, N.W., Washington, DC 20580.

NOTE: A consent agreement is for settlement purposes only and does not constitute an admission of law violation. When the commission issues a consent order on a final basis, it carries the force of law with respect to future actions. Each violation of such an order may result in a civil penalty of $11,000.

Source: Federal Trade Commission, www.ftc.gov.

of a person's rights, the individual is entitled to a hearing under the Due Process Clause of the Fifth Amendment for federal agencies and the Fourteenth Amendment for state agencies. The development of administrative rules follows the commercial development of the American west, tragedies of transportation accidents, development of the federal government as collector of revenues, government as benefit provider, and the populist rebuttal to the exploitation of the farmer by the rail trust.[20]

Regulatory law and administrative law, as stated earlier, work in tandem, but are not the same thing. *Congress does not like controversy.* Congress is a provincial political institution. In other words, members of Congress do not enjoy conflict-laden issues where they are likely to have constituents split over the solutions. Each member of Congress comes from a narrow, provincial, political base. Each member of Congress looks out for his or her district's narrow economic interests and not those of the entire nation. Partly because Congress is composed of politicians representing 535 political jurisdictions, they pass laws that do not speak clearly. It is not difficult, therefore, to explain the presence of vague, ambiguous, and general laws that allow human discretion.

Administrative agencies serve to interpret the vagueness, ambiguity, and generality of these laws. For example, the FCC, by rule, restricts the number of commercial broadcasting stations a private corporation may operate. The IRS, by rule, determines which groups in society must pay or are exempted from paying taxes. The FCC creates communications law; the IRS makes tax law. Independent regulatory commissions, cabinet agencies, independent agencies, public corporations, and the EOP have similar functions.

THE ADMINISTRATIVE PROCEDURE ACT

The Administrative Procedure Act, although not a comprehensive code of administrative procedure, provides a general framework of fundamental importance. The APA, in the minds of some authorities, serves as the "Magna Carta of Administrative Law." Regulatory law regulates citizen behaviors; administrative law oversees the administrative discretion of bureaucrats.

Judges interpret legal statements and prescribe the procedures that agencies and their employees follow. Judicial interpretation originates from Constitutions; primary, but not exclusive, origin for interpretation comes from due process clauses. Judges also interpret administrative procedure statutes, if applicable; some clauses within a statute require agencies to follow certain procedures, including conducting a full hearing of the concern. Administrative law, meanwhile, applies legal principles originating from statutes, common law, constitutions, and regulatory law.[21] Public administrators, as implementors of regulatory law, implement rules. The terms rule and regulation are nearly synonymous. Unless rules are successfully undermined in a lawsuit as unconstitutional, rules have the force of law. What is a rule? The APA defines a rule as:

> *the whole or a part of an agency statement of general or particular applicability and future effect designed to implement, interpret, or prescribe law or policy or describing the organization, procedure, or practice requirements of an agency and includes the approval or prescription of the future of rates, wages, corporate or financial structures or reorganizations thereof, prices, facilities, appliances, services or allowances therefor or of valuations, costs, or practices bearing on any of the foregoing.*[22]

TYPES OF AGENCY RULES

There are four types of agency rules. Legislative or substantive rules, presuming they are authorized by statute, do not exceed or contradict the statute, and are applied according to correct procedure, having the force and effect of law. Interpretative rules advise clientele on what the agency interprets a statute or regulation to mean. Interpretative rules examine the construction of a law that an agency administers. Procedural rules regulate an agency's internal practices. All agencies establish rules governing their own procedures. General policy statements are philosophical commentary and are not accountable to the rule-making provisions of the APA. Procedural, interpretative, and general policy statements are published in *The Federal Register*.

Source: Stanley A. Reigel and P. John Owen, *Administrative Law: The Law of Government Agencies* (Ann Arbor, Mich.: Ann Arbor Science, The Butterworth Group, 1982), 39–59.

The first of the two types of rule-making delineated by the APA is informal or "notice and comment" rule-making. The characteristics of this procedure are advance notice and public participation. Notice of proposed rule-making gives the time, place, and nature of the rule-making proceeding, refers to the authority, or statute, under which the rule is proposed, and includes the terms or substance of the proposed rule or a description of the subjects and issues therein.

The second type of rule-making, "on the record" formal rule-making, occurs when a "trial-type" hearing precedes rules. The trial-type hearing is an adversarial process entailing production of evidence, testimony by witnesses, cross-examination, and representation by counsel. The more formal requirements apply when a statute determines that rules must be cited "on the record after opportunity for an agency hearing." *The Federal Register* and *The Code of Federal Regulations* publish notices of proposed rule-making. The Federal Register Act of 1935 established a system of federal rules publication. The act designated *The Federal Register* as the official publication of federal rules, regulations, orders, and other documents of "general applicability and legal effect." On March 14, 1936, *The Federal Register* began publishing every day, Monday through Friday. In 1936, *The Register* published 2,619 pages of rules, orders, and other actions. In 1980, or more than forty years later, *The Register* totaled more than 87,000 pages.[23] After each year, the issues of *The Register* are bound and indexed. The regulations published *The Federal Register* for the preceding year are codified with regulations previously issued and still in effect. *The Code of Federal Regulations*, a collection of paperback books grouped together by agency, is divided into fifty titles, as each title more or less represents a particular agency or a broad subject area. Table 12-5 illustrates *The Federal Register* format.

TABLE 12–5 Proposed Rules

This section of *The Federal Register* contains notices to the public of the proposed issuance of rules and regulations. The purpose of these notices is to give interested persons an opportunity to participate in the rule making prior to the adoption of the final rules.

DEPARTMENT OF TRANSPORTATION

Federal Aviation Administration
14 CFR Part39
[Docket No. 98-NM-132-AD]
RIN 2120-AA64

Airworthiness Directives; Airbus Model A300, A310, and A300-600 Series Airplanes

AGENCY
Federal Aviation Administration, DOT.

ACTION
Notice of proposed rulemaking (NPRM).

SUMMARY
   This document proposes the adoption of a new airworthiness directive (AD) that is applicable to certain Airbus Model A300, A310, and A300-600 series airplanes. This proposal would require a one-time operational test and repetitive functional tests of the free fall control mechanism of the main landing gear (MLG), and corrective action, if necessary.

DATES
   Comments must be received by June 15, 1998.

ADDRESSES
   Submit comments in triplicate to the Federal Aviation Administration(FAA), Transport Airplane Directorate, ANM-114, Attention:Rules Docket No. 98-NM-132-AD, 1601 Lind Avenue, SW, Renton, Washington 98055-4056. Comments may be inspected at this location between 9:00 a.m. and 3:00 p.m., Monday through Friday, except Federal holidays.
   The service information referenced in the proposed rule may be obtained from Airbus Industrie, 1 Rond Point Maurice Bellonte, 31707 Blagnac Cedex, France.

FOR FURTHER INFORMATION, CONTACT:
   Norman B. Martenson, Manager, International Branch, ANM-116, FAA, Transport Airplane Directorate, 1601 Lind Avenue, SW, Renton, Washington 98055-4056; telephone (425) 227-2110; fax(425) 227-1149.

Continued

SUPPLEMENTARY INFORMATION:

Comments Invited

Interested persons are invited to participate in the making of the proposed rule by submitting such written data, views, or arguments as they may desire.

Comments are specifically invited on the overall regulatory, economic, environmental, and energy aspects of the proposed rule.

Availability of NPRMs

Any person may obtain a copy of this NPRM by submitting a request to the FAA, Transport Airplane Directorate, ANM-114, Attention: Rules Docket No. 98-NM-132-AD, 1601 Lind Avenue, SW., Renton, Washington 98055-4056.

Discussion

The Direction Generale de l'Aviation Civile (DGAC), which is the airworthiness authority for France, recently notified the FAA that an unsafe condition may exist on certain Airbus Model A300, A310, and A300-600 series airplanes. The DGAC advises that during training flights on two Airbus Model A300 series airplanes, the flight crew reported difficulty in extending the main landing gear(MLG) by means of the free fall control mechanism of the landing gear. The free fall control mechanism allows the flight crew to extend the landing gear in the event of failure of the hydraulic system that normally is used to extend the landing gear. A functional test of the free fall control mechanism on both airplanes revealed that this mechanism was rigged incorrectly, which caused the cockpit control handle of the free fall control mechanism to reach its mechanical stop before the MLG was released for extension by free fall.

Malfunction of the free fall control mechanism, if not corrected, could result in the inability to extend the MLG in the event of failure of the hydraulic extension system.

FAA's Conclusions

These airplane models are manufactured in France and are type certified for operation in the United States under the provisions of section 21.29 of the Federal Aviation Regulations (14 CFR 21.29) and the applicable bilateral airworthiness agreement. The FAA has examined the findings of the DGAC, reviewed all available information, and determined that AD action is necessary for products of this type design that are certified for operation in the United States.

Explanation of Requirements of Proposed Rule

Since an unsafe condition has been identified that is likely to exist or develop on other airplanes of the same type design registered in the United States, the proposed AD would require accomplishment of the actions specified in the AOT' and the service bulletins described previously.

Cost Impact

The FAA estimates that 24 Model A300 series airplanes, 41 Model, A310 series airplanes, and 61 Model A300-600 series airplanes of U.S. registry would be affected by this proposed AD. The cost impact of the proposed operational test on U.S. operators is estimated to be $22,680, or $180 per airplane. The cost impact of the proposed modification on U.S. operators of Model A300 and A300-600 series airplanes is estimated to be $356,150, or $4,190 per airplane. The cost impact of the proposed modification on U.S. operators of Model A310 series airplanes is estimated to be $220,990, or $5,390 per airplane.

Regulatory Impact

The regulations proposed herein would not have substantial direct effects on the States, on the relationship between the national government and the States, or on the distribution of power and responsibilities among the various levels of government. For the reasons discussed above, I certify that this proposed regulation: (1) Is not a "significant regulatory action" under Executive Order 12866; (2) is not a "significant rule" under DOT Regulatory Policies and Procedures (44 FR 11034, February 26, 1979); and (3) if promulgated, will not have a significant economic impact, positive or negative, or a substantial number of small entities under the criteria of the Regulatory Flexibility Act.

List of Subjects in 14 CFR Part 39

Air transportation, Aircraft, Aviation safety, Safety.

The Proposed Amendment

Accordingly, pursuant to the authority delegated to me by the Administrator, the Federal Aviation Administration proposes to amend part 39 of the Federal Aviation Regulations (14 CFR part 39) as follows:

PART 39—AIRWORTHINESS DIRECTIVES

1. The authority citation for part 39 continues to read as follows: **Authority:** 49 U.S.C. 106(g), 40113, 44701. **$39.13 [Amended]**
2. Section 39.13 is amended by adding the following new airworthiness directive: **Airbus Industrie:** Docket 98–NM–132–AD.

Issued in Renton, Washington, on May 7, 1998.
John J. Hickey
Acting Manager, Transport Airplane Directorate, Aircraft Certification Service
[FR Doc. 98–12807 Filed 5–13–98 8:45 am]
BILLING CODE 4910–13–U

Source: *The Federal Register,* 63, 93 Thursday, 14 May, 1998: 26742–26744.

RESTRAINT AND EXPANSION

Between 1970 and 1980, as measured in constant dollars, regulatory budgets nearly quadrupled. For example, during the decade of the 1970s, the FTC perceived its legislative mandate as a consumer police officer for the economy. For every six persons employed in federal regulatory activities in 1980 there were five employed in 1984. By 1988, the nation's federal regulatory agency employed 9 percent fewer persons than in 1980. The decline in regulatory staffing between 1980 and 1988 occurred in Consumer Safety and Health, Job Safety and Other Working Conditions, and Industry-Specific Regulation. With a 14 percent reduction in real terms from 1980 to 1984, regulatory budgets declined in the early 1980s.[24]

THE FEDERAL REGISTER AND THE CODE OF FEDERAL REGULATIONS

The Federal Register, published daily, Monday through Friday, provides a uniform system for making available to the public regulations and legal notices issued by federal departments and agencies. These include Presidential proclamations and Executive Orders and federal agency documents having general applicability and legal effect, documents required to be published by act of Congress and other federal agency documents of public interest.

The Code of Federal Regulations is a codification of the general and permanent rules published in The Federal Register by the Executive departments and agencies of the federal Government. The Code is divided into fifty titles which represent broad areas subject to federal regulation. Each title is subdivided into chapters which usually bear the name of the issuing agency. Each chapter is further subdivided into parts covering specific regulatory areas.

The Federal Register and The Code of Federal Regulations must be used together to determine the latest version of any given rule. Each volume of the Code contains amendments published in The Federal Register since the last revision of that volume of the Code. Source citations for the regulations are referred to by volume number and page number of The Federal Register and date of publication.

In the early 1980s President Reagan realized cuts in federal regulatory budgets, but these early reductions were more than countered by steady spending increases in the president's second term. In real dollars, the federal government spent 10 percent more on regulation in 1988 than was appropriated in 1980. The EPA, the largest of the regulatory agencies in terms of budgeting and staffing, experienced a 25 percent decline in spending on research and development in the 1981–1984 period, but Reagan was unable to convince members of Congress to keep EPA's regulatory budget at a low ebb. During the Reagan years, real spending for this agency increased by almost $1 billion, an increase of 63 percent. Growth in regulatory spending during the Reagan era increased by 62 percent in Finance and Banking, 34 percent in General Business, and 30 percent in Environment and Energy.

Therefore, the 1980s constitute an era of regulatory contradictions, restraint, and expansion in the financing of regulations and the workforce committed to such activities. For example, in General Business, the Antitrust Division of the Department of Justice and the FTC had a real spending cut by more than 25 percent since 1980, whereas the International Trade Administration and the International Trade Commission had a boost in real spending by 139 percent since 1980. The inconsistent efforts of the Reagan administration to reduce the size and costs of the regulatory establishment placed additional emphasis upon improving the substantive aspects of the statutes themselves, which empower agencies to make regulations. In other words, the quality of regulations are as important as the quantity of them.[25]

ADMINISTRATIVE RESPONSIBILITY

Administrative responsibility incorporates accountability, competence, fairness, and responsiveness. *Accountability* is answerability, answering, in particular, to someone or something outside the organization. Accountability also refers to direction and control, for if things go wrong, someone is held liable. *Competence* implies expertise, prudence, and care for consequences rather than negligence. Recognizable objective standards guide the formulation and implementation of public policy. *Fairness* combines the individual concern for due process with the notion of justice and is designed to protect the individual from arbitrary and capricious decisions. *Responsiveness* acknowledges an organization's yielding to citizen demands for policy change and entails initiation of proposed solutions for problems.

Source: Paul N. Tramontozzi with Kenneth W. Chilton, *U.S. Regulatory Agencies Under Reagan, 1980–1988* (St. Louis, Mo.: Center for the Study of Business, 1987), 11–14.

THE STAGES OF RULE-MAKING

Rule-making is easier understood by perceiving developments as a sequence of activities. All eleven stages are affected by the stages preceding it.[26]

Stage 1: Origin of Rule-Making Activity. Congress is the true origin of rule-making. No rule is valid unless it is authorized by law prescribed by Congress. The rule exists to promote a statutory purpose. The degree of agency discretion, procedural requirements, and volume and frequency of rules to be produced are matters dealt with in Stage 1.

Stage 2: Origin of Individual Rule-Making. Deadlines and hammers are prominent in this stage. Hammers provide that statutes will take effect on a certain date if the agency fails to issue an alternative regulation. Hammerers are used to convince agencies to expedite the rule-making process. Internal and external sources are available when rules are not explicitly mandated. Internal sources of ideas are political leadership, senior career service personnel, advisory committees, program office staff, office of the general counsel, field staff, and enforcement officials. External are not confined to the public sector. However, the White House, Congress, agencies, and citizen action are primary sources of ideas for writing better rules. The APA permits anyone to petition an agency to make a rule.

Stage 3: Authorization to Proceed with Rule-Making. This stage includes a priority-setting system and agency approval process. By establishing priorities throughout its jurisdiction, an agency controls the types of rules and sequencing of rules. Priority setting enables the agency to determine how it will respond to external demands and how the agency's resources devoted to rule-making will be allocated. Mechanisms to authorize rule-making vary dramatically. Some are highly structured and rigid. Others are permissive.

Stage 4: Planning the Rule-Making. Who in the agency is responsible for developing the rule, what is the objective of the rule being written, and how the public will be involved are pursuits of this stage. The content may not be determined at this stage. But the quality of work accomplished in this stage influences the ease and speed in which rule-making is carried out. Goals of the rule, legal requirements, technical and political information requirements, and participation plans occur at this stage. The securing of necessary resources and assignment of staff also take place at this juncture along the rule-making pathway.

Stage 5: Developing the Draft Rule. Collection of information, analysis of information, impact studies, internal consultations, informal external consultations, draft language of preamble and rule, and implementation plan dominate the activities of this stage. Impact studies include the following inquiries: Will the rule have an effect on the physical environment? Will it have a disproportionate impact on small businesses and other entities? Does it curtail in any way the normal legal prerogatives of state and local governments? Will it necessitate the collection and reporting of additional information?

Stage 6: Internal Review of the Draft Rule. Internal reviews occur horizontally and vertically. The horizontal review takes place across the agency. Various offices determine if the proposed rule has any effect on the areas under their jurisdiction. The influence of particular offices depends on the relative power that particular office enjoys in the bureaucratic pecking order. Vertical reviews involve supervisors and senior officials. Rules are developed at a relatively low level of the agency. This review allows supervisors and senior officials to monitor the consistency of agency programs.

Stage 7: External Review of the Draft Rule. The Office of Management and Budget, Congress, interest groups, and agencies participate at this stage of rule-making. OMB affects the substance and process of rules. If other agencies are affected by the contents of a new rule, they may be asked to examine the proposed new rule. Congress and interest groups will be consulted on the contents of the draft rule.

Stage 8: Revision and Publication of a Draft Rule. The guidelines of *The Federal Register* must be met. The specifications of *The Register* may require agencies to resubmit draft rules, thereby meeting the stringent guidelines of *The Register*. This stage is routine in rule-making but should not be underestimated.

Stage 9: Public Participation. This stage includes the receipt of written comment, conduct of public hearings, review and analysis of public input, and draft responses to public input. The choice between written comment and conduct of public hearings is more a matter of politics and public relations than the quality of input expected. In this stage, the agency must manage the receipt of comments, ensure that those submitted are retained, and then make them available in a location accessible to citizens.

Stage 10: Action on the Draft Rule. This stage is crucial. All essential technical and political information have been collected, and all internal and external constituencies have been heard from. For still-unfinished rule-making, several alternative paths may be taken:

1. When no changes are needed, the agency has succeeded in producing a draft that can stand as is. All that remains is the preparation of the appropriate notice for *The Federal Register* and final clearance by the OMB.

2. When only minor revisions are needed, those drafting the rule may circulate it for another round of internal and external reviews. If the revisions are minor, they will be made as a matter of form. Review of the final rule by the OMB is required, however.

3. Another round of participation is pursued only when comments by the public are unclear and raise issues that cannot be resolved internally. Usually, the notice issued will ask the public to respond to a specific set of questions.

4. When major revisions are needed the agency will, in effect, reproduce the process starting with Stage 5, because the changes constitute a new proposed rule.

5. Abandoning the rule-making and starting over is a more extreme version of option 4. Here the agency is convinced that its work was for naught and begins anew.

6. A rule-making is abandoned altogether if the agency is convinced that its decision to write a rule was wrong. It will notify the public that no rule will be issued through a notice in *The Federal Register.*[27]

Stage 11: Post-Rule-Making Activities. If rule-making works to everyone's expectations, this stage is not active. If rule-making is flawed, lawsuits are probable. Most rule-making alternatives are less dramatic, however. Staff may be called on to reinterpret vague or unclear provisions of a rule. Parties affected by the new rule may file petitions for reconsideration. Frequently agencies issue technical corrections or amendments of flawed rules. Rule-making is not a process that has a definite start and finish. Aspects of rules may be challenged and altered at any time in this process.

ADMINISTRATIVE RESPONSIBILITY: PROFESSIONALISM, PARTICIPATION, AND PUBLICITY

In casting about for answers to the question of responsibility, we are at the outset likely to come across the phrase, *"the public interest."* Many see the entire solution to the question neatly encapsulated in this phrase, as though an administrator need only resolve to serve the public interest and his or her problems concerning responsibility will vanish.

This solution, like so many other easy solutions to difficult problems, raises more questions than it answers. The most basic is this: *What is the public interest?* Walter Lippman once claimed that "The public interest may be what men would choose if they saw clearly, thought rationally, and acted disinterestedly and benevolently.[28] This leaves us with the task of defining "clear" vision and "rational" thought, concepts that, in practice, seem susceptible to varying interpretations. Even deciding what course of action is "benevolent" and "disinterested"

TYPES OF ACCOUNTABILITY

There are four types of accountability. *Bureaucratic accountability* entails an organized and legitimate superior/subordinate relationship with close supervision or a
surrogate system of standard operating procedures or clearly stated rules and regulations. *Legal accountability,* similar to bureaucratic accountability, is grounded upon
relationships between a controlling party outside the agency, typically composed of
lawmakers, and members of the organization. Bureaucratic accountability portrays
a hierarchical relationship, grounded upon the ability of supervisors to reward or
punish subordinates, while legal accountability presents a relationship of two relatively autonomous parties, involving a formal or implied trustee agreement between the public agency and its legal monitor. *Professional accountability* relies upon
skilled and expert employees for providing appropriate solutions. Deference to expertise within the agency is the key to professional accountability. *Political accountability* asks: Whom does the public administrator represent? The general public,
elected officials, agency heads, agency clientele, special interest groups, and future
generations constitute potential constituencies. The key relationship is between the
public administrator and his or her constituents.

Source: Barbara S. Romzek and Melvin J. Dubnick, "Accountability in the Public Sector: Lessons from the
Challenger Tragedy," *Public Administration Review* 47, no. 3 (May/June 1987): 227–238.

---

may produce more controversy than it settles. "It may be somewhat difficult for
some readers to accept the conclusion that there is no public interest theory worthy of the name," concluded political scientist Glendon Shubert.[29]

Another maxim that often presents itself is "following one's conscience." This,
too, fails to furnish a usable guideline. The enforcers of the Inquisition who burned
thousands of heretics at the stake felt they were following the most lofty appeals to
conscience. The same can be said for so many other appalling actions that people
have perpetrated on others. As Carl Friedrich noted, "Autocratic and arbitrary
abuse of power has characterized the officialdom of a government service bound
only by the dictates of conscience.[30] While Friedrich rules out the use of conscience
as a means of ensuring responsibility, he does have some positive ideas to offer in
its place. "We have a right to call such a policy irresponsible if it can be shown that
it was adopted without proper regard to the existing sum of human knowledge
concerning the technical issues involved; we have also a right to call it irresponsible if it can be shown that it was adopted without proper regard for existing preference in the community and more particularly its prevailing majority.[31]

In keeping with this admonition, Friedrich sees the solution to the question of
administrative responsibility lying in two areas: *professionalism* and *participation.*
Professionals usually have been conditioned to uphold certain standards, and
they usually subscribe to a code of ethics that governs the practice of their profession. As Friedrich sees it, professionalism constitutes something of an "inner
check" on administrative irresponsibility. Participation, meanwhile, means that

administrators must consult more interests and listen to more points of view. Allowing divergent parties to share in decision-making should make that process less arbitrary and subjective and more responsive and responsible.

To Friedrich's twin safeguards of professionalism and participation can be added a third protective device: *publicity*. Directing the public spotlight onto administrative decision-making should make such decision-making more responsible. Secrecy has rarely led to improved administrative decisions or better administrative behavior.

Professionalism, participation, and publicity do not in themselves guarantee responsible administration. Professionals can act irresponsibly, and shared decision-making can produce irresponsible decisions. Publicity can, on occasion, distort an administrator's perspective, because what is immediate "good press" is not always most beneficial to the public. These caveats notwithstanding, these three "Ps"—professionalism, participation, and publicity—provide a basis for better public management. As they become more a part of bureaucratic behavior, such behavior may move closer toward meeting the desires and demands of the American people.

SUMMARY

- The fragmentation and personalism of our political system makes the typical administrative agency an isolated entity, continually developing and maintaining sources of support. Administrators assume an activist role in developing that support. *Size, dispersion, degree of organization,* and *degree of passion, enthusiasm,* and *zeal* contribute to the effectiveness of an agency's clientele.
- Regulations take force because the market or markets fail or otherwise do not work effectively. U.S. regulatory activities began with the establishment of the Interstate Commerce Commission in 1887. Information is a scarce commodity. Decision makers cannot collect all relevant information. They act in a state of partial ignorance and uncertainty. They use the best source of information available: *what just has happened.* Government oversight and information occur in this perspective. Railroads, motor carriers, and airlines were deregulated. Public choice assumes that rational individuals pursue their own interests.
- *Advisory committees,* complaint handling, and public hearings play roles in developing strategies for support by clientele. *Advisory committees* serve as a two-way transmission system for communication, bringing clients' concerns to the agency and bringing the agency's problems to the clients.
- Two developments increase clientele effectiveness and influence in U.S. public bureaucracies. The *orientation* and *structure* of public agencies based on interest groups, or clientele, and the *administrative decentralization* of program functions enhance the power of clientele.
- The full scope of *regulatory power*—in addition to the power to formulate rules—includes the authority for interpreting laws and regulations, enforcing rules and regulations, trying cases concerning violations of those rules,

holding hearings for investigating and adjudicating such circumstances, and imposing sanctions on violators. Administrative regulatory power combines legislative, executive, and judicial powers.

- *Operational costs* for the federal regulatory establishment for fiscal year 1999 is $17.9 billion. Spending and staffing at the sixty-one regulatory departments and agencies are divided into two categories: *economic* and *social regulations*. Total staffing for economic regulation in 1999 was 29,836, a 1.3 percent increase over 1998. Total staffing at social regulatory agencies was 98,091, a 0.9 percent increase over 1998.

- *Economic regulation* is the more traditional, industry-specific form of regulation. These regulators employ economic controls such as price ceilings and service parameters. These departments and agencies regulate a broad base of activities in particular industries. Examples of economic regulatory agencies are the Federal Communications Commission (FCC), the Federal Deposit Insurance Corporation (FDIC), and the Federal Trade Commission (FTC).

- *Social regulation* focuses on achieving cleaner air, equal employment opportunity, safer work environments, and consumer safety. Social regulatory departments and agencies are limited to a specific issue, but their prerogatives include regulatory powers that penetrate and spread through industry boundaries. Illustrations are the Environmental Protection Agency (EPA), the Drug Enforcement Agency (DEA), and National Labor Relations Board (NLRB).

- *The Federal Register* provides a uniform system for making available to the public regulations and legal notices issued by federal departments and agencies. *The Register* includes presidential proclamations and Executive Orders and federal agency documents having general applicability and legal effect.

- *The Code of Federal Regulations* is a codification of the general and permanent rules published in *The Federal Register* by the executive departments and agencies of the federal government. *The Federal Register* and *The Code of Federal Regulations* are used in tandem to determine the latest version of any rule or regulation.

- Administrative power expands as the power and responsibilities of government expand. An industrialized, urbanized, interdependent society requires a more active role for government. The United States is a *regulatory state* where nearly all activities of organizations and individuals are part of administrative regulations and controls. There are three types of regulatory behaviors: *economic, social,* and *subsidiary.*

- Rule-making and adjudication are not the same. *Rule-making* is general and focuses upon the future. *Adjudication* is particular, focusing upon the present or the past. Administrative agencies interpret vagueness, ambiguity, and generality of laws; public administrators, as implementors of regulatory law, interpret rules. The terms "rules" and "regulations" are synonymous. There are four *types of agency rules:* legislative, or substantive, rules; interpretative rules; procedural rules; and general policy statements.

- *Administrative responsibility* entails the ideas of accountability, competence, fairness, and responsiveness. Executive control, pluralism, professionalism, and representative bureaucracy are especially important for achieving administrative responsibility. There are four types of *accountability:* bureaucratic, legal, professional, and political.
- *Professionalism, participation,* and *publicity* contribute significantly to administrative responsibility and provide a sound basis for better public management.

The following case portrays the social regulatory process in action. The case welds together the many subtle and not-so-subtle issues associated with public policy analysis and regulation. This topic is an interesting one, and although the topic might seem to be somewhat parochial in nature, it does cross the progrowth versus environmental impact; rural versus urban tensions; small versus large producer; and the old style versus new style technological and value concerns associated with livestock production in the United States.

CASE STUDY

Pigs, People, and Pollution.[32]

Country singer Willie Nelson led a march of angry independent hog farmers, rural activists, and environmental advocates to the makeshift platform that had been hurriedly erected on the steps of the state capitol. "We are declaring war on the corporate swine who are destroying the American hog farmer," proclaimed the seasoned populist singer and Farm Aid organizer to the large crowd of cheering, slogan-chanting, and placard-carrying protesters. As Nelson spoke of the erosion of the traditional, small family farm and the emergence of modern, corporate-owned, large-scale hog production factories, a thunderous applause, punctuated by boisterous shouts, erupted from the crowd. After all, they were there to protest policies that would allow large companies, many from other states, to set up their own hog raising facilities that confine thousands of animals to cages (3½ ft. x 7 ft.), located in dimly lighted hog barns.

Protestation and demonstration

The protesters had firsthand experience dealing with the megahog confinement facilities that had begun to dot the rural landscape. They had seen the farrow to finish operations and smelled the rancid odor that literally steamed off the open, aerobic manure lagoons and fouled the countryside breezes. They knew that a single corporate farm could raise nearly 10,000 pigs at one time, thereby replacing nearly 100 family-operated hog farms. Family farmers worried that they would be pushed completely out of the hog industry and they believed that a few extra pennies spent at the grocery store was a small price for the consuming public to pay for a pound of pork. Certainly, they mused, this is a paltry sum to pay to maintain "the most efficient food producer in the world—the American farmer."

Speakers at the rally proclaimed, "If thousands of farmers are forced to quit raising hogs on their own farms, they will stop paying taxes, stop buying products in town, and become unemployed. These corporations don't care about the schools, small businesses, churches, and families in local communities. They don't care to be good stewards of the land like an independent farmer. They only want to fatten their balance sheet by monopolizing your hog industry." Another said: "There are no simple, practical, and cost-effective methods to eliminate odors from livestock systems," and "I don't want to live next to a hog farm." Acknowledging where he lived, he further stated "that this hog industry is big, but hogs always stink." One disgruntled farmer said that "Right now, the big hog operations are using other people's air to dispose of their odors. They can't do that with the water anymore, or they pay for it." And a farm woman said "They're going to stink us out of house and home. You'd better not hang your clothes out to dry."

Environmental advocates also spoke at the rally about animal waste, water pollution, and odor problems caused by large, industrial hog operations. "Corporations are poisoning the landscape by pouring millions of gallons of raw pig sewage on the land, which ends up in the water we drink. The odor from these farms is so concentrated that the chemical emitted from the hog feces is actually absorbed into your bloodstream! Anyone who supports these huge hog cities should be forced to raise their family downwind from one of these operations!" A community organizer chimed in with his concerns, saying "We want research that will actually solve problems for America's family hog farmers and rural community, not more research for high cost, polluting, inhumane, stinking factory farms."

In addition, pleas were made that the government do a better job of testing the soil for nitrates, fecal chloroform, chloride, and other chemicals found in manure; that the government and industry do a better job of finding engineering and design solutions to the problem of water and odor pollution; that the techniques of enzyme treatment of hog waste lagoons (which cause a crust to be formed over the manure lagoons) be explored; and that aerobic and anaerobic lagoons, slurry storage systems, bubbleless oxygenation, and the common options of spraying the liquid manure on fields or knifing it into the soil be evaluated for their effectiveness. In the final analysis, those with ecological worries knew that there was no magical "foo-foo dust" that would kill the odor.

Task force addresses concerns: A political nightmare

Governor Jake Duroc was well aware of the controversy that hog confinement centers had caused in his state and knew that these factory farms had to be addressed. He was under increased pressure to allow large operations into the state to protect his state's position as a leader in the area of hog production. Other states were recruiting corporate hog operations in an effort to stimulate jobs and to attract packing plants—economic activity that translated into jobs. He also was well aware that the neighboring competing states were less concerned about the ecological problems and saving the family farm than they were about the prospects of attracting jobs for the unemployed. Governor Duroc asked himself how his state could compete, yet protect family farmers, local economies, and the environment? If the state doesn't adapt, he thought, what are the long range consequences? In the final analysis, the governor's advisors had informed him that there would be little "political hay" to be made on this one.

To help the governor sort out the policy issues, problems, and alternatives, he decided to commission a "blue ribbon" task force (The Swine Production Task Force) comprised of economists, university professors, industry experts, family farm advocates, rural development professionals and agricultural business leaders. The task force was given the charge to come up with a set of recommended policies that would make the state competitive, yet maintain the quality of life for independent farmers and rural communities. After all, Governor Duroc stated, many of these problems would need to be addressed by the state legislature and find their way into a set of state laws and regulations.

Briefing the swine production task force

The Swine Production Task Force was thoroughly briefed by members of the governor's cabinet on the modern hog industry versus the old, traditional, highly protected hog industry. It was informed that a number of competing, dynamic tensions needed to be examined: The issue of market structure and market power versus odor and pollution; large versus small hog producers; corporate versus sole proprietorship production; community versus community and state versus state concerns; and the economics involved in the hog industry restructuring itself, especially as the pork industry entered a global market.

The governor's staff specifically emphasized quality of life issues, clean air, water, and safe soil, and how policies that might protect the environment must at the same time provide a favorable economic environment for large-scale livestock production. Of course, members of the task force knew that large-scale hog production was dependent on a supply of labor, a readily available and stable source of feed grain, access to pork processing facilities, and the ability to assure an adequate supply for packing plants.

Importance of hogs to community

The briefing provided much new information to the task force. The background history of the hog industry was carefully presented. They were told that "Hogs in the state outnumber people four to one and represent $12 billion of annual economic impact; that nearly 95,000 workers were employed in the hog industry." They were also told that "Hogs had been traditionally raised in small numbers (two-thirds of the hog farms raised fewer than 100 stock) on family-owned farms. Farmers either produced their own hogs through breeding sows (female hogs), thereby producing litters of eight to ten pigs every six months, or by purchasing young pigs on the open market and feeding them until they had reached a market weight of approximately 200 pounds."

It was explained that the farmer sold his hogs to a local company or a meat packing plant (processor) that paid a price based on the national market price of hogs. The price was strictly determined by the demands of the packing plants versus the supply of hogs ready for slaughter. In payment for their standing livestock, the farmer would then buy new hog production equipment, feed, and other family consumer goods from stores located in their own community. In summation, the secretary of agriculture stated: "Hogs are the backbone of the rural economy."

Emergence of the corporate farm

As the briefing continued, members of the task force became increasingly aware of the many organizations (public, private, and nonprofit), that had a major interest on how pork production problems were to be resolved. One speaker handed them a listing of potentially concerned parties (see Exhibit 1). At first, the task force members could not fathom why organizations as diverse as the Little Brown Church in the Vale, the American Heart Association and the Department of Justice would have an interest in the pig business.

The basis for these multiple interests in the industry emerged as the briefing continued. The task force was informed of the national trend toward the large corporate farms that raise thousands of hogs at one location—corporate-investor-owner forms of production or modern-day pig factories. Industrial mass production could take advantage of high technology, labor-saving equipment, plus more efficient use of the work force made up of specialists and laborers. The result of using state-of-the-art scientific husbandry and economies of scale in agricultural production had the potential of completely changing the landscape of the hog industry from many thousands of family-run, diversified farms to several hundred corporate facilities. They were told: "An operation of this mega-size can make an agreement or contract with the packers to provide a specific number of hogs at a predetermined time. The packing companies can specify the quality of meat that will be needed, thereby providing a better match between the production of pork and consumer preferences for taste, cooking time, cholesterol, and texture." The prospect of what might happen if packaging companies were to build large hog operations and completely vertically integrate the production process, although this practice had been outlawed in several states, was becoming a real issue.

A look at the numbers

Additional statistics presented confirmed the trend toward fewer, larger operations. The number of hog farms nationwide had fallen from 900,000 in 1970, to fewer than 250,000 in 1995, and is expected to drop, by the year 2000, to about 100,000. The task force learned that the number of farms had fallen in their state from 150,000 in 1954 to just 29,000 today, while simultaneously, the number of hogs produced had grown from 12 million to 14 million. Responding to these figures, one member of the task force, an economist, stated that, "If pure market forces are allowed to take their natural course, family-sized operations will continue to dwindle because corporate operations can raise hogs at 75 percent of the cost of the traditional farmer. As more hogs are raised by larger producers, market forces will eventually drive the cost paid for a 'finished' hog below the small producer's cost of production."

Handling the problem of waste

The cost of production was not the only factor that the task force had to consider. Waste from large hog operations also posed a significant environmental problem. A hog produces fifteen pounds of waste per day, four to five times the amount produced by a human. Thus, a 10,000 head operation produces the same amount of waste as a city of 50,000.

Smaller farms are able to recycle their animal waste by applying it as fertilizer to their cropland, which, in turn, is used to raise the feed grains fed to their hogs or sold to the local elevator. Corporate operations, due to their large herd size, collect

EXHIBIT 1. LISTING OF SELECTED AGRIBUSINESS, GOVERNMENTAL, ENVIRONMENTAL AND "GRASSROOTS" ORGANIZATIONS WITH AN INTEREST IN HOG CONFINEMENT, ODOR, AND POLLUTION POLICY

American Cyanamid
American Heart Association
Arens Implement and Motor
    Company
Campaign for Family Farms and the
    Environment
Carroll's Foods (2nd in U.S. pork
    production)
Center for Rural Affairs
Citizens for Community
    Improvement
Continental Grain Company
Corn Growers Association
County Board of Supervisors
    (Judges or Commissioners)
DeKalb Service
Department of Conservation
Department of Economic
    Development
Department of Health
Department of Natural Resources
Department of Wildlife and Fisheries
Dow Chemical
Farm Bureau Federation
Farmers Union
Friends of Rural America
Hormel Meat Packing
Illinois Corn Growers Association
Iowa Beef Processing
Iowa Pork Alliance
Iowa Pork Producers Association
Iowa State University
Jimmy Dean Sausage Company
John Deere Corporation
League of Municipalities
Little Brown Church in the Vale
Meyer's Livestock and General
    Hauling Company

Minnesota Pork Producers
    Association
Murphy Farms (first in U.S. pork
    production)
National Association of County
    Officials
National Catholic Rural Life
    Conference
National Farmers Organization
National Pork Board
National Pork Producers Council
National Rural Conference
National Swine Research Center
Pig Improvement, Inc.
Pioneer Hi-Bred International, Inc.
Pork Producers Association
PrairieFire Rural Action (rural
    advocacy group)
Premium Standard Farms
Purdue University
Sierra Club
Southwest Quality Pork (a farmer-
    owned cooperative)
State Extension Service
State Legislature
State Senate
U.S. Army Corps of Engineers
U.S. Department of Agriculture
U.S. Department of Commerce
U.S. Department of Justice
U.S. Environmental Protection
    Agency
U.S. House of Representatives
U.S. Meat Export Federation
U.S. Senate
University of Minnesota
World Pork Expo Conference

animal waste in large, open earthen lagoons. Then it is applied, often with large sprinklers, to the surrounding land in much higher concentrations than is needed for crop fertilization. Of course, the problem of nitrogen run-off into adjacent rivers, lakes, sloughs, streams, and other water supplies must be considered. Also, the odor from the open lagoons, coupled with the smell that comes from the surrounding land covered with liquid manure, can pollute miles of the country. The members of the task force were further informed that the chemicals emitted from hog feces are believed to cause physical and mental ailments, including hog odor being absorbed into lungs, blood, and fat, and leading to anxiety, depression, and the loss of enjoyment of life.

Building consensus

Governor Duroc returned to the task force during the closing session and again explained how much importance he would place on their work and recommendations. He assured them that the complete resources of his office and the executive branch would be made available to the members of the task force. "This issue," he stated, "is of great interest to me and to the state legislature. I'm counting on you to help us solve this litany of problems that you have heard about today, and to do so fairly and quickly." The task force then decided to have an open meeting in which all interested parties could present their views.

The public forum

At the first public forum, passions ran high as farmers and citizens spoke of the quality of life they felt would vanish if small farmers were not protected. "How can farmers help keep the rural communities alive if the state stabs a pitchfork in our backs by promoting corporate farming? We thought the people we elected to office were on our side, not the side of big agribusiness," testified one small farm advocate. Others in the audience gave examples of how local rural economies were made stronger by the presence of small farmers in contrast to those states dominated by corporate farms. "The money just doesn't trickle down to the local community when it comes to the large swine companies," reported a university economist who specialized in rural economic development.

In sharp contrast, representatives of large hog operations emphasized that the shift to large, corporate farms offers the consumer a better product at a lower cost. "Corporate operations can control their product insuring a better tasting, lower cholesterol, safe product available to consumers at a lower cost. If we don't allow the free market to operate, then pork will lose market share to other meats like chicken, which is not raised in this state," reported a pork industry leader.

State economic development professionals said that other states were promoting the large operations and greatly increasing their percentage of the national pork market. "If we don't take action to promote or at least tolerate large operations, North Carolina and Missouri will receive all of the new business, leaving us with nothing."

The economic development specialist further stated that "North Carolina increased their breeding stock by 25 percent last year while we lost 18 percent. Large hog producers offer decent paying jobs too. One company located twenty miles beyond our southern border employs 1,500 persons with an annual payroll of $35 million. That's over $23,000 for a person living in a low cost, rural area. Besides, the state university is working on ways to control the odor and pollution, and only the large operations will be able to afford this new technology. We can't afford to be left behind."

Odor and pollution issues were also raised during the public forum and became the most controversial part of the meeting. Everyone in the rural community is affected by the "smell of hogs." The task force was told that several lawsuits regarding odor and water quality were pending. "The cost to the state's environment is not counted in the cost of production," testified a representative of a major environmental group. Horror stories of waste-filled streams and overpowering odors that ruined the quality of rural life in those areas dominated by large hog farms were reported. One farmer from the southern part of the state, who had traveled a considerable distance to attend the meeting, said he observed that someone had placed a large sign in a field adjacent to the highway which stated in large blue and red letters: "Duroc and Hog Factories = Environmental, Economic, Social Damage," which some in the room responded to with a loud "Amen!"

Rural residents and environmental interest groups testified that they wanted stricter rules that would protect the quality of rural life and the environment. A state senator said that pig farmers with larger operations should be made to "meet clean water standards comparable to those in place for municipal sewage treatment plants," because they produce an equivalent amount of waste. One spokesperson indicated that the corporate community wants laws preventing "nuisance lawsuits" against farms that follow the state regulations regarding waste disposal. "We are perfectly willing to follow the law and pay for developing reasonable waste disposal systems," testified the president of a major corporate hog firm that wanted access to the state.

A variety of new laws regulating location of operations and waste handling were then discussed. The task force could readily see that new, stricter regulations on the hog industry would also affect the small farmers, thus placing them at a further disadvantage because they are less able to afford the new technology required for regulatory compliance.

Additional testimony was provided by two young farmers who held diametrically opposed positions. Peter Vanderhout stated, "If we don't put a halt to these corporate mass productions, we'll all become unemployed or low-paid workers—just like living in a Domestic Banana Republic! What kind of priorities does this state have if it is willing to drive reasonably middle-class families off their own farms—some of which have been in the family for generations—and into the 'soup kitchen' or unemployment line? We've already experienced what happens to our local merchants when the giants like Wal-Mart come in—they're squashed like a bug and so will we."

In marked contrast, Jack Thompson, a young, entrepreneurial, owner-producer of a large confinement operation suggested the potential for hogs in the state was unlimited. "This is hog heaven," he boldly declared. "Yeah, unless the small farmer gets with the agenda and begins to use the new technology that is available and drop these worn-out, traditional values and ideas, we're going to drive him out of the hog production business. We know that the only thing that is constant is 'change,' but these folks protesting want the protection of the state and federal government. They don't want to and they can't compete with those of us into modern agricultural technology. You know, we aren't talking about growing flowers—we're talking about raising hogs and making a profit on our investments."

The public hearing took most of the day and the members of the task force were thankful that the interested public had attended the meeting and expressed their views. There was little doubt that whatever they recommended, it would have profound implications on the combating interests. Last, before adjournment, the task force was given material that a member had received from a professor who had attended the International Roundtable on Swine Odor Control. The literature reported that "long-term exposure to hog odor can lead to depression, anxiety, confusion, and a lack of energy."

The task force had heard earlier testimony about the impact of hog odors on the human psyche and physiology, and they had studied an earlier report that linked hydrogen sulfide, a compound found in manure, to nearly twenty deaths at hog operations in the state since 1978. Even an odor tax on large hog lots and municipal sewage treatment plants had been proposed by a university professor. The taxes would be paid by the polluting producers and given to adjacent landowners depending on the level of odor in the air as measured by a "dynamic olfactometer."

Wrap up: Where do we go from here?

As the meeting wound down, a member of the task force quipped that he read a local newspaper article where the scientists who research pig odor refer to their group as the "Manure fraternity," and that an agricultural specialist said: "We tell our friends, 'It may be manure to you, but to us it's our bread and butter.' " Not to be outdone, another member said "On a lighter note, did you see the story about how angry the National Pork Producers Council is with the former Republican U.S. Senator Alfonse D'Amato? He apparently made up his own lyrics to the 'Old McDonald Had a Farm,' in protestation to the lack of progress that had been made on the budget bill. The lyrics were considered derisive to the pork industry that has been trying to sell a leaner cut of meat to the world that has become more concerned about fat in their diet." He went on to quote the senator: "President Clinton had a bill. E-I-E-I-O. And in that bill was lots of pork. E-I-E-I-O. New pork here, Old pork there. Here a pork, there a pork. Everywhere pork, pork. . . . " What really made the council take note is when the director of the Pork Information Bureau heard a senator proclaim, "I don't want any pork. I don't want any pork chops. I don't want any pork ribs."

The chair of the Swine Production Task Force scheduled the next meeting to be held in two weeks and asked the members to study the Administrative Plan of Action that staff had quickly assembled based on the testimony. The chair then entertained a motion for adjournment.

At their third meeting, the Task Force went right to work and considered the massive amount of information they received from the public forum, the testimony and supporting materials submitted from a plethora of interest groups, and the pile of reports that had come in from the various state agencies. In examining the issues, the task force discussed the pros and cons of the issues, problems, and concerns that surrounded the production of pork in the state. Finally they compiled a number of policy options and their perceived impact on stakeholders (see Exhibit 2). They felt confident that they had identified the major policy options. Now the difficult part of their charge was about to begin—the preparation of a final report that would include a set of recommendations on which the members had consensus.

EXHIBIT 2. SWINE PRODUCTION TASK-FORCE
ADMINISTRATIVE PLAN OF ACTION

Selected Objectives

1. Determine if there should be a minimum distance requirement between hog facilities of a specific size (5,000 or more?); earthen manure lagoons; and neighboring houses, businesses, and public use areas. Should these same standards be applied to large-scale turkey and chicken production factories?

2. Explore the need for legal protection from "nuisance lawsuits" for hog producers who follow the law.

3. Discuss the feasibility and desirability of creating an indemnity fund to pay for cleanup of hog operations if they go bankrupt or leave the state.

4. Determine if large confinement centers should be exempt or nonexempt from local government (county) zoning regulations and exclusively regulated by the state. How will local citizens prevent the depreciation or erosion of their property values?

5. Research what must be done to make sure small producers are fairly paid by packers and have access to markets as provided for by the U.S. Packers and Stockyards Act.

6. Research and determine the standards required to protect the environment, such as set back requirements from waterways, streams, aquifers, and wells; owner submission of a manure management plan that specifies the volume of manure that may be spread per acre dependent on season of the year, slope of the land, kind of application, and type of soil.

7. Examine if "odor shares" might be bought and sold by livestock producers much the same way that "pollution credits" are exchanged (traded, paid-for, etc.) on the open market by polluting industries.

8. Research if any cases dealing with large livestock confinement operations had been adjudicated at the state level and determine their final disposition (if any), on such issues as mental anguish, loss of enjoyment of life, deprivation of property, stress, nuisance, damage to health, groundwater pollution/contamination, and waste spills and waste cleanup.

QUESTIONS AND INSTRUCTIONS

1. If you were Governor Jake Duroc, what considerations would go into forming a "blue ribbon" task force to study hog confinement operations in the state (size, interests represented, demographic characteristics of members, regional representation and the like)? Why are these representativeness concerns important? Please elaborate.

2. From a public policy perspective, what are the likely interests of the agribusiness, governmental, environmental, and "grass roots" organizations listed in Exhibit 1. Please place them into categories of interest and develop what might be their major concerns. How would you satisfy these competing concerns through the use of administrative procedures and regulatory law? Please elaborate.

3. From a policy perspective, what are the tensions that exist between urban and rural sectors, corporate and family values, between economic growth advocates and environmental protection activists? Between higher quality pork production and lower consumer costs?
4. Should the commission take into account the value of "quality of life" in their recommendations? If so, how should it be measured? How can quality of life be improved? Please be specific.
5. Should the commission be influenced by the concerns of outside states competing for a larger share of the hog industry market? How can they compete successfully with other states if they recommend policies that promote small, family-run operations?
6. Should the commission offer multiple options for the governor to consider or should it attempt to present a single, unified answer to the question of corporate hog operations versus family-run farms?
7. Evaluate the matrix that presents the task force's policy options (see Exhibit 2) and their perceived impact on stakeholders. In what areas do you believe it is adequate? Are there any deficiencies? If so, please correct them.

INSIGHTS-ISSUES / PIGS, PEOPLE, AND POLLUTION

Clearly and briefly describe and illustrate these concepts, issues, or points. Interpret the word "role" as meaning impact, application, importance, effect and/or illustration of certain facts, concerns, or issues from the case study.

1. Role of market failure, or when normal operations of the marketplace fail to protect the citizenry from actual or potential abuses of power by business and/or corporate firms. Explain.
2. Role of an advisory committee/task force as illustrated by the "blue ribbon" task force (The Swine Production Task Force). What were its impacts? Explain.
3. Role of industry economic factors for prompting prospects for economic regulations? Illustrate.
4. Role of industry social factors for prompting prospects for social regulations. Illustrate.
5. Roles of professionalism, participation, and publicity. Was the "public interest" served? Explain.

ENDNOTES

1. Daniel J. Gifford, *Administrative Law: Cases and Materials* (Cincinnati: Anderson Publishing Co., 1992), 1–9.
2. Dennis L. Mueller, "Public Choice: A Survey," *Journal of Economic Literature* 14, no. 2 (1976):395.

3. Lief H. Carter, *Administrative Law and Politics: Cases and Comments* (Boston: Little, Brown, and Company, 1983), 14–39.

4. Florence Heffron with Neil McFeeley, *The Administrative Regulatory Process* (New York: Longmans, 1983), 1–23.

5. Douglas Costle, "In Defense of the Public Service," *Public Administration Times* (1 May 1980): 3.

6. Murray Weidenbaum, *A New Approach to Regulatory Reform* (St. Louis, Mo.: Center for the Study of American Business, 1998), 2–3. See also Thomas D. Hopkins, *Regulatory Costs in Profile* (St. Louis, Mo.: Center for the Study of American Business, 1996).

7. Heffron with McFeeley, *The Administrative Regulatory Process*, 6.

8. Melinda Warren and Kenneth Chilton, *The Regulatory Legacy of the Reagan Revolution: An Analysis of 1990 Federal Regulatory Budgets and Staffing* (St. Louis, Mo.: Center for the Study of Business, 1989), 9–12. See Melinda Warren and Barry Jones, *Reinventing the Regulatory System: No Downsizing in Administration Plan* (St. Louis, Mo.: Center for the Study of Business, 1995), 8–20.

9. Thomas D. Hopkins, *Regulatory Costs in Profile* (St. Louis: Center for the Study of American Business, Policy Study Paper Number 132, August, 1996), pages 3–12; Murray Weidenbaum, *A New Approach to Regulatory Reform* (St. Louis: Center for the Study of American Business, Policy Study Paper Number 147, August, 1998), 2–8.

10. Hopkins, *op. cit.*

11. Douglas R. Wholey and Susan M. Sanchez, "The Effects of Regulatory Tools on Organizational Populations," *Academy of Management Review* 16, no. 4 (October 1991): 743–767.

12. Melinda Warren and William F. Lauber, *Regulatory Changes and Trends: An Analysis of the 1999 Federal Budget* (St. Louis, Mo.: Washington University, 1998), 1999 Regulatory Report.

13. Melinda Warren and James Lis, *Regulatory Standstill: Analysis of the 1993 Federal Regulatory Budget* (St. Louis, Mo.: Center for the Study of American Business, 1992), 1–2, 5, 7–9. See Warren and Barry Jones, *Reinventing the Regulatory System*, 8–20.

14. Wholey and Sanchez, "The Effects of Regulatory Tools," 743–767.

15. Warren and Lauber, *op. cit.*

16. Ibid.

17. Heffron with McFeeley, *The Administrative Regulatory Process*, 347–371.

18. Warren and Chilton, *1989 Federal Regulatory Budget and Staffing: Effects of the Reagan Presidency* (St. Louis, Mo.: Center for the Study of Business, 1988), 4. See Warren and Jones, *Reinventing the Regulatory System* 8–20.

19. Warren and Chilton, *1989 Federal Regulatory Budget and Staffing*, 4; Warren and Jones, *Reinventing the Regulatory System*, 8–20.

20. James T. O'Reilly, Administrative Rule Making: Structuring, Opposing, and Defending Federal Agency Regulations (New York: McGraw-Hill), 4–6.

21. Lief H. Carter, *Administrative Law and Politics: Cases and Comments* (Boston: Little, Brown, and Company, 1983), 14–39.

22. Administrative Procedure Act, P.L. 404, 60 Stat. 237(1946), 5 U.S.C.A. 551.

23. William F. West, *Administrative Rule-making: Politics and Processes* (Westport, Conn: Greenwood Press, 1985), 17.

24. Murray L. Weidenbaum and Ronald J. Penoyer, *The Next Step in Regulatory Reform: Updating the Statutes* (St. Louis, Mo.: Center for the Study of Business, 1983), 24–32.

25. Paul N. Tramontozzi with Kenneth W. Chilton, *U.S. Regulatory Agencies Under Reagan, 1980–1988* (St. Louis, Mo.: Center for the Study of Business, 1987), 11–14.

26. Cornelius M. Kerwin, *Rulemaking* (Washington, DC: CQ Press, 1994). See O'Reilly, *Administrative Rulemaking*, 90, 131.

27. Kerwin, *Rulemaking*, 84.

28. Walter Lippman, *The Public Philosophy* (Boston: Little, Brown, and Company, 1955), 42.

29. Glendon A. Shubert, Jr., *The Public Interest* (New York: Free Press, 1952), 223.

30. Carl Friedrich, "Public Policy and the Nature of Administrative Responsibility" in *The Politics of the Federal Bureaucracy*, ed. Alan A. Altshuler (New York: Dodd, Mead, 1968), 417.

31. Friedrich, "Public Policy," 417.

32. C. Kenneth Meyer and Thomas F. Sheehan, professor of Public Administration and chair, Department of Public Administration, College of Business and Public Administration, Drake University, Des Moines, IA, 50310, and Lance Noe, School of Public Administration, College of Urban and Public Affairs, Florida Atlantic University, Boca Raton, FL, 33301, written for *The Craft of Public Administration,* 7th edition. The authors retain all copyright privileges.

INDEX

D

E

R